THE LIGHT OF BATTLE

THE LIGHT OF BATTLE

EISENHOWER, D-DAY, *and the* BIRTH *of the* AMERICAN SUPERPOWER

MICHEL PARADIS

MARINER BOOKS
New York Boston

 For information, address HarperCollins Publishers, 195 Broadway, New York, NY 10007.

HarperCollins books may be purchased for educational, business, or sales promotional use. For information, please email the Special Markets Department at SPsales@harpercollins.com.

FIRST EDITION

Designed by Renata DiBiase
Chapter opener illustrations by Carol Wong

Library of Congress Cataloging-in-Publication Data has been applied for.

ISBN 978-0-358-68237-0

24 25 26 27 28 LBC 5 4 3 2 1

To Zelda XIV

Today, war—and even a single battle—is so extensive in its physical ramifications alone that thousands of eyewitness accounts would be required for anything approximating a full picture. Fortunately, today, war is the most thoroughly and impartially documented aspect of human life. The historian of Overlord, for instance, would start out with the study of the doctrinal developments, based on World War I, in the professional schools of the United States and Britain; continue through the vast amount of planning done in the U.S. and the U.K. prior to D-Day, all summed up in the final Overlord forecast. Unless all that happened before the first man touched the beach were studied, the leader of combat operations could not be fully understood and grasped.

—DWIGHT D. EISENHOWER

CONTENTS

General Strategy of Overlord in Conjunction with Anvil (Later Dragoon)

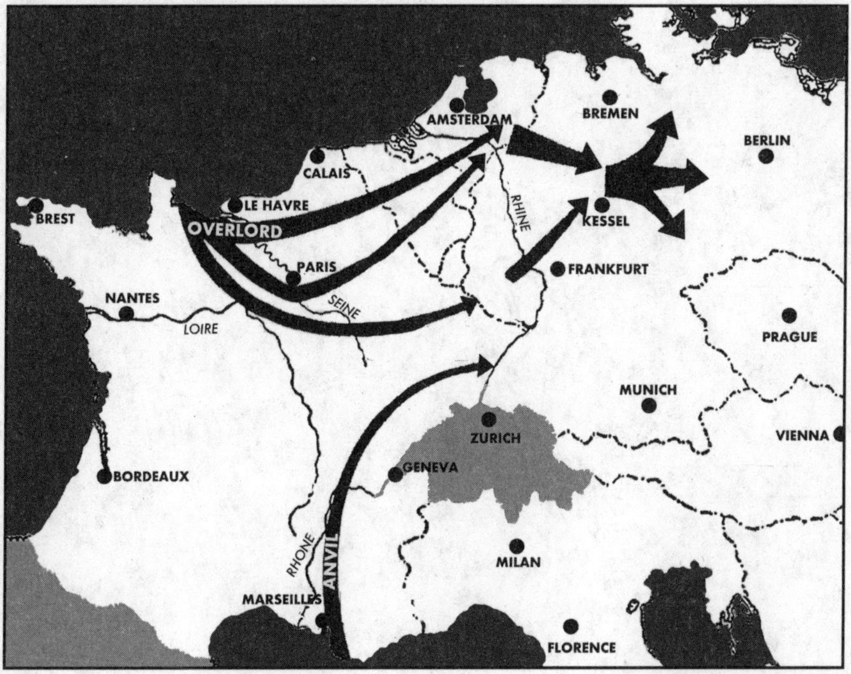

Courtesy of the author.

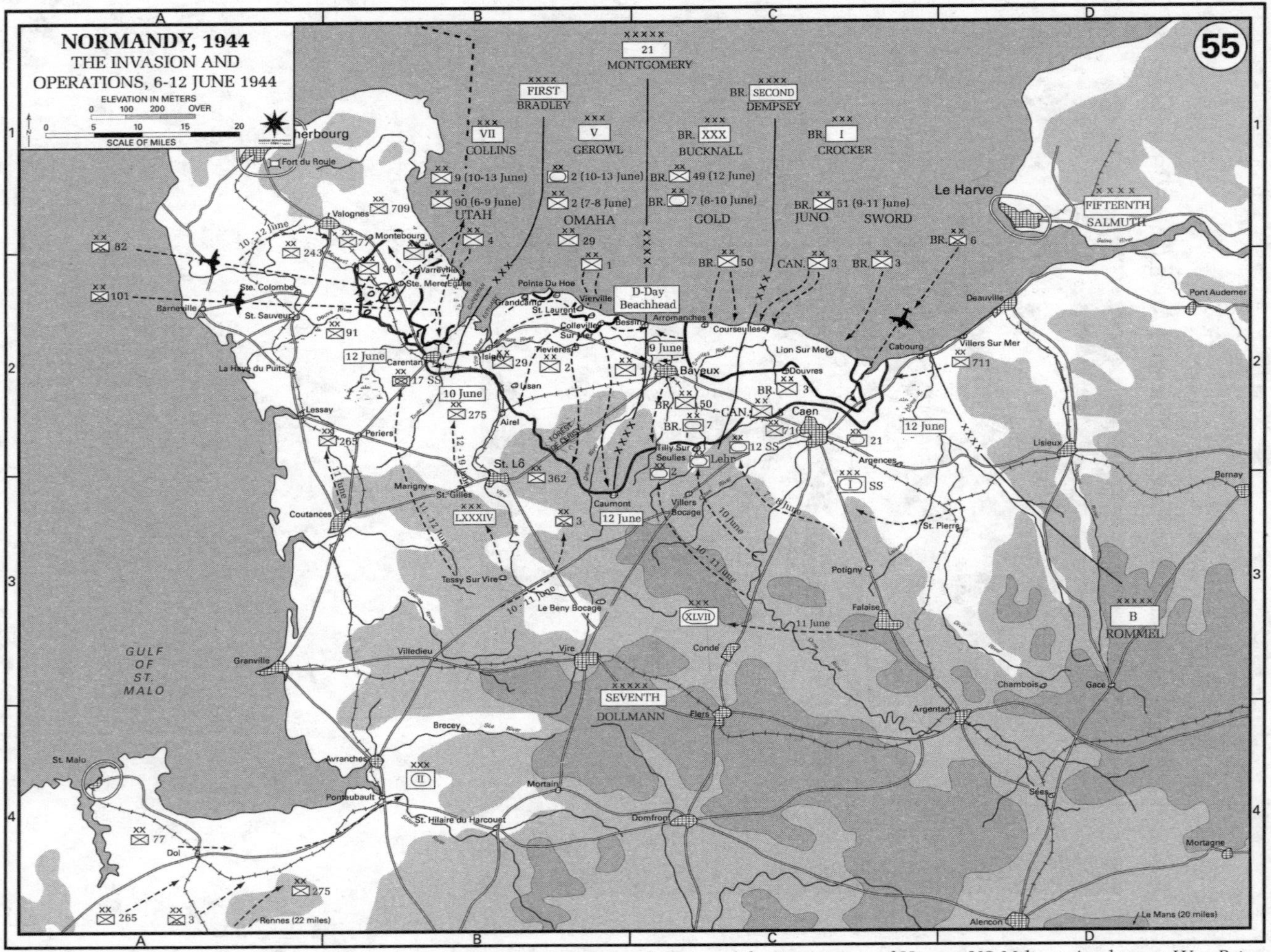

Courtesy of the Department of History, US Military Academy at West Point.

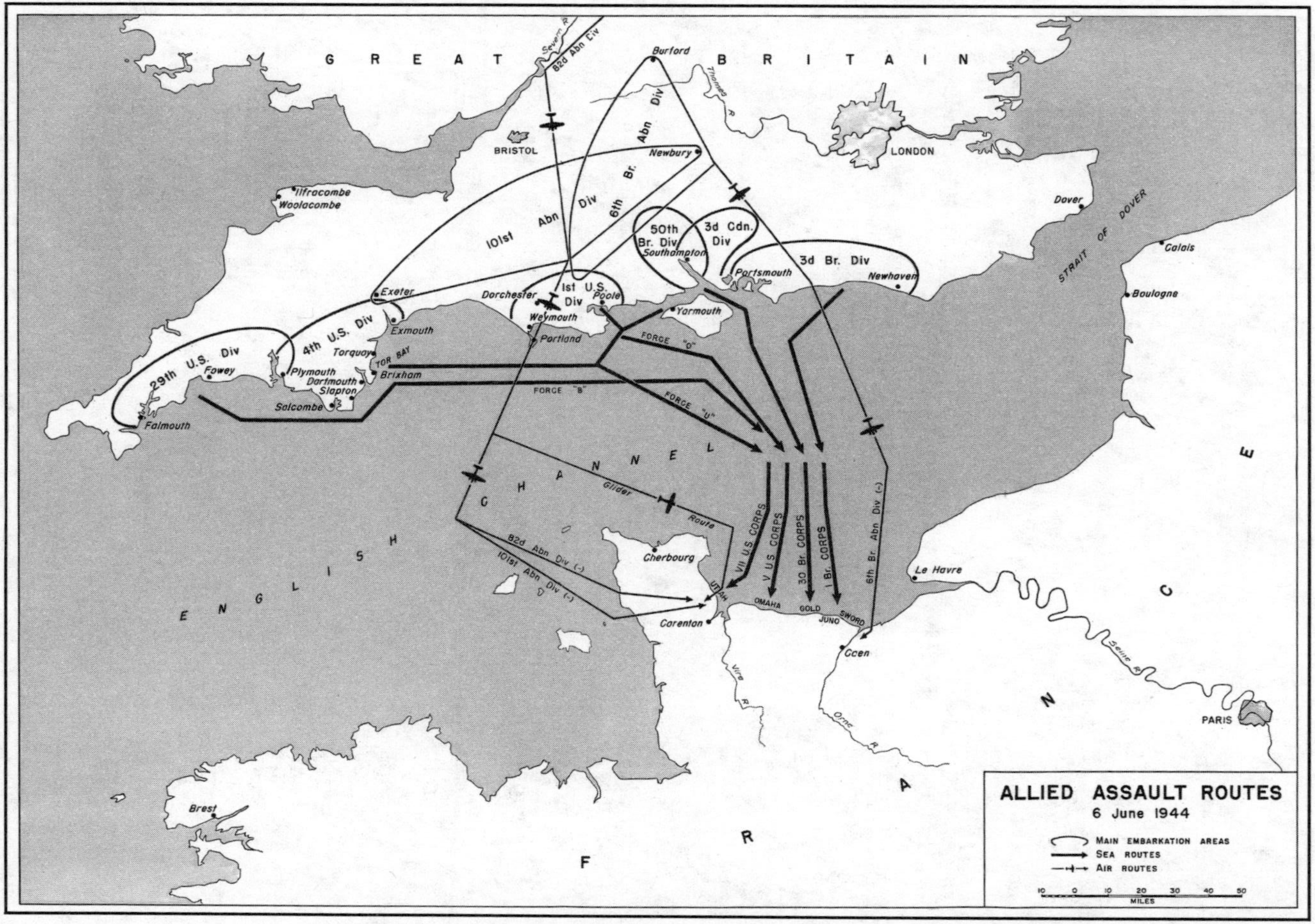

Courtesy of the US Army Center of Military History.

THE LIGHT OF BATTLE

Winston Churchill

PROLOGUE

ANYONE EVER ASKED remembered that it was so, so loud. It was the kind of loud that just shook the thoughts right out of your head. Guns were always loud. But there was something about being on the water in a little boat under a canopy of 12-inch, 10-inch, 6-inch, and 12-pound shells.

Since before dawn, four battleships and four cruisers had been pummeling one little strip of the coast, a shrubby cove barely 350 yards across. The cliffs ahead rose about a hundred feet above the beach and were still cast in shadow as the sun rose behind them. The cliffs seemed to liquefy under the onslaught, and red clay seeped out in rivulets of dust between the rocks. It was as if the earth itself were bleeding.

Then, the barrage stopped. Everything was silent. Clouds of red clay thinned into the air and all was peaceful. The only sounds to disturb the calm of dawn were the nervous shufflings of hundreds of young, cherry-faced men crowded into boats as they headed to shore and the lapping of the sea.

Then there was a shot. A single rifle shot. It splashed into the water next to a boat that was only a hundred yards from landfall. The young, cherry-faced men jeered in the evident belief that it had not been luck, but the incompetence of the enemy, or maybe even divine providence, that had directed that bullet harmlessly into the water. It was barely a moment. Short enough to flash a contemptuous smile.

But then, the slumbering cliffs erupted. The sea seemed to boil, spurting up flicks of water with every missed shot, as bullets rained back from the cliffs like sleet and overwhelmed whatever shelter that luck or providence might provide.

Young, cherry-faced men slumped forward to the right and to the left in their crowded boats. There was nothing dramatic, heroic, or tragic about it. Just a man upright at one glance, slumped forward with a red stain on his shirt at the next. In one boat that almost made it to land, a sergeant major who waxed his mustache into points stood up, took a bad one in the belly, and slumped forward. Next to him, an enlisted looked over the side of the boat, took one above the eyebrow, and slumped forward. Six weeks earlier, they had been home with girlfriends, moms, and wives, looking sharp in their brass buttons and puttees. Now their commanding officer was looking at them all slumped forward in their red-stained shirts, unable to think of anything except for Rudyard Kipling's poem "If—," and its opening lines, "If you can keep your head when all about you/Are losing theirs."

Major Thomas Frankland had joined the first wave along with General Steuart Hare, a lean Etonian whose skin had weathered fighting for the Empire throughout south Asia and who was now tasked with leading the king's army over the narrow strip of beach ahead. Their boat was a few hundred yards back from the vanguard, and though there to lead this battle, Frankland and Hare found themselves helpless to do anything for the young, cherry-faced men under their command, except to press on.

With the sun in his eyes, it was difficult for Frankland to see what was happening exactly. The boats ahead had just stopped fifty or so yards from shore. There was splashing over the sides, as men went overboard, weighed down by seventy-pound packs. The faces of some burst up to the surface. Others just disappeared.

The happy few who made it overboard and kept themselves from drowning were making hopeful progress. They waded inland, waterlogged and exhausted, but dogged and almost to dry land. But then, those happy few stumbled, splashing face down into coils of barbed wire that had been hiding below the waves. Those ensnared looked as if they were battling a nest of sea serpents, kicking and thrashing, only to be pulled under the moment a wave or a bullet from the cliffs knocked them off balance. As one man drowned in the tangle, another could be seen climbing over him only to gnarl himself in another row of wire, and then another man over him. These men had been friends.

On the right and center of the cove, the beaches were soon choked by a flotsam of once cherry-faced young men, who drifted out and back with the tide like washed-up garbage. Their blood dyed the ocean around them a dark crimson that soon stained sand beneath the roll of the tides. Seeing the massacre ahead, Frankland ordered the boatsmen to turn toward the left edge of the cove, where the cliffs offered a modicum of cover.

Frankland was prepared to distinguish himself that morning. He had been commissioned as an officer in the Royal Dublin Fusiliers at nineteen and spent the past sixteen years in the British Army. His soft chin, large Irish ears, and fashionably trimmed mustache did not give him the most martial appearance. But he was from a military family. His older brother was a captain in the army, and they had both fought in the Boer War. His father, who had only died two years earlier, had risen to the rank of colonel, and his grandfather had been knighted after fighting in the victory against Napoleon at Waterloo. Frankland was comfortable with danger, even going so far as to earn his pilot's certification a year and a half earlier, at a time when aviators still had the bravado (and life expectancy) usually associated with barehanded snake handlers.

Upon hitting a sheltered spot along the shore of what had been codenamed "W Beach," Frankland charged forth as Steuart Hare rallied his men in a ferocious drive up the flank of the cliffs. Frankland personally shot three Turks as they stormed forward as if to prove that victory always went to the bold.

But then Hare took one through the calf. The charge faltered and Frankland helped drag Hare to a ditch, where the general nearly bled out as Frankland dressed his wound as tight as a tourniquet.

Frankland raced back down to the beaches, where the wounded lay about with holes in their shins and windpipes and stomachs and spines. Those still able to fight were sheltering under cliff edges and in ditches, struggling to get the sticky ocean-soaked sand out of their rifles. Some tried to pick the sand out grain by grain with their fingertips. Some furiously kicked at the bolts until they sprung open. Others tried to piss the sand away.

Frankland ran back up to check on Hare, who asked how things were. Frankland said they were making progress, and Hare told him to send a report back to headquarters. "Lancs getting on all right," Frankland wrote out in a hasty message. "General wounded."

Frankland tried to assess their situation coolly. The cliffs had been dug through with trenches, giving the Turks an extraordinary defensive advantage. It was hard to know where they even were. The gunfire echoed between the rocks in an incessant static that faded and grew louder in random waves, only to be punctuated by a sickening burst each time a boat or a foot or an elbow fumbled onto one of the mines hiding in the sand.

Frankland pulled out his binoculars to look for a vulnerability through which he could mount another charge. It wasn't more than a second before a few opportunistic bullets cut through his forehead, neck, and heart. Frankland slumped onto the ground. It was not yet nine in the morning.

As the day wore on, the fury of battle reached its culmination and gave way to standoff. The air grew cold and drizzly. Snipers took potshots at any carelessly exposed skin, and often a lone Turk manning a trench would hold out for hours until being gunned down at close range by a pistol.

The day of the invasion, April 25, 1915, the Turks had twenty thousand lightly armed men on the Gallipoli Peninsula and fifty large guns. The British had the firepower of the Royal Navy and sixty thousand British Army regulars. By midnight, though, Sir Ian Hamilton, the commanding general of the British forces in what would come to be called the Gallipoli campaign, issued an order that would define the months ahead: "Dig in and stick it out."

THE BRITISH PLAN had been for the navy to bombard the Turkish defenses, clearing the way for the army to land on six beaches around the Gallipoli Peninsula, to push quickly inland, and to then link up on the grassy plateau above. Once secured, Gallipoli would give Britain near-total control of the Dardanelles Strait and force Turkey's capitulation in what was then called the Great War.

On a map, it all looked not just easy, but obvious. Britain could capture Constantinople, a city as old as civilization, and set another jewel in the crown atop the Pax Britannica. A southern line of supply could be opened with Russia before the czar's forces became exhausted on the eastern front. And with the Ottoman Empire defeated, the British could press their advantage through the Middle East to Palestine.

Maps, though, can be deceiving. As Steuart Hare would write, reflecting on that day, "Any fool can see what would be a good thing to do—there are probably more than one—but the difficulty is in deciding whether what would be advantageous can be done or not." Britain's War Office had estimated that taking Gallipoli would be achieved in a day and result in five thousand casualties. Instead, there were thirteen thousand casualties in the landings alone, and by January 1916, when Britain evacuated Gallipoli in unqualified defeat, there would be sixty thousand more.

For the men pinned down around Gallipoli's perimeter, those nine months were long and desperate. The beaches and coves the British had captured became overcrowded colonies that visitors described as "a giant shipwreck." Resupply from the sea was slow and inadequate. The wounded languished waiting for evacuation. And the fight to make any progress inland was as bitter and futile as crossing no-man's-land on the western front.

The forty-six-year-old commander of the Eighth Manchester Regiment, Lieutenant Colonel Donald MacCarthy-Morrogh, had served with distinction for twenty years in the British Army. He was sent to Gallipoli in July 1915 and was excited for the opportunity, writing home, "I am off to the Dardanelles, where I have been promised a command." Soon, even he had lost faith. While his wife, Vera, was home in Ireland with their four children, MacCarthy-Morrogh spent his tenth wedding anniversary raging into his war diary at the incompetence of his superiors.

Journalists were forbidden from writing anything but stories of British gallantry. But the truth eventually found an unlikely fissure in the wall of censorship.

Keith Murdoch, a young Australian reporter, was an unembarrassed champion of the British Empire and the Gallipoli campaign. Murdoch had produced a film entitled *A Hero of the Dardanelles* and, eager to chronicle the heroism of the Aussies on what came to be called ANZAC Cove, he donned a pith helmet and set off for the Adriatic. Stunned by what he saw, Murdoch went to London in late September 1915 and wrote the full, scandalous truth about the campaign's mismanagement and failures in the form of a twenty-five-page letter to the Australian prime minister. Murdoch made sure the letter circulated widely among London's political insiders and the square-jawed Aussie briefly became a minor celebrity in the heart of the empire.

In the history of war, no single piece of journalism has ever had such an immediate and decisive effect. Not only did Britain abandon Gallipoli within months, Murdoch's letter all but ended the political career of Britain's First Lord of the Admiralty, the mastermind of the operation and its ardent political patron: Winston Churchill.

Churchill derided Murdoch's letter as rank gossip and remained convinced that a decisive investment would turn the tide, not just of the Gallipoli campaign, but of the war. To his still young and ambitious mind, Churchill was convinced that winning Gallipoli would break Britain free from the wasteful madness of the western front, where what passed for military strategy involved throwing the flower of Britain's youth at German machine guns in the hope that the kaiser would eventually tire of it all.

But the truth of Murdoch's letter resounded. By November 1915, Churchill was forced to resign, and the men he had sent to Gallipoli would spend the remainder of the year trying to survive in the damp and cold. On November 23, 1915, the day Donald MacCarthy-Morrogh's oldest child, Kathleen, turned seven, he wrote bitterly that it had been "a cold hard day. The wet night last week has told on the men." Three dozen had fallen deathly ill.

In the first draft of history, Churchill bore the blame for the disaster. Resenting this, he would spend the next half decade writing a two-volume account of the First World War, entitled *The World Crisis*. Published in 1923 and by turns revealing and defensive, clear eyed and adolescent in its self-pity, Churchill devoted the second volume mostly to Gallipoli. He would later joke that people should "leave the past to history, especially as I propose to write that history myself." And in *The World Crisis*, Churchill wrote the history of a man who was right in principle and betrayed by forces outside his control.

Benefiting from his singular eloquence, as well as the passage of time, Churchill would succeed beyond his most grandiose ambitions in rehabilitating his reputation as a leader in times of crisis. But the words "Gallipoli" and "the Dardanelles" would remain cautionary epithets, much as the word "Munich" would become by the time Churchill returned to power as prime minister in 1940. Hastings "Pug" Ismay, one of Churchill's closest friends and advisers, would always remember the stories from Gallipoli. "The sea," he would say, "was red with blood for fifty yards."

WHAT MADE THE Gallipoli operation innovative was that it attempted to overcome the brutal advance in military technology wrought by the invention of the machine gun and modern artillery. With men no longer able to charge across open plains without being ground like waste meat, Gallipoli was a sea battle against land. Ships against forts. Nimble naval power that could annihilate a clear path for the army to stroll ashore. And over the following decades, in every school in which military strategy was taught in the English-speaking world, that idea came to be seen as the "folly of follies."

George S. Patton conducted a detailed study of Gallipoli for the US Army in 1936. Part of the problem, Patton thought, was the culture of the British Army, which was so rigidly bureaucratic that it couldn't press an advantage when the opportunity arose. But Gallipoli revealed that certain problems were inherent to such an operation. An amphibious invasion against a coastline defended with modern weaponry without the cover of darkness gave extraordinary advantages to the defenders. Naval power could do little to dislodge dug-in positions. And, as the Turks had proven, a handful of riflemen in trenches could cut the invaders down like grass as they stumbled onto foreign beaches saturated by saltwater and sand. Charging up a defended beach in broad daylight, Patton concluded, was as futile and suicidal as sprinting across no-man's-land.

Patton's bleak conclusion was shared by almost every serious military theorist of the era. The US Army would not adopt any doctrine on amphibious warfare until 1941, and even then, its investment was limited to a perfunctory cribbing of research from the Marine Corps. The Marines, whose very reason for existing had been their capacity to attack from sea to land, had studied Gallipoli intently and sought to show that the problems that bedeviled the British were solvable (and, by extension, that the Marine Corps had not become obsolete). Even still, the Marines' solutions to all those bedeviling problems were bewildering in their cost and complexity. To land on a hostile shore in daylight might be possible, but it required a delicate coordination of air, sea, and ground forces that had never been achieved and that, to any knowledgeable person, looked utterly infeasible.

In 1939, Dwight Eisenhower was asked to write a report assessing the threat the Japanese posed to the Philippine archipelago. Then a lieutenant colonel with only modest prospects for future advancement in the army, Eisenhower was reassuring. If the Philippine Army focused on defending the country's coastlines, it would be nearly invulnerable to invasion. "There is one line, and one only, at which the defending forces will enjoy a tremendous advantage over any attack by land," he wrote. "That line is the beach. Successful penetration of a defended beach is the most difficult operation in warfare."

Eisenhower warned that if the Japanese penetrated the coastal defenses at any point and succeeded in establishing a foothold inland that they could resupply, then the American-backed Philippine Army would lose 90 percent of its defensive advantage. To prevail, he therefore advised, "the enemy must be repulsed at the Beach."

Eisenhower had spent most of the previous decade as the second in command to Douglas MacArthur in the Philippines, which was then America's largest colony, but scheduled for independence in 1946. Soon after he finished his report, Eisenhower returned to the United States, and MacArthur, who had officially retired from the US Army in 1937, stayed behind to serve as a field marshal in the Philippine Army. It was a lucrative and self-anointed honor of which Eisenhower would remain forever dubious. But it meant that MacArthur would be the man responsible for defending the archipelago if Japan ever did attack.

Two years later, the Imperial Japanese Army landed at five points around the island of Luzon, the heart of the Philippines. Little had been done to harden Luzon's coastal defenses and the Japanese quickly penetrated inland. At the time, Eisenhower was on the War Department's planning staff in Washington, working directly for Army Chief of Staff General George Marshall.

Eisenhower was critical of MacArthur for not making a "better showing at the beaches and passes." But he did everything he could to get MacArthur the firepower needed to stall the Japanese advance. MacArthur escaped from the Philippines in March 1942 under direct orders from President Franklin Roosevelt.

Little did Eisenhower know, either in 1939 when he wrote his report on the defense of the Philippines, or in 1942 when he watched its recommendations ignored, that before long, he would be the one attempting to launch the most difficult operation in warfare. It would be on a continental scale. It would involve the coordination of air, naval, and ground forces from a dozen countries. And it would be against the most well equipped, battle-hardened, and ruthlessly dug-in enemy the world had ever seen.

PART ONE

KEUREN

George Marshall

CHAPTER 1

CHURCHILL WAS PREDICTABLY late. Eisenhower, though, was always adamant about being on time. He had gotten up before dawn and driven through a rainstorm to catch his flight from Algiers to Malta. The flight was delayed due to weather until near noon, but Eisenhower stuck it out, all with a cold brewing in his head, because Churchill wanted to meet before the big conference in Cairo and, over and above the fact that he was Eisenhower's superior, Winston Churchill was also the prime minister of the British Empire.

Only after Eisenhower arrived in Malta that afternoon did he learn that the weather had also delayed Churchill's flight from Gibraltar. But instead of waiting for the weather to clear, as Eisenhower had done, Churchill opted to sail to Malta instead, a comfortable two-day voyage through the Mediterranean, which, in the middle of November, was as temperate as an English springtime.

It was certainly possible that Churchill was making Eisenhower wait out of spite. They had not seen each other in person for quite a while, and the last time they had communicated about anything, Eisenhower had pissed him off. That September, the British had taken the initiative on what they saw as a target of opportunity in the Aegean. The Italians had surrendered that summer and the British made a move to occupy the Dodecanese, an

Italian archipelago just south of Gallipoli, whose most prominent member was the island of Rhodes.

The British had succeeded in taking the island of Kos, but soon the Germans used their air superiority and the British were holding on by a thread. Churchill had asked Eisenhower to send in reinforcements from the Allied forces in Italy and North Africa, but Eisenhower saw that it was a losing bet. He did not say as much. Instead, he informed Churchill that the Dodecanese were outside his area of authority. That was technically true. He was an Allied commander, serving jointly between the British and American governments, and his area of authority was limited to North Africa (up to the border of Egypt), Sicily, and the Italian peninsula. The Aegean was too far east.

"All I am asking for," Churchill wrote to him, "is the capture of Rhodes and the other islands of the Dodecanese."

Eisenhower, though, continued to resist and persuaded his American superiors to tie his hands. Ultimately, President Roosevelt had to step in, cabling Churchill that "I do not want to force on Eisenhower diversions which limit the prospects for the early successful development of the Italian operations to a secure line north of Rome."

Even after Roosevelt's intervention, Churchill had kept at it, asking that the question be considered again. Eisenhower continued to demur that it would have to be approved by the Combined Chiefs of Staff, the joint war council of British and American military leaders. Churchill called his bluff and proposed that the Combined Chiefs grant Eisenhower authority over the whole Mediterranean. No decision had yet been made on the proposal. But just before Eisenhower had left for Malta, the Germans had expelled the last of the British forces from the Dodecanese.

Churchill's voyage to Malta was scheduled to stop over in Algiers. Eisenhower could have flown back to meet him but opted to take the two days to sleep off his cold. It was his own fault. He had gone out partridge hunting with Walter Bedell Smith, whom everyone called "Beetle." Beetle was formally his chief of staff, and though probably the single person closest to him in Algiers, the two never really connected as buddies outside work. That didn't stop them from trying, though. Hence, the hunting trip. But the weather had been miserable, and they'd gotten soaked to the bone. Predictably, Eisenhower came down with something.

When not in bed resting off his cold, Eisenhower was treated to one of the ancient jewels of the British Empire. Malta was a strategic hub for the Royal Air Force (RAF), and impressively dressed RAF airmen could be seen throughout the island's mosaic of limestone villages, forts, churches, and ancient ruins, all set off from one another by citrus orchards and potato fields. A maze of tunnels had been carved into its foundation over the centuries, a tradition the British had revived in earnest once the threat of German bombardment loomed.

As it happened, W. Averell Harriman was making his own stopover in Malta. Eisenhower had first gotten to know Harriman in the summer of 1942, after General Marshall sent Eisenhower to London as the American commander of the European Theater of Operations, or "ETO."

Harriman was about Eisenhower's age, but the lives that had brought them together on Malta could not have been more different. Harriman had grown up in the same circles as the Roosevelts, a blue blood in Gilded Age New York. He left a career in finance after growing his family's already considerable wealth to become the president's bagman in matters of high diplomacy. Eisenhower had grown up in Abilene, Kansas, where the blood was red and often cast against the umber gray of well-used farm tools. The closest thing to gilded in Abilene was the yellow-green grass that ran along the banks of Mud Creek.

Harriman had what he thought was some juicy gossip to share with Eisenhower. Roosevelt, Harriman said, was planning to appoint General George Marshall to lead the invasion of Europe and to strike the final blow against Hitler. Harriman said all this with that telltale accent of the northeastern aristocracy of his day. His unhesitating confidence that he knew all there was to know meant that his heavy black eyebrows almost never moved when he talked.

This gossip, however, was stale. Of course it would be Marshall. General George Catlett Marshall was the most respected military man in the United States, if not the world, and arguably more powerful than Roosevelt on matters of war and peace. It had gotten to the point that if Marshall came asking for something on Capitol Hill, lawmakers would demand to know if he wanted it or if he was "speaking for the president." Marshall had the power to kill a whole initiative simply by saying that he was there at Roosevelt's behest. But if he wanted it, he got it. Democrat or Republican, Marshall was the one man whom everyone agreed with.

In fact, Eisenhower had all but ensured that General Marshall would lead the invasion of France. Back in February 1942, Eisenhower had been promoted to head the army's War Plans Division, which was expanded and reorganized as the Operations Division the following month to serve as the War Department's command post in Washington. Eisenhower had basically drafted the two-stage strategic plan for winning the war in Europe that the Allies were now launching. The first stage was a gradual, but massive, buildup of American military personnel and firepower in the United Kingdom, an operation code-named "Bolero." Then, at stage two, the Allies would reach "the critical point in our war effort," and mount an invasion of France across the English Channel, when it would be necessary for "the Chief of Staff, himself, to proceed to London and take over command."

The real juicy piece of gossip that Harriman offered, though, was what Roosevelt was planning to do once General Marshall came to England. Harriman told Eisenhower that it had been discussed in detail and the only man that Churchill would accept as the new army chief of staff was . . . well . . . Dwight D. Eisenhower.

It was the top job in the US Army, and Eisenhower was obviously flattered. The president of the United States and the prime minister of the British Empire not only knew who he was, but bandied his name about with George Marshall's.

Despite Harriman's evident satisfaction at being the first to know what was what, Eisenhower had already heard that this was a possibility. The secretary of the navy, Frank Knox, had visited Algiers in October and told Eisenhower in confidence that he was in line to be chief of staff. Beetle had heard similar rumors during a trip to Washington earlier that month, and Harriman now seemed to confirm it.

It was a tremendous honor and would give Eisenhower the chance to get back to his wife, Mamie, whom he had not seen for eighteen months. The day before Eisenhower left for Malta had been Mamie's birthday. November 14, one month exactly after his. He had just turned fifty-three, she was now forty-seven, and they had been together for twenty-seven years and four months. He had proposed on Valentine's Day, which added another fourteenth on the calendar to celebrate. He had asked for her hand and presented a miniature version of his West Point class ring, a military academy tradition. Mamie had balked, though. She would agree to marry him only if he gave her a full-size West Point class ring. It was that kind of pepper that had charmed Eisenhower when they first met, and he duly obliged.

He had sent Mamie two pairs of silk Italian stockings for her birthday, which he jokingly called the "socks" she had requested. He also took the time to write her a long letter about his day-to-day life as the Allied commander in Algiers. He went into detail about his "happy family" of staff, his "Official Family," while mindfully assuring her that "you're often talked about."

There was Butch, the charming former CBS News executive, Harry Butcher, to handle his diary and visitors. There was Ernest "Tex" Lee, to manage the office and transportation. There was Mrs. Kay Summersby, "my driver & secretary" whose duties in addition to chauffeuring were limited to handling the "unofficial mail from unknown people." There was Mickey McKeogh, whom Mamie had first hired to do odd jobs around their house in the summer of 1941. Now Mickey was Eisenhower's personal orderly and "chief factotum."

Rounding things out, there were some "stenographers and clerks," whose names Eisenhower couldn't quite recall, a few "WACs," and the kitchen and housekeeping staff. Chief among those was Corporal Henry Clay Williams, who dressed in an immaculate white jacket and would announce meals with a pomp befitting a president; and Sergeant John Moaney, who was his personal butler and the most furiously loyal member of his Official Family. "That is the whole group. All are nice—and I think are personally devoted to me. So far it's been quite a happy family."

Eisenhower spent most evenings with Butch, Kay, and a rotation of old buddies, such as Georgie Patton, and Everett Hughes, who served as Eisenhower's deputy theater commander, and who could all reliably round out a bridge game, share a film, or unwind with a drink. The folks back in Kansas might not approve, but who could fault the man leading the Allies to victory against Hitler for enjoying a highball of whiskey in the privacy of his Official Family?

Eisenhower had been in the Mediterranean for over a year and felt that he had learned something. He knew the geography, the people, the politics. He had spent months developing a relationship with Pietro Badoglio, who now headed the anti-Fascist Italian government. They were making progress up the boot toward Rome. All of that and more made the prospect of being promoted to the top job in the army an honor that Eisenhower dreaded.

Leaving now would not only throw all of Eisenhower's successes to chance, but it would also deprive him of even-greater victories ahead. He had wanted to be a general since he was a little boy, and that did not mean politicking from an office in the Pentagon. It was not even obvious that he would survive in the job. Being chief of staff meant that he would be in the extremely awkward position of supervising George Marshall in Europe and his other former boss and mentor, Douglas MacArthur, in the Pacific. Even if Roosevelt declared him Sultan, no one would back his judgment over that of his ostensible subordinates to the east and west.

The threat of promotion was enough to make Eisenhower regret having given up his former job as the army's commanding general for the European Theater of Operations. Eisenhower had basically created that job too and designed it to ensure that whoever occupied the position would play a leading role in the invasion of France. Its major responsibility was to manage the massive logistical demands of the Operation Bolero buildup in the United Kingdom. While still head of the Operations Division, Eisenhower had gone to England in the spring of 1942 on a fact-finding trip to figure out why Operation Bolero was having difficulty getting off the ground. He came back and recommended that the American general then in charge be fired, concluding, "It is necessary to get a punch behind the job or we'll never be ready by Spring 1943, to attack. We must get going!"

At the time, Eisenhower had been an important, but entirely deskbound brigadier general. General Marshall had even told him to expect spending the rest of the war at his desk. But then Marshall took his recommendation, fired the American commander of the European Theater of Operations, and picked Eisenhower to replace him. That day was the first time in a decade that Eisenhower had imagined big things for himself. In his diary he wrote, "If U.S. and U.K. stay squarely behind Bolero, it will be the biggest American job of the war." He scolded himself for nurturing the fantasy that he might even be the one to lead the invasion of Europe. But, if he did a good job with Operation Bolero, Eisenhower would be the natural person to serve as General Marshall's second in command.

A lot, though, had changed over the intervening eighteen months. The biggest was that Eisenhower's initial plan for invading France in 1943 had been postponed in favor of expelling the Axis powers from North Africa, an operation code-named "Torch." The buildup under Operation Bolero would continue. But the Allied invasion of France across the English Channel was deferred indefinitely.

With the switch to Operation Torch, Eisenhower took a chance on getting himself closer to the action. When asked for his thoughts on who should lead the invasion of North Africa, Eisenhower took the uncharacteristic step of including his own name on the list, along with those of Omar Bradley and George Patton. He was not particularly qualified for the job. He had never served as a field commander, and never fired a shot in anger. But he was well liked by the British, who saw him as General Marshall's "well trained and loyal subordinate." And so, he got the chance he had dreamed of since he was a little boy, to lead men in battle.

Becoming the supreme commander for Operation Torch had given Eisenhower the lofty title "Commander-in-Chief, Allied Forces, North Africa," but it meant that Eisenhower was replaced as the commanding general of the European Theater of Operations by another protégé of General Marshall, Jacob Devers. Operation Bolero was now Devers's responsibility, meaning that Devers—not Eisenhower—would be the inevitable deputy when Marshall came to England.

Chatting with Harriman in Malta, though, gave Eisenhower a glimmer that he might avoid exile to the Pentagon. Roosevelt, Harriman explained, was "very reluctant to allow General Marshall to leave Washington." In addition to being indispensable, Roosevelt was facing opposition on Capitol Hill and from the rest of the Joint Chiefs of Staff, who doubted that Eisenhower was up to the job. It was nothing personal. But the sun never set on the American military. There was no one, not even Roosevelt, who had Marshall's literally global understanding of the war. Admiral Ernest King, the head of the navy, had told Roosevelt with usual bluntness, "We have the winning combination here in Washington. Why break it up?"

No one knew, really knew, what Roosevelt would do. Even his wife would complain that the president had a unique talent for convincing everyone that he agreed with them. The key was that he always listened to everyone. And when they sought his approval, Roosevelt would mumble ambiguously as he nodded his head, being careful to never actually say yes or no. Just an ambiguous mumble and a nod, which meant nothing more (at least to him) than that he had listened carefully.

But if Roosevelt didn't give General Marshall the job, that created an even bigger problem over who would get it. That question was on Churchill's mind as well, when he finally arrived that Wednesday evening.

CHURCHILL WAS INCUBATING a cold of his own. But he was in a jaunty mood and seemed to have let go of any grudge over the Dodecanese. It had been a little more than a year since the Allies had invaded North Africa and, there being something of a lull in the war, the prime minister was keen to relish their achievements. And as if to show that bygones were bygones,

Churchill even presented Eisenhower with a special variation of the "Africa Star" medal that he had ordered to be made just for Eisenhower and his British deputy in North Africa, General Harold "Alex" Alexander.

Churchill had been a legend for as long as Eisenhower knew who he was. They had first been in the same room together around Christmas 1941, though Churchill had no reason to remember. He was there with the top British military brass for the Washington Conference, at which the United Kingdom and the United States formally joined their collective strength into a working military alliance. That was where the Combined Chiefs of Staff was created. Cochaired by British Field Marshal John Dill and American Admiral William Leahy, both éminences grises, it paired the heads of the British and American armies, navies, and air forces into a global war council against the Axis powers. The Combined Chiefs would supervise the war and across the world "supreme commanders" would be appointed to lead joint operations in different theaters.

Formally a collaboration among equals, America was decidedly the junior partner in the endeavor. To be sure, Roosevelt had worked to rally the United States' vast industrial capacity into the "Arsenal of Democracy." But the British Empire claimed twelve million square miles of the earth's surface and nearly a quarter of its people.

It was not just that Britain, led so iconically by Churchill, had stood alone in staring down Hitler. It had stood for something while America stood on the sidelines. An Australian historian of the British Empire captured this sentiment in the 1943 book *Argument for Empire*. "In an illiberal age, the British government has retained liberal ideas about public opinion and truth." Though the product of a bit of horse trading, it was thoroughly unsurprising that the first supreme commander, whose mandate covered a swath of southern Asia from Burma to the Philippines, was British.

The first time Eisenhower was introduced to Churchill was during his fact-finding trip to England back in the spring of 1942. He received an invitation to a party at the prime minister's country retreat, Chequers, where he was, in truth, something of plus-one to the actual guests, such as Averell Harriman. That night, the Royal Air Force had conducted its largest air raid over Germany to date, against the city of Cologne, and the guests stayed up late into the night to find out the results.

It wasn't until Eisenhower returned to London as the commander of the European Theater of Operations that Churchill made him the guest of honor at Chequers. It was July 5, and despite having celebrated the previous day's holiday, Eisenhower suffered a severe case of Anglophilia.

The Chequers estate dated back to 1060, six years before the Norman Conquest. Churchill had put Eisenhower up in Chequers's grand manor house, itself dating to 1480. His room was dominated by an imposing portrait of Oliver Cromwell and an enormous canopy bed made of ornately carved black oak. On the finely inlaid wood desk, there was a book on the history of Chequers, which offered the stories behind its furniture, art, and legendary occupants. As he leafed through it, Eisenhower saw a chapter on the very room in which he was standing. This had been the bedchamber of Oliver Cromwell, whose son-in-law had been a prior owner and who, at least according to the book, had worked at the inlaid wood desk.

Dinner had not been until nine at night, after which Churchill invited Eisenhower to his private movie theater to watch *The Tuttles of Tahiti*. The combination of the lubricated dinner and the ribald comedy put everyone in a good mood, and Eisenhower stayed up with Churchill until two thirty in the morning in awe of the man's limitless energy, never stopping, interrupted constantly by aides with reports from around the empire, and always happy to pour another. When the news was good, Churchill became incandescent. When the news was bad, he was dour. Back and forth, covering every conceivable point on the globe.

It was then that Churchill had worked Eisenhower over on the desirability of invading North Africa or Norway, instead of France. A cross-Channel invasion, Churchill thought, would be slaughter. "We are not strong enough, either in the air, or on the ground, or with landing craft to make the operation a success and stay on the continent this year."

Eisenhower, who as the Operations Division chief had helped draft the plan to invade France, tried to argue. Didn't the same also apply to invading North Africa, or Norway? And wasn't part of the goal to help the Russians? If they attacked North Africa, Eisenhower doubted if that "would divert from the Russian front a single German division or a single German airplane."

Churchill confidently assured him that the Germans would counterattack wherever the Allies attacked. And the French in North Africa would not fight Americans. The English, of course, were different. The French would fight bitterly against the English. That tradition was over a thousand years old (not to mention Britain's rather merciless sinking of the French fleet in

North Africa back in 1940). But the Americans and the French were old friends, as the previous day's anniversary was a reminder.

Eisenhower was less sure, but it was the middle of the night. Churchill could have kept going. Eisenhower could not.

Before getting into his enormous canopy bed, though, Eisenhower realized that Mickey had forgotten to pack him his pajamas. Churchill thought nothing of it, and saw to it that Eisenhower got one of his nightshirts. Now, alone in Oliver Cromwell's bedroom, Eisenhower undressed and discovered that the shirt was both too short and so large that it billowed around him. Thinking it better than nothing, Eisenhower went to sleep.

That night, Eisenhower had a nightmare that he was being strangled. Trying to keep up with Churchill's drinking certainly did not help. But Eisenhower was also, at that moment in his life, suffocating under the strain. He had spent the majority of his career as the quintessential staff officer; the planner of other people's decisions. Being in command was something else. It meant being throttled from all sides by incessant demands.

In his first week in the United Kingdom, Eisenhower had been flown to Scotland, Ireland, and the south of England, and met with politicians, ambassadors, generals, and admirals, not to mention an uncountable number of people claiming to be well-wishers. On July 4, he had been invited by the US ambassador, John Gilbert Winant, to what he was told would be an intimate, if ironic, celebration of American independence that, upon his arrival, he discovered involved a receiving line of 2,560 people each seeking to make an impression. He wrote to Mamie that he had become "a bit of a diplomat-lawyer-promoter-salesman-social hound-liar (at least to get out of social affairs)-mountebank-actor-Simon Legree-humanitarian-orator and incidentally (sometimes I think most damnably incidentally) a soldier!" He was desperate for just a moment to think.

In his nightmare, Eisenhower clawed at his neck and felt the noose tightening. The shock of it startled him awake. And when he reached for where the noose had been, he found Churchill's oversized nightshirt, which had rolled up his body and become tangled around his neck. He pulled himself free and slept the rest of the night naked in Oliver Cromwell's bedroom, relieved to be alive, but furious at Mickey.

Eisenhower awoke the next morning at 7:45 beneath the portrait of Cromwell looking down at him. Cromwell, as always, bore the snarl of a man who seemed to have just smelled burning trash.

Churchill was nowhere to be found, but his staff had prepared Eisenhower a breakfast of fried eggs and ham and arranged for a guard of honor to perform a stunning series of drills before he left later that morning. Eisenhower couldn't help but notice that every single one of the soldiers in the guard of honor was taller than he was.

A LOT HAD changed over the ensuing year and a half. Despite a less than impressive start with Operation Torch, Eisenhower had succeeded in leading Allied victories across the Mediterranean by holding together a rickety coalition of British and American air, sea, and ground forces. He was being talked about for big things. But Eisenhower was still awed by Churchill's imperturbable confidence, his ease in knowing that he was Winston Leonard Spencer Churchill.

Eisenhower had heard that when Churchill visited the White House the previous summer, he also had forgotten his pajamas. But instead of borrowing something, he just strutted around his room nude, regardless of the time of day. Supposedly, Roosevelt had rolled in on him and Churchill just stood there in his naked cupid glory, saying, "As we said last night we have nothing to conceal."

It was not just Churchill, though. The British Empire remained a thing of awe. Churchill was in Malta, a British possession, on his way to a conference with Roosevelt that would take them first to Cairo, in the British territory of Egypt, and then on to Tehran, which Britain and the Soviets had jointly acquired in 1941. The day Churchill arrived in Malta, Eisenhower had received a cable from Roosevelt warning that the location of the conference in Cairo had been compromised. The Nazis might be infiltrating the ancient city with spies and assassins. But this was not an insuperable problem, as Roosevelt himself suggested. They could simply divert a thousand miles deeper into Africa to Khartoum, in the British possession of what is today Sudan. Churchill was doubtful that Khartoum had adequate accommodations. But there was always Malta. Churchill was already there.

Eisenhower recommended keeping things in Cairo, just with added security. But the very problem and its many solutions took for granted that they all could go anywhere for thousands of miles in nearly any direction without ever leaving the realm of the British Empire.

At dinner, Churchill was fully clothed and as keen to talk about the plan to invade France as he had been back at Chequers a year and a half earlier. Now the operation was code-named "Overlord." The original plan had been for a Brit to lead the invasion. It was launching from England, after all, and

Churchill confided to Eisenhower that he had promised the position to Sir Alan Brooke. The Chief of the Imperial General Staff, Brooke was the head of the British Army and George Marshall's counterpart on the British Chiefs.

That would have left Eisenhower in the Mediterranean, where he was happy. And it would have made Alan Brooke happy too. But Roosevelt had reopened the subject at the Quebec Conference that summer and indicated his strong preference for an American commander, given the size of the American contribution to Operation Bolero and, not for nothing, 1944 was an election year. Churchill had readily agreed in exchange for making British generals the supreme commanders in Southeast Asia and the Mediterranean. Operation Overlord would be something for the history books. But when it came down to it, Asia and the Mediterranean were of greater importance to the empire than France. Churchill mentioned to Eisenhower under his breath that it had been quite awkward to break the news to Alan Brooke, who took it rather badly.

There was still a back-and-forth, though, because of how important General Marshall was in Washington. One idea was to put Alan Brooke in command of the invasion and to make Marshall's role as supreme commander more remote, more ceremonial. This would leave Eisenhower in the Mediterranean, but Churchill didn't like the idea, if only because it would make a mess of the Combined Chiefs of Staff system.

Another idea being floated was to put a British general, such as Sir John Dill, in the ceremonial position as supreme commander, with American generals in charge of different regions around Europe. But General Marshall, at least, did not seem to like that proposal. Churchill added, gratuitously, that if the supreme commander was to be an American, there were only two men he would accept: Marshall or Eisenhower.

Churchill's suggestion that Eisenhower could do the job was not entirely serious, though it had been floated before. Back in September, the syndicated columnist David Lawrence, who had known Eisenhower's brother Milton for years, made a conspicuous point of noting that, if General Marshall was "needed more at Washington than in Europe, then General Eisenhower would seem to be the logical choice for over-all commander." But that was just a journalist's armchair speculations.

"With General Marshall in command," Churchill announced to the table, "we shall have no fear but that the operation will have an abundance of American power." He then turned to Eisenhower rather apologetically. "Eisenhower," he said, "I'm sure you realize, my dear General, that we are quite happy with you, but it would obviously be unfair to us to be foreclosed from both major commands in Europe."

Eisenhower forced himself to agree amicably.

But Churchill remained unconvinced about the wisdom of invading France. He portended the "Channel tides running red with Allied blood" and "Beaches choked with the bodies of the flower of American and British manhood." He had long preferred attacking Germany from the south, what he rather casually referred to as the "soft underbelly of Europe." He envisioned the Allies working like Phoenicians from the Maghreb to Sicily to the Dodecanese archipelago and then into the mainland of Europe via Greece or, ideally, the Balkans.

Churchill was preparing to go to Cairo for a fight, convinced that the Allies should press their advantage and to make the Mediterranean the central front of the war. Should Churchill get his way, Eisenhower could stay put in the Mediterranean, and not suffer a return to a desk in Washington.

Franklin Roosevelt

CHAPTER 2

"WILL PROCEED TO Cairo as planned," President Roosevelt cabled from the USS *Iowa*, just as Eisenhower was getting back to Algiers. It was a good thing too. Eisenhower's cold was not getting better, and even the thought of all that it would take to redirect an entire summit to Khartoum in two days was daunting.

Eisenhower had gotten word only a few weeks earlier that Roosevelt was coming. Henry Morgenthau, the treasury secretary, had come to North Africa to assess the economic situation and handed Eisenhower a personal note from the president. "Don't tell anybody," it had said, "but it is possible that I may see you in a little over a month—probably in north Africa. My best wishes to you."

Eisenhower flew to Oran, Algeria, to welcome not just Roosevelt, but nearly everyone in the United States government who mattered when it came to waging the Second World War. General Marshall was there, along with Ernest King for the navy and Henry "Hap" Arnold for the air force, as well as William Leahy, the American cochair of the Combined Chiefs. There were also Brehon "Bill" Somervell and Charles "Savvy" Cooke, who were each responsible for ensuring that everything the army and navy needed was built and delivered; Harry Hopkins, Roosevelt's "special envoy," who was more aptly described as the president's right hand for nearly everything that mattered; Wilson Brown, the president's naval aid; Edwin "Pa" Watson, his de facto chief of staff; and Ross McIntire, his personal physician.

Transporting all this brass and their staffs, a total of ninety-three people who each required baggage, lodging, food, and a demonstration of comfort that matched their self-importance, required nine dedicated aircraft, fifteen cars, and two GMC 6×6 "Jimmy" trucks. The operation to assemble all these giants together in North Africa and then safely deliver them to the summit with the British in Cairo was given the self-aware code name "Operation Adult."

The USS *Iowa* had been a floating war cabinet for the previous week. At 888 feet long, a beam of more than 108 feet, and square footage spanning 9.5 acres, it was the largest man-o'-war in the US fleet. A lucky U-boat could have decapitated the whole of the American command. And just five days earlier, it seemed that such had been the fate of the free world when a torpedo nearly missed. It had been a tense moment, with the explosion under the water and the urgent announcement, "This is not a drill." The torpedo, though, was not German but an accidental fire from a nearby American ship.

The *Iowa* approached the Barbary Coast at 7:15 a.m. It was a cool fifty degrees, and the sky was blindingly clear. It was a break from the soupiness that had pervaded Oran for the previous few days.

Eisenhower was intent on personally welcoming the president and escorting him for the fifty-mile drive to La Sienna airport. The Secret Service had objected and Eisenhower had gotten his back up. This was his theater. But before things turned ugly, Butch intervened with his trademark charm to negotiate the Secret Service into "permitting" it.

Eisenhower stood on the docks with two of the president's sons, Elliott and Franklin Jr. Both were serving in North Africa. Eisenhower did not know Franklin Jr. well, but Elliott had become a regular pal. He was a frequent guest at Eisenhower's villa in Algiers, since he could more than hold his own in a game of bridge. He was also a fun guy to be around. A colonel with the Army Air Forces, Elliott had a reputation for risk-taking that put his superiors, most particularly Jimmy Doolittle, in a constant state of anxiety over whether they would be responsible for the loss of the president's son. Eisenhower, though, had little reason to give Doolittle any sympathy. Eisenhower had to regularly scold Doolittle to stop flying on missions with his men.

Through binoculars, Eisenhower could make out the shape of a man being lowered into a whaleboat next to the USS *Iowa*. Even at a distance, he was unmistakable. *That's Roosevelt.* With his cigarette holder jutting up from that singular chin, there was no one else it could be.

For the next twenty minutes, Eisenhower's welcome party watched as the president reclined with the sun and wind bathing his brow and the snowcapped Atlas Mountains in the distance. And then, just before nine, there it was. The smiling face of Franklin Delano Roosevelt.

"Roosevelt weather!" the president said with a jaunty wave to all those who had come to greet him. Eisenhower crowded into the car with the president and his sons, and the motorcade thundered through the streets of Oran, a swarm of motorcycles, Secret Service cars, followed by more cars, then another swarm of motorcycles, followed by more cars. All along the streets and at every curve and intersection were soldiers standing sentry and ever-growing crowds eager to see the fuss.

Roosevelt was ebullient. He chatted with his sons about the news from home and his anticipation of the days ahead, particularly getting the chance to meet Joseph Stalin for the first time. But it was more than that. There was a sense that after two brutal years of war, victory was at hand.

"The war—and the peace. Can you wait, Ike?" Roosevelt asked, bringing him into the conversation.

"Just about, sir," Eisenhower replied awkwardly.

Eisenhower did not really know the president he had served all these years. In the 1930s, Eisenhower was not a fan. He was quiet about it, seeing as he was only a major in the army at the time. But, if asked in private, he would say, "I think Mr. Roosevelt is a mediocre man who has a pleasant-sounding voice on the radio."

Their first meeting had been brief. Eisenhower had gone in to see him for a ceremonial farewell with Mark "Wayne" Clark, who had been one of Eisenhower's best friends and his partner in mounting the invasion of North Africa. Churchill had been in Washington, and Roosevelt made a point of saying how impressed he was by Eisenhower's younger brother Milton. There were, the president explained, four different departments in the midst of an "inter-bureau war" over where Milton, the boy wonder, should go. It was taking up all his time, the president joked.

"My brother is a very able man," Eisenhower said stiffly.

"I am well aware of that fact," Roosevelt replied. "That was the whole reason for the war."

They had met again, also briefly, at the Casablanca Conference in January 1943. Roosevelt had taken the chance for daylong tours with Wayne

Clark and George Patton. Eisenhower, though, had garnered little more than Roosevelt's disdain, given the lack of progress. Eisenhower had been sick with the flu and was all nerves knowing that his "neck was in a noose." An operation that was initially expected to last weeks had been dragging on for months. Even General Marshall thought he was out of his depth. Eisenhower had heavy-handedly imposed censorship to thwart negative publicity, which soon became its own negative publicity. And then there was the Darlan affair.

At the outset of the North Africa campaign, Eisenhower had reached a negotiated settlement with Admiral François Darlan, an unapologetic collaborator and anti-Semite with blood on his hands for what would in time be called the Holocaust. Eisenhower thought that the French were an "extremely legalistic race—they insist on legitimate succession of power." Darlan would therefore stay in control of French civil affairs in North Africa in exchange for complete surrender. To Eisenhower, the deal was obvious and those who were in the know had anticipated it for months. It offered the chance to capture Tunisia quickly. "Whatever would help at the moment," Eisenhower would explain. "You have to do that when you're in command. You have to think logically."

But then Tunisia remained out of reach. Having yielded none of its objectives, the deal began to stink. Everyone with an opinion denounced it as contrary to the very values the Allies were fighting for. And the Oxbridge set, who held their posts in His Majesty's Foreign Office like their memberships in any one of London's other invitation-only clubs, relished the chance to tut-tut their callow American cousins for their amateurish play at the gentleman's game of Olde World diplomacy.

Wayne Clark had negotiated and signed the deal. But Eisenhower took full responsibility. The press seemed to turn on him overnight, and Eisenhower grew cynical about how everyone was now competing to demonstrate their dislike of François Darlan in a competition of virtuous loathing.

Eisenhower smiled his way through it, but it destabilized him. He thought of what his son must be thinking, and even made a point of writing him a letter with the joking assurance, "You are learning that it is easy enough for a man to be a newspaper hero, one day, and a bum the next. The answer is that just as one must not let his head get swelled too much by a bit of a claim, he must not be too upset and irritated when the pack turns on him."

At the Casablanca Conference, Eisenhower took the chance to apologize personally to Roosevelt. "Generals could be repudiated and fired," he told the president, "but governments could not afford to make such mistakes."

Roosevelt laughed him off and told him that he should "go ahead and make mistakes." He could be "reasonably sure that he would be backed up." *Reasonably.*

Roosevelt's willingness to forgive had no doubt been helped by Darlan's assassination on Christmas Eve 1942 by hitmen tied to the French general in exile, Charles de Gaulle. At Casablanca, Darlan was in the past. But Roosevelt was less forgiving about the future.

"How long'll it take to finish the job?" demanded Roosevelt.

"Can I have one 'if,' sir?" Eisenhower asked.

Roosevelt scoffed.

"With any kind of break in the weather, sir," Eisenhower said, "we'll have 'em all either in the bag or in the sea by late spring."

"What's late spring mean? June?"

"Maybe as early as the middle of May. June at the latest."

Roosevelt was less than impressed, and the British were proposing various ideas to sideline Eisenhower and take over the North Africa campaign themselves. A few days later, when General Marshall suggested that Eisenhower be promoted to the rank of four-star general to give him more authority when dealing with his British counterparts, Roosevelt had been snide. The president said that he would approve a promotion for Eisenhower only "when there was some damn good reason to do it."

At the White House Correspondents Dinner the following month, Roosevelt made a show of his faith in Eisenhower, saying, "I spent many hours in Casablanca with this young general—a descendant of Kansas pioneers. I know what a fine, tough job he has done and how carefully and skillfully he is directing the soldiers under him. I want to say to you tonight—and to him—that we have every confidence in his leadership." But Eisenhower knew, everyone knew, that he was hanging by a thread.

Since then, Eisenhower had earned his fourth star. And he had made good on his promise of victory in North Africa, just ahead of schedule. On May 9, 1943, the American army under Omar Bradley captured Tunis. Bradley sent Eisenhower a cable saying simply, "Mission accomplished." Less than a week later, a quarter-million Axis soldiers surrendered in the last act of the North Africa campaign.

That Roosevelt was now calling him "Ike" was certainly a good sign. But unlike Churchill, the president called everyone nicknames. The only exception was General Marshall, and that was not for a lack of trying. When Marshall became chief of staff, Roosevelt had asked, "Can I call you George?" Marshall had responded, "It's General Marshall, sir."

Roosevelt respected Marshall's formality, at least to his face. Behind his back, Roosevelt had devised code names for the men running the Allied war, each glibly taken from the house staff at his country home in Hyde Park. Churchill was "Moses Smith," after one of Hyde Park's long-term tenants. Marshall was code-named "Plog," after Hyde Park's superintendent. And betraying his view of the man he was now chummily calling Ike, Eisenhower was christened "Keuran," the name of Plog's assistant.

When they arrived at the airport in Le Sienna and drove up to the waiting C-54s, Roosevelt brought Eisenhower onto his plane and left Marshall to fly behind him in Plane 2. Within fifteen minutes, Plane 1 was in the air, and they tracked the coast, escorted by fighters, as they flew the three and a half hours to Tunis.

The flight was more turbulent than expected due to crosswinds. The view was clear, though. And from overhead, it was easy to see why the fighting had been so much more bitter than expected in the optimistic days of November 1942. The terrain was hilly. There were few real roads and fewer places to take cover. There was almost no water to be seen, save for the ocean.

Eisenhower got the sense that Roosevelt was sizing him up, asking him his thoughts on various things military, and not. At one point, Roosevelt even brought up Kay Summersby. How's that "British girl"?

THE PRESIDENTIAL AERO-CADE reached El Aouina airport near Tunis around two p.m. The wreckage of the vanquished Luftwaffe still littered the tarmac. The usual paranoia of the Secret Service had led to a swap in the landing order, so that Plane 2, carrying General Marshall, was directed to land first, making old Plog the royal taster. When the presidential plane finally taxied to a stop, a clutch of soldiers busily assembled for Roosevelt. Eisenhower was the first to step out and looked about until he spotted Kay with the car.

Roosevelt was wheeled down behind him and lifted into the back seat. But before Kay could drive away, a Secret Service agent stopped the car.

"You can't drive," he told her sternly. "The sergeant will take over!"

Kay got out, a sergeant got in, and they were off.

It was twelve miles to Carthage and the route took them past all the ancient ruins. When they reached the famous amphitheater, Roosevelt asked to stop to get a better look, just like any other tourist. He had never been to this legendary part of the world. And there it was.

They eventually pulled up to a villa on the shore of the Gulf of Tunis between the cobblestoned Sidi Bou Said neighborhood to the north and the mythic Carthage to the south. It had been the German commander's residence during the Axis occupation of Tunisia. When Eisenhower had taken it over, it was rechristened the "White House." With Roosevelt in town, it was only fitting that Eisenhower cede it to the White House's usual occupant.

They were in the library of the White House, and Eisenhower was standing by the fireplace when Butch came in. Eisenhower gravitated toward fireplaces, not the least because it gave him a discreet place to dispose of his cigarette butts. Kay had just driven Butch, Harry Hopkins, and Ernest King from El Aouina, and she was waiting outside if Eisenhower needed her.

Roosevelt took conspicuous delight in the news of Kay's arrival. He told Butch to go fetch her. And before long, there she was. Tall and slim with dark hair and wise eyes, an Irish Catholic whose peppy insouciance could be lethally charming.

Eisenhower was prone to puppy love. He still wrote a schoolboy's quantity of exclamation points in his letters to Mamie. And Kay was a very easy woman for an old and lonely dog to love.

After knowing her only a few months, Eisenhower had confided to his buddy Everett Hughes that whenever he saw her, "I want to hold her hand." In public, Eisenhower kept a poker face and seemed to treat Kay the same as everyone else. But he would subtly slip her little notes when he was thinking of her, saying things like, "Irish, How about lunch, tea & dinner today? If yes: Who else do you want, if any? At which time? How are you?" He thought of her as one of the closest people to him in the world.

"Mr. President," Eisenhower announced, "this is Miss Kay Summersby, the British girl you asked about."

"I've heard quite a bit about you," Roosevelt said, shaking her hand. "Why didn't you drive me from the plane? I've been looking forward to it."

"Mr. President." Kay blushed. "Your Secret Service wouldn't let me drive!"

"Would you like to drive me from now on?"

"It would be a privilege, sir."

"Very well. You should drive me then. I'm going on an inspection trip soon." Roosevelt gave Kay a friendly that-will-be-all-dear nod, and she went back outside. He then turned to Eisenhower and invited him to join him for an intimate dinner with his two sons and a few carefully selected guests. But, the president insisted, Eisenhower needed to be sure to bring Kay along as his date.

GENERAL MARSHALL WAS not invited to dinner. Nor were Ernest King or Hap Arnold. In fairness, the rollicking dinners Roosevelt enjoyed throwing were not the kind of thing Marshall seemed to enjoy. Marshall could dominate any room with the look on his face. But there was a reticence to him, a shyness in social settings, that confounded Eisenhower.

Eisenhower wasn't sure if there was anyone in the world whom General Marshall would call a buddy. Marshall had only ever called him "Ike" once, by accident, and then repeated the word "Eisenhower" half a dozen times to make sure he understood it was a slip. And Eisenhower, like the president, only ever called him "General Marshall."

With the president in the White House, Eisenhower was sharing a villa with Marshall, as well as King and Arnold, that for some reason had gotten the name Times Square. It was usually occupied by the famous stunt pilot—now general for the Army Air Forces in the Mediterranean—Jimmy Doolittle.

When Eisenhower got back to Times Square, Marshall, King, and Arnold were enjoying a few drinks as they waited to get dinner with Butch. King, faithful to the navy's reputation, had pulled ahead in the number of pours and was keen to gossip. Faithful to his own reputation, Marshall slowly sipped a single glass.

King brought up the scuttlebutt on everyone's lips. Who would lead Operation Overlord?

"This is the President's decision," Marshall said. "I haven't a thing to do with it."

"Well, General," Eisenhower quipped, "if you haven't, it's certain that I haven't a thing to do with it."

Eisenhower had gotten to know the bony-faced King at the start of the war, when he was working under Marshall in Washington. He had thought little of King's intelligence, and even less of his bullying pettiness. In his diary, Eisenhower had written after one particularly long day, "One thing that might help win this war is to get someone to shoot King." The man seemed allergic to cooperation, even when it was in his interest.

So it was a bit of a surprise when King started gushing about how much he would miss General Marshall. "We now have a winning combination," he said. "Why do we want to make a radical change? Each of us knows his own role; each of us has learned how to work with the others." Turning to Eisenhower, King added, "Why doesn't the President send you up to Overlord and keep General Marshall in Washington? Marshall is the truly indispensable man of this war."

It was as if King were giving a toast. Hap Arnold agreed. And Marshall stayed implacable as always. (Those who knew him, however, knew that when Marshall was feeling pressed, the corners of his mouth would pull into what could only be described as a pained smile.)

Eisenhower, for his part, kept his genial poker face and King boozily apologized for putting Eisenhower on the spot, assuring him that he didn't have to say anything.

Eisenhower tried to change the subject. He shared the gossip he had gotten from Churchill about Alan Brooke and his disappointment at not getting to command Operation Overlord. General Marshall couldn't help but laugh at the irony. Brooke had long opposed the invasion of France and by all lights continued to oppose it. Funny how a heroic opportunity can change a man's opinion of a situation.

Eisenhower bid his betters a good night and King walked him out, saying, "I hate to lose General Marshall as Chief of Staff, but my loss is consoled by the knowledge that I will have you to work with in his job."

Eisenhower flashed an embarrassed glance at Marshall, who had not yet said anything to Eisenhower about his being promoted to chief of staff. Marshall just sat stone-faced, his glass of sherry still quite full, as Eisenhower blushed his way out the door.

DINNER WAS AT eight. Roosevelt was keen to have Kay sit near him and peppered her with questions: How had she been during the Blitz? What were the roles of British women in the war? Were women in the factories? What about women bus conductors, known as "clippies"? How had that all worked?

Kay was full of opinions. She had driven ambulances for the Motor Transport Corps throughout London during the Blitz. She came from a military family. Her father, Donald MacCarthy-Morrogh, had served in Gallipoli, when she was six. He died young, though not in Gallipoli. He lived until 1932, the last time Kay had been back to County Cork, or to Ireland, for that matter.

Eventually, Kay felt bold enough to ask a question in return. "Mr. President, will there ever be conscription of women in the United States?"

"No." Roosevelt shook his head. "I'm afraid not. The country would never stand for it."

Roosevelt mentioned that he was due to leave first thing in the morning for Cairo, and Eisenhower interjected.

"A night flight, Sunday night, would be better, sir. Getting you to Cairo in the morning."

"A night flight? Why? I particularly wanted to get a view of the road the battle took, from El Alamein."

"Too risky, sir. We don't want to have to run fighter escort all the way to Cairo, it'd just be asking for trouble. Quite apart from that, the night flight is a much smoother trip."

"But . . ."

"The night flight is S.O.P., sir."

"Standard operating procedure, Pop," Elliott chimed in.

"Thank you," Roosevelt said to his son. "There are a few bits of Army slang with which the Commander-in-Chief is familiar." He then turned back to Eisenhower. "Okay, Ike. You're the boss. But I get something in return."

"What's that, sir?"

"If you're going to make me stay over at Carthage all Sunday, you've got to take me on a personally conducted tour of the battlefields—ancient and modern."

"That's a bargain, sir."

EISENHOWER GOT BACK to Times Square around 10:30. He slept fitfully that night. He got out of bed and milled about in the dark. At one point, Butch found him and asked if he was all right. It was quarter past four in the morning. Eisenhower offered the alibi that he was just looking for an alarm clock. The president was staying, but most everyone else was leaving at 7:30 that morning, and he wanted to see General Marshall to the airport.

They were all up at 5:30 and Eisenhower got in the car with General Marshall to El Aouina. He had asked Butch to take Ernest King and Hap Arnold separately, so he could have a chance to talk to Marshall alone. He and Marshall communicated nearly every day. But the two hadn't gotten to speak in person since before the invasion of Sicily the previous summer.

With Marshall, that mattered. The man was circumspect like a mob boss. He was not only oblique when he wrote, but on the phone, he was so concerned about eavesdroppers that he would talk in impromptu code words that were so opaque, Eisenhower could barely understand him. One time, when he was still in Washington, Eisenhower had become so confused that he just walked around the corner to Marshall's office to confirm what his boss wanted.

"By god," Marshall scolded him, "I spend all this time trying to save you time and you come in here. What is a telephone for?"

"By god," Eisenhower shot back playfully, "it takes me longer to interpret what you are trying to say than to get in here."

General Marshall glowered back and, safe in the privacy of his office, clarified what he wanted in proper English.

With the conferences in Cairo and Tehran coming up, there was a lot that Marshall wanted Eisenhower to know. In particular, he wanted Eisenhower to feel confident that the U.S. Chiefs were fully behind him on the Dodecanese, and that he should not take Churchill's tantrum to heart. American interests in the eastern Mediterranean, he said cryptically, "did not necessarily parallel Britain's."

One thing Eisenhower had not expected was to hear that there was an issue with Mark Clark, who was now leading the American side of the offensive in Italy as the commanding general of the Fifth Army. Marshall wanted Eisenhower to know, presumably on the assumption that he would let his buddy Wayne know, that Marshall was annoyed.

Since the war began, the press had made all sorts of generals and admirals into celebrities. Eisenhower was no exception. His name was in the newspaper almost every day. But Eisenhower was savvy enough to convey a Kansas-bred humility, even embarrassment, about being in the limelight that kept things dignified.

A year earlier, *Life* magazine had done a glowing profile timed to the invasion of North Africa, which opened, "When General Dwight David Eisenhower is confronted by a piece of bad Army paper work or muddled thinking, he does not growl nor explode after the fashion of some other generals. He sighs gloomily, 'That's too complicated for a dumb bunny like me,' or 'I'm just too thick-headed to understand this damn thing. You'll have to make it simpler.'" The piece continued from there, celebrating his "wholesome informality" and how he saw himself as just part of a team.

It was quite another thing to be seen to be enjoying or, worse, seeking celebrity. Marshall thought that was unseemly. They wore a uniform for a reason.

It was not entirely Clark's fault. Five years younger and five inches taller than Eisenhower, he was the only senior general in the army whom the press could honestly package as a heartthrob. What caught Marshall's unforgiving eye was Clark's wife. She was gallivanting around the country making speeches in which she would read from their love letters and parade the pair of pants he had worn during a swashbuckling secret mission in Algiers as if they were a piece of the True Cross. She would say hammy things like, "Mark always wears the pants in our family anyway," and "General Clark lost his pants but annexed Africa."

Clark was becoming the butt of jokes. "Publicity"—Marshall grimaced—"is harmful."

AROUND NOON, KAY drove Eisenhower to the White House to pick Roosevelt up for his tour. Telek, the dog they had adopted into their "Official Family," was in his usual spot in the front with Kay.

As they pulled up, they discovered that the Secret Service had escalated an afternoon of nearby sightseeing into a modest ground offensive. There were more than a dozen cars, jeeps, Jimmy trucks, a weapons carrier, and a swarm of motorcycles poised to make the advance with them. The president, though, was all smiles as he was placed into the back of Kay's Cadillac with his eldest son, Franklin Jr. And soon they were off with one truck of military police ahead of them and another on either side with eight MPs on motorcycles buzzing about to clear traffic as they went through the winding streets of Tunis.

The six months of American presence led inevitably to the gray-marketing of equipment, so that Arabs and French soldiers alike walked about in sold-off uniforms. But ancient Carthage was everywhere: the amphitheaters and temples, marble sculptures of pagan and then Christian and then Muslim religious imagery, old grain vaults, old villas. It was a place where history was all around. Broken stone ruins from the time of Hannibal next to the charred steel of burned-out tanks from the time of Hitler.

Eisenhower had originally promised to take Roosevelt to Bizerte, the city north of Tunis, where the victory in North Africa had been clinched the previous May. But the Secret Service had objected. And so they traveled south into the countryside toward Medjez El Bab. Among the groves of olives, oranges, figs, and grapes were stores of bombs and ammunition, spread over miles to minimize losses in case of an air raid. It was astonishing how few scars of battle remained. Country people in red turbans and long gowns leading their centuries-old country lives, shepherds tending flocks, farmers tilling with horses and oxen. Eisenhower attributed it to precision bombing. The only signs of the extraordinary battle that had been mounted across this place were the occasional husks of tanks, trucks, and other detritus and roped-off plots, marked with the skull and crossbones and the word MINEFIELD.

Like a mine, Telek popped from the front seat with Kay into the back seat. Eisenhower caught the dog midair like a wide receiver.

"I am sorry, Mr. President."

"Come on boy!" Roosevelt said, calling the excited dog over. Roosevelt loved Scotties and asked if Telek was British or American.

Eisenhower revealed that he had come from a mixed marriage. "Trouble is," Eisenhower added, "he's more devoted to Kay than to me. She looks after him so much. Still, I guess I think as much of him, Mr. President, as you do of Fala."

Roosevelt visibly relished the chance to have the dog in his lap. Telek was an active, spoiled, and consequentially mischievous boy, whose wake of chaos was protected from criticism by Eisenhower's unqualified love. He had been a member of the Official Family for nearly the entire war. When Eisenhower arrived in London in the summer of 1942, he had been put up in a lavishly gilt room, suite 408, at Claridge's, which made Eisenhower uncomfortable. He wanted something that looked more American and less like a parlor in which the Marquis de Sade might entertain.

Butch found a Tudor country house in London's outer borough of Kingston upon Thames that was nestled within ten acres of trees, English lawns, and hedges. It was named Telegraph Cottage from when it was part of the semaphore network throughout England, and it became the castle for Eisenhower's Official Family, which was made complete when Kay brought home the dog as a gift for his fifty-second birthday. Eisenhower had named him after Telegraph Cottage and, as Kay would brag, after her: "Tele-K."

Telek, Roosevelt, and Eisenhower sat together in the back, talking about the North Africa campaign, the difficulties of the terrain, and the even greater difficulties of some of the people involved. When Germans under the command of the notorious "Desert Fox," Field Marshal Erwin Rommel, broke through at the Kasserine Pass, the French general Henri Giraud, who had been America's great hope for the future of a Free France, had come storming into Eisenhower's office wailing, "We've lost Tunis!"

Eisenhower had projected the excessive calm that comes easily when confronting a frantic. "No we haven't. We haven't lost anything. Look at the map. Look at the terrain. Even if we weren't able to oppose Rommel with any stronger forces than have faced him thus far, he hasn't enough stuff to follow through. He'll get caught and stopped in the pocket below Kasserine." Thanks to a massive artillery bombardment, the prediction had proved true.

The "bloody nose" Eisenhower took at the Kasserine Pass, though, still smarted. He blamed his subordinates, but never out loud. He instead publicly blamed himself for overextending his strength.

They passed members of a Bedouin tribe with a camel caravan, and before long, there was Hill 609. Shaped like a weathered arrowhead, Hill 609 was a shrubby near-mountain, reaching 2,400 feet high with a clear view of Tunis from its heights. The US Army had tried to take it for three days, with 183 men killed, 1,594 wounded, and 676 captured. It had been the site of the heaviest concentration of artillery fire of the war.

As they continued south, they soon reached Medjez el Bab. Roosevelt spotted a grove and directed Kay toward it, saying, "That's an awfully nice place. Could you pull up there, child, for our little picnic?" Kay promptly turned off the road and the president's convoy abruptly followed.

Eisenhower stepped out, and as he rummaged for their lunch, the head of the Secret Service came running over in a fury. The sudden turn had caused him to lose part of the convoy down the road, and he was frantically assembling guard positions all around their autumn picnic.

"Child," Roosevelt said to Kay, indifferent to the commotion, "won't you come back here and have lunch with the dull old man?"

Kay was flattered and Eisenhower passed them chicken sandwiches through the window, apologizing that there were no vegetables, given the risks of the local water.

Roosevelt was again all questions for Kay, and asked about Dick. Kay's fiancé, Dick Arnold, had been young and exceedingly handsome. Kay was madly in love and Eisenhower had personally approved their request to marry back in March 1943. But then Dick had tragically died after stepping on a mine in North Africa.

As Roosevelt and Kay enjoyed their chicken sandwiches, Eisenhower wandered off to look at some burned-out tanks in the woods. The rest of the convoy also took the chance to mill about the now-quiet battlefield. At one point a squadron of fifty-one medium bombers flew overhead in a V formation, returning from a mission. There were gaps where the planes that had not made it home should have been.

When Eisenhower returned to the car, Roosevelt asked, "Ike, if, one year ago, you had offered to bet that on this day the President of the United States would be having his lunch on a Tunisian roadside, what odds could you have demanded?" The president's only disappointment was that the invasion of North Africa had happened just after the 1942 midterm elections. He gossiped about his disagreements with Churchill, but then was sure to add, "No one could have a better or sturdier ally than that old Tory!"

They were interrupted by Pa Watson, Roosevelt's de facto chief of staff, who cheerily presented them with a horseshoe he had found. Such was the mood that afternoon, that a vice admiral who had been in command in the Pacific when the Japanese attacked Pearl Harbor was as giddy as a young nephew at the discovery of a lucky souvenir. And both Roosevelt and Eisenhower were delighted to pose for a picture celebrating the find.

The convivial mood was broken, though, when the head of the Secret Service came back. "Mr. President, we've been here longer than I like. We should go on now."

Roosevelt shared an eye roll with Eisenhower, and said, "You are lucky you don't have the number of bosses I have."

Kay turned west and then north along the Medjerda River, following the path Africanus Scipio had taken when leading the Roman legions to Carthage at the end of the Second Punic War. Carthage had been subjected to unconditional surrender. And Roosevelt wondered aloud whether any of the battles from the Punic Wars had taken place on the same battlefields as those on which the Allies had fought the Germans.

Eisenhower said he doubted it. Most of the fighting against the Axis had been in the mountains. The terrain would have been bad for Hannibal's war elephants.

Roosevelt lit up at Eisenhower's enthusiasm for and encyclopedic knowledge of ancient military history. Eisenhower had admired Hannibal since he could remember. When he was a boy, the editor of a local newspaper back in Abilene had given him a copy of Thomas Arnold's *Life of Hannibal*. He had a restless boy's fascination with the pagan glory of ancient Greece and Rome, a fascination his very religious mother found so troubling that she locked his books away in a closet (that he would then break into whenever she was out working in the garden). Hannibal had always been a favorite, particularly because his greatness had carried through history even though he had been "written about only by enemies."

Roosevelt was as keenly interested, if not more, in the battles of ancient Carthage as the battles Eisenhower had personally led. And Eisenhower was happy to hold forth with the excitement of the boy he had been, when hiding in his mother's closet. They speculated in earnest about where the

Battle of Zama must have taken place. No historian, so far as Eisenhower was aware, had pinpointed the precise location. But he and the president considered the various contenders as they drove along assessing whether the terrain was suitable for the charge of elephants.

Roosevelt mentioned that he was planning on sending General Marshall to England to lead the invasion of Normandy. He could tell that Marshall clearly wanted it and deserved it. But Eisenhower suspected Roosevelt was conflicted.

"Ike," he said, as if trying to convince himself, "you and I know who was the Chief of Staff during the Civil War. But practically no one else knows, although the names of the field generals are household words. I think that George Marshall is entitled to establish himself in history as a field general."

Roosevelt was ultimately a political animal, though, and the amount of scandal that picking Marshall to lead Operation Overlord invited was a cost that weighed on him. He then broke the news that he was planning on bringing Eisenhower back to Washington to be acting chief of staff. Precisely what "acting" meant was not entirely clear. But Roosevelt wanted him to come personally to Cairo to brief the Combined Chiefs.

Eventually, they reached the crossing at Djedeida and, before long, were back at the White House at close to eight in the evening. Roosevelt and Eisenhower shared a smile. And with a glint in his eye, Roosevelt grabbed him by the arm.

"You know, Ike—I'm afraid I'm going to have to do something to you you won't like." The president let the anxiety linger in the air as if he was considering what he was about to say. "I know what Harry Butcher is to you, Ike. Well, despite the fact that he's your right arm—anyway your left—I may have to take him away from you."

"Well, sir . . ." Eisenhower's smile flattened a touch.

"The point is," Roosevelt assured him, "Elmer Davis has turned in his resignation again. What would you say if I drafted Butch to take over the job?" Butch had been an executive at CBS before the war and would be a natural replacement to head the Office of War Information.

"Well, Mr. President—I won't pretend it wouldn't be tough. But if you need him, if you give the word, the answer is, sure, go ahead."

Roosevelt grinned with satisfaction. "I'll see, Ike. Maybe it won't be necessary. I'll let you know. If you mention it to Butch, be sure and tell him that he was Elmer's own choice for the job. In any case it won't be definite till January."

Soon, Roosevelt was aloft for Cairo.

George "Georgie" Patton

CHAPTER 3

THE DAY BEFORE he was due to leave for Cairo, Eisenhower received a short cable from General Marshall: "Wide publicity in this country on alleged incident in which General Patton is reported to have struck a soldier in the hospital." Eisenhower knew exactly what this was about.

On August 3, 1943, George Patton had been visiting the wounded at a hospital in Sicily. One of the wounded, a private by the name of Charles Kuhl, was not wounded—at least visibly. Kuhl was a carpet layer from Indiana, who had been admitted to the Ninety-Third Evacuation Hospital for severe diarrhea. His original diagnosis was "exhaustion (fear)."

Patton questioned him, and Kuhl said that he "was nervous and couldn't stand it up there." Unknown to either man at the time, Kuhl was in the early stages of malaria.

This admission of weakness provoked Patton to slap him and then spout a fountain of profanity. He reportedly told Kuhl, "You're going back to the front lines and you may get shot and killed, but you're going to fight. If you don't, I'll stand you up against a wall and have a firing squad kill you on purpose." And when this threat failed to have the desired effect, Patton reached for his pearl-handled revolver and threatened, "I ought to shoot you myself, you God damn whimpering coward."

Patton apparently thought the experience was worth repeating, and a week later, at yet another evacuation hospital, reprised the scene on another private, Paul G. Bennett, slapping him twice, calling him a "God damned coward," and a "yellow son of a bitch," before ordering the staff not to admit him to the hospital. Between these episodes, Patton issued a personal order to his commanders that men were not allowed to go to the hospital "on the pretext that they are nervously incapable of combat" and further directed that all cowards be returned to their units.

Those who knew—and liked—Patton called him "Georgie" and understood that the outrageous things he said were mostly for a reaction. General Marshall, who had been a friend of his for decades, would say that Georgie tended to "curse and say a hymn," and he usually had a glint in his eye as he looked to see who was in on his joke.

Georgie was one of Eisenhower's oldest friends. They had met after the First World War, when Eisenhower was sent to Camp Meade in Maryland, where the army had relocated its Tank Corps. Eisenhower had tried desperately to get deployed during the Great War. Instead, the army sent him to Camp Colt in Gettysburg to help stand up its new Tank Corps. There had been no real tanks to train with, but he made use of the old Civil War battlefield to get his men as able as they could be to use a new technology that was still decades before its prime. Georgie, though, had been stationed with the American Expeditionary Forces during the war, where he got to know the French Renault tanks, and came to Camp Meade evangelical about their capabilities.

Georgie was also a West Pointer, though a half decade older than Eisenhower, and had grown up in California as a member of the western United States' small but self-confident new-money aristocracy. The son of a successful and politically connected lawyer from Pasadena, Georgie swaggered with the ease of his family resources, rode the large stable of horses he collected, wore clothes tailored in London, boots cobbled in Rome, and, like Wild Bill Hickok, kept two Colt pistols on his hips that were decorated with ivory grips personally customized in Connecticut.

Back then, Eisenhower had also been something of a self-styled cowboy. Eisenhower was born the year the Census Bureau declared the frontier closed, and grew up in Abilene, a town that had been for a moment in time, and forever in legend, synonymous with the Old West. Growing up, Eisenhower had known old-timers who claimed to have been cowboys in the bad old days that had brought Wild Bill Hickok to town. Legend had it that Abilene was where Wild Bill crossed a cross-eyed drifter by the name of Jack McCall, who would later shoot him in the back of the head with a Colt .45 as Wild Bill held two pair, aces over eights; his last hand of poker in a Deadwood saloon.

When Eisenhower was a boy, he went by the name Dwight, and Abilene was the farthest thing from the Old West. Wild Bill had been dead twenty years, and largely thanks to the influx of God-fearing River Brethren that made up young Dwight's extended family, Abilene had reformed itself into a paragon of temperate middle-American respectability with a zeal achievable only by the converted. Nevertheless, Abilene's association with the immortal memory of Wild Bill Hickok guaranteed that its history would always be there under its sleeves like an old tattoo. And to those outside Kansas—really, outside a day's ride of Abilene—few would have had any reason to know the town had reformed its ways, given that every mention of it in *Collier's*, the *Saturday Evening Post*, or any pulp western magazine was as the fabled cow town, where whiskey and whores asked the same price, justice demanded a quick draw and clean shot, what you did mattered more than who you were, and the only mortal sin was to shoot a man in the back.

Young Dwight and his brothers lived through those stories, such as the one in which Wild Bill killed six men when he first came to Abilene. The local sheriff claimed to have served with Buffalo Bill Cody in the Civil War and would regale young Dwight with yarns about fighting in the border towns, riding across arid country for days without water, and how the taste of a stream could make a thirsty man drunker than whiskey.

At Camp Meade, Eisenhower and Georgie Patton became fast friends. They loved to bullshit. They reveled in their insurgent status, as believers in tanks. They rode horses, bootlegged bathtub gin, and played at gunslinger (though found themselves disappointed by the apparent lack of bandits on Maryland's country roads). And over the years, Georgie had looked out for Eisenhower and was always keen to be the special kind of mentor a charismatic older brother could be.

Eisenhower had almost ended up working for him back in 1940, when Patton was leading the Second Armored Brigade. Eisenhower jumped at the chance to do some real fighting if war broke out, but was diverted by the army to roles where his unique talent for staff work could be put to use. With their traditional roles reversed, and Georgie now working for Eisenhower, their relationship remained close but became strained. There was just something about Georgie that made Eisenhower more abrupt than he might otherwise want to be. Georgie was always up to something, always stirring things. It was part of his battlefield brilliance. But it was hard to take from a subordinate, and Georgie never quite accepted the idea that he was Eisenhower's subordinate.

As a result, Eisenhower could be petty with him. Just days into the Sicily campaign, he visited the Seventh Army's headquarters, where Patton had excitedly laid out maps to show him the progress he was making. But before he could start, Eisenhower could not help but hector him about sending situation reports on time, as a good subordinate needed to do.

There were more serious things too. On a single day, two different components of Patton's command in two different parts of Sicily murdered seventy-three prisoners of war in cold blood. Patton had reportedly tried to rally his men by telling them, "When we land against the enemy, don't forget to hit him and hit him hard. We will bring the fight home to him. We will show him no mercy. He has killed thousands of your comrades, and he must die."

That much may have been written off as Patton being Patton. But he hadn't stopped there. "If you company officers in leading your men against the enemy find him shooting at you," he had continued, "and, when you get within two hundred yards of him and he wishes to surrender, oh no! That bastard will die! You will kill him. Stick him between the third and fourth ribs. You will tell your men that. They must have the killer instinct. Tell them to stick him. He can do no good then. Stick them in the liver. We will get the name of killers and killers are immortal."

General Omar Bradley, whom Eisenhower had promoted over Patton as the commander of II Corps, asked him about this. Patton dismissed it all as "probably an exaggeration" and suggested forging the report to say that the prisoners had been killed trying to escape. Otherwise, Patton warned, "it would make a stink in the press." Bradley had refused and instead referred the perpetrators for prosecution as war criminals. The incident remained largely out of the press. But slapping around shell-shocked American soldiers was a problem of a different political magnitude.

Two reporters, Merrill "Red" Mueller and Demaree Bess, had come to Eisenhower with the story within a few days of it happening. Eisenhower had gotten to know both men well, and they warned him that it was going to be ugly. There were a lot of witnesses and a lot of people who wanted to see Patton go down. There was no way to spike the story. And their guess was that when it ran, it would end Patton's career.

Eisenhower sent Patton a hectoring letter. He told him to stop wearing his Colt revolvers and "acting like a madman." The press, he warned, was all over him and would like nothing more than to write exposés. But Eisenhower decided to protect him.

Eisenhower had long understood that being friends with everyone gave few people a reason to want to screw him. And being friends with the press was especially important. He went personally to Red and Bess, and asked "as a friend" for them to kill the story. He wasn't going to censor them. But he was asking for a favor. The fighting in Sicily was over by that point. Patton was not needed in the field. But, Eisenhower explained, he needed Patton for "cover."

The Germans could not stop thinking about George S. Patton. They were terrified of the guy. Everywhere he went, the Germans thought it was America's next move. And that was valuable. Eisenhower promised that Patton would apologize and that he had also asked Robert McClure to do an assessment. McClure was Eisenhower's public relations man and the bearer of bad news whenever the press was concerned. McClure had convinced him that the "story could be kept under cover."

Red and Bess disagreed. They promised they were not just out for a scoop. They were just offering friendly advice. "It would be better to break it now." But Eisenhower pressed them and they obliged him the favor.

Why did he go to such lengths to protect Patton? Eisenhower would say that he was "the only General who could inspire men to conquer." He would never say it to Georgie's face, but always to people who would inevitably pass the compliment along. And when General Marshall submitted George S. Patton's name for promotions that September, after the slapping incident had been papered over, Eisenhower had gone to bat for him, writing, "I do not see how you could possibly submit a list for permanent Major Generals, on combat performance to date, and omit his name."

"There are men who parade their fault blatantly, so that when you first meet them you know their fault," Eisenhower would say. "Their virtues may be deeply hidden and harder to find. George Patton is such a man. You can't be with Patton five minutes but what you know that here is an impulsive, over-dramatic man of erratic judgment on many things. Yet Patton has great virtues. He's a splendid man for any operation, military operation, where you need lots of dash and go."

When Eisenhower finally got to talk to him about it in person, Georgie had dolefully handed him a letter explaining himself. Eisenhower put the letter into his pocket. Georgie claimed he was "putting on an act" to cure them. He wanted to shock them out of their stupor. He had given a similar excuse to Bradley, saying he "could not understand why anybody who had an opportunity to fight would not fight." He was trying to make the young man angry enough that he would want to fight somebody. Though he was also the first to admit that seeing healthy-looking men convalescing amid the horribly wounded "made him see red."

Eisenhower broke the news that he had appointed inspectors to conduct a formal investigation. The two went back and forth for nearly two hours, with Georgie apologizing for acting "precipitately" but doing little to hide his disgust with the investigation. Eisenhower tried to convince him that he was looking out for him, that the investigation would protect him if the story ever got out. But Georgie was suspicious about whose career Eisenhower was protecting.

Things had been cool between them since then. Georgie had joined Eisenhower and Kay for dinner soon after Eisenhower's birthday that October. Georgie enjoyed raising his eyebrows at their relationship. When Eisenhower had brought Kay to observe combat operations in Italy the previous month, Georgie had mused aloud that "she must be a most necessary driver." And at dinner, he put on his usual show, provoking Eisenhower to lose his patience.

Why are you "always acting a part"? Eisenhower had snapped. Do you have some kind of "inferiority complex"?

It was inevitable that the story of Patton slapping soldiers around would break. Drew Pearson, the muckraking journalist known for writing the "Washington Merry Go Round" column, opened his radio show saying, "Here is a story which I don't like to tell, but in wartime we have to let the chips fall where they may." Pearson then described Patton's behavior in vivid detail and speculated that soldiers were no longer willing to fight under him. Pearson then reported that Eisenhower had "severely reprimanded" Patton, who "wouldn't be used in combat anymore."

With the press about to feed, Eisenhower sent Georgie a heads-up. "A very vicious and exaggerated version of the Sicilian hospital incident was broadcast two days ago by Drew Pearson from Washington. It resulted immediately in a flood of messages from the press associations to their representatives here demanding confirmation or denial."

Feed they did. It was soon in all the papers. The *New York Times* ran it as a front-page story. Newspapers were printing interviews with Charles Kuhl's parents. Senator Claude Pepper from Florida called for Patton's court-martial and lambasted Eisenhower for tolerating the abuse of American soldiers. The Republican whip in the House called for an inquiry. Drew Pearson called for the incident to be submitted to the Truman Committee, the Senate's tenacious watchdog against wartime fraud, waste, and abuse. Red Mueller was outed as having sat on the story and did a broadcast to defend himself, saying that he was breaking his silence now "not to supply fuel to gossip-mongers. I am only interested in proving that no American commander, particularly General Eisenhower, would condone rough treatment of any soldier."

General Marshall had assured Eisenhower that "we will support your stand in the matter." But with so much in flux, it was not at all clear how deep that support was. It was the biggest political scandal to embroil Eisenhower since the Darlan deal. And it gave ammunition to his rivals.

Joseph McNarney had served for more than a year under General Marshall as the deputy chief of staff. He had been in Eisenhower's class at West Point, where he was known as the "silent one" and was the kind of merciless son of a bitch whom Marshall liked; a real "hatchet man." And, not without encouragement from Marshall, McNarney also expected his next big move to be as army chief of staff. Roosevelt's promises during their tour of Carthage notwithstanding, McNarney was poised to get the job if Eisenhower became politically unacceptable.

Butch, Eisenhower's ostensible naval aide, encouraged his boss to do a press conference. Better to get out ahead of everything than let the story spiral. But Eisenhower was tired. His cold was relentless. And given everything else that was going on, he made the judgment that it was better to lay low. And so, Eisenhower told Beetle to handle it.

Beetle, never a master of subtlety, issued a blunt denial: "General Patton has never been reprimanded at any time by General Eisenhower, or by anybody else in the theater." This was, of course, a lie and exposed as such by the following morning. Beetle brought the clippings to Eisenhower.

"Well, I certainly messed that one up," he said apologetically. The story was now escalating into a broader exposé on the credibility of the War Department.

"For God's sake," Eisenhower scolded Beetle, "never lie to the press. Say nothing, perhaps—but don't lie." He then took a beat and looked at Beetle.

"Oh, well, Beedle, I'll allow you one mistake a year." But it was now Beetle's mess to clean up.

The irony was that Beetle and Georgie hated nearly everything about each other. Nevertheless, Beetle dutifully prostrated himself before the press, reminded them of George S. Patton's great accomplishments, and assured them all that Patton had made "full and complete amends." He then made himself look even more like a weasel by defending his previous denials on the technicality that Eisenhower had not formally reprimanded Patton under military law. He then added that Eisenhower had "mercilessly castigated" Patton to make clear "exactly what he meant and felt."

Before leaving for Cairo, Eisenhower sent Patton an "eyes only" message. "It is my judgement," he wrote, "that this storm will blow over." The best thing to do was to lay low and give his side of the story to the press off the record. Eisenhower hastened to add, though, that it was all a reminder of "the necessity for acting deliberately at all times and avoiding the giving way to impulse."

Alan Brooke

CHAPTER 4

THE LAST TIME Eisenhower had been asked to present to the Combined Chiefs was nearly a year earlier, at the Casablanca Conference in January 1943. He had not impressed. He was there to brief the Combined Chiefs on the "situation in North Africa," which at that moment was a literal quagmire. Bad winter weather had turned the scrubby plains of the northern Maghreb into mud, which funneled vehicles of any kind onto congested and unreliable roads that were easily targeted from the air. Until that changed, any major advance west toward Tunis needed to wait.

Anticipating the impatient groans this would elicit, Eisenhower had come up with an alternative plan for an American division to mount an attack from southern Tunisia, where the terrain was better, on the port city of Sfax. When it was his turn to speak, he had barely laid out the plan before Alan Brooke cut in to vivisect it as an amateurish tabletop exercise.

Eisenhower had first met Alan Brooke at the Washington Conference in December 1941, when the Combined Chiefs of Staff was formed. Eisenhower had been in Washington barely a week and was eager to see the famous Churchill up close. But it had been Brooke, with his close-clipped mustache and eyes that suggested he found nearly everything tedious, who really impressed Eisenhower most: articulate, quick, a commanding knowledge of military history.

Eisenhower, for his part, had made no impression on Alan Brooke either then or the second time they met, a few months later. And since Eisenhower's selection as the Allies' supreme commander in the Mediterranean, Brooke remained convinced that Eisenhower's inexperience was the only thing notable about him.

What if, Alan Brooke had asked at the Casablanca Conference, the Germans counterattacked in force? Had Eisenhower looked at a map? He would be encircling his own forces with far-larger German divisions to his east and west. Had he coordinated this plan with the British contingents in the area? If the weather made it impossible for the British forces in the north to move west for two months, then Eisenhower would have no reinforcements until at least March 15. Right?

Eisenhower was forced to agree, but said he hoped the British forces might break through before then and that the American division could conduct an "active defensive" against any German counterattack in the meantime.

Well, Alan Brooke had then asked, wouldn't two months of an "active defensive" risk exhausting that force, leaving them little fighting power when reinforcements finally did come, assuming of course that they were not annihilated before then by the vastly superior German numbers?

Eisenhower bled out. He rambled on for minute after uncomfortable minute about every aspect of the war in North Africa. No one had come to his defense or the defense of his Sfax plan. He was just unceremoniously excused.

When seeing Georgie Patton at the Casablanca Conference, Eisenhower confided that he thought his "throat [was] about to be cut." He was left on his thread, though, ironically thanks to Alan Brooke.

"I am afraid," Alan Brooke had concluded, "Eisenhower as a general is hopeless!" But he did give Eisenhower credit for "the charm of his personality." And he also understood that Britain—and he—could wield more power by "flattering and pleasing" his country's American allies than humiliating them.

Alan Brooke proposed allowing Eisenhower to fail up, enhancing the nominal prestige of his position as supreme commander and giving him a British deputy to do the bothersome business of directing the armies where to go and what to do. Brooke selected Harold "Alex" Alexander, a legendary British general, who was more than happy to take the reins of the actual war fighting, while Eisenhower did the upstairs work in what Brooke sarcastically called the "stratosphere and rarified atmosphere of a Supreme Commander."

Soon, all the senior commanders in North Africa were British, except for Eisenhower. And Alan Brooke was content in the knowledge that the British would remain in actual command of the war while the Americans failed to "fully appreciate the underlying intentions."

Intentions are one thing, however. The intervening reality was that Eisenhower and Alex became a genuine team. They were nearly the same age, which gave them a common sense of being yoked by their respective elders on the Combined Chiefs. Alex was an aristocrat, but he shared Eisenhower's self-effacing manner, which made his boundless energy and conspicuous talent hard to resent. He had gone to Cambridge, making him the butt of endless jokes for having been Jawaharlal Nehru's "fag," a not entirely dignified term used to describe the mentee to an upperclassman. His only flaw, such that Eisenhower could see, was that he lacked the ability to put on a hard game face when dealing with subordinates.

As a team, though, Eisenhower and Alex integrated the American and British militaries to a degree that no one had imagined possible. And the results came quickly as the mud in Maghreb hardened. By spring, they had cleared the Axis powers out of North Africa. By summer, they had led the Allied conquest of Sicily. By fall, after a high-risk amphibious landing in Salerno, southern Italy was in Allied hands and Mussolini was exiled to running a rump German puppet government from a resort town on Lake Garda.

As the conflict over the Dodecanese had just shown, having Alex as deputy did not turn out to give Alan Brooke or the British the control they perhaps assumed they would have. And by November, Brooke would write in his diary that seeing Alex "fills me with gloom, he is a very, very, small man, and cannot see big." This was always Brooke's go-to insult. Whether it was Eisenhower, or Churchill, or Alex, the slight was invariably someone's "lack of vision." But Alex had garnered an extra lump of Brooke's disdain for having "always sought someone to lean on," particularly if that person was General Dwight Eisenhower.

EISENHOWER FLEW TO Cairo on a Tuesday night, sharing his C-54 with Elliott Roosevelt and his Official Family, to whom he had offered the trip as something of a vacation. The sun was rising over the great Egyptian plain as they approached. In the orange light, Egypt was a sea of desert that abruptly bloomed into a fantastic green along the Nile River delta. It was as if some eccentric painter had grabbed the most brilliant emerald hue on the palette and slashed a triumphant brushstroke down a sheet of cheap packing paper. Dotting the landscape, small as toys, were the mythic pyramids. And the opaque purple waters of the Nile ran south to north as if to accentuate the strangeness of flying into a place so ancient that the authors of the Bible wrote in awe of its antiquity.

Eisenhower was scheduled to present on Friday afternoon and so had two days to enjoy Cairo, where nightclubs, hotels, bars, and everything else were "going full swing." The Mohamed Ali Club was sumptuous. Anything and everything was for sale. The prices, though, left Eisenhower purchasing only a bit of fresh fruit. Kids hitched rides by playfully jumping onto cars' running boards. Beggars, suffering from the signs of hookworm, milled about in an inescapable cloud of hashish smoke. The Nile itself was dense with felucca boats, which cast the same silhouettes across the same riverbanks one would have seen in the time of the pharaohs.

Thursday was Thanksgiving, and Alan Brooke arranged for a church service in Cairo's cathedral to welcome his American cousins. That night, there was a large feast followed by a screening of Billy Wilder's *The Major and the Minor*, starring Ginger Rogers. Even the weather welcomed: warm but not hot days and cool nights, which made for heavy, restful sleep.

Friday afternoon, before his presentation to the Combined Chiefs, Eisenhower met with General Marshall. While Eisenhower had been enjoying Cairo, Roosevelt had met Chiang Kai-shek for the first time and received official confirmation that Stalin would arrive in Tehran that weekend. Eisenhower asked why Stalin was willing to meet now in Tehran, when he had refused to come to Casablanca. Marshall smiled and said, "That's one thing you and I don't have to bother our heads about." The conference between the Combined Chiefs was also in full swing and turning out to be contentious.

As Eisenhower's time approached, General Marshall escorted him to the president's suite in the ambassador's villa in Mena, on the western edge of Cairo near the pyramids. When they arrived, Roosevelt was sitting in a broad easy chair with his back to a large spray of flowers. He had a small box in his hand and flipped it open to reveal the Legion of Merit.

The Legion of Merit had been created at the beginning of the war as the most democratic of the military decorations. Given irrespective of service or rank, or even nationality, for exceptional service to the country, it was modeled on the French Legion of Honor, which Henri Giraud had awarded

Eisenhower earlier that year complete with awkwardly received kisses. Elliott Roosevelt had gotten word to his father that the Legion of Merit was the one medal that Eisenhower really wanted.

Roosevelt had Pa Watson read the citation as Eisenhower stood straight as a cadet. He then told Eisenhower to step forward and pinned the medal on his chest. "You deserve this," Roosevelt said, "and much more, Ike."

"It's the happiest moment of my life, sir," Eisenhower said, holding back tears. "I appreciate this decoration more than any other you could give me."

THE COMBINED CHIEFS meeting was already underway in a closed session on Southeast Asia. Eisenhower was then called in. He entered flanked by the head of his air and naval forces in the Mediterranean. Alex would have been there too, had he not fallen ill just before.

The tension in the room could be tasted. The British and Americans had been at odds for days over strategy all around the world and nowhere more intensely than the Mediterranean. Churchill had been pressing for unified command over the Mediterranean, lamenting the five thousand British soldiers lost in the Dodecanese debacle and blaming it on the fact that Eisenhower "had the forces but not the responsibility." And as expected, Churchill and Alan Brooke were seeking to reopen the debate over whether to launch a cross-Channel invasion. He proposed that the Allies instead commit to taking Rome in January, Rhodes in February, and from Rhodes to the Dardanelles, or to the Balkans, which Churchill had sold as "a common front with the Russians."

Churchill insisted that he did not oppose Operation Overlord. "Overlord remained top of the bill," he said, if only to placate his American allies. "But this operation should not be such a tyrant as to rule out every other activity in the Mediterranean." Overlord should be a coup de grâce, Churchill insisted, once Germany had been weakened from below. If the Americans insisted on a precipitous invasion of Normandy, Churchill warned, "The Channel will be a river of blood."

It was the same old argument. During a conference in Algeria in the lead-up to the invasion of Sicily, Alan Brooke had pulled Eisenhower aside to make the same case against the invasion of France. The "European fortress" was invulnerable to attack from the west, he warned. But even if the invasion were successful, Brooke asked, what would that leave the Allies? A land war in northern Europe? That could easily become a "very costly stalemate or even worse."

Avoiding all-out land battles was the core of British strategic doctrine ever since the Treaty of Versailles. Only fight small battles against small enemies. And if the enemy is large, devastate their ability to fight from afar until they are small.

As far as Brooke was concerned, it was better to use the Allies' air superiority to burn Germany to the ground while "nibbling around the edges." "Thrust and peck" to keep the Germans off balance and then go for the kill once "German morale had cracked."

There were other, usually indirectly stated, reasons that the British preferred to expand the Allied presence in the Mediterranean over an all-out land war across northern France. Britain had been at this a long time, whether it was the Vikings, the Normans, the Spanish, the Hundred Years' War, the Second Hundred Years' War, or the skirmishes with the Thugs, the Ghazis, the Zulu, and the Boers. Britain had not become Great by betting everything on a war to end all wars. The one time it had, look what happened: A generation dead in trenches. The Irish, who had fought valiantly for the empire, revolting and then breaking away.

Alan Brooke was convinced that Germany would lose. They were encircled, they were bleeding, and they had tens of millions of Russians advancing on them. He was frustrated that "Eisenhower does not begin to realize the possibilities that lie ahead of us in this theater."

Churchill had a clear vision too, as Pug Ismay would describe it, of getting the British "established in the Balkans before the Russians, and Tito could come in." The opportunity was there to bring the whole of the Mediterranean, from Gibraltar to Gallipoli, into the realm.

This was also precisely what Roosevelt feared. "We must realize," he told his commanders, "that the British look upon the Mediterranean as an area under British domination." If America helped conquer Rhodes, Churchill would declare, "Now we will have to take Greece." It was the logic of imperialism and endless in its ambitions.

Invading France from the west was, Roosevelt would say, "The way to kill the most Germans, with the least loss of American soldiers." That was the only goal the Americans had in mind. "I see no reason for putting the lives of American soldiers in jeopardy in order to protect real or fancied British interests on the European continent. We're at war, and our job is to win it as fast as possible, and without adventures."

It had fallen to General Marshall to be the heavy throughout the Cairo Conference. Churchill had at one point insisted that further operations against Rhodes were necessary because "His Majesty's Government can't have its troops staying idle." Churchill gripped his lapels for stentorian effect.

"God forbid, if I should try to dictate," Marshall had said, "but not one American solider is going to die on that goddamned beach."

It was unclear how Eisenhower would fit into this debate. And in a room that was poised to explode, Eisenhower was simply poised. He recounted the year's successes and the paths ahead with a mastery of not just the physical terrain, but the political. He expressed no opinion on the invasion of France, other than to say that he had already accounted for the transfer of personnel to England in doing his planning for the war in Italy. All he needed was landing craft.

Eisenhower then outlined what he saw as the most valuable strategic objective in the Mediterranean: the Po Valley. The northern Italian province of Lombardy was a crossroads into the Balkans, France, and the heart of Germany. Taking it would put every option on the table. But to do that, he would need more resources. And even with those resources, he felt the need to add—though without mentioning Churchill's expectation that Rome could be taken in a matter of weeks—that it "would be quite impossible to reach the Po by 15 January." In his experience, the success of amphibious invasions depended on the weather as much as the degree of German resistance. And so, any prediction of quick success had to be qualified by the possibility that the Germans and the weather might have different plans.

Alan Brooke asked the first question. And he took the chance to clarify that Churchill's projection for victory in January was to the Pisa-Rimini line (in other words, just Rome), not all the way up to the Po Valley. He then asked, with that in mind, how support could be given to the partisans in the Balkans.

Eisenhower replied with a cartographer's mastery of what would be involved. To create a tenable supply line to the Balkans, they would need to get to the Po line and then build small garrisons in the Adriatic. If they got only as far as Rome, then it would not be possible.

There were no more questions. Eisenhower then gave his air and naval chiefs a moment in the spotlight and took his leave.

When the door closed, a room full of men in their sixties, who were deliberating on the future of the free world, "almost resulted in a brawl." General Marshall and Alan Brooke got into what Brooke described that night as "the father and mother of a row!" This went on until nearly five in the evening, with none of the major questions resolved before they all headed the following day to Tehran.

Katherine "Kay" Summersby

CHAPTER 5

EISENHOWER WAS NOT important enough to go to Tehran and enjoyed Friday-evening drinks at the Mohamed Ali Club with William "Wild Bill" Donovan, the head of the Office of Strategic Services (OSS). Wild Bill had gone to law school with Roosevelt and, by all appearances, looked like he was a senior partner at some white-shoe Manhattan firm. But somehow, from the expedition against Pancho Villa to the Cairo Conference, the blue-eyed man from Buffalo had an uncanny ability to be where whatever was happening was happening.

General Marshall ordered Eisenhower to take a few days off. And so the next day, Eisenhower took his Official Family to Luxor. His air chief, Arthur Tedder, had told him to fly along the Nile to the Valley of the Kings, so they could see all the ancient sights from the air. Enjoying a bird's-eye view was complicated, however, by the fact that the flight was bumpy and hot, leaving all concerned thinking of little other than being on the ground.

In Cairo, the army had assigned Eisenhower a villa, failing to account for his Official Family. That made for close living and a bit of awkwardness as Kay and the other women on his staff shared a room on the bottom floor. But in Luxor, where the ancient city of Thebes once stood, they were treated to rooms in the storied Luxor Hotel on the banks of the Nile, a hotel whose grandeur rivaled the ancient Luxor Temple next door.

That night, Elliott Roosevelt joined them, having flown down from Cairo at Eisenhower's invitation for a grand sightseeing tour before Elliott was due to join his father in Tehran. A sergeant traveling with Elliott had been a pianist for Kay Kyser's big band and played for a few hours on the hotel's upright piano. The music echoed under the ceiling that soared above. And Dwight Eisenhower, a middle child from Abilene, Kansas, just sat back and let the music wash over him in the comfort of a grand lounge in a grand hotel in an ancient part of the world grand enough to be marked on a map as the place for kings.

Eisenhower almost had to wonder what his father would think. His mother would have probably liked it. Though ardently against the pursuit of earthly rewards of any kind, Ida Stover Eisenhower appreciated nice things, and most of all the sound of a well-played piano. Her prized possession was an ebony piano that she had bought with her inheritance after her father died. And despite never having more than exactly enough money for the family, his mother cherished and cared for that piano like an eighth child.

Eisenhower's father, though, was different. David Eisenhower never drank, never smoked, and was opposed to gambling on emphatic principle. The principle, it seemed, was that he despised fun. Even the single bottle of whiskey kept in Eisenhower's childhood home was reserved strictly for medical emergencies. And despite a few bouts of scarlet fever, and a gangrenous knee injury that nearly took Eisenhower's leg as a boy, the bottle had never been opened.

Eisenhower's father had been obsessed with Egypt. Not so much the actual place, but its mythological and, to his father, literal significance as a biblical terraform. It was a place where God had taken a direct interest in the activities of his creation, leading Moses and the Israelites to the promised land. And it was where the Old Testament appeared to offer prophecies of Judgment Day. "In that day," the Good Book declared, "shall there be an altar to the Lord in the midst of the land of Egypt, and a pillar at the border thereof to the Lord. And it will be for a sign and for a witness to the Lord of hosts in the land of Egypt; for they will cry to the Lord because of the oppressors, and He will send them a Savior and a Mighty One, and He will deliver them."

Eisenhower's father had been born the summer after the Battle of Gettysburg in a River Brethren community not seventy miles away. The River Brethren were a temperate, pacifist branch of the Mennonites who thought the "possession of property a divine virtue and to be accomplished by hard work." David was a teenager when the Eisenhower clan moved to Dickenson County, Kansas, just as Abilene was putting its years as a cowboy town to bed.

The Eisenhower family became locally prominent as successful farmers and then landowners, and David Eisenhower grew up in relative prosperity. But he cultivated a contempt for the farmer's life and was, by all accounts, a man embittered by everyone's failure to recognize that he had figured it all out, even if precisely what "it" was remained more an impulse than a concrete idea. David Eisenhower attended, but then dropped out of, Lane University, where he had met Ida Stover, to go into business. That business failed, as did a few other ventures and schemes David pursued, sentencing him to live out his days making ends meet as someone else's employee, raising a family in a house purchased for him by his father.

David was a man convinced that there was some secret to it all and was fanatical whenever he thought he had found it. Eugene V. Debs toured through Abilene in 1900, packing the local theater to standing room only, and crowing, "I find a very strong Socialist sentiment in Kansas; many tell me they will support the movement." In 1903, David ran for the Abilene school board as a Socialist and lost 146 to 27.

Failing in the pursuit of earthly rewards, David turned just as fanatically toward heavenly ones. He worked as a technician at the local Belle Springs Creamery, a venture founded by fellow River Brethren. He would get up at five in the morning, build a fire in the potbellied stove, and then call up for the boys. Once assembled in the kitchen, David would read from the Bible, and do a blessing before breakfast. He'd get home around six for supper, read the Bible, and then before bed, wind the clock, whose ticking resonated throughout their little house all through the night. Among the courses offered at Lane University had been Greek, the original language of the New Testament, and David kept a copy of a Greek Bible that he would conspicuously endeavor to read.

The religiosity of the Eisenhower household eschewed religion. Church was not a regular habit, but the Sabbath was scrupulously observed. The boys were not allowed to play sports, and their aunt Amanda, David's sister, insisted on dragging them to the Brethren in Christ Sunday school.

David's willingness to dispense with church and other Christian ceremonies was largely attributable to his and Ida joining the Bible Students movement in 1895. "It isn't a religion," was the motto. "It's worship."

A mystical form of Christianity, the Bible Students movement was founded by Charles Taze Russell, a controversial and quintessentially American figure, one of the great charismatic speculators who founded Great Awakening religions. Russell had become fascinated by pyramidology and the writings of John Taylor and Charles Piazzi Smyth. Like those who devised theories about the celestial significance hidden in the dimensions of prehistorical ruins like Stonehenge, Smith devised the "pyramid inch" and "pyramid cubit," and elaborated the correlations between thousands of measurements taken from the Great Pyramid of Giza and the relative position of the earth, the sun, and the poles.

The first volume of Russell's multivolume series, *Studies in the Scriptures*, was entitled *The Divine Plan of the Ages and the Corroborative Testimony of the Great Pyramid in Egypt, God's Stone Witness and Prophet*. Russell used pyramidology to show that the dimensions of the pyramid mapped to major events in the Bible and subsequent history. To demonstrate his revelation, Russell included numerous diagrams and a large foldout "Chart of the Ages," mapping the dimensions of the pyramid to the epochs of history and the prophecy that Judgment Day was near.

"The Pyramid witnesses," Russell wrote, "that the close of 1914 will be the beginning of the time of trouble such as was not since there was a nation—no, nor ever shall be afterward." David copied the chart, enlarging it to a massive sixteen-square-foot scale. It was the most prominent thing anyone would see in the living room of the Eisenhowers' little farmhouse.

David Eisenhower was a very certain man. Predictably, that made him an angry man. And, just as predictably, a violent man. He could be indiscriminately so toward children, his own or others. When Eisenhower was six, his father was arrested and found guilty of beating a neighbor boy, whom he perceived had done some wrong.

Six or seven years later, Eisenhower and his older brother Edgar had gone home for lunch and David, home from work for some unknown reason, found them in the barn. Eisenhower remembered, "His face was black as thunder." David grabbed a leather tug, hooked Edgar by the collar, and began whipping him in a frenzy. Eisenhower shouted at his father to stop, hoping their mother would hear and intervene. When she didn't come, Eisenhower grabbed his father from behind. It was the first time in his life that he recalled standing up to the man, who turned toward him, tug in hand, threatening, "Oh, do you want some more of the same?"

Eisenhower avoided getting beaten that day. In his memory it was because he had said, "I don't think anyone ought to be whipped like that, not even a dog." But who knew? For the rest of his life, Eisenhower would rationalize his father's abusiveness as the discipline that a house of rowdy boys needed. But his brother Edgar would say their father acted that way because he was "weak."

David Eisenhower died in 1942, searching for an answer that never came. Russell claimed that Judgment Day, the end of the modern world, would come in October 1914, which correlated with "the floor-line measurement of the Grande Gallery in the Great Pyramid." But then the world continued as it was. David unsuccessfully lobbied Kansas' Republican senator for a job in the nearby post office and then went to work for the local gas company, where he became the record keeper for its employees' pension, insurance, and savings plans.

Charles Russell died in 1916, and for the next decade, the Bible Students splintered, with various groups reinterpreting the prophecy hidden in the Great Pyramid, setting the date of Armageddon back to 1918 and then 1925. The Watch Tower Society, the organization Russell founded, then abandoned the Great Pyramid's divinity in 1928, with the new leader of the organization, Joseph Rutherford, announcing in a nationwide radio address that the pyramids were created by the devil. Soon after, Rutherford rebranded the Watch Tower Society as the Jehovah's Witnesses.

Along the way, David left the Bible Students because, his son Edgar would say, "he couldn't go along with the sheer dogma." Ida, though, saw to it that David received a Witness funeral when he died in March 1942. The ceremony was conducted by Dr. J. L. Thayer, a dentist who opened a practice in 1902 above Hubbard's Bookstore in Abilene and had remained close to Ida over the years. He was a popular lecturer of the Bible Students' message, and continued through the 1920s on topics such as the "Millions Now Living Will Never Die." He gave his own radio address in the fall of 1928, entitled "Jehovah God, the People's Friend," which was adapted from the broadcast given by Joseph Rutherford the previous summer.

A local paper noted David's death as significant because he was the father of Milton Eisenhower, the little brother who cast a grand shadow over the Eisenhower family at that point. Another remembered him as having been "connected with United Companies for several years, notable for the success of the six sons of the family," and "respected for his courtesy, sincerity and fidelity to every trust."

Eisenhower had been working eighteen-hour days for General Marshall at the time, and Ernest King had driven him to distraction on something that day. He got the call from Mamie at his desk. A telegram had just arrived from Abilene. Mamie was full of sympathy, but he told her that he had to get back to work. And he did. No one in the office knew anything was wrong. And as if Mersault, Eisenhower wrote in his diary, "Father died this morning. Nothing I can do but send a wire."

Later, Eisenhower felt compelled to write, "I loved my dad," and he described how he wished to be back in Abilene to console his mother. But he wrote stoically, "We're at war. And war is not soft, it has no time to indulge even the most sacred emotions."

Work prevented Eisenhower from going to the funeral. To mark the day his father was buried, he closed the door to his office for a half hour and wrote a private eulogy praising his father as an honest man with prairie values. "I am proud he was my father! My only regret is that it was always so difficult to let him know the great depth of my affection for him." Work was also the reason that eighteen months later, Eisenhower found himself sitting next to the president's son, enjoying a bit of piano music in the Luxor Hotel.

THE FOLLOWING DAY, as promised, Eisenhower treated his Official Family, along with Elliott Roosevelt and his entourage, to a tour of Luxor, the tombs of the pharaohs, and the Temple of Karnak, all conducted by an archaeologist who was an old friend of Arthur Tedder. He even showed them into the newly discovered tomb of King Tut, and all along the way explained how these relics and monuments, which nearly all predated the Bible, had been built by men. These men were artisans, who learned their craft, who kept regular hours, and who would even go on strike. They used delicate tools and expensive paints, such as the blue that had lost none of its luminance over the millennia.

At times, Eisenhower could lose himself in the presence of history he had known only through books. But, try as he might, he could not help thinking about work and his dread of being "promoted" back to Washington. He perseverated about what news would await when Roosevelt returned from Tehran and nagged Elliott, hoping perhaps that the message would get through to his father, about how he preferred to serve in the action, rather than at a desk in Washington.

Elliott more than got the point and after the third or fourth time Eisenhower brought it up, he grew awkward about it. "The Joint Chiefs will surely consult you, sir," Elliott eventually said with a placating *enough already*, "before they take any final action."

ELLIOTT LEFT FOR Tehran the next day and Eisenhower returned to Cairo, where he met a Franciscan priest, Father Pasquale, who offered to take Eisenhower on a tour of Jerusalem. And so Eisenhower flew with his Official Family across Lake Tenes, tracing Moses's biblical path out of Egypt to the promised land, a rolling strip of low hill valleys, scattered olive groves, and mimosa trees between the Mediterranean and the Dead Sea.

Jerusalem, monochromatic in its trademark limestone, was a maze of alleys and deep doorways that brought right to mind how intimate the battles that had unfolded there since antiquity must have been. As a religious experience, though, it was disappointing. The ruins seemed more ruined and the hawkers crowded out whatever sense of spiritual awe one might have otherwise felt around the Church of the Holy Sepulcher.

The monks came tromping out of the monastery without a hint of piety, and Pasquale introduced them all to Brother Francis, "a bouncing little man, full of fun, from Kansas." Brother Francis grabbed Eisenhower by the elbow and showed him all around the streets jammed with beggars and hawkers, who had made a business of the tourists for millennia. Eisenhower was recognized a few times and given beads, postcards, trinket crosses, and other tat for which he would smile gratefully. Eventually, he slyly leaned over to Kay and said, "Guess I've got a free ticket to heaven!"

In River Brethren Sunday school, the theme had always been damnation and hellfire. Even then, Eisenhower never quite got it. How could something burn forever? Everything he and Edgar had ever burned went right to ash. Real hellfire was the sound of his mother's voice when she would quote the Bible at him when he was in trouble. It was always somehow worse than the whippings his father might give him; to hear those archaic names paired with line numbers, confirming the wrong he had done down to the chapter and verse.

But here, in the actual place of the crucifixion, carnival barkers offered a step-right-up chance to touch the rocks at the foot of Calvary. Kay, raised a good Irish Catholic, could not resist commenting on how the whole scene was as tacky as the Blarney Stone. Though this was nothing compared with her rants about how many of the ancient artifacts of Christianity were now in the hands of Muslims. Even the Mount of Olives, from which Christ was to have ascended into heaven, was occupied by a mosque.

They left Jerusalem for Cairo that afternoon. It took longer to fly in and out than they had spent in the Holy Land. From Cairo, Eisenhower would return to Algiers to await his orders home.

Before leaving Cairo, though, Eisenhower was relieved to get word that there would be no immediate change in his status. He should still be prepared to go to Washington, but it wouldn't be for at least ninety days. Decisions were still being made.

Mamie Eisenhower

CHAPTER 6

EISENHOWER RETURNED TO Algiers the morning of December 1, 1943. He spent most of the next week moping around, dreading news of his imminent return to a desk in Washington. It would be a giant desk, and the idea that he could fill General Marshall's chair was a compliment that no one, including himself, fully believed. Even his title was likely to be "*Acting* Chief of Staff," a reminder to everyone that he would be only minding the store.

Eisenhower joked to Butch that he would not need to bring any of his staff to Washington, since he would be "carried up to Arlington cemetery within six months." Butch reassured him that he would be right there with him; though he was keeping his options open. Butch took the chance that week to write discreetly to Steve Early, Roosevelt's press secretary, to let him know of his interest in the president's offer to move to the White House if Eisenhower was sent to the Pentagon.

Eisenhower's dour mood was not helped by the fact that, for the first time in two years, he did not have much to do. The previous two weeks had made him feel as if his feet were in the middle of quicksand. But now his feet were firmly on the ground in a comfortable place where he was in charge. There were things he needed to do. But they were all routine things. None was particularly important. And none was urgent. With all the "important personages" flying in and out, his most urgent task was to be the "travel agent in chief," and the most important thing ahead of him was another trip to Tunis to welcome Roosevelt back from the Tehran Conference like a four-star concierge.

Eisenhower began to wonder if he had become addicted to what he called the "eternal pound, pound, pound," which felt like a burden as it pummeled him, but left life feeling dimmer the moment it stopped. He first noticed it in the lead-up to Operation Torch and how it made time itself a thing he noticed only when relevant to planning. Without it, what did he have? Would he become a "nervous wreck" or "wholly unfit for normal life"? He joked in a letter to Mamie that "being lazy by nature, I think there is hope for me."

It had been two weeks since he received a letter from Mamie. She sent him a copy of a letter dated 1918, written by a soldier he had commanded when he was stationed at Camp Colt in Gettysburg. "Our new Captain," it gushed, "Eisenhower by name, is I believe one of the most efficient and best army officers in the country." It spoke admiringly of Eisenhower's football player's build. "He knows his job, is enthusiastic, can tell us what he wants us to do, and it's pretty human, though wickedly harsh and abrupt." An old family friend had sent it to Mamie, who thought he might get a kick out of it.

Camp Colt had been where Eisenhower and Mamie had first really lived together as a family. The previous summer, he had been stationed at Fort Oglethorpe, Georgia, to help train the one million draftees who had been inducted to fight World War I. He was sleeping in a tent when he got the news that Mamie had given birth to his son. He sent a telegram, and then a letter that rambled with excitement. "Gee! I'm crazy to see you," he wrote. "I've sent you 100,483,491,342 kisses since I've been gone." He threw out baby name suggestions, and closed by saying, "Millions of kisses & lots of love to you & 'Muvver.'"

Mamie had named their boy after his father on the spot, Doud Dwight Eisenhower. He was Little Ike, and soon just "Icky." Eisenhower had first met Icky after Christmas, when he was granted emergency leave to visit Mamie, who had come down with influenza. He fell in love instantly and was overjoyed when they got to live together as a family at Camp Colt that summer.

The most brutal part of World War I for Eisenhower had nothing to do with the trenches on the western front. Instead, in October 1918, the Spanish Flu burned through Camp Colt like a firebomb. There were more bodies than coffins. Doctors tried anything. Those who fell ill did so seemingly at random and died just as absurdly. After the first wave of deaths seemed to have abated, another crashed over the camp. And because Camp Colt was in the early stages of closing down, the nursing staff had already transferred out. Medical care, such as it was, fell to the Red Cross, who set up a hospital in a nearby school and the local community rallied to provide bedding, hospital supplies, broth, and jelly to care for the ill.

Outwardly, Eisenhower thanked the people of Gettysburg for their "kindness and sympathy" and did what he could to take charge of the situation. He put the camp under lockdown and forbade social gatherings. But inwardly, he was terrified for his Mamie and Icky. He asked one of the doctors on post for help and was given an apothecary's chest worth of sprays and syrups to ward off the dread disease.

Perhaps by black magic, they worked. Nearly two hundred of his men were dead. The mortality rate was better than many army camps whose commanders were not as quick to take the virus seriously. But Eisenhower was just grateful that Mamie and Icky had been spared.

"I miss you terribly," Eisenhower wrote Mamie, as he waited for Roosevelt's arrival in Algiers. "What is going to happen as a result of all rumoured changes in command, etc., I don't know. But no matter what does happen—I do hope I can have a visit with you before too long. I know I'm a changed person—no one could go through what I've seen and not be different from what he was at the beginning. But in at least one way I'm certain of my reactions—I love you! I wish I could see you an hour to tell you how much!"

Eisenhower consoled himself by reflecting on how lucky he had been. In just two years, he had gone from lieutenant colonel to full general. He had gotten his time in the sun. And who knew? Maybe he would be a good Acting Chief of Staff. Though try as he might, he hated the thought of it. It was like being taken off the field during a winning game.

There were glimmers of hope. When the Tehran Conference concluded, the British and Americans reconvened for a few days in Cairo. Elliott Roosevelt skipped this leg and came back to Algiers eager to share all the gossip.

Churchill, Elliott said, had made a mess of things, and the friction between Churchill and General Marshall became socially uncomfortable. Churchill kept reproposing his schemes and Marshall would—all to the apparent delight of Uncle Joe Stalin—sternly dissect Churchill's proposals with the impatience of a piano teacher.

Roosevelt had asked Stalin for the Soviets' position on the Allies' next strategic move. Stalin brooked no doubts. Proceeding through the Alps was treacherous, and more investment in the Mediterranean was a waste. The key was France, though Stalin recognized that the fighting would be bitter.

"The Channel is such a disagreeable body of water," Roosevelt mused. "No matter how unpleasant that body of water might be, however, we still want to get across it."

"We were very glad it was an unpleasant body of water at one time," Churchill had quipped.

According to Elliott, Roosevelt said his biggest accomplishment was "making clear to Stalin that the United States and Great Britain were not allied in one common block against Soviet Union. I think we've got rid of that idea, once, and for all. I hope so. The one thing that could upset the apple cart after the war, is if the world is divided again, Russia against England and us."

On the last day of the Tehran Conference, the date for the invasion of France had been set: May 1, 1944. Stalin liked it because it was May Day. And the invasion would not just be in the north across the Channel, but also in the South of France from the Mediterranean. This second operation, code-named "Anvil," would complete a continental-size pincer maneuver that would divide the German defenses in an unwinnable two-front war.

The Combined Chiefs still had not figured out who would be in charge. The latest rumors were that General Marshall would go to London six to eight weeks before the invasion to serve as the Supreme Commander for Europe, with Alan Brooke as the subcommander for the cross-Channel invasion. If that panned out, Eisenhower would likely stay in the Mediterranean to fight up the boot of Italy and maybe even lead Operation Anvil. But nothing was certain yet.

TO KEEP HIMSELF busy, Eisenhower dictated letters. It was faster than writing by hand, but he spoke fast, smoked profusely as he spoke, and paced around the room as he smoked. He had gained a reputation for being short-tempered with his exhausted stenographers, who at least had enough sense not to transcribe every four-letter word that fell off his tongue. When called on his behavior, at the very least the prolificacy of his vocabulary, Eisenhower would just shrug and say "Shit, I don't curse. I just use some words as adjectives."

Georgie Patton, who was something of a poet in his use of short words, had written recommending a book, *The Greatest Norman Conquest*. What the Normans did, Georgie wrote, "was nothing, both in extent of territory and in time to what you have done in the past year." He then closed, "I suppose what I have just written sounds like either bullshit or bootlick, but that is not the fact. The fact is that whereas it took some 900 years for the Normans to receive the credit due to their efforts, I trust by this letter to do my small part in sending you the credit while you are still alive and able to enjoy it."

Eisenhower welcomed Georgie's bootlick, given the renewed furor over his slapping subordinates, and took the chance to assure his old friend, saying, "I think I took the right decision then and I stand by it. You don't need to be afraid of my weakening the proposition in spite of the fact that, at the moment, I was more than a little annoyed with you."

Eisenhower wrote to Kay's mother about how she was feeling. Kay had stopped writing home the previous summer, in the depth of her depression over Dick Arnold. And so Eisenhower picked up the correspondence, if only to assure her mother that her daughter was in the company of friends. He wrote to his brother Milton, who was now the president of Kansas State University, sharing his thoughts on how "in education lies the true answer to most of the world's ills." He wrote to his son, who was in his final year at the military academy, commiserating over the petty annoyances of a West Point education. And he wrote to Mamie's father about how busy he had been.

Restless, he wrote to Mamie every day, fantasizing about the quiet life they could enjoy in retirement in "a little place far away from cities (but with someone near enough for occasional bridge) in the field in which to shoot a few birds once in a while—I think that's roughly my idea of a good life." Then, on Monday, December 5, 1943, he wrote Mamie a love note in which he promised to dictate a long chronicle of his travels and experiences over the previous few weeks. He planned to do it after he got back from Tunis, where he was due to fly the following day as part of his four-star concierge duties.

EISENHOWER WAS UP sufficiently early Tuesday morning to get to Tunis by nine thirty, which would leave plenty of time to welcome Roosevelt that afternoon. Breakfast had not yet been laid out, leaving him to do nothing but smoke, bullshit with Butch, and wait for the day to begin.

Eisenhower had moved into his Algerian villa a year earlier. The water and gas mains had been destroyed by German bombing, and his first breakfast had been cooked in the dining room fireplace. It was not Telegraph Cottage, but it had its own dreary charm, at least to Eisenhower. It was more modest than the vast mansion that Beetle had requisitioned. But the view from the terrace over the palm trees would be easy for him to miss.

The phone rang. Butch went over to get it. It was Beetle. Butch handed Eisenhower the receiver.

A cable, Beetle told him, had come in the night before from General Marshall. It was official. Eisenhower was being replaced in the Mediterranean by a British officer. This was the bad news Eisenhower had been dreading, and earlier than expected. Beetle then started complaining about Churchill. The prime minister was insisting that Beetle stay in the Mediterranean for continuity instead of letting him be a part of Operation Overlord. Beetle was distraught. He told Eisenhower that he wanted to go with him to London.

To London?

Yes, to London. It was right there at the end of Marshall's message. "The possibility has been considered of leaving Smith in the Mediterranean until sometime in February or March, and then his joining *you* in the United Kingdom." Eisenhower had been picked to command Operation Overlord.

ROOSEVELT LANDED IN Tunis late in the afternoon, and Eisenhower joined the president for the drive to the White House.

"Well, Ike," Roosevelt said teasingly, "you'd better start packing. You are going to move." The president let the words hang in the air, leaving Eisenhower to doubt for a moment what he was suggesting. "You are going to command Overlord."

The Combined Chiefs had agreed that Eisenhower should take command in London effective the first of the year, and that he should be given the title of "Supreme Commander, Allied Expeditionary Force," or "Supreme Allied Commander" for short.

"Mr. President," Eisenhower said, "I realize that such an appointment involved difficult decisions. I hope you will not be disappointed."

"I cannot spare Marshall from Washington," Roosevelt explained.

That night, Roosevelt invited Eisenhower to a dinner served by two Italian prisoners of war, who acted as waiters under the watchful glare of the Secret Service. Scenes from the Tehran Conference were reenacted with dramatic reminiscence, and toasts were made to anything that would give everyone a reason to drink. Roosevelt held forth on what a sight it was to see the Nazi retreat in North Africa. Thousands of miles of broken-down tanks, cars, equipment, and debris. That was all that remained of the Nazi Afrika Korps. Roosevelt waxed about how he had decided to launch Operation Torch, though the president's memory of his own foresight and initiative was rather different from what Eisenhower remembered.

The following day, Eisenhower dutifully served as Roosevelt's four-star concierge, escorting the president to Malta to present Field Marshall John Standish Surtees Prendergast Vereker, Sixth Viscount Gort, a testimonial of friendship from America to Malta, and then on to Sicily to award the Distinguished Service Cross to Wayne Clark. Roosevelt was also supposed to present Beetle with the Legion of Merit, but the moment the award was to be presented, Beetle had absconded somewhere. Roosevelt had planned to fly on to Marrakesh, but due to equipment failure, returned to Tunis, stayed overnight in the White House, and then left the next morning to complete his journey home to the United States.

It was all the "eternal pound, pound, pound" that Eisenhower had complained to Mamie about earlier that week. But in the private moments in between, Roosevelt confided in Eisenhower about the challenges ahead, in ways that suggested Roosevelt no longer thought he was just Plog's assistant.

"Poor dear old Winney is getting pretty difficult," Roosevelt warned him, "but Uncle Joe and I see eye for eye."

Roosevelt was wary of British intentions. He had taken to instructing Americans sent to London that they were to have "the office open at 9am, an hour before the British, and to never have tea at 5pm." Roosevelt was steadfast in his belief in the alliance with Britain. But he fretted that Churchill's "Empire ideas are nineteenth century, if not eighteenth or seventeenth. And we're fighting a twentieth-century war. Thanks be to God, the balance has shifted somewhat; it's no longer quite a war for survival; but it was a close thing, a very, very, close thing; and one of the principal reasons it was a close thing lies in their assumption of the eternity of Empire."

EISENHOWER STAYED IN Tunis after the president left, since Churchill was due to arrive the next day. And again, the prime minister was late, his trip being delayed until Saturday.

As Eisenhower waited, he received a cable from Roosevelt asking whether he wanted to postpone his transfer to London until after he had captured Rome. He signed off, "I enjoyed our day together ever so much. Good luck."

Eisenhower did not hesitate. "The date for the capture of Rome is so indeterminate," he replied the same day, "that we should go ahead with plans looking toward a transfer shortly after the first of the year." There might be progress by then but Eisenhower did not want to get bogged down in Italy and give the president a reason to reconsider his decision.

Walter "Beetle" Smith

CHAPTER 7

EISENHOWER HAD HOPED to see General Marshall. But then came word that Marshall changed his travel plans. Instead of returning to Tunis, he went east to the Pacific.

It certainly smacked of a grudge, but then Eisenhower received a letter, personal from General Marshall. Inside was a note in Marshall's handwriting, reading, "From the President to Marshal Stalin, The appointment of General Eisenhower, to command of overlord. Operation has been decided upon. Roosevelt." The word "immediately" had been inserted before the word "appointment." At the bottom, Marshall added, "Dear Eisenhower, I thought you might like to have this as a memento. It was written very hurriedly by me as the final meeting broke up yesterday, the president signing it immediately. GCM."

In his excitement, Eisenhower wrote his son a letter. He was appropriately discreet, given that his new position was still a government secret. But he could not resist the chance to brag to his boy. "For your very private information, it is possible that you may see some orders come out that will affect me. Don't be excited and don't for one second try to interpret them as anything but complete and official stamp of approval on everything I have tried to do." He then beamed that while he "did not give the matter any publicity, the President in person, just recently awarded me yet another decoration and pinned it on me himself when he was in Cairo—so you can see that everything is OK."

Eisenhower had earned that stamp of approval, not because of his battlefield cunning, but because he had built the perfect team to fight an allied war. Looking forward to Operation Overlord, Eisenhower's top priority was building the right team because if he had learned anything over the past year, it was that putting the right people in the right positions was the most important decision he made. People were policy.

The previous February, Erwin Rommel's Afrika Korps had humiliated America's II Corps at the Battle of the Kasserine Pass. Eisenhower took the defeat as an opportunity to replace the commanding general, Lloyd Fredendall, with George Patton, along with Omar Bradley as Patton's deputy. They hadn't lost a battle since.

Eisenhower's instinct was to keep his winning team together as much as possible, particularly when it came to his British commanders. And just as important, he wanted to preserve a unified command. Overlord was a far vaster operation than anything he had ever attempted. But he still wanted a single allied commander in chief for each domain: air, ground, and sea without any national distinctions. That was how he had organized his headquarters throughout the Mediterranean, and he did not want to have to manage separate British and American "army groups" for Operation Overlord.

Part of the reason was to ensure a truly allied effort. He didn't want the battlefield divided into national fiefdoms as it had been to disastrous results in World War I. It also made practical sense, given the geography of northern France. "The front," he wrote to General Marshall laying out his organizational plan, "is so narrow that the employment of two separate tactical air forces at the beginning is unthinkable."

For his ground commander, there was no one better than Harold "Alex" Alexander. And for the air chief, there was no one better than Arthur Tedder.

Tedder had the airman's usual swagger and was apt to be spotted speeding behind the wheel of his little French sports car. He was one of Britain's great aviation heroes, having led the air campaign in the victory over the Germans at El Alamein in October 1942. But unlike the typical airman, Tedder's swagger did not bleed into insufferable arrogance. He had taught Eisenhower an enormous amount about airpower without lording his encyclopedic knowledge of the subject over Eisenhower with condescension. If anything, Tedder was understated to the point of diffidence and had become, over the previous year, one of Eisenhower's most trusted friends.

Eisenhower knew these men and what they could do. There was no British-American line between them.

For the navy chief, there was also no one better than Andrew Cunningham, who had served in that role throughout Eisenhower's greatest successes in the Mediterranean. Cunningham, though, had been promoted that October to the position of first sea lord, meaning he was now Ernest King's counterpart on the British Chiefs of Staff. Second best, though, was Bertram "Bertie" Ramsay. A steel-trap mind, and a meticulous planner, he was an éminence grise in the Royal Navy, and his storied career spanned the Gallipoli campaign to orchestrating the evacuation of Dunkirk. He had served under Cunningham in the Mediterranean for the past year and Cunningham had personally recommended him to be the naval commander in chief for Overlord.

Just as important as Eisenhower's commanders in chief, if not more important, was his personal staff. These were the people truly closest to him, day-to-day. That meant, of course, the pillars of his Official Family: Butch, Kay, and Telek. But he also knew that he needed Beetle Smith, who, Marshall would say, "did the dirty work for Eisenhower."

Beetle was outwardly everything Eisenhower could not be if everyone was going to like Ike. Where Eisenhower's broad, boyish smile could disarm anyone, the dimple in Beetle's chin somehow seemed like an obscene gesture. Beetle had very large chips beneath the three general's stars he now wore on his shoulders. But he had earned them. He had dropped out of school at sixteen to enlist as a private in the Indiana National Guard and then pulled himself to the top like a drowning man by always getting the job done.

When Beetle made people's toes sore, Eisenhower would always defend him, saying that the man's grandfather had served in the Prussian army. But even more than his ability to do what Eisenhower could not, or at least should not do, Beetle knew his stuff. "Staff is an extension of the commander's brain," Beetle would say. "I think almost exactly like Eisenhower, on purely military matters." And of the most value, with yes-men everywhere Eisenhower looked, Beetle was still willing to have a drag-out argument if he thought Eisenhower was wrong about something.

Eisenhower also needed James "Jimmy" Gault, who had joined the Official Family that summer. He was Beetle's opposite in every meaningful respect. An Eton- and Cambridge-educated Scots Guardsman, Jimmy was technically Eisenhower's British military aide, but his real job was to be a fixer and a British-to-American translator. Jimmy was cartoonishly British. His whole face talked through his mouth, a narrow slit that was prone to purse tightly with all the manners someone speaking the King's English should display. He would tolerate the nickname "Jimmy," at least from Eisenhower, but not the American-flavored "Jim," which provoked Butch to call him nothing but "Jim."

The only thing Eisenhower lacked was a stenographer who could keep up with him. When he had imagined the general's life as a child, he had no way of knowing that most of his days would be filled by reading and sending messages. Long and short, personal and top secret, cables, letters, and VMail, for himself or for everyone, to and from points all around the globe: Eisenhower was in a near-constant state of conversation with people who were elsewhere. He would laugh that back in Abilene anyone who talked to himself this much was showing "a sure sign of senility." But now here he was, filling his days smoking, pacing, and losing his patience with exhausted stenographers.

With the move to London, things would be moving even faster. Robert McClure, who headed up public relations, supposedly had a great secretary: Mattie Pinette. Eisenhower decided to give her a shot.

Mattie arrived, a self-possessed woman in her early forties with short curly hair sprouting out from under her standard-issue Women's Auxiliary Corps (WAC) cap. Eisenhower welcomed her and said he was looking for a new stenographer. It was a demanding job and few lasted long. Was she interested?

Mattie was uncowed and so Eisenhower asked if she would be willing to submit to a test of her stenography skills.

Of course, she said, and pulled out her pad.

Eisenhower then paced about the room, dictating a usual message, plump with military jargon and needless abbreviations, between puffs on a fresh filterless Camel, rattling it all off as rapidly as he thought the words. All the while, Mattie scribbled on her pad. At no point, did she ask him to slow down or to repeat anything. She just continued to scribble until he stopped. That was it.

Mattie politely excused herself from his office and Eisenhower turned to other things. After a while, though, he noticed that she never returned. Was she still typing? He opened the door of his office and looked out. Mattie

Pinette was gone. Had she quit? Already? Eisenhower then saw, on the desk outside his office, a sheet of paper. It was the message he had dictated. It was perfect.

CHURCHILL ARRIVED SATURDAY in his custom Lancaster around nine in the morning. He looked terrible. The cold he had been suffering in Malta had gotten worse.

That night, Eisenhower joined the prime minister for dinner, which did not start until eight thirty, with the expectation that it would last until everyone except Churchill had collapsed. But everyone was tired, Churchill most of all. His voice was hoarse and lacked his usual pugnacity.

Eisenhower took the opportunity to announce some of his personnel demands as the new Supreme Allied Commander. Among them, he insisted, in order of priority: First, Telek would remain his dog and be exempt from the usual six-month quarantine for animals entering the British Isles. Second, Beetle would remain his chief of staff. And third, Jimmy Gault would remain his British military aide.

Absolutely not, Churchill scowled. This was an absolute red line. This was still the British Empire, after all. Telek would have to quarantine. Even the King's dogs had to quarantine. With respect to the rest, Churchill was willing to relent, including on Beetle. He suggested, though, that Eisenhower wait and see before bringing too many of his people along with him. There were already a lot of very qualified people in London, who had been working on Operation Overlord for nearly a year.

After the Casablanca Conference, the Allies had created an organization in London called the Chief of Staff to the Supreme Allied Commander, or "COSSAC" for short. COSSAC had prepared a detailed plan coordinating air, sea, and ground forces to punch through the Normandy coast. Roosevelt and Churchill had personally approved the plan when they met in Quebec the previous summer. And COSSAC had been building, organizing, and storing everything needed to implement that plan under the command of the British general Frederick "Freddie" Morgan, who had been assigned to lead COSSAC on the assumption that he—not Beetle Smith—would be the chief of staff when the Supreme Allied Commander arrived.

Freddie Morgan had a reputation as a superb military planner, though profoundly unlucky in his assignments. He seemed always to be put in charge of operations that were later tabled through no fault of his own. Given Morgan's depth of knowledge, Eisenhower wanted to keep him.

Though again, in another turn of bad luck for Morgan, that meant a demotion to being Beetle's deputy and a cut in pay.

The bigger personnel problem Eisenhower confronted, or at least a more sensitive one, was what to do with Jacob Devers. Another protégé of General Marshall, Devers was hand-selected to command the European Theater of Operations in April 1943. This was the very job Marshall had sent Eisenhower to do back in June 1942, before Eisenhower took command in the Mediterranean. That meant Devers was expected to play a significant part in the invasion. But Eisenhower did not particularly know or, for that matter, like Devers.

General Marshall had sent Devers to North Africa early in 1943 to assess the shortcomings in Eisenhower's use of tanks, no less. And Devers was full of critiques. When he became commander of the European Theater of Operations, Devers had never let his overriding importance to the "overall war effort" go unnoticed. The previous summer, when Eisenhower was leading the hot point of the war in Sicily, he had requested four heavy bomber groups to be temporarily diverted south to provide air support. Devers vetoed the request on the ground that the heavy bombers were committed to bombing strategic targets in Germany. "I must be guided by the greatest damage to the German enemy," he replied to Eisenhower, as if retaking the Mediterranean from Axis control was an Anglo-American hobby. "I must never lose sight of the imminence of Overlord."

Devers's heart was set on commanding the First Army, the American ground force that would be invading Normandy. Omar Bradley was in command of the First Army on an interim basis, and there was an assumption that Devers would replace him at some point. But in addition to the personal things, Eisenhower was not convinced Devers was up to the job. He had no combat experience. True, the same could have been said of Eisenhower, but the Combined Chiefs had just declared the invasions of northern and southern France the "supreme operations for 1944." Too much was at stake for on-the-job training.

Eisenhower had seen Patton while escorting Roosevelt to Sicily and asked his advice on what to do with Devers. Patton and Devers had been classmates at West Point and worked together for decades.

It was the first time Eisenhower had seen Georgie since the slapping incident hit the news, and Georgie presented him with a fine pair of $7.10 Italian boots as a gift. It was an unnecessary kindness, Eisenhower assured him. He was already planning on giving Patton an army to take into France.

Georgie was predictably delighted and told Eisenhower not to waste his time with Devers. He thought the man was useless, though his opinion was colored by General Marshall having promoted Devers over Patton to lead the army's armored forces back in 1941.

Eisenhower did not want Devers leading an army and he sure as hell did not want him back-seat driving in London as the commander of the European Theater of Operations. So, Eisenhower decided to propose a swap. Eisenhower would retake command of the US Army in the European Theater of Operations, which would add to his troubles, since being theater commander would make him responsible for the management of the US Army at the same time he would be orchestrating the most difficult military operation in human history as the Supreme Allied Commander. But Eisenhower had worn both hats in North Africa and enjoyed considerably more authority as a result, since being the one who approved promotions and decided courts-martial ensured that his orders were more apt to be followed—at least by American soldiers.

If Eisenhower took over as the commander of the European Theater of Operations, Devers could then take over as the commander of what had become the Mediterranean Theater of Operations. And when a British general took over Eisenhower's present job as the supreme commander for the Mediterranean, Devers could become the American deputy.

In principle, the deputy job should have gone to Wayne Clark, who was due for a promotion. But Eisenhower figured his old buddy Wayne would prefer to lead the invasion of southern France anyway. Operation Anvil offered a lot more glamour than doing staff work as deputy to a British general.

Eisenhower wrote a lengthy letter to General Marshall outlining his plan. Devers, he said, would be "superfluous in the UK" and should be sent to the Mediterranean. He also put in a formal request for Patton. He acknowledged that it was a sensitive subject, but defended the choice, saying, "I have no intention of throwing valuable men to the wolves merely because of one mistake."

Harry "Butch" Butcher

CHAPTER 8

THE DAY AFTER Churchill's arrival, Hap Arnold, the head of the Army Air Forces, paid his own congratulatory visit to Eisenhower. He had just come from Naples and the central Italian front, where Wayne Clark was slogging up the boot of Italy toward Rome.

Clark had led the landings at Salerno, code-named Operation "Avalanche" back in September 1943. The beaches were weakly defended and the initial buildup looked promising. But a few days in, the Germans counterattacked in force. Things had been pretty touch and go, but mercifully, the weather cooperated and Eisenhower was able to send in paratroopers as reinforcements. Within a few weeks the Germans had pulled back and the Allies controlled the bottom half of the Italian boot, including the port city of Naples.

The fighting north toward Rome, though, had been slow. And Hap Arnold's description of what he saw at the front was like a Wilfred Owen poem.

"Modern battle," Arnold wrote in his diary, "Jeeps and mud, trucks and tanks, more mud, trucks and road jams, bridges and culverts blown out by bombs and demolitions of the Germans, bomb holes, mine holes, railroad ties cut in two by German heavy ploughs pulled by locomotives. Villages and towns, demolished, partly demolished. Destruction and devastation everywhere. Mud and more mud. Trees cut down by explosives to block the road.

"A tank blown to bits from running over mine, five bodies lying in small pieces on the ground. Civilians, men and women, clinging to desolated and despoiled houses, and mud, mud, mud. The Germans over the hill, watching us, perhaps, wondering who could be so foolish to come up there."

With only two weeks left in the Mediterranean, Eisenhower flew to Caserta, Italy, to see the front for himself. Butch and the whole Official Family had gone ahead to prepare his headquarters, an ornate villa overlooking Napoli harbor, christened the Della Ortensie. Wayne Clark was waiting for Eisenhower when he arrived.

Looking to the future, Wayne was eager to be done with Italy and to take Eisenhower up on the chance to lead the invasion of the South of France. It would make them something of a duo again, like they had been in Washington at the start of the war. He warned Eisenhower, though, that to do Operation Anvil properly, they should abandon the plan being considered to invade Anzio further up the boot of Italy. Code-named "Shingle," the invasion was an end run around the German resistance Wayne was facing in his drive north toward Rome. If the Allies' goal was capturing Rome, Operation Shingle made sense. But if France was the prize, and they were set on invading the French Riviera by May 1, they would need to start moving landing craft out of Italy by the end of January.

It was not realistic, Wayne thought, to expect the invasion of Anzio to wrap up in a week or two given how slowly things were moving through the Italian mud. To show Eisenhower what he meant, Wayne took him on a jeep tour of the front. Wayne was confident that they were making progress. But the endless rain made everything a miserable slog.

Things would be better, Wayne said, if he had control over the air forces. The bombing of Italy the summer before Operation Avalanche had been devastating, as anyone entering the Napoli harbor could still see. But without the ability to continue to bomb where and when he needed to bomb, the Germans simply regrouped and resupplied after each day's battle, ensuring that the next day's battle would be just as brutal. It takes everything you have to kill what refuses to die.

EISENHOWER RETURNED FROM a long and discouraging day to an old stone hunting lodge that Butch had found in the hills around Caserta. For the few days he would still be supreme commander for the Mediterranean, this would be his official residence in Italy. It was the kind of retreat Eisenhower always enjoyed, and he plopped down into a comfortable chair next to the giant Italian stove that kept the cold out.

Eisenhower had promised to take the whole Official Family to Wayne Clark's command tent that evening for a proper Italian dinner. Tired as he was, though, he would've been content to just sit, smoke, and sleep. But then Mickey came storming down the stairs.

"There is a rat in the general's bathroom!"

The frenzy made it sound as though the rat were armed with a carbine. Telek had discovered it, but had been held at bay by Mickey, who feared Telek's life as a spoiled lap dog had failed to prepare him for a fight to the death with a rat that had lived through Operation Avalanche.

The excitement got Eisenhower out of his chair. With father-knows-best élan, he grabbed his revolver and went upstairs to show everyone how it was done back in Abilene. It would be the first firefight of his military career.

Eisenhower moseyed through his new bedroom, a vast bedchamber with an enormous fireplace perfect for pitching cigarette butts. And then to the bathroom, which was up a few steps and, he discovered, the size of a closet. The rat had holed up behind the sink.

Eisenhower got a bead on him and fired. The rat, evidently unarmed, did not return fire, but instead took evasive action and scurried up the toilet pipe. Eisenhower fired three more times, succeeding only in clipping the little guerrilla's tail and blowing pieces of Italian porcelain onto the floor.

Low on ammo, Eisenhower finally got a body shot. The rat stopped scurrying. On closer inspection, though, the rat was only wounded. Mortally, perhaps, but still clinging to life. Then, *whomp!* Butch finished him off with a log from the fireplace. It takes everything you have to kill what refuses to die.

GOOD TO HIS word, Eisenhower treated his Official Family to a seven-course feast, complements of Wayne Clark. Elliott Roosevelt even joined. And that night, Eisenhower went to bed content that he had done good by his people.

As he closed his eyes, the phone rang throughout the entire house. Someone answered, and it stopped. He breathed in the darkness and the sounds of the forest as he waited for sleep.

The phone rang again. He was jolted, but just as quickly as it started, the ringing stopped. There was another long moment. At last, it was quiet.

There he was, lying in a large, comfortable bed in the Italian countryside. He was—at least temporarily—the master of a hunting lodge that some Italian noble had built how many hundreds of years ago in a bedroom that was decorated for a caesar. There were elaborate murals on the walls. There was even one on the ceiling, painted so that the light fixture hung from the navel of Cupid like an umbilical cord. The bedroom was cold, but nothing like the cold he had grown accustomed to in his shared bed as a boy in Abilene, where he would always be the last out of bed after the father called up. Eisenhower lay there beneath Cupid, finally drifting to sleep.

The goddamn phone rang again. This time, in a rage, he grabbed the receiver and shouted, "For God's sake, the goddamn phone rings every time I am about to go to sleep. Can't something be done about it?"

A sheepish voice that sounded conspicuously like Elliott Roosevelt apologized that he had gotten the wrong number.

Eisenhower returned to bed still hot. He tried to slow his heart rate down. He was determined to get some sleep. The room was quiet again.

Then, he heard a creaking. Then a snap. Then a crash as the bedposts buckled. He was suddenly part of a pile on the floor. He checked himself. He was unhurt. And so, he left the problem for tomorrow and went to sleep.

THERE WERE ALL sorts of problems that he could leave for the proverbial tomorrow. A cable had come from the Combined Chiefs instructing him to make no promises to the Turks about future operations in the Aegean. An important point no doubt, but his eyes were tired, and the thing at the front of his mind was how annoying it was to read in cable-ese, where words were abbreviated and abbreviations, to include punctuation and numbers, were written out as words. CMA for comma. PD or just X for period. PARA for a new line. BAKER for B. CHARLIE for C. And CHARLIE CHARLIE for the Combined Chiefs.

"Goddamn," he said, "I get tired of having to read all these Charlie, Charlie, in these repeated messages."

The day after the Battle of the Rat, Eisenhower drove with Beetle the seven hours to Bari for a meeting with Pietro Badoglio on the future of Allied operations in Italy. The rain and the mountain roads made for a tedious drive home, which was made all the more tedious by the fact that they had driven the same distance in the other direction earlier that day.

Eisenhower invited Beetle to dinner that night once they dried off. Beetle, though, declined, saying he was tired. There was something in the tone of Beetle's voice, a certain self-assurance, a forgetting of his place. Combined with a long car ride in the rain something spiked in Eisenhower.

You know, he said to Beetle, it is very discourteous to decline a dinner invitation from a superior officer.

Beetle chaffed at being scolded like a truant West Point cadet. He then threatened to quit. It was best if his superior officer was going to talk to him that way.

"Fine," Eisenhower snapped back. Beetle could stay with Devers in the Mediterranean. It would make Churchill happy.

They stewed in the rain and in the car, until Beetle relented and apologized. All was forgiven, Eisenhower promised. But a grudge chilled the rest of the ride back and they went their separate ways when they got to Caserta.

It was not long, though, before Beetle returned. There was a cable from General Marshall. It wasn't good. Marshall was insisting that the United States have its own army group separate from the British. And, what was more, Marshall wanted Devers to command it, or at least one of its major components.

Eisenhower and Beetle worked out a reply, explaining the reasons for consolidating British and American forces, so that they could fight with the coordinated efficiency that they had achieved in the Mediterranean. But whatever the structure, Eisenhower was adamant that the American ground commanders needed "combat experience in this war." If there was to be a US army group, the man to lead it was Omar Bradley, not Jacob Devers. Brad, as Eisenhower called him, had been a classmate at West Point and, as far as Eisenhower was concerned, was so well balanced, and well rounded, that his biggest flaw was lacking any flaws Eisenhower could identify.

It was already after five in the evening. And as he and Beetle worked over the text of their reply to Marshall, another urgent cable came through. This one was directly from Roosevelt. "Please inform the French Committee as follows: 'In view of the assistance given to the Allied Armies during the campaign in Africa by Boisson, Peyrouton, and Flandin, you are directed to take no action against these individuals at the present time.'"

It was all over the news that Eisenhower and Beetle had missed during their long car ride back and forth to Bari. Charles de Gaulle, the leader of the French Committee of National Liberation, had just ordered the arrest of several former Vichy officials, including Pierre-Étienne Flandin, the former prime minister; Pierre Boisson, the former governor-general of French West Africa; and Marcel Peyrouton, the former interior minister.

Eisenhower was stunned. These three men had been indispensable in helping Eisenhower conquer North Africa. Boisson, in particular. They had trusted him.

Churchill was still in Tunis convalescing with pneumonia. "I am shocked," Churchill cabled Roosevelt. This was a matter of the empire's prestige. Churchill had personally assured these men of their safety if they supported the Allies in the fight for Tunis. "Count on me," Churchill had said.

What was De Gaulle doing? The previous summer, the British, Canadian, and Soviet governments had recognized the French Committee as France's government-in-exile. Roosevelt had refused to go that far, recognizing only its authority to administer France's newly liberated colonial territories. Now De Gaulle seemed to be intent on finding ways of sticking his thumb in Roosevelt's eye.

Eisenhower and Beetle thought about what to do. Sending Roosevelt's demand to the French Committee would only escalate the situation. "There was a chance," Beetle recognized, "that the French would ignore us and shoot the people anyway, and thus give us a black eye." And then what?

Beetle devised a plan. He would go back to Algiers the next day to try to negotiate with the French and see if he could persuade Churchill to tone it down. Meanwhile, Eisenhower should stay in Italy and go somewhere he would be hard to reach. That way, if the president reacted badly to being second-guessed, Eisenhower could disavow what Beetle had done in his absence. Eisenhower agreed.

With Beetle on his way to Algiers, Eisenhower sent a cable to the American liaison to the French Committee, saying, "I can visualize nothing less than the gravest possible consequences if the French National Committee undertakes to try and judge French citizens prior to the establishment of a free and national French government." He then replied to Roosevelt, notifying him that he was at his "advanced headquarters in Italy where I am visiting the front." He assured the president that he was "profoundly disturbed" by De Gaulle's actions and was sending Beetle to Algiers immediately to take charge of the situation.

The next day, with Beetle in Algiers, there was another message from General Marshall. It was an "eyes only" cable, in which Marshall said that he was "seriously concerned" and accused Eisenhower of trying to "gut the Mediterranean headquarters and leadership, leaving a most complex situation" for his successors. Marshall then reiterated his opposition to sending

Devers to the Mediterranean and proposed leaving Beetle there instead, at least for another few months, since Freddie Morgan was "a very capable officer and almost seems more American than British."

If that were not enough, Eisenhower then received notice that the British had blocked his request to have Harold "Alex" Alexander as his overall ground commander. Eisenhower knew there was opposition, not the least from Alan Brooke. But as early as that morning, he had hoped his request for Alex would be approved.

Churchill, though, had sent his final decision to Roosevelt the previous day. Alex would stay in Italy. The British ground commander for Operation Overlord would be Bernard "Monty" Montgomery.

Eisenhower knew this was a possibility. But Monty? The only man Monty respected was Alan Brooke, who by turns was also Monty's greatest patron. Brooke had been grooming Monty for this moment, and now it had arrived.

"Monty," Eisenhower would say behind closed doors, "was a little man, little physically, little mentally, little in every way." Now that little man would be the most important general under his command.

Douglas MacArthur

CHAPTER 9

EISENHOWER SPENT HIS last day "at the front" in Italy on a goodwill trip to the island of Capri. The Army Air Forces in Europe, under the command of Carl "Tooey" Spaatz, had requisitioned the island as a rest camp.

It was Christmas Eve, and he brought along Butch and Kay, as well as Mickey and Pearlie Hargrave, a WAC on his staff to whom Mickey had just gotten engaged. Capri was a forty-five-minute boat ride from Naples and they were all enthusiastically greeted by the island's mayor, who bore an uncanny resemblance to Fiorello La Guardia. A young local girl presented Eisenhower with a bouquet of flowers in celebration of his visit and Eisenhower was given the grand tour.

Capri was an island of wildflowers and bleach-white villas with terracotta roofs. It had rained the entire time Eisenhower was in Italy, but Capri was all sunshine. Its water so clear, blue, and at ease that staring into the sea felt like the childhood memory of lying in the grass beneath a quiet summer sky. Eisenhower had no problems in Capri. There was no war in Capri.

As the tour went on, Eisenhower saw a conspicuously large villa overlooking the sea. It was a palace that would have comfortably suited Emperor Claudius during his exile in Capri two millennia before.

"Whose is that?" he asked.

"Yours, sir," the tour guide told him.

Then, an even grander palace, more than three times the size of the first, came into view. "And that?"

"That one belongs to General Spaatz."

The answers bothered him. They both looked like something Douglas MacArthur would insist on living in.

Of all his mentors—and he had many—none had taught Eisenhower more about the appeal and fatal flaws of the megalomaniac than did Douglas MacArthur. Eisenhower had first gone to Washington when he was thirty-nine and brimmed with all the naive confidence of a man turning forty. His brother, Milton, was already a star in the capital's elite circle of apolitical politics: executive-branch appointees and their staffs, who were overconfident in their competence and eye-rolling in their contempt for the hurly-burly of deal-making, compromise, favor-trading, and electoral politicking that made democracy feel burdensome. Eisenhower quickly joined in.

"Things are not going to take an upturn until more power is centered in one man's hands," Eisenhower wrote after Roosevelt's election. "For two years I have been called 'Dictator Ike' because I believe virtual dictatorship must be exercised by our President. So now I keep silent—but I still believe it!" Eisenhower even came to admire Benito Mussolini, if only because El Duce was "an able administrator."

It was perhaps inevitable that Eisenhower would be one of the many who were awed by Douglas MacArthur. The scion of a storied military family, top of his class at West Point, hero of the Battle of Veracruz, a general at thirty-eight, superintendent of West Point at thirty-nine, chief of staff of the army at fifty. When in his dress uniform, MacArthur's medals and awards ran up to his neck. The only thing MacArthur lacked was humility. And by the time Eisenhower angled his way into MacArthur's inner circle in 1932, MacArthur had already taken up the habit of referring to himself in the third person. Eisenhower was enthralled at being part of MacArthur's "gang."

In the summer of 1932, veterans of World War I established a massive encampment in Washington, DC, to protest the lack of pay and benefits, which in the throes of the Great Depression, had left many destitute. MacArthur led the army, against the president's orders, on a violent assault against the encampments of the so-called Bonus Army, which included driving tanks through the nation's capital.

Eisenhower would later claim to have opposed the crackdown. But at the time, he was literally shoulder to shoulder with MacArthur and wrote the report justifying MacArthur's actions. The ensuing political controversy was intense, and in his diary, Eisenhower wrote, "As Gen. MacA's aide took part in Bonus incident of July 28, a lot of furor has been stirred up, but mostly to make political capital. I wrote the General's report which was as accurate as I could make it."

Eisenhower had happily followed MacArthur to the Philippines, where Roosevelt gave MacArthur a mandate to stand up the Philippine Army, so that it could defend itself by the time the archipelago was scheduled for independence in 1946. With the imperial status of a colonial military governor, MacArthur's feral charisma soon curdled into the vaingloriousness and paranoia of a tinpot dictator.

The president of the Philippines, Manuel Quezon, chaffed at MacArthur's increasing demands, particularly after acceding to MacArthur's insistence on being anointed a field marshal of the Philippine Army at a salary of nearly $4,000 a month (the modern equivalent of a million dollars a year). This was over and above the various perks and privileges MacArthur had been already given, such as the grand suite in one of Manila's most exclusive apartment buildings.

MacArthur, in gratitude, called Quezon a "conceited little monkey" and grew increasingly indifferent to the ostensible duties of his field marshalship. That left Eisenhower as diplomat and producer of actual results. By the time Eisenhower left the Philippines, MacArthur was spending at most an hour a day in the office and doing little more than scheming new ways to add yet more plumage to his well feathered nest.

Eisenhower was willing to forgive nearly anything, and to overlook almost any character flaw. His closest friends and mentors had been racists, imperialists, and, at least in Georgie Patton's case, borderline sociopaths. But the people who kept Eisenhower's respect were all committed to duty. The only thing Eisenhower could not forgive was indifference to doing the job you were there to do.

Eisenhower's contempt for MacArthur grew raw as the dead end that every dictatorship inevitably reaches came clearly into view. Eisenhower was racked with self-pity, and blamed himself for being seduced by MacArthur at the cost of the best years of his life and what in 1940 seemed like his career. Eisenhower's contemporaries from West Point had all begun to surpass him, while he was marooned with a megalomaniac who had no sense of shame, let alone duty. Eisenhower still garnered a letter from MacArthur upon his departure that lauded his "superior professional ability, unswerving loyalty and unselfish devotion to duty." But the experience left him spent.

It was appropriate, and inevitable, that MacArthur and Marshall hated one another. They were the same age. MacArthur had gone to West Point, Marshall to Virginia Military Institute. They were heat and light, glory and honor, charismatic leadership and selfless service, the generalissimo and the soldier. True to form, when Marshall was appointed chief of staff, MacArthur took it as a personal insult. And just as true to form, when MacArthur escaped from the Philippines with a vow to return in 1942, Marshall drafted his commendation for the Medal of Honor. Marshall did not think it was particularly deserved. But he knew America needed a national hero. And so, he did it.

It was seductive being in a place like Capri, just as it was seductive to be in the orbit of someone like MacArthur. It was easy to forget that the smiles and the flowers were being given to him not because of his personal greatness, but because he was the vicar of the powerful force that had dropped bombs from airplanes, laid waste to the ships in the Napoli harbor, and had sent so many young men to slog it out in the mud.

If generals could live like this, sleeping beneath frescoes, it was easy to see how wars could go on forever. But seeing those pompous villas on Capri and being told that one was his, shook Eisenhower. He sent off a letter ordering Wayne Clark to "abolish all personally assigned villas."

Eisenhower left Italy for North Africa on Christmas morning. It was time to smite the gray sea with his oar.

Bernard "Monty" Montgomery

CHAPTER 10

CHURCHILL WAS LOOKING better. The fortnight convalescing in the White House had done him some good. Alex and Tedder were there to celebrate the holiday along with Maitland "Jumbo" Wilson, whom Churchill had selected to replace Eisenhower as the supreme commander for the Mediterranean. Churchill toasted to everyone's health (not the least being his own).

With Britain now firmly in command of the Mediterranean, the main topic of discussion was whether and how to open a second front farther up the Italian boot at Anzio, Operation Shingle. The only concern Eisenhower raised was Wayne Clark's worry over landing craft. Given the scale of the invasion plans for France, they would need to start moving landing craft into position for the Overlord and Anvil operations in the second half of January.

Eisenhower left after lunch and was back in Algiers that evening. There were other things, urgent things, that needed his attention, even on Christmas. The most pressing was Charles de Gaulle.

Beetle had spent the previous two days lobbying Churchill to temper the confrontation with the French. Churchill had gone off hot, which both prompted and permitted Roosevelt to do the same. As far as Roosevelt was concerned, De Gaulle was Churchill's creation, and had long been suspicious that Churchill was intent on installing De Gaulle as a kind of Cromwell for France. And Roosevelt's suspicions of De Gaulle had hardened into disdain after Churchill arranged for them to meet at the Casablanca Conference, which ended up having all the warmth of a mistress being introduced to a wife. Roosevelt probably welcomed Churchill's outrage over De Gaulle's arrest of the Vichy turncoats as a chance to finally rid himself of an over-tall Napoléon.

Beetle, though, prevailed on Churchill to cool things down. If Eisenhower delivered Roosevelt's ultimatum, De Gaulle might hasten to execute the collaborators, which would be "a direct slap that the President of the United States could not accept." Roosevelt would be then forced to refuse to deal with the French Committee, and maybe even stop arming the French altogether, at the very moment he and Eisenhower were hoping to have the Free French forces assist in the invasion of France.

Churchill begrudgingly agreed to take a more diplomatic approach and to urge Roosevelt to do the same.

All while keeping Eisenhower willfully blind, Beetle persuaded the French to accept a face-saving compromise. De Gaulle would postpone the trial of the collaborators until after France was liberated or treat the case as a civil investigation, which would then be terminated for a lack of evidence. In the meantime, the collaborators would be kept comfortable under house arrest in Algiers.

Deal in hand, Beetle had cabled General Marshall on Christmas Eve pressing him to persuade Roosevelt to agree. But there was still no word from the president.

There was also still no further word from General Marshall on Eisenhower's personnel proposals. Marshall had never hesitated to disagree with Eisenhower, and Eisenhower knew not to take it personally. In fact, Marshall had disagreed with Eisenhower the very first time they met.

It was the late 1920s. As an up-and-coming officer, Eisenhower was given the cushy job of traveling to France to assist General John Pershing in writing his semiofficial memoir of America's involvement in World War I. Pershing was the doyen of the army, and Marshall had been his longtime aide. Pershing's flair as a military commander, however, did not endow him with much talent as a writer, and Eisenhower suggested some edits. Pershing was supportive and told Eisenhower to take the edits to Marshall, who thanked Eisenhower for sharing his ideas, and left the draft as it was.

This disagreement over the people who would be the backbone of Eisenhower's team for Operation Overlord was different. And it mattered more. General Marshall had spent months anticipating taking command in

England and had clearly formed his own ideas about how to invade France. That opportunity of a lifetime now having been taken from him, Eisenhower found it hard to shake the feeling that Marshall was more than a bit chapped, seeing his protégé trying to go his own way. It was still Marshall's ultimate call. But Eisenhower had to figure out a way of persuading his mentor to trust him and his judgment about who he needed doing what.

It was a lonely way to spend Christmas, and Eisenhower found himself feeling homesick. Everything felt off. Mamie had sent him a portrait of herself in a leather folder frame, suitable for all his traveling, and Mamie's parents, who always spoiled him at Christmas, sent him a care package stuffed with a scarf, handkerchiefs, playing cards, a toothbrush, toothpaste, his favorite soups, soap, buttons, a polish set, and all sorts of sundry things to make him feel more at home. It was a wholesome companion to the presents from Field Marshall Aleksandr Vasilevsky, Russia's chief of staff, who sent him vodka and cigarettes.

THE FOLLOWING DAY, things finally started breaking Eisenhower's way. Roosevelt agreed to the backroom deal Beetle had cooked up with the French, though he still insisted that the United States' "alarm" at the situation be communicated to De Gaulle personally.

There was still no word, though, from Marshall. Eisenhower wrote him a lengthy cable that began apologetically. He did not mean to be presumptuous but was offering only "my personal views as to the most satisfactory arrangement for Overlord command." He made clear that he had "no objection to accepting" any of Marshall's ideas. While he made his case for Omar Bradley, he also conceded "I am not as well acquainted" with Devers. He closed by saying, "I repeat my readiness to accept your designations and give those officers every encouragement and opportunity."

Eisenhower was running late that morning for his last press conference in the Mediterranean. He duly apologized when he arrived and announced that his main reason for being there was "to say goodbye to you fellows, as a personal thing, and moreover to express, if I could, a little bit of appreciation that I owe you fellows, and the way you've acted in this theater."

The first question was a friendly one. "Here for the benefit of those who are accredited here, and are likely to remain here, will there be any good stories within the next six months?"

"If the Mediterranean isn't fighting like hell in the next six months I'll be surprised," Eisenhower said. "Don't think the Mediterranean theater is just going into a state of slumber, a drunken stupor. No, sir, they are going to be fighting. You bet they are!"

Clare Hollingworth, a British reporter, asked the next question. Hollingworth was a legendary war correspondent, famous for breaking the news of Germany's invasion of Poland. Monty had expelled her from his command the previous spring, evidently on the ground that he did not think women should be near the front.

"I'm new to this theater," Hollingworth said disarmingly, "and I haven't followed all the campaign. I should like to ask the following question: I have heard a lot of criticism for our landing in Salerno, instead of higher up."

"I have read serious criticism that we went to Salerno myself," Eisenhower said, his jolly holiday-season mood fading. He then explained the geography, the intelligence, and all that went into his thinking, adding, "I say simply this: any commander who will send the vast surface fleet, by that I mean a surface fleet carrying soldiers and supplies, few of which can be warships that could defend themselves relatively easy, and to go under the enormous land based aircraft—that commander ought to be relieved before he starts his planes."

"Couldn't you have occupied Corsica?" Hollingworth asked, following up.

"We didn't have Corsica then," he replied. "We got Sardinia later. The Germans saw it was silly for them to stay there any longer. How long would it have taken to build them up as an air base from which you could operate? Time is what you're always fighting for and more. Time's what you can't afford. That's always the most important thing in war. To take Sardinia and Corsica, then start to build them up as air bases, that was time."

"On the other hand," Hollingworth continued, "it seems difficult to take Rome from the south. Looking back through history, I don't find any invaders who took Rome from the south."

"There are lots of things done in this war that have not been done in history," he snapped before stopping himself. "I don't mean that to be sarcastic. Everybody must realize that war never produces a maximum effort that is sustained over a great period of time after a battalion has fought to its extreme limit for three days or three nights, someone has to go there and relieve it. You haven't got the resources. It is easy for people to sit back and draw arrows on a map but you got to produce the means to make that arrow a reality."

The subject changed to the French and another reporter caveated his question, "This may be more of a question of politics than military . . ."

"War is nothing but an extension of politics to the field of force," Eisenhower said, without missing a beat. And after some back-and-forth on the status of the fighting in Italy, he was asked about his new job.

"General," one reporter asked. "As you know some people contend that a great part of the knockout can be done by air. I wonder whether you would care to give any impression as to how far that may prepare for the final blow?"

"I am convinced that we must do everything possible to intensify the bombing effort against Germany, because there are certain periods of the year when bombing is our best way of striking. I do not subscribe to the belief that by bombing alone, you can conquer a nation with the resourcefulness and strength of the German nation."

"Would you give us a statement on what you think we will look at next year at this time?"

"You know," Eisenhower began mischievously, "I don't like to pull my punches; so I'll tell you this, and you can quote me."

Pencils were poised. One of Eisenhower's quirks, which he shared with Roosevelt, was that he hated the thought of being quoted off the cuff. If anything was to be put in quotation marks next to his name, he insisted on running it through the public relations office first. The newly minted Supreme Commander, Allied Expeditionary Forces, it seemed, had a new confidence to speak his mind publicly.

"We will win the war in '44," Eisenhower said with brio. It was a nice grace note on which to end the year.

"You mean the German war?" Clare Hollingworth interjected.

"We will win the European war in 1944," he clarified.

Then from the back of the room, another correspondent followed up. "Do you think the European war will *end* in 1944?"

"European war is never going to end," he chuckled, before adding, "that's not for quotation. I mean the one we are fighting now. It is my conviction that the allies will win the European war in 1944."

"How long do you think the Japanese war will last after that?" Hollingworth asked.

"I really don't know. This is something even the people who are most familiar can't tell," he said. "But we will win that one and after we get loose on this one they will know someone hit them.

"I must say," Eisenhower concluded as he prepared to leave, "I appreciate the association with you and I hate to be leaving you fellows—maybe I'll be seeing you again. All the way from Darlan on down you have been very understanding and cooperative."

As Eisenhower left the briefing, Butch pulled him aside. "Win the war in '44"—wasn't that being a bit optimistic? Maybe they would win the war in 1944, but this was the kind of quote that could haunt him.

Eisenhower knew Butch was right and so dictated a press release for the correspondents to use in its place: "It is my conviction that the allies will win the European war in 1944. The only thing needed for us to win the European war in 1944 is for every man and woman, all the way from the front line to the remotest hamlet of our two countries to do his or her full duty."

Not quite a grace note, but it would keep him out of trouble.

WHILE EISENHOWER WAS with the press, Beetle had been meeting with De Gaulle and Henri Giraud. They, on behalf of the French Committee, agreed to put Free French forces under Eisenhower's command for the invasion of France. The one condition was that they would play a prominent role in the retaking of Paris. All that was left was for Eisenhower to seal the deal with a little personal diplomacy before he left Algiers.

With one prima donna under control, at least for the moment, Eisenhower and Beetle turned to another: Monty.

Monty had been Alex's instructor at the British Army's staff college, and Monty never let Alex forget it. Eisenhower had met Monty at a farmhouse in southern England back in May 1942. Monty was conducting exercises with British and Canadian forces, and Eisenhower and Wayne Clark were invited to observe.

At a briefing, Eisenhower and Wayne sat in the back and Eisenhower was impressed by Monty. He was energetic and knew his stuff. At one point, Eisenhower reached for a Camel. He offered one to Wayne, who passed, and then smoked as he listened to Monty demonstrate a degree of decisiveness and a mastery of the details that Eisenhower could not help but admire.

But then Monty abruptly stopped. He sniffed from his proud beak of a nose, and demanded, "Who's smoking?"

"I am," Eisenhower confessed.

"Stop it," Monty scolded him. "I don't permit smoking in my office."

Eisenhower put out the cigarette, redirecting its flame into his veins, which reddened his face with a combination of embarrassment and fury.

Monty had been the ground commander for the British Army's great victory at El Alamein. It made him a national hero beyond reproach. But in private, even this victory was begrudged. Arthur Tedder, with obvious self-interest, attributed the victory to superior airpower. "German communications had been wrecked, and that had forced Rommel's retreat," he would say. "El Alamein was won before Monty's ground forces had even begun to move."

Tedder, like every Brit, was dutifully quick to lavish praise on Monty regardless of what they thought of him. But it always irked Tedder that Monty had never once recognized the air force's role in bringing the Germans at El Alamein to heel.

Monty had been one of Eisenhower's principal British subordinates for the past year. And when Eisenhower forced himself to assess Monty objectively, he gave him credit for being the kind of commander who inspired the men under him. Even Monty's preening for the limelight could be viewed—generously, at least—as a strategy to bolster the confidence of his men.

Monty was, despite their many differences, a lot like Patton. Their main difference was their reputations for risk taking. Monty was cautious and Patton was not, which was one of many reasons why Monty's men loved him, and Patton's often hated him. The rivalry between the two men had become notorious with Patton losing no opportunity to remind everyone that his army had outrun Monty's to Messina and ultimate victory in Sicily. When Georgie heard that Monty would be taking the lead for Operation Overlord, he fretted that Monty's tendency to plan everything "down to the last shoelace" would sap the invasion of the energy it would need.

Eisenhower had asked Monty to come to Algiers that afternoon to discuss the way forward. Monty was due to visit Churchill, who had moved to a villa in Marrakesh after Christmas to rest up for the New Year. And wholly apart from their less than friendly personal history, there was reason for concern.

Monty's greatest patron, the only reason he had been selected to lead the ground forces into Normandy over Alex, was Alan Brooke. Eisenhower had every reason to fear that Monty was there as a stalking horse for Brooke, who, like Churchill, continued believe that the Mediterranean was a more worthwhile investment than the invasion of France.

Things were, of course, too far along to cancel Operation Overlord outright. Churchill had begrudgingly accepted that much at Tehran. But the weeks and months ahead would be full of tense negotiations over how big an investment the Allies would allow it to be.

The previous May, when the Combined Chiefs had ordered Freddie Morgan's COSSAC to develop a plan for a cross-Channel invasion, Freddie's primary objective was capturing a port. Twenty-nine army divisions—a division being approximately fifteen thousand men with supporting matériel—would then mount the land campaign through that port, into France, and on to Germany. But capturing a port was no simple task.

The northern coast of France was not like the coasts of North Africa, or even Sicily or Salerno. Once the Germans had expelled the British from Dunkirk in 1940, Hitler had sought to create "Fortress Europe" and fortified the coast into what came to be known as the "Atlantikwall." The Atlantikwall was not a metaphor. It was a real, intricate system of fortifications into which Germany had poured 142 million square meters of concrete across the northern coasts of France, Belgium, Denmark, Germany, and Norway and which promised certain, violent death to anyone foolish enough to lay siege to Fortress Europe.

The Atlantikwall's principal line of defense consisted of beach defenses fortified by concrete and armor. The concrete was six feet thick at its strongest points and no less than three feet thick elsewhere. And the concrete used to build bunkers that served as headquarters along the Atlantikwall could be ten feet thick.

Between all of this were minefields that spanned fifty to three hundred yards, seawalls and roadblocks that spanned from six to ten feet high and three to eight feet thick. The beaches themselves were fortified with barbed wire, ditches, and steel obstacles, many of which were embedded just below the sea line to gore landing craft before a single man could reach dry land. Open fields near the shore bristled with row upon row of pikes that jutted five to fifteen feet and were booby-trapped with 105mm shells to shred any poor son of a bitch who tried to land in a glider or parachute.

Behind all of that was a mass of firepower concentrated on and immediately behind the coastal beaches. Mobile reserves were stationed at strategic points inland, ready to mount a concentrated counterattack within days, if not hours, of any attempted Allied invasion. And if that were not enough, Hitler had just made the Nazis' most dynamic general the Atlantikwall's lead sentry: Erwin Rommel.

Freddie Morgan's planners had studied the coastline carefully. The most obvious target was Calais, a peninsular port near the Belgian border, just west of Dunkirk, that also offered the closest point in France to England. But its obviousness to the Allies made it equally obvious to the Germans, who had spent the previous two years protecting it with the biggest bricks in the Atlantikwall. What was more, even if Calais itself could be taken, its location at the tip of a peninsula made it vulnerable to being choked off from the French interior.

Similar concerns led Freddie Morgan's planners to rule out Cherbourg on the tip of the Cotentin Peninsula, which delimited the western coast of Normandy. It was a weaker point in the Atlantikwall, but the terrain was not flat enough to establish airfields, and the Germans could quickly tie a defensive tourniquet around the base of the peninsula to choke off any advance inland.

That left the coastal plain of Calvados, just east of the Cotentin Peninsula, whose capital city of Caen was only twelve miles inland. The Germans had largely neglected Caen, an old stone citadel of a city, as well as its rural surroundings, which offered square miles of potential airstrips. From Caen, the Allies could rapidly break west to capture the ports in Brittany, south to liberate Paris, and east to outflank the German positions on Calais before driving into Berlin.

Freddie Morgan's concept was therefore simple. Break through the Atlantikwall in a hard initial shock just north of Caen and then race to get as many men and supplies across the Channel and though the breach as possible. The main limitation was the material resources the Combined Chiefs had made available, landing craft in particular. So, the COSSAC plan focused on taking Caen the first day and then concentrating Allied forces into defensive positions to allow time to build up. To do that, they would drop two divisions of paratroopers onto Caen the night before, and then hit its beaches with three divisions in an initial wave, followed up by two more divisions in a second wave the same day.

Eisenhower had first seen the COSSAC plan the previous October and was told that Freddie Morgan had designed it based on Eisenhower's successes in the invasions of the islands of Pantelleria and Sicily. Eisenhower, though, thought the plan was "fairly weak," and that Freddie Morgan's planners had drawn the wrong lessons. Neither island had been robustly defended at the beaches and Sicily had been a slog even still. Had the Italians and Germans been better equipped and more determined on the beaches, Eisenhower could have faced the same disaster the British suffered at Gallipoli.

The best intelligence was that the Germans had four divisions in and around Caen and could double that within a few days. Under the COSSAC plan, the Allies could get at most six divisions onshore in the first two days of fighting and at most twelve within the first five days. Gallipoli showed that the Germans would have extraordinary advantages in defending against any amphibious invasion attempted in broad daylight. Being equally matched, therefore, invited Allied defeat.

The assumption that the Germans could only double their forces in the first few days after the invasion was also optimistic. So was the assumption that the Allies could double theirs. What if there was bad weather? What if the Germans proved uniquely effective at sinking landing craft? What if Allied losses were high? What if the Germans choked off the exits from Caen's beaches?

Once on land, it would be a race. The German Seventh Army was deployed in Normandy and would rush reinforcements to the coast. That meant the Allies had to stream not simply enough men, but also tanks, weapons, and supplies across the Channel faster than the Germans could move them over land.

Limiting the front to Caen's beaches made the whole operation too weak and too narrow. If they were going to break through the Atlantikwall with any hope of breaching Fortress Europe, they would need overwhelming force. Operation Overlord would have to be bigger and wider.

Beetle felt the same way. Three divisions, he thought, was puny. They'd had more than that in Sicily and Salerno. In talking it over, Eisenhower figured they would need ten or twelve divisions to even have a chance. But doubling the size of the invasion would require a lot more resources of every kind, most especially landing craft. That meant taking what was needed from where it could be found. And the closest place to find landing craft was the Mediterranean.

Overlord, in other words, would have to be a greedy tyrant indeed. Eisenhower and Beetle needed to persuade Monty to give his full-throated support to making Operation Overlord everything Churchill feared it would become.

MONTY ARRIVED IN the afternoon and, standing five inches shorter than Eisenhower, looked up as he always did with a reproving expression. Thin to the point of bony, with deep-set gray eyes and a sweeping arch of a nose, Monty had a vulturine appearance that seemed to have been formed by his personality. He was on his way to visit Churchill in Marrakesh to review the

COSSAC plan, ostensibly for the first time. Churchill wanted to present Monty the plan himself in order to get his honest opinion, uncolored by the views others might have.

Eisenhower was all charm and told Monty that he wanted him to be the "head soldier and to take complete charge of the land battle." There would be, in other words, no British and American army groups. There would be a single unified ground commander for the largest amphibious invasion force in modern history. And Eisenhower wanted Montgomery of El Alamein to be that commander.

This was, to be sure, how Eisenhower had initially imagined the role of ground commander when he thought Alex would fill the job. But a single ground commander was not something Eisenhower was technically able to promise. The COSSAC plan, as jointly approved by Roosevelt and Churchill, was organized around British and American army groups. Marshall had proposed Devers to head the American army group. And even the official announcement of Monty's selection had been careful to say that he would be the commander of the "British and Canadian expeditionary group under Eisenhower."

But Marshall had not rejected Eisenhower's proposal just yet. And so, it was at least something Eisenhower felt he could still promise, if it meant getting Monty invested.

Monty loved the idea. As he would say, "War is history and history is built upon war." And in command of a multinational coalition in the decisive battle of the greatest war humankind had ever seen, Monty would be building great history.

Eisenhower was also sure to alert Monty to the "fairly weak" size of what COSSAC had planned. He was humble about it, acknowledging that Freddie Morgan had made the "best possible use of the material that could be made available by the proposed target date." But the plan was "weak in numbers and frontage."

"I'd like to assault with twelve divisions if I could," he told Monty. "But I must have at least five, five divisions the first assault and two to follow up." Otherwise, they would be courting disaster and a tremendous loss of life. And that touched a nerve for Monty that made it impossible for him to disagree.

To those who disdained him, Monty's reputation for being exceedingly cautious was simply a function of being paranoid about losing his reputation as a victorious general. "No risks. That's Monty's motto," Tedder would say. "No Risks."

That was unfair, though, and Eisenhower knew it—even if begrudgingly. Monty had a near-magical way of winning the loyalty of the British Tommies because he genuinely cared about them. He had been in the trenches during World War I, been wounded at Passchendaele, and had dedicated his life to his men. He had gotten married at forty, though lost his wife in a tragic accident soon after their tenth anniversary, in 1937. His only son, now fifteen, was away in a posh public school and Monty had little interest in keeping in touch. His sole interest was the men under his command. When asked why he never remarried, he would say that he "wasn't interested in girls."

Monty's caution on the battlefield was as much attributable to the fact that he put a premium on their lives as it was to anything else. He knew that his men would accept casualties if they were necessary to victory. And he knew they would do nothing he asked if they thought he was throwing their lives away. That is why he would say "his chaplains were more important to him than his artillery."

Eisenhower told Monty that he wanted him "to take complete charge of the initial land battle." He wanted Monty to work with Beetle once they both got to London after the New Year to figure out how to broaden the front. They needed a strong plan. And Eisenhower added that he hoped Monty wouldn't mind taking control of things as the Supreme Allied Commander's "deputy" until he arrived in England the second week of January.

Monty readily agreed. He was on the team.

BEETLE LEFT FOR London the next day and Monty returned to Italy to say farewell to his men. Eisenhower caught up on the pile of cables and letters from the previous month.

A message from De Gaulle had come in, saying that the French Committee "has full confidence in you in the employment of the French forces that it is placing under your command for the next allied operations." Eisenhower replied, thanking him for his "very understanding attitude toward these matters," and adding that with his imminent departure for London, "I do hope that you and I can find it mutually convenient to have at least a short meeting before I go."

There was also a message from Jacob Devers. Eisenhower had cabled him the day before, saying that he looked forward to getting his input on "personalities or plans." Devers had replied right away. "I am looking forward with real pleasure to your arrival," he wrote with newfound obsequiousness. He then offered a few opinions of the people in London. "Morgan fine personality, the best British Officer I deal with," and "You will need Bedell Smith." And he expressed his eagerness to see Operation Overlord through, saying "I can be of most use as the Commander of the First Army Group."

Eisenhower opted not to reply right away. He cabled General Marshall yet again to clarify "my conceptions for initial command arrangements" and, in particular, his reasons for not wanting American and British army groups. He neglected to mention that he had already promised this to Monty. But he tried to make the case for it and assured Marshall that once in France, the British and American forces were likely to regroup along national lines for the charge into Berlin.

The difficulty and danger of the task ahead was becoming more apparent each day. As he was writing yet another cable to Marshall, an intelligence report came in from Madrid. The Germans were building massive cement platforms along the Channel coast. These, it was believed, would serve as launching pads for the Nazis' newest secret weapon: fifteen-ton, rocket-propelled glider bombs that could soon be raining down on London with such ferocity that the Battle of Britain would seem like a fond memory.

Charles de Gaulle

CHAPTER 11

THE NEXT MORNING, at breakfast, Butch was in a jolly mood. Eisenhower, though, was feeling impatient. He got up from the table and called over to his headquarters to see if anything had come in overnight. Something had. There was a message from General Marshall.

The secretary responsible for monitoring the cable traffic, who had seen Eisenhower's many unanswered pleas to General Marshall over the previous few weeks, said, "You got everything you wanted."

Eisenhower couldn't help but smile as the secretary read the message. Patton could go to England. Devers could go to the Mediterranean. Clark could lead the invasion of southern France. Bradley could lead the American side of the invasion of northern France. Marshall said nothing about Eisenhower's proposal to unify his command and dispense with the plan to have separate British and American army groups, but as far as the US Army was concerned, Eisenhower could have his team.

The whole tenor of General Marshall's message was surprisingly conciliatory. He suggested the names of generals he knew and trusted for some of the other positions Eisenhower had to fill. But, Marshall said, whether Eisenhower chose to use them was "your affair." He then concluded by saying, "I suggest that you either come straight to the United States from Africa or if you go to England, report here shortly thereafter to make the necessary contacts with the War Department, to see your family, and to get at least a brief rest."

Eisenhower did not waste a second in replying to General Marshall to confirm all his choices. He then concluded, "With regard to my visit home I feel that for the moment it is an impossibility. I truly hope that February or early March will afford me such an opportunity."

Eisenhower then replied to Jacob Devers who had just received the order from the War Department officially sending him to the Mediterranean. "Thank you very much for your telegram," Eisenhower wrote. "I learned that you have been designated as the American commander for this theater, a position which I assure you will be most important and interesting." Eisenhower then proceeded to explain why he would be taking few, if any, of Devers's many suggestions on how to conduct Operation Overlord and closed by asking him to forward a message to Beetle that would leave no doubt in Devers's mind that Eisenhower was why Marshall had exiled him to the Mediterranean.

Perhaps sensing that he had come off a bit too cocky to General Marshall, Eisenhower quickly sent him a second cable, taking one of Marshall's suggestions, and asking that Courtney Hodges be sent to England to provide seniority and experience to his team. And Eisenhower soon learned that had been too cocky.

In short order, General Marshall cabled back, ordering him to report to Washington. "You will be under terrific strain from now on," Marshall scolded him. "I am interested that you are fully prepared to bear the strain and I am not interested in the usual rejoinder that you can take it. It is of vast importance that you be fresh mentally and you certainly will not be if you go straight from one great problem to another. Now come on home and see your wife and trust somebody else for twenty minutes in England." It was a useful reminder that General George C. Marshall never truly "suggested" anything.

BEFORE LEAVING FOR Washington, Eisenhower took the chance to seal Beetle's deal with Charles de Gaulle. He had met De Gaulle during the whirlwind days of July 1942. Churchill had given De Gaulle haven after the fall of France and when General Marshall was in London to debate the relative merits of invading France or North Africa that summer, De Gaulle had come to give a presentation on how the Free French could support the Allied side. The tall heron of the French Resistance had been given no reason to suspect that Eisenhower was important.

Eisenhower understood better than most that the United States' long-standing national friendship with France was a complicated one. While most Americans waxed misty about Lafayette and Yorktown, Eisenhower remembered the parts of the Franco-American relationship typically erased from grammar school history books. The Quasi-War, in which the United States sided with England against Napoléon, France's neutrality during the US Civil War. There was no natural, inevitable affinity between any two governments. And De Gaulle was just as apt as Eisenhower, when asked about Franco-American cooperation, to cite the Prussian military theorist Karl von Clausewitz: "War is politics carried on by different means. Each time we make wars of coalition, we have difficulties between allies, because they have different political desires."

After Darlan's assassination, De Gaulle wrote to Eisenhower that the murder was "a most definite warning." A warning of what? "A warning of the incalculable consequences inevitably resulting from the lack of national authority in the midst of the greatest national crisis of our history."

Over the previous year, Eisenhower had been forced to endlessly mediate between Henri Giraud, whom Roosevelt and the State Department had backed to lead the Free French, and De Gaulle, who would announce himself by declaring, "*Je suis ici en ma qualité de Président du Gouvernement français*" (I am here in my capacity as president of the French government). In that time, Eisenhower had learned to reflect De Gaulle's grandeur back with it-is-what-it-is sympathy, and De Gaulle's grasping for the reins of history with the avuncular candor of a simple soldier whose hands were tied. De Gaulle would predictably storm out when he did not get his way, but just as predictably would come back after some rococo compromise garnered him Eisenhower's assurance that he was not *not* the president of France.

From Eisenhower's perspective, Henri Giraud was no easier a personality and, despite Roosevelt's hopes, lacked either the charisma or cunning to become a viable alternative to De Gaulle. France under Vichy had become a mess of factions, and the best intelligence was that De Gaulle was the only consensus figure. And De Gaulle's celebrity was neither an accident nor undeserved. De Gaulle had led some of the French army's only tactical victories against the German Blitzkrieg in 1940, successfully rallied some of France's African colonies against Vichy after his exile to London, and—as perhaps the brightest jewel in the crown of resistance that he placed upon his own head—De Gaulle walked around under a death sentence that the Vichy government had imposed upon him in absentia.

De Gaulle was the only man who had the support of both the Communists on the left and the monarchists on the right. These factions saw their support as transactional, to be sure, and De Gaulle as a temporary figure who would bridge the dark days of Vichy to their desired France of the future. But the key thing was, whatever their long-term motives, they supported De Gaulle.

Upon greeting De Gaulle in Algiers, Eisenhower laid the Kansas on thick, as if they were old hunting buddies. Butch joked afterward that it had been a "love fest" complete, in the French custom, with kisses.

Eisenhower reminisced about what a challenging year it had been. The politics were a tricky business, and Eisenhower said that he was doing the best that a simple soldier from Kansas could. He told De Gaulle that he had made a lot of mistakes along the way, and that he was mighty sorry for them. But he was thankful for help he had received from wise, experienced men like De Gaulle, who had the grasp of the situation that he, as a simple soldier from Kansas, did not have.

De Gaulle swelled with appreciation and replied, in English, "You are a man." Eisenhower assured De Gaulle that the American army would not enter Paris without the French army beside it. While he could not speak for Roosevelt, Eisenhower had no interest in working with anyone in France other than De Gaulle and his French Committee.

In turn, De Gaulle pledged his full support. And he reiterated his promise to Beetle that no action would be taken against the collaborators he had arrested until a properly constituted French government had been formed in France.

De Gaulle said the only differences between them were imposed by "*la situation très compliquée dans lequel se trouvent nos deux pays*" (the very complicated situation that our countries find themselves in). "*Mais tout cela n'est que momentané*" (But all this is only temporary), he continued. "*Quand nous aurons gagné la guerre, il n'en restera plus trace, sauf, naturellement, pour les historiens*" (When we have won the war, there will be no trace of it, except, of course, for historians).

EISENHOWER WAS SET to leave for Washington on New Year's Eve. Stalling, he spent the morning soaking in the bathtub. There were so many urgent and important things he needed to do in London. The British Chiefs of Staff were insisting on their own personnel choices. They were not only foisting Monty on him, but also refusing to let Arthur Tedder be the air chief. Instead, they wanted to keep Trafford Leigh-Mallory, a fighter pilot who had gotten settled as Freddie Morgan's air chief and was a favorite of Churchill's. Tedder, they were proposing, could be made a deputy under Eisenhower, though what that meant beyond adding yet another general to the org chart was unclear.

Beetle was by that point in London and wound up about it, leaning on Eisenhower to get himself to the United Kingdom as soon as possible. These personnel debates were wearing on Eisenhower. It was such a high-profile opportunity that every ambitious military man with any pull was now lobbying for a starring role in Operation Overlord. The question was, what could he do about it? All he wanted was people he could trust doing the jobs he could trust them to do.

As he soaked, Eisenhower called out to Mickey, who was getting ready to go to London as his advance man. How was packing going?

"I'll be ready to leave for England as soon as you've left for the States, sir."

Eisenhower sat and thought in the bath. "How long would it take you to pack for Washington?" he asked Mickey, figuring his "chief factotum," who always did the job Eisenhower trusted him to do, deserved a brief rest too.

"I can leave in ten minutes!" Mickey replied.

AT ELEVEN THIRTY that morning, Eisenhower, Butch, and Mickey flew to Marrakesh. It was six in the evening by the time they landed. Rather than continue on across the Atlantic, Eisenhower drove to Taylor Villa, where Churchill was staying with his wife, Clemmie. The prime minister was still recovering from his pneumonia and was just finishing up with his doctor when Eisenhower arrived. "The Prime Minister is up to his old tricks," the doctor said as he left. "He won't let me read the thermometer."

Churchill was jovial on the eve of the New Year. He pressed Eisenhower to spend the night at Taylor Villa, but Eisenhower graciously declined. He had an early flight and was already staying with his people at the Mamounia, a hotel in Marrakesh.

Well, in that case, Churchill insisted, stay for dinner. As it happened, Monty had just arrived with his aide-de-camp, or "ADC," and Churchill was adamant that everyone ring in the New Year together. He was preparing some punch.

Monty had arrived tired and disagreeable. When Clemmie casually told his ADC that she looked forward to seeing him at dinner, Monty snapped, "My ADCs don't dine with the Prime Minister."

"In my house, General Montgomery," Clemmie replied with a scowl, "I invite who I wish and I don't require your advice."

Churchill dominated the discussion with his plans for the invasion of Anzio. The taking of Rome, Churchill relished, would be a historic moment. It would be "acclaimed in the future as a great success."

The prime minister's zeal made Eisenhower uneasy. Churchill's great literary imagination inevitably made him obsess about "eccentric operations." Gallipoli had been such an operation. In a great novel, it was always a daring, counterintuitive strike that won the day, like some quirky clue through which Sherlock Holmes unraveled a mystery. Reality rarely proved as romantic. But even after Gallipoli's hard lessons, Churchill wrote of the invasion with the same literary zeal. "The masterpieces of military art," he wrote in *The World Crisis*, "from which have been derived the foundation of states and the fame of commanders, have been battles of manoeuvre in which very often the enemy has found himself defeated by some novel expedient or device, some queer, swift, unexpected thrust or stratagem."

Eisenhower warned Churchill that they would need good weather. The success in Salerno had been entirely contingent on the weather. Bad weather would limit air support and slow the rate of resupply. If landing craft were short, they would risk annihilation if Alex could not get the ground forces that were already around Naples to link up with those landing at Anzio.

Eisenhower's unwillingness to share Churchill's enthusiasm for the Anzio operation prompted the prime minister to goad him. Don't let your reputation for success make you cautious, Churchill said.

Eisenhower joked that he was usually accused of recklessness, so was glad to be "balancing the scales."

After dinner, Monty announced his desire to go to bed. He wanted to read the COSSAC plan carefully and also knew that Churchill would keep the party going late. Churchill then used his prerogative as the leader of the British Empire to declare the New Year early so Monty could join him in singing "Auld Lang Syne." Eisenhower left before the new British New Year, preferring to return to the Mamounia to toast the dawn of 1944 with Mickey, Butch, and a few glasses of champagne.

They left Marrakesh before five in the morning. The C-54 took off in the dark, and made its first stop, at Terceira Island, in the Azores, six hours later. As they approached, about three miles off the island of San Miguel, an anti-aircraft battery opened fire. They were far enough away that there was no damage, but the friendly fire from the Portuguese was certainly unnerving. The British had acquired the base from the Portuguese the previous October on the condition that it not be given over to the Americans. This, however, proved a short-lived prohibition that was all but abandoned by New Year's Day.

After a three-hour layover, they took off again, this time for the British island of Bermuda, and the American air base that Roosevelt had negotiated to get in 1941 in a trade for Lend-Lease aid. They arrived at dinnertime, joined by the base's American commander, who was happy see Eisenhower off for the four-hour flight to Washington, DC.

Eisenhower was dreading the return to Washington. Part of it was that he wanted to be in London to get things under control. But things had also been icy with Mamie. He was wistful about the last time he saw her. She had walked him to the car as he left for his flight to London. He had gotten in, reached out the window, grabbed her wrist, and kissed her hand. "Goodbye, Honey." Mamie then stood by the flagpole near their house on Fort Mayer and waved as his plane passed overhead. He loved her so much. He sent her a cable the moment he had landed. "Because of you," he wrote, "I've been the luckiest man in the world for twenty-six years—love Ike."

That was a year and a half ago, and it had been a long year and a half. She had not written to him in weeks. The last he had heard from her was a curt cable, notifying him that she had returned to Washington after a visit to West Point. He cabled back, "Delighted to receive your teletype several days ago, as I had come to believe that you had retired into a convent."

For day-to-day things, there was a desk at the War Department, where they could call to leave short messages. But Mamie didn't do that very often either. And regardless, sundry messages to some desk clerk in the War Department were hardly the medium for a great love affair. He wished Mamie wrote more, and when he was feeling particularly neglected, he would mention it in one of his letters to his son, hoping, perhaps, that it would indirectly shake some word from her.

Eisenhower's letters to Mamie were syrupy sweet in their boyishness. It was difficult to imagine Erwin Rommel scrawling "Happy Birthday!!!" in the margin of a letter and then underlining it twice. But Eisenhower's notes to her were often goofy and always warm.

Mamie's letters, when they did come, could be a little more unpredictable, particularly when Kay was at the front of her mind. Eisenhower was always careful about how he mentioned Kay. Where he would use other people's first names and nicknames, he would usually refer to her as "Mrs. Kay Summersby" in his letters to Mamie. Calling her "Mrs." was a bit misleading. It was perfectly correct, since a woman did not cease to earn the title "Mrs." after a divorce, and Summersby had been her married name. She no longer went by Miss Katherine MacCarthy-Morrogh, after all. But "Mrs." was not a title he was apt to call Kay to her face. "Lieutenant," maybe. "Kay," more often. "Irish," when he was feeling playful.

When he had acquired the silk Italian stockings for Mamie's birthday, he had also given Kay a pair, which he tactfully neglected to mention in his birthday letter to his wife. Instead, he apologized that he had come up with only two pairs. "It was the best I could do," he fibbed, "but if I can get some more I will." Had she known, Mamie's jealousy could be something out of the Iliad.

When *Life* magazine ran a human-interest story about the WACs working on Eisenhower's staff, the reporter had featured "the irrepressible Kay Summersby, Eisenhower's pretty Irish driver," who enjoyed a few more photographs than her colleagues over the winking caption describing her as "the beauteous Kay." Mamie noticed.

"I love you all the time," Eisenhower reassured her. "Don't go bothering your pretty head about WACs. So *Life* says my old London driver came down! So she did—but the big reason she wanted to serve in this theater is that she is terribly in love with a young American colonel and is to be married to him come June—assuming both are alive. I doubt that *Life* told that!" At the time, this was—more or less—true.

Kay was a lot like the Mamie whom Eisenhower had met in 1916. Mamie was saucy. Her eyes grinned slyly. And Eisenhower liked saucy.

"Now, Miss Doud," he had warned Mamie as he took her on a tour of Fort Sam Houston, "this is an Army post, and the men in the barracks are not expecting ladies. I suggest you keep your eyes to the front."

Mamie immediately took to glancing with a defiant flourish to her left and right as they strolled. "And what are you going to do about it?"

All Eisenhower could do was beam his broad smile at the woman he would soon ask to become his wife.

PART TWO

DWIGHT

Fox Conner

CHAPTER 12

THE SKY WAS dark out the window on the flight north from Bermuda. It was the darkest time of the year. Abilene's winters had long nights, short days, and bitter cold. The only heat in their little home when he was growing up had been the potbellied stove in the kitchen. In the mornings, when his father would call up "Boys!" to get them out of bed, Eisenhower and his brothers would wriggle to get dressed in the warmth still trapped under their blankets.

There were no festivities in the Eisenhower home to warm the season. The Bible Students were adamant that Christmas was a pagan ritual, and a materialistic one at that. Eisenhower did not really know Christmas in its All-American yuletide joy until he had been brought into Mamie's family, with all its warmth and cheer. Mamie's father, John Doud, whom everyone called "Poopua," had made a small fortune in the meatpacking business. It was not as posh as mining by the standards of Colorado high society, but it had assured his family all the comforts of the aspiring new-money aristocracy.

It was only when Little Icky was born, that Eisenhower got a glimpse of the ecstatic wonder a child could feel at the pagan rite of being spoiled rotten as the grown-ups sang strange songs and seemed curiously overjoyed despite how cold and dark it was outside. As Little Icky was approaching his fourth Christmas, the season had been especially spectacular.

Little Icky had spent the summer with Mamie's parents, Poopua and Miss Min, as Eisenhower and Georgie Patton refurbished the ramshackle housing they had been afforded at Camp Meade. When Little Icky arrived that fall, he was the big man on campus. He was at that bewitching age when a child's unembarrassed excitement at tanks, football, and parades is infectious. He delighted in the company of the neighbor's dog, Sandy. And he was a charmer, somehow picking up the phrase "See you later" whenever he said goodbye.

Little Icky became the Tank Corps' mascot, and when he turned three that September, the home Eisenhower had spent the summer building for them was filled with toy tanks, stuffed animals, drums, horns, and everything else a boy could want to clutter the floor. Eisenhower's Tank Corps soldiers had even made Little Icky a child-size uniform, complete with overcoat and cap.

Little Icky had proved his value as a mascot. The fall of 1920, Eisenhower coached the Tank Corps football team to a perfect season, giving up only two touchdowns in six games. General Samuel Rockenbach, the army's Tank Corps commander, praised Eisenhower's success as "based on those elements which insure success in war and peace."

It was the happiest time of Eisenhower's life. He had a happy family, in the way that all happy families are the same, and between his army major's pay and a bit of support from Poopua and Miss Min, they were as comfortable as they had ever been. Eisenhower even hired a nanny, marking the first time he had been able to give Mamie a taste of her pre-army life. They hosted Sunday buffets and receptions for visiting higher-ups, at which Mamie charmed her husband's professional patrons. And Eisenhower relished finding himself in a position for which he had no experience or training: being a dad.

Just before Christmas that year, Mamie had left Little Icky with the nanny to go shopping in Baltimore. When she came home, Little Icky's stomach was bothering him. The doctor came by and said not to worry. Little Icky had probably just eaten something. He started getting feverish and so Eisenhower and Mamie let him spend the night in bed with them to keep him cozy. But by morning, his fever was worse and they decided to take him to Camp Meade's hospital.

Eisenhower carried his son down the stairs, and as they passed the

Christmas tree, Little Icky pointed to the red tricycle waiting for him there. Eisenhower consoled him that it would still be there when he got back.

Camp Meade's hospital had been hastily built during the First World War. Much of it, including the porch around its perimeter, was still just nailed-together lumber. But that did not seem to matter. Little Icky was getting better, and it was increasingly difficult to keep him in bed. Whenever someone turned a blind eye, Little Icky would just get up and wander down the hall. But then a doctor from Johns Hopkins gave them the diagnosis: scarlet fever. No more wandering the halls. Little Icky needed to quarantine.

The hospital put him in an officer's room and kept the door locked. That left Eisenhower and Mamie standing on the porch outside in the cold, doing their best to entertain Little Icky through the window. There was no real reason to worry. Eisenhower's little brothers, Milton and Earl, each had contracted scarlet fever as young boys. They had both recovered, though Milton was always a scrawny kid after that. But so what if the same was true for Little Icky? He might never grow big enough for football, but everyone always said that being scrawny was what made Milton the brain of the family.

Little Icky also seemed to be doing just fine. But then he developed tonsillitis, and then an ear infection, and then sepsis. He grew listless and frail, all alone in his bed. Mamie couldn't bear it. She went home and came down with something. The doctors said it could be pneumonia. Whatever it was, it kept her in bed, or at least away from the hospital. And that left Eisenhower alone in the cold and in the dark on that porch of hastily nailed-together timber.

All the doctors could offer Eisenhower was a chair. All he could do was make silly faces to cheer Little Icky up and wave in those moments when his son had enough of a spark to look up at him. He couldn't take his son's little hand into his own as he slept. He couldn't brush the sweat-soaked hair away from his forehead. He couldn't hug him close and tell him all his wishes would come true, that it would be all right, that there was a red tricycle waiting for him under the Christmas tree. All he could do was make faces and wave in the cold and in the dark.

As things turned worse, the doctor let Eisenhower come to the door and call in a few words to let Little Icky know his father was there and that he loved him. But he never got to hold him again.

It was ten p.m., January 2, 1921. Once he was gone, the shock that made it feel all so unreal hardened inside Eisenhower. He raged at himself for every day that he had taken his son for granted. He thought about the happy, rambunctious little boy dressed in his little uniform, riding in the tanks as if "he was just one of the boys." He thought about how happy and how proud he was. And it broke his heart.

Mamie couldn't talk about it, and they never did. The Tank Corps formed an honor guard to escort Eisenhower, Mamie, and the coffin to the train station, where they rode to Denver for the burial. Mamie's family held the funeral in the same room where Eisenhower and Mamie had been married five years earlier. They boarded the train back east to Camp Meade, stopping over in Chicago for a night, where they didn't sleep.

When they arrived back home, the men in the Tank Corps had made a chest for Little Icky's belongings. Sandy, the neighbor's dog, had been hit by a truck while they were away, which was just as well.

Eisenhower tried to keep busy, focusing on the things he could do something about, mostly the bills. The bitterest one was the bill for fifty dollars from the nurse they had hired to take care of Little Icky in the hospital. She had worked for only four days.

Eisenhower started working as late as he could. Outside, he could smile and be Ike. Inside, the only word he could find to describe his grief was "insurmountable." He would come home and see Mamie late in the evening and they would talk about anything other than the obvious. It was always hardest at night. In bed, they would lay sleepless and quiet with Little Icky haunting their home, waiting in his empty bed to be tucked in or comforted after a bad dream. And Eisenhower would get up early, go to work, and come home as late as he could in the evening.

THE COLD AND the dark seemed to never lift that year. That summer, Eisenhower got unwittingly wrapped up in an army embezzlement scandal and faced court-martial. In a single year, he lost his son and the happiness of his marriage. And it looked not only as if he would lose his nascent military career, but that he might also serve prison time.

But then, in December, the investigation against him was abruptly closed. On December 7, 1921, he got an order, direct from General John Pershing, chief of staff of the US Army, to report to the Panama Canal Zone "for duty as executive officer of the 20th Infantry Brigade."

Eisenhower and Mamie left in the middle of January, sailing over the ocean from the mid-Atlantic's winter and into the chthonic Panamanian heat. Mamie hated it immediately—and, in fairness, there was almost nothing to like.

Eisenhower was stationed at Camp Gaillard, which sat atop a muddy and precarious cliff that dropped steeply down into the low waters of the Panama Canal. It had been clear-cut from the surrounding jungle, which remained intent on retaking its lost ground. The only road connecting Camp Gaillard to the rest of Panama was in constant danger of sliding into the canal. And its brown wood and brick buildings were constructed with little structural regard for the stresses of the local climate. The vines strangling the beams of the porch peeled back the screens to welcome in the lizards, snakes, and other crawling fauna eager to reclaim the home as rightfully theirs.

Mamie was pregnant again, and the humidity was so intense that she cut the long hair she had worn since girlhood into a curly bob. Their bedroom had the permanent scent of kerosene, which they applied liberally to the bed frame each week to keep down the bedbugs. And then there were the bats. The French had imported bats to keep the mosquito population down, and, like any invasive species, they proliferated. As night fell over the canopy of trees, the bats would swarm out and bombard the screened-in porches in a torrential flapping.

One night, when a bat had made its way into their bedroom, Eisenhower drew his saber to engage it in single combat. Eisenhower lashed around their room, flailing as if battling an unseen hydra, until a lucky stroke felled the intruder. In the decades to come, Eisenhower and Mamie would tell it all as a funny story. But the stories were happy only in hindsight.

Their unhappiness together in Panama was loud and recurrent enough to raise eyebrows in the claustrophobic community of Camp Gaillard. After four months, Mamie had enough and left to be with her parents in Colorado. If nothing else, Camp Gaillard's clinic was no place to have a child if you could avoid it. It was in such disrepair that the roof was buckling, which made it leak profusely whenever it rained. And, as far as Mamie was concerned, Panama was no place to live if you could avoid it.

For Eisenhower, his serving the next three years at Camp Gaillard was also not, on the face of things, time well spent. It was a marginal military installation and, most of all, boring. It had been one of the first Marine encampments in what soon became the northeast bank of the Panama Canal and was given over to the army, when the Marines were redeployed to

Mexico in the hunt for Pancho Villa. Most of the enlisted soldiers assigned to the Twentieth Infantry Brigade were Spanish-speaking Puerto Ricans and the officers were English-speaking gringos. That made the military's already rigid caste system even more brittle and surrendered all hope of any esprit de corps.

The most interesting operation that happened during Eisenhower's time in Panama was a naval exercise in which the United States fleet shelled the decommissioned USS *Iowa*. Camp Gaillard was otherwise notoriously riven with vice. All sorts of people lived in nearby bungalows, leading to a robust black market for rum, gambling, and prostitutes. In the secluded, steamy jungle, Camp Gaillard was at the center of a sodomy "crisis" that alarmed the higher-ups in Washington, with the handful of Panamanian outposts accounting for three-quarters of the army's sodomy prosecutions.

The camp's commander, who had personally requested Eisenhower, was General Fox Conner. A rigid man in his way, he was a Scotch-Irish career soldier. He grew up in Reconstruction-era Mississippi as the son of a teacher who had gone blind after being shot in the head during the Battle of Atlanta while serving as a private in the Confederate army. Known for having a fearsome intellect and an extraordinary career, Conner inspired neither warmth nor loyalty in most of those who served under him.

To get the disciplinary problems under control General Conner ramped up courts-martial and ordered his subordinates how to vote and what sentences to impose, threatening them, "If you don't vote as I direct, I will know exactly who voted wrong." This was, strictly speaking, illegal. But, in big things and small, General Conner disdained legalistic technicalities that got in the way of what he considered his overriding duty to get results as an army commander.

Eisenhower's principal job was to be his "hatchet man," and his daily chore was writing the order of the day, stating what needed to be done, who was to do what, and how success was to be measured. It was inane busywork in a place with nothing meaningful to do. But still, General Conner demanded that Eisenhower write it all out each morning and bring it to him for review, scolding Eisenhower pitilessly to say things more clearly, to think it all through more precisely.

Eisenhower never called him anything other than General Conner, even long after Eisenhower had gotten his fourth star, and therefore significantly outranked him (General Conner having retired in 1938 as a major general). Eisenhower knew how to live under the authority of a stern man. He had survived a childhood under the roof of David Eisenhower. And he learned the virtue of being a yes-man, or more generously, the self-discipline to fit in.

When a friend from West Point who was stationed in Panama complained about one of General Conner's new policies, Eisenhower offered some career advice. "I'll tell you my guiding philosophy," Eisenhower advised. "When I go to a new station I look to see who is the strongest and ablest man on the post. I forget my own ideas and do everything in my power to promote what *he* says is right."

General Conner's outward rigidity, though, was thin. He had his view of things, and he was dead certain that he was right. But he was just certain that he might be wrong. He regularly lectured at the Army War College and had the reputation of being one of the army's "brains," which in every generation is a double-edged compliment. He read everything that might provide insight on the vocation of being a soldier. Even Shakespeare, he told Eisenhower, offered insight, because when Shakespeare wrote about Julius Caesar or King Richard, "Shakespeare undoubtedly was describing soldiers he knew at first hand."

General Conner had accumulated a massive library, which he insisted the army transport with him, including to Panama. Perusing the shelves, there were books in German and French. There were the blue leather-bound Harvard Classics, colloquially known as the "Dr. Eliot's Five-Foot Shelf of Books," which included works by Plato, Epictetus, Marcus Aurelius, Darwin, Plutarch, Homer, Machiavelli, Locke, and Hume. There were countless military histories and novels. Eisenhower had never seen so many books that were the property of one man.

One evening, General Conner asked Eisenhower if he liked to read. Did he read military history?

Eisenhower had loved history as a child, but West Point had drained the great body of military history of all its blood. Take Gettysburg. At West Point in the years before Douglas MacArthur had overhauled its curriculum, the Battle of Gettysburg was reduced to memorizing the order of battle and mapping the location of each unit at each hour. It left Eisenhower bereft of why anyone had done anything.

As they chatted, General Conner pulled a few books off his shelf. One was *The Crisis*, by Winston Churchill (an American of the same name), a historical novel set in Missouri that presented the American Civil War as a continuation of the conflict of ideals at the heart of the English Civil War two hundred years earlier. Another was Mary Johnston's *The Long Roll*, about the men from a Virginia regiment who fought under Stonewall Jackson. Though fiction, both would tell Eisenhower more about the Civil War than any map. He also handed him a copy of the *Exploits of Brigadier Gerard*, a somewhat comic tale about the Napoleonic wars by Sir Arthur Conan Doyle.

Eisenhower drank them all down. When he returned them, General Conner handed him some heavier reads about the military history of those periods. He gave him the memoirs of Ulysses S. Grant and Philip Sheridan, and some of John Codman Ropes's volumes on the Civil War. He then gave him Comte de Paris's *Army of the Potomac* and the accounts of Gettysburg written by the British general Arthur Lyon Fremantle and the Union general Frank Haskell. Each time, when Eisenhower returned, General Conner probed him, not on dates, but on decisions.

"Why did Lee invade the North a second time?"

"Why was Meade successful?"

"Why did Lee choose to fight at Gettysburg?"

"What were Lee's alternatives?"

He told Eisenhower to think not as a student, but as a general. And soon the Battle of Gettysburg was real. Eisenhower had lived there and knew the terrain. Reading the accounts from all the different perspectives, he came to see the why behind all those points on the map.

Nearly every day, Eisenhower and General Conner were apt to go out on horseback, inspecting the Canal Zone. They both chain-smoked, and in those long hours, Conner would question Eisenhower about his most recent reading like an Oxford don conducting a tutorial. In the evenings, they would sip a few and continue the conversation deep into the night over a chessboard.

Eisenhower redecorated the second floor of his kerosene-smelling house like a war room, covering the walls with maps to plot the great campaigns of history. General Conner was a keen student of Napoléon, and there on the walls, Eisenhower plotted out the movements at Austerlitz and Marengo. Eisenhower grew particularly fascinated by Napoléon's fateful campaign in 1814, the failure of which led to his exile on Elba.

Frederick the Great's 1757 victory at the Battle of Leuthen in the Seven Years' War was one of General Conner's favorites because it both informed and illustrated the ideas of Karl von Clausewitz. The single most important book, Conner told him, was Clausewitz's *On War*. Over the course of the nearly three years they spent together, Eisenhower felt as if he had read the book three times.

Eisenhower studied W. F. Reddaway's account of the Battle of Leuthen and admired Frederick's surprise flanking attack against the Austrian army, which was twice the size of the Prussian forces Frederick commanded. Frederick had tricked the Austrians into believing he was mounting an attack on their right, and then executed a massive surprise attack with the full force of his army on the Austrians' left. This victory was written into German strategic doctrine in principles like "It is an art to concentrate all available forces for the decisive stroke"; "Numerical inferiority is offset by greater mobility"; and "The most important means to success is always surprise of the enemy." It all illustrated Clausewitz's three essential strategic principles: (1) concentrate at the point of the decisive blow, (2) do not lose time, and (3) follow up success by vigorous pursuit.

Thinking deeply about the distant past kept Eisenhower busy enough to avoid thinking too much about the recent past. And General Conner was more than happy to keep Eisenhower's mind busy. One of the titles that Eisenhower would remember for the rest of his life was General Conner's book of Friedrich Nietzsche, the German philosopher.

Nietzsche wrote the kind of books that felt like a gun in the hand. The journo-pugilist H. L. Mencken had popularized the philosopher in 1907 with a biography that celebrated Nietzsche's unsentimental gaze. In 1910, Mencken rode the wave of popular interest he started with a collection of Nietzsche's writings titled *The Gist of Nietzsche*. The opening passage, from *Human, All Too Human*, was a paean to seeing the world as it is, not as it should be: "Convictions are more dangerous enemies to truth than lies. He who has attained something of intellectual freedom cannot regard himself otherwise than a wanderer on earth, and not as a traveler toward some goal, for none exists. But he will have his eyes open and watch what happens in the world."

Nietzsche reproached those looking for meaning in their struggles to value the struggle itself. "Democracy immediately ceases to mean freedom as soon as it is attained," he lamented. "But democracy produces quite different effects so long as it is being fought for; it then, in fact, furthers freedom in a powerful manner." Nothing was more powerful, once aroused, than the drive toward freedom.

"Warfare prepares a man for freedom," Nietzsche continued, as if writing a battle cry for the soldiers of democracy. "For what is freedom? The will to be responsible for oneself. The will to keep one's distance. The will to become indifferent to hardship, severity, privation, to life itself. The will to sacrifice men to one's cause—and oneself, too. Freedom implies that manly instincts, which delight in war and victory, have dominion over all other instincts, including the instinct to be 'happy.' The man who is truly free treads under foot that contemptible species of security dreamt of by shopkeepers, Christians, cows, women, Englishmen and other democrats. The free man is a warrior!"

Nietzsche was great for aphorisms, and there was nothing that General Conner loved more than a good aphorism, writing many gems himself on the problems of leadership. "Always take your job seriously," Conner would say, "never yourself."

Of all the topics that General Conner directed his intense and learned mind to solving, leadership was his life's work. "A few men are born leaders; perhaps one every century or two." But leaders could be made, he believed, so long as they lived by the "square deal." "Play no favorites. Let your standards, step by step, be higher and higher and hold everyone to those standards without fear, favor, or affection," he would instruct. "Your own attitude, deportment, state of mind, language and every element of your personality are important in determining the leadership you may attain. If you are habitually late for duty or work, careless or indifferent, you can expect nothing else from others. And if you are loud mouthed, vulgar, or abusive, others will go you one better."

Despite his own difficulties in dealing with people—or perhaps due to the clarity of a hypocrite's insight—General Conner understood the centrality of the human element in warfare. "In spite of the long standing advice, 'The proper study of mankind is man,'" he wrote, "nothing is more neglected than training in the handling of men."

"General," Eisenhower asked at one point, "what is the first and greatest quality of a good staff officer?"

"A ready grin."

In between communing with the great dead minds of the past, General Conner would share his own experiences, having been at Pershing's right hand in France during the Great War. Conner had planned the war's two major American operations, Saint-Mihiel and Meuse-Argonne. He had been wounded on an inspection trip and wore his scars as proof that a commander needed to be out in the field, to not rely on reports.

The Great War was the first time, really, that the US Army had to fight in any significant size beyond America's shores. When the American Expeditionary Force belatedly arrived in Europe, there was not even a clear idea of how the basic divisions of the army should be staffed and organized. The French had their ideas, the British had theirs, and Conner was left to devise American doctrine on the fly.

General Conner had hated the allied nature of the command. "The ulterior motives of the several members of a coalition," Conner concluded, "formed the principal obstacle to securing either Unity of Direction or Unity of Command." Each nation fought with an eye toward its postwar position. The challenge was "how do you get allies of different nations to march and think as a nation?" His answer was bleak. "Only an actual or a threatened catastrophe is likely to bring about anything approaching either Unity of Direction or Unity of Command."

The Great War was where General Conner had gotten to know George Patton, who was always jealous of Conner's beautiful shrapnel wounds. That was also where he had met George Marshall, who became Pershing's deputy in the War Department. Marshall was, he told Eisenhower, "nothing short of a genius."

"When war comes again, and it is going to come, and it will probably be in your time" Conner advised, "you can do no better than to try to tie yourself to General Marshall because there is a man who can fight the war, because he understands it." And he did not think it would be too long. "The Treaty of Versailles is an unacceptable thing. You can't hold a proud people down like that."

General Conner was set to leave Panama a few weeks before Eisenhower, and as they parted ways, he poured his protégé a whiskey. "Goddammit, Eisenhower, Anglo-Saxons don't kiss each other on the cheek but I am just sorry we are parting. Let's have a drink."

EISENHOWER FELT A lifelong desire to impress General Conner with his accomplishments, like a son seeking the validation of a remote and deeply admired father. He returned from Panama in September 1924 with a new son of his own, John, a new marriage with Mamie, and a new sense of focus.

General Conner used his magic to get Eisenhower a spot at the army's prestigious Command and General Staff School in Leavenworth, Kansas. It was where the top officers from across the army went to learn both the fundamentals of command and, just as important, how to be a "staff officer," the solider next to the commander, who knew how to ensure that every command was followed.

Eisenhower was insecure about his ability to make good. His grades at West Point had been middling and he said as much to General Conner.

"You will recall that during your entire service with me I required that you write a field order for the operation of the post every day for the years you were there," Conner wrote to him. "You became so well acquainted with the techniques and routine of preparing plans and orders for operations that included their logistics, that they will be second nature to you. You will feel no sense of inferiority."

Eisenhower threw himself into the work, writing to Georgie Patton to get his notes from when Patton took the course a few years earlier. Leonard "Gee" Gerow was also in the class.

Eisenhower had been with Gee in San Antonio, his first assignment out of the army. It was where he met Mamie. At the time, Eisenhower had a reputation as a "woman hater," his heart having been recently broken by Gladys Harding, whom Eisenhower would pine for as "the prettiest girl in Abilene." After an intense summer romance, Gladys had declined his invitation to become an army wife, preferring to tour the country and its big cities on her own dime as a professional pianist. Gee had been one of the first to see Eisenhower's heart reassemble just a few months later, when Eisenhower introduced him to a saucy young debutante from Denver by the name of Mamie Doud.

Back together at Leavenworth, Eisenhower and Gee filled ashtrays until one or two in the morning in the upstairs study, where Eisenhower had created a personal map room like the one in Panama. When the final grades were posted, the name Dwight D. Eisenhower was in the number one spot (Gee was eleventh).

Mamie's parents sent telegrams of "Congratulations" and "Hurrah." Georgie congratulated him with the backhanded compliment that he needed to "stop thinking about drafting orders and moving supplies and start thinking about some means of making the infantry move under fire."

If anyone ever asked, Eisenhower would deny studying much at all. And from that moment, he began to get a reputation for "divine destiny." He might've been paddling through life as hard as he physically could withstand. He was plagued in the years to come by chronic stomach troubles and lower back pain that his doctors would attribute to "a neurotic element." In the Philippines, it had gotten so bad that he spent a week in the hospital for gastroenteritis after his stomach bloated out, he would say, "like a dying frog." The doctors almost put him under for surgery before it suddenly and embarrassingly resolved itself. But except for a few conspicuous flare-ups, all of that was kept inside. On the surface, Eisenhower seemed to move through life as smooth as a mallard.

Mamie and Gee's wife became close. And in the early 1930s, the two couples formed the center of a regular social circle in Washington, DC. They would host parties when big football games were on the radio, and between cigarettes and cocktails, Eisenhower and Gee would move the players back and forth on a large map of the field to illustrate the plays as they unfolded. They jokingly called themselves "Club Eisenhower," and with John running the house, it was the first time since Camp Meade that their home had been filled with the happiness of family.

IT WAS ALMOST midnight. Eisenhower awoke as his plane descended toward Washington, DC. He had spent the whole first day of 1944 in motion. He looked down to see the city's lights exploding through darkness.

"Has someone gone crazy?" he thought. For the past year and a half, he had grown accustomed to the night being pitch-black as a precaution against air raids. How uncanny it felt to suddenly be in a place that, for all practical purposes, was at peace.

Eisenhower and Butch drove together to Wardman Park, an apartment building, where both of their wives were living. Mamie and Ruth Butcher had waited up for them. And when the door opened, Butch and Eisenhower presented Junior and Rubev, the children of Telek and Caacie, Butch's war dog. Both puppies promptly peed on the rugs.

Bernard Baruch

CHAPTER 13

THE RETURN TO Washington introduced Eisenhower to the Pentagon. When he left back in 1942, the War Department still worked out of the old Munitions Building, a hideous and crumbling office complex around the block from the White House on the National Mall. The year before, however, General Marshall and the secretary of war, Henry Stimson, had moved across the Potomac River to the tan brick labyrinth that had been newly constructed next to Arlington National Cemetery.

To maintain secrecy, General Marshall's personal aide, Frank McCarthy, met Eisenhower at Wardman Park's back stairs and drove him in an unmarked black car to a private entrance at the Pentagon, where he was taken in a private elevator to the office suite shared by Marshall and Stimson.

Eisenhower had not seen General Marshall since Cairo and had every reason to wonder where he stood with his old mentor. Marshall never expressed to Eisenhower, or to anyone else, a desire to lead the invasion of Fortress Europe. When Eisenhower had asked him about it, all he said was, "This is something for our superiors and I have nothing to say." But Marshall wanted it. Everyone knew that. And he deserved it too.

As late as the first week of December, Frank McCarthy was scheduled to go to England in advance of General Marshall's arrival. And yet, back in Tehran, Roosevelt had changed his mind. Roosevelt went to see Marshall and had all but offered the job to him. Marshall just had to say he wanted it. But Marshall insisted on taking himself "wholeheartedly" out of the deliberations. In that case, Roosevelt had said, "I feel I could not sleep at night with you out of the country." Marshall fell on his own sword and urged the president to appoint Eisenhower instead.

Eisenhower had kept General Marshall's note, the draft of the cable from Roosevelt to Stalin, announcing his selection. He had it framed and told Marshall as much. But whether Marshall was pleased to have cultivated a grateful protégé or resentful that Eisenhower's name would forever mark the liberation of Europe, no one could tell. That was the thing with Marshall. He never complimented Eisenhower to his face, except for one time he slipped and said, "Well, you're not doing so badly, so far." Did it matter that Marshall was denied the opportunity that should have been the culmination of his career? It seemed to matter least of all to Marshall. It was what Eisenhower always admired most about him: his superhuman ability to keep his personal feelings out of mind. He was the truest soldier.

Marshall called Eisenhower back to the United States ostensibly to get some rest. And Frank McCarthy had given Eisenhower an itinerary that would take him to visit his son at West Point, his mother in Kansas, and a resort in White Sulphur Springs, West Virginia, for a few days' getaway with Mamie.

But General Marshall really wanted to talk to Eisenhower behind closed doors and to say things that he should not write down. In particular, he wanted to warn Eisenhower about Churchill. Marshall did not think he could be trusted. Churchill was a canny political operator and never took no for an answer. There was no reason to think that he had a change of heart about Operation Overlord and, regardless of what he said, he could be expected to use every means available to force Eisenhower's hand. When Marshall had expected to be Supreme Allied Commander, he had prepared himself to go public if the British were unwilling to go "all out" in the war against Germany.

General Marshall had been thinking about the invasion of France for a long time. And he chaired a series of meetings for Eisenhower at the Pentagon with everyone he thought might be essential to its success, because if there was one thing George C. Marshall knew how to do, it was run a meeting.

Without any notes, Marshall would proceed methodically and decisively through a mental agenda that hit every salient point. And once he had scratched every line off his mental list, he would say, "Any questions or comments?" He would let a few seconds of silence pass and then be up and out of the room before anyone had a chance to say anything irrelevant.

The meetings were not simply General Marshall's way of educating Eisenhower. He also made sure Eisenhower was seen by everyone who mattered to the military. Marshall had spent decades becoming one of the most trusted men in Washington. Eisenhower, to the extent he was known at all, was viewed the way Roosevelt had viewed him before their tour of Carthage the previous November. Eisenhower was Plog's assistant; likable Ike from Kansas. He needed to be seen as the Supreme Allied Commander.

That evening, General Marshall feted Eisenhower as his secret guest of honor at the Alibi Club. The oyster dinner was joined by the ranking members of the House and Senate Military Affairs Committees, top officials in the War Department, and other wartime luminaries. Marshall introduced Eisenhower to the literal smoke-filled backroom, along with two more of the army's newest stars from the Pacific. There was J. Lawton "Lightning Joe" Collins, who had just led the Twenty-Sixth infantry across Guadalcanal, and George Kenney, who had made a name for himself as the Army Air Forces' most brilliant innovator.

The man Eisenhower was perhaps most impressed to see, however, was Bernard Baruch. He had met Baruch, at least from afar, a decade and a half earlier, when he had come to Washington at the end of 1929 to work for General George Moseley, the assistant secretary of war. It was the first time Eisenhower had been in the proverbial room where it happens, and a major issue of the day was the relationship between business and the military.

In 1930, Congress created the War Policies Commission to examine how the United States could "promote peace" and prevent war profiteering. Eisenhower was on the commission's staff, which meant he had to sit attentively through two weeks' worth of testimony from seemingly everyone in America who thought he knew something about war. Many in the parade of speakers were religious, socialist, or other ideological "pacifists." (Eisenhower, at this point in his life, would routinely put the word "pacifist" in punishment quotes.) They spent their allotted time inveighing against war and trumpeting pet causes, such as the abolition of the military, joining the League of Nations, liberating the Philippines, abolishing the Monroe Doctrine, and recognizing Soviet Russia.

Eisenhower developed what would become a lifelong, eye-rolling impatience for people who dedicated themselves to symbolic politics. It was not that he doubted their sincerity, at least in most cases. It was that they seemed completely disconnected from the world as it was and appeared to give no thought to the prosaic problem of how to bring about the utopia they imagined. It was all too reminiscent of the abstract world his father insisted on living in, a world that had made his father neither happy, nor provided for his family.

But then, as if cutting a cool breeze into the dank, hot air, there was Bernard Baruch. The fabulously wealthy New York financier was full of specific ways to prevent war profiteering without the complete reimagining of America's government and the abolition of private property. He offered specifics on how price controls could be used to minimize inflation, price gouging, and the ballooning of debt. It didn't ring in the ears like Fiorello La Guardia's proposal to amend the Constitution to "give the government the broad, all-sweeping powers that it needs to take over property, nationalize industry, stop speculation, and suspend all normal gains and profits; nothing short of that will equalize the burdens of war." But Baruch spoke with a crisp specificity about the world as it was and how it could—and could not—be made better.

Eisenhower had been completely taken by the clarity and precision of Baruch's practical line of thought. It also did not hurt that Baruch had the confidence of someone with an astronomical fortune—the kind of money that no one back in Abilene could have imagined. Baruch seemed to have the real world figured out. And now, as General Marshall's secret guest of honor, Eisenhower was shucking oysters at the same table as the man.

General Marshall interrupted the dinner so everyone could hear from his golden boys. First, he called over to Joe Collins to let the table know how things were going at Guadalcanal. Then, Marshall turned to George Kenney, who had captured an airfield from the rear in Papua New Guinea using paratroopers. "I truly don't believe that another air force in the world today could've put this over as perfectly as the Fifth Air Force did," Kenney would say. It was clockwork: 1,700 men and 15 tons of supplies. There was even a group of Australian gunners who at the last minute demanded to be dropped as well. These guys had never worn a parachute, but they suited up, jumped out with their guns, and were in the fight within an hour.

As Kenney continued at length, as he was wont to do, General Marshall interrupted. Tell them about the ice cream, Marshall suggested.

Kenney explained that not only had the airfield been captured that very day, but it had been such a clean operation that the paratroopers got to enjoy some ice cream that very night.

General Marshall then turned to Eisenhower, who held forth for nearly a half hour, detailing his successes and trying to live up to Kenney's heroics. And with Baruch at the table, Eisenhower's mind turned to the business of war. The most difficult question, Eisenhower said, was not what the Germans were doing, but what the Americans were doing.

"What about the strikes?" he asked.

That November, coal miners had gone on strike, followed by steel workers in December. More than 4.5 million man-days had been lost and that, Eisenhower said, slowed the production of the planes, the landing craft, and the tanks he needed to win. Just the uncertainty over what would get made gave the Germans an incentive to keep fighting, since for all the destruction that the air forces had done to Germany's war machine with bombs, labor and management were doing to America's war machine with bickering.

Marshall then stood up and proposed a toast. To Eisenhower. And then, he added, to Roosevelt. All stood with him.

John Eisenhower

CHAPTER 14

THAT NIGHT, EISENHOWER'S buzz from the Alibi Club had barely time to clear before Frank McCarthy picked him and Mamie up and took them to George Marshall's private train car for the night journey up the East Coast to West Point. John had entered the military academy in 1941, so he should have been a junior. But in 1942, West Point shortened the curriculum from four to three years, meaning that John was now, at the age of twenty-one, due to graduate on June 6, 1944.

Eisenhower had first pulled into the gothic gray granite West Shore Railroad passenger station on June 14, 1911, five months before his twenty-first birthday. He was a tall, gawky Kansan then. His modesty would compel him to tell people that he had applied to the service academies because they offered a poor boy the chance for a free education. But he had dreamed of going to West Point for nearly as long as he knew it existed. He would tell Beetle, "I had never wanted to be anything but a soldier." In private, he would confess that finally going to the Military Academy was "not a decision; it was an instinctive desire that I followed persistently until I had attained it."

When Eisenhower was ten years old, the *Saturday Evening Post* began a yearlong series celebrating West Point's upcoming centennial. The inaugural issue featured a cover illustration of sharply dressed cadets standing in a defensive circle, rifles up and out like a sea urchin. Inside it regaled readers with stories of "plebe life," rife with hazing, drills, "unlimited fighting but no complaints" as young men began the "climb to greatness."

West Point also had a storied reputation for the thing Eisenhower cared most about as a boy: football. In 1905, when elite football was still a college game that yielded more than a dozen annual fatalities, the colleges convened in New York to discuss whether the game should be reformed, or even abolished. The *Literary Digest* reported that the conference "was dominated by West Point," whose representatives took a hard-line position not only against abolishing football, but also against making its rules too soft. "West Point did not want all the roughness taken out of the game," the article recounted, "for some knocks and bruises were necessary to the sport."

No one from Abilene had been selected for West Point in fifteen years. And scoring the appointment required political connections not readily available to the son of a religiously pacifist creamery mechanic, whose only political association had been with the Socialist Party. Eisenhower tried to build his own political connections while still in high school under the tutelage of Joe Howe, the publisher of the *Dickinson County News*. Howe had given one of Eisenhower's close friends, John "Six" McDonnell, a job setting type after Six's father died. Eisenhower would come visit Six after school and look through all the newspapers that came in, or the latest books from the big-time publishers, who had sent them to Joe seeking "the small town view of the publication." When Joe asked Eisenhower what his interests were, Eisenhower replied, "I like to read about what is going on outside of Kansas." Joe was happy to cultivate the young Dwight's curiosity and Eisenhower gravitated to him as a mentor. Indeed, Joe had been the one to lend him the *Life of Hannibal*.

Throughout high school, Eisenhower spent many afternoons at Joe's with a gang of friends, who christened themselves the "Knights of Honor." This was something of a riposte to Abilene's cool kids, whose families lived in the mansions along Buckeye Avenue and called themselves the "Bums of the Lawsy Lou."

In his senior year, Joe encouraged Eisenhower to give a speech at the Young Men's Democratic Club. Choosing to title his address "The Student in Politics," the young Dwight used the occasion to attack partisanship as the reason for the Republican lock on Kansas and lambasted the Republican Party for becoming lazy and corrupt. He spoke admiringly of the Square Dealers and Insurgent Progressives and the reformers trying to remake the

Republican Party from within. But he mused to the gathered Democrats that, like any other young student in politics, "he admires these men greatly, but he cannot help but remark that they are fighting for many of the principles which the Democrat Party advocates." He then concluded, "With the Republican Party splitting up, and the number of honest and fearless ones tending towards democracy, the Democrat Party deserves his first look. And since the first vote generally determines his political standing, we find one more intelligent young man enlisted under the standard of democracy."

Joe Howe published Eisenhower's speech on the front page with a handsome picture of the up-and-comer. But being a Democrat in Kansas, which had never elected a Democrat to a full term for any national office in its history, did not give Eisenhower the kind of political connections he needed to get into West Point.

Eisenhower found his opportunities limited after high school. He graduated in 1909, the same year as his older brother Edgar. They had a handshake agreement that they would each take turns, year by year, in college, while the other worked to pay for tuition. As the older brother, Edgar took the first year at college, going all the way to Ann Arbor and enrolling at the University of Michigan. Eisenhower sent Edgar two hundred dollars to pay his way. Edgar, though, became reluctant about returning to Abilene to keep his part of the deal. That left Eisenhower, for the foreseeable future, working in the same creamery as his father, still playing football for Abilene High School, and facing the dead end of his life.

Eisenhower remained friends with Six, who would cover for him at the creamery when he wanted to go make out with Esther Baumgarth. And he told Six of his dream of going to West Point. But Six didn't know anything about it. Neither of them knew really anything other than Kansas.

By chance, an old friend from the wealthy side of Abilene's tracks, Swede Hazlett, had come back to town. They had lost touch in high school after Swede's father sent him to a boarding school in Wisconsin. Upon graduation, Swede was selected for the US Naval Academy, but had failed the entrance exam and so had to spend a year back home studying to take it a second time.

Swede traveled in Abilene's uptown circles, where the Republicans lived, such as Charles Harger, who published the *Abilene Daily Reflector*, the Republican rival to Joe Howe's *Dickinson County News*. Eisenhower had indirectly known Harger in high school, when he served with his daughter on the yearbook staff.

Eisenhower rekindled his friendship with Swede, who made a habit of visiting Eisenhower during the night shift at the creamery. They would goof off, play poker, boost some ice cream, and mostly just bullshit. Eisenhower was curious about how Swede had gotten into Annapolis, and Swede encouraged Eisenhower to give it a shot. They could go together and become sailors.

"What chance have I got?" Eisenhower had asked him.

What did he have to lose? Swede told him to write to the state's congressmen and ask.

Eisenhower gave it a shot. He expressed his desire to go to either Annapolis or West Point. (He also lied about his age, saying that he would be turning nineteen that October instead of twenty, since Annapolis put an age limit on its cadets.) He then went to local businessmen with impeccable Republican credentials to write him letters of support.

The only response he got was from one of Senator Joseph Bristow's aides, formulaically thanking him for his letter and assuring the young Dwight that "your application will be filed along with those the Senator already has on hand." Then Eisenhower saw an article in the paper. Senator Bristow was an antipatronage crusader and had been the political architect of the Seventeenth Amendment, requiring senators—the ultimate patronage job—to stand for popular election. True to his ideals, the paper reported that Bristow planned to select his nominees to West Point and Annapolis through a competitive exam. And so, Eisenhower sent another letter asking to compete for the nomination.

This time, Bristow wrote back personally telling Eisenhower to not get his hopes up. The article had perhaps overstated Bristow's commitment to unadorned meritocracy. But he was holding a competitive examination in Topeka at the beginning of October and was happy to give Eisenhower a shot.

Eisenhower would forever credit Swede Hazlett, who became one of his few true lifelong friends, with his having gone to West Point. He scored second among the applicants for West Point and top among the four who also applied to Annapolis. It was October 24, 1910, ten days after his twentieth birthday, when Eisenhower got the letter. Senator Bristow was sending in his name "as my nominee for the vacancy in the West Point Military Academy occurring next spring."

Swede was disappointed and Eisenhower acted disappointed that their fantasy of going to Annapolis together was now dashed. He told Swede that he had gotten the top score on Bristow's test and that the senator wanted the top student to take the West Point exam.

Swede told him to write to Bristow to ask him to reconsider, but Eisenhower muttered that he was "not looking any gift horse in the mouth."

Eisenhower told his parents of his selection, but the subject was taboo. He left Abilene when his father was at work. His mother went onto the porch with his younger brother Milton, who was no more than twelve at the time. She stayed there as Eisenhower walked uptown to the train station, carrying his suitcase. She stood like stone until her son was out of sight. Then, Milton told him later, she went inside and sobbed.

ARRIVING AT THE West Shore Railroad passenger station back in 1911, Eisenhower was decidedly not in Kansas anymore. His would be the largest class to graduate from West Point at the time and include the first Puerto Rican and the second Filipino. In the years to come, it would be dubbed "the class the stars fell on" for how many of its cadets—including Omar Bradley—would become army luminaries. The farm boy from just near the geographic center of the continental United States was graduating as part of a new and broader America.

The West Shore Railroad passenger station was near the banks of the Hudson, and Eisenhower had to lug his suitcase up the steep hill in the early-summer sun. When he reached the top and passed through the gray granite gates of the United States Military Academy, the upperclassmen charged, screaming orders at him and the other cadets in what seemed like a wall of gray-clad chaos.

"What am I doing here?" he wondered. His clothes were cheap and ill fitting, marking him, as they had in Abilene, as God-knows-who from God-knows-where. He was a gangly 152 pounds and was so lacking in any sense of rhythm that he could not even march in time.

What Eisenhower lacked in worldly grace, he soon realized he could make up for with the broad smile he had inherited from his mother as well as the cachet of not being from Kansas, so much as being from Abilene. If there was one town in all of Kansas that young men from as far as the Philippines recognized, it was the legendary saloon town where Wild Bill Hickok had been sheriff, where the law was found in holsters, and where a real man always maintained his cool swagger, whether sitting at the poker table or drawing up in a duel. His humble origins hidden by the equalizing gray of his cadet uniform, Dwight from Kansas acquired a swagger, crooned cowboy ballads loudly off-key, and started introducing himself as "Ike."

With his gang of friends back at Joe Howe's printing shop, he had assumed the silly nicknames of "Ugly Ike" and "Little Ike." He and his older brother Edgar had been inseparable as kids, and fought constantly, which naturally made Edgar "Big Ike." "Big Ike" and "Little Ike" were a recurring character type at the time, typically as minstrel characters who were always at odds. In 1909, around the same time Eisenhower and his older brother adopted the nicknames, Joseph Cotter published the popular book of poems *A White Song and a Black One*, which featured the poem "Big Ike and Little Ike," a comic tale written in dialect of two Ikes who get drunk and try to lynch each other over a woman. Eisenhower's high school yearbook entry read, "Little Ike, now a couple of inches taller than 'Big Ike,' is our best historian and mathematician. President of the Athletic Association 09, football 07, 08, baseball 08, 09."

At West Point, Eisenhower was just Ike. It was a name that, in western pulp fiction, always went to big men, who were at home on the land, talked salty, and though lacking the refinement of city folk, were always on the right side when things got real. The quintessential Ike was the antihero of Ralph Connor's popular novel *The Prospector*. Published when Eisenhower was fourteen, it combined football and the western, and featured a cowboy named Ike, who kept a wad of tobacco in his cheek, who gambled, smoked, and swore prolifically (always written as "blank blank"), who "had a fondness for words not usually current among the cowboys," and for whom "religion, with all its great credos, with all its customs, had simply no bearing."

At West Point, Eisenhower relished the chance to be an outlaw within the safe confines of a disciplinary system that was so tight, the smallest assertion of wit or individuality counted as rebellion. He rolled his own cigarettes because unlike pipes or cigars, cigarettes were the only form of smoking the rules forbade. He hustled his classmates at poker, also forbidden, which was the most authentic part of his Abilene cowpuncher persona, having learned the game as a boy from an old trapper who also taught him the rudiments of living off the land. When a yearling ordered him and a fellow plebe to report to his room in "full-dress coats," Eisenhower convinced his accomplice to join him in stripping naked, so they could duly appear in only their full-dress coats. When asked to explain himself, Eisenhower replied like a genie, "Nothing was said about trousers, sir." He was even given demerits for smiling.

THOSE WHO KNEW Eisenhower back then would say "he loved life and people and didn't seem to be very ambitious." What need did he have to be? He loved being at West Point. It gave him the chance to become the kind of man he had always wanted to be, even if the only thing the academic side of his education taught him was that supposedly educated men could be idiots.

While it failed to cultivate a love of learning, West Point gave Eisenhower the structure to cultivate himself. Nowhere was this more significant than in football. At five feet, eleven inches, he was comparatively tall, leading to his assignment with F Company, which was full of football players. He had played in Abilene, though was known more for his willingness to take the pain needed to play rough than for his athletic grace. But through that same grind, he put on twenty lean pounds over his freshman year and got himself on the varsity squad as a sophomore.

Eisenhower's first chance to play was in the first game that year against Stevens. West Point won, 27–0, and Eisenhower quickly developed a reputation as a line smasher, particularly in the game against Yale, whose defensive line that year was assumed to be a stone wall. Then, that November, Eisenhower's name found its way into the *New York Times* for the very first time, when West Point played an immediately legendary game against the Carlisle Indian School.

If the West had closed in 1890, the year Eisenhower was born, it was only because it had been slammed shut by decades of brutality between the US Army and the country's diverse Native American tribes. Army v. Carlisle was a pantomime of that conflict a generation later, and on Carlisle's side, an opportunity for revenge.

Eisenhower was fielded as halfback in what quickly became a bare-knuckle slugfest. In a shining moment, Eisenhower pulled off a twelve-yard rush, West Point's first (and nearly only) successful rush of the game. This provoked a fistfight between West Point's rear guard and Carlisle's halfback, who got himself ejected. West Point's team captain was then ejected at the start of the second half for slugging Carlisle's left tackle.

Eisenhower's star might have shone more brightly that day had he not been positioned opposite Carlisle's Jim Thorpe, whom the *Times* gushed was the "athletic marvel of the age" and who, over the following eighty-eight years, would never be dethroned as the greatest American athlete of the twentieth century. Eisenhower's twelve-yard first down was downright adorable next to Thorpe's fifty-five-yard touchdown on the punt return. Each Army cadet on the field took a shot at stopping Thorpe, and each flopped or flailed fecklessly onto the field until it looked like the Little Bighorn. "Thorpe went through the West Point line like it was an open door," the *Times* wrote. Trying to stop him was "like trying to catch a shadow."

Eisenhower caught that shadow once. He and a teammate planned to give "that Indian," as they called Thorpe, the "high-low," a tackle designed to cut a man in half. When Thorpe came through, unstopped by the line, Eisenhower's high-low succeeded in knocking him down. But Thorpe got right back up. And on the next play, he ran the ball ten more yards. This, while Eisenhower and his teammate were pulled from the rest of the game because they knocked their heads together giving Jim Thorpe the high-low.

West Point did not get a single first down in the entire second half. Carlisle won, 27–6. In another life, Eisenhower's respectable performance in a legendary game might have cut him a path to becoming a professional athlete. Before West Point, Eisenhower had thought of trying to make it as a major-league baseball player. His hero was Honus "the Flying Dutchman" Wagner, a shortstop for the Pirates who offered hope to those with conspicuously German names that they too could be a superstar. And he had made some cash playing professional baseball outside Abilene, which he forever kept as a poorly guarded secret, since (as Jim Thorpe would later discover), doing so would have disqualified him from playing under West Point's amateurism rules.

The next game, against Tufts, ended Eisenhower's athletic career, and nearly his military one as well. Eisenhower got knocked in the knee. He stayed in the infirmary until the swelling subsided and was sent on his way. Then, as if nothing had happened, he reported to cavalry training, where he was ordered to do the "monkey drill," which required a cadet to jump off and then vault back over a horse. To do it right, you wanted to hit the ground hard with your heels so that the recoil sent you back over the horse. Eisenhower hit the ground hard. And as soon as he did, his knee just crumpled. He was again rushed to the infirmary, where it took another four or five days to straighten the leg out. He would never play football again.

Laid up for months, Eisenhower entered a deep depression, what he called his "Blue Devils." He felt helpless, and given his upbringing, that made him feel worthless. And he considered resigning from the army preemptively, since it was unlikely to commission him as an officer due to physical disability.

Eisenhower had no intention of returning to Abilene. His plan was to make his way to Argentina after graduation. The country had fascinated Eisenhower since boyhood as a place that was more "entrancing than Europe." The Argentina of young Dwight's imagination was a place like that described in "The Pampas Hunters," a story in the dime western magazine *Beadle's Boy's Library of Sport, Story and Adventure*, which told the tale of Jack and Monte, two American boys who struck out for the great Argentine pampas, where the "people—Gauchos and Indians—lead a life as free as the exhilarating air they breathe; they have the blue vault of heaven for a roof, and the most beautiful carpet that Nature ever spread yields joyously to their lofty tread." With the collapse of the Spanish Empire at the turn of the century, South America was billed in magazines as a peaceful and prosperous land of opportunity, with boosters hailing the beginning of the "Pan-American Era."

As he recovered, Eisenhower forced himself to stay active and stay involved. His best friend at West Point was not a fellow cadet, but the trainer at the gym, an Irish immigrant named Marty Maher, who took care of his knee and helped him get back into shape. His outlaw persona notwithstanding, Eisenhower developed a reputation as an active, school-spirited student. He even served on the yearbook staff. His own entry gave his nickname as Ike and read, "At one time he threatened to get interested in life and won his 'A' by being the most promising back in Eastern football—but the Tufts game broke his knee and the promise. Now Ike must content himself with tea, tiddledywinks, and talk, at all of which he excels. Said prodigy will now lead us in a long, loud yell for—Dare Devil Dwight, the Dauntless Don."

Eisenhower also stayed close to football. He coached the junior varsity team and joined the cheerleading squad. That put him on the sidelines when Army was famously drubbed his junior year by Notre Dame, which deployed a then-revolutionary forward pass strategy enabled by the adhesive hands of Knute Rockne. As both men grew more famous over the years, rumors circulated that Eisenhower and Rockne had met for a boxing match. It was a total fantasy, but a legend that Eisenhower was slow to debunk.

West Point's quick adoption of Notre Dame's strategy led it to victory in the Army-Navy game. And despite his short career on the field, Eisenhower's natural talents off the field were such that by his senior year, he was made an assistant coach.

Coaching football was a skill that the army prized greatly in that era;

enough to turn a blind eye to Eisenhower's knee injury. The army had football teams all around the country, and before television left everyone to watch football, regular people played it to win. Eisenhower came to believe that "football, perhaps more than any other sport, tends to instill in men the feeling that victory comes through hard—almost slavish—work, team play, self-confidence, and an enthusiasm that amounts to dedication."

Looking back over his life and the development of his own thinking about how to be a leader, the lessons only a football coach could learn were as significant as the lessons Eisenhower drew from Clausewitz, Nietzsche, or any of the other great thinkers in General Conner's library. On his very first day at the Command and General Staff School at Leavenworth, the commandant had even introduced military leadership by saying, "A football team composed of individuals of medium ability, indoctrinated in teamwork and led by a real leader, will beat a team of hastily assembled stars, all wanting to carry the ball individually in eleven different directions."

Eisenhower's coach at West Point, Ernest Grave, was a major in the army himself and wrote about the connections between generalship and football in a book entitled *The Line Man's Bible*. "The all important idea," Graves wrote, "is conveyed in one word, viz. simplicity. Napoleon's maxim of war that simplicity is a prime requisite applies throughout the game of football. Simplicity in planning, and simplicity in execution are essential to success."

Planning, Graves wrote, was key, as was the discipline of committing plans to writing. Changes to meet conditions on the ground were always easier to make and more readily understood than trying to coordinate a group of men to do anything by improvisation. As Eisenhower would later expand upon the idea, "Plans are nothing, planning is everything." It was a sentiment also captured in a classic book of the time, *Football without a Coach*, written by the famed founder of American football (and ace bridge player) Walter Camp: "Master every detail."

Graves also firmly believed that leadership was first and foremost about taking responsibility. "It is up to the coach to make the men into players and if they do not become good, it is his fault and his fault alone." And when it was time to act, it fell to the coach to take charge. Graves instructed coaches to say to their squads without a breath of hesitation, "All right. Let's go."

IT SEEMED AS if everyone Eisenhower knew had a son at West Point: Patton, Gruenther, Truscott, Clark, Bradley, Doolittle. Doolittle's son had made something of a reputation for himself as a boxer.

Eisenhower's son, John, had neither the build nor temperament for boxing or football. He had also gotten into West Point the old-fashioned way, with the help and support of Eisenhower's politically connected younger brother, Milton, who had served as a surrogate father to John throughout his adolescence. Speaking of West Point, John would say, "This place made my dad."

John worried and delighted his father the way only a son can. Eisenhower wrote to him often, and as John progressed as a cadet, he would share his thoughts and vulnerabilities with a candor he afforded no one else.

The last time Eisenhower had gone up to West Point to visit was back in March 1942. He was still working on General Marshall's staff. After three months of eighteen-hour days, seven days a week, Marshall had just told him, "I want you to know that in this war the commanders are going to be promoted and not the staff officers." Marshall then opined at length on his reasons, seemingly indifferent to the fact that he was belittling all the sacrifices Eisenhower felt he was making. Eisenhower's father had died just two weeks earlier and he had not even gone to the funeral. "Eisenhower," Marshall had concluded, as if the gut punch was necessary at this point, "you're not going to get any promotion, you are going to stay right here on this job and you will probably never move."

Eisenhower tried to keep a poker face. "I simply don't care," he told Marshall, before storming out of his office.

The indignity of it had burned Eisenhower for days. By turns, he felt sorry for himself and angry at himself for wallowing in things he could not change. He had gone to visit John in the midst of it all, and confided his disappointments. He was sorry to let his boy down about the fact that his old man was not ten feet tall. He was going to be a brigadier general at a desk in Washington through the war, not some hero on the cover of *Life* magazine.

That, of course, was one of the many false dusks of Eisenhower's career, a fact that John appreciated far more than his father ever could. The last time they had seen each other was at the end of June 1942. John had a brief stint of leave before his father left for London. Eisenhower hadn't been feeling his best after a series of inoculations and was running a fever.

"What's your job going to be over there?" John had asked.

"Well, I'm going to be boss," Eisenhower replied, as if it were obvious.

"Are you—?"

"I'm going to be the commanding general."

"My God!" John said, eyes wide.

Eisenhower was giddy when John started West Point. He reminisced about his own time there, heavily sanitized for his son's consumption, and gently chided his boy against getting too many demerits, since that would count against his final class standing (failing to mention, of course, the prodigious number of demerits he had accumulated).

John would say that his father never talked to him about anything until he was fourteen. But upon his entering West Point, Eisenhower was delighted to have something to share and offered John his thoughts on training, tactics, strategy, or anything military in the hope of having the understanding, if not interest, of his son. He could offer words of soldierly advice, such as, "The only unforgivable sin in war is not doing your duty when you know what it is. To attempt to say that the duty is unimportant or inconsequential, and therefore, one may neglect it, is to be guilty—at least in principle—of the biggest crime a soldier can commit." And he could talk to his boy as if he were the heir apparent to the family shop, such as in the early days of the North Africa campaign, when Eisenhower told John to brush up on his Mediterranean geography "because someday I will want to talk over this campaign with you and get your idea as to whether or not we did it correctly."

EISENHOWER HAD NINE hours to spend at West Point, though to maintain secrecy, he was confined to the anonymity of General Marshall's private train car. Eisenhower asked if someone could bring him some whiskey.

Francis Wilby, the superintendent of West Point, dropped by for a short visit. And West Point's barber came to give Eisenhower a fresh haircut. John had not been told his father was coming, just that he was to report to a train car down by the West Shore Railroad station. And when he arrived, he bore an uncanny resemblance to his father, though was a man all his own.

John was two inches taller, and more than a few pounds leaner, much thinner than his father had been at his age. He didn't have his father's stomach and back problems or his bad knee. But he had a chronic ear issue. His eyesight was also beginning to fail, though he hated the thought of glasses.

Eisenhower had gained some weight and aged a bit since they had last seen each other. He also had grown more impatient.

Eisenhower would get giddy thinking about seeing his son, but for some reason, tended to tense up when they finally were in the same room. John's shortcomings, no matter how minor, always seemed to demand stern correction and John would admit to being a "little afraid" of his father. Growing up, he would say, "Everything had to be the old man's way; strict." Eisenhower's temper was terrifying, though he never laid a hand on his son the way his own father had so often done. For a while, John came to resent his father's public reputation for "affability" and "sociability," saying that at home, "Mother makes the house revolve around him. He just sits back and lets it revolve. He's very good-natured at home as long as everything goes his way."

Eisenhower would often find himself falling into the role of hectoring quizmaster or coach, drilling John the way the voice in his head had always drilled him. He couldn't help himself. And he always felt remorse about it, when he sensed its effect, when he sensed that he had put John down. In one letter, Eisenhower assured his son, "Please don't take me too seriously when I ride you a bit on your academics—you have only to look over my own record to know that I wasn't a particular star in most subjects."

But in the train car together, despite their long absence from one another, or perhaps because of it, Eisenhower fell into the same old traps. He was incurably impatient with John's seeming lack of drive to use all the advantages he had been given, whether it was in football or school or anything else. And he returned to a recurring conversation over what specialization John intended to choose in the army once he graduated. "Infantry or artillery?" John was almost reticent in the way he spoke, which contrasted sharply with his father's increasing tendency to speak from his throat.

"Infantry," John said.

Eisenhower then started talking up the artillery. And when John seemed to lean then toward artillery, Eisenhower, as if on cue, started expounding on the virtues of the infantry. The only thing Eisenhower was dead set against was John joining the paratroopers. They had a lot of glamour, given how dangerous the job was. But, at least out loud, Eisenhower worried about John's ear condition.

In his own way, Eisenhower was trying to engage with his son. But he failed to see how indistinct a son's feelings of admiration and intimidation could be. Mamie thought he was acting too keyed up and restless and at one point, scolded him for being so distracted and abrupt.

"Hell," Eisenhower snapped, "I'm going back to my theater where I can do what I want."

There was so much going on outside that stuffy train car that Eisenhower needed to know. And other than perhaps Beetle, he did not know whom he could trust. General Marshall had given in on Devers, but he clearly had his own ideas for how the invasion of France needed to go. It was no accident that Marshall had invited Joe Collins and George Kenney to dinner the night before. These men had gotten the job done, and quickly enough for everyone to enjoy some ice cream. Would Eisenhower?

Before they returned for Washington, a whole case of whiskey was delivered. The B&O Railroad's chef also prepared a delicious dinner for them to enjoy in the dining car. John was allowed to invite some of his friends, sworn to secrecy, to share the meal.

As they dined, Eisenhower playfully asked John and his friends what he should do in Europe. He was struck, though, by how humble and serious they were in giving him their answers. But, of course, they should be. In six or seven months, they and their classmates would go from fretting about demerits and the loss to Navy at the close of the 1943 football season (in their own stadium, no less) to leading a unit on the front line, probably under the command of their classmate's dad.

Henry "Hap" Arnold

CHAPTER 15

BACK IN WASHINGTON, Eisenhower went to the White House. The president's schedule had been cleared since before the New Year due to a "cold." When Eisenhower arrived, he was shown into the president's bedroom. Roosevelt, he was told, was getting over the "flu germ." But the man he saw was almost unrecognizable. The iconic Roosevelt face sagged. Where was the bounding colossus of charm from just a month earlier?

Eisenhower tried to lighten the mood and recounted the story about Churchill hiding the thermometer from his doctor. Roosevelt laughed. "My God," he said, "I do it myself." He didn't trust the doctors to tell him the truth either.

Roosevelt had signed a portrait for Kay that Eisenhower had requested. All the rumors about Eisenhower and Kay had been swirling long before the president's visit to Tunis. And Roosevelt had come away suspecting the rumors were all true. He could see how attractive Kay was and, perhaps, had an old politician's sixth sense for how people related to each other. It certainly did not make Roosevelt think the worse of Eisenhower. How could it? If anything, it made Eisenhower more relatable. And, given Eisenhower's implacable cool as Roosevelt showered shameless attention on Kay whenever the three of them were together, Eisenhower had proved that his broad, boyish smile could be one hell of a poker face.

Eisenhower stayed with Roosevelt for about an hour and brought him up to speed on all that had transpired. Roosevelt remained deeply suspicious of De Gaulle. "The French just had to have their own opportunity to decide what they want to do," the president said. The country was going to be weak, and Roosevelt feared that De Gaulle would seize power like Napoléon and attempt to retake its colonies for the sake of French imperial prestige.

"Well," Eisenhower said, "France probably wanted to retain her position."

Roosevelt was not sympathetic. "The poor Indo-Chinese," Roosevelt had come to believe, "had nothing done for them during a hundred years of French responsibility, no education, no welfare. They were just as poor as they had ever been, and there was no reason why this state of affairs should be allowed to go on."

At the Casablanca Conference, Roosevelt had made an effort to warm to De Gaulle, telling him, "I am sure that we will be able to assist your country in re-establishing her destiny."

De Gaulle had huffed and then demanded the return of French colonies at the end of the war. Roosevelt had just spent dinner with the sultan of Morocco imagining together a future for his country free of European domination, one in which Morocco could develop its own natural resources for its own benefit. The suggestion of simply returning it to France as if to a landlord repulsed Roosevelt.

Roosevelt had vented to his son, "Don't think for a moment, Elliott, that Americans would be dying in the Pacific tonight if it hadn't been for the shortsighted greed of the French and the British and the Dutch."

BACK AT THE Pentagon, Eisenhower confronted more diplomatic problems to weigh on his mind. Though the sensitivities over prestige were intramural, instead of international.

General Marshall had arranged for a meeting with Hap Arnold. Eisenhower had gotten to know Arnold well in early 1942 and liked him. They had spent a few Sundays together studying geography down to the mountain ranges, peninsulas, and atolls that might become crucial to winning a world war. But personal friendship went only so far when ambitions were at stake. And Marshall was emphatic. Eisenhower needed to get control over the air forces—*all* the air forces.

It was a sensitive subject. Since the summer of 1942, the air forces had started dividing themselves between "tactical" and "strategic." The tactical air forces were the light bombers and fighters whose goal was to provide air support to soldiers on the ground. The strategic air forces were the heavy bombers that could fly deep into the European interior with enough large bombs to rubble whatever lay below.

The division had become an ideological debate about the future of warfare. At Leavenworth, Eisenhower had been taught to think of all airpower as tactical. It was a tool for a ground commander to use in support of ground troops. This was army doctrine. But there were those who had come to believe as an article of faith that bombing could be strategic, that with enough airpower, you could win a war without having to bother with tactics as primitive as putting men in boots on the ground you sought to conquer.

During the First World War, when airplanes were spectacularly glamorous but, in truth, useful for little more than reconnaissance, true believers saw the future of the technology in grandiose terms. The Italian Giulio Douhet wrote the Old Testament of airpower, *The Command of the Air*. In the past, Douhet wrote, "the battlefield was strictly defined; the armed forces were in a category distinct from civilians, who in their turn were more or less organized to fill the needs of a nation at war." The airplane made this all obsolete. In the future, the battlefield was the air and everything under it. Wars would be won or lost by bombing the enemy, its industrial capacity, and its civilian population into submission.

Just as the navy owned the sea, and the army owned the land, the believers in airpower saw the skies as a new domain of warfare with its own needs, its own doctrine, and its own objectives that, not coincidentally, would give airmen something to own.

The British were the first to embrace the idea, creating the Royal Air Force, or RAF, in 1918, which quickly became jealously separate from Britain's army. In 1942, the British appointed Arthur "Bomber" Harris as the head of the RAF's Bomber Command. Harris wanted it known that "he intended to be a real Commander in Chief of the Air." He was a fanatical believer in strategic airpower and not only promised to win the war against Germany single-handedly by annihilating it from the air, but to do so by June 1944.

The United States was slower to embrace airpower, though in the 1920s, a brigadier general named William "Billy" Mitchell wrote his own three-hundred-page testament, *Winged Defense*, in which he promised that, "No longer will the tedious and expensive processes of wearing down the enemy's land forces by continuous attacks be resorted to. The air forces will strike immediately at the enemy's manufacturing and food centers, railways, bridges, canals, and harbors." Through bombing alone, victory would come because "the losing side will have to accept without question the dominating conditions of its adversary."

Mitchell became a cult figure for a small but influential group of instructors at the US Army's Air Corps Tactical School, who converted a generation of airmen into lifelong disciples of strategic airpower. And though the Army Air Forces, as it was now called, remained technically part of the army, the disciples of Billy Mitchell saw the war as a golden opportunity, not simply to prove the good news to be true, but to declare the independence of a US Air Force.

At the Casablanca Conference a year earlier, the Combined Chiefs decided to give strategic bombing a chance. In May 1943, they gave the RAF's Bomber Command and the United States' Eighth Army Air Force a joint mandate to destroy German industry and the Luftwaffe, under the code name "Pointblank." Then, at Cairo, the Combined Chiefs had agreed to make Tooey Spaatz into Bomber Harris's effective equal by rechristening the Eighth Army Air Force as the "US Strategic Air Forces in Europe."

Eisenhower had thought Spaatz was a great choice for the job. A year ahead of Eisenhower at West Point, he had fought as an airman in France during the First World War and had been ruthlessly effective in leading bombing operations in North Africa. Except for his being prickly about the correct pronunciation of his name ("spots," not "spats"), Eisenhower admired Spaatz as one of the most unshakable people he had ever known. He trusted his judgment, but Spaatz was also an evangelical believer in Billy Mitchell's gospel of strategic bombing. And that could be a problem for Operation Overlord.

As a direct mandate from the Combined Chiefs, Operation Pointblank effectively made the strategic air forces independent of Eisenhower's nominal supremacy as the Supreme Allied Commander. If Eisenhower needed heavy bombers to prepare the battlefield for the invasion of France, all he could do was make recommendations to the Combined Chiefs. And the Combined Chiefs would, in turn, consult with Bomber Harris and Tooey Spaatz on whether the diversion from Operation Pointblank was worthwhile. Even if they agreed, the bureaucracy of it would cost Eisenhower precious time and attention. And there was no reason to think they would ever agree. Harris had a reputation for refusing to agree with anyone on anything, and both Harris and Spaatz continued to insist that, given free rein, strategic bombing would force Germany to surrender in a matter of months. Nothing, in other words, was more worthwhile than Operation Pointblank.

General Marshall would say, "The air people thought this and that and did a lot of wishful thinking." He was also wary of their ambition to declare their independence and their related impulse to bloat their budgets. It was one of the reasons he had warned Eisenhower not to let Spaatz gold-plate his new headquarters after being elevated to lead the newly created US Strategic Air Force. The Army Air Forces were already soaking up more than a third of the army's budget, and that did not account for all the guns, bombs, and logistics costs, which still fell on the overall army's ledger. Its procurement budget over the previous year was more than the navy and the "Army Ground Forces" (as the actual army had come to be called) combined.

Yes, airplanes were expensive. But there was a growing complex of relationships between the air forces and the aviation industry, which kept drawing the unforgiving glare of the Truman Committee. Take the B-29. The contracts had been cut to build a new Superfortress to replace the B-17 Flying Fortress almost four years earlier. But so many experimental technologies and platinum finishes had been crammed into its development that barely a dozen B-29s were airworthy.

General Marshall told Eisenhower that when he had anticipated being the Supreme Allied Commander, he was going to insist on nothing less than direct command over all the air forces, tactical and strategic, British and American. He was prepared to take the issue to the press if he had to and force a choice between him and the air force prima donnas. Marshall could do that. Eisenhower, though, could not. He was not George Marshall. And so, Eisenhower outlined his plan for the invasion of France and tried to persuade Hap Arnold that unified command over the heavy bombers was crucial to its success.

The Sicily campaign had shown that the careful coordination of air and ground forces was key to striking hard enough. As just one example, Eisenhower had been able to order the bombing of Pantelleria soon after the fall of Tunis in May 1943. The heavily fortified island stood between North Africa and Sicily, and the heavy bombers pummeled the island's defenses so thoroughly that the Italians surrendered the moment the first landing craft reached its shores. That not only neutralized a threat, it enabled the Allies to use the island as a launching pad against Sicily a month later.

Eisenhower needed to have the same flexibility in the invasion of France.

"When a battle needs the last ounce of available force," Eisenhower would explain, "the commander must not be in the position of depending upon request and negotiation to get it. It was vital that the entire sum of our assault power, including the two Strategic Air Forces, be available for use during the critical stages of attack."

Hap Arnold agreed, at least in principle. Though a hand-anointed acolyte of Billy Mitchell, Arnold was not a zealot. Rather jovial by nature (hence the nickname "Hap," short for "Happy"), Arnold had succeeded in the War Department as a conciliator, as keen to sell ground force commanders on the value that air forces could provide above all that ground, as he was to gain bureaucratic independence for the air forces themselves.

Arnold was eager to have a unified commander over air operations in England, if only to better manage things. The fixation on Operation Pointblank was leaving 70 percent of the Allied bomber capacity sitting idle at any given time due to things as fickle as the weather. Arnold hoped that consolidating command would give air operations the "necessary drive." That was why they had created the Strategic Air Command, and at Cairo, the understanding had been that the Supreme Allied Commander would ultimately take command of all the air forces.

There were issues, though. Arnold had been fine with having a British officer serve as Eisenhower's air chief, even though the United States was producing nearly three times the number of aircraft as the British were and, given that the British refused to bomb during the day, taking more of the risks. But given the size of the US contribution, Arnold insisted that Eisenhower's command over the strategic air forces include all the air forces, British and American. That would be controversial. Charles Portal, Hap Arnold's British counterpart, had resisted any consolidation of command over the strategic air forces at Cairo. On the bright side, though, Leigh-Mallory was a favorite of Churchill, who, Arnold said, would be key to overcoming any lingering resistance among the British Chiefs.

Arnold also thought that Eisenhower needed a concrete plan for how he would use the strategic bombers. Operation Pointblank had a year's worth of planning and momentum behind it. Without a plan of his own, Eisenhower would just be arguing on principle, and arguments on principle never got very far.

General Marshall then called George Kenney into the meeting. Kenney had gained complete air supremacy in the South Pacific, and Arnold wanted him to tell Eisenhower how to get it done in Europe. Kenney explained his thinking on all manner of air tactics, such as his development of fuse-less bombs that detonated on impact. Eventually sensing, perhaps, that Eisenhower was in no mood to be told how to do his job at that moment, Kenney stopped himself, saying the wars in Europe and the Pacific were "entirely different and being fought against opponents, who were also quite different in their methods, their military, intelligence and capacity, and their psychology." Kenney said he, therefore, "could not presume to tell either Eisenhower or Spaatz how to fight their war."

That was, however, precisely what Arnold—and Marshall—had called Kenney in to do. And Arnold suggested that Eisenhower bring one of Kenney's men, one of his "spark plugs," onto his staff in England.

Kenny offered to send Freddy Smith, who could explain everything to Tooey Spaatz, airman to airman. Freddy was getting pretty burned out in the tropics and needed a break anyway.

Eisenhower, of course, welcomed him as if he had a choice in the matter.

EISENHOWER WAS DUE to leave that evening for White Sulphur Springs as part of his Marshall-ordered vacation with Mamie. But before he left, he shot Beetle a cable, obliquely hinting at the trouble they faced from the air forces and telling him to put Tedder on the job of getting a plan in place. He signed off, letting Beetle know, "I am leaving the city for a few days but essential messages can reach me."

The moment the cable was sent, Eisenhower was handed a long message that Beetle had just sent from London. The good news was that Monty was all in. "Montgomery insists on a strengthening of the assault to at least five divisions and a broadening of the base from at least twenty-five to approximately forty miles."

The bad news was that the only way to get the landing craft needed for the invasion of northern France was to abandon the simultaneous invasion of southern France. To have Operation Overlord, they needed to cut Operation Anvil. They could still make it look like they were going to invade southern France. But with all the resources being drawn into preparations for the invasion of Anzio, there were not enough boats in the water.

Milton Eisenhower

CHAPTER 16

THE ARMY HAD taken over the Greenbrier Hotel in White Sulphur Springs, West Virginia. For two days, Eisenhower and Mamie were under strict orders, direct from General Marshall, to relax. But for those same two days, Eisenhower was eager to hear back from Beetle, who had gone to Marrakesh to meet with Churchill.

They had driven overnight Wednesday. And on Saturday, Eisenhower was granted a reprieve from relaxing. Frank McCarthy landed in White Sulphur Springs just before noon with a C-47 to take Eisenhower to Kansas. When Marshall had ordered him home, Eisenhower's main request had been to see his mother, since the last time he had been to Kansas was in June 1941. His visits to Abilene had become fewer and further between over the years, and the last true family reunion, when all the brothers were together, had been in 1926. They took a family portrait in which everyone glowered at the camera in the finest traditions of the American gothic. The only exception had been Dwight, who wore his army uniform, black riding boots polished to a high shine, and a wide, winking grin.

After returning from the Philippines, Eisenhower made more of an effort to visit Abilene after seeing how feeble his parents were getting. And since his father had died, he had wanted to go home to be with his mother. She was losing her memory and rapidly becoming frail. His older brother Edgar had persuaded Naomi Engle, a fellow Bible Student in her sixties, to stay with her, and Eisenhower sent money to his younger brother Roy, who lived in the neighboring town of Junction City. Roy was a "little jolly fat fellow" and perfect for keeping their mother's spirits up, but he had died suddenly, in June 1942, just as Eisenhower was leaving for England.

Ida Stover Eisenhower, who had spent thirty years shepherding half a dozen boys through a very small house, soon found herself in a sadly quiet world. "I feel lost," she would say. "With them all gone now, nothing seems real anymore. They're all so far away, about all I have to look at is their pictures."

Eisenhower tried to imagine his mother happy, collecting flowers in pots and arranging them by the big bay window to fill the living room with color. He kept in regular touch with Naomi Engle, who promised to read his mother his letters and to respond with updates. In the summer of 1943, Eisenhower wrote his mother a long and affectionate letter. "He sounds so sincere," was her reaction. In true Eisenhower fashion, she always reacted to his flattery as if it was just words, or at least as if she had to act that it was just words to prevent feeling the words too deeply.

Mamie opted to stay in White Sulphur Springs, blaming her heart murmur for not wanting to fly. Eisenhower was supposed to land in Kansas in the afternoon but the flight got delayed; he ultimately landed at Fort Riley after seven that night and then drove to Milton's house in Manhattan, Kansas.

Milton had brought their mother from Abilene, and there was a bit of a question about whether she would remember her Dwight.

"You know who I am?" Eisenhower asked.

"Of course, I know who you are."

"Well, who am I?"

"You don't need to ask me that, I know who you are."

And they laughed. His mother always laughed when she couldn't call something to mind, which meant that she was laughing more and more. Her memory was failing her. But, in a blessing, her memories of suffering seemed nearly gone. She missed her Dwight, as she insisted on calling him. Though she worried he was too occupied by the pursuit of worldly honor, at the expense of his immortal soul, and she never fully came around to the idea that he was a military man.

When reporters asked her the obvious question about how a pacifist raised one of the most powerful generals in all of human history, she would say, "I hate war, and war is wrong. I was born in war country during civil war times. My mother grieved herself to death when I was 11 because of the war. I have hated war since then." She never criticized her Dwight. But the most encouraging words she would ever offer for the daunting task he confronted was, "Well, since they got this thing started, it's about time they got it finished!"

Milton had tried to make the occasion a warm homecoming. Mamie's parents flew in from Denver, and Eisenhower's older brother, Arthur, and his wife, Louise, also made the trip from Kansas City. Arthur's presence was a bit of a surprise. As the oldest, he was the most like their father and seemed perpetually suspicious that his younger brothers were grubbing for his money. As Eisenhower became more famous, though, Arthur started taking more of an interest in family.

Milton was, as ever, a charming and gracious host, and Eisenhower brought Junior the puppy as a gift for Milton's kids, Buddy and Ruth. Mamie had not warmed to the love child of Eisenhower's English dog, particularly after he had introduced himself by soiling her rugs. Eisenhower presented Junior to his niece and nephew, claiming that Telek, the puppy's father, had been a gift of the British as a token of Anglo-British friendship.

Born when Eisenhower was nine, Milton had always been the smallest of the boys. He was, though, insatiably ambitious. Long after Eisenhower had left, Milton cut his teeth as a reporter, working for Charles Harger's *Abilene Daily Reflector*. He had an instinct for the press and went to Washington, DC, in the 1920s, where he became a wunderkind in the still-mysterious art of public relations. Not yet thirty, he was appointed as the director for information for the singularly powerful Agriculture Department, which at the time controlled nearly 10 percent of the federal budget. Milton handled the press and supervised the steady stream of pamphlets, reports, and books designed to convince the Congress and the public of the wisdom of America's farm policy. This was no easy task in the era of the Dust Bowl. And as a true sign of Milton's talents, Roosevelt kept him in the job to help sell the New Deal.

The age gap was such that Eisenhower and Milton had never really known each other until the early 1930s, when Eisenhower moved to Washington. Milton had a house near Embassy Row, and would offer advice on the reports Eisenhower was being tasked with preparing for the War Department. Milton was a natural at the politics of Washington, the kind of person who seamlessly garnered invitations to the White House, regardless of whether the president was named Coolidge, Hoover, or Roosevelt. He would bring Eisenhower to all the best parties and Eisenhower developed a reputation around the capital's swell set as Milton's friendly older brother.

Milton's reputation was for getting messy things done without making a mess. At the start of the war, Roosevelt put him in charge of the War Relocation Authority, responsible for interning tens of thousands of Japanese Americans. It was a dirty job and Milton knew it.

When asked about it, all Milton would say was that it was "purely a military decision, approved by the President." Privately, though, he told Roosevelt as early as 1943 that young Japanese American citizens were "living in an atmosphere for which their public school and democratic teachings have not prepared them. It is hard for them to escape a conviction that their plight is due more to racial discrimination, economic motivations, and wartime prejudices than to any real necessity from the military point of view for evacuation from the West Coast." Milton recommended that the government move away from the use of concentration camps, lest there be the "creation of a racial minority problem after the war which might result in something akin to Indian reservations."

Milton quickly got himself out of the nasty business of running concentration camps. In the summer of 1942, Roosevelt made him the Associate Director of War Information, a job for which he was ideally suited and eager to apply the "science of propaganda warfare" to the interests of liberal democracy. "Strategy and tactics," he would say, "must be worked out as meticulously in propaganda warfare as in military warfare." And he was great at it.

Milton's key insight was that a neutral press—and more important, the appearance of a neutral press—was a powerful way to persuade the public. He sought, and succeeded, in making America the source of foreign countries' foreign news. This led in 1943 to the creation of Voice of America, which soon had twenty-three transmitters broadcasting news and entertainment across the world in twenty-seven languages. Milton gloated that Germany complained about how much American news was now a part of Swedish news. Milton's ideas fit perfectly with Roosevelt's ambition to ensure that America's face abroad had a broad and trustworthy smile.

Milton had left the government to become the president of Kansas State University, where he was now pursuing donors to create an Institute of Citizenship. Just before he left for the United States, Eisenhower had opened a letter from Charles Harger, the staunchly Republican publisher of the *Abilene Daily Reflector*, reporting on Milton's popularity at the university. Harger also mentioned that two different authors were now making their way around Kansas, working on biographies of Eisenhower that played up the "home boy makes good" Horatio Alger theme.

Eisenhower had replied to Harger, playing up the character. "It will take a very imaginative writer to make anything very spectacular out of a plain farmer boy type such as I am." It was, of course, the only thing he could say as a Kansan, certainly to a fellow Kansan, just as he wrote to Joe Howe, the staunchly Democratic publisher of the *Dickinson County News*, that "if the home folks try to high hat me and call me by titles instead of Dwight, I will feel I am a stranger."

Ostentatious modesty was a Kansan's mark of belonging just as the stiff upper lip was to the British. In 1896, the Kansan William Allen White wrote the famous screed "What's the Matter with Kansas?," in which he wrote of the state's singular self-loathing pride, "Go into any crowd of intelligent people gathered anywhere on the globe, and you will find the Kansas man on the defensive." To be a Kansan was to insist you were not all that much to go on about.

The more famous Eisenhower became, he dutifully exaggerated the mediocrity of his life and accomplishments all the more. Upon his selection to be the Supreme Allied Commander, Butch prepared a bio for the press that gave Eisenhower's résumé as having worked "as a cowpuncher, professional baseball player, farmer, and finally, in the refrigerating industry." It said he had planned to go to the University of Kansas, but was then appointed to West Point as if by accident.

It was a persona, to be sure. But Eisenhower was genuinely uncomfortable with fame. There was something ridiculous about it and especially those who sought it. Wayne Clark's wife parading around the country with a raggedy pair of his pants? Publishing their love letters for popular entertainment? It chilled the bones. And it was all so fickle.

One of Eisenhower's recurring laments in his letters to John was how "it is easy enough for a man to be a newspaper hero one day, and a bum the next. The answer is that just as one must not let his head get swelled too much by a bit of acclaim, he must not be too upset and irritated when the pack turns on him."

In another letter, Eisenhower raged about newspaper columnists who attacked him for his willingness to cut deals with men like François Darlan. "I have been called a fascist and almost a Hitlerite," he fumed to John. "Actually, I have one earnest conviction in this war. It is that no other war in history has so definitely lined up the forces of arbitrary oppression and dictatorship against those of human rights and individual liberty. My single passion is to do my full duty, and helping to smash the disciples of Hitler."

What had made Milton a wunderkind was that he was a Kansan untroubled by fame. Since the advent of the radio, mass media was an extraordinary new source of power. That was what the fascists had understood so well. But being a Kansan, Milton understood that a message was far more likely to take root if it seemed like a plain statement of common sense. And by the same token, celebrity was far more durable if it seemed unbidden. Even the way Milton dressed reflected his genius for how to be seen. He had that subtle intuition into what shirt went with what tie and what jacket, so that he looked impeccable while still seeming plain, modest, and effortless.

Eisenhower stayed the night at Milton's. It was a quick visit. He had hoped to stay longer, but there were reports of bad weather and in Kansas, in the middle of January, bad weather could keep every plane and every train stuck where they were. So, Sunday morning, he flew off again and returned to Mamie at White Sulphur Springs in the late afternoon.

Brehon "Bill" Somervell

CHAPTER 17

THERE WAS LITTLE about the return to his spa vacation that was restful. While in Kansas, Beetle had finally cabled back about the meeting in Marrakesh. Churchill had apparently taken a firm decision on launching the Anzio operation on January 22. Beetle had mixed feelings. "The operation is risky and is, in effect, a gamble on the weather, but it is a calculated risk, and in my opinion, the results, if successful, are well worth the risk involved." The cost, though, would be landing craft.

Frank McCarthy also called to check in. Among the various issues, there was a rumor circulating about the army running brothels in Salerno and Palermo, "including one that was allowing the mixture of the races." He was certain that it was just a nasty rumor, but he wanted Eisenhower to at least know that a potential scandal was brewing.

Then there was a cable from Monty, confirming what Beetle had said respecting his enthusiasm for expanding the size of the invasion. But, Monty added, the only way to accomplish this would be canceling the simultaneous invasion of southern France, Operation Anvil. "If we do not get the Anvil craft then I consider the chances of quick success are not good."

Dealing with all of this from White Sulphur Springs, with all the delays in getting updates and replies to his messages, was not restful. After two days, Eisenhower and Mamie took a private train car back overnight to

Washington, where they were picked up in a discreet black sedan, ushered to the back steps of Wardman Park, and then up to Mamie's apartment just in time for breakfast. Eisenhower did not stay long. He had an appointment with the president that morning, followed by more meetings at the Pentagon.

At ten thirty, Eisenhower met with Roosevelt at the White House. The president was looking much better and ribbed Eisenhower over whether he liked his big new title. Eisenhower joshed back that he liked being the Supreme Allied Commander, it had "the ring of something like Sultan."

The night before, Roosevelt had delivered the State of the Union address. "This nation," he had begun, "in the past two years has become an active partner in the world's greatest war against human slavery." It was an ambitious and visionary speech, pressing Congress to pass an "economic Bill of Rights" that guaranteed Americans a right to work, shelter, health care, and education.

Roosevelt also articulated a new vision of the world, proclaiming, "The best interests of each Nation, large and small, demand that all freedom-loving Nations shall join together in a just and durable system of peace." Security, both political and material, was the only way to secure a lasting peace. It was a vision of a rules-based world, where imperialism was a thing of the past, and where the money now squandered on a bomber could be used to build thirty schoolhouses. "Freedom from fear," he said, "is eternally linked with freedom from want." China, Russia, Britain, and the United States were "truly united" in this vision, he said. But Roosevelt knew this was only true at the highest level of generality, even between America and Great Britain.

Since the Atlantic Charter in the summer of 1941, the United Kingdom and the United States had worked shoulder to shoulder as the central pillars of the United Nations. But would that last?

Eisenhower certainly thought so. It was naive, perhaps, and certainly superstitious, but he carried three lucky coins, one British, one American, and one French. No doubt he would carry a ruble too if someone gave him one.

Roosevelt, though, was unconvinced. And it was unclear if anyone other than Eisenhower and his three lucky coins could hold the alliance together. As Eisenhower himself had once said to General Marshall, "The seeds for discord between ourselves and our British allies were sown as far back as when we read our little red history school books."

There were reasons beyond the control of any one person why the Anglo-American alliance might not only work but endure. Britain in 1944 was far more democratic than the Empire of King George III in 1776, and the United States was a far more mature (indeed imperial) world power than the revolutionary republic that had spent the prior century sowing rebellion from Ontario to Venezuela to Oregon. The two countries—largely—shared a language and the liberal government traditions of Magna Charta and Francis Bacon. And the British needed the American "arsenal of democracy" to have any chance of defeating the Axis, just as the Americans needed Britain's global imperial network.

But there were so many points of possible failure that any one disagreement, over Lend-Lease aid, over war strategy, over personnel, over logistics, over the two countries' domestic or diplomatic politics, could be the crack that crawled like a spiderweb until the whole common edifice shattered. Americans had every reason to suspect that Britain was seeking to expand its empire with Uncle Sam's money and the blood of its sons. And the British had every reason to suspect that America was either woefully naive about the world or seeking to gobble up Britain's imperial possessions for itself.

All of this had been on display in Cairo and Tehran. For whatever bygones-will-be-bygones Churchill had offered Eisenhower in Malta, the prime minister was embittered by the United States' willingness to let the British be humiliated in the Dodecanese. Behind closed doors, he had gone on a "long tirade on evils of Americans." At one point, he floated the idea of presenting an ultimatum at Cairo, saying that "if you won't play with us in the Mediterranean, we won't play with you in the English Channel" before Alan Brooke warned him off such a move.

By the same token, Roosevelt was growing increasingly weary of Churchill's imperial pretentions. In between meetings with Chiang Kai-shek that Churchill thought were a waste of time, Roosevelt tried to explain to the prime minster why he was so adamantly behind an independent and decolonized China. "It was better," Roosevelt suggested, "to be friends than enemies with a country of four hundred million souls," to which Churchill grumbled derisively, as he always did, about Roosevelt's romantic attachment to the "pigtails," "Chinks," and "little yellow men."

For the alliance to work, to really work in ways that the Anglo-Franco-American alliance never did during the Great War, there needed to be that ever elusive element of mutual trust. That was the only way the allies could "march and think as a nation."

Eisenhower, though as American as Kansas, was an incurable Anglophile the moment he arrived in London back in 1942. His favorite book was Sir

Arthur Conan Doyle's *The White Company*, about a band of English archers in the Hundred Years' War. "So they lived, these men, in their own lusty, cheery fashion—rude and rough, but honest, kindly and true," the book closed. "The sky may darken, and the clouds may gather, and again the day may come when Britain may have sore need of her children, on whatever shore of the sea they be found. Shall they not muster at her call?" It was as rousing an appeal for Albion as the hymn "Jerusalem."

Eisenhower's love for things English raised more than a few American eyebrows. It made Patton so furious that he lamented, "I wish to God he was an American." But it worked. The British loved Eisenhower back and trusted him, giving the benefit of the doubt, rather than suspecting the worst of their American cousins. Even Alan Brooke, who never missed an opportunity to slight Eisenhower's qualifications for anything, readily admitted that he had a genius for fostering the alliance between Great Britain and its former colony.

It was one of the reasons Roosevelt had selected Eisenhower over General Marshall to be the Supreme Allied Commander. At Cairo, Roosevelt felt saddled playing "peacemaker." He came away telling his son, "It seems pretty clear that Winston will refuse absolutely to let Marshall take over." Marshall knew his stuff and was a man of principle. No one could doubt that. But those very traits stiffened the backs of his British counterparts. "It's not that he's argued too often with the P.M. on military matters," Roosevelt added. "It's just that he's won too often."

The Tehran Conference was a meeting not just of three military allies, but of three profoundly different systems of government. Roosevelt was now thinking about the need for America to have a distinct role in the postwar world. And that needed to start with Germany.

The rough plan had been to divide Germany into three parts. The Russians would take the east, the British would take the northwest, and the Americans would take the southwest. Roosevelt had thought better of the arrangement, though. "The Southwest," Roosevelt said to Eisenhower, "had nothing but scenery and tourists." He wanted the northwest. That would put America in charge of Germany's industrial region, including the Ruhr.

"It's none of my business," Eisenhower told Roosevelt, "but it seems to me that Germany should be run as a unit, and not by zones of occupation." When Hitler was gone, Eisenhower, or his successor, should run the military occupation of Germany long enough to get a friendly government in place, and then go home. It would be a mistake to divide Germany. If nothing else, putting the United States singly in charge of northwest Germany would saddle it for years, if not decades, with keeping a large American army in central Europe. We would own the place. With Russia and Great Britain occupying the other two-thirds, the United States would be stuck, since it hardly seemed feasible or advisable to stand up a German army capable of defending the American sector on its own.

"No," Roosevelt said, ending the discussion. "I am committed to that. I am going to get the northwest."

Eisenhower sensed that he had violated one of the most important pieces of wisdom he had given his son on dealing with superior officers: "Do not be too free with advice."

BEFORE EISENHOWER LEFT, Eleanor Roosevelt dropped in to give him some pleasantries, and the next day and a half were a blur of meetings—not just with General Marshall, but also with Harry Hopkins and Henry Stimson; Generals Brehon "Bill" Somervell, Thomas Handy, and John Hull, as well as Admirals Henry Hewitt and Charles Cooke; and for good measure, Elmer Davis, the director of War Information.

Eisenhower was shown maps of southern France and the planning that had been done for Operation Anvil. He was shown the newest tank technology. And Dr. Vannevar Bush, a long bony presence with round spectacles, who headed the War Department's Office of Scientific Research and Development, described the most recent intelligence on the Germans' flying bombs. Hap Arnold, who called them the "Drones," would estimate, "If the Germans were as efficient as we were in our fabrication, they could produce the 'Drones' with about 2,000 man hours and at a cost of about $600.00. They could launch them from the tracks at a rate of about 1 every 2 minutes per track. With 48 tracks they are supposed to have serviceable—24 per minute—1440 per hour or 14,000 in 24 hours." Dr. Bush, though, was more concerned about the possibility that even a few of these Drones could be equipped to shower London with poison gas.

All Eisenhower could say to all of this was, "You make me scared."

The main issue Eisenhower faced, though, was logistics. Part of that was getting enough of what was needed built. General Marshall did everything he could to build more, faster. And he wanted Eisenhower's help. Almost nothing got the industrial wheels turning faster, he told Eisenhower, than good movies. "The leader in a democracy has to keep the people entertained. That may sound like the wrong word, but it conveys the thought," Marshall would explain. "People demand action." The workers at plants around the country turned more bolts, hammered more nails, and cut more steel when they could see the fruits of their labors in a celluloid glow.

Filming combat was, therefore, a weapon of its own, and Marshall told Eisenhower to ensure that there was as much footage as possible of "actual combat scenes involving men, equipment, armored vehicles, and weapons in actual operation," "scenes showing casualties during and immediately after action," and the "results obtained by American artillery, aerial bombs, hand grenades, mortars, and other destructive weapons."

But logistics was not simply about having enough. "There are now more than fifty divisions in the United States which we wish to deploy as soon as possible in addition to those already overseas," Marshall observed during the meetings with the Soviets at Tehran. "The military problem, therefore, resolves itself almost entirely into a question of shipping and landing craft." Marshall mused that "prior to the present war I never heard of any landing-craft except a rubber boat. Now I think about little else."

The British, as far as General Marshall was concerned, did not understand logistics. Equipment was scattered all over the country. And Bill Somervell, who ran the army's procurement process, told Eisenhower that he needed to give his logistics people the same status as his battlefield commanders. Bill recommended that John "Cliff" Lee, who had been the head of logistics (or "services of supply") in England, should be promoted to lieutenant general. This was a war being fought with supply lines.

Everyone was receptive to Eisenhower's proposed expansion of the invasion. The trouble, though, would be the logistics. Eisenhower needed more landing craft than were currently projected to be in England. And, in particular, he needed more Landing Ship Tanks, or "LSTs." Jokingly referred to as "large, slow targets," LSTs were oceanic pack mules. Longer than a football field with a box-shaped body, they were so utilitarian that each was named not in honor of a hero or a celebrated place, but by number. So, instead of the USS *Arizona*, men would serve on the USS *LST 507*.

As unlovable as they were, LSTs were the only reason an army could land on a hostile shore and have any hope of avoiding the fate that befell the thousands of men cut down at Gallipoli. In fact, the stalemate at Gallipoli was the reason things like the LST were invented. British landing forces in 1915 had relied on rowboats that became death traps for the men trying to get ashore. But as weeks turned to months, and the Turks still held much of the high ground, British ingenuity was put to the problem of how to resupply the shores without similar bloodshed. By the summer of 1915, the British had engineered armored barges, nicknamed "Beetles," whose spoon-shaped bow could be run up onto a beach and then opened into a ramp. The Beetles were one of the only reasons the British could evacuate Gallipoli in January 1916 with as few casualties as they suffered in retreat.

The Beetles solved the problem of getting men to the water's edge safely, but that was only half the problem. With modern defenses, such as machine guns, an exposed beach was a no-man's land if the men charging onto shore had no tanks. Eisenhower had thought about tanks for nearly his whole career and understood their power as the modern equivalent of Hannibal's war elephants: the only way to drive into heavily defended positions and to shield men as they advanced. But offloading a multiton block of steel from a ship onto a beach was no simple task. In assessing the failures at Gallipoli from the vantage point of the 1930s, Patton had concluded that amphibious invasions were largely doomed because getting tanks into action on a hostile shore was too slow and too exposed.

That changed with the LST, which could drive toward the shore in relatively shallow water and then beach itself by throwing its anchor and using the drag to pitch its belly up onto the sand. Its yawning mouth of a gangplank could then open and pour out as many as twenty battle-ready Sherman tanks in minutes.

From at least late January 1942, Eisenhower had uniquely understood the urgent need for landing craft. It had been his job to plan the war in the Pacific, and looking at the map, with its speckle of near indiscernible islands of enormous strategic value, he immediately saw that the war might be won by whichever side could get men and equipment on and off those specks quickly. It had been one of his greatest bureaucratic frustrations during his time working for General Marshall. The navy loved battleships. The army loved tanks. The air forces loved bombers and fighters. But there was no love for landing craft. And so, no one in a position to lobby wanted to spend their budget on building LSTs.

As late as May 1942, Eisenhower wrote out with escalating exasperation the basic questions that remained unresolved. "Who is responsible for building landing craft? What types are they building? Are they suitable for cross channel work? Will the number of each be sufficient?" Eisenhower had been at his wits' end. "How in the hell can we win this war unless we can crack some heads?"

General Marshall ultimately did crack heads and tasked the single-minded Bill Somervell with getting American industry in the business of building landing craft. The results could be stunning, as was seen with the development of the LCI, or Landing Craft Infantry. The idea for it was first drawn up in early 1942 as a smaller LST that could quickly belch a hundred combat-ready men onto a beach. The British director of ship construction, whose nickname was the "director of ship obstruction," insisted that only a craft suitable for thirty men could be built.

The project stalled until the summer of 1942, when a British navy planner had mentioned it to Marshall during a Friday meeting. The following Monday, word had come back that Roosevelt approved the construction of two to three hundred LCIs. The first twenty arrived in England four months later and had continued to sail across the Atlantic ever since.

In the first full year of the war, the United States had manufactured 9,488 landing craft. In 1943, the number had risen to 21,535. By the end of 1944, the country was on track to nearly double that. There were tens of thousands of LSTs, LCIs, and an alphabet soup of other landing craft being built and shipped to battlefields all around the world. Eisenhower's challenge was persuading the Combined Chiefs to send them to England, instead of to the Mediterranean or the Pacific, where the Marines were hopping their way across increasingly well-defended islands toward the Japanese archipelago.

Eisenhower's meetings at the Pentagon convinced him that with a bit of patient negotiation, he could get more landing craft for the Normandy invasion. The navy was willing to make concessions from the Pacific, given the president's strong support for the invasion of France. Whether that would last or be enough was unclear. But what General Marshall made crystal clear was that Monty and Beetle's proposal to abandon the simultaneous invasion of southern France was unacceptable.

There was more to Operation Anvil than military tactics. There was, for one, a need to get the French into the war. The French Resistance was strongest in the South of France, and there were two Free French army divisions in the Mediterranean being trained and equipped at great American expense. Their participation would send a clear message to ordinary French citizens, who might still need to be persuaded that an Anglo-Saxon invasion of their country was preferable to a Teutonic one.

The bigger issue, though, was that Roosevelt had promised Stalin an "all out" effort in France. Russia had been battling on the eastern front at a scale inconceivable to the Allies. Millions of Russians were fighting millions of Germans, from Ukraine to the Baltic. From the moment the United States entered the war, the goal had been to keep Russia in the fight, and to prevent Germany from sending those millions of fighting men west. A simultaneous amphibious invasion on the northern and southern French coasts would be a demonstration to Russia—indeed to the world—of Allied military power and resolve. It would show Stalin that the United States was a peer to be trusted and respected. Shrinking the operation, by contrast, would show America failing to deliver on its promises. And whether the reason was that it could not be trusted, or that it didn't have the wherewithal to follow through, was irrelevant.

Before leaving for London, Eisenhower cabled Monty, saying that he was on his way to London and asking Monty to wait before he made any recommendations. He assured Monty that the "desirability of strengthening Overlord is universally accepted." But he needed to remember that Operations Overlord and Anvil were two arms of the same attack, and that the invasion of southern France should be abandoned only "as a last resort."

Eisenhower then shot another cable to Beetle, telling him to stall Monty. They needed to keep something called Operation Anvil in the works. There were politics involved. The Combined Chiefs had not even given their official approval to the near doubling of Operation Overlord. Until then, Eisenhower suggested, it was better to see what resources they could quietly siphon off from the Mediterranean than to force a debate that Eisenhower could not win.

PART THREE

SUPREME ALLIED COMMANDER

Betram "Bertie" Ramsay

CHAPTER 18

EISENHOWER, BUTCH, AND Mickey boarded a C-54 in the evening and spent the next day hopping across the Atlantic, first to Bermuda, then to the Azores, and then on to Prestwick, Scotland. Things with Mamie had not been left on good terms. She told him not to come back again until the war was over. In time, she would soften what she meant, saying she did not want to say goodbye again. But the two weeks they had been together had not made for a happy reunion: the constant travel, Eisenhower's long days at the Pentagon, and his distraction when they were together. She felt jilted by everything. When he told her about meeting Eleanor Roosevelt, Mamie was insulted that she had not been invited.

Eisenhower was still not over his cold. In her own way of reminding him that she loved him, Mamie gave him a bag of vitamin-fortified chocolate and a sack of pecans, so he could eat something good for him. And Eisenhower regretted how things had gone with his family from nearly the moment he left.

When Eisenhower landed in Prestwick, Jimmy Gault was waiting for him. The fog in London was too thick to fly south, so Jimmy had arranged for Eisenhower to get his own private railcar, named the *Bayonet*. It was a long ride and the farther south the *Bayonet* chugged, the denser the fog. It was an hour to midnight before the *Bayonet* finally pulled into London, nearly forty-eight hours after Eisenhower had left Washington. As he collected himself and his things, Eisenhower noticed that the bag of pecans and vitamin chocolate from Mamie had gone missing.

London was always dark at night due to the blackout and famous for its fog in the best of times. It was always worse in the winter, since the famous "London fog" was a euphemism for a caliginous smog of chimney smoke, motor fumes, humidity, and coal ash. Eisenhower had never been to England in the winter, and the fact that the seat of the British Empire was shrouded in total blackness upon his arrival felt like an omen. But Kay was there, waiting to pick them up in an olive-green Packard.

With her usual vivacity, Kay made light of it all, saying it was "a real pea souper." She was refreshing that way. But she was not just the bubbly Irish who put everyone in a good mood. Eisenhower recognized the loneliness beneath her infectious smile and they had been through a lot together. Eisenhower had been the one to break the news that Dick Arnold had been killed, on June 6, 1943. Kay was inconsolable, throwing what Butch called an "Irish tantrum" for the ages. She blamed Eisenhower and accused him of sending Dick to die, as if he were David sending Uriah to be killed by the Ammonites. Eisenhower did not blame her. He knew that kind of pain.

Eisenhower did whatever he could for Kay. He helped her get her finances in order. He even tried to find a job on his staff for her. He gave her time and space to grieve that he never gave anyone, not the least himself. But he also knew that it was the quiet times that let the mind dwell on what was lost. So he shared his most private cure for pain: stay busy. She was, he told her, "very necessary," and he gave her as many things to do as he could find, even when she wasn't very good at them.

Eisenhower would say that he never got over Little Icky's death, just that he grew better at being "philosophical about it." Over time, Kay also got better at compartmentalizing her grief. And they grew closer. Before Eisenhower had left for Washington, he gave Kay a postcard from the Garden of Gethsemane. It had been the only contemplative spot they could find in Jerusalem. On the back, he wrote, "Good night! There are lots of things I could say—you know them. Good night."

Seeing her through the English fog for the first time in almost three weeks, Eisenhower joked, "Now I know I'm back in London. Think you can make it, Kay?"

Kay took the question as a playfully insulting challenge and drove through the murk of London's streets by memory, as if doing some blindfolded magic trick.

Eisenhower, Butch, Jimmy, and Mickey stayed dead quiet, knowing that a bus or a lorry or anything could emerge suddenly from the London fog, leaving no one enough time to stop. Then, Kay pulled over. She got out and within a few steps disappeared. A moment later, she reappeared, beaming with pride.

"Here it is! This is 20 Grosvenor!" The Supreme Headquarters, Allied Expeditionary Force, or "SHAEF."

Grosvenor Square had been, since the American Revolution, the center of the official American presence in London. It was a block of comparatively tall redbrick office buildings with gabled roofs built around a six-acre garden that made it look like a massive college quad. Eisenhower's office had been in the same building in the summer of 1942, which led Butch to jokingly rechristen Grosvenor Square, "Eisenhower Platz."

Eisenhower went to his new office to see if there were any urgent or important cables and, there being nothing that could not wait until the next day, he returned to Kay and the Packard. Jimmy told Kay to drive toward Berkeley Square and Chesterfield Hill, where they finally reached Hayes Lodge, a stately townhouse Jimmy had let for Eisenhower, complete with a massive living room, a fireplace for cigarettes, seven bedrooms, two bathrooms, and staff quarters in the basement. Kay had somehow gotten them all there safely.

EISENHOWER'S FIRST FULL day in London was a Monday. Technically, he was still only the "acting" Supreme Allied Commander and his headquarters only "interim." The Combined Chiefs were still negotiating the terms of his appointment. But there was nothing interim about the demands of that first week.

Photographers swarmed to capture the new commander at his desk. Mattie and Butch both suggested that he write a prepared statement for the newsreel and he quickly dictated a minute and a half's worth of remarks to Mattie, who typed it all out and handed him the final product. He reread it and left it on his desk. Thinking he forgot it, Mattie grabbed the speech and raced to bring it to him, only to find Eisenhower delivering it from memory, near verbatim.

Eisenhower closed with a paraphrase of Nietzsche. "I have complete confidence that the soldiers and airmen and all the civil populations of the United Nations will demonstrate once and for all that an aroused democracy is the most formidable fighting machine that can be devised."

Eisenhower met with the COSSAC planners, including Freddie Morgan, who was still technically his chief of staff. Beetle was back in North Africa and would not be getting into London until the following day. Morgan had taken the initiative to have a new emblem made for SHAEF that was jointly designed by two British and American soldiers. It was a black sable with a rainbow arching across the top. In the middle was a flaming crusader's sword to symbolize SHAEF's mission of liberating the world from the darkness of fascism. Eisenhower readily approved.

There was a ream of messages to review and dictate, and Mattie quickly proved her salt. Eisenhower sent a short note to Mamie, letting her know that he had arrived. "While our visit together was often interrupted, and the pain of parting was as bad as ever, I am still glad I made the trip. I feel much better after having those 10 days with you." He sent another to Jacob Devers, apologizing that he had been too busy to come to Algiers on his way back from Washington, but inviting him to London. "I will always be ready to meet your ideas and intentions in a cooperative spirit in all tasks in which we may have a common interest. Good luck." He then went over his personnel needs and sent another cable to Devers asking for some of his former men to be transferred from the Mediterranean.

There was fan mail and hate mail to answer. A resident of Surrey, appropriately named Burn, wrote that while "I offer you personally a welcome to England, I do not do so as commander-in-chief of the allied forces, because I consider that either General Montgomery or Alexander should have held that position."

Eisenhower dictated a phlegmatic Kansan response. "I am the first to agree with you that any one of the generals you suggested and possibly even any one of the number would have been a better selection than that actually made for the accomplishment of my task," he said. "However, I hope you will agree that as long as this duty has been placed upon me by Great Britain and the United States, I have no recourse, except to do my very best to perform it adequately."

It was doubtful Monty would have said the same about him. And Eisenhower was beginning to rue the intensity of his Christmas charm offensive against the British general. It certainly had its desired effect. Monty was all in on Operation Overlord. But the picture Eisenhower painted of his authority went to Monty's head.

Before Eisenhower had arrived in London, Monty had recommended the cancellation of Operation Anvil to the British Chiefs. He then issued a press release, saying, "I came home the other day from Italy to take command of the British army and the American army of which General Eisenhower is the Supreme Commander, and he has put one army, the First American Army, under me for the battle. We are going to fight and that is a very great honor for me."

The press were certain to ask Eisenhower about it. Who was really in charge? And, there being no time like the present, Eisenhower stood for his first press conference just before lunch.

The room had been decorated with the Soviet, American, and British flags and a wall-sized map of the world's many battle fronts. Eisenhower took his position behind an enormous wooden desk whose high polish gleamed.

"Because none of you fellows have chairs, I think I had better stand today. I haven't any startling announcements to make that will make any headlines, but my principal purpose in asking you to come and see me today was to give you my idea of the place in my Headquarters I have for accredited correspondents.

"When a correspondent is accredited to my Headquarters," Eisenhower warned them, "he becomes a quasi–Staff Officer of mine." But, he hastened to add, "There is one thing that will never be censored in my Headquarters—any criticism you have to make of me—that will never be censored you can be sure. But, on the other hand, and to go back to my original theme, we are partners in a great job of defeating the Axis. You have got your job, and I have mine."

"Now as far as I am concerned," he continued, "I will mount the cross. I will sit down and you fellows can go to town on me. Any questions?"

"Sir, could you tell us who is to be the Commander of your troops—general Montgomery's opposite number?"

"Actually, there is still a little bit of a question as to how the details I think are going to be organized. I don't know who. Has General Bradley's name ever been released here at all?"

"It is well known that he is here, but it hasn't been released."

"General Omar Bradley is now my senior American Ground Commander in Theater."

"Can that be published?"

"Yes, that can be published."

"That means then, sir, he will be General Montgomery's opposite number?"

"If I were you, I wouldn't go too far into laying that out. Actually, and this is for your very secret information, I could really make quite a speech on my opinion of some of the people that have been given to me, and I am an intense admirer of all of them. But since to enumerate anything is always to exclude everything else, I think it would be a little bit unfair for me to say what I think of some of these people. But I will just tell you this: I am delighted—I am highly pleased."

Eisenhower told them not to "go off the end of a limb" in saying who was in charge of whom. The last question of the day, though, returned to who was in charge of whom.

"General can you tell us what the position is in regard to the Strategic Air Forces as far as your command is concerned? There has been some confusion about it."

Eisenhower did not want to answer, so he got verbose. He waxed at length and abstractly about the complexities of joint command, always prefacing his most inane statements with "this is confidential again," before veering stream-of-consciousness through various topics until it was apparent that the room was so exhausted that the question was forgotten. He then abruptly stopped talking without ever once even mentioning the strategic air forces or, for that matter, the flying of airplanes, and asked, "Are there any other questions?"

None forthcoming, Eisenhower bid them all a jaunty goodbye.

EISENHOWER OBSCURED THE truth about who would be in charge of what because he still did not know himself. He got a better sense the next day, when Beetle finally got to London. Beetle was a bit punchy because his plane had buzzed the island of Guernsey on the way. Had the Germans noticed, they could have easily shot him down.

Beetle had a long talk with Churchill about who was going to control what and thought the prime minister was talking out of both sides of his mouth. To Beetle's face, Churchill assured him that he supported Eisenhower having supreme command over everything, including the strategic air forces. But Churchill had said the opposite to Bomber Harris. It was a bit classic, but Eisenhower assured Beetle that Churchill would go "all out" when it mattered.

Asked how things were going in North Africa, Beetle said that everyone was all geared up to launch Churchill's new pet military project: the invasion of Anzio. The final decision to launch had been made by Churchill himself after one of his epic dinners. The thing was, Beetle said, Jumbo Wilson—the man responsible for leading the invasion—had already gone to bed. "After all," Beetle said, "he is getting old." And so Jumbo found out about Anzio the next morning, and he wasn't that interested. He was all focused on the Balkans, and Tito's guerrillas.

Beetle had also taken the chance to talk to Jacob Devers. His impression, in one word: "lightweight." Devers had pissed and moaned to Beetle about how Eisenhower was taking all the best people. He had even assigned an officer to investigate whether Eisenhower was sabotaging him. Devers was gearing up to fight tooth and nail over every request Eisenhower made.

Devers is just not a team player, Eisenhower lamented.

Eisenhower needed team players, if only because his team was now so monstrously large and his schedule so mercilessly full. His second full day in the office, Eisenhower met with Sidney Negrotto, the war room commander; Edwin L. Sibert, from the intelligence section; Omar Bradley, the commander of the First Army; Alan Kirk, the admiral in charge of the US naval contingent; Robert Crawford, from the logistics and supply section; John Watson Gibson, the British engineer supervising the construction of something called "Mulberries"; Freddie Morgan, who had been running COSSAC; Harold Stark, the admiral in charge of all US naval forces in Europe; Kenneth Anderson, the commander of the British Second Army (whom Monty was about to replace with Miles Dempsey); William Phillips, Eisenhower's special diplomatic adviser; Cliff Lee, his head of operations, the Services of Supply; Robert Littlejohn, Cliff Lee's quartermaster; and finally John Crane, who was planning for the occupation of Rome.

Eisenhower paid his "duty" call to King George VI, who asked him to sign a card for his aunt, who collected autographs. And Eisenhower introduced himself to more than a hundred senior members of Freddie Morgan's COSSAC staff, who were now his senior staff at SHAEF, praising all the work they had done, and telling them if there was trouble ahead, he was there to help.

There was already trouble. Beetle had an altercation with Alan Brooke, after Brooke also accused Eisenhower of raiding all the talent from the Mediterranean. It got nasty and while Brooke relented on at least a few of the people they wanted transferred, Brooke had also lodged a formal complaint about Beetle's discourtesy. Eisenhower would have to patch things up.

And in another sign that the "eternal pound, pound, pound" was only going to get faster and louder in London, Roosevelt had sent a personal request. The crown prince of Norway wanted American help. The Germans had occupied the country since 1940, but there was a chance they might soon evacuate to consolidate their forces on the continent. In such an eventuality, could the Americans send some army divisions to Norway? Roosevelt wanted Eisenhower's opinion, signing off, "It was grand to see you the other day. All the good luck in the world. FDR."

It was not the first time the president had tried to send Eisenhower on an errand. In their brief and inauspicious meeting the year before at the Casablanca Conference, Roosevelt had told him to send a regiment to Dakar. Eisenhower had respectfully informed the president that Dakar was way outside his area of authority, but Roosevelt persisted. Eisenhower then did what he would ultimately do when Churchill was after him to send men to the Dodecanese and told the president he would comply as soon as the order came through the Combined Chiefs.

As expected, the question never arose again. But given the faith Roosevelt had now personally put into him, and the need to keep the president's trust, Eisenhower ordered a comprehensive study. Given how stretched he was in getting the manpower and resources to invade France, the answer was easy to guess. But he wanted to give Roosevelt the benefit of being seen to try.

THERE WERE SO many uncertainties. No easy answers. And everything he did was now subject to intense scrutiny in the press.

Despite filibustering the question at his press conference that Monday, the press' newest pseudo-scandal to cover was why Eisenhower had not been given command of the strategic air forces. Trying to get that command was only harder if it became a political story, since any compromise would be seen as a concession on principle. Eisenhower could only speculate about who had put reporters on to the story.

Then there was the news from home. The Associated Press had done a whole feature about his supposedly secret trip to Kansas. It charmed readers with the story of a regular American who called Kansas home and, despite the weight of the free world resting on his shoulders, thought nothing about going thousands of miles out of his way to be good to his mother. The only thing missing from the story was apple pie, though the lede highlighted his mother's insistence on cooking dinner for "my boy."

Eisenhower could see Milton's fingerprints all over it. Even the dateline was given as "Manhattan, Kansas." He seethed at his brother. What was private, like family, should be private. But he also had to worry about General Marshall. The last thing he needed was a stern rebuke for using government aircraft so that he could parade his mother around to the press like Wayne Clark's pants.

Frederick "Freddie" Morgan

CHAPTER 19

ON FRIDAY OF that first hectic week, Eisenhower convened the first meeting of his commanders in chief. Kay drove him to Norfolk House, an eight-story redbrick office building that had been constructed on the site of the Old Saint Albans House, where King George III had been born on May 24, 1738. Parking was reserved in order of precedence, and as Kay pulled up to the front, to the space of supreme precedence, they found a black Rolls-Royce that had been polished to a mirror shine. Monty.

Kay threw an Irish tantrum. She was so enraged, in fact, that it spared Eisenhower the trouble of getting angry himself.

"That's OK now," Eisenhower said, calming her. "Don't say anything. It just doesn't matter."

Monty had seized the mantle of his position with gusto. His return to London had been the return of a golden bull intent on leaving none of the china acceptable for sale. Taking command of the British 21st Army Group, he had replaced nearly all the officers of significance with his men from North Africa.

Monty's specific role and authority in SHAEF was somewhat ambiguous. The Combined Chiefs never approved the creation of an overall headquarters for ground forces, and the British were running embarrassingly short of the manpower needed to create such a headquarters in any event.

But that did not prevent Monty from declaring to Freddie Morgan within days of his arrival that, from then on, Monty would "command his administration." This left Freddie to write to COSSAC's staff, "I have not the foggiest idea what he means, or what this expression means, but he seems to be entirely satisfied with it."

Over the course of three days at the beginning of January, Monty and Beetle had worked all day, every day, with COSSAC's planning staff to figure out how to expand Operation Overlord. It was not a simple matter of driving 150,000 men over Caen's beaches instead of 100,000. There were only a limited number of exits off those beaches. If they landed across forty miles instead of twenty-five miles, as COSSAC had proposed, the bottle would be bigger, but the neck would be the same size. And it might make things worse. A massive buildup on the beaches could create traffic jams that would be vulnerable to attack and might actually slow the speed at which tanks, trucks, equipment, and men could squeeze into the French interior.

Solving the problem over those three days, Monty displayed all the tedious arrogance and relentless brilliance that made him so frustrating and so effective. As exhausting as he could be—and he could be very exhausting—Monty's impatience with bureaucracy and deficit in traditional British manners had arguably saved his country from dying of imperial sclerosis. Centuries of storied traditions had turned the British Army into a tight, top-heavy gentleman's club, full of "chaps, who went in because it looked nice to wear a uniform, and have a title." This meant, as a rule, that hierarchies were rigid, dissent was rude, and those in charge were painfully mediocre.

At the start of the war, the British Army was beset by all the pathologies of the country's broader class system. And like every class system, it depended on the principle of distrust. At places like Sandhurst, the United Kingdom's elite military academy, officers were taught to specify orders down to the finest detail, as if programming a machine. It was a theory of command that assumed the lower classes, who filled out the enlisted ranks tasked with following those orders, could hardly be trusted to know what was right. The results had been nearly catastrophic during the retreat at Dunkirk. An order had gone out that no bridge should be destroyed without a commanding officer's permission. As a result, only one bridge was blown up to slow the German advance and only then because a lance corporal had risked court-martial and violated the order.

Monty had been full of these prejudices as a young officer. During World War I, he thought little of his men, who had all come from the lower classes.

But Monty had come to regard his subordinates not just with more respect over time, but with genuine affection as he matured as an officer and witnessed their bravery and sacrifices during World War II. Unlike many of his contemporaries, Monty had been eager to learn from the near disaster at Dunkirk. Alan Brooke saw the best in Monty and promoted him, essentially giving him carte blanche to go through the ranks of British officers, almost platoon by platoon, to get rid of the dead wood so that the empire could take the war to Hitler.

For the three days that Monty and Beetle worked with COSSAC's staff, Monty badgered his way to a plan that would work. The COSSAC planners had proposed a three-division assault to ensure the capture of Caen. Monty, though, was confident that two divisions would suffice. He wanted to divide the landing forces to hedge against the possibility of strong German fortifications in any one point and to create more openings for a buildup. They also needed a shot at reaching a real port. Caen, for all its many advantages, particularly in setting up landing strips, was nowhere near a port.

COSSAC's planners had, of course, thought of that. Freddie Morgan credited an American sailor on his staff, Hughes Hallett, with having devised an ingenious solution. After a long planning session, Hallett had joked, "Well, if we can't capture ports we must make one." After looking into various options, including just sinking a massive number of ships around Normandy to calm the seas, COSSAC went forward with the joke and devised an enormous and intricate system of breakwaters and floating piers that were given the jolly code name the "Mulberries."

It was one of those preposterously grandiose and eccentric ideas that Churchill loved the moment he heard it. As a result, the Mulberries had been under construction for months and would, when assembled and towed across the Channel, provide two miles of flexible, floating bridgeways capable of offloading ten thousand tons every day.

Monty, though, was unpersuaded that the Mulberries were enough. If nothing else, it was foolish to make the success of a campaign dependent on the realization of a joke taken seriously. And so, he proposed sending the rest of Allied forces to other points along the Channel coast as far west as Brittany or as far east as Dieppe, a small port town just to the west of Calais.

Dieppe was a sensitive subject. The day after Hitler turned east to invade Russia in 1941, Churchill proposed dividing the Führer's attention with a raid on Calais, "something on the scale of twenty-five thousand to thirty thousand men—perhaps the Commandos plus one of the Canadian divisions." The plan had been studied but then abandoned in February 1942, only to be revived a few months later as a test run for a larger-scale invasion.

At the time, Gallipoli remained the only large-scale amphibious invasion since the advent of the machine gun, and there was a desire to see what lessons had been learned. Dieppe was chosen because it was one of the few beaches within the then-existing range of British fighter aircraft.

Eisenhower had been in England for less than a week when he was briefed on the plan, which included a token force of thirty American commandos. Eisenhower contemplated participating himself, in what he wrote excitedly to General Marshall would be "the first offensive action by Americans in this theater in this war."

Monty had played a key role in the planning of the operation along with Trafford Leigh-Mallory, who received great credit after the fact for the Royal Air Force's performance against the Luftwaffe. The plan had been based on the Gallipoli model of a massive predawn naval bombardment, followed by a beach landing, and then a frontal assault. It was not a deeply considered plan, but the Canadians, who had been impatient to see action, readily committed a division to it.

The invasion of Dieppe was originally set for July, but there had been a monthlong postponement due to weather. The delay demoralized the men, who spent an uncomfortable few days locked down inside transport ships. It also created more opportunity for leaks, to the point that the *Daily Telegraph* crossword puzzle offered a six-letter clue the day before the invasion was finally launched whose answer was "DIEPPE."

The invasion was at dawn, and it was just after lunchtime when the commanding general sent the grim news back on a pigeon: "Very heavy casualties in men and ships. Did everything possible to get men off but in order to get any home had to come to sad decision to abandon remainder."

More than nine hundred men were killed, with overall casualties exceeding five thousand. A dozen planes were lost, as well as a destroyer, five tank landing craft, and twenty-eight personnel landing craft; an overall loss percentage of 28 percent. With the capture of so many men and so much equipment, the Germans were afforded the clearest picture of Allied capabilities since Dunkirk. The performance of the Royal Air Force notwithstanding, it was a disaster, good only for the lessons learned.

Adding another attempt at Dieppe to Operation Overlord was, therefore, unappealing for many reasons. And the German defenses made it too risky to go as far west as Brittany, which was already an overstretch of the air forces' range.

COSSAC's planners had drawn the same conclusion many months before. The farthest west the Allies could realistically go was the Cotentin Peninsula, which delimited the western boundary of the Normandy coast and offered the port of Cherbourg at its tip. There were two beaches suitable for landing on the eastern coast of its base: the broad, sandy Varreville Beach, and the narrow, rocky Saint-Laurent Beach farther east. Soon, these beaches would be code-named "Utah" and "Omaha."

As COSSAC's planners had also concluded many months before, attacking those beaches verged on suicidal. Utah Beach, in particular, was extremely hazardous. It was separated from Omaha Beach by the Douve estuary, meaning that the two landing forces would be cut off from one another until they made it deep inland. And Utah Beach was cut off from the rest of the mainland by the Merderet River and its floodplain, which the Germans had graciously flooded, choking the exits from the beach into a few narrow bottlenecks.

The risks inherent to landing on Utah could be lessened if an airborne division or two were dropped inland around the town of Sainte-Mère-Église. The paratroopers could protect the bottlenecks and harass the Germans defending the beach from the rear. The risks to the paratroopers would be enormous, but Monty and Beetle both thought those risks worth it.

The only question left was organization. Given that American forces were already amassing on the southwest coast of England, taking the Cotentin Peninsula would fall to Omar Bradley. He could divide the American forces, hitting Utah and Omaha simultaneously, then link up to drive south and west. Monty's 21st Army Group would then attack the beaches north of Caen like a trident, with the British Army attacking Ouistreham Beach (code-named "Sword") and the Asnelles Beach ("Gold"), and a Canadian contingent driving through the middle of the spear at Courseulles Beach ("Juno"). From there, they would strike south, take Caen, and "prevent any interference with the American army from the east."

This division, with the Americans in the west and the British and Canadians in the east, achieved the near doubling in size that Eisenhower wanted. And it subtly helped to solve the more sensitive problem over whether the British and American forces should be divided into army groups. With the ground forces naturally dividing along national lines, driving in opposite directions, more than ten miles apart, there was now a clear boundary and, therefore, less need for a single headquarters to coordinate.

It had been a messy three days. Monty blasted the inadequacy of COSSAC's planning, and Freddie Morgan's people, in turn, critiqued all the flaws in Monty's impossible suggestions. It was impolite. It was uncomfortable. But it did the job. Even Beetle was impressed. A plan had taken shape.

Monty was happy to take credit. He presented the plan from then on as the "Montgomery Plan." That chafed the egos of Eisenhower, Beetle, Freddie Morgan, and countless other COSSAC planners. But if calling it the Montgomery Plan meant that Churchill, Alan Brooke, and the rest of the British brass would get behind it, then the Montgomery Plan it was.

EISENHOWER ASSEMBLED WITH all his commanders in chief in room 126 of Norfolk House at ten thirty sharp. Room 126 had a high ceiling and white walls covered near to the top with a facade of dark oak wainscoting, which gave the room the appearance of a gentleman's library. Heavy blackout curtains covered the windows, and maps of various scales and sizes were propped up against the walls. The heavy oak conference tables were covered in blue-green baize and decorated with a scattering of ashtrays shaped like pinion gears.

The whole team was there. Beetle and Monty, and also Arthur Tedder. There was Bertie Ramsay and his staff for the naval forces, Trafford Leigh-Mallory and his staff for the tactical air forces. And Tooey Spaatz and his staff for the strategic air forces.

They posed together stiffly in front of a giant map of western Europe for the press photographers, whose flashbulbs looked like a meadow of lilies. They obliged when the newsreel cameramen asked them to make it appear as if they were discussing important things for the B-reel. Eisenhower awkwardly dragged his hand down the middle of France as everyone looked on, and when his hand reached Provence, he thew an is-that-enough look back at the camera.

Finally, the door closed, the press was gone, and Eisenhower got down to business. Freddie Morgan had one of his people give an overview of COSSAC's original plan. Then Monty took the floor to boldly pronounce its many flaws. They needed, he declared, "to strike hard and deep." To do that, he presented the Montgomery Plan to replace COSSAC's plan, which he said was not "a sound operation of war." Monty then added that they should attack as scheduled at the beginning of May to provide the longest opportunity for summer ground fighting.

There were, no doubt, still challenges and risks. "The Mulberry," Monty thought, "is still an untried expedient." The condition of the beaches was also uncertain. COSSAC's planners had noticed the problem only two months earlier. According to some medieval maps, Normandy had been a peat bog, meaning the beach might be pocketed with quicksand.

Monty concluded, though, by saying that he was the ground commander and was confident that he had solved the ground war problems. He could not solve the naval and air problems. The navy needed to secure landing craft, for which Monty proposed reducing Operation Anvil to a feint. And the air forces needed to support the invasion forces and to cripple the railways surrounding Normandy for a radius of 150 miles. "It remains to be seen," Monty said, summing things up, "whether the Navy and the Air would be able to meet these requirements."

Eisenhower made a show of his agreement with everything Monty had just said. But he cautioned against recommending the elimination of Operation Anvil to the Combined Chiefs, at least not yet. "We must remember," Eisenhower said, "that the Russians had been led to expect that operation would take place; and in addition, there would be at least seven American and seven French divisions, which would remain idle in the Mediterranean, if Anvil did not take place."

"The biggest problem," Eisenhower added, "was the question of lift." For that reason, they should be open-minded about delaying the invasion until June. If a few weeks delay offered the possibility of more landing craft, that was preferable to abandoning Anvil.

Bertie Ramsay gave the naval picture. His principal concern was the Mulberries. "To complete two artificial ports within a space of seven days," he said, "involved the transport across the channel of over 1,000,000 tons of material in some 400 to 500 separate tows, some of which would be as heavy as 6000 to 7000 tons." That was extraordinary. And the problem would become even more extraordinary with the proposed expansion of the operation. A coordinated attack with that many men in two different places would require the creation of two more naval assault forces. "This increase would lead to serious congestion along the south coast of England," making the navy easier pickings for the Luftwaffe.

Then there was the weather. As currently organized, the navy could launch on twenty-four hours' notice. Adding two more assault forces, spread over the entire southern coast of England, could stretch that out to sixty hours. Predicting the weather a day in advance was difficult enough. Predicting the weather *three* days in advance was impossible.

And then there was the lack of landing craft. They would need forty-three more LSTs, and nearly two hundred more smaller landing craft. But it was not simply a matter of having the ships in England. It was a question of manpower. The British had recently demobilized an entire Royal Marine division to reassign men to landing craft. Even if they canceled Operation Anvil, the landing craft would still not be ready to sail until June. "Our resources for maintenance and repair of craft," Ramsay said, "were already fully stretched."

On that optimistic note, Trafford Leigh-Mallory spoke last on behalf of the air forces. He started from the premise that it was necessary to attain air superiority. Operation Pointblank had succeeded in reducing German air production by half. But they would have to accept that "it was unlikely that the decisive battle in the air would take place until the day of our assault; we would fight for our superiority, then, and we would likely achieve it."

Leigh-Mallory had concerns. As the only commander at the table to have stayed on from COSSAC, he felt he had an understanding of the terrain and complexities of the operation that others might underestimate. And Monty's demand for the destruction of all French railways within a 150-mile radius of Normandy was a bit ambitious. To do what was necessary, Leigh-Mallory proposed delaying the invasion until June, so they had more time to bomb and get additional aircraft for close air support.

With everyone having staked out his position and, just as important, his turf, Eisenhower called a recess and told everyone to come back at three that afternoon. They needed to make a recommendation to the Combined Chiefs, and with all that had been said, they needed to come to consensus.

EISENHOWER HURRIED OUTSIDE, where Kay was waiting, beaming her coy Irish smile. The parking space of supreme precedence was now occupied by his olive-green Packard.

It was hard to be too excited about winning a parking space. He had a one thirty appointment with Churchill. Bertie Ramsay and Leigh-Mallory had raised doubts about the operation that could encourage Churchill to revive his long-standing opposition.

Eisenhower's stomach was bothering him again. He wasn't quite a "dying frog," but there were so many unknowns. Could he sell the Combined Chiefs on the Montgomery Plan? And could he get the landing craft he needed to pull it off?

Monty's answer was the obvious answer: cancel Operation Anvil. In principle, Eisenhower did not disagree. The previous October, when Eisenhower was still in charge of the Mediterranean, the Combined Chiefs had asked him to study the feasibly of invading the South of France. He had examined the options closely with some of COSSAC's planners, and his basic conclusion was that it was a bad idea. There were sixty German divisions around the Mediterranean that could be moved into southern France with relative ease. Depending on the timing, even the perception that an invasion of southern France was being planned could have the perverse effect of drawing more Germans into France in advance of the cross-Channel invasion. He had, ironically, advised that it was preferable to launch amphibious strikes in northern Italy to support the ongoing ground offensive he had been waging toward Rome.

But now, he was the Supreme Commander, Allied Expeditionary Force. If he was going to get the Combined Chiefs' support for anything he needed, such as getting control over the strategic air forces, he could not very well pick a fight over Operation Anvil, with all its political ramifications.

Kay drove him to 10 Downing Street, where Churchill was waiting. It was Eisenhower's first chance for a one-on-one meeting with Churchill since coming to London. The prime minister was over his pneumonia and ebullient. His newest pet project, the invasion of Anzio, was set to launch the next day, which seemed to put him in a generous mood.

"The cross-channel effort," Churchill proclaimed, to Eisenhower's great surprise, "represented the crisis of the European war." Churchill assured him he was eager to support Eisenhower "to the limit" and "prepared to scrape the bottom of the barrel in every respect in order to increase the effectiveness of the attack." There were other plans on the drawing board. But this was, Churchill repeated several times, "the crisis of the European war."

Eisenhower returned to Norfolk House, where the key point of contention was what recommendation to make about Operation Anvil. Bertie Ramsay said that whatever the decision, he needed all the landing craft in England no less than four weeks out from D-Day. For that reason alone, he suggested, and ultimately everyone agreed, to recommend that the invasion be postponed until June.

Given the decision to postpone, Eisenhower persuaded the room that the fate of Operation Anvil should be left for another day. Rather than make a firm recommendation to the Combined Chiefs, he would simply insist that the expanded plan be approved and that the invasions of northern and southern France be treated as a whole. That would reassure the US Chiefs, who were adamant about Operation Anvil, but also create space later so that resources could be drawn from one to ensure the success of the other. And Eisenhower told his assembled commanders in chief that in making that case, he would include a strong statement that Operation Overlord was the "crisis of the European war, both for the U.S. government and the British government; that it must not fail, but must be a complete success."

THAT WEEKEND, ORDERS went out for Operation Anvil. George Patton was ordered to London to take over the Third Army and ceded command of the Seventh Army to Wayne Clark, who would lead the invasion of southern France with the Free French forces. Wasting not a moment, Georgie cabled Eisenhower asking to take his entire senior staff from the Seventh Army with him. The request would have to be approved by Jacob Devers, who until that point had either blocked or ignored almost every similar request Eisenhower had made.

The first reports from Jumbo Wilson about the Anzio invasion also came in that weekend. "Landing was a complete surprise and opposition negligible. No violent enemy reaction so far." The good news was well timed, because Eisenhower had to meet again with Churchill, this time with Alan Brooke. Eisenhower presented the Montgomery Plan and suggested that at least some landing craft might have to come from the Mediterranean. Alan Brooke was in full agreement, particularly on the understanding that this was Monty's plan. Eisenhower, Brooke remained convinced, "has got absolutely no strategical outlook and is really totally unfit for the post he holds from an operational point of view. He makes up, however, by the way he works for good cooperation between the allies."

Things were looking up. Mamie had finally written. And Jimmy Gault had convinced the current tenant of Telegraph Cottage to permit Eisenhower to return to his favorite country home, where he could smoke in peace by the fireplace.

Sunday night, Eisenhower worked carefully with Monty and Beetle to craft the proposal to the Combined Chiefs. They sent it at an hour to midnight. "This operation marks the crisis of the European war," it declared. "Every obstacle must be overcome, every inconvenience suffered and every risk run to ensure that our blow is decisive. We cannot afford to fail." Eisenhower assured the Combined Chiefs that the invasion could be launched on May 1 as scheduled, but suggested that a month's postponement would be acceptable if it ensured the delivery of the additional forces requested.

Sending the proposal made Eisenhower anxious. He had made the case, but who knew what the Combined Chiefs would do? He consoled himself by committing his anxieties to writing. "Whatever my orders are, I'll carry them out—but I am convinced that the original plan does not carry enough strength in the control wave." If he had the resources, he knew he could win. But that was a big if.

Jacob Devers

CHAPTER 20

MONDAY MORNING, EISENHOWER reconvened with his commanders in chief in a meeting that was far more freewheeling than it had been the previous Friday, when the cameras were there and everyone was feeling scripted. There was discontent with what Eisenhower had sent to the Combined Chiefs and its wholesale embrace of the Montgomery Plan, without reflecting any of the concerns Leigh-Mallory and Ramsay had raised.

Sensitive to these complaints, Eisenhower made a point of saying at the outset that "everyone's views would be respected," and that "no one's views would be considered sacrosanct." He was just looking for the right answer. They were "one team."

Eisenhower did his best to keep to his agenda, but Leigh-Mallory had concerns. Would there be enough aircraft for the airborne operations? He was also pessimistic about the plan to drop airborne forces behind Utah Beach. The paratroopers would need to be resupplied. They couldn't just be left stranded back there.

Eisenhower took the opportunity to express his full agreement with Leigh-Mallory's concerns and endeavored mightily to get through his agenda. Before they adjourned, he reminded everyone that they were "one family with no individuals with any aces up their sleeves." He wanted every member of his staff to "hang together and for no one on his staff to begin to think that he knows something the others do not."

That afternoon, Kay gave him what he needed most: a true and trusted friend. She drove him to the quarantine kennels to visit Telek. The poor guy's cage was dismal, though someone had decorated it with a large portrait of Eisenhower to keep him company. Eisenhower was sad at the prospect of five more months' incarceration for his little friend.

The press was there, but Eisenhower shooed them away. He blamed Butch for "over-publicizing" their goddamned dogs. He wanted something, anything, to himself.

AS JANUARY TURNED to February, there were air raids on London nearly every night. Beetle became the butt of many jokes for his skittishness. Churchill had requisitioned an air raid shelter near Hayes Lodge with plenty of room for Eisenhower and his staff. But Eisenhower never slept in it on principle, or at least to dare the devil. Nazi air raids had nothing on the "eternal pound, pound, pound" of his daily life.

Crashing through the Atlantikwall was astonishingly complex. It was not one operation, but thousands of them, and planning each and its coordination into a singular whole was monstrous in its difficulty. For the ground operations, Monty had adopted what he called the "syndicate" method. He broke the overall plan down into twenty-five subcomponents, with a planning staff assigned to each. Roads and bridges, reinforcements, mounting the armies on the beach, communicating—every component of a massive logistical machine down to the smallest detail. And the smallest details could be maddening. Given the fears of quicksand, they had sent frogmen to swim to shore at night, through mines and obstacles, to report back priceless intelligence on beach conditions that anyone taking a summer vacation could have offered five years earlier.

Monty's approach to solving these problems created its own problems. Without a SHAEF headquarters for the overall ground commander, Monty ran the planning operation out of his British 21st Army headquarters in London, which had the effect of cutting out the Americans almost entirely. Omar Bradley naturally resented this and, making matters worse, Brad's US First Army headquarters was 140 miles away, in Bristol. To solve this problem, Eisenhower created the First US Army Planning Group, based in London, so that Brad's people could participate in the syndicate meetings.

Coordinating the two army cultures was a challenge all its own. The

British, for example, could never understand how the Americans used so much paper for everything. Why did every thought or discussion have to be memorialized in carbon copy triplicate? But eventually Monty and Brad's people realized that they largely spoke the same language. And the result was the Initial Joint Plan, consolidating all twenty-five syndicates into an overall picture of the invasion. It was ambitious and nothing if not optimistic. It even set out "stage lines" on maps that reflected the ground to be captured by various deadlines. Monty would take Ouistreham, Caen, Trévièrs, and Isigny within two days, and Brad would take the Cotentin Peninsula within twelve.

If cooperation between the armies was a challenge, coordinating the navies was a nightmare. Save for Gallipoli, neither Eisenhower, nor any other soldier of his era, had much in the way of an education on amphibious warfare. And combined exercises between the US Army and the US Navy were exceedingly rare, if only because of the budgetary red tape in an era when the army and navy were two different cabinet departments.

Brad, at least, had experience leading the landings in Sicily and a good working relationship with the American naval commander, Admiral Alan Kirk. But overall naval command was in the hands of Bertie Ramsay, and the only thing to foster any spirit of cooperation between the British and American navies was the innate belief that all sailors have in their superiority to the fellows in the army.

The British and American navies had different schemes for marking beaches, different naming conventions, different approaches to gunfire control, and different communications protocols. At first, even the colors used to label Normandy's beaches were different.

Culture, though, was the biggest difference. The American navy's approach to planning was to state objectives at the top level and then delegate the details for achieving those objectives further and further down the chain of command to ensure maximum flexibility and ownership. The British, by contrast, planned everything from the top, down to the smallest turn of the rudder, and once in place, the plan became the law.

The Royal Navy's confidence in its methods and its wariness of American attempts at innovation sprang from the same source. When Bertie Ramsay had joined the Royal Navy at the turn of the century, it was twice the size of the next two largest naval fleets combined. The British controlled ports and territory on every continent, including Antarctica, and maintained a cable network that circumnavigated the globe, making London the world's most important hub for banking, insurance, politics, and trade. Rivals such as

Russia, France, Japan, and Germany, which all had their own designs in Asia, the Middle East, and Africa, had been stifled in their ambitions by British naval power. The Anglo-American alliance that was now preparing to cross the English Channel had become possible at the turn of the century only because Great Britain had voluntarily relinquished naval dominance over the Caribbean.

From the start of the war, the Royal Navy had risen to the occasion. It tripled and then quintupled its production of ships, such that more than two hundred and thirty British vessels were rolling out into the sea each year. It had all but wiped the Kriegsmarine off the surface of the Atlantic, leaving Germany to rely on what were effectively guerrilla attacks from U-boats and night raids by fast-moving E-boats, which by the middle of 1943 had largely been contained into the Channel.

The US Navy, however, had rapidly become unlike anything the world had ever seen. The United States was soon producing ten times the number of ships as Britain. In 1943 alone, the United States poured 2,654 new vessels into the ocean. The American navy was soon three times larger than Britain's. And it was eager to innovate, whether it came to operating at high speed, or launching aircraft, or refueling, or recovering at sea. This left Alan Kirk resentful of the diplomatic need to honor what he felt were outmoded British traditions.

Similar resentments festered between the air forces. Part of that was Leigh-Mallory, who tested even Eisenhower's bonhomie. Leigh-Mallory had gotten where he was because he had a brutally efficient mind and was completely intolerant of vagueness. When he asked for plans, he demanded precise timetables. But even those who liked Leigh-Mallory acknowledged in an honest moment that he was insufferably condescending. If it were just Leigh-Mallory, then that would be one thing. But the strategic air forces also seemed to demand Eisenhower's constant conciliation, with Tooey Spaatz complaining that he had to add "Air Ministry" to his communiqués reporting on entirely American bombing operations over Germany, when Bomber Harris never bothered to even mention the Americans.

Even Eisenhower's American allies seemed intent on making his life harder. Eisenhower sent Jacob Devers yet another cable, saying "assignments can no repeat no longer be delayed." He felt he had gone out of his way to be cooperative. When Devers had asked for personnel, Eisenhower had replied that all but Gee Gerow were available. But then Devers continued to stonewall his requests. Eisenhower eventually sought General

Marshall's intercession. He did so tactfully and indirectly, knowing that Devers was one of Marshall's guys. But he made a point of adding that he was "a bit puzzled" by Devers's delay in getting the personnel decisions finalized.

Devers finally responded, denying nearly all of Eisenhower's requests. "Sorry we could not do it 100%." Devers then added that when it came time to invade southern France, "you may count on me to be in there, pitching with one idea, to assist you." Eisenhower rolled his eyes and forwarded the message to Beetle, who wrote back, "This is just swell. I love this 'one idea to assist you' stuff."

It was all so much so fast. Eisenhower wrote to Mamie that he felt like "a flea on a hot griddle." It was like when he had arrived in London in 1942. He had no one to go home to and Mamie did not write often, even back then. Butch had been his only family, and he felt as if he was "just jumping around like a Jack-in-the-Box." He had been so overwhelmed that he wrote to General Conner in desperation. "I find it difficult at times to separate the wheat from the chaff among opposing views presented, I believe, with full honesty of purpose." It was nearly two months before he received a reply.

"Organization," General Conner advised him, "is largely a matter of the problems to be solved." Eisenhower just needed to keep his eye on what was important, which in Conner's opinion, was keeping Russia fighting. "Your present detail was, and is, widely approved," he assured his protégé. "No better choice could have been made."

The encouragement helped, as did Butch, who put a filter on the incessant parade of visitors demanding Eisenhower's attention. Butch would intercept anyone who dropped into Grosvenor Square, have a friendly chat, and only when he knew what they wanted (and whether it was worth Eisenhower's time), would he send them in, telling Eisenhower right up front what decision needed making.

Eisenhower gradually grew more confident. He was still pulled in every direction, but he had a better sense of what to prioritize and what to ignore. But that had been nothing compared with what Eisenhower confronted from the moment he returned to London that January. Sensing that he was losing control of his time and his ability to think clearly, he told Tex Lee, his aide-de-camp, to stop scheduling afternoon meetings when possible. He also knew that he needed to get out of downtown London, and the claustrophobic confines of Eisenhower Platz.

Omar Bradley

CHAPTER 21

AT THE END of January, Omar Bradley invited Eisenhower on a trip to Slapton Sands, a beach community in Devon that was surrounded by a muddy clutch of farms and hedgerows, ancient churches that claimed Saxon roots, and pubs with names like the Claycutter's Arms. It had been an anonymous hamlet until September 1943, when its locals were informed that their sleepy little town had been indefinitely requisitioned by His Majesty. The reason, its locals were told, was top secret. That secret was that Slapton Sands bore such an uncanny resemblance to the Normandy coastline that it was as if the English Channel were just a river between the two banks.

The British had constructed mock-ups of the known shore defenses, which looked more horrifying in person and more daunting the deeper one went inland. The men hitting the beaches would have to first overcome a field of underwater mines, then crawl through belts of barbed wire that were fortified with the occasional pillbox, then cross another minefield, and then scale or break through a fifteen-foot concrete wall that was twelve feet thick at its base. Assuming a man made it through all that, he would find himself in a shooting gallery of concrete-reinforced pillboxes. The Atlantikwall, indeed.

On the day Eisenhower and Brad visited, the British were conducting a demonstration of the duplex drive (or "DD") tank, a Sherman tank with an inflatable life vest bolted onto it. It was an ugly monster, but in testing, it could be reliably dropped into the ocean and then putter itself onto the beach, where it became an ordinary Sherman tank. Eisenhower ordered three hundred produced.

Brad was less enthusiastic about newfangled contraptions. He just wanted more tanks, and his biggest concern was ensuring that enough ammunition got onshore. That could be done with low-tech ferries, like the ones commuters might use to get their cars across the Hudson River between New Jersey and Manhattan. Fill them up with ammo and tow them ashore. If they could get a few East Coast cities to ship some commuter ferries over, problem solved.

Eisenhower thought the world of Brad. They had been in the same company for their last three years at West Point. Eisenhower had even written Brad's yearbook entry, saying, "His most prominent characteristic is 'getting there' and if he keeps up the clip he's started, some of us will one some day be bragging to our grandchildren that 'sure, General Bradley was a classmate of mine.'" He was known for being the clearest speaker and thinker in the army. Some would say "his weapon of command is understatement." And Brad cultivated his image as a gruff combat soldier. Looking at a picture of himself, with the scar on his cheek from a bayonet fight in World War I, he'd say, "That's not how I look. That's how I feel."

Brad thought little of Monty, but he was so understated that few knew it. He was also one of the few people immune to Eisenhower's likability. But he was trustworthy because nothing seemed personal. Even Beetle admired him. He was, in almost every notable respect, the opposite of Patton. He wore no sidearms. He bore no swagger. He did not bully. All he did was move about entirely confident of being in charge.

GEORGIE, AS IT happened, had just arrived in London, though his presence was technically a secret. He was as cantankerous as ever. Upon hearing that Beetle had been promoted to three-star general, Georgie's eye-rolling reaction was, "God Bless Us All."

Eisenhower broke the news to Georgie that despite what he may have suggested when they met in Sicily, Patton would not be given a direct role in the D-Day landings. The plan was instead for him to come over to France a few weeks after the invasion, and to lead the Third Army into Brittany to establish America's Atlantic ports.

Georgie complained that he was getting "nothing for Sicily." How could the honor of leading the First Army go to his former subordinate? "Bradley," Georgie would grumble, "is a man of great mediocrity." And he groused that the generals that Brad would be commanding across the Channel were all novices. But George S. Patton would, of course, do his duty.

Eisenhower was glad to have Georgie as part of the team. He was one of the few men whom Jacob Devers had let go without a fight. All Eisenhower asked him to do was to remember to count to ten "before issuing an order or taking abrupt action."

Eisenhower invited Georgie to dinner the night he arrived. It was an Official Family dinner with Butch, Kay, Jimmy, and Mattie Pinette.

Mattie turned out to be a perfect new addition to the Official Family. She had been and would be far more than a stenographer. Growing up in Maine, she spoke French fluently, and went to college, where she got a degree in business. She was never interested in getting married. Instead, she worked at the Bureau of Aviation in the 1930s before joining the WACs in 1942. She was as accomplished as a self-made woman could be in 1944 and had no patience for anyone who couldn't take care of themselves. She teased Jimmy about how Scots Guardsmen looked like Russians in their ornate red uniforms, which Jimmy took in cheerful stride. And while she acknowledged that Butch was both handsome and charming, her favorite pastime seemed to be getting Butch riled up arguing politics.

At dinner, Georgie sought to impress everyone, Mattie included, from the moment he arrived. It was the full George S. Patton show. By turns profane and obsequious, blunt and sly, he kept his posture tumescently erect. He regaled his audience with all the military history he had been reading, such as the exploits of the Normans, and admonished everyone at the table that they should never question Eisenhower, because he was "the most powerful person in the world." The only thing missing from the table was Patton's high-polished helmet.

In the right mood, and in the right context, Eisenhower enjoyed the George S. Patton show. When relaxed, the two were as warm as brothers. But Eisenhower was not relaxed. And Georgie made Eisenhower bristle the way only an older brother can.

At one point Georgie misquoted a verse from the Bible and Eisenhower corrected him. There was something sharp in Eisenhower's voice as he did it that chilled the room. Georgie grumbled that Eisenhower was showing off because Kay was there.

Without directing a word at his old friend directly, Eisenhower went off on a rant about how important it was for generals in London to conduct themselves with dignity. Take Cliff Lee. John Clifford Hodges Lee had earned the nickname "Jesus Christ Himself," both for his daily church attendance and his self-righteous belief that being in command of the services of supply made him the divine dispenser of all US government property. Lee had arrived in London in May 1942 and soon after, created a small fiefdom for himself, moving his headquarters a hundred miles west to a spa town in the scenic Cotswolds.

As far as Eisenhower was concerned, Lee was a prime example of how generals were getting too fat and happy. Lee had requisitioned an eleven- or twelve-car private train just for himself. How did that look? The world was watching. And generals needed to start acting like it.

Eisenhower's rant had all the passive-aggressive piety that Georgie simply lacked the self-regulating neurons to resist. Georgie vowed to be on his absolute best behavior now that he was in the capital of the British Empire, and vowed that if he were to do anything that might draw negative attention to himself, to Eisenhower, or to the US Army, that he would be careful about where he did it, and would sure as hell "not choose a hospital."

ON THE FIRST of February, word came back from the Combined Chiefs. They had agreed to all of Eisenhower's proposed changes to Operation Overlord. The following day, Churchill treated Eisenhower to one of his epic dinners at Number 10, this time joined by King George.

The king was the guest of honor, but it was Churchill who held court. "Politics," he took the chance to say, eager to share his newest bon mots, "are very much like war, we may even have to use poison gas at times."

A manic diversity of topics was on Churchill's mind. There was the cover plan for Operation Overlord that COSSAC had devised. These dramatic and clever sorts of things were Churchill's favorite part of warfare. "There is required," he believed, "not only massive common sense and reasoning power, not only imagination, but also an element of legerdemain, an original and sinister touch, which leaves the enemy puzzled as well as beaten." At the Tehran Conference, the prime minister had waxed eloquent that the "truth deserves a bodyguard of lies." Uncle Joe, who shared the prime minister's enthusiasm for duplicity, took the chance to describe the various Potemkin armies that the Russians had created, complete with dummy tanks, aircraft, and landing fields.

Freddie Morgan's planners had devised a plan that would include not just these kinds of decoys, but an entirely fictional First US Army Group, or FUSAG. Like Frederick the Great at the Battle of Leuthen, they were doing everything possible, including real bombing operations, to make it seem as if

FUSAG were leading a massive invasion force toward Calais on Germany's right so they could mount a massive surprise attack with the full force of the Allied army on Germany's left.

Churchill was tickled by everything except the name that COSSAC had given the cover plan. "Messpot." A code name, in Churchill's view, should inspire. Overlord. Neptune. *Messpot?* He personally asked Freddie Morgan to fix it. And two weeks later, he got his wish. The cover plan was now Operation Fortitude.

Italy was at the top of Churchill's mind, and the table conversation turned to whether the Allies should drop their support of the king of Italy and Badoglio in favor of other Italian factions. "Why break the handle of the coffee pot at this stage and burn your fingers trying to hold it?" Churchill said. "Why not wait till we get to Rome and let it cool off?"

Churchill continued like this for hours, just as he had when Eisenhower first got to London, and Eisenhower was bewildered all over again by the prime minister's stamina. It was always that way. If someone suggested that it was time to go to bed, Churchill would mutter, "Very well if you don't care about winning the war, go on to sleep."

Well past midnight, debating the ideal time to launch Operation Overlord became something of a parlor game. Some said it should be before the harvest. Some said it should be close to the vernal equinox. Churchill lost his patience. "Well," he asked, "what I would like to know is, when did William cross?" There was a moment of doubtful silence.

"Sir," Pug Ismay chimed in, "I think it was 1066."

Churchill slammed his fist on the table, "Dammit, everybody knows it was 1066. I want to know what month and what day."

There was another moment of doubtful silence. No one knew. A table of men who had spent their entire adult lives studying history's wars were at a loss. Churchill huffed, "Class dismissed."

King George took his leave of the table at one in the morning, and Eisenhower was keen to seize the opportunity to go to bed. But before he could go, Churchill called him back.

The prime minister was worried about the Anzio operation. In just two weeks, he was hearing that eight thousand men had been killed, another forty thousand wounded, and another twenty thousand were either missing or taken prisoner. For all of that, there was almost no progress inland. There had been so much promise after the initial successes, and growing frustration that the advantage had not been pressed. It was turning into another Gallipoli.

Leonard "Gee" Gerow

CHAPTER 22

EARLY THE NEXT morning, Eisenhower boarded the *Bayonet* for a groggy trip to Plymouth to see Gee Gerow, the commander of the US V Corps. Under the plan now in place, the two prongs of the American attack on Omaha and Utah Beaches would be carried out by two army corps, V Corps and VII Corps. A corps commander was responsible not just for the infantry divisions that would be storming the beaches with rifles in hand, but also the Army Ranger battalions doing the commando work, the armored divisions driving the tanks into battle, the barrage balloon battalions obstructing enemy bombers overhead, the paratroopers dropped behind the lines, and the sappers, who would be some of the first men on shore, to clear the path for everything else. A corps commander's job, in short, was to drive the war machine from the front line.

But Eisenhower had a problem. Patton was right. Neither Gee Gerow nor Roscoe Woodruff, a West Point classmate of Eisenhower's who commanded VII Corps, had led an army in the field. Woodruff had briefly fought in World War I as a junior officer. But being a company commander in the trenches was nothing like commanding an entire corps in Operation Overlord.

Marshall had sent Joe Collins, the hero of Guadalcanal, to Europe. Collins would be perfect to lead a corps. Eisenhower was desperate to get Lucian Truscott transferred from Italy to be a corps commander. He had sent Devers multiple requests, touting Truscott as "exceptionally well-experienced in planning and executing an amphibious assault." Truscott had not only distinguished himself in the amphibious invasions of North Africa, Sicily, and Salerno, he was a genuine expert on the problem of overcoming minefields and beach obstacles, having spent most of 1942 studying the problem from every conceivable angle. Truscott, though, was among the many men whom Devers had refused to let go.

Beetle doubted whether Gee Gerow had the drive to be a corps commander. General Marshall also had his doubts, as well as his own favorites, such as Courtney Hodges and Leslie McNair, old army hands who had been part of Marshall's circle for decades. But Eisenhower wanted to give Gee a shot.

Gee had done so much of the planning for the assault that it seemed foolish to send him away. He was also one of Eisenhower's oldest friends. They had drifted apart since the days of Club Eisenhower in the early 1930s, but still took the time to write when congratulations or happy birthdays were due. In fact, the previous fall, Gee had paid a visit to Algiers and was one of the few people to tell Eisenhower to his face that he—not Marshall—should be put in charge of the "big push" into Europe. And it was not because they were friends, Gee said. It was because Eisenhower had earned it.

Gee had been promoted to lead V Corps the previous July, though he confided in Eisenhower at the time a bit of reluctance. He had spent most of the war building up the Twenty-First Infantry Division, which was a component of V Corps, and still had never seen combat. He had been hoping "to lead it in at least one good fight."

Eisenhower discussed the selection of the corps commanders for Operation Overlord with Omar Bradley. They agreed that of the two, Woodruff should be replaced by Joe Collins. The assault on Utah Beach was far more complex and risky than the straightforward drive across Omaha Beach was expected to be. The Utah landing required coordination with an airborne drop as well as unpredictable terrain. It was the job Eisenhower had originally wanted to give Lucian Truscott. And so, with Collins in charge of VII Corps, Gee could stay in place and lead the assault on Omaha Beach.

Eisenhower's train arrived in Plymouth on a cold, windy morning. Gee welcomed him and his entourage at the platform, and the two spent the rest of the day driving between the various locations where Gee's men were training. V Corps was made up of mostly National Guard soldiers from Maryland

and Virginia, who had arrived in England in 1942 and stayed there, garnering the derisive nom de guerre, "England's Own." The only part of V Corps that had seen any action was the First Infantry Division, known as the "Big Red One." Yet, in part because of the personnel battles with Devers, the Big Red One was led by a new commander, who had not led men in combat since World War I.

At each stop, Gee's men assembled for a formal review and Eisenhower spoke from a partially memorized script of sorts that he was getting adept at meaning every time he said it. "You are the ones," he would say, "who must and will win this war." His remarks, brief and plainspoken, were always apt to provoke an ovation.

Eisenhower would then tell the men to break ranks so he could get a good look at them, saying something like, "I wonder whether I could expedite this by asking you to forget any orders you have received so far today and break ranks and gather around here so I can talk to you. Standing out there you remind me too much of a firing squad." It was a leadership trick that he had copied from Monty.

Eisenhower envied the electric effect Monty had on his men, but he made the trick his own, developing a folksy patter and mingling about, shaking hands, asking where everyone was from. "Is there anyone here from Kansas?" He'd pick men randomly to connect with, asking what job they did back home. He'd ask how the food was. Eisenhower was maniacal about the quality of the mess halls and always made a point of inspecting the food the men were getting.

The most important thing for a commander to do, Eisenhower would advise his son in one of his many letters on military leadership, was to take care of his people. Were they fed? Was their clothing warm? Did they have good shoes and socks? How were their feet? It was the small stuff that was not in the training manuals but to him was the essence of leadership.

Eisenhower was not there to be their buddy. But unlike, say, Patton, Eisenhower thought there was nothing to be gained from intimidating them. And so, when he sensed that some young man was feeling self-conscious about meeting the Supreme Allied Commander, he'd crack a dreadful joke from his growing catalog of dreadful jokes.

He'd tell the one about the two soldiers who saw a four-star general drive by in a limo. "Boy, that's the job I'd like in the army," one said. To which the other replied, "Oh, I don't know. There's disadvantages. For one thing, you'd never be able to look forward to a promotion."

Or, if Eisenhower wanted something a little ribald, he'd tell the story of the "Mae West," the nickname given to the standard-issue life preserver that inflated on a soldier's chest. "The British soldier," he would say, "was seen blowing up his Mae West in the morning. Someone asked him what he was doing. 'Blowing it up,' the soldier replied. 'This is the only bloody air support I'll get today.'" He'd take the laugh, since everyone always laughed, and then get more serious. "Well, men, I can tell you that *you* are not in the position of that soldier. You'll *have* air support."

And if he was particularly keen to rev the men up, he would say that he looked forward to seeing them in Berlin, where he promised everyone champagne, "even if I have to buy it myself." As they left Plymouth that evening, Butch joked that, given the number of times he repeated that line, Eisenhower was running up a pretty big champagne bill.

Not missing a beat, Eisenhower smiled and assured Butch that, when they reached Berlin, there would be "plenty in the contingent fund to buy champagne."

Getting out of London and meeting all these young men quickly became Eisenhower's favorite part of the job. It was invigorating. It inspired him. It not only made the constant bullshit in London more bearable, it made it worthwhile. And getting that fresh air was important, because the bullshit was piling higher.

Ernest King

CHAPTER 23

EISENHOWER WAS TRYING to deliver the young men he had just promised champagne safely into France. But Roosevelt, his commander in chief, was refusing to give him the authority to coordinate that invasion with the French.

Eisenhower had maneuvered to try to force the issue through military channels. Upon arriving in London, he wrote an urgent request to the Combined Chiefs "that General De Gaulle be asked to designate an individual or group of individuals with whom I can enter into immediate negotiations. The need for prompt action cannot be overemphasized."

The maneuver worked, to a point. The War Department sent Eisenhower a cable "informally" giving him permission to coordinate with the French Resistance, even if it involved working with representatives from De Gaulle's French Committee. He was told that an official directive would be forthcoming, but Roosevelt continued to stall any decision that might help De Gaulle consolidate power.

Eisenhower did what he could do "informally." He quietly set up a meeting with representatives of the French Committee in London, which opened a back channel to Marie Joseph Pierre François Koenig. The French Committee had selected Koenig to lead the Free French army and De Gaulle was sending him to London, to also serve as his personal envoy, which would require Koenig to wear two not entirely compatible hats.

Koenig was one of the most able French generals to defect from the Vichy regime. An aristocrat, born in Normandy (Caen, no less), he had been a career officer. But when his country capitulated to the Nazis, Koenig fled to Britain on a fishing boat and joined De Gaulle. In 1942, Koenig achieved fame and glory at the Battle of Bir Hakeim, where he pinned down Erwin Rommel's Panzerarmee Afrika for more than two weeks with a small brigade of fewer than four thousand Frenchmen. It was the first major break in Rommel's momentum and paved the way for the British victories at El Alamein, where Koenig also led his brigade to victory.

Despite all this, Koenig was something of a provocative choice as De Gaulle's envoy in London. Monty despised him. Just weeks before Eisenhower launched the invasion of North Africa, Operation Torch, news leaked to the press that Koenig was having an affair with his driver, a British nurse whom he called "La Miss." The prudish Monty was uncompromising. De Gaulle promoted Koenig away from Monty's battlefield, forcing him to leave La Miss behind.

Koenig was among the most direct, practical, and military-minded Frenchmen Eisenhower had ever met. There was none of the pompous preening of Charles de Gaulle or Henri Giraud. Instead, with blond hair, a soft chin, and blue eyes that were quick to smile, Koenig carried himself with the aloof confidence of a man who was born knowing exactly what his very long name was and all that to which it entitled him.

Koenig's people did not press Eisenhower on the extent of his mandate from the Combined Chiefs or demand that Eisenhower make political commitments. Instead, they laid out what was possible, and what the Free French would need to help the Allies liberate Koenig's hometown. In Normandy, they said, things would be difficult. The Germans understood their vulnerability and had sought to evacuate or otherwise neutralize Normandy's fighting-age male population. That meant the only things that could realistically be done there were sporadic acts of sabotage.

Deeper into France, though, the Resistance was larger and better organized. They could cut communication lines, power lines, railroad tracks. They could commit the kind of persistent sabotage that maddened the Germans. And deeper still into France, once you started getting into the mountainous areas in the south, they could mobilize the Maquis, a loosely defined term for the hundred thousand Frenchmen who operated as terrorist groups and were always delighted to pick off the odd German soldier who had wandered dangerously from his herd. They were hard to control, but easy to arm. And best of all, the Germans hated them so much that they spent far more hunting the Maquis down than it cost the Allies to support them.

Koenig was confident that they could carry out large-scale, coordinated guerrilla actions to assist the invasion. What the French needed from the Americans were two things: weapons and transportation. And so, Koenig's people asked Eisenhower with a refreshing bluntness: Where did he want the Resistance to fight and what kind of weapons would he be able to give them?

The honest answer was that, given the "informality" of his authority, Eisenhower did not have a good answer. Over the previous year, Wild Bill Donovan's Office of Strategic Services had been air-dropping aid to the French Resistance, but on a scale that amounted to 10-15 percent of what Britain's Special Operations Executive was doing. Neither of these clandestine organizations were under Eisenhower's command. That meant Eisenhower lacked the ability to promise Koenig much of anything.

THE GROWING QUAGMIRE in Italy was realizing all the fears that had led Churchill to oppose the invasion of Normandy. The casualties were astronomical. The men were stuck in dug-out positions, succumbing to cold and trench foot. And the longer it dragged on, the more it threatened the viability, not just of Operation Anvil, but of Operation Overlord.

The planning for the simultaneous invasion of Normandy and the South of France had all proceeded on the assumption that the landing craft used to invade Anzio would be freed up by the end of January. But those landing craft remained essential to getting supplies and reinforcements to the men who were pinned down. There were only two solutions, and both were bad. The Combined Chiefs could go back on the expansion of Operation Overlord, which the British Chiefs might welcome, given their long-standing skepticism of the cross-Channel invasion. Or they could cancel Operation Anvil outright.

Eisenhower wrote to General Marshall on February 6, saying, "I believe that the late developments in Italy create the possibility that the necessary forces there cannot be disentangled in time to put on a strong Anvil." The fact that the Allies were bogged down meant that the Germans were also bogged down in Italy, and so that would compensate at least somewhat for the absence of a new front in the South of France. But they needed the landing craft more in Normandy, and they needed certainty about what they would have.

The same day, Churchill sent a message to Roosevelt asking for a high-level meeting of the Combined Chiefs in London to decide where landing craft should go. Privately, Eisenhower wrote, "Anvil is doomed. I hate this," and his old disgust with Ernest King raged back. The only reason there was a shortage in landing craft was because the US Navy was hoarding them for their "private war" in the Pacific.

King had been pressing the Combined Chiefs to shift the Allies' focus to "all out war" against Japan since as early as January 1943. But the navy's interest in the Pacific had been overweening from the start. The Pacific had been the stage for some of the greatest naval battles in military history.

In the summer of 1942, King had succeeded in scuttling plans to build nearly two hundred large landing craft, including one hundred LSTs, in favor of building more traditional warships. The navy naturally also had more sympathy with the Marine Corps' insatiable appetite for landing craft, as they island-hopped to the Japanese mainland. That November, when the Allied leaders were deliberating the risks of the Normandy invasion in Cairo, the Marines had mounted the first seriously contested amphibious landing of the war against the Pacific atoll of Tarawa. In January, the Marines led the amphibious invasions of the Marshall Islands, which remained ongoing, and planned to continue that summer into the Mariana Islands of Saipan, Guam, Tinian, Peleliu, and Anguar.

As far as Eisenhower was concerned, King's focus on these specks of volcanic rock was as ridiculous as it was selfish. The invasion of Normandy was, he vented in a memo to himself, the "critical phase of the European war." They were proposing to send 176,475 men and 20,111 vehicles onto five narrow strips of intemperate beach that were being defended from the sea, air, and land by one of the most formidable militaries ever raised, all within twelve hours. They needed "lift." The invasion, he wrote, "should have every resource the two nations can produce until the moment when the invading force is firmly established on the continent."

As things stood, Eisenhower was only on track to have 191 LSTs and 120 LCIs, as well as 778 of the smaller Landing Craft Tanks (LCTs) and a few dozen other landing craft. Based on the planners' estimates that was only enough to move 143,235 men and 17,591 vehicles. They were short 47 LSTs and 81 LCIs. These were not impossible numbers. Eisenhower just wanted six months in which he could get all the resources he needed. Was that too much to ask?

Apparently, it was. General Marshall sent his response and was in a sarcastic mood. He mused about how ironic it was that the Americans and the British had switched on the relative merits of conducting operations in the Mediterranean and Normandy. And with Eisenhower pressing for the cancellation of Operation Anvil, Marshall wondered if his protégé had contracted a nasty case of "localitis."

General Marshall told Eisenhower to think longer term. Rome was bound to fall. What then? If they abandoned Operation Anvil now, they would have an enormous force in the Mediterranean just sitting idle. The British would undoubtedly seize the chance to open a new front in the Po Valley or Yugoslavia or God-knows where. As far as Marshall was concerned, they should commit to doing everything necessary to make both Operations Overlord and Anvil a success. Eisenhower's impatience, Marshall said, made him wonder if "the pressures on you have not warped your judgment."

The charge of "localitis" struck a nerve. Accusing Eisenhower of being an Anglophile was the go-to insult for any American who wanted to vent resentments against him. Georgie Patton had even ragged on him for wearing suede shoes, as if doing so was the same as pissing tea on the grave of George Washington.

Eisenhower spent the next morning composing as tactful a response as he was capable. The result was a long and rambling argument for putting everything into Normandy. He was not, he protested, succumbing to localitis. He had just come to recognize that Operation Overlord was where the war against Hitler would be won or lost. From D-Day and for two months after that, "this thing is going to absorb everything the United Nations can possibly pour into it."

That afternoon, Eisenhower had Beetle call Thomas Handy in Washington. Handy was Marshall's deputy, and Beetle assured him that Eisenhower was fully committed to Operation Anvil. The issue, Beetle came to learn, was that the planners in Washington didn't trust the British numbers. All their estimates pointed in the same direction: more landing craft. The British, Handy told Beetle, were wasting space and being too fussy about how many men could fit on an LST. Before Ernest King was willing to divert anything from the Pacific, he was going to insist that not a square inch be spared.

The next day, there was no response from General Marshall to his rant against the charge of "localitis." Eisenhower sent a more conciliatory message, apologizing for going off hot and assuring Marshall that he would never surrender his convictions "merely in the interests of local harmony."

Beetle made another call to Handy in Washington, who had done some investigating. It was not simply a matter of how many men could fit on a ship. The British also took a more conservative view of how many landing craft would be "serviceable," meaning fit to sail. American planners had estimated that each landing craft could make at least three laps across the English Channel before needing repairs. More laps, more men ashore. The British, though, proceeded on the assumption the landing craft needed to be retired for repairs after only two laps.

Handy told Beetle that, as far as the US Chiefs were concerned, the invasion of Normandy needed to be an "all out" operation. There was no keeping the powder dry. If a landing craft could sail, it should sail. And so, Eisenhower should plan accordingly.

GENERAL MARSHALL, EVIDENTLY still concerned about Eisenhower's untreated localitis, sent a note to the British Chiefs agreeing to Churchill's proposal for a Combined Chiefs meeting in London. But there was a catch. Rather than come himself with Ernest King and Hap Arnold, Eisenhower was being directed to negotiate not in his capacity as the Supreme Allied Commander, but as the "representative of the U.S. Chiefs of Staff."

General Marshall was, in effect, ordering Eisenhower to get back on side. And if that message was too subtle, Marshall sent Eisenhower notice that Admiral Charles Cooke and General John Hull were on their way to London to "assist Eisenhower, in a purely advisory capacity." Not coincidentally, these two men had been King's and Marshall's principal planners for the European war.

Being the Supreme Allied Commander and the representative of the US Chiefs put Eisenhower in the awkward position of wearing two not entirely compatible hats. He went that afternoon to meet with the British Chiefs, still wearing his Supreme Allied Commander hat, to discuss whether they would be amenable to his returning a few days later wearing the hat of the designated representative of the US Chiefs. He went with Beetle and Arthur Tedder and had Beetle do the honors of explaining the American navy's objections in what came to be called the "Battle of the Numbers."

The British were getting their backs up, and so Eisenhower interjected that he thought these problems were all solvable. He asked Andrew Cunningham if he was willing to sit down and draw up plans that might satisfy the US Navy's concerns. He mentioned that Cooke and Hull were on their way and if they could be persuaded, King and Marshall would likely be as well.

Cunningham was happy to do it.

Eisenhower's real question was whether the British Chiefs were firmly behind the expansion of Operation Overlord, even if it meant that Overlord would, to use Churchill's phrase, become a tyrant in its demand for resources.

Alan Brooke was adamant. Monty was right. It was, Brooke said, "absolutely essential to widen the bridgehead as much as possible." The only reason to invade the South of France at the same time as Normandy, as far as Alan Brooke was concerned, was to divide the German defenses. "Instead of being ordered to plan Operation Anvil," he suggested, "General Wilson should be told to put proposals for containing the maximum German forces in the Mediterranean theater."

Eisenhower welcomed Alan Brooke's rather zealous conversion to Operation Overlord, but suggested that the US Chiefs would likely demand something more definitive. But the most important thing, in the short term, was to get some basic agreement on the numbers. He would do that as the Supreme Allied Commander. Once that was done, he would change hats and come back.

COOKE AND HULL arrived the following Sunday like Rosencrantz and Guildenstern, and Eisenhower welcomed them to London like his most excellent good friends. Eisenhower took the chance to make his pitch. Whatever other demands the navy might have in the Pacific, Eisenhower needed more landing craft, and he needed them quickly. Beetle then took Cooke and Hull to Norfolk House to confer with the planning staff and arrive at some consensus on what the numbers really were.

Before they left, Hull handed Eisenhower a top-secret, personal, eyes-only, confidential letter that General Marshall had given to him to hand-deliver. Eisenhower opened it. Perhaps it contained some words of encouragement? Or an unofficial suggestion of what the navy might really be willing to commit? No, it was neither of these things.

"My dear Eisenhower," it began ominously. It was not that General Marshall never addressed him in this way. But the usual was either "Dear Eisenhower" or just "Eisenhower." General Marshall was looking to get his way.

When he had anticipated becoming the Supreme Allied Commander himself, General Marshall explained, he wanted to try something innovative with the paratroopers. Doctrine was to use airborne forces tactically; to do what Eisenhower had planned to do by sending the 82nd and 101st Airborne divisions behind Utah Beach. Marshall, though, wanted something bolder, like what George Kenney had done.

What if, General Marshall proposed, they could make the battlefield truly three-dimensional? What if, as Eisenhower's men were establishing the beachhead at Normandy, the airborne divisions could instead be dropped deep inside France, more than a hundred miles farther inland, around the town of Évreux? What if, he suggested, the airborne forces could establish an airhead to go with the beachhead, a landing strip so that Allied air forces could quickly get on the ground and resupply? It would be a third front opened from inside France.

The idea excited General Marshall, and he envisioned it not only being a complete surprise, but also directly threatening Paris and the crossings of the Seine. "The trouble with this plan," General Marshall confessed, "is that we have never done anything like this before." But then he added, "frankly that reaction makes me tired." In addition to Cooke and Hull, Marshall revealed, he was sending two more officers from the Pentagon to brief Eisenhower in detail. He wanted, in a word, for Eisenhower to show that he could get some ice cream.

Eisenhower thought the proposal was terrible. It was obvious to anyone who understood the scale of the European theater, its geography, and its logistics. But it was General Marshall's idea. So all Eisenhower could do was patiently wait for the architects of this awful plan to arrive and then provide Marshall with a deferential explanation of why he was not going to maroon a few thousand Americans deep inside enemy territory for some ice cream.

MONDAY MORNING, EISENHOWER sat down with Cooke and Hull, as well as Bertie Ramsay and some of the relevant staff from SHAEF. He opened the meeting saying that they needed to figure out a way of getting the landing craft for Operation Overlord, hastening to add in the presence of Rosencrantz and Guildenstern, that they also needed to leave enough in the Mediterranean for Operation Anvil.

Cooke offered some numbers he had calculated. If they assumed 95 percent of the landing craft they had were serviceable on D-Day, they had 172 LSTs, 131 LCIs, and 685 LCTs. That was enough "lift" for 168,200 men and 19,800 vehicles. With the expansion of the invasion size, they needed enough lift to move 176,200 men and 21,000 vehicles. And if they were frugal in how they used space—requiring men to double-bunk, for example—

they could do that with 214 LSTs, 174 LCIs, and 661 LCTs. Those were reasonable numbers.

Eisenhower asked Bertie Ramsay what he thought. Couldn't they just stuff more into the LSTs?

"Questions should not be confined to the assault only," Ramsay said, "but should be directed at the build up as well." Ramsay turned the floor to his chief of staff, who expanded on that, saying, "We could not justify the risks of heavier losses on D-Day. With overloaded vessels on D-Day, the probable heavy personnel losses would seriously affect the assault on the shores."

"Why," Eisenhower asked, "would attacks be more serious on D-Day than on succeeding days?"

"The dangers were two-fold," Ramsay's man explained. "The primary danger being air attack and the other coastal gunfire."

There was a third danger as well, on the army side. Monty had sent word that he did not want his men double-bunking. They would be at sea for several days before landing and would not be in top condition when they hit the beaches.

Beetle scoffed like a Prussian at Monty's complaints about comfort, saying he was "unable to understand why the troops could not forgo their comforts when submarine crews were often required to undergo such conditions for a considerably longer period of times."

The seemingly practical question of how many men could fit on an LST risked becoming an argument over principle, and so Eisenhower ended the discussion for the time being. He told Ramsay to coordinate with Monty on what needed to be done to get more men on fewer ships. Given the risks, he also asked Ramsay to see if the navy could make additional battleships available to intensify the bombardment.

Even assuming all that worked to save space, however, Eisenhower still had a problem. He still faced a shortfall of 42 LSTs.

"There was a possibility," Cooke suggested for the first time, "of providing an additional 10 LSTs which might be withdrawn from the training program in the United States." Cooke then added, somberly in the way any salesman does when claiming that a customer is picking his pocket, "if this were done, the training program in the United States would suffer very seriously."

What would be the shortfall if they got the ten LSTs from the United States? Ramsay asked.

A navy staffer chimed in: "There would still be a shortage of 32."

"How many LSTs were allocated for Anvil?" Eisenhower asked.

Another navy staffer answered: "77 had been committed."

In that case, Eisenhower suggested, couldn't they send some of the smaller landing craft that would not work well in the Channel due to the sea conditions down to the Mediterranean, where the waters were calmer? They could swap them out for as many as twenty-two LSTs, leaving the overall lift for Operations Overlord and Anvil the same. That would cut the deficit down to ten LSTs. And that, Eisenhower said, was something that he, as the representative of the US Chiefs of Staff, could recommend.

Operation Overlord was "the all-out operation." The risk they would be running—and he was clear eyed about it—was that if they took twenty-two LSTs from the Mediterranean, Jumbo Wilson would "undoubtedly conclude that Anvil could not be undertaken." But that was a fight for the future.

BACK AT THE office, Eisenhower sent a cable to General Marshall, summarizing the day's discussions, noting "already the great value of sending Cooke and Hull here has become apparent. I am fully prepared to accept many of their recommendations." But he warned that there remained significant uncertainty.

The only certainty, he realized at that moment, was that every day he would face "unceasing pressures and responsibilities." He mulled over how to deal with it all. Smoking was not the answer, though he was not about to stop. Staying sane was a question of mental discipline. "Think only of essentials," he told himself. "Get basic things started right, with the right people in charge of each important activity." To do that, to keep his head clear, he realized he had to "watch my disposition just as I do my diet."

Eisenhower noticed that it was Valentine's Day. He had not heard anything from Mamie in two weeks. But he wrote with all the uxorious glee he always put in his letters to her. It had been twenty-eight years, he recalled, since he had "brought out the West Point class ring to 1216 McCullough, proud as a peacock!" He mused about his day and his stresses and his getting out of shape. But, he concluded, "maybe on next Valentine's Day, I can crack your ribs instead of hurting your eyes with scrawl like this—I love you—always."

Walter White

CHAPTER 24

EISENHOWER WAS SET to present his proposals to the British Chiefs the following Saturday. In the meantime, the planning staff would continue fighting out the Battle of the Numbers. He tried, as much as he could, to spend the intervening week on matters that were less urgent, but more important.

Eisenhower had seen cable traffic between Roosevelt and Churchill, arguing over the plans for the postwar occupation of Germany and Europe more generally. Churchill was resisting Roosevelt's new demand for northern Germany. Not only would it lead to the crossing of logistical lines, Churchill argued, but the north was the British sphere of influence. It was as if Britain were demanding to occupy Mexico while telling the United States to occupy Brazil. The exchanges grew increasingly testy, with Roosevelt flatly telling Churchill, "I am absolutely unwilling to police France, and possibly Italy and the Balkans as well."

Eisenhower had his own idea for the postwar era: just leave. He reached out to General Marshall to try and broker a compromise. The British, he wrote, would always have a "transcendent interest" in northern Germany. Making it an American zone of occupation would create all sorts of headaches, if only because the British, Belgian, and Dutch air forces would want to use the airspace. What if, instead, Roosevelt proposed keeping US forces in Germany, "only so long as the Allied principle of unity of Command is observed"? Should Great Britain "decide that she wanted to control any specific major portion of Europe strictly from London, then we should simply withdraw." Military withdrawal did not mean an American retreat to isolationist irrelevance. America had the money and industrial base that Europe would need to rebuild. Without a single American boot on the ground, Eisenhower said, America would still be "strongly represented in the *whole* controlling system." It was the best of both.

The brief reprieve from daily crises had given Eisenhower a chance to think bigger. But the reprieve was short lived. That same week, Butch woke him up in the middle of the night. Alex, Butch said, was looking to pin the quagmire in Anzio on the Americans. Butch handed him a cable that had been sent directly to Alan Brooke blaming the stalemate on Major General John Lucas, the commander of America's VI Corps. Alex asked if he could replace Lucas with a British commander, or if an American, then a real "thruster," like Patton.

Alex had not consulted with any of his American commanders in the Mediterranean. It was a power play that would give him an American goat to sacrifice for the failures of the previous month. But it could also create a wound of resentments in the Anglo-American alliance that, if left to fester, could make Eisenhower's life harder.

Eisenhower called Alan Brooke and told him that any switch from a British to an American commander in the middle of a crisis would be "unwise, to say the least." Eisenhower said he would be happy to make Patton available for a month, but only so long as Jacob Devers requested him. He could not be seen as interfering with Devers or Wayne Clark's management of their command.

Georgie came by Grosvenor Square at eleven the next morning. Eisenhower looked wryly at him. "I'm afraid you will have to eat crow for a little while."

"What have I done?" Georgie asked.

"You may have to take command of the beachhead in Italy and straighten things out."

"It was not eating crow," Georgie crowed, "but a great compliment."

Eisenhower handed him the cable from Alex. Eisenhower would never ordinarily agree to putting Patton under British command, but for a month, perhaps, it could work. Could he put the fight back into the fight?

Georgie asked whether Eisenhower would give him his full backing. "Otherwise, I would be made a goat."

Eisenhower assured him that he had his back and would report the whole thing personally to General Marshall.

Georgie beamed like he had licked a lollipop. His hope of being the savior of Anzio was short lived, however. Within a day, Alex gave a press conference, at which he attacked the press for presenting bad news negatively and announced that Lucian Truscott would take over VI Corps.

THE NEXT DAY, yet another festering problem of Allied cooperation began to seethe. De Gaulle, with the support of the British, had proposed to set up a tripartite committee in London to coordinate the delivery of weapons to the French Resistance. The US Chiefs rejected the proposal out of hand, passing the responsibility to Eisenhower, who still lacked a formal directive authorizing him to coordinate with the French.

The last thing Eisenhower wanted to do was govern France, just as he had no interest in governing Germany. Civil affairs, as it was called, was a military nightmare. The responsibilities were seemingly endless.

Before leaving for London, Eisenhower had been asked to resolve a severe food shortage in Sicily that was on the verge of triggering riots or even a famine. The American soldiers were also increasingly undisciplined, enraging the Neapolitan people, who were justifiably sensitive about US soldiers knocking around in a two-thousand-year-old antique store.

In North Africa, internecine violence had been rampant and "the Jew-Arab question," Eisenhower would say, "It's dynamite." The Germans had spread a rumor that Eisenhower was Jewish and planned to impose a Jewish government. "If the Arabs had once got the idea that the Jews would be put over them, they'd have gone on a massacre," Eisenhower said. "And the Jews themselves knew it." The experience had dramatically shaped Eisenhower's views of the limits of military power: "You can't drastically reform everything at once. The world moves forward in little steps." And those steps were especially little when forced at the point of a foreign army's gun.

Eisenhower needed only to look out his window in London to see how difficult the basic problems of government were. Tens of thousands of American soldiers arrived each month, making the United Kingdom the reluctant landlord to a million and a half mostly young American men. With numbers like that, there were more than a few bad apples, and it did not take long for American soldiers to get a reputation for hassling British women, plying underage girls with alcohol, and even barging into homes on the assumption that their very Americanness made them welcome. They were not.

Within days of Eisenhower's arrival in London that January, there had been the condom controversy. American soldiers were leaving condoms everywhere: parks, sidewalks, churchyards. They were left wherever they had been used, no matter how briefly, before being discarded like a soggy pea pod. To the British, every soggy pea pod was a reminder that there was likely a British woman, often a girl, at the scene as well.

People tried to make light of the indignities suffered by His Majesty's dominion. But little indignities were the thousand cuts that could destroy an alliance. And so, Eisenhower saw to it that a memorandum was sent out, by his judge advocate general, Edward Betts, an Alabama lawyer, whose main job it seemed was to bring Eisenhower a list of all the worst things that soldiers had done that week. The memo admonished American soldiers to dispose of their soggy pea pods discreetly, out of respect for their hosts.

Then there were the crimes, such as the twenty-one-year-old private who had just been sentenced to hang for robbing and then strangling a British cabbie to death. Because Eisenhower was also the commanding officer of the US Army, European Theater of Operations, these cases were all his responsibility. Betts would bring each case to him to review. Each one that involved a British citizen was a potential diplomatic flashpoint. And there was no diplomatic flashpoint more frustrating, more explosive, and more embarrassing, than America's "color problem."

It was said that "the Negro question is the hyphen in Anglo-American relations." In his first press conference in London, back in 1942, one of the British correspondents pressed Eisenhower on America's practice of racial segregation and the obvious irony of a segregated army claiming to fight against fascism. Eisenhower was caught flat-footed. He said he was just following orders. But he felt the tension enough that, when Butch got wind that the censors had blocked stories criticizing America's "color problem," Eisenhower overruled them. "Might just as well let the American public know what the problems are and our success or failure in meeting them."

Eisenhower was and would remain ambivalent about racism. He had the casual prejudices of a man born in 1890. He thought nothing of referring to Black people as "darkies," at least in private company. And he had risen up through an army under mentors who were committed and vocal racists. General Conner was a Mississippian, who pronounced the "e" in the word "negro" as if it were an "i." And Eisenhower's path to MacArthur, who certainly seemed to believe that light skin was one of his many signs of superiority, had been laid by becoming a protégé of George Moseley.

Moseley had a crank's obsession with immigrants and spent the 1930s using his public profile as one of America's leading generals to campaign against Jewish refugees, arguing they should be forcibly deported, detained in concentration camps on a remote Hawaiian island, or at the very least sterilized upon arrival, lest the United States be swamped by "defective civilian manpower." By 1939, his eugenic ambitions grew higher, stumping a "humane" final solution to the so-called Jewish problem. "In my opinion," he would say, "the greatest boon which could come to the world today in advancing civilization, eliminating war and raising moral standards at home, would be the elimination of all Jewish blood from the human race. That is a large order, but still it is possible of accomplishment by the humane method of sterilization." He despised Bernard Baruch as "a very dangerous Internationalist" and, perhaps unsurprisingly, privately came to think that Hitler had a point.

Eisenhower never shared these views. Hitler always revolted him in large part because of the Nazis' "blood purges" of the Jews. He was also friends with Jews in Manila, at a time when the Philippines was exploring whether to offer safe haven to refugees. He had worked for years, side-by-side with Filipinos, who were earnestly trying to build their country, and one of the hottest rages his son ever saw him fly into was when he caught his son aping the casual racism that led most Americans in the Philippines to condescend to their "Little Brown Brothers." John was just a teenager and had asked his father, trying to be funny, "What time are your Googoo friends to arrive this evening?"

"They're not Googoo friends," Eisenhower exploded. "They're nice people!"

Eisenhower was even willing to challenge his old mentor Moseley. "I am not one of those who would attempt to ascribe to the Filipino any racial defect which would make it impossible for him ever to become a good officer," he wrote to correct Moseley. "Genghis Khan produced one of the finest military machines the World has ever seen, and the only material he had was nomadic tribesmen in Central Asia."

Eisenhower had been underestimated enough for coming from the wrong side of Abilene's tracks to know that who you were said little about what you could do. Merit was merit. A lifetime of competition against men like "that Indian," Jim Thorpe, had proved in the scorecard that European ancestry offered no advantages in getting across the goal line.

Eisenhower did not really care about race. But he also rarely cared that others cared. Georgie Patton could say some of the most vulgar things ever said about Arabs, Blacks, Jews, and Asians. It might make Eisenhower cringe. But that was true of a lot of what Georgie said. Racism was a personality quirk, a taste he didn't share.

Being the governor of a million and a half Americans stationed in England, however, made that indifference untenable. About 10 percent of Eisenhower's men were Black, and the mistreatment of those soldiers had provoked his first diplomatic embarrassment with the British. In August 1942, American officers were going around and ordering pubs, restaurants, and cinemas to refuse service to Black soldiers when white patrons were present. The British Home Office sent an emphatic message to the country's constabulary forbidding "any discrimination as regards to treatment of coloured troops."

Eisenhower responded to the British government, saying—implausibly, given the official segregation of the army—that "this policy of nondiscrimination is exactly the policy, which has always been followed by the United States Army." He then issued an order to his subordinate commanders that struck an initially placating tone that reflected his ambivalence—or at the very least awkwardness—in having to address the issue at all.

"The presence of Negro troops in this theater," he wrote, "creates a problem of interracial relationships, much different from that in the United States. There is practically no colored population in the British isles." Eisenhower worried about what Black soldiers dating white British girls might unleash.

But having made the decision that nondiscrimination was the rule, Eisenhower's actions to enforce that rule were categorical and blunt. He prohibited racial discrimination in the granting of passes or the visiting of local pubs and then prohibited overt expressions of racism with the threat of court-martial. "It is absolutely essential," he ordered, "that American officers and soldiers carefully avoid making any public or private statements of a derogatory nature concerning racial groups in the United States Army. The spreading of derogatory statements concerning the character of any group of United States troop, either white or colored, must be considered as conduct prejudicial to good order and military discipline and offenders must be promptly punished."

Eisenhower would say that his rule was simple. "People that were good enough to fight were good enough to be treated properly." The problem, though, was that they weren't being treated properly. And more than two years into the war, the American color problem in the United Kingdom had gotten worse.

When Jacob Devers took over the year before, nondiscrimination remained the rule officially, but unofficially segregation became tolerated, if not encouraged. Before the war, and in command of Fort Bragg in North Carolina, Devers had betrayed no qualms about enforcing the absolute segregation that existed under both army policy and state law.

Race relations in the United Kingdom deteriorated under Devers. In the summer of 1943, a white colonel sent a memo to subordinate officers entitled "Leadership of Colored Troops." "Colored soldiers are akin to well-meaning, but irresponsible children," it explained, warning that "they cannot be trusted to tell the truth, to execute complicated orders, or to act on their own initiative, except in certain individual cases." It then went on to itemize and endorse various racial stereotypes that were "peculiar characteristics of the colored race," and advised, when making promotion decisions, "the real black bosses should be picked rather than the lighter 'smart boy.'" The memo provoked such a scandal, among white and black soldiers, that Devers ordered it recalled. But he did nothing to punish its author under Eisenhower's antiracism policy.

Fights, many bordering on riots, between Black and white soldiers became common. It reached the point that, the previous September, a group of Black soldiers mounted an armed revolt against the military police in protest of the segregation that the local army commander had imposed in Cornwall. Devers's response was to welcome Jim Crow to the United Kingdom under what came to be known as the "Blacks Tuesday, Whites Wednesday" policy.

NO ONE HAD thought to add America's color problem to Eisenhower's worries since his return to London. But then on Friday, the day before he was scheduled to negotiate the future of Operation Anvil with the British Chiefs as the deputized representative of the US Chiefs, Cliff "Jesus Christ Himself" Lee came into his office and introduced him to Walter White.

Eisenhower had heard the name before. The previous summer, he had received a letter of introduction from Wendell Willkie, the famed American entrepreneur who unsuccessfully ran as the Republican alternative to Roosevelt's third term in 1940. Willkie introduced White as "one of the foremost citizens of our country. In service to his cause he is the most disinterested representative of any group I know in America. In addition he is a highly intelligent, delightful and attractive gentleman."

White was of mixed ancestry, and his light complexion and blue eyes enabled him to pass as white, to the point that he was able to personally infiltrate the Ku Klux Klan. He was also not above making the obvious joke about his last name.

The executive secretary of the NAACP, White got an army press pass to report for the *New York Post* and *Life* magazine on the experience of Black soldiers around the world. He had arrived in London just after the New Year and enjoyed a German air raid his first night. After that, he traveled more than 1,700 miles, visiting army bases throughout England, Scotland, Wales, and Northern Ireland to interview soldiers.

White wrote a report for Eisenhower and the War Department that stated the problem unflinchingly. "We may," he wrote, "win the war and lose the peace." The American practices of segregation and discrimination were defining features in how the foreign press covered America, not just in Axis-controlled media, but also in India, the West Indies, Africa, and the United Kingdom. The Italians, the North Africans, the British, White wrote, "have found it difficult to understand why some American soldiers should be so violent in their hatred of other American soldiers, especially when all of them are fighting in a common cause."

White saw a conundrum. The United States was "fighting a war for freedom" with "two armies—one white and one Negro." The perception of America as a racist country was the single greatest obstacle to the creation of the "American Century" that, for every other reason, should be inevitable.

Cliff Lee arrived with White just fifteen minutes after Eisenhower got to the office that morning. Eisenhower's plan had been to spend the day preparing for Saturday's big meeting with the British Chiefs. He had a long meeting with Admiral Cooke scheduled at noon, and that evening he would be heading to Norfolk House to meet with his commanders in chief, including Monty, who was feeling jilted for having been left out of the Battle of the Numbers.

Eisenhower's impulse was to avoid the issue and to placate White quickly out of his office. Practical problems, even of the human sort, could command Eisenhower's seemingly inexhaustible attention. Abstract problems bored him to near immediate impatience. And since his days on the War Policies Commission, Eisenhower had an allergy to people he thought were conflict entrepreneurs, who talked—and only talked—about abstract problems precisely because their insolvability provided job security for people whose only skill was talking.

Eisenhower was therefore gracious to White, but shrugged that he was just a soldier. Social policy was not something he did. He told White a story about a journalist who had come from New York when he was back in North Africa. "He told me my first duty was to change the social thinking of the soldiers under my command, especially on racial issues." Eisenhower waxed incredulous. "I told him he was a damn fool—that my first duty is to win wars, and that any changes in social thinking would be purely incidental. Do you think I was right?" Eisenhower asked White, almost accusingly.

White, who was deferential but no shrinking violet, said with his faint hint of a Georgia accent that he "saw merit in the other man's point of view." White, whose self-effacing charm was perfectly tuned to soften Eisenhower's defensive crouch, continued by saying, of course wars had to be fought to be won. But, White added, "we must not fight them solely for the sake of making wars."

It was a sentiment with which Eisenhower could blandly agree, but he did not have the time or patience to discuss abstract platitudes. He changed the subject to something personal, to charm White or perhaps to just filibuster the further discussion of a problem he did not want. He told White about his recent trip to Washington and how he'd sneaked away to see his mother. It had been a short trip. But he was grateful for it. She was getting old and he wasn't sure how long she had left.

Eisenhower then moved to wrap up the meeting by turning to White's report. White had found that "the overwhelming majority of the white American soldiers in the ETO [European Theater of Operations] are decent, fair-minded individuals." But "a smaller percentage have brought strong racial prejudices with them to the ETO from the United States and persistently stir up friction." American officers were stoking British fears and ignorance, spreading rumors that "all Negroes have tails, that they are savage, diseased, illiterate, and will rape their women."

The mayor of one English town had told White that his constituents were "frightened when they heard that Negro troops were to be sent there. For days the British avoided even walking close to Negro soldiers. But one morning the Lord mayor was greeted with a pleasant 'good morning, sir,' by one of the soldiers." The man had been startled that the soldier could speak English. Now imagine, White suggested, what impact that had not just on the relations between Americans and their British hosts, but what stories like that did to the morale of Black soldiers.

White recounted being asked by some Black soldiers, "What are we fighting for? Were we sent to the ETO to fight the Nazis—or white soldiers?" Did Eisenhower really want a civil war inside his army?

Eisenhower was, of course, sympathetic. Of course . . . Of course . . . But what could he do about it? Being a general gave him no power to revolutionize the hearts of men.

White, though, was not asking for that. He was concerned with practical problems, which Eisenhower had the power to solve, often easily.

Why were the "overwhelming majority of the Negro troops," White asked accusingly, "assigned to service units"? White had met a Black soldier who said, "It is hard to identify one's self with fighting a war when all he does is dig ditches, and lay concrete." Think about how demoralizing that was to a man who had come to Europe to fight. "None of the glamour, excitement of war. Educated men digging ditches, building runways in mud and darkness."

Black men could fight. Just look at the Negro Ninety-Ninth Pursuit Squadron in Italy. Ernie Pyle was reporting that 70 percent of the men in the trucking units in Anzio were Black. That was one of the most dangerous jobs in the war. White's reasoning was simple: "As men approach actual battle and face the dangers of combat, they tend to discard many of the prejudices and preconceived notions they formerly held."

Eisenhower found himself stunned into agreement. He mentioned to White that he had served with Black soldiers throughout his career. It made sense to make them a part of the liberation of Europe.

White was pleased to hear that. There had been two Black divisions training in the United States for the past two years. White suggested bringing at least one of them to Europe.

But that was not the only problem Eisenhower could do something real to solve. Look at how Black soldiers were covered in the press. Look at how white soldiers were trained to interact with Black soldiers. Given Eisenhower's influence, if not his explicit control over these things, more could be done to counter the use of inflammatory stereotypes that reinforced prejudices.

Or, look at positions of leadership. As best as White could find, there was not a Black soldier above the rank of captain in a theater that was clogged with colonels and generals. It was hard to avoid the impression that Jim Crow had come to England, when every man who could tell a Black soldier what to do was white. Role models were important, as much to white soldiers as to Black. Eisenhower could do something about that. White suggested that Eisenhower could even put "a Negro of sober judgment of rank of at least full colonel" on his own staff to set an example.

Or, look at the way military discipline was enforced. White said that Black soldiers were court-martialed more often and given higher sentences. That was not just unfair, it fostered deep distrust, particularly when most of the military police were white. White had found that in the few places where Black and white military police patrolled together, there was less "inter-racial friction." Why not implement that everywhere?

White was not selling symbolic politics. He offered solutions that made sense of the real world. It was the same clarity and precision of thought on a seemingly abstract issue that Eisenhower had admired when he first saw Bernard Baruch. Eisenhower promised White that he would implement his ideas to the extent he could, and to investigate whether there was unfairness in the military justice system.

Cliff Lee gave the signal to White that it was time to go, and White began to get up. But Eisenhower waved Lee off and gestured White to sit down.

What caused all this tension? Eisenhower asked. It made no sense to him. Why couldn't these men see that they were on the same team? Why did some units work well, while others didn't? Eisenhower looked at White, not as an activist full of abstract platitudes, but as someone who could tell him the answer to a question he could not get his mind around.

White's answer was simple: It was the officers. If the commander of a unit had character and treated all his subordinates without discrimination, that set the tone and it was followed. If the commanding officer brought his own prejudices or was weak in the face of his subordinates' prejudices, it was only a matter of time before you saw a fight or a riot, or some other opportunity for friction. Equality flowed from the top down.

White credited, for example, Eisenhower's directive abolishing "off limits" areas in towns and pubs. He suggested that the directive be enforced, since a lot of the lower officers had gotten used to violating it. Those were the kinds of things that mattered.

Eisenhower told White that he had to turn to other things that morning. But he invited White to grab a bite to eat later that day to continue their conversation.

The meal was an example of White's basic, and fundamentally hopeful, finding that prejudice was not inevitable, or even desirable to most people.

Talking to one American officer, White had been told "two men having a friendly drink together is not news; while one man objecting to having a drink in the same pub is news."

The problems Eisenhower confronted, though, seemed endemic. A survey of enlisted soldiers showed that only 36 percent of Black and 12 percent of white soldiers thought units should be integrated; 40 percent of Black and 81 percent of white respondents favored segregated PX facilities; and 48 percent of Black and 85 percent of white soldiers favored segregated service clubs. As they ate, Eisenhower expressed his gratitude to White and emphasized that his own philosophy was "teamwork." It was teams that succeeded. He hoped that everyone could work together regardless of race or anything else.

Cliff Lee chimed in that there was no "Negro problem" in Europe. There was an "American citizen problem." And in a letter thanking White for the visit, Lee told him that his proposed reforms were being put in place and echoed Eisenhower's hope that "progress is being made. What we all seek is evolution, not revolution."

Andrew Cunningham

CHAPTER 25

FRIDAY EVENING, EISENHOWER greeted his commanders in chief at Norfolk House. Everyone knew the issue at that point. Landing craft were finite, and they needed to figure out how they could launch the simultaneous invasion of northern and southern France with what they had. Eisenhower then had Beetle explain how they could make up for the shortfall with a combination of reshuffling, more aggressive accounting of serviceability, and stuffing landing craft until their seams split.

Monty took the opportunity to reiterate his opposition to the plan he had seen earlier in the week. That plan would have reduced the target number of LSTs from 217 to 210, and the number of LCIs from 174 to 144. "The 21st Army Group was unwilling to accept the original plan," Monty said. "But after further consideration and discussion, we're now willing to accept a compromise." That compromise meant accepting a reduction in LCIs on the condition that twenty LSTs be drawn from Operation Anvil. Six large cargo ships would then be sent to the Mediterranean to make up for the lost LSTs. And the rest of the shortfall, which depending on how they counted it would be anywhere from fifteen to twenty-two LSTs, would be filled with a combination of accounting tricks and overloading. Monty agreed to all of this on principle, but wanted Bertie Ramsay's candid view of whether it was feasible.

"From the naval point of view," Ramsay replied reluctantly, "every endeavor possible under the circumstances have been made in order to reach a solution." But he would be remiss if he didn't add that all the tricks they were using "added to the complexity of an already complex naval situation."

Eisenhower understood the qualms and reassured everyone that "he would explain to the British Chiefs of Staff that these proposals included an understanding that it may be necessary at a later date to withdraw additional ships and craft from the Mediterranean."

Beetle handed out a memo summarizing the proposal that he suggested Eisenhower present to the British Chiefs the next day. They read it out line by line, and all was fine until Beetle got to a paragraph that said a final decision on the allocation of landing craft should be postponed until April 1. Eisenhower interrupted.

What was that about? "I am unable to understand the reason for this delay," Eisenhower said. "It is essential that a decision be made at this time."

All eyes were on Beetle. The issue, he said, was uncertainty about Germany's intentions. "German strength in the West, particularly the mobile divisions, might be increased to such an extent that Overlord would be impracticable." That might, in turn, "require shifting the weight of the attack to the Mediterranean." In other words, if the Germans got any stronger in northern France, the Allies might need to reduce the Normandy invasion, or even cancel it. "We may be confronted with the fact that Anvil may be the only feasible approach to gaining a foothold on the continent."

Eisenhower wanted that paragraph cut. "We should make the decision now," he scowled.

Privately, Monty pressed Eisenhower to go bold and to recommend, in his capacity as the Supreme Allied Commander, at least, that Operation Anvil be abandoned. Monty had just had lunch with Churchill at Chequers, and the prime minister was fully behind focusing on the Normandy invasion. "I recommend very strongly," Monty confided, "that we now throw the whole weight of our opinion into the scales against Anvil. Let us have two really good major campaigns—one in Italy, and one in Overlord."

THE NEXT MORNING, Eisenhower greeted the British Chiefs wearing his hat as the representative of their American counterparts. He handed out the revised version of the memo Beetle had written, specifying how landing craft could be divided between northern and southern France without fatally compromising either. He repeated the American position on the necessity of a two-pronged attack. According to intelligence sources, he said, "a two prong assault on France would result in much greater support from the French resistance groups, particularly in the south, where French resistance was strongest." To do this, they had to make sacrifices and accept "every possible risk in respect of Overlord" while also avoiding interfering with the campaign in Italy.

Alan Brooke was incredulous. Planning for the two-pronged attack was already interfering with the campaign in Italy. Divisions were being trained for amphibious operations rather than being sent to the front. And if they continued planning to launch Operation Anvil on the existing timetables, it would continue to drain more from Italy. "The trend of operations in Italy was becoming increasingly unfavorable to the prospects of Anvil." Brook then added that "the proposals now submitted by *General Eisenhower*" would just make it worse.

Beetle defended his memo and his numbers, despite having never been especially enamored of Operation Anvil. And having only his one chief of staff hat to wear that morning, Beetle nudged the British Chiefs to support the cancellation of Operation Anvil by reminding everyone that to prepare for the invasion of the South of France, "two divisions should come out of the line in Italy now."

Andrew Cunningham, mindful of his nation's policy of not abandoning the Mediterranean, said that he doubted whether it was even possible to withdraw twenty LSTs, get them to the United Kingdom, and then repair and refit them in time. He said that he had been under the impression that the Americans were going to send twenty-six new LSTs to England, rather than the Mediterranean, to make up the shortfall.

Admiral Cooke chimed in to defend the plan, saying that Ramsay had approved the withdrawal of the twenty LSTs. General Hull then took the chance to emphasize that the United States was sending more men to the Mediterranean to make Operation Anvil a success. But Alan Brooke was dismissive. If they canceled Operation Anvil, as he thought they should, they could still do something later after the invasion of Normandy was underway. Why create a crisis now?

Eisenhower, though, was disturbed by what Cunningham had just said and wanted to focus on the LST question. If they canceled Operation Anvil today, Eisenhower asked, was Cunningham saying that they could not get the LSTs that were currently in the Mediterranean for Operation Overlord?

If Anvil were canceled, Cunningham said, "every effort would be made to return these ships from the Mediterranean and to see that they were, as far as possible, manned by experienced crews." The phrases "every effort" and "as far as possible" leapt out.

"If a decision were taken not to undertake this operation," Eisenhower said, "then Overlord should be strengthened by such landing ships and craft." He took a breath and then took off his US Chiefs hat for a moment.

"Owing to developments in the situation in Italy, it might no longer be practicable to undertake Anvil," Eisenhower admitted. He emphasized that this was only his personal opinion, but that is what he thought. And whatever everyone else thought, they needed to decide quickly.

Eisenhower's personal opinion was all Alan Brooke needed. The British Chiefs formally and "emphatically recommended that any idea of an Anvil to synchronise with Overlord should be abandoned."

Eisenhower left the meeting weary. He reported back to General Marshall on everything that had transpired, as well as his personal doubts. It was not what Marshall wanted to hear. But Marshall was always telling Eisenhower that he needed to use his own best judgment. Even when throwing around accusations of localitis, Marshall had promised, "I will use my influence here to agree with your desires."

EISENHOWER WOULD PUT General Marshall's promise to the test twice that day. Back from his meeting with the British Chiefs, Eisenhower finished a lengthy memo offering his bleak assessment of Marshall's ambitious, Kenney-inspired proposal to vault paratroopers a hundred miles into France. By writing a memo, instead of a cable, Eisenhower could be confident that Marshall would not receive it for at least a few days.

Eisenhower began tactfully, of course, writing, "I agree thoroughly with the conception." But, he added, "I disagree with the timing." He had spent nearly two hours going over the proposal with its architects that week. The main issue was mobility. This wasn't World War I. Speed was everything, and they had not yet developed reliable ways of dropping tanks and jeeps and other hardware that would be needed to equip airborne forces to move once they were on the ground. Airborne forces scattered hundreds of miles inside France without any armor, and with minimal weaponry and sparse provisions, would be sitting ducks.

Eisenhower sympathized with General Marshall's eagerness to envelop the Germans, since traditionally a smart commander would always retreat rather than risk being surrounded. Eisenhower had seen war change, though.

Just look at Anzio. On paper, it had been a textbook case of a threatened envelopment that should have made any rational German commander retreat. But the Germans ignored the textbook and ferociously counterattacked, pinning the landing forces down near the coast. The only reason disaster had been averted thus far was because the Allies could resupply from the sea, which not coincidentally was causing the present shortage in landing craft. Airborne forces a hundred miles away from Normandy would be isolated, immobile, and quickly starved. "There must," Eisenhower explained like a defiant pupil, "exist either the definite capability of both forces to combine tactically, or the probability that each force can operate independently without danger of defeat."

Eisenhower got that George Kenney had pulled off something similar in the Pacific. And everyone got ice cream. But Europe was not the Pacific. The distances, though the same in inches on a map, were vastly larger at the scale of reality. German radar coverage and the Luftwaffe's efficiency posed astronomical risks, particularly to airborne operations. Eisenhower assured Marshall that he was keen to learn from Kenney's innovations. But not all lessons translated. "The resistance to be expected by our landing forces at the beaches is far greater than anything we have yet encountered in the European War." The airborne forces were already anticipating massive losses, both to the men jumping and to the planes dropping them.

Eisenhower confessed that he might be thinking too conservatively and assured General Marshall, "I instinctively dislike ever to uphold the conservative as opposed to the bold." The risks, though, did not make sense. It was not what Marshall wanted to hear, but that was Eisenhower's best judgment of the battlefield.

Everett Hughes

CHAPTER 26

DISAGREEING WITH GENERAL Marshall, particularly so directly, did not come easily. Marshall was not just Eisenhower's greatest benefactor, he loomed as large as his shadow. He was one of the only people in Eisenhower's adult life to never call him Ike. Marshall was formal that way, of course. But it also had a subtle way of penetrating Eisenhower's "Likable Ike" persona.

Marshall seemed completely unaware of the effect he had on people. Back at the start of the war, one of Eisenhower's subordinates, a man by the name of R. W. Crawford, had been working hard on an issue, and Eisenhower gave him the honor of being the one to brief Marshall on it. Under Marshall's cool glower, however, Crawford got flustered and rambled until Marshall lost patience and Crawford was dismissed.

Once Crawford had left the room, Marshall told Eisenhower, "I don't want that man around. He just stumbles and fumbles around."

"General," Eisenhower said incredulously, "did you ever talk to him?"

"Yes."

"Most of these people are scared to death of you."

"Who could be frightened of me?"

"By god," Eisenhower said, "R. W. Crawford is."

Eisenhower was where he was because of General Marshall. Beetle too.

And he had spent the whole war living up to his reputation as Plog's assistant. Back in September, he wrote to Marshall, saying, "I wouldn't even know how to proceed here if I didn't have the assurance of your firm backing and your complete understanding behind me every minute of the day." True to form, Marshall was apt to get annoyed by Eisenhower's obsequiousness and would tell him, in so many words, "Man up." With the Battle of the Numbers and all the other burdens Eisenhower had been shouldering, though, his reputation as Marshall's amiable administrator felt increasingly like a yoke.

As much as he hated to admit it, Eisenhower resented the swashbuckling press coverage given to people like Georgie and Monty and Kenney. The press was always touting their "initiative" and "boldness" while crediting Eisenhower for his "friendliness in welding an allied team." No one seemed to understand—and more selfishly, no one gave him credit for—his boldness, his initiative, his genius for the battlefield. He had ordered the integration of American forces into the British battle lines, which led to the victory in Tunis. He had ordered the surprise attack on Pantelleria, which made Sicily possible. He had gambled on the weather and won victory at Salerno. And somehow, he had developed a reputation for being a timid, military accountant, a nice guy whom everyone liked, but who just stood around like a cheerleader.

Eisenhower wrote all these frustrations down to help expunge the thoughts from where they were festering in his mind. "It wearies me to be thought of as timid, when I've had to do things that were so risky as to be almost crazy.—oh hum—."

At the same time, when newspaper columnists began to criticize Jumbo Wilson for lacking Eisenhower's boldness, Eisenhower felt embarrassed. He reminded himself that good press rarely did any good for anybody and sent Jumbo a short note of encouragement, saying, "All your last year's team mates now in the UK are following your operations with keen realization of the innumerable obstacles you are encountering and with complete faith in your ability to overcome them."

BRIGHTENING EISENHOWER'S MOOD, Everett Hughes had just arrived that weekend. A few years older than Eisenhower, Everett had been an instructor at Leavenworth during Eisenhower's fateful year there. They both found themselves in Washington in the early 1930s, and Everett and his wife, Katie, or Kitten, became regulars at Club Eisenhower.

Hughes's role as Eisenhower's deputy theater commander in North Africa was a job with ambiguous responsibilities that naturally overlapped with Beetle's role as chief of staff. Beetle and Everett bitterly jockeyed for position on Eisenhower's org chart. Unlike Beetle, though, Everett Hughes was not widely respected.

Eisenhower had spent the previous month trying to persuade Jacob Devers to approve Hughes's transfer to London, and General Marshall had intervened to share some gossip, saying that Hughes was a royal pain in the ass. That was, of course, true. But like Beetle, he was also a loyal pain in the ass. And of greatest importance, he was a buddy and a great bridge player. A big man with ice blue eyes and a full head of hair, Everett was one of the only people Eisenhower trusted with personal things, outside of Butch and the rest of the Official Family.

Everett had arrived in London in the middle of the night, and was dogged by a cold. It was something Eisenhower knew that he would have to get used to, just as Eisenhower did. Eisenhower offered him the job of being Patton's chief of staff, since they were good friends, but Everett immediately passed on being responsible for Georgie. Eisenhower asked if he would be content being a "special assistant," Eisenhower's eyes and ears in the European Theater of Operations, and Everett was more than happy to do it.

They had dinner that night with Kay, Butch, and Mollie Ford, Butch's "Red Cross Girl." Mollie had gotten the nom de guerre from her job at the desk of the Red Cross Club in Algiers. She had succumbed to Butch's charms and was now very openly his mistress. Butch planned to divorce Ruth after the war to marry Mollie, who had become good friends with Kay.

Like a good friend, Mollie was protective of Kay and, therefore, never quite got along with Eisenhower. Eisenhower had made no great promises to Kay about leaving his wife, the way Butch had done. But that did not stop him from carelessly musing about a future with her and running away to Tahiti when the war was over.

Mollie also thought that Eisenhower acted more jealous than a married man had a right to be. One example was the whole thing with Red Mueller, the reporter. He had come to London from Algiers and started paying a lot of attention to Kay. Eisenhower couldn't stop himself from making snide remarks to her about it.

"Why are you so jealous," Kay had scolded him, "when you have nothing to be jealous about?"

Mollie naturally took Kay's side.

Eisenhower was cold in a petty way toward Mollie. The welcome dinner for Everett, whom Butch's wife, Ruth, joked was a "worn out wolf" himself, got awkward. And Eisenhower got annoyed with Butch for bringing her.

THE NEXT DAY was all bad news. No one in the United States was on Eisenhower's side, no one. Roosevelt had seen his objections to the division of Germany. "Sit tight" the president replied. "I do not intend to use Americans to keep the peace in Southern Europe after the war ends." Roosevelt had also been briefed on the debate over Operation Anvil, prompting him to remind Eisenhower, "We are committed to a third power, and I do not feel we have any right to abandon this commitment for Anvil without taking the matter up with that third power."

General Marshall and the rest of the US Chiefs were also unhappy with him. "You were delegated to represent United States Chiefs of Staff in conference with British Chiefs of Staff on question of Overlord—Anvil," Marshall scolded him. The US Chiefs rejected the British proposal to cancel Operation Anvil and were also unimpressed with the compromise Eisenhower had tried to work out. Instead, the US Chiefs agreed to send seven LSTs—not ten—from the United States to England, as well as more than sixty-five other landing craft. But that was all conditioned on the British Chiefs agreeing to proceed with Operation Anvil as planned. The only ground given was a willingness to defer a final decision on the launch date, as Beetle had conspicuously suggested, to April 1, 1944. Eisenhower was then ordered to either persuade the British Chiefs to agree or to formalize the disagreement between the two nations.

From the other direction, Monty not only wanted the invasion of southern France canceled, he wanted it canceled immediately and badgered Eisenhower as if he could simply resolve it with a smile. "If the decision is postponed," Monty inveighed, "it will be impossible to make the best use of the additional craft, and moreover the last moment alteration in the plan may lead to heavy and inadequate preparations with consequent risk of confusion."

Eisenhower attempted to call Monty but was told he was unavailable. So he wrote Monty a letter, telling him that he shared Monty's concerns, and tried to convince the stubborn son of a bishop of the wisdom of patience. If Italy suddenly resolved itself, then Operation Anvil would be the only way they could force the Germans to divide their forces in the defense of Paris and the path to Berlin.

The only thing everyone agreed on was the need for an immediate decision. But to get what he desired from opposing sides, who were both unwilling to agree to give him what he asked for, Eisenhower needed to keep the negotiations going. To do that he began each round of the negotiation, every cable, every conference, every discussion, by saying the time had come to make a final decision, given that everyone agreed on that. And when he sensed that he couldn't get what he needed in that round of the negotiation, he made sure to end on something, anything, everyone could agree on, even if the only thing anyone could agree on was the need to come to an agreement eventually.

Like a recurring argument in a strained marriage, the Battle of the Numbers had ceased to be about LSTs and the relative merits of invading the French Riviera. It was about the power and prestige of two nations that had both changed profoundly in the two years since they had joined together in a common cause. It was a fight over who needed whom more. For Eisenhower, that fight was destructive and irrelevant. The bottom line was that they still needed each other if they had any hope of breaking through the Atlantikwall. And he had the thankless task of holding an increasingly unhappy couple together.

Eisenhower returned to Alan Brooke and the rest of the British Chiefs, who had read the latest counterproposal from Washington. He made a show of agreeing that the battle in Italy needed to take precedence. But, he warned, the Americans were prepared to withdraw from the Mediterranean entirely if Operation Anvil were canceled.

Alan Brooke took an uncharacteristically conciliatory tone, saying he "agreed very largely with the views expressed by General Eisenhower." But he continued to insist that "operations in Italy should have the first call on all our resources in the Mediterranean."

Eisenhower searched for a compromise and, rather duplicitously, suggested that the British Chiefs did not need to agree to a massive invasion of southern France. They just needed to agree to something called "Operation Anvil." So why not just agree with the US Chiefs to wait to see how Italy went over the next month? In the meantime, given that determining the precise where and when of Operation Anvil would be deferred until April 1, they could free up more resources for Jumbo Wilson in Italy.

"If General Eisenhower agreed, that the operation known as Anvil need not necessarily be mounted on a scale of ten divisions, and need not necessarily be mounted against the South of France," Alan Brooke said, then the British Chiefs were "prepared to agree."

Without mentioning his suggestion that Operation Anvil might not involve what everyone had assumed to that point Operation Anvil involved, Eisenhower tried to sell General Marshall on the compromise. It would, at least, keep the negotiations going.

Trafford Leigh-Mallory

CHAPTER 27

THAT NIGHT, EISENHOWER went to dinner with Tedder, Beetle, Andrew Cunningham, and the whole cohort with whom he had fought in North Africa, to smoke, drink, and celebrate having done what seemed impossible at the time. Eisenhower had not expected anything, but then Cunningham got up to speak.

"Today," he said in his peculiar Irish-Scottish-Royal-Navy-man's brogue, "is George Washington's birthday, but I hasten to assure our guests that that is not the true reason which has led us to ask them to honor us with their company. Indeed, it might be that George Washington would witness this gathering here tonight with considerable concern, but hardly as much as that which must be caused to George III to know that the staff of an American General is installed in the house built on the site of one in which he was born."

Cunningham went on to celebrate Eisenhower's appointment to lead the war in Europe and to reflect on the previous two years. Things had seemed so daunting, and everyone doubted whether Eisenhower was up to the job. "What sort of man is this American General who has been entrusted with the command of this great enterprise?" Now, though, there were no such doubts: "No one will dispute it when I say that no one man has done more to advance the Allied cause."

Cunningham then read from his dispatch back to the War Cabinet on the success of the Mediterranean campaign from October 1943. It was this very success that had propelled Cunningham to the top spot in the Royal Navy.

"I feel that it should be placed on record that there reigned a spirit of comradeship and understanding which provided that vital force which brought success to our undertaking," Cunningham had written. "The embodiment of that spirit was exemplified in our Commander in Chief, General Dwight Eisenhower. We counted it a privilege to follow in his train."

Cunningham presented Eisenhower with a silver salver, an exact copy of an artifact from 1750. On the front was engraved "General Dwight D. Eisenhower, Commander-in-Chief, Allied Forces, North Africa, 8 November 1942–8 January 1944. A token of admiration and affection from some British officers of Allied Force Headquarters." On the back, Cunningham, Tedder, and all the other major British officers from the North African campaign (except for Monty) had engraved their signatures.

The churlish part of Eisenhower's mind thought it would make a splendid card or cocktail tray. But these glib thoughts were just a defense against how much it meant to him. It was one of the nicest things he had ever been given and was preceded by what felt like the nicest speech ever given about anyone. He welled up and felt embarrassed. He had trouble believing that anyone thought he deserved any of it. He thanked everyone as best as he could without cracking.

Eisenhower awoke early the next morning and admired the gift. He held it between his hands, letting the light reflect back at him. There was a smudge, a thumbprint on the front. He took the edge of his bed sheet and polished until it gleamed cleanly back at him. He wanted to preserve it as it was. Like a championship trophy, he looked down at the names of men whom he had grown to trust and who trusted him. He had done what General Pershing could not do, and what General Conner thought could not be done. He had built a genuine team of Allies. And together, they had changed the tide of the war.

Eisenhower thought about putting the platter in a glass case, just like a trophy. He wanted glass on both sides, so that the names of these men could be seen as clearly as his own name on the front.

Eisenhower felt embarrassed for how awkward he had been the night before and contacted the Parker Pen Company with a request to make custom fountain pens, complete with special bottles of ink. He had nine made altogether. Four for Cunningham and his commanders in chief in North Africa, and five for his staff. He gave one to Kay with a note saying, "In your own important sphere your services have been of inestimable and constant value. I thank you very much and hope that this little pen will remind you of my gratitude." He also gave one to Beetle, with the begrudgingly sentimental note, "I have so often tried to express to you my feelings of admiration, as well as personal and official obligation, for the great service you performed."

THE WARM FEELINGS did not last long. That Saturday, Eisenhower called a commanders-in-chief meeting. Apparently Jumbo Wilson had sent a cable to the British Chiefs. Had anyone seen it?

Beetle said that he had not, but understood that Jumbo was making the case against Operation Anvil. It was a tedious argument of insidious intent.

"How long," Eisenhower asked Ramsay, can the navy "wait for additional craft to become available if Anvil were definitely canceled?"

Ramsay said it depended. He had been working out all the details of the naval plan, and it was nearly complete. But it would be useless if Operation Anvil were canceled, since that would change what was available.

Beetle interrupted. He had just been handed a message from the White House.

"Conclusions," it read, "have been agreed by the Combined Chief of Staff and approved by the President and Prime Minister." A deal had been reached. It was Eisenhower's deal. Italy would, for the time being, take precedence in the Mediterranean. Eisenhower would get some, but not all, the LSTs he wanted for Normandy. And Jumbo Wilson was directed to prepare for undetermined "amphibious operations in the Mediterranean," preferably Operation Anvil. They would then reassess on March 20.

Beetle read that to mean that if Operation Anvil was canceled on the twentieth, the extra landing craft would go to Operation Overlord for sure. Then they wouldn't have to double-bunk and overload and do all the other crazy things they had contrived to stretch the numbers.

Monty took that as his cue. Why wait? The time had come to cut Operation Anvil loose so that they could finally plan for a "real and proper Overlord."

They were deferring to the end of March, Eisenhower said, in the hope that Italy might get better. The cable was a signal, though, that the US

Chiefs had also come to see the inevitable. Maybe Monty was right, Eisenhower suggested. Maybe he could send a personal telegram to General Marshall "stating it was his view that Anvil was impossible."

Beetle wasn't so sure. If Eisenhower sent that message, it would look like they were just changing their minds back and forth. They had gotten the deal they asked for.

"Full Overlord must be planned now," Monty snapped.

Then plan it, Beetle snapped back. They had the "lift" they needed. Just add the extra they might be able to scavenge from Operation Anvil as additional flexibility.

Eisenhower agreed with Beetle. It was better to just "saw wood" for a little while longer.

Leigh-Mallory had concerns. Did they even want more landing craft? The Germans had gotten very good at the so-called pathfinder technique, in which scout aircraft dropped colored flares to guide the larger bomber forces to targets. If they used those techniques to target ports like Southampton it could be disastrous. And it would be worse if the ports were more congested.

Was Leigh-Mallory proposing, Eisenhower asked, that they did not want the landing craft they had been begging to get for the past month because the Luftwaffe was getting stronger? What the hell were the air forces doing? Jimmy Doolittle had just launched what soon came to be known as "Big Week." It was an onslaught comprising 3,300 sorties and the dropping of 6,000 tons of concussive force across Germany. The whole point of that mission, and of Operation Pointblank, was to neutralize the Luftwaffe. Doolittle was reporting that they had shot down more than five hundred German fighters out of the sky. And yet, the Luftwaffe was getting stronger?

It was more, Leigh-Mallory said carefully, "an increased effort rather than an increase in actual strength."

Eisenhower was unclear what he was supposed to do with Leigh-Mallory's problem spotting, and so he turned back to the landing craft they might get if Operation Anvil was canceled.

It posed a major planning problem, Ramsay said, if he did not know precisely how many landing craft of what kinds would be available. He had just done a whole plan based on the existing numbers.

Couldn't the navy, Eisenhower asked, just operate on the assumption that there would be something between what they had now and what they might get if Operation Anvil were canceled?

Ramsay grimaced at the prospect of planning in the face of uncertainty.

If he was going to plan each turn of the rudder, he needed to know how many rudders would need to turn. But he promised to consult with his staff and determine a consensus figure.

Eisenhower looked around the room. "What other courses of action can we take while awaiting the Combined Chiefs of Staff decision on Anvil?"

"None," Beetle said. But he promised to chase down a copy of Jumbo Wilson's cable to see if it clarified anything.

From the sea, Eisenhower turned to the air. What was the status of the air plan? Eisenhower needed a fixed plan if he was going to persuade the Combined Chiefs that he should have control over the strategic air forces.

"The Air Plan will not be ready for a few days," Leigh-Mallory explained. He needed "additional time to consult with his railroad and transportation experts."

Insofar as the air plan was still in flux, Ramsay took the chance to raise his lingering concerns about Leigh-Mallory's plans for air support on the beaches. "It would be necessary," Ramsay said, "in order to achieve a successful assault, to neutralize the coastal defense batteries by heavy bombardment from air and sea." Ramsay spoke from experience. He had been at Gallipoli. They needed to complement the horizontal attack from the sea with the vertical attack from the air.

Monty fully agreed. His ground forces needed air support. Otherwise, the landing would be suicidal.

Leigh-Mallory disclaimed any responsibility. People needed to understand, he said, that "total air effort for Overlord was a fixed quantum, and that it was for the three services to consider together how it should be allocated to the best advantage." He had his ideas, but ultimately it was something that needed to be decided through consensus.

Well, Eisenhower said, in that case, consider it together. Meeting adjourned.

Arthur Tedder

CHAPTER 28

THE MONTH OF February had been brutal, on Eisenhower's mind, on his health. He was drinking more and smoking three packs a day. He knew the smoking was prolonging his never-ending cold. He also knew that chain-smoking was not a good look for an international role model. He had experimented with a cigarette holder like Roosevelt's to make it classier, but the simple fact was that he relished the habitual vice of it. He liked rapping his fist on whatever furniture was at hand to knock the ash off onto the carpet. He liked pitching his butts into his fireplace. And he liked lighting up another.

London winters were grim under the best of conditions. It was never quite as cold as an American winter. But the snow fell fast and heavy like rain, and the brevity of the sun's appearance low in the sky somehow made the chill all the more biting. Add to that the blackouts at night, which had not stopped Germany from rounding out the month with an onslaught of air raids like the city had not seen since the Blitz in 1941. In just a week, nearly seven hundred people were killed, and close to three thousand injured.

Churchill invited Eisenhower and Beetle over for dinner on what should have been the end of a dismal month had the leap year not prolonged it further. The prime minister was in a foul mood and eager to blame everyone for everything. The Italian campaign had become a sinkhole and Jumbo

Wilson was urgently demanding more LSTs. But that was hardly the only problem.

The British had sent two divisions of colonial soldiers from New Zealand and India to try to cross the Rapido River after two American divisions had failed. The colonial soldiers had also failed, and so now another American division, along with some French and Polish soldiers, were going to make a third attempt. More than ten thousand men had already been killed, not to mention those captured, or missing, or wounded.

At ten that evening, they all retired to the Map Room for a meeting with the British naval commanders on what kind of naval gunfire they could bring to bear on Normandy's beaches. An aerial reconnaissance report from earlier that day had shown that the Germans were constructing new underwater obstacles along the coastline.

Churchill had been heartened by the American success in the landing on the Marshall Islands. The US Navy had made extensive use of close-range fire to break a path through the beaches. The problem, though, was that the ships approaching Normandy would have to stay seven to eight miles from the coast. The waters around Normandy were much shallower, and full of mines.

Bertie Ramsay's solution, though not perfect, was to bombard the beaches in phases that would hopefully make the best use of the battleships and cruisers they could bring within range. The discussion of what was possible with naval bombardment led inevitably to the role of airpower. Here, again, was the problem that Eisenhower had arrived in England assuming would be his biggest and most challenging.

Eisenhower still did not have a final air plan. Part of the reason was the endless debate over Operation Anvil. The expansion of Operation Overlord had created a greater demand for everything, including airpower, and Eisenhower had requested three additional squadrons to be transferred from the Mediterranean. On its own, this request was nowhere near as controversial as the greedy scramble for LSTs. But, given the inevitable bureaucratic tendency for decisions to lump together, the delay in one caused a delay in the other. And official approval of the squadrons' transfer became a victim of the slowest common denominator.

Nevertheless, when consolidating control over the air forces came up, Eisenhower told Churchill that it was time to make Leigh-Mallory the overall air commander in chief, to include the strategic air forces. A memo on how the strategic bombers could be used most effectively in support of the Normandy invasion had been circulating for a few weeks. The targets made sense: twenty-five Luftwaffe airfields within a 130-mile radius of the beaches, the dozen or so coastal batteries, and the beach defenses. The most controversial parts of the proposal, though, were railway targets in northern France and Belgium, the bombing of which would come to be called "the Transportation Plan."

Arthur Tedder deserved significant credit for the idea. The thing that made the invasion of Normandy so risky was the Germans' ability to march more men to northern France faster over land than the Allies could sail them across the English Channel. Victory would go to the swiftest.

The Allies had refined the process of loading landing craft, traveling to shore, unloading, and traveling back to load again, down to the second. But the efficiency with which enormous steel machines could be moved through space had natural limits. That meant Eisenhower could have thousands of LSTs and still lose because they could only ever get men and equipment on shore so fast.

To win the race, they had to also slow the Germans down. Tedder had thought about the problem as an airman. There had been some tentative proposals drafted by Freddie Morgan's planners at COSSAC for targeting French roads and railways. But the plans seemed rather weak, since the few meters of railroad track that would be gnarled by even a direct hit (and very few hits were ever direct) could be repaired in a matter of hours.

Tedder therefore asked some British railway engineers, "What attack would hurt them most?" Their answer: repair facilities. "If you destroy those, the network will soon be paralyzed."

To take them out, air planners estimated that they would need to drop at least four 500-pound bombs per acre to devastate the railway stations where these repair shops were located, as well as the nearby warehouses, power stations, oil stations, office buildings, water towers, and communication hubs, not to mention the various homes in which the railway workers lived. Given the size of these targets, and the distances involved, only the heavy bombers could do it. And to do it properly, they would need to redirect about 90 percent of the airpower currently dedicated to Operation Pointblank.

Churchill balked at the thought of Leigh-Mallory commanding the RAF's Bomber Command. Arthur Harris would never stand for it. "Why did we give you Tedder?" the prime minister asked sourly.

"Why?" Eisenhower asked back. Eisenhower had wanted Tedder to be the air chief only to have Leigh-Mallory forced on him by Churchill. Eisenhower tried to explain his vision for combining the air forces, but Churchill was not in a listening mood. Knowing that once Churchill took a position, he was immovable from it, Eisenhower played for more time, assuring the prime minister that they were in the final stages of drafting the air plan.

THE NEXT DAY Eisenhower told Tedder to get the air plan finished immediately. They needed to win this bureaucratic fight. Tedder needed no convincing. He had some research done, which showed that Operation Pointblank would reduce German production by 7 percent at most by May. They needed something that would work in the time they had.

Eisenhower also needed no convincing. Back in 1919, he had participated in an army caravan whose goal was driving across the United States. He had been appalled by the state of America's roadways, writing that the roads in the Salt Lake Desert were a "succession of dust, ruts, pits, and holes" which had made them "almost impassable to heavy vehicles." If they could use airpower to turn the highways and byways of northern France into something like western Utah, then the men on Utah Beach might just have a better chance of surviving.

They needed to make their case, Eisenhower told Tedder, before Churchill was "in this thing with both feet." Another meeting with Churchill, as well as with the full complement of British Chiefs, was scheduled for ten p.m. the next day.

That meeting began with yet another discussion of landing craft and the failures at Anzio. "We hoped to land a wildcat that would tear out the bowels of the Boche," Churchill grumbled. Instead, "we have stranded a vast whale with its tail flopping around in the water." To help the whale, the British were now proposing to redirect even more landing craft to Italy.

Churchill's position on the air forces had also hardened. As far as he was concerned, the RAF Bomber Command should remain independent. It would work collaboratively, of course, to assist Operation Overlord. But it should stay under Bomber Harris's command.

Eisenhower became indignant. This went back on the directive the Combined Chiefs had approved at the Cairo Conference. Everyone had already agreed, he insisted, that he was to be given command of all the air forces, including the strategic air forces, in the run-up to D-Day.

Charles Portal, the chief of the Royal Air Force, stopped Eisenhower right there. Portal had negotiated the directive on the "Control of the Strategic Air Forces in Northwest Europe and the Mediterranean" and it was far less categorical than Eisenhower had been led to believe. The directive dealt only with the US strategic air forces, not the RAF.

Portal had opposed the consolidation of command "on principle," but signed off on the directive because the United States was free to organize its military however it saw fit. In case Eisenhower had forgotten, he was in the heart of the British Empire. Would he also insist on authority over Britain's Coastal Command? Should the British government delegate to him the responsibility of defending England?

Eisenhower took the point. He was not asking for control over the Coastal Command. But, he insisted, the RAF Bomber Command was an "important striking force." He could not face Hap Arnold, let alone General Marshall, if Britain was unwilling to go all out for Operation Overlord, and—more to the point—all in with him. It would be a vote of no confidence in his leadership and, Eisenhower added, he would simply have "to go home."

Churchill softened his stridency. He was not trying to drive Eisenhower back to America.

Portal also took a breath and suggested that, in principle, Eisenhower could be given some kind of role in directing Bomber Command's operations in the lead-up to D-Day.

Seeing the opening for compromise, Churchill told them to work it out. If they came to an arrangement, he would back it.

EISENHOWER WENT TO Tedder's house to strategize. The main problem was personalities. There was no way that either Harris or Spaatz would ever agree to Leigh-Mallory being in charge. They could solve that by putting Tedder in charge. But would Leigh-Mallory agree to be demoted?

He might quit, Tedder said.

Would that be the worst thing? Eisenhower gradually came to the view that "Leigh-Mallory was simply incapable of handling the air show. He didn't know strategic bombardment and he didn't know tactical air power." There was a vacancy in the Far East, and Leigh-Mallory could go there without any loss of face. Tedder could then become the commander in chief of the air forces.

Tedder, though, liked being Eisenhower's deputy. He was also apt to be generous to Leigh-Mallory. He was not so bad, Tedder thought. He was one of the few people, certainly senior people, to consistently work into the night. He knew his details. And when asked whether he was willing to accept Tedder as de facto head of the air forces, in order to give Eisenhower control over the strategic air forces, Leigh-Mallory was happy to go along if that was what it took to get the job done.

Before Eisenhower and Tedder could write up their proposal, Charles Portal sent Eisenhower a letter. Eisenhower's suggestion that he would ask to "go home" appeared to be reverberating. The most important thing, Portal wrote, was for Eisenhower to know that the objections to giving him control over Bomber Command were "either organisational or constitutional, and in no way implies any lack of confidence in you or your Deputy." Portal therefore proposed a compromise. What if Operations Pointblank and Overlord were officially deemed of equal importance? The directive could then authorize "the continuation of Pointblank in parallel with the other air operations in more direct support of Overlord," as the basis on which Eisenhower could be given "such use of the strategic bombers as may be necessary to execute the Overlord cum Pointblank plans."

Eisenhower hated the suggestion. The Combined Chiefs had declared the amphibious invasions of France the "supreme operations for 1944." He was not about to relegate the importance of his own operation in favor of a giant experiment the air forces were conducting to see if they could win a war by bombing. And Portal's message, read between the lines, suggested that he did not have to. Portal would not have felt the need to emphasize the degree of British "confidence" in Eisenhower if, when push came to shove, and the choice was between him or Harris, Eisenhower would be the one to go home.

Eisenhower was tired of the air forces' "constitutional" sensitivities. And he was tired of the arrogance. Hap Arnold had just sent Freddy Smith, the "hot shot of Kenney's," as his "special representative on the broad subject of the defeat of the German Air Force," with instructions to Eisenhower, "Please see that he has complete access to all air activities; surely all of our activities and, if possible, all RAF." Eisenhower also had to keep reminding Jimmy Doolittle to stop flying on missions with his men, and Doolittle would moan that Eisenhower was preventing him from doing the thing he did best.

Eisenhower called Tedder and told him to persuade Charles Portal to agree to a draft directive that made three points clear: (1) Tedder would be in overall command of the air forces; (2) Operation Pointblank would continue, but only subject to the needs of Operation Overlord; and (3) Eisenhower would have command over all the strategic air forces necessary to carry out Operation Overlord.

Tedder doubted that Portal would go that far. Harris certainly wouldn't. There were sensitivities.

"Now listen Arthur," Eisenhower snapped. "I am tired of dealing with a lot of prima donnas. By God, you tell that bunch that if they can't get together and stop quarreling like children, I will tell the Prime Minister to get someone else to run his damned war—I'll quit."

Tedder tried to calm him down. He could not be serious.

"I will ask to be relieved and sent home."

Tedder talked to Harris, airman to airman, and Harris was not budging. He had promised Churchill that Operation Pointblank could win the war by June 1944, and Churchill had told him to go for it.

"In that case," Tedder told Harris, "you must go."

Faced with the ultimatum, Harris blinked. He wanted to stay and said, as long as he did not have to answer to Leigh-Mallory, he would agree.

Portal agreed the next day. He had a few small edits to the draft Tedder had prepared, and asked that Eisenhower's "responsibility for supervision of air operations," would commence only once the air plan was finalized. But they had a deal.

Eisenhower told Portal that it was "exactly what we want." He then sent the revised draft to Beetle to double-check if he was missing anything.

"I think this is excellent and a most fair solution," Beetle replied.

With that last loose end tied up, Eisenhower officially sent each of his commanders in chief their orders for D-Day. Omar Bradley, though technically under Monty, received orders too. A courier brought the orders to each of them, requiring a signature. Monty had his chief of staff sign. Bertie Ramsay, already confident that he knew what he needed to do, signed without reading them. And Leigh-Mallory had concerns as he scrutinized each line, making several suggestions for revisions, including to punctuation. When the courier informed him that these were the final orders and no further changes were possible, Leigh-Mallory looked at the man sourly and, with painstaking care, signed his name. Operation Overlord was on.

PART FOUR

SOLDIER OF THE EMPIRE

Joseph Lawton Collins

CHAPTER 29

IT WAS A Friday afternoon and Eisenhower left the office early to accept an invitation from the groundskeeper of Richmond Park to get some fresh air. "No man ever thinks clearly when he's angry or when he's fearful," Eisenhower would say. "Therefore, placidity of mind is as important in the commander as is moral courage."

Richmond Park was close to Telegraph Cottage, as well as Eisenhower's new offices at Wide Wing. Eisenhower never did, nor would, like city living and had been looking forward to moving his headquarters out of downtown London from the moment he arrived. They had made the move from Grosvenor Square to Wide Wing the second week of March and Eisenhower celebrated the chance to be out in the "country."

Like the Pentagon, Wide Wing was a half hour drive from the intrigues and oversight that came with being in the capital. It was also just as deliberately ugly as the Pentagon, with just-to-the-point architecture that reminded everyone who entered its flat gray walls that no one would be there unless there was a job to do. Eisenhower's offices were part of the same complex in which Tooey Spaatz had set up the Strategic Air Command, which was convenient now that Eisenhower, or Arthur Tedder at least, would be directing his operations.

Moving to Wide Wing also helped make the incessant flow of daily visitors more deliberate. If someone wanted to claim Eisenhower's attention, it took something to venture out to the London suburbs that popping into his office at Grosvenor Square did not. And if it wasn't worth coming to Wide Wing, they could just dial Kingston 7777 to ring up his office. Then they could learn from Eisenhower's staff that the Supreme Allied Commander was not available at that moment, because if it wasn't worth their time to come to Wide Wing, it probably wasn't worth his time either.

The move itself contributed little to Eisenhower's placidity of mind. All week, he found himself shuttling back and forth to Grosvenor Square for all sorts of things that demanded his presence, and occasionally his attention. But with the air forces question finally resolved by Friday morning, Eisenhower's afternoon was now free to take the Richmond Park's groundskeeper up on his offer to explore its vast acreage on his personal horse.

It was a nice-enough day, and Eisenhower knew he needed the exercise as much as he needed the fresh air. Horseback riding through the countryside back in Algeria had been his favorite way to escape his worries. He would go out at least a few times each week. He never could quite get used to the glare of the North African sun. But the vast, flat, arid plains reminded him in a nostalgic way of Kansas. And the freedom of it and the intimate reconnection to nature offered him the same rare chance for serenity that it gave to the gunslingers in the horse opera westerns that littered his bedside table.

Kay would often come along. They both enjoyed long, meandering rides, though they had to be vigilant about causing a scandal. Kay would have to gallop away whenever it looked as if they had stumbled on some American soldiers who might get to talking about seeing their supreme commander out alone with a beautiful young woman, astride an Arabian.

Eisenhower loved horses. The Eisenhower family had a workhorse on the farm back in Abilene. But the horse that had stolen Eisenhower's heart had been the fourteen-year-old gelding he was assigned back in Panama named Blackie. He was an ugly, clumsy plow horse, well past any prime he might have had. He had a short, thick neck and an enormous head that made Blackie look like a mule. Eisenhower had gotten him because no one else wanted him. But he intuited that Blackie was a smart boy that no one had given a real chance.

Over weeks and then months and then years of riding through the Panamanian rainforest, often in deep conversation with General Conner, Eisenhower grew to love that horse. They rode for hours every day among the ceiba, mahogany, and cocobolo trees. In the shade, Blackie's hooves could disappear into the ferns and knotgrass, and in the sun, his horseshoe prints would crush down into the damp earth between the spike rushes. The two trusted one another enough to amble through the rockiest jungle.

Before he left Panama, Eisenhower entered Blackie in an equestrian competition in Balboa. It seemed as if everyone assumed he was playing a prank until his proud, ugly horse won a yellow ribbon. Eisenhower took the win as affirmation of a hope he had kindled since childhood: "A difficult boy can become a fine man."

The groundskeeper's horse had nothing on Blackie, and the amble around Richmond Park in mid-March, with its leafless old-growth oaks, matted wintering grasses, and sedge that had turned khaki in the cold, was not nearly the escape that his rides through Panama and Algeria had been. He was still in London, and the bridle path was lined with anti-aircraft installations, which made the groundskeeper's horse jittery. He was also escorted through the park by the groundskeeper's assistant. Not that he minded the company. Eisenhower liked people. But since his return to London, he had become a global celebrity and had learned that privacy means something different for the truly famous.

Eisenhower confronted a visual reminder of his growing fame every time he walked into his new office in Wide Wing. When he had arrived in London, a single filing cabinet was all he needed for his personal correspondence. But soon, he needed another, and then another, to hold all the paper coming in at him. It seemed as if anyone Eisenhower had ever met was now writing to him. Old acquaintances from Abilene recounting stories of his childhood for which he had only the sketchiest memory. He was unflaggingly affable in his replies, but every time he got a follow-up letter that passive-aggressively chided him for failing to respond to a previous missive more promptly ("I am not sure if you received my prior letter . . ."), what was left of Eisenhower's good humor curdled.

It struck him how different the tone was from the letters he sometimes got from mothers, who never played up some long-ago encounter to insist they were his old friend. They were just desperate for word about a child who was missing in action. They always apologized for adding to his burdens. And he knew what they were going through. He knew how desperate they were, how single minded a parent becomes when afraid for a child. They were the people most entitled to demand his attention given what the army had asked of them, but they betrayed the least amount of entitlement. He always made sure to personally respond to them as soon as he could, if only to assure them that he was looking into it.

Eisenhower wrote to Mamie about it, saying, "I begin to think that the more people suffer, the more truly considerate they become. Well, maybe I don't know exactly what I do mean!"

Four different biographers were now digging into Eisenhower's family and friends back in Abilene. He was deeply ambivalent about it all. On the one hand, he cringed at the thought of all these busybodies rummaging around in his past for "human interest" material. On the other, he knew history and knew that he was now a part of it. He had always enjoyed reading Julius Caesar, with his eye for detail and the dispassion with which he wrote about events in which he was a central player. He admired the fact that Caesar was "interested in the entire scene of the Gallic and Civil Wars—the customs, manners, practices of all the participants."

Eisenhower had already thought, albeit vaguely, about writing his own Caesar-esque memoir of the war. He knew books would be written. One of the reasons he brought Butch over to England back in 1942 was to keep a daily diary for posterity. Now Butch was in talks with publishers about writing a memoir. His brother Milton was keen to make Butch's book a blockbuster and had offered Butch exclusive access to the brothers' childhood reminiscences.

Butch tended to think that it was better to give the childhood anecdotes to the real biographers who were already hard at work. He asked Eisenhower about it.

"Let the biographers work for the stuff they get," Eisenhower said. He was delighted by the idea of Butch writing his biography.

Butch, though, was reticent. He was keeping the diary, but he wasn't a biographer. There would be biographies. Why not try to shape them?

Butch was not the only person to whom Milton was offering special access. In fact, he was thinking far bigger than a simple biography. A few weeks earlier, Milton had taken the occasion of George Washington's birthday to deliver a speech on America's "spiritual greatness" (a phrase that would loom large for Eisenhower in the years to come).

Milton was far from the first big thinker about America to see that the country was on the verge of something great. In 1940, the publisher of *Time* magazine, Henry Luce, had inaugurated the coming "American Century." It was a time of gloom and ambivalence with the United States buffeted by a world at war, though not fully in it, and riven with partisan divisions. Luce saw an opening for a uniquely American internationalism that broke with the empires of the past, in favor of an "internationalism of the people, by the people and for the people." It was a vision of America leading the world with "jazz, Hollywood movies, American slang, American machines, and patented products." It was an empire built on the universal appeal of individualism, prosperity, and plain old American fun.

For Milton, the American Century needed a foundation firmer than the global allure of Coca-Cola and making a buck. The war was a contest of ideas. It was the Atlantic Charter against *Mein Kampf*. "Our intellectual heroes," Milton said, "are such men as Tom Paine, Washington, Emerson, Jefferson, Lincoln, John Dewey. Theirs are such men as Machiavelli, Nietzsche, Pareto, and Spengler. Where we are believers, they are cynics." The American Century needed a new birth of freedom, rooted in those parts of the country's history that "fused idealism and hard headed practicality."

"When we look deeply and honestly into our American past, we find that material progress has been much admired, but only as an expression of spiritual greatness." And the great hero of that past, in Milton's telling, was George Washington, the one man who stood above the partisans and profiteers, "steadfast in his determination to fight on," who could unify a divided country around a Constitution dedicated to the pragmatic goal of making a more perfect union. "He alone, by virtue of the universal esteem in which he was held by his fellow countrymen, was able, as chairman, to hold the constitutional convention together, while the great work was done."

"It was inevitable," Milton added, "that he should become, under the new Constitution, the first president of the United States."

Milton saw more clearly than anyone that his brother could be the inevitable hero of the new American Century. It was the end of an era that stretched back to the beginning of recorded history, where power scowled and the men who wielded it strode the earth posing at every moment for the marble statue that would be sculpted of them. Roosevelt's meretricious charm had broken with this past. And Eisenhower was poised to fully embody a new kind of political leadership that fused power and likability: a general who smiled.

Milton had been reaching out to publishers to sell them on the idea. It would capture the reader's attention by building on the "drama in the fact that Ike was born in an honest, pioneer, educated, peace-loving family and grew up to command a mighty allied army." But it would not just be a yarn about

Eisenhower's life. It would be "a book of character and family as an expression of American democracy." And Milton had the perfect man to write it.

Ken Davis was a young, aspiring novelist who had been working as Milton's assistant at Kansas State. Milton had asked him if he was interested in writing Eisenhower's biography, but Davis was reluctant. He thought of himself as more of a novelist and philosopher than hagiographer. But Milton could be very persuasive. He told Davis that he had asked him, and only him, because he thought there should be a book about his brother with "more literary quality and more social and historic significance than the kind of hack jobs which are likely to flood the market later on."

Davis soon found himself at the center of a bidding war between major New York publishers. Doubleday ultimately offered a $4,000 advance. And Davis's literary agent stirred up interest from *Life* and the *Saturday Evening Post* to serialize the finished product.

Doubleday held out the prospect of more money if the book was an authorized biography, but Milton refused. It would be unethical, he told Davis, "for the family to favor publicly one book over another, since this would be lending the General's prestige (if indirectly) to one commercial product over all others, so to speak." Of course, it would also compromise the book's credibility as a work of candid history. If Eisenhower would be presented to America as the soldier of democracy, like George Washington, he could not very well crown himself with that title.

Milton, though, promised plenty of help, including in getting Davis a pass from the army to travel to England. Milton told Davis to have Doubleday make the request for a press pass through official channels. Milton would then privately ensure the request was favorably reviewed. But it was important, Milton emphasized, for things to be seen as going through the ordinary channels.

Eisenhower learned of Davis only when he received a letter from Milton, who promised that everything was being done behind the scenes, and that no one from the family would have any acknowledged connection to the project. But, he asked, should Davis's request come across his desk, "I hope you will give that request, serious consideration."

Eisenhower still preferred to have Butch write his biography. But Milton could be very persuasive.

EISENHOWER'S FAME WAS such that he was invited to be the guest of honor at Sandhurst's so-called passing-out day, the day when cadets graduated and became officers in the British Army. The invitation had been extended by Major General Evelyn Fanshawe, the commander of the Royal Armoured Corps Training Establishment, responsible for training Britain's future tank officers.

At 11:50 sharp, Sandhurst's army band began to play the general salute, and Eisenhower stood on the steps of the neoclassical Old College Building, stiff at attention, giving a proud salute to each squadron of cadets that marched past, in tight rows, black berets, rifles on the left shoulder, and right arms arrow-straight as they whipped up and back in unison. When the band got to the end of the general salute, and the parade was not yet over, it struck up a rendition of the "Stars and Stripes Forever."

Eisenhower then walked down the steps, where he was given the honor of presenting "the bands," the awards given to the top cadets. He shook their hands and gave words of congratulations, each young face looking back at him the way his son's might. Eisenhower then walked back up to the Old College steps to make a few commencement remarks. He had nothing written and there was no podium from which to read a speech if he wanted. There was just a bouquet of microphones, fields of young cadets, and a cameraman attempting to be inconspicuous to his right.

Eisenhower stood with his hands locked behind his back. There was no broad Eisenhower smile. "I'm keenly sensible," he began, "of the honor that General Fanshawe has done me, a foreigner, by asking me down here to witness the Passing Out review of a class from this famous Military College. Yet, on your soil, I do not feel particularly a foreigner or a stranger. Since 1812, there has been no question, no difference arising between our two countries that hasn't been capable of amicable settlement. Within one lifetime, your nation and mine have twice found themselves partners in war.

"In this war, more than any other in history, I think that we find the forces of evil more distinctly arrayed against those of decency and respect for humankind, than ever before. We are on the side of decency, and democracy and liberty." He looked out at their faces and tried to offer words of advice for the challenge ahead of them.

"Young men have this war to win," he told them. "Upon your shoulders rests the greatest responsibility of all." He closed with one of his stock lines: "If I could have my wish as I stand here today, feeling honored as I do on the tribute paid me, I would say this: If I could only meet you all somewhere east of the Rhine . . . and"—he fumbled over his words for a moment—"and renew the acquaintanceship of this pleasant morning. Good luck."

Eisenhower then stepped to the side, and the graduating cadets marched past him, up the steps and into the Old College Building, as the band played the mournful melody of "Auld Lang Syne." He found himself thinking about war's mindless cruelty. All these young men, bravely walking into the Old College Building as if into a shared mausoleum.

Eisenhower thought of Mamie and John, who was less than three months away from his own graduation. It seemed as if something was fundamentally wrong with humanity. "One would feel that man's mere intelligence to say nothing of his spiritual perceptions would find some way of eliminating war," he confided to Mamie. "But man has been trying to do so for many hundreds of years and his failure just adds more reason for pessimism when a man gets really low!"

All anyone could talk about was what a great speech he had given to the cadets at Sandhurst. Kay was mobbed by people asking for a copy, and delighted at their bewilderment when she told them he'd just spoken from the heart. And Eisenhower's face was, of course, all broad smiles as he shook their hands.

But a few days later, Eisenhower wrote to General Marshall asking if an exception could be made to policy. He asked if John could come for a brief visit to England that June for the month of leave that West Point cadets were given upon graduation. Eisenhower made sure to emphasize what a good experience it would be for a young officer. But the truth was, he confessed, "I think, at times, I get a bit homesick."

FOR ALL OF war's senseless cruelty, few would ever understand that one of the most violent military operations in history turned on the outcome of a form of military planning that Butch called the "transatlantic essay contest." By raw volume, the precise number of landing craft Eisenhower would be allocated, and the fate of Operation Anvil, proved to be the most costly in terms of ink, carbon paper, and blood pressure. By March, everyone was fretting over the most recent tables itemizing the quantity and readiness of not just rubber boats, and not even just LSTs, LCIs, and LCTs, but also AGCs, LCMs, LCVPs, LCPs, LCVs, LCSs, LCCs, LCFs, and LCGs, as well as APAs, AKAs, and XAPs.

Things had become so dire in Italy that Jumbo Wilson was demanding to keep both landing craft in the Mediterranean and the long-range fighter aircraft Eisenhower needed in England. As the March 20 deadline for Eisenhower's final recommendation approached, he gently tried to prepare General Marshall to accept the inevitable about Operation Anvil. What remained unclear was what the Combined Chiefs would do.

The Allied essay contests then hit a new low, when the subject turned to Eisenhower's command over the strategic air forces. He had overcome long-standing British opposition to any arrangement that would put Bomber Harris's operations under anything but British control. He would have "responsibility for supervision of air operations out of England."

But then a cable came in from the US Chiefs. They agreed with Eisenhower's proposal except for one word. The proposal gave Eisenhower "supervision" over the air forces, not "command." If US Strategic Air Command was going to be subject to Eisenhower's command, Hap Arnold remained opposed to anything less for Britain's Bomber Command. General Marshall agreed and thought the deal Eisenhower had struck was ridiculous, saying for the record (to ensure that Eisenhower saw it) that "he did not want any commander to supervise in battle, he wanted him to command."

Accusing Eisenhower of "localitis" was demeaning. But accusing him of merely "supervising in battle" was castrating. Eisenhower distanced himself from the word "supervision," and told General Marshall that he was "astonished" the British would be reluctant to "accept the word 'command.'"

The perverse irony was that as long as the semantic distinction between "supervise" and "command" remained the subject of epistolary debate within the Atlantic alliance, Eisenhower had neither. That not only prevented any actual progress on things like the Transportation Plan, but it also forced Eisenhower to endure Monty's condescending tirades about the need for air support, as if Eisenhower disagreed.

ON MONDAY, MARCH 20, Eisenhower had his first commanders in chief meeting in Wide Wing's just-to-the-point conference room, C4-Room 8. They recommended, to no one's surprise, that Operation Anvil be reluctantly canceled. Eisenhower and Beetle then rushed to meet Churchill for lunch in London.

When they arrived, Churchill was irate. Was it the essay contest over landing craft? The essay contest over air command? No. It was the French.

De Gaulle's people had executed Pierre Pucheu, a former Vichy bureaucrat who had switched sides after Eisenhower had invaded North Africa. Henri Giraud, with full support from the Allies, had promised Pucheu amnesty. And here De Gaulle had executed him as a traitor. The trial had been a media circus, with Pucheu denouncing his prosecution in the press as "the first of a series of purges" in De Gaulle's quest to conquer France.

The move had come just as Roosevelt and Churchill were close to agreeing on the directive that would empower Eisenhower to deal officially with the French. The subject had been the focus of its own transatlantic essay contest for the past two months and equally turned on the choice of a single word. Roosevelt proposed saying that Eisenhower "may" coordinate with the French Committee of National Liberation. Churchill wanted it strengthened to "shall."

"May" or "shall." "May" or "shall." Week after week, a dispute over a modal verb had left Eisenhower formally permitted to do nothing except keep open friendly lines of informal communication with Joseph Koenig. With the execution of Pucheu, De Gaulle seemed intent on proving all of Roosevelt's suspicions correct.

Churchill had made promises and knew, or at least thought, that he could work with De Gaulle. Things had been going so well. In September, the Soviet Union had recognized the French Committee as the legitimate government of France, and Churchill's foreign secretary, Anthony Eden, had welcomed the news on the floor of Parliament. Roosevelt's intransigence was increasingly hard for anyone to defend. All sorts of governments-in-exile had been recognized as legitimate, even though they governed little more than a townhouse in London. The French Committee operated from Algiers, which was recognized as French territory, administered much of the French Empire, and maintained an army, a navy, and an air force that was fighting alongside the Allies in Italy.

But maybe Churchill was wrong. It wasn't just Roosevelt who was suspicious of De Gaulle. The US ambassador in Algiers had studied the question closely and concluded that most of the political actors still inside France saw the French Committee as "mediocre men who will be brushed aside and play no role after the liberation of France." He warned that "so far as possible, we should avoid intervention in French affairs, and leave the settlement of those affairs to the French themselves. Our entire experience in intervention in the affairs of other countries, setting up governments, and supervising elections in Central America and the Caribbean has been pretty disastrous. There is no reason to believe it would be any better if we tried it in France."

Backing an exile like De Gaulle could even alienate the resistance fighters who had stayed in France to oppose the Germans with their lives. As soon as the exhilaration of liberation had ceased, France could quickly fall into a civil war. This would be Eisenhower's problem, but he still had no official authority to solve it.

EISENHOWER AND BEETLE then made the half-hour's trip back out to Wide Wing. It was still only Monday. He saw Butch when he got back, who asked how it went. All Eisenhower could say was, "I get so weary of these things."

There was, however, yet more bad news. Letters Eisenhower had written to his mother had been published in a newspaper back in the United States. It was the very thing that had set General Marshall off about Wayne Clark, and it came at the very moment Marshall was chiding him for being content to "supervise" his battles. He wrote a hasty message to Marshall apologizing and disavowing having anything to do with it.

Eisenhower stewed. He had made so much progress on everything that mattered. He had done his duty. But all the things that were out of his control, all the transatlantic essay contests, were taking their cumulative toll. Eisenhower wrote a long memo pouring out his frustrations. There were half a million Germans waiting to kill every Allied soldier who tried to breach the Atlantikwall. If Normandy turned into Anzio, they would lose hundreds of thousands of lives. The Russians would have every reason to cut a separate peace with the Nazis. And Fortress Europe would become the citadel of fascism for a generation.

To have any hope of success, Eisenhower needed certainty, not more goddamned essays. He needed to know how many landing craft they would have. He needed the legal authority to deal with the French. And he urgently needed the military authority to control the air forces. For General Marshall to leave all that unresolved and then nitpick him over the distinction between "supervision" and "command," was frivolous madness.

Eisenhower then concluded, "If a satisfactory answer is not reached I am going to take drastic action, and inform the Combined Chiefs of Staff that unless the matter is settled at once, I will request relief from this command."

The next morning, Eisenhower got word that the essay contest over his control of the air forces had been won. The great transatlantic alliance had found the semantic midpoint between "command" and "supervision" in the word "direction." The strategic air forces would fall under Eisenhower's "direction."

All Eisenhower could do was say "Amen!"

EISENHOWER BEGAN A two-day train tour with Churchill and Omar Bradley of some of the American forces stationed around the United Kingdom. He needed to get away. And it was not just the endless haggling that had taken a toll.

There was new intelligence on the Germans' flying bombs, warning that any moment the Germans could begin raining fire down onto Britain's ports. There was a cryptic message from General Marshall, ordering him to meet with a major by the name of A. V. Peterson, who was being sent to brief him on "certain materials which might be used against your Armies in a landing operation." Then there was the alert from Clayton Bissell, the head of intelligence at the War Department about a package full of documents marked "BIGOT," the classification code word for Operation Overlord, that had been found in a post office in Chicago addressed to a house in the city's German neighborhood. "At least twelve unauthorized civilians known to have had access to contents of package in this country. Five of these known to have been aware of contents."

The first stop on the *Bayonet* was Berkshire, fifty-five miles west of London, at the Newbury Racecourse, where the 101st Airborne Division was training. The start of the war had led to the creation of a new class of soldier, the paratrooper. The Germans had used paratroopers with stunning success in the Blitzkrieg of 1940 and 1941. Airborne operations had been a fascination of General Marshall's since the start of the war, and Eisenhower had been intrigued by their possibilities too.

There was a glamour in being a paratrooper, the kind of glamour that aviators claimed in World War I. It was the glamour that comes from being at the vanguard and having such an astronomically high chance of being killed that to volunteer as a paratrooper was case-closing proof of a man's iron balls, and to survive was case-closing proof of having been selected as an immortal hero by the gods of war. It was enough to make even George Patton queasy when his son—two years behind John at West Point—expressed an interest in becoming a paratrooper.

Churchill led the review through the rows of helmets, punctuated by the occasional beret. The prime minister lumbered a bit and walked with a cane. He had been looking more worn down. But Churchill could still work the crowds like a veteran pol, and like Roosevelt, made a special point of seeking out and graciously giving his regards to Kay, doffing his bowler hat, and proclaiming, "My dear!"

During a presentation of the various weapons they would be taking across the Channel, they were presented with an 81mm mortar.

"This 81, using this new ammo," Eisenhower told Churchill, "has a range of about 3,000 yards."

"Excuse me, sir," a corporal interrupted, "it's 3,250 yards."

Churchill and Eisenhower shared a grin.

"Look, soldier," Eisenhower played, "you wouldn't make a liar out of me in front of the prime minister for 250 yards, would you?"

Up close, it was obvious why so many of the men inside those helmets and berets were convinced of having been divinely chosen for immortality. None of them had been alive very long. They had not yet realized that death did not care if you believed in its permanence. These were the very young men whom General Marshall had attempted to goad Eisenhower into dropping far behind enemy lines just because George Kenney had gotten some ice cream.

When the formal review was complete, the men broke ranks, gathered round, and Churchill stood before a microphone to make a few remarks.

"Soon you will have an opportunity of satisfying your faith in all those inspiring phrases of the American constitution and striking a blow which, however it may leave the world, will, as we are determined, make it a better, broader world for all." They were there, he added, "for a cause, which is greater than either of our two countries have ever fought for in bygone times."

"I thank God you are here," Churchill closed. "I wish you from the bottom of my heart good fortune and success."

Within minutes, C-47s flew overhead in formation, dropping 1,500 paratroopers with gliders towed behind. At a distance, it was a spectacular rain of red, yellow, white, and green parachutes falling to earth like confetti.

A little after six in the evening, Eisenhower, Churchill, and everyone else was back on the *Bayonet*. They were joined the next day by Joe Collins, to inspect some of VII Corps, whom he would be leading across Utah Beach.

VII Corps had some of the new American carbines, and Churchill asked if he could shoot one. In short order, Manton Eddy, the commander of the Ninth Infantry Division, had three targets set up at three distances. Twenty-five yards for Churchill, fifty yards for Eisenhower, and seventy-five yards for Omar Bradley. They each pinched off fifteen rounds, though Eddy was smart enough to have the targets taken away before each man's grouping could be inspected.

The press photographers delighted in the shots of the prime minister and the Supreme Allied Commander drawing up next to one another. Churchill also wanted to try out the tommy gun, and the mood of the day was captured perfectly in a single shot of him holding the tommy gun at his side, insouciant cigar dangling from his mouth, and smirking at the camera like Al Capone.

Churchill again spoke movingly, promising the men that he would "back General Eisenhower with all he had got."

The days had been long, and Churchill made sure that the two nights they all spent on the *Bayonet* together were even longer. There was brandy to be had. There was also champagne that Eisenhower had ordered special for the prime minister. And everyone was invited. Jimmy, Mattie, Kay, even Churchill's daughter Sarah made an appearance.

There was nothing the prime minister relished more than the chance to regale everyone with stories of his adventures, from when he was serving in Egypt or when he was a reporter in Cuba and South Africa. He was also keen to grill Joe Collins about how things were going in the Pacific.

After a few, Churchill took the chance to let loose on why they needed to cancel Operation Anvil. It was like that late-night debate he forced Eisenhower to have at Chequers back in July 1942, when the Allies were divided over whether to cross the Channel or to invade North Africa. Churchill was confident that he would win this debate as well.

Eisenhower, of course, agreed that Operation Anvil should be canceled. But with Omar Bradley, Joe Collins, and so many other Americans within earshot, Eisenhower made sure that everyone could hear him making the case that the US Chiefs would want to hear him making in Operation Anvil's defense.

Churchill always got dour when thinking about the invasion of France. It was easy to forget that the British had been at war for more than four years, a period that included disasters and devastation that made Pearl Harbor look trivial. Churchill, like the British more generally, had become "casualty conscious," and would inevitably start to portend "Channel tides running red with Allied blood," and "beaches choked with the bodies of the flower of American and British manhood." He was, Pug Ismay said, "haunted by the twin horrors of the Dardanelles and Passchendaele."

Churchill just didn't see it. He couldn't understand why the invasion of Normandy would work. It was always the same recurring argument.

"My dear General," Churchill would say, "if by the time snow falls you can have restored her liberty to our beautiful Paris, I shall proclaim to the world that this has been the best conceived and most remarkably successful military operation of all history."

Eisenhower's response was also always the same. "Mr. Prime Minister, I assure you that we are going to be on the borders of Germany by Christmas and if Hitler has any sense whatsoever he will see the hopelessness of his situation and surrender."

To which Churchill would reply, "Ah, it is well for Generals to be optimistic, otherwise they would never win a battle. But what I have said stands."

Eisenhower pressed Churchill on his persistent pessimism. Why voice these doubts, particularly in front of so many people who were committing their lives to its success?

Churchill got a mischievous smile on his face. It was history. "I'd not want history to record that I agreed to this without voicing my doubts."

As they rode together in the dark through the English countryside, Churchill overheard someone say, "Shoot, if you must, this old gray head."

The prime minister looked up, eyes wide, and began to recite "Barbara Frietchie" by John Greenleaf Whittier from the beginning:

Up from the meadows rich with corn,
Clear in the cool September morn,

The clustered spires of Frederick stand
Green-walled by the hills of Maryland.

Churchill then continued, reciting the whole of the poem to its end.

Peace and order and beauty draw
Round thy symbol of light and law;

And ever the stars above look down
On thy stars below in Frederick town!

The *Bayonet* was soon filled with poetry, all recited from memory and all with the gusto that only a few bottles of champagne can muster. Churchill excitedly delivered Bret Harte's "The Reveille."

Hark! I hear the tramp of thousands,
And of armed men the hum;
Lo! a nation's hosts have gathered
Round the quick alarming drum,—
Saying, "Come, Freemen, come!
Ere your heritage be wasted,"
said the quick alarming drum . . .

And after each verse, he would add with the excitement of a schoolboy who had just learned the poem, "The drums! The drums! The drums!"

Charles Portal

CHAPTER 30

EISENHOWER HAD SECURED his authority to "direct" the air forces. But Tooey Spaatz and Bomber Harris made a rear-guard effort to limit what Eisenhower could direct them to do. If they could persuade the Combined Chiefs to disapprove of the Transportation Plan—the targeting of bridges and railways into northern France—then airmen could reclaim their independence to continue Operation Pointblank, because Pointblank would be the only operation they were authorized to carry out.

What made the endless arguments with the air forces so tedious was that Eisenhower was being forced to argue over the future with people who had nothing but contempt for the past and who confused the clarity of their vision with the inevitability of a future world that they lacked the humility to see would be much messier than any grand theory might predict. General Conner, who revived Eisenhower's deep respect for the lessons of history, would always say, "War is essentially friction and change. The only way of avoiding changes in a plan is to plan to stay home." Eisenhower would come to understand that his esteemed mentor had missed something with this aphorism. For as complicated as war became, "The only constant is man." And if there was one thing that could be predicted about people, it was that they will always find ways to make every grand theory about what they will do look ridiculous.

Strategic bombing was a grand theory of warfare that made perfect sense when looking at maps and charts. If war could be reduced to a handful of industrial variables, then bombing those numbers down to zero would work. But if war was determined by the ingenuity of people bent on survival, then winning on paper was worth as much as the paper those maps and charts were printed upon.

The argument over Operation Pointblank culminated in a showdown upon Eisenhower's return to Wide Wing. It was a grand conference, chaired by Britain's Air Chief, Charles Portal, at which Spaatz, Harris, Tedder, Leigh-Mallory, and Eisenhower could plead their cases to verdict.

Like Henry VIII on the throne at Westminster, Portal said little at first. Tedder made the opening case, being sure to start with points on which everyone agreed. The biggest among those: the need for air superiority. Those aspects of Operation Pointblank whose purpose was to ground the Luftwaffe would continue no matter what. The only question was what they should be using the Allies' strategic bombing capacity to do. Tedder said the best and only realistic option was the Transportation Plan.

The goal, Tedder emphasized, anticipating Spaatz's objections, was not to "prevent all traffic getting through." Rather, the objective was to disrupt and "canalize" Germany's reinforcements. Without hampering German reinforcements in this way, Tedder was convinced that they would have "no chance of success."

Portal then spoke. The Transportation Plan, Portal said, "would have a most serious effect on the efficiency of the enemy railway system. It was essential, however, to be certain that what was left would not be adequate for the amount of movement which the enemy would find necessary in the first few weeks of the battle." Assume, for example, they succeeded in reducing railway traffic to 20 or 30 percent of its former amount. The Germans would still have plenty of capacity to move what they needed. Was that really worth the investment, and the significant diversion away from Operation Pointblank?

Assuming the intelligence estimates were right, Tedder said he was "fully convinced the plan would have a military effect." The goal, Tedder reiterated, was to slow everything down.

Eisenhower echoed Tedder's basic point that anything was better than nothing. "The first five or six weeks of Overlord," he said, "would be the most critical for the Allied armies, and it was essential that we should take every possible step to ensure they got ashore, and stayed ashore. The greatest contribution I could imagine the Air Force making to the same was that they should hinder enemy movement."

No one disagreed with that, interjected Major General John Kennedy, the man Alan Brooke had sent as his representative. The question was whether the operation was "too ambitious." Did they really think they could disrupt the entire northern European railway system? And if they couldn't, he added, "if it did not come off completely, then the whole effort might've been wasted." Look at Italy. They had been bombing Italian railroads day and night. Why would the effort be any more effective in France?

"Everything I have read," Eisenhower said, defending Tedder, "has convinced me that apart from the attacks on the Luftwaffe, the Transportation Plan was the only one which offered a reasonable chance of the Air Force making an important contribution to the land battle during the first vital weeks of Overlord; in fact, I do not believe that there was any real alternative."

Tooey Spaatz took that as his opening to speak up. There was an alternative, Spaatz announced. He had circulated a memo before the meeting. He called his alternative to the Transportation Plan, "the Oil Plan."

As laid out in Spaatz's memo, there were twenty-seven oil refineries and other processing facilities that accounted for "approximately 80% of total synthetic production and 60% of readily reusable refining capacity." They were poorly defended and vulnerable to attack. The loss of oil would hit the Germans' blood supply, and if the Russians succeeded in cutting off the industrial areas in Ploeşti, hitting Germany's western oil refineries could bring the whole war machine to a halt. By hitting just twenty-seven targets hard enough, Spaatz insisted, they could win the whole war from the air.

The Oil Plan, Portal said, intrigued, was worth considering. He turned to the representative from the Ministry of Economic Warfare. What effect would it have?

There would be a 25 percent reduction in German oil capacity, he estimated, in about six months.

Six months?

"There would certainly be some effect noticeable in the west for five months after the plan began to be put into effect."

So, Portal said, "this showed conclusively that the Oil Plan would not help Overlord in the first few critical weeks. It was, rather, a longer-term plan, which might have greater overall effects on the course of the war as a whole than the Transportation Plan, but it would be six months before these were felt appreciably." Couldn't they just postpone the implementation of the Oil Plan, Portal asked, until after Overlord?

"I entirely agree," Eisenhower said, the jaws of victory closing down. "The Oil Plan should be considered as soon as the first critical situation and Overlord has passed."

Spaatz began to flak, throwing up a series of practical objections to the Transportation Plan that Tedder answered until Spaatz was out of ammunition.

Portal had a final question, though. The targets for the Transportation Plan, the rail facilities and the like, were in cities. Had they thought about civilian casualties? "This was naturally a matter of some concern to His Majesty's Government," Portal said, "and the Cabinet ought to be given an opportunity to consider the implications." Perhaps they could warn the French?

Eisenhower didn't have an answer. But he promised that he would take the issue seriously as they began to implement the attacks on France. The Transportation Plan, under Eisenhower's direction, was a go.

Then, that evening, Eisenhower got a cable from General Marshall. The US Chiefs had finally come to a decision on landing craft. Eisenhower would get the twenty-four LSTs and other landing craft he had requested for the Normandy invasion. They would begin the voyage up from the Mediterranean within the week. But the US Chiefs wanted Operation Anvil to be postponed, not canceled. And to sweeten the deal, Ernest King had agreed to replace what was poached from the Mediterranean with landing craft that had been earmarked for the Pacific. The only condition was that the British agree to set a firm date of July 10 for Operation Anvil.

It was another moment for Eisenhower to say amen. If the deal held, Eisenhower would get the landing craft needed to give Operation Overlord a real punch. And even postponed by a month, Operation Anvil would still have nearly all its desired effect. The mere presence of yet another Allied invasion force building up in the Mediterranean would compel the Germans to continue to divide their strength.

By then, Eisenhower knew enough to never take comfort in anything being finally settled. But there was something invigorating about the war. Even when people disagreed, there was a shared sense of purpose. What they were doing mattered, and that made everything seem brighter. It drove Eisenhower to want to visit even the most far-flung corners of the United Kingdom in order to meet the young men and women who shared that common endeavor with him.

Carl "Tooey" Spaatz

CHAPTER 31

A ROUTINE DEVELOPED for Eisenhower's trips out on the hustings. If it was far, Eisenhower, Mattie, and Kay would load into the *Bayonet*, sometimes with Butch or Jimmy. Kay would make sure the Packard was put aboard with care, and they would chug along the British countryside. Kay would drive with Mattie in the front seat as navigator between the various posts, leaving Eisenhower to sprawl out in the back and think about whatever the passing scenery brought to mind.

They would make these trips even in the cold. Even in the rain. It was especially important then because, Eisenhower had come to realize, the whole point was showing these young men that he was really there. He had initially thought these reviews were self-indulgent, and certainly for many other generals he knew, they were. But he hoped that his willingness to be there with them, even in the cold, even in the rain, made them feel safer.

On one particularly grueling trip, Eisenhower, Mattie, and Kay ventured south, driving 120 miles in a single day to visit various components of Gee Gerow's V Corps. Among them were the First Infantry Division, the Big Red One.

An undercover officer had infiltrated the Big Red One, dressed as "Private Arthur Goodwin," to report on what being a replacement in one of its units was like. Among his principal discoveries was that the army's efforts at civic education were not being received as planned.

A captain had conducted an "Army Talk" titled "The Nature of a Free Man." When the captain asked at the end, "What will you do when you hear there's an armistice?" the typical responses ranged from "go home and get drunk for six months" to "go home and kiss the Statue of Liberty."

"Do you mean," the captain had asked, "after seeing your buddies killed, you're not going to do something not to have to go through all this again?"

The responses again ranged from "Let's line up them Germans and mow them down" to "I say lead them—don't push them."

Private "Goodwin" was taken to a Nissen hut that formed the men's barracks. The walls were papered with cartoons and pinups from *Yank* magazine and hand-written combat glossaries: "*Halt! Wir da?*—Halt! Who's there?" "*Ruhe!*—Shut up!"

In another Nissen hut, Private Goodwin was warned, "You're in the infantry now, brother. There's a coffin built and waiting for you." He asked what that meant and the soldier replied, "Haven't you heard? There's going to be an invasion. In two weeks. And we're going to be the first to hit the foul beach!"

When the men weren't being fatalistic about being killed, they were celebrating their inevitable triumph in France and indulging in the spoils of war.

"How do you say 'I love you?' in French?" one asked.

"All the French I know is *beaucoup vino*."

It was cold and rainy as Eisenhower mingled with the Big Red One himself. And with all the speech-making in the misty English winter, his never-ending cold flared up again and his voice started growing hoarse.

Gee Gerow made it worth his while, though, treating Eisenhower, Mattie, and Kay to a delicious dinner of wild pheasant. One of Gee's men had a habit of poaching game in the nearby woods.

"You know you're not supposed to do this," Gee confessed, "but every now and then, he does it and there's nothing I can do about it."

"If he can shoot Germans as well as he can pheasants," Eisenhower joked, "we are bound to win the war."

Eisenhower had been looking forward to seeing Gee. His return to London had given them the chance to spend real time with one another for the first time in many years, really since the days of Club Eisenhower back in the early 1930s.

Their friendship had been strained after that. When Eisenhower shipped off to the Philippines with MacArthur, Mamie had stayed behind and continued their old Washington social life with the Gerows. Mamie's refusal to come to Manila had been one of the major rifts in their marriage, and the resentments came to a boil when Gee's wife died of cancer. Within a few months, Eisenhower was hearing all sorts of rumors in Manila about Gee and Mamie being seen out together and returning home to the Wyoming alone.

When Mamie finally did come to Manila, Eisenhower confronted her, saying, "I gather I have grounds for a divorce, if I want one." Precisely how intimate Mamie and Gee's friendship had been remained unsaid. Though Mamie was unusually upset when she heard that Gee had remarried a few months later. "That rascal!" she had said bitterly.

While Eisenhower was stagnating in the Philippines, Gee's career blossomed. He ascended the ranks to the point that in 1941, General Marshall selected him to run the War Plans Division at the precise moment the United States giant was waking from its slumber. Gee modernized the army's planning process to meet a real world that looked very different than it did the last time the army had fought a war.

After Eisenhower left for the Philippines, they had not really seen each other or spoken for almost a decade. But then, Eisenhower had picked up that fateful phone call from Beetle.

It was less than a week after Pearl Harbor. One of Gee's deputies had died in a plane crash, and Eisenhower was ordered to Washington to take his place. Eisenhower had been the chief of staff for the Third Army at the time.

"How long?" Eisenhower had asked.

"I don't know," Beetle said. "Come on."

"What kind of duty? Office duty where?"

"The Chief says for you to get on a plane and get up here."

Eisenhower left that day with Mickey in tow. All the planes had been grounded due to cloud cover, and so Eisenhower arm-twisted a lieutenant into flying them from San Antonio to Dallas, where they boarded a train that got them to Washington two days later.

It was a Sunday morning when Eisenhower arrived, and General Marshall had engaged in no pleasantries. He just glowered at Eisenhower and said, "Look, there are two things we have got to do. We've got to do our best in the Pacific and we have got to win this whole war. Now how are we going to do it? Now that is going to be your problem."

Wayne Clark had recommended Eisenhower for the job. Marshall did not really know Eisenhower, except for his unappealing connection to Douglas MacArthur. But Marshall kept a list of officers whose names had come to his attention, names he would also strike off when they came to his attention for the wrong reasons. Eisenhower's name had been on Marshall's good list as among the people who stood out during some maneuvers the army had conducted in Louisiana the previous year. And so, Marshall had Beetle make the call.

Patton always teased Eisenhower with the nickname "Divine Destiny," or "Destiny" for short. It was his backhanded way of suggesting that Eisenhower had leapfrogged him through the grace of chance as opposed to merit. But in the case of Gee's and Eisenhower's parallel careers, it was true. Had the dice of the universe flown ever so slightly higher, it would have been Eisenhower impressing Gee on a drizzly day in April with some wild pheasant.

Barely two months after that fateful call from Beetle, Gee was pushed out and Eisenhower was promoted to take his job in the rechristened Operations Division. It was Eisenhower's first appearance in the *New York Times* since the brief mention of his being steamrolled by Jim Thorpe. He was introduced to the world in the paper of record as the man who "worked closely with General MacArthur in planning the defense moves put into effect by the Philippine defenders since the Japanese invasion." This was two days before Roosevelt would order MacArthur to flee the archipelago.

Gee's departure had nothing to do with his talent for the job. He had arguably done more faster with less than any other man to hold the position. He just happened to be on the wrong side of destiny.

On November 27, 1941, when Japan broke off peace negotiations, General Marshall had been away from the War Department observing army maneuvers in North Carolina. That left Gee in charge, and he had sent a message out to commanders in the Pacific: "Japanese future action unpredictable but hostile action possible at any moment."

"Report: Department alerted to prevent sabotage," had been the reply from the commander in Hawaii.

Gee scrawled his initials on the reply perfunctorily, as he did to scores of messages every day. He hadn't noticed that the commander in Hawaii had failed to appreciate the urgency of the situation.

Then on December 6, 1941, two messages to the Japanese embassy in Washington were intercepted. The first notified the embassy of an urgent fourteen-point message to deliver to the American secretary of state. The first thirteen points were decoded and translated that evening. It was a long inventory of Japan's grievances.

Beetle had been in the office that evening and told the courier that General Marshall was out for the night. If it was urgent, the rule was to hand-deliver the message to Marshall at home. But since the rest of the message had not yet been decoded, Beetle told the courier to put it in the safe, so that Marshall could see it in the morning.

The courier warned Beetle, "It's very important."

But Beetle told him to wait.

The fourteenth part of the message arrived at eight a.m. the next morning, when General Marshall was out on his usual Sunday horseback ride. Then at nine a.m., two more intercepts came in, directing the Japanese ambassador to deliver the fourteen-point message at one p.m. and to destroy their cyphers as well as all secret documents.

Gee had called Marshall at home alerting him of the need to come in, and Marshall got to the office around eleven thirty. When he read all that had transpired, he immediately saw that this meant war and that Japan was planning something for one o'clock. He scrawled out an alert that was sent just before noon, but it was too late. Zeros were already closing in on Honolulu.

Gee willingly took the fall for the army's failures before Pearl Harbor. Politicians needed a goat, and General Marshall was too indispensable for the buck to stop with him. It could just as easily have been Beetle. But it had been Gee's initials on that message from the commander in Hawaii, meaning that it was Gee who found himself repeatedly called to explain his failure to see Pearl Harbor coming.

It was something that could only be called an oversight in the hindsight hunt for scapegoats. Eisenhower's initials made it onto dozens, if not hundreds, of pieces of inane bureaucratic effluvia every day. But Gee became a political vulnerability, and so, he was sent out to the field. On merit that overcame his luck, Gee had risen back up. Now he was a front-line commander in the battle that could begin the end of the war.

BACK IN LONDON, Churchill invited Eisenhower and Beetle to lunch. Conversation dwelled on the political constraints that seemed to frustrate their ability to achieve their common endeavor. As large a figure as Churchill cut on the world stage, he was still a parliamentary politician and had just called a controversial confidence vote on amendments to a law guaranteeing pay equality for teachers. He won the vote overwhelmingly and was pleased with himself. The press, though, was mocking the prime minister for tying such a consequential decision to such a trivial piece of legislation, calling him Cromwellian for treating every point of disagreement as a mortal showdown.

Churchill was unembarrassed. "On the eve of the invasion," he said, "it would be foolhardy to let people over the world believe the government of Britain was hanging only by a thread."

Eisenhower didn't get it. Why not just call a confidence vote on the war?

But Eisenhower was being naive. Churchill had easily survived a no-confidence vote on the war back in July 1942, but it was still embarrassing. And after two more years of war, his opponents were stronger. With things in Italy, and so many Americans overstaying their welcome, why on earth would he force his backbenchers to take a vote on that?

Churchill's newest maneuver, unseemly as it might have been, had insulated his government from any serious political attack for the foreseeable future. With any luck, it could take him through the end of the war without having to face the voters.

Eisenhower had his own political problems. Upon returning from his trip to see Gee Gerow, he had gotten wind of a magazine story in *Collier's* predicting catastrophe at Normandy. It went into graphic detail about the hazards of the Atlantikwall and then mused on the probability of disaster. "It is an axiom of amphibious warfare that casualties increase relatively to the number of troops landed. If we land 200,000 men on our initial assault, we must expect well over 50 percent casualties. If we land a million men, the percentage of casualties will rise sharply."

The article fed into growing political opposition in the United States to investing any more blood or treasure in Europe. Japanese advances on the Asian continent were provoking headlines like "Demand to Beat 'Japan First' Sweeping the Nation." A Gallup poll showed that most Americans now doubted that Eisenhower would, in fact, win the war in '44. And Senator Albert Chandler, the chair of the Military Affairs Committee, promised congressional action to force Roosevelt to turn away from the European sinkhole that had been sold to America by "British propagandists."

Churchill grinned as he heard all this. "Sometimes," he mused, "it would be advantageous to have the powers of a Hitler."

The issue, though, was serious. The political tide was stiffening Ernest King's spine when it came to the negotiations over landing craft. Eisenhower was adamant that the British Chiefs needed to agree to set a deadline on

Operation Anvil. While the landing craft for Operation Overlord was no longer an emergency, they still needed to ensure that German defenses in France were divided.

Churchill showed Eisenhower a draft telegram from the British Chiefs. They had agreed. They had finally reached a deal.

Churchill had also agreed to give in on the French question. Eisenhower had made no secret of the fact that he thought De Gaulle was his only viable partner in France. And whatever concerns there might be about De Gaulle himself, the intelligence on Koenig was all positive. Confident, then, that in Eisenhower's hands the word "may" would pose no serious risk to Churchill's longer-term interest in a Gaullist France, Churchill begrudgingly agreed. He would drop his demand for "shall." All that was left was for the Soviets to sign off.

Leaving 10 Downing Street, Eisenhower was buoyed by more good news that had come in from the War Department. After an investigation, the spill of the highly classified BIGOT documents in Chicago was under control.

Eisenhower took the momentary quieting of the "eternal pound, pound, pound," to respond to letters, even from very old and out-of-touch friends who had suddenly found themselves thinking of him. He wrote to Mamie about John. And he wrote to John, telling him not to fret too much about what his specialization in the army would be and—between the lines—apologizing for riding him about it during their brief time together after New Year's, since he would always be proud of him no matter what.

The biggest decision Eisenhower had to make, at least for a few days, was to grant Butch his request for a two- or three-month tour aboard a command ship. Butch aspired to play a direct role in the invasion on D-Day. And so, Eisenhower begrudgingly agreed.

But then, Eisenhower got a letter from Churchill, raising an issue that had not come up at their lunch a few days earlier. There had been a cabinet meeting about the Transportation Plan. "In view of the fact that scores of thousands of French civilians, men, women and children, would lose their lives or be injured," Churchill told him, the issue required more deliberation.

The question had been referred to the Defence Committee. The Foreign Office and State Department would need to come to agreement on the diplomatic implications. And Churchill would send a personal message to Roosevelt. "Would it not," he added, "also be necessary to consult General de Gaulle and the French National Committee of Liberation?"

Eisenhower worked with Tedder on the reply. They tried to play up the prime minister's oft-repeated worries about the Channel running red with blood. The Transportation Plan, he insisted "made feasible an operation which might otherwise be considered extremely hazardous, if not foolhardy." Eisenhower did not gainsay the risks to the French, but he thought the people opposed to the Transportation Plan, like Spaatz and Harris, had ulterior motives to exaggerate those risks. And even if they were right, "the French people are now slaves. Only a successful Overlord can free them. No one has a greater stake in the success of that operation than have the French."

There was nothing else Eisenhower could do, except go for an afternoon ride with Kay in Richmond Park to clear his head.

Arthur Peterson

CHAPTER 32

IT WAS NOT unusual, and not always unwelcome, for General Marshall to send people to advise Eisenhower. There had been Cooke and Hull to advise on the landing craft negotiations. There had been the air force generals sent over to persuade him of Marshall's airborne scheme.

April was full of such visitors. There was General William Borden from the Ordinance and Chemical Warfare Service. Borden had spent the summer developing mortars and rockets with special fuses that made them more effective against pillboxes. In the battle for Kwajalein, he had found that the only effective way of clearing out pillboxes was to use 4.2-inch mortar rounds full of high explosive and white phosphorus. One of Borden's newest creations was the T15 90mm antitank gun, which could punch through steel as if breezing through a paper target. Eisenhower asked when he could get one of these new "super guns," and Borden said they would be available that summer. Eisenhower shook his head. He planned to "have the Germans licked by then."

There was the undersecretary of state, Edward Stettinius, who came to London to discuss the planning for postwar Europe. Eisenhower tried to persuade Stettinius to soften Roosevelt's demand for "unconditional surrender" to help him get the Germans licked in the first place. Without the promise of a future for "good Germans" and the not-so-good-but-not-evil

Germans, the whole continent would become as bitterly fought as the Marshall Islands had been.

Then there was the visit from the assistant secretary of war, John McCloy, and General Joseph McNarney, which Eisenhower took to be a "tidiness inspection" from General Marshall. Their arrival happened to coincide with Exercise Thunderclap, a daylong presentation of the invasion planning by Eisenhower's commanders in chief. Monty gave a two-hour presentation that played to Eisenhower's sensibility by emphasizing the efforts of the "Allied Team" and Eisenhower's role as "captain of the team." The mood was collaborative, which certainly made Eisenhower look tidy. Even Churchill came by to show his support, using his time to remind everyone to be aggressive so that things would not stall as they had in Anzio. "This is an invasion," Churchill said. "Not a creation of a fortified beachhead." Churchill relished the thought of how the "Germans will suffer very heavy casualties when our band of brothers gets among them."

Exercise Thunderclap broke up just before six at night, and all the VIPs went for a late dinner at one of the Hill Street restaurants in Mayfair. McNarney was, as always, eager to find fault and all but blamed Eisenhower for the mess in Italy, accusing him of failing to set up an efficient system for replacing casualties. Patton, who also enjoyed the gourmet dinner, could not resist the chance to pile on. Replacement was key to victory. "A shortage of 10% in personnel reduces the effectiveness of a division about 20% and as the losses increase, the efficiency decreases in almost geometrical ratio." Under his breath, Georgie seemed to imply this would all be obvious if Eisenhower had ever spent time commanding a battlefield.

This touched a very raw nerve. The main reason there were manpower problems in Italy was because of the uncertainty over Operation Anvil and nearly every day, Eisenhower plodded through round after round of negotiations, eking out incremental agreements at each turn to settle things once and for all. Maybe the replacement problem would not be so difficult, Eisenhower said, if the Combined Chiefs had not been "off again, on again, gone again, Finnigan" on Operation Anvil.

Then there was the visit of John Lucas, who had been relieved of command in Anzio. He told a very different story about its failures and put together a presentation complete with charts, maps, and an hourlong lecture he called "The End Run That Was Blocked." As Lucas described it, the Anzio campaign was half baked from the beginning. The Allies lost the initiative because they could not build up fast enough to match the Germans' mobilization of reinforcements. They had also massively underestimated how dug in the Germans were. The battle for Cassino, he said, had become like Verdun. They had bombed the city to near annihilation, but it did nothing, because the Germans had an extensive system of tunnels where they took refuge during the bombing, only to come back out to fight as soon as it was over.

When Lucas was done, a violent argument broke out over who was to blame, with some accusing Lucas of just having lost his nerve. But Eisenhower thought his insights were invaluable and asked him to make the same presentation throughout the United Kingdom, particularly to Omar Bradley and George Patton. Mistakes were inevitable. But they were inexcusable only if they were made for a second time.

LUCAS NOTWITHSTANDING, THE parade of mandatory visitors was rarely a good use of Eisenhower's time. There were always urgent new problems that he did not even know he previously had. And none loomed larger than the increasingly dire picture of what lay on the other side of the English Channel.

The British had secretly developed a machine called Colossus that could decode the radio traffic sent between Berlin and Field Marshal Gerd von Rundstedt, Hitler's overall commander for France, Belgium, and Holland. In the middle of March, the British finally agreed to share these intercepts. Code-named "Ultra," they gave Eisenhower a tap on the man on the other side of the Channel.

One of the first messages deciphered was a report back to Hitler warning that the long-awaited Allied invasion was imminent. The good news was that Operation Fortitude had convinced Rundstedt that the main target was Calais. The bad news was that he had also concluded that Eisenhower planned to land on Normandy.

In response, the Nazis were submerging more obstacles along the beaches that limited his options for how and when to attack. There were stakes prickling up like pikemen and "Element C" obstacles, massive steel tangles that could pin down a tank or gore through the belly of a landing craft overhead. There were the Hedgehogs, the Tetrahedra, and the I beams planted deep into the sand like rows of teeth. And scattered about all these steel claws were land mines to skin anyone who tried to slip through.

Complicating all this further, there was a twenty-two-foot differential between high and low tides. In an ideal world, the Allies could land at high tide, so they could get deeper inland before exposing their men to enemy fire. The German obstacles made that impossible, since the sappers from the Allied engineer battalions couldn't do anything about obstacles that were submerged below two feet of water. They would have to come in at low tide. But at low tide, the beach extended an additional half a mile out to sea, leaving the men storming it more exposed to enemy fire and more vulnerable as the water behind them rose at an average rate of two inches every ten minutes until high tide.

THE DAY AFTER his tidiness inspection by Joseph McNarney, Eisenhower dutifully met with a man General Marshall had sent, evidently about beach obstacles, with the admonition that "This matter is of the highest order of secrecy." It was a Saturday and Eisenhower made it his last meeting of the afternoon.

A rather bookish-looking major in his early thirties had come to Wide Wing and introduced himself as Arthur Peterson from Chicago. The only thing initially remarkable about the man was that he was just a major. There was no shortage of lesser generals eager to tell Eisenhower what he needed to know, especially something so important and secretive that Eisenhower had to speak to him alone.

Peterson had nothing to offer on the Tetrahedra or the Element C obstacles. His area of expertise was rather different. The need for secrecy was due to his working for a special research program the president had created back in 1942 called the Laboratory for the Development of Substitute Materials, or the "Manhattan District" due to its origins at Columbia University. Some just called it the Manhattan Project.

Physicists, Peterson was keen to explain, were now in universal agreement that all matter in the universe was made up of atoms and that atoms were composed of a positively charged nucleus surrounded by a cloud of negatively charged electrons. The electron cloud was the source of an atom's chemical properties: Why is a lead bullet softer than a copper one? Why does TNT explode? But when it came to the basic things—questions like Why is lead also *heavier* than copper?—those were the properties of the nucleus.

Over the past generation, physicists had revealed the architecture of the nucleus and decoded the invisible forces that in any previous century would have been damned as witchcraft. When released, some of those forces could be thousands of times more powerful than TNT. Others were more mysterious.

German physicists had been at the forefront of the study of the atom for decades, and once the war started, Hitler brought those men together in a special project of their own, called the Uranium Club. A leader of the club was Werner Heisenberg. Born in 1901, the year the first Nobel Prize in Physics was awarded to the German scientist Wilhelm Röntgen, for the discovery of X-rays, Heisenberg won the Nobel himself at the age of thirty for unraveling the mysteries of the subatomic quantum world. Under Heisenberg's direction, the Germans had started seeing success in large-scale experiments with self-sustaining nuclear reactions. And in September 1941, Heisenberg had met with his old mentor, the Danish physicist Niels Bohr, in Copenhagen, where he revealed how close the Germans were to building an atomic bomb.

The British had been hard at work on their own research into nuclear weapons, code-named "Tube Alloys," which became an Allied joint venture once Roosevelt signed off on the Manhattan Project. As it happened, Niels Bohr, whose mother was Jewish, had been secreted into Britain in 1943 and was now in the United States with Albert Einstein, Enrico Fermi, Edward Teller, John von Neumann, and dozens of other genius refugees from Hitler's anti-Semitism, who were putting their collective mind toward turning nature's most fundamental forces into a bomb that could consume cities.

Such a bomb had been a speculation of science fiction since Eisenhower was still a cadet at West Point. In *The World Set Free*, H. G. Wells imagined a future in which nuclear weapons were so devastating that humanity finally came to its senses, abandoned war, and lived in eternal peace. There was no room for techno-optimism, however, if such a weapon fell into the hands of the Nazis, who were always touting their newest "secret weapons" for world domination. The week before Pearl Harbor, newspapers in Fascist Spain had heralded the power of Germany's secret weapons, and in particular "la bomba atómica," that would secure victory for the eternal Reich.

Eisenhower had left the War Department for London before the Manhattan Project came under the army's supervision in August 1942. The following month, though, General Marshall had told him to develop plans to target the Norsk Hydro electric plant in the Norwegian town of Vemork. The details were deliberately vague, but he told Eisenhower that the plant was producing heavy water, a crucial precursor to "the development of fission bombs based upon uranium." Eisenhower was assured that "our own scientists are making progress along this line," but warned that "whichever nation can put fission bombs of this character in use will have a destructive agent which may determine the final outcome of this war."

By the time Eisenhower had returned to London, the Norsk Hydro plant had been driven out of operation thanks to the efforts of the British Special Operations Executive and a healthy dose of American strategic bombing. Eisenhower had no need to be kept abreast of the nuclear arms race while leading the campaign in the Mediterranean. But now here was Peterson, the first direct confirmation that nuclear weapons were real, that the Germans might have them, and that they presented dangers H. G. Wells could scarcely have imagined.

Peterson explained that he had come to the United Kingdom as part of something called Operation Peppermint, and that his expertise was not so much in the creation of nuclear bombs. His specialty was poisons—radiological poisons.

"It is possible for a new type of weapon to be used by the Germans before or during the invasion," Peterson warned. "The weapon is the use of materials having radiations similar to those of radium." Peterson handed Eisenhower a report he had written: "Manual on Use of Radioactive Materials in Warfare." Twenty-eight typed pages, it contained a brief master class on the principles of atomic radiation, complete with a diagram depicting Niels Bohr's model of the atom.

The first study of the problem had been released just days after the attack on Pearl Harbor. Scientists working for the National Academy of Sciences hypothesized that the byproducts from even small nuclear reactions could form a poison capable of contaminating large areas. Then in the summer of 1943, the head of the Manhattan Project warned General Marshall that, given what was known about the Uranium Club's progress, "it would be possible for the Germans to produce large quantities of radioactive material (with an effective life of about 20 days) some time in 1944." If they did, they could drop radiological dust on London like a poison gas.

Peterson and other Manhattan Project scientists had conducted experiments to assess the viability of radiological poisons in battlefield conditions. The good news was that they need not worry too much about radiological bombs falling on London. It turned out radiological materials did not lend themselves to being dispersed in the air at lethal concentrations like a poison gas. The bad news, though, was that they were extremely effective as defensive weapons. Sprinkled on the ground, they could form a subatomic minefield that could not be seen, smelled, heard, tasted, or felt. They left no burns. They caused no immediate pain. But they guaranteed death, disability, and if nothing else, panic.

Peterson was full of new jargon. "The roentgen," he explained, "is the commonly used unit of radiation absorbed, and a person exposed for 24 hours to 1 gram of radium at a distance of ten feet (in air) is said to have been exposed to one roentgen." What was generally called radiation was two different kinds of energy ray, gamma and beta. Beta waves were like fire and could leave skin lesions that refused to heal, but only at exposures of 3,000 to 6,000 roentgens. The gamma rays, though, could kill at just a tenth of that.

Experiments showed that infinitesimal amounts of radioactive dust spread over soft ground produced potentially lethal concentrations of gamma rays up to three feet in the air. "One day's exposure (100 roentgens to the whole body) would result in temporary incapacitation, a lesser period of exposure in incapacitation to a lesser degree, and one week's exposure in death." No one would notice at first. The effect was slow and insidious. Those exposed would feel fatigued. Their blood cell counts would fall. Their skin would become red and then begin to tan, like after a sunburn. Hair would fall out. The sweat glands would fail, leaving the skin dry and cracked. Fingernails would become brittle. Men would become sterile.

"There is no accurate way of estimating what the Germans may be able to do or what progress they have made along these lines," Peterson concluded. "It is definitely established, however, that they have known for several years of the processes used to manufacture these materials and that they have gone to considerable effort to obtain certain materials required in their production." Chemical companies connected to the German government, such as Auergesselschaft and Roges mbH, had been purchasing hundreds of tons of uranium.

According to Peterson, "no moral issue will influence the use of these materials as a weapon on the part of our present enemy." From his perspective, it was simply a matter of capability. Could the Germans get enough material and deploy it effectively?

"Our intelligence, as well as that of the British, believe that the manufacture of radioactive materials on a sufficient scale is improbable," he concluded. "However, the problem cannot be ignored."

But what did "improbable" mean? Lots of improbable things happened.

Experts inside the Manhattan Project estimated that the odds were about 10 percent. That was better than the odds of getting two pair in a hand of poker.

What could be done? Could the sappers do something to clear the radiation while they were clearing the mines and beach obstacles?

Peterson's experiments had found that flushing a contaminated surface with water had shown some promising effect, at least so long as the surface was smooth and hard.

But what about sand?

"No decontaminating methods are known."

Was there anything that could be done to protect the men? Special clothing?

"No effective protective clothing for personnel seems possible of development."

The only effective way of protecting anyone was to identify radiation as quickly as possible and to avoid it. That was what Operation Peppermint was all about. Getting the equipment and knowledge in the right places to determine whether and where the Germans had used radiological weapons.

Peterson explained that there were two known ways to detect radiation in the environment. The simplest was photographic film. When exposed to radiation, even when still inside the can, film turned as black as if someone had taken a picture of the sun. The other was expensive, delicate radiation detectors.

Peterson revealed to Eisenhower that four officers who had been assigned to innocuous-seeming jobs throughout the European Theater of Operations since December were secretly operatives for Operation Peppermint. They had radiation detectors and were on the lookout for indications of radiation. Every time a German bomb dropped on the United Kingdom, one of them was apt to try to do a test. There were also fifteen hundred lightproof, airtight canisters of film distributed around Great Britain to be developed at regular intervals in search of any telltale blackening.

As the Supreme Allied Commander, Eisenhower had the discretion to inform those—and only those—who he believed needed to know. Operation Peppermint was not something to be written about, only spoken about. The matter was so sensitive that Peterson had to get the personal signature of anyone who had viewed the documents he carried.

THE FUNNY THING was that just a few days before, Everett Hughes had come back with some eyes-and-ears recommendations. Eisenhower was always looking for unvarnished advice and had asked Hughes to sniff around for problems that people would be scared to bring to him directly. A big one,

Everett found, was stovepiping. There were so many components with so much overlapping responsibility that people felt the need to make themselves indispensable by hoarding information. Everett recommended that more information be pushed down "to the lower echelons and to the men who are going to have to do the work."

Now Eisenhower was discovering that he had been stovepiped. There were men under his command whose true mission had been kept from him. Jacob Devers had been orally briefed on these men's "special additional duties" before he was sent to the Mediterranean and had never thought to inform Eisenhower. Even Edward Betts, the judge advocate general with whom Eisenhower spoke every week about the latest courts-martial, had been brought in on the secret a few weeks earlier, when the American ambassador in London needed legal advice on how to discreetly buy uranium from the Belgian Congo.

Eisenhower contemplated what to do with his newest secret. He told Peterson to brief Beetle as well as his heads of intelligence (G-2), John Whiteley, and operations (G-3), Harold "Pink" Bull. Eisenhower did so, knowing that informing Whiteley altered the nature of the secrecy problem. Whiteley was British.

The British, it turned out, wanted information about the Manhattan Project and Operation Peppermint distributed no further in the absence of any specific intelligence indicating the Germans were preparing to use such weapons. Eisenhower and Beetle conferred on what they should do. It was something they should at least tell Monty; maybe Omar Bradley, Jim Collins, and Gee Gerow too. They deserved to know what they and their men might be walking into.

But then Eisenhower changed his mind. Deserving to know did not mean they *needed* to know. What value would there be in telling them of a risk that they could do nothing about? Eisenhower decided to tell them that there was an operation called Peppermint underway and that the details were closely held. But that was all.

To take advantage of everyone's eyes and ears, alerts went out that concealed their ulterior motive. "A few cases of mild disease of unknown etiology have been reported," the theater surgeon informed his medical staff. They should therefore report any cases of soldiers showing "Fatigue, Nausea, Leukopenia, Erythema."

Another message was sent out from the director of the Army Pictorial Division. "A survey is being conducted by this Office concerning the matter of fogged emulsion on film and paper." Anyone who discovered blackened film should report. Similarly vague messages had gone out back in December and January. But other than a few reports of exposed film, nothing had been discovered, at least not yet.

Eisenhower had been let in on one of those secrets that, once known, make the world look different. Peterson could have just as easily revealed that the Nazis had weaponized time travel, or invisibility, or human-animal hybrids, so that Eisenhower's men might be beset by hyena-swine and wolf-bear men on Normandy's shores.

It was one of those secrets that made people out of the know seem like ancient ancestors who still believed the earth was flat. He had no way of knowing in that moment how central this new, mysterious technology would be to his life, or how central he would be to it. And he had no way of knowing if atomic weapons would be just another bullet, or something that would leave war without any logic whatsoever.

But the fact that something so profound could be revealed to him on a Saturday afternoon by an army major demonstrated that meticulous planning for every contingency had its limits—and for that reason, it was all the more necessary to do. The only way they could be ready to adapt to the unknowns awaiting them was by ensuring that everyone, all the men who had to do the work, down to the buck privates and swabbies, were fully prepared for the knowns.

Hastings "Pug" Ismay

CHAPTER 33

IT WAS ANOTHER week before the question of Operation Anvil was finally resolved. It was the lowest point yet in the Anglo-American alliance. The US Chiefs put a new condition on their willingness to send landing craft from the Pacific. Jumbo Wilson would have to turn toward making Operation Anvil his top priority as soon as he linked up all the Allied forces on the Italian boot. There would be no great push to Rome.

Churchill had balked at being blackmailed and personally intervened, saying he did not want Jumbo Wilson "falling between two stools."

Eisenhower had been cut out of the negotiations and when he found out about Churchill's ultimatum, he cabled General Marshall, near begging him to reach a deal. He blamed the British for their stubbornness but pleaded for the long view. He then worked with Pug Ismay on a draft of a memo that Eisenhower could send to the US Chiefs, proposing a compromise that would salvage the deal and let everyone save face. But it was too little, too late.

Before Eisenhower could send his proposal, the US Chiefs walked away from the negotiations. Jumbo Wilson would have to make do with the landing craft still in the Mediterranean, and Eisenhower would have to hope that the continued fight for Italy would prevent the Germans from turning all their forces north to defend the Atlantikwall.

The whole experience had left everyone bitter. "History will never forgive them," Alan Brooke said of his American counterparts, "for bargaining equipment against strategy and for trying to blackmail us into agreeing with them by holding the pistol of withdrawing craft at our heads!"

Eisenhower was also embittered by the thought that it was a sign of Roosevelt shifting to a "Pacific First" strategy because it was an election year. Eisenhower got plenty of political gossip from Edward Stettinius. There was talk that Roosevelt might bow out of the race. Some were even suggesting he do it at the Democratic Convention and at the same time nominate General Marshall to be president. The Democrats would not only win, Stettinus said, Roosevelt would go down as the greatest president in American history.

As things were, no one was sure Roosevelt could pull off an unprecedented fourth term. His health was failing. His vice president, Henry Wallace, had become a liability with the southern Democrats. Then there was the MacArthur factor. The newspapers had been awash in political intrigue after MacArthur's letters with a Republican congressman came to light, welcoming efforts to nominate him in opposition to Roosevelt and comparing himself to Abraham Lincoln. Their publication forced MacArthur to backtrack, disclaiming any intention to "seek public office," but the damage was done.

Over evening drinks in Telegraph Cottage, Butch guessed that this all helped explain Roosevelt's turn toward the Pacific. He had to placate MacArthur and probably wanted to make a big push over the summer to get "a few victories against the Japs."

"If Overlord failed," Eisenhower said, "the president couldn't possibly be elected."

This all made Churchill's rather unseemly finagling of a confidence vote a few weeks earlier seem all the wiser in retrospect. And the more Eisenhower got to watch Churchill the politician up close, the more he admired him.

At one of their regular lunches, Churchill revealed that there was a problem with the Mulberries. The British Admiralty had issued a discouraging report on their progress. Two massive caissons, which had been given the nicknames Phoenix and Whale, were the central pillars of their design. And the Mulberries were a central pillar of the Allies' plan for success. These artificial harbors were the only way they could move the astronomical quantity of tanks, trucks, men, and supplies that would be necessary to prevent the Normandy beachhead from bogging down as Anzio had.

The Germans knew that too. Lord Haw Haw, the British traitor, had even incorporated the Mulberries into his propaganda broadcasts. "You think you are going to sink them on our coasts in the assault?" he said. "We'll save you the trouble. When you come to get underway we're going to sink them for you."

Construction of the caissons was behind schedule, not for lack of material, but of man-hours. It was, in short, a labor problem in a political climate where scolding organized labor to work harder was as useful as scolding a thunderstorm to keep the noise down.

Churchill had a plan to make his own weather, though. He wanted Eisenhower to come to the cabinet meeting that evening and give a report on the importance of the Mulberries. Then he wanted Eisenhower to offer a few US engineer regiments to get the work done if necessary.

"Of course," Eisenhower said. "They will be available tomorrow."

"Oh, no, General," Churchill said slyly. "I just want you to offer them, not to send them."

As planned, Churchill opened the meeting and grumbled about the slow progress of the Mulberries. It was a litany of despairs. There were no more men to do the work. The bottom of the barrel had been scraped to splinters. Churchill then turned to Eisenhower. How would this affect things? Were there any solutions?

Eisenhower took his cue. The Mulberries were essential, he explained. "If they could not be ready unless we speeded up production by using more manpower, I would volunteer a number of efficient US Engineers for British use." The men, he explained, were in the middle of training exercises, but the Mulberries were more important.

"It seems," Churchill said, "that our Commander-in-Chief is the only one present who can produce a constructive idea. We thank him for his generous offer, especially because its acceptance would interfere with his necessary military program."

"But, Gentlemen," Churchill groaned, "are we to admit that the British Government is so helpless, so unimaginative, so lacking in determination, that it cannot, except by calling upon our Allies, carry out a simple duty that it took upon its own shoulders? I cannot believe that we are so stripped of resources that we cannot fulfill our pledges, made in good faith to our partner in this great enterprise. I want each person here to make another survey of the capacity of his organization and expect to meet with you here tomorrow, when we shall produce a solution to this problem, which I refuse to admit is unsolvable."

Sure enough, the Ministry of Production came through and found a special labor force of three hundred extra men to ensure that the Mulberries would be done on time. Churchill rang Eisenhower the following day: "Everything was on the track."

Eisenhower admired the maneuver the way an athlete admires the subtleties of another's game. In the half century in which he had made his own way in the world, Eisenhower had grown confident in his ability to play bureaucratic politics. He was less sure, though, that he was cut out for the grander stage of electoral politics.

Bureaucratic politics had, until recently, allowed him to enjoy importance with substantial privacy, even anonymity. Now the details of his life were being picked through, and he was having to send letters to relatives reminding them to be discreet in what they told sleuthing reporters and biographers. His brother Edgar could not help but tease him for his newfound celebrity. Looking back on their childhood, Edgar said he could think of various "instances that have some connection with your present character development," adding that "some of the stories that I remember are not the kind I should tell." The time Eisenhower knocked him unconscious with a baseball bat, for example, was a story he had no intention of having immortalized.

Since his return to London, Eisenhower had become the kind of public figure who shook a lot of hands. He had already conducted dozens of inspection trips, mingling his way around the United Kingdom. He was frequently the guest of honor at major public events, including that year's championship football (soccer) match at Wembley Stadium between Chelsea and Charlton Athletic. The crowd of ninety thousand hailed Eisenhower as he went onto the field to shake hands with the teams before the game, and after Charlton won, it was unclear who was honoring whom when Eisenhower presented the team's captain with the Champion's Cup.

Eisenhower had shaken so many hands over the previous two months that it hurt. Literally. Each new paw was now giving him a wince of pain, such that it was getting hard to even write with a pen. Thankfully, he had Mattie, but Mamie never let him forget the one time he sent her a dictated letter. And so, he toughed it out with her as his penmanship deteriorated into a scrawl, and he wrote to her about his fantasies of leaving public life after the war, perhaps taking to writing full-time, and seeing the world. "Baghdad, Rangoon, Sydney, Tahiti, Quito, Brazzaville, and Timbuktu. I'd like also to travel throughout Russia. Would you?"

It was easy, and dangerous, to fall for the hype. Eisenhower was getting asked more often about whether he would run for president. It took little more than looking at MacArthur to see how entertaining such ideas could distract him. "No wartime soldier," he concluded, "can retain his military effectiveness if he becomes tied up in the public mind with political problems." Whatever ambitions he might nurture for a future political career, the advice he wanted Roosevelt to hear applied to him categorically. If Overlord failed, he would never be elected to anything. And as he understood more than anyone, Operation Overlord could fail.

"We are not merely risking a tactical defeat," Eisenhower wrote to a friend back in Washington, "we are putting the whole works on one number. A sense of humor and a great faith, or else a complete lack of imagination, are essential to sanity." It irked him how many people—high-level, responsible people—acted as if victory were guaranteed. It was the same kind of hubris everyone had back in January before the Anzio invasion, when they predicted that Rome would fall in February. Even the best plans executed by the best men could fail because of something as simple as the weather. And not the kind of political weather that a savvy operator like Churchill might be able to influence. The actual weather.

John "Cliff" Lee

CHAPTER 34

IN BATTLE, THE weather was a terrain that you could not plan for by looking at a map. But that did not mean you could not plan for it. When Eisenhower arrived in London, there was no centralized office for meteorology. He fixed that problem and the task was assigned to Dr. Martin Stagg, a tall and meticulous Scot who had worked in the British Air Ministry's Meteorological Office.

Eisenhower asked all his commanders in chief for the "minimum operating weather conditions requirements" for the invasion. The navy needed minimal fog and maximum visibility. The army needed dry ground and low wind, to keep the seas calm, and because the invasion was going to be in two waves, they also needed a day that had two low tides while the sun was up. The air forces needed cloud cover no lower than 3,000 feet for the bombers during the day and calm air with low, thick clouds the previous night for the airborne forces, ideally a night with a late-rising full moon, so the approach could be made in darkness, but the men could drop with some sense of where the ground was.

Stagg had his staff do the calculations, and they estimated that those conditions could be expected to occur together once in a century. But, if the invasion was to happen in the next six weeks, Stagg said that June 5 would be the least-worst choice. They could push it as far as June 7, but then things got dicey. After that, the seas, the sun, and the moon would not align again until the end of June.

For the weekly commanders in chief meeting on April 17, Eisenhower added a new seat at the table for Stagg. He wanted the weathermen to know they mattered and, just as important, to face the same pressure to perform.

"As you all know, when the time comes to start Overlord we are going to have to rely very much on the weather forecast, so I want to hear what our weather experts can do," Eisenhower said. "Now, Stagg, go ahead."

Stagg stood up and peered around the table from his blue eyes, a visibly cowed civilian who had only recently been stuffed into a uniform. Eisenhower smiled back at him encouragingly.

Stagg then began to speak in a quiet brogue. He predicted the following week would have fair weather.

Eisenhower asked him how confident he was.

Not confident, Stagg replied.

Tedder asked about visibility in France on Thursday and Ramsay asked specific questions about sea conditions around the Breton Peninsula.

Stagg answered, but always with uncertainty.

That uncertainty gave Eisenhower confidence. Stagg knew the details, would explain the reasons for making one prediction or another, but then would highlight all the things that could go the other way. He knew enough to know what he did not know. He was realistic without being indecisive.

"Whenever you see a good spell that would be suitable for Overlord coming along during the next month," he told Stagg, "I want you to tell us: give us as much notice as you can."

The meeting then turned to other matters, but before they adjourned, Eisenhower announced that Stagg would present the weekly weather forecast at the end of each commanders in chief meeting. If failure or success was going to turn on the uncertainties of the weather, they would at least know how uncertain they should be.

THE NEXT WEEKLY commanders in chief meeting was long. Omar Bradley and Tooey Spaatz attended, and discussions about the use of airpower predominated, including the continuing controversy over French casualties. Though initially skeptical of the casualty protections, Spaatz had seized the issue and was now warning Eisenhower, "Many thousands of French people will be killed and many towns will be laid waste in these operations," being sure to add that pursuing Operation Pointblank "better achieves the basic aim of maximum direct assistance to Overlord." Eisenhower, though, remained unmoved.

With Brad there, Beetle had also added a cryptic item to the agenda: "Enemy secret developments." He did not indicate that there was anything specific to worry about. But Beetle wanted to raise the possibility that there might be weapons they hadn't seen over there. If that turned out to be the case, they should have "plans for securing enemy secret weapons and equipment for study."

Stagg was then called up to give the weather report. His prediction of the previous week scored about 70 to 75 percent. Not bad, but they needed better. Exercise Tiger was about to begin, making Stagg's prediction for the upcoming week of more than academic interest. It would be the largest rehearsal for the most dangerous and uncertain part of the Normandy invasion: the taking of Utah Beach.

The most recent estimates projected casualties on Utah Beach of 15 percent, three times higher than Omaha. And that did not include the expected 9 percent loss of men who never made it ashore, nor did it include the paratroopers being dropped inland. The three miles of the Slapton Sands beach, which was backed inland by the Slapton Ley, narrowed the exits from the beach just like the flooded marsh behind Utah. It was perfect to simulate the terrain. They had even embedded mock pillboxes into Slapton Sands, old tank turrets that the naval gunners could use for target practice. And Eisenhower wanted to hear Stagg's forecast.

Stagg confidently said that the weather would be good on Wednesday, but then deteriorate on Thursday, with intermittent moderation in the weather Friday until Saturday.

"Aren't you sticking your neck a little far out?" Beetle asked.

"Some of my colleagues," Stagg replied, "would certainly have been content to stop at Wednesday or even Tuesday; but you asked for a forecast from four days beginning on Wednesday and we have done our best to produce it."

THE FOLLOWING EVENING, Eisenhower boarded the *Bayonet* with Omar Bradley, Arthur Tedder, and Gee Gerow, en route to Slapton Sands. He stopped in Wilton along the way to visit the Southern Base Section of Cliff Lee's services of supply network. The Southern Base Section was the hub of the logistics and marshaling work being done for the invasion. Eisenhower was taken on a tour of its war room, where he could see the scale models of the supply lines. It was enough to forgive Cliff "Jesus Christ Himself" Lee for any sins he may have committed. The man had built Eisenhower an engine for the greatest war machine the world had ever known.

The American military did not have the most men. The Russian army was more than twice as big. The Americans did not even have the best weapons. The British Spitfire and the German Messerschmitt were faster than anything the United States put into the air. The German MG 34 and StG 44 were lighter, more reliable, and far more powerful than even the best American rifles. All things being equal, a division of German Tiger tanks should win every battle against a division of American Shermans. But all things were not equal. And the charts and graphs and maps and scale models in this room showed why.

Everything was systematized and optimized for scale, like some enormous Ford factory line. At the beginning of the war, the British proposed shipping American truck parts to the United Kingdom, since shipping a whole truck would waste valuable cargo space. But relying upon mechanics to assemble them from scratch in Britain was too slow. By 1944, the army had mastered the process of breaking American trucks down into a few standardized subassemblies that fit snugly into standardized shipping containers that were floated across the Atlantic to Britain where they could be rapidly reassembled by two mechanics following standardized instructions.

America did not need to have the most or the best, so long as it could ensure what was needed to win was in the right place at the right time. And if there was one thing a country born out of the search for El Dorado had mastered, it was getting what was wanted to those who wanted it as quickly as the weight of the world could be lifted to get it there.

THE WEATHER WAS beautiful the day Exercise Tiger's landings on Slapton Sands were scheduled to commence. The water was smooth and clear, the sun bright. Hardly typical for the English coast in April, but not unwelcome.

A few weeks before, the Combined Chiefs had finally settled on the naval resources that would be dedicated to the invasion. There would be six battleships, two monitors, twenty-two cruisers, and ninety-three destroyers divided into five attack divisions, each in support of one of the five beaches. By April 26, thousands of ships, large and small, had been conspicuously berthed at every suitable hitch from Milford Haven to Harwich, with more in reserve in Humber, Belfast, and the Clyde.

Bertie Ramsay's operational orders for Operation Neptune, the code name for the subpart of Operation Overlord dedicated to punching the first holes through the Atlantikwall, formed a cinder block. Three inches thick, twenty-two chapters, each with its own appendices, it was a monument of planning down to the last turn of the rudder.

The navies were divided along national lines, with the Royal Navy in control east of Port-en-Bessin and the US Navy controlling the west out toward the Atlantic. Don P. Moon, who impressed Bertie Ramsay as a "fine type of U.S. officer," would command Force U, dedicated to Utah Beach, and the naval component of Exercise Tiger.

The goal of Exercise Tiger was to coordinate naval, air, paratrooper, and landing forces on the beaches of Slapton Sands in as close to "actual war conditions" as possible. It was a two-day operation, with D-Day set for April 27 and H-hour for the landing at seven thirty in the morning. The 101st Airborne would conduct a "simulated" drop behind Slapton Ley four hours before landing. These simulated jumps were called "GMC jumps," since they involved being driven to the drop site and jumping off the back of a truck.

Fighter-bombers would attack inland an hour before landing. There would be a barrage of live naval fire "upon beach obstacles from H-50 to H-Hour." Then men would land on the beaches, the obstacles would be disabled, and the simulated Atlantikwall would be breached. The following day, D+1, additional LSTs would land on Slapton Sands, disgorging more men, vehicles, and supplies to stress test the army's and navy's ability to manage the traffic. All told, Moon's armada for Exercise Tiger would comprise twenty-one LSTs, twenty-eight LCIs, and nearly two hundred other landing craft.

Exercise Tiger had gotten off to an inauspicious start. A few days earlier, there had been a simulated "bombing" of the docks around Plymouth as the army and navy loaded thousands of men, vehicles, and supplies for the landings. In the fog, the traffic got jammed, and during the "bombing," thirty-seven transport trucks were "annihilated," leading to hundreds of "casualties" and a three-hour delay as the "wreckage" was cleared and the roads "repaired."

But D-Day would be the real test, and so Eisenhower got up before dawn, Kay drove him the twenty-minutes to Dartmouth, and he was welcomed aboard USS *LCI 495*, which had been prepared to host him and some of the other top brass.

By 6:30 a.m., they were deep into the bay with a clear view of the coast.

But then nothing happened. At 6:50 a.m., the scheduled naval bombardment began to spectacular effect. But ten minutes later, it stopped. Apparently, Moon had postponed the start of the exercise by an hour at the last minute because a group of landing craft was running behind schedule.

Fifteen minutes later, bombers began flying overhead. The day before, Arthur Tedder had treated everyone to a demonstration of the awesome effectiveness of airpower against beach obstacles. There was therefore a bit of anticipation to see more fireworks on Exercise Tiger's D-Day. But as plane after plane droned past, none dropped any bombs.

In dribs and drabs over the next hour, landing craft could be seen dawdling through the bay toward the beaches. At 8:21 a.m., the lion's share of the landing craft finally started getting close to shore.

Air raid sirens then began to wail. Actual German reconnaissance planes started buzzing overhead. It took another eighteen minutes for the all-clear to sound. By then, the landing craft started lowering their gangplanks to launch the amphibious trucks, the DUWKs (or "ducks"), which bobbed when they splashed into the water and began puttering, seemingly at the pace of a real duck, toward the shore.

Before long, a ribbon of smoke could be seen coming up from one of the DUWKs, which was soon followed by a yellow buoy popping out, alerting everyone that the DUWK was foundering. One of the small landing craft nearby diverted from its path and came to the rescue.

Finally, men started hitting the beach, the sappers from the engineer brigade out front fixing explosives to obstacles and cutting a path. Though "hitting" was the wrong word. "Strolling," "ambling," "lumbering": those words more accurately captured the urgency with which the men galumphed ashore. Had there been real Germans on the beach, there would have been little left of the men on the beach to bury.

It was a disaster. When that *Collier's* article had come out a month earlier, Eisenhower tasked Omar Bradley with tamping down the panic, and Brad had gone around England making speeches, saying that the casualty estimates swirling around were "tommyrot." But watching this slow, confused muddle, and thinking about everything the Germans had prepared and might be preparing, one could be forgiven for thinking that 50 percent casualties looked optimistic.

For all the planning that had been done, for all the ships, the men, and the planes, for all the lessons learned from disasters like Gallipoli, maybe Churchill was right. America may be the best at getting the right thing to the right place at the right time. But the best might not be enough to break through the Atlantikwall.

EISENHOWER DID NOT have time to ruminate for long. Almost as soon as he was back on land, there was a call from Beetle. General Marshall had sent an urgent message from Washington. It was Patton again.

"Newspapers today," General Marshall wrote, "carried glaring reports of General Patton's statements reference Britain and America's rule of the world. We were just about to get confirmation of the permanent makes. This I fear has killed them all."

Patton had been invited to a reception at the British Welcome Club. When asked by the host to offer a few remarks, he had said, "Until today, my only experience in welcoming has been to welcome Germans and Italians to the 'Infernal Regions.' In this I have been quite successful, as the troops whom I have had the honor to command have killed or captured some 170,000 of our enemies." As was often the case, that much may have been written off as Patton being Patton. But he hadn't stopped there.

"I feel," he had continued, "that such clubs as this are a very real value, because I believe, with Mr. Bernard Shaw, I think it was he, that said the British and Americans are two people separated by a common language, and since it is the evident destiny of the British and Americans, to rule the world, the better we know each other, the better job we will do."

Georgie had, evidently, neglected to mention the Russians, stoking the Soviets' recurring—and not entirely irrational—paranoia of Anglo-American duplicity. It might have gone unnoticed, but it echoed, near verbatim, a similar faux pas by Foreign Secretary Anthony Eden made the month before. Eden had ducked a question in Parliament regarding the recognition of De Gaulle's French Committee by saying that "the whole question is now under examination by His Majesty's Government and the United States Government," again notably neglecting to mention the Soviet Union. And as if to leave no room for misunderstanding, Eden had emphasized that "the *two* Governments are examining the position together, and whatever we say and do, we shall say and do together." The Soviets were justifiably livid at their exclusion from the table at the very time they were driving the Germans back to Berlin.

The irony was that the Russians had recently awarded Eisenhower the Order of Suvorov, First Degree. Named after General Alexander Suvorov, who led the Russian invasion of Berlin in 1760, it was first bestowed on

Soviet general Georgy Zhukov in the final week of the Battle of Stalingrad. It was the second-highest military honor the Russians awarded, and the State Department had sent a cable delighted to accept it on Eisenhower's behalf. It was a gorgeous object, a gold cross nearly two inches wide, though the best part of it, as far as Eisenhower was concerned, was that it entitled him to ride the Moscow subway for free. With Eden, and now Patton, Russian goodwill overtures to tighten the alliance were being met by Anglo-American slaps at the very time the Russians' battlefield successes gave them increasing leverage over the future of the war.

Eisenhower told Beetle that he would deal with Patton when he got back. He also told Beetle to call Georgie and tell him to keep his mouth shut. He was no longer to make any public remarks on any subject without first submitting them in writing for approval.

When Eisenhower saw Brad, he told him the latest. "I'm just about fed up," Eisenhower said. "If I have to apologize publicly for George one more time, I'm going to have to let him go, valuable as he is. I'm getting sick and tired of having to protect him."

Brad agreed.

EISENHOWER RETURNED TO the *Bayonet* for the trip back to London that evening, and was soon joined by Brad, Tedder, and Gee. The mood was like in a locker room after a playoff loss. The sorry display that morning had hit Gee especially hard. D-Day for his own rehearsal of the invasion of Omaha Beach, Exercise Fabius, was a week away.

Gee wanted to know who delayed everything at the last minute and why. "Never change the time once it is set," he said, as if declaring one of the noble truths. "Too much confusion arises." As he ranted, Butch came in. Butch had been with the navy most of the day observing from another one of the LCIs. Gee asked Butch, accusingly, why the navy had delayed the landing.

Butch shook his head. He didn't know.

For all the worrying about Utah Beach, Gee thought he could see unique dangers at Omaha that everyone was underestimating. On a map it looked straightforward. It even divided neatly with nice straight lines, cutting the beach into sectors and subsectors from west to east like a literal piece of cake. But Gee had studied the terrain more closely. The whole beach was surrounded by cliffs that were up to 110 feet tall and almost certainly capped by German guns.

Gee planned to use the Rangers to scale the cliffs as quickly as possible.

They were experimenting with grappling hooks, though he found that firemen's ladders worked well. The trick was figuring out how to mount them on the DUWKs so they could get to shore in one piece. That was the thing, though. Simple solutions. The British, as far as Gee was concerned, were always coming up with new contraptions that made things more difficult.

Brad agreed. All he wanted was more tanks. They didn't have to float, or flail, or do anything special. They just had to reliably fire a 75mm shell.

Gee was also fretting about the beach obstacles and was contemplating sending bulldozers out in front. The Nazis had been cheap and just jammed old French train tracks into the sand. A bulldozer could chew right through a train track. It was the mines that were the trouble.

Tedder reminded Gee that he would have airpower directed at those obstacles. With their new short-fused bombing techniques, they could set the mines off in chain reactions and simultaneously clear a path. All Gee had to do was get his men through the hole within about one or two minutes after it was created.

Gee scoffed. The navy wouldn't give him a window of any less than three to four minutes to be anywhere. That was the best they could do, they said, because of the tides.

They needed to do better, Tedder said. For airpower to be useful at all, Gee's men would need to land within about forty-five seconds of a bombing run. Too much later, the obstacles would move around under the water. Any earlier, Gee was liable to find his men above the obstacles and under the bombs.

Eisenhower told Gee to be "optimistic." Hell, he should be "cheerful." Behind him, Eisenhower said, was "the greatest fire power ever assembled on the face of the earth."

Gee said he wasn't being pessimistic. Just "realistic." He wanted to know the worst that could happen "so that every preparation that could be thought of would be made."

Dr. Eugene Eckstam

CHAPTER 35

WHILE EISENHOWER SLEPT on the *Bayonet*, the remainder of Don Moon's forces continued on their way around Lyme Bay toward Slapton Sands to complete what was left of Exercise Tiger the following morning. Dr. Eugene Eckstam was the medical officer on USS *LST 507*.

Dr. Eckstam had just finished medical school and accepted a commission with the US Naval Reserve. He had reported to the Great Lakes Naval Training Station in Illinois to do induction physicals, of which he would say, "I became an expert in hemorrhoids, hernias, and right ears." Stated more frankly, that meant a daily procession of nearly two thousand young men's assholes, balls, and right ears.

This might have been how Dr. Eckstam spent the "Great World War II," a job only slightly more glamorous than "shoveling shit in Louisiana." But then he got orders to report to Long Island to head up a so-called Foxy 29, the medical unit for a ship.

In early March, Dr. Eckstam became part of the maiden crew of *LST 507*, which looked like a clean trash barge, and embarked for the southern English port at Brixham. The work of a Foxy 29 doctor was not all that different from performing induction physicals, except that the procession of assholes, balls, and right ears was now assessed for fresh cases of venereal disease.

On April 24, Eckstam boarded *LST 507* with 164 fellow Navy sailors and 282 Army soldiers, who brought dozens of DUWKs, tanks and jeeps, enough gasoline to service a small town for many months, and a youthful delight at the chance to enjoy a few days' boat voyage slowly circling Lyme Bay in unseasonably beautiful weather.

There was little in the way of real work to do. There were not even safety drills. The soldiers on board spent their productive time learning to translate "head" as "latrine," and to pop the CO2 cartridges that inflated the life belts in case of emergency.

The rest of the time was whiled away in a mostly friendly rivalry with the sailors on board, having food fights in the mess hall, dancing to banjos, guitars, and improvised jeep-hood drums, dressing in drag to add a feminine flavor to festivities, and putting hairy knuckled hands on hips to form conga lines around *LST 507*'s decks. The only thing to distinguish the voyage of *LST 507* around Lyme Bay from any other leisure cruise was the official absence of alcohol.

Dr. Eckstam had gone to bed the night of April 27, knowing that the next morning *LST 507* would offload the DUWKs, the soldiers, and the sense of revelry onto Slapton Sands. But then at 1:35 in the morning, there was a furious knocking against the hull that echoed through the ship. Then, into the vigilant silence it left behind, the *wamp-wamp-wamp-wamp-wamp-wamp-wamp* of the alarm to general quarters deafened every corner of everything. Dr. Eckstam slung his standard-issue gas mask over his shoulder, grabbed his life belt, and funneled out of his quarters into *LST 507*'s now crowded corridors.

As the sailors scrambled their Mae Wests on, the alarm was matched by the bowel-shaking *bomp-bomp-bomp-bomp-bomp-bomp-bomp* of the ship's 40mm guns blasting into the darkness. Seeing some shipmates, Dr. Eckstam said, "They had better watch where they were shooting or someone would get hurt." There was no reason to think this was not all part of Exercise Tiger. Live fire was part of the plan to stiffen the men's nerves.

"I guess they're trying to make it as real as possible."

The general-quarters alarm had been blaring away for half an hour. Dr. Eckstam was making his way to the stairs to go topside when *BOOM!*

It was so sudden and so loud, Dr. Eckstam had no chance to be frightened. In fractions of a second, the lights had gone out and he had no sense of where his body was in space until spikes of blunt pain stabbed through his knees. He had fallen forward onto the hard steel deck. The pain was so intense that the professional part of his brain immediately feared how serious his injuries might be.

Dr. Eckstam got himself up and tried to make his way forward. He came to the hatch leading out to tank deck, where all the DUWKs, full of fuel, had been packed, ready to drive out onto Slapton Sands that morning. It was as if opening a doorway to hell. The fires were so bright in his eyes, the heat so intense against his skin, and the panicked wails of the men burning to death inside so chilling that he slammed the door and bolted it shut. He did not look back. He told himself that navy protocol was to "dog the hatch" if the ship was at risk of sinking. That's all he had done. There was nothing he could have done. He had done what he was supposed to do.

Dr. Eckstam finally made it topside, where he found his fellow doctor on board, Dr. Ed Panter. The stern and bow had been severed in two. He and every other man who had gotten topside could do nothing but watch as the fires within the ship burned, cooking off ammunition and cans of gas in morbid fireworks that burst in random paths out from *LST 507*.

The fires soon became too hot to withstand. Dr. Eckstam and Dr. Panter cracked the CO2 canisters on their life belts and climbed down the stern into the water. Dr. Eckstam's life belt jerked up his under his armpits as the weight of his body went into the sea.

The ocean was as cold and black as the sky. The current swirled a stew of jagged debris and burning engine oil around the sinking wreckage of *LST 507*, threatening to leave a man drowned, frozen, gored, and burned to death all at once. Dr. Eckstam struggled to swim with Dr. Panter away from the sinking ship. But the strap from the gas mask kept tangling him.

"Why are you dragging that gas mask?" Dr. Panter asked.

"Don't we have to account for it?"

"Toss it!"

They swam until they reached a raft with what seemed like a hundred men trying to hold on. Men hung in rings around whatever could keep them buoyant. A tight ring of men with their hands on the raft with a wider ring holding on to whatever strap or clothing would keep them tethered to the center, with wider and wider rings of men hoping that the links in their chain would not break.

Some tried to make a swim for it, got lost in the dark and cold, then floundered in panicked screams until they fell quiet. Some bargained for their lives, offering driftwood for a life vest, betting on which would keep their heads above water longer. Some, closer to the raft, threatened mutiny to those inside, with soldiers telling sailors to swim because they were "fish-like," or another yelling at Clarence Ellis, a steward's mate on *LST 507*, "Get that nigger off there!"

The darkness over the sea was broken by volleys of red and yellow tracer fire, LSTs burning, and stars shining in an otherwise clear sky. The light from all that shimmered was eclipsed by waves of acrid black smoke. A few flashes from a searchlight even came across the water from a fast-moving boat that quickly left, seemingly uninterested in the men's plight.

Dr. Eckstam went numb. The next thing he sensed was his knees again. The sun was coming up. There were American voices. He was on the deck of an LST.

In the dawn light, the sea was littered with naked purple men, bobbing with the current among body parts, crates of oranges, and DUWKs, all floating by as if washed away in a flood. Small American landing craft circulated with their front ramps down, scooping up bodies. The HMS *Saladin* was supposed to have been escorting *LST 507*. When it finally arrived, it scattered corpses in its wake.

Dr. Eckstam analyzed why he had survived. He thought of the choices he had made and the choices the dead had made. There were the men who stripped down and jumped into the ocean, as if diving into a pool. His choice to wear his clothes must have insulated him, whereas they froze. He had stepped carefully into the water, where others had jumped in headfirst, not realizing that the life belt around their waist would slip right off their legs. He had dropped his gear, except for that gas mask, where others had put on their packs, only to find that they were so top heavy, their life belts flipped them and pinned their heads upside down, leaving their frozen legs floating above the surface like wilted lily pads.

Hundreds of men had made thousands of choices. Someone had made the choice to launch two lifeboats off *LST 507* before it sank, saving dozens of men on board. Someone from the British navy had made the choice to send the alert that a pack of German Schnellboote (what the Allies called E-boats) had been spotted in Lyme Bay. But someone had also made the choice not to send the message on the frequency used by the US Navy. And someone from the US Navy made the choice not to keep track of radio traffic on the frequency used by the Royal Navy. Someone made the choice to order the nearby American ships to not heed the distress calls, so as not to delay the completion of Exercise Tiger again. But at 4:35 a.m., the captain of *LST 515* made the choice to defy that order and rescue survivors.

Nothing had gone according to plan. And so, life and death, success and failure, all had to come down to individual choices. Soon after *LST 507* was hit, the E-boats hit *LST 531*. It sank within minutes and nearly everyone on board died. In the confusion, *LST 496* began opening fire on what it thought was an enemy vessel. It had been shooting at *LST 515*, the only American ship to rescue anyone. It saved 132 men, including Dr. Eckstam.

EISENHOWER AWOKE ON the *Bayonet*, which pulled into London early the next morning. He had an early meeting at 10 Downing Street, where Churchill was waiting for him in the prime minister's Map Room. Churchill had a cabinet meeting scheduled for noon and wanted to give Eisenhower the courtesy of letting him know. There had been an intelligence report on the French reaction to the bombing. All the intelligence pointed to the same conclusion: "there were too many civilian casualties."

A raid in Paris a few days earlier had killed more than 120 people, prompting one Parisian informant to say, "They bring us liberation with wooden crosses." The Vichy government was taking full advantage.

Sure, Americans might be flying most of those planes and dropping American bombs. But they were taking off from British soil. And with Bomber Harris's reputation, the Brits would receive the blame. He could not justify so many civilian casualties for an operation that hardly seemed like a wise use of strategic bombers to begin with.

This set off an argument that would run for days. Eisenhower tried to reason with Churchill. While the casualties should not be ignored, Eisenhower insisted, the Transportation Plan was achieving "a high degree of success." Anything that disrupted the Germans' ability to counterattack was tantamount to adding divisions of Allied forces onto the beaches. It was zero sum.

Couldn't the bombers just focus on "bases, troop concentrations and dumps," Churchill asked.

Where did the prime minister think those were? Dumps were near marshaling yards. Troop concentrations were near villages. If they bombed those villages, they would probably kill four Frenchmen for every German. Was that better? Was that more humane?

Churchill was unpersuaded. The reputation of the British Empire was at stake.

IT HAD BEEN a long and dispiriting few days, and Eisenhower spent Friday afternoon chatting with Butch, who was atypically dour. From what Butch could see during his time aboard ship, the junior officers were "green as corn" and the senior officers were "fat, gray, and oldish. Most of them wear the Rainbow Ribbon of the last war and are still fighting it." Butch was an optimist by nature, but he was shaken by what he had seen. This all could fail.

The phone rang as they chatted. It was Beetle again. At 4:10 that afternoon, Joe Collins had sent out a message. German E-boats had attacked Exercise Tiger. Two LSTs sunk. Another seriously damaged. Casualties were unclear but could be in the hundreds. "This reduces our reserve of LSTs for the big show," Beetle added, "to zero."

Eisenhower absorbed the information. "Get off a cable to the Combined Chiefs," he told Beetle, "advising them of the loss."

The next day, Eisenhower cabled General Marshall that the loss of the LSTs "was not a restful thought to take home with me." Assessing the situation, "we are stretched to the limit in the LST category, while the implications of the attack and the possibility of both raiders and bombers concentrating on some of our major ports make one scratch his head." He then added, "Apparently we lost a considerable number of men."

Bertie Ramsay followed up with Eisenhower a few days later, with a revised picture of how significant the loss had been. The investigation was ongoing, Bertie said, but the casualties were likely higher than the three to four hundred initially reported. Much higher. The number of dead alone exceeded six hundred. And while those dead were a tragic loss, the 243 men still missing was a potentially catastrophic one. Ten of the missing officers had BIGOT clearances. They knew the plans for D-Day. And there were Ultra intercepts. One of the E-boats had sent out an order: "*Gefangennahme schwimmender Seeleute*" (Capture floating sailors).

Edward Betts

CHAPTER 36

EISENHOWER WAS INUNDATED with hard questions. That was the life of a general, and he had spent fifty years studying how to find the best answers to hard questions, understanding that the battlefield would often prove the best answer to be wrong. But he had no way of knowing, when he was reading the exploits of Hannibal, Caesar, and Alexander the Great, how vexing finding the best answer could be when the question was justice. Not justice in some grand philosophical sense. Rather, the brass tacks of adjudicating what to do with people who did what they shouldn't have done.

These judgment calls were always complicated by his overriding mission to win the war. Omar Bradley had come to him with the case of General Henry Miller. Miller had been at a dinner on April 18 at Claridge's, and during a boozy rant, mentioned the projected date of D-Day at least three separate times. He had been loud enough for waiters to hear.

Eisenhower had gone to West Point with Miller, and would say that he was a "hell of a good friend of mine." But Miller was not an indispensable man and his loose lips were potentially lethal so close to D-Day.

The ten officers with BIGOT clearances who had gone missing during Exercise Tiger had potentially exposed the whole plan to the Germans. Monty had ordered his American staff officer, Major Ralph Ingersoll, to investigate, and there were reports that the E-boats had indeed been searching for survivors to take prisoner. Monty faced the real question of whether Operation Overlord needed to be called off. There were no Ultra intercepts about the Germans having taken any prisoners, but even one captured man could expose the whole operation. There was therefore nothing short of relief, morbid as it was, when the tenth dead body was found.

This was far, however, from the only spill of precious BIGOT intelligence to places where the enemy could find it. There had been, of course, that careless soldier who accidentally mailed invasion plans to a German neighborhood in Chicago. But there was also a story circulating about a dozen copies of the Overlord outline plan being knocked out of a window of the War Office and onto the streets of London. Whether or not that story was true, it easily could have been. Operation Overlord was becoming a secret so oceanic in scale that it was bound to find cracks through which to leak out.

A memo circulated with the list of the officers who had a "complete knowledge of Overlord." It ran six pages with two columns per page, listing generals down to lieutenants. But it seemed as if everyone knew. Even *Time* magazine promised its readers in early May, "Between now and D-Day, each correspondent will be given his assignment in secret." Eisenhower had his intelligence chief interview each section chief about their security protocols. Each headquarters was now responsible for monitoring careless conversations in restaurants, bars, or even cars driven by uncleared drivers. The phones were also to be monitored intermittently, and inspections would be done constantly to uncover any mishandling of sensitive information.

That still left the question of what precisely to do with General Miller. He had written a letter of apology and explanation. But Eisenhower sent him home and made sure everyone knew why. "An alleged serious violation of military security by a General Officer of the Allied Expeditionary Force has resulted in the relief of this officer from his command and his being placed under close arrest."

In balancing fairness and winning the war, it was an easy call. It was a bit unfair, since the consequences to Miller were far greater than the damage he caused. But publicly beheading a general reverberated down to the lowliest buck private, reminding them all to keep their goddamn mouths shut. If just one man was deterred from making a catastrophic slipup, that was far more valuable than anything Miller could ever do.

WITH GEORGIE PATTON, what was fair and what was needed to win the war was flipped. Eisenhower drafted a cable to General Marshall recommending that Patton be relieved of command. But before he could send it off, Everett Hughes dropped by to plead Georgie's case.

"Why can't he shut up?" Eisenhower asked. He showed Everett the cable sending Patton home.

Georgie was, Everett reminded Eisenhower, "a nervous, fidgety and temperamental race horse, which would kick his trainer, get his front feet into the manger, and bolt his food." Now, Everett continued, straining his metaphor, "the trainer has to avoid being kicked." But if he did, the horse would win him some races.

Eisenhower, though, was tired of being kicked.

Everett then pulled out some papers. Two full pages, with a stack of attachments and witness statements, making out Georgie's case like a lawyer. Georgie claimed to have an alibi. He had been misquoted. His true remarks were, he claimed, "it is the evident destiny of the British and Americans, *and, of course, the Russians*, to rule the world." That was what the witness statements confirmed. It was all just a misunderstanding whipped up by yellow muckrackers.

Even still, Georgie had told Everett to pass along the message that he wanted to have his name withdrawn from the promotion list, if that would help get other men promoted. He had no ambitions except "to kill Germans and Japanese in the command of an army. I cannot believe that anything I have done has in any way reduced my efficiency in this particular line of action."

"Oh hell," Eisenhower said, as he tore up the cable sending Patton home.

It was obvious that Georgie had, true to form, said exactly the wrong thing, no matter how many "witnesses" he had cajoled into covering for him. But he *was* indispensable, where Miller was not.

To make Operation Fortitude convincing, SHAEF had created an entire command structure (an order of battle) for the fake First US Army Group (FUSAG), staffed by real generals and including some real commands, such as the Third Army. In support of FUSAG, the navy created three fictitious naval assault forces that generated hundreds of hours of meaningless wireless traffic that made it appear that they were mobilizing for a massive invasion of Calais. And to make FUSAG seem all the more menacing, it was commanded by the one American general whom the Germans feared as much as the Allies feared Erwin Rommel: George S. Patton. At that very moment, Patton was pinning hundreds of thousands of Germans down to the east of Normandy by dint of his mere presence in England.

It wasn't fair to let Georgie slide—again—for running his mouth off. But it might win the war.

The whole truth was, also, that Eisenhower owed him; he really owed him. Part of that, as anybody knew, was that Eisenhower's great successes in North Africa and then Sicily would not have been possible without Patton's relentless drive to victory. But it went deeper than that.

Back in 1921, a few months after Little Icky died, that embezzling scandal was closer to ending Eisenhower's career than he would ever admit. It was a petty thing. In the summer of 1920, when Little Icky was in Denver and while Eisenhower and Georgie were refurbishing their houses at Camp Meade, Eisenhower had continued to submit claims for a childcare credit the army offered to parents who lived off post. It seemed at least arguable that since Little Icky was not living on base, he still qualified for the extra $250.67. The army, though, disagreed.

Eisenhower had turned himself in. There had been an investigation of a lieutenant for doing the same thing, and wanting to get out ahead of any issue, Eisenhower came clean and paid the money back. His commanding officer, General Rockenbach, knew him, liked him, and decided to let him off with a reprimand. But then an assistant inspector general from the War Department decided to make an example out of Eisenhower.

In October 1921, Eisenhower was charged with fraud against the government and conduct unbecoming an officer and a gentleman. General Rockenbach tried to protect him with a military law loophole. Under Article of War 104, the reprimand he had given Eisenhower was technically punishment, and as such appeared sufficient to bar further prosecution under the principle of double jeopardy. That technicality was good enough for General Rockenbach to recommend to the War Department that the case be dropped.

The assistant inspector general was undeterred, however, and requested a formal opinion on the question from the War Department's judge advocate general. In a single year, Eisenhower's entire life seemed as if it were falling apart. The only thing that had saved him, albeit indirectly, was Georgie Patton.

In the middle of November, while the question of Eisenhower's court-martial was pending with the judge advocate general, General Conner had dropped into John Pershing's office to say farewell on his way to Panama. Two days later, he followed up with a formal request to Pershing, asking for Eisenhower to be his deputy.

General Conner's request was tantamount to divine intervention. It was by all appearances an absurd thing for someone as esteemed in the army as General Conner to have done for a very junior officer with no wartime experience, middling grades at West Point, and who was facing potential court-martial. But General Conner knew and trusted Patton. And as General Conner's wife would always remember, when Georgie prayed for an intercession on behalf of Eisenhower, General Conner granted the tempest-tossed young man another chance.

A few weeks later, the judge advocate general ruled against Eisenhower and the assistant inspector general recommended prosecution, because Eisenhower was "charged with offenses of the gravest character, for which he might not only be dismissed from the service, but imprisoned." On December 7, 1921, however, the order came, granting General Conner's request, direct from the desk of General John Pershing.

This boon could protect Eisenhower from even the most tenacious scrivener from the inspector general's office. The assistant inspector general was forced to settle for the inclusion of an admonishing letter in Eisenhower's permanent record.

The biggest obstacle to protecting Georgie from his gaffe about the Russians was General Marshall's ire. Patton was one of the most divisive figures in Washington, and his latest gaffe was poorly timed because his name had been on a list of officers the Senate was considering for permanent promotion. Now the promotions were held up, making Marshall's thankless life all the harder.

Eisenhower, though, could not be seen as trying to protect Patton. Not again. And so, Eisenhower drafted a letter lashing the paint off Georgie. "I have warned you time and again against your impulsiveness in action and speech and have flatly instructed you to say nothing that could possibly be misinterpreted either by your own subordinates or by the public," he wrote. "I am thoroughly weary of your failure to control your tongue and have begun to doubt your all-round judgment, so essential in high military position."

Eisenhower forwarded a copy of the draft to General Marshall, adding "investigation shows that his offense was not so serious as the newspapers would lead one to believe, and one that under the circumstances could have occurred to almost anybody." He then put the decision in Marshall's hands. George Marshall had known—and liked—George Patton for decades. Patton had even taken Marshall, along with Fox Conner and John Pershing, on a tour of Camp Meade to show off the army's new tanks, soon after Eisenhower's arrival in the autumn of 1919. Marshall knew the balance of Patton's virtues and flaws as well as anyone. If anyone was going to end Patton's career, it should be Marshall.

Eisenhower called Beetle, telling him to order Georgie to come to Wide Wing on Monday. He had time on his schedule either at 11:00 a.m. or 3:00 p.m.; it was Georgie's choice.

Eisenhower then wrote yet again to General Marshall, performing the utmost pique. "On all of the evidence now available I will relieve him from command and send him home unless some new and unforeseen information should be developed in the case." But he then probed the extent of Marshall's outrage, suggesting that "there is always the possibility that this war, possibly even this theater, might yet develop a situation where this admittedly unbalanced but nevertheless aggressive fighting man should be rushed into the breach."

Monday morning, Georgie arrived early and waited conspicuously outside Eisenhower's office, dressed in full battle rattle. He was seen in at 11:00 a.m. sharp and was visibly on edge. Eisenhower told him to sit down.

"George, you have gotten yourself into a very serious fix."

"Before you go any further," Patton interrupted, "I want to say that your job is more important than mine, so if in trying to save me you are hurting yourself, throw me out."

"I have now got all that the army can give me." Eisenhower shrugged. "It is not a question of hurting me but of hurting yourself and depriving me of a fighting Army Commander." These incessant controversies, Eisenhower explained, "have shaken the confidence of the country in the War Department." Despite everything, though, Eisenhower told his old friend, that he was still pulling for him. It was in General Marshall's hands now and there was nothing he could do. But he had recommended that if he was to be sent home, that he not be demoted to colonel, which was Patton's permanent rank.

Don't bother, Georgie said. He would rather be demoted to colonel and would then demand to be reassigned to command one of the assault regiments on D-Day. That was his right as a soldier.

Don't be so dramatic, Eisenhower told him. If it was up to him, George S. Patton would command an army. There was no need for threats.

"I am not threatening, but I want to tell you that this attack is badly planned on too narrow a front and may well result in an Anzio, especially if I am not there."

"Don't I know it," Eisenhower said, "but what can I do?" It was an old plan, drawn up by the British—who did not want to invade in the first place, and had agreed to expand the front as much as they did only because Monty had owned the idea.

There needed to be a ninety-mile front, Georgie said.

Returning to the issue at hand, Eisenhower warned him that he would be getting a rather "savage" letter, but not to take it to heart. It was an election year, and the administration could not be seen as having no control over its generals. And they would know soon if Marshall decided to let him stay.

The whole thing made Georgie recite Kipling to himself.

If you can make one heap of all your winnings
And risk it on one turn of pitch-and-toss,
And lose, and start again at your beginnings
And never breathe a word about your loss

General Marshall put Patton's fate back in Eisenhower's hands the next day. "The decision is exclusively yours. My view, and it is merely that, is that you should not weaken your hand for Overlord." He then added, in case the implication was lost, "Incidentally, the numerous editorials, while caustic regarding his indiscretion, lack of poise or dignity suitable to his position, and have not demanded his release from command. Do not consider War Department position in the matter. Consider only Overlord and your own heavy burden of responsibility for its success. Everything else is of minor importance."

Eisenhower called Georgie to tell him everything was OK. He would have an admonishing letter put in his permanent record that Eisenhower would send by cable. The cable was stern enough to satisfy any critic who might later read it.

Henry Stimson, the secretary of war, wrote privately to Eisenhower. He had been watching the whole controversy unfold and just wanted to let him know that the "judicial poise and good judgment, as well as the great courage which you have shown in making this decision, has filled me with even greater respect and admiration than I had for you before—high as that has always been."

ADJUDICATING PATTON'S CASE required savvy, but in the end, it was not hard. The hard cases, the really hard cases, were those in which it was unclear what was fair or what was best for winning the war. And the hardest of the hard cases were the ones that dredged up America's old "color problem," whose ugly and often wanton violence unnerved those who were otherwise eager to like America with the suspicion that there was something vicious lurking behind all those quick American smiles.

Eisenhower had implemented nearly all of Walter White's recommendations. He had abolished the Jim Crow rules that Jacob Devers had put in place back in October, and further directed that "any person subject to military law who makes statements derogatory to any troops of the United Nations will be severely punished for conduct prejudicial to good order and military discipline." And he requested that the Ninety-Second Division, the Buffalo Soldiers, be sent to Europe.

Eisenhower also approved new training materials titled "The Command of Negro Troops." Cliff Lee saw to it that 200,000 copies of the pamphlet were distributed throughout the European theater. Twenty-eight pages long, it instructed that "colored Americans, like all other Americans, have the right and duty to serve their country to the very best of their individual abilities." It embraced the liberal notion that "no statement, beginning 'all Negroes' is true, just as no statement, beginning 'all Frenchmen,' 'all Chinese,' or 'all Americans' is true." It cautioned readers against using derogatory language, even in jest, saying that terms such as "boy," "Negress," "darky," "uncle," "Mammy," "aunty," and "nigger are generally disliked by Negroes."

The pamphlet also encouraged commanders to be sensitive to "conflict of ideas within the Negro group, and within the mind of many an individual Negro soldier," torn between patriotism to America and hostility borne out of American prejudice, which limited "their participation in the life of the country." There was no greater symbol of this conflict, it instructed, than the "double V campaign," under which Black soldiers would flash the "V for victory" sign with both hands for double victory: one for winning the war, and the other for winning equality.

Black military police were being integrated into patrols, and there was evidence of this having the desired effect. In early April in the village of Hook Norton, near Oxford, a near riot broke out after rumors circulated of a Black soldier having been lynched by some white southern soldiers in the nearby town of Chipping Norton. Black soldiers organized to march, with the rallying cry "Let's go to Chipping Norton." One even succeeded in boosting a truck.

"We have been pushed around so much now from town to town," one said. "It's something had to happen sometime."

A Black military policeman, though, was able to keep the riot from escalating, which created time for the allegedly lynched soldier to come to Hook Norton to prove he was very much alive. Hook Norton was, in some respects, a success story, certainly compared with the spirals of racial violence the army had seen the previous year. But things were not all happy and bright. Once the riot had been quelled, the Black soldiers in Hook Norton were forced to parade in front of their white officers, who picked ten out as the goats to be court-martialed for disorder. There was a perception, and a reality, of unfairness in the court-martial system.

Some commands, including Patton's, were experimenting with ensuring that at least one Black soldier served on any court-martial involving another Black soldier being tried for a serious offense. But the problem was starkest and potentially most explosive when it came to the prosecution of rape, which in the army was punishable by death.

Since Eisenhower first took command of the European Theater of Operations in the summer of 1942, fifty-three soldiers had been charged with rape, and nearly all the victims were British civilians. Half of the soldiers charged were Black. Where a white soldier had a one in four chance of being convicted, a Black soldier's odds were three in four. And only one soldier—also Black—had been sentenced to death for rape, a sentence that was commuted just before Eisenhower's arrival back in January.

As Eisenhower was deciding what to do with the Patton and Miller cases, the case of Privates Willie Smith and Eliga Brinson also demanded his attention. The facts of the case were brutal. The accusation was that the two Black soldiers had smashed a bottle over the head of an American soldier and kidnapped his sixteen-year-old British girlfriend as they left a pub in Gloustershire. The kidnappers then gang-raped the girl in a nearby cemetery. The evidence pointing to Smith and Brinson as the perpetrators was circumstantial. The girl couldn't identify them beyond their being Black, and the evidence against them boiled down to footprints that arguably matched their boots, traces of blood and semen on their clothes, and weak alibis. Both men also had criminal records, having been convicted of petty military crimes in the past.

Eisenhower was not particularly disposed toward the death penalty. In one case, a private with the Big Red One had been sentenced to be shot for cowardice after abandoning his post and hiding during the Battle of El Guettar the previous spring. His commanding officer had approved the sentence, but Eisenhower commuted it to life.

Eisenhower was also not opposed to the death penalty either. The army had conducted executions in England with some regularity. There had been three hangings and one firing squad since Eisenhower had taken command. But these had all been murder cases.

Was it fair to execute these two men? Would it help win the war? The best answer to either question was unclear.

Smith and Brinson's trial had made the front page of the local paper. Their death sentences, however, made news across the United Kingdom, and the case became a diplomatic issue. This was, in part, because the British had abolished the death penalty for all but murder. But the real issue was a clash of values and the dangerous social forces the case seemed to unleash.

"People who live in or around a safe English village should be prepared to admit that the Americans, with the teeming millions of blacks in their midst, must know a good deal more about the colour problem than we in England can ever know," a letter to the editor in Gloucestershire's local paper wrote. "Their form of justice may be stern, but it is undoubtedly necessary. When that justice is applied as in the present case, to the upholding of the protection of young English womanhood, it should evoke thanks, and not squales of ignorant protest." Another wrote, "American negroes have been warned that the punishment is death if they violate our English women. It is the same law in their own country."

The case of Smith and Brinson seemed to be proof that the Americans who were disembarking at British ports by the thousands had spread their "color problem" to the seat of the empire like plague-infected rats. It got to the point that the foreign secretary, Anthony Eden, was challenged in Parliament by members of the opposition who condemned the trial of Smith and Brinson as both a case of "racial persecution" and contrary to British law.

Eisenhower asked his judge advocate general, Edward Betts, to conduct a study into the use of the death penalty for rape and whether these perceived disparities between Black and white were real. He also told Betts to draft personal responses to all the letters of protest, defending the fairness of American justice. But that such a defense needed to be mounted only highlighted the fact that America's ugly "color problem" was also Eisenhower's problem.

Marie Joseph Pierre François Koenig

CHAPTER 37

THAT OLD, FAMILIAR tension was building. It had been the same before the invasion of North Africa, the invasion of Sicily, and then the invasion of Salerno. Each time, the anticipation put everyone on edge. The pressure inside Eisenhower's head had gotten to the point that his ear started ringing and it wasn't going away. He was no use to anyone if he was overwhelmed. But how could he not be?

There was another Ultra intercept from Rundstedt warning Hitler of the potential for attacks against Normandy. The Germans were moving in reinforcements, including Panzer divisions around Caen, and reconnaissance flights farther inland spotted a new crop of "Rommel's asparagus," tall poles topped with mines, primed to detonate if clipped by a glider or an unlucky paratrooper.

There was also an intelligence report suggesting that the Germans were preparing to defend the Atlantikwall with botulinum, which it described as "one of the most deadly toxins known to science." If inhaled or injected in any quantity, a person would first find that they could no longer swallow, then that their vision was doubling, then that they were paralyzed, and finally that they could no longer breathe.

Then there were the inklings of unknowns. Irwin Rommel was now bragging that his forces along the Channel coast were being equipped with "new and surprising weapons." A British pilot then spotted a "most colossal white explosion" during a night mission off the coast of Calais. No one could account for it, and there was speculation that it might be the Germans' newest "secret weapon." Had the Germans succeeded in their quest for an atomic bomb?

Eisenhower had received no further word about Operation Peppermint and struggled to weigh the odds. Had Eisenhower received no further instructions from the Combined Chiefs because they had concluded the odds remained low? Or was he being kept in the dark, the way he was keeping Monty and Brad in the dark, because the odds were high and there was nothing he could do even if he knew?

Eisenhower wrote to General Marshall personally, all but pleading for some certainty on the potential nuclear threat. "I have assumed that they consider, on the present available intelligence, that the enemy will not implement this project," he wrote. He then added that based on this assumption, "I have not taken those precautionary steps which would be necessary adequately to counter enemy action of this nature." But all he got back was more silence.

Eisenhower was weary. He could still muster the energy to meet a moment, to flash his broad, likable smile, or to say some disarming thing. But it was getting harder to bounce back. There were so many things, from so many different directions, some urgent, some important, some neither, some both.

Eisenhower thought hard about his own thinking and how to make the best decisions he could without becoming overwhelmed. He needed to compartmentalize. And the only way to do that was to make it as easy as possible to focus on the problems in front of him that could be solved. He made it a practice to have only one piece of paper on his desk at a time. And he tried to be disciplined about protecting time during the day to think, to get outside in the fresh air.

Kay helped. And Butch helped. After a few weeks shipboard, Butch thought better of leaving the catbird seat just to say he had done a stint at sea. Eisenhower was glad to have him back. Butch's dirty jokes over drinks and cigarettes at Telegraph Cottage, rides with Kay through Richmond Park, hands of bridge with the Official Family, and a stack of pulp westerns were all he had to clear his mind.

Butch had also brought back good news. The week after the disastrous Exercise Tiger, Butch had enjoyed a front-row seat for the final and largest of the rehearsals, Exercise Fabius. It rehearsed the landings on all three of the British and Canadian beaches as well as Omaha Beach. By all measures, it was a resounding success. There were only two reported casualties. One soldier came down with pneumonia and another junior lieutenant somehow got himself shot in the ass.

The weather had been horrible, though even that was a good sign. At the commanders in chief conference that week, Stagg had predicted bad weather, giving Eisenhower the chance to postpone the operation by a day with plenty of notice. If Exercise Tiger had bode poorly for the already high-risk landing on Utah Beach, Exercise Fabius offered some hope that the landings on Gold, Sword, Juno, and Omaha might go off without a hitch.

THE RESULTS OF Exercise Fabius constituted the first really encouraging news on the prospects for the Operation Neptune part of Operation Overlord. But as Churchill had said, the goal was "an invasion, not a creation of a fortified beachhead." To prevent Normandy from stalling like Anzio, Eisenhower had to slow the German counterattack, and the way to do that was the Transportation Plan.

Eisenhower had tried to be sensitive to the concern over casualties. He assured Churchill that they would organize the bombing so that the largest number of casualties would be deferred until the week before D-Day, when the diplomatic attention would be distracted by the actual invasion. Harris, Spaatz, and Leigh-Mallory were under orders that in the "selection of targets for attack those with the lower estimated civilian casualty figures are to be given priority."

But the War Cabinet voted against the Transportation Plan nevertheless and Churchill wrote to Roosevelt, saying, "The War Cabinet is unanimous in its anxiety about these French slaughters, even reduced as they have been, and also in its doubts as to whether almost any good military use could not be produced by other methods."

Churchill's latter point, about "other methods," got to the irreconcilable heart of the controversy: Operation Pointblank. To those baptized into the faith of strategic bombing, the frustration was raw. They believed they were being denied the chance to win the war. Even those who did not share their absolute faith in strategic bombing, such as Alan Brooke, thought options like Tooey Spaatz's Oil Plan showed bolder vision. And while Operation Pointblank caused extraordinary civilian casualties, those civilians were largely German. And who cared if they complained?

Britain had to care, however, when the French Committee complained.

And complain it did. It protested that "the losses and damage that the aerial bombardment have brought for the population seem out of proportion to the military results obtained." It proposed a reorientation of the bombing and, if nothing else, asked to have input on the selection of targets and means of destroying them. Eisenhower, however, still had no official authority to invite that input.

The Combined Chiefs had permitted Eisenhower to informally coordinate with Koenig, but solely in Koenig's capacity as the head of the French military mission in London, not in his role as De Gaulle's political envoy. Whenever they met, Beetle would have to ask Koenig, "Which hat are you wearing today?" The answer would make all the difference.

Beetle was increasingly pessimistic. As he saw it, they had a 50/50 chance of holding on to the beachhead once the Germans counterattacked. They needed more support from the other side. They needed French cooperation. And Beetle leaned on Eisenhower to try to get more leeway. But there was nothing more Eisenhower could do in the never-ending essay contest over "may" versus "shall."

Churchill's capitulation notwithstanding, De Gaulle had gone on record opposing both "may" and "shall." The only acceptable terms, he insisted, were the French Committee joining the Combined Chiefs as an equal. And it remained unclear whether the Soviets, who recognized the French Committee as the only legitimate French government, would undercut De Gaulle and agree to "may."

What little "informal" influence Eisenhower had was solely due to Joseph Koenig being the man in the middle. Eisenhower kept Koenig more in the loop than he was probably permitted to be, at least officially. He did so even though it sometimes came back to bite him, such as when the press reported that Eisenhower was critical of Roosevelt's hard-line stance against De Gaulle. This, in turn, forced Eisenhower to reassure General Marshall that it was an "absurd allegation" and to lament that "any newspaper can be allowed to insinuate that commanders in the field are tacitly insubordinate."

Koenig was also stretching the very outer limit of his authority in keeping the lines of communication open with Eisenhower. It was a problem of Eisenhower's own making. All through April, he had lobbied Churchill to cut off diplomatic travel and uncensored communications from London for all except Canada and the United States, "countries whose troops are participating in 'OVERLORD.'" Churchill had relented after overcoming significant opposition from the Foreign Office. Predictably, De Gaulle exploded and ordered Koenig to cut off all communications with Eisenhower in return, which Koenig honored with the same fidelity that Eisenhower honored Roosevelt's demands about De Gaulle.

With the controversy over the Transportation Plan roiling, Eisenhower hosted Koenig and four of his officers from the French mission for a Saturday lunch reception at Wide Wing. The conversation involved little more than pleasantries, which were made even more superficial by the language barrier. Eisenhower had lived for more than a year in France, and his mentor General Conner was a bona fide Francophile. But Eisenhower never had a knack for languages and could never say more than a few perfunctory words. But that did not prevent the hour from being convivial, and Eisenhower came away feeling that Koenig was a man he could still trust.

The following Monday, Eisenhower notified the Combined Chiefs that he intended to tell Koenig "the name of the country in which the main attack will take place and the month for which it is scheduled." That, in turn, set off a new round in the essay contest over how much coordination of what kinds Eisenhower could have with which French. It was enough that Eisenhower warned the Combined Chiefs that "the limitations under which we are operating in dealing with the French are becoming very embarrassing and producing a situation, which is potentially dangerous." That, in turn, provoked Roosevelt to admonish Eisenhower that he was not permitted to engage in any political dealmaking with De Gaulle.

Eisenhower looked for ways of doing covertly what he was not permitted to do officially. In the middle of April, he had managed to get official authority to direct the activities of the Office of Strategic Services' operations in Europe. British influence over the French was due in no small part to their providing more direct military aid to the France Resistance. Orders of magnitude more. And De Gaulle went out of his way to remind the world of that fact whenever he got the chance.

Eisenhower used his newfound command over the Office of Strategic Services to change that. By June, American aid to the French Resistance would be double that of the British. The OSS was in the process of dropping two dozen agents into France to coordinate and, in many cases, to do the sabotage attributed publicly to the homegrown French Resistance. Another operation, the "Green Plan," involved infiltrating the French railway union so that French Committee loyalists were put in charge of managing the rail traffic around Normandy. The OSS was embedding agents in the Maquis. And Eisenhower had doubled the number of planes dedicated to the 801st Bomb Group, a covert OSS operation, whose payloads were not bombs.

By the end of the month, the 801st Bomb Group was on track to drop 3,000 rocket launchers, 16,000 carbines, 125,000 grenades, and more than 25 million rounds of ammunition, to go with the 60,000 boxes of cigarettes, 40,000 tins of corned beef, and 11,000 pairs of wool socks being dropped on France, Belgium, and the Netherlands. Mixed within were also a few dozen "bodies"—the manifest euphemism for secret agents.

EISENHOWER AND BEETLE cultivated considerable mutual trust with Koenig. But, as the French Committee's fierce opposition to the Transportation Plan laid bare, that mutual trust had not translated into real influence.

That was the biggest seeming difference between the United States and Great Britain. America had far more resources. And that mattered, as the spat over the LSTs had demonstrated. But the British were still the masters of influence.

Churchill understood influence. That was why he had picked De Gaulle and shepherded him past his many French rivals. After World War I, and for much of the following decade, the British government had proceeded on the assumption that its next great power war would be with France. Now, by cultivating De Gaulle, Churchill was on the verge of turning one of Britain's oldest imperial competitors into a client state.

Churchill had somehow managed to turn even the LST question back in his favor. A few weeks after the US Chiefs pulled out of the negotiations over Operation Anvil, Churchill started putting momentum behind a new operation to invade Bordeaux that the British could do with the landing craft already at their disposal. Like an audience member picking a card from a magician's deck, Ernest King returned to the negotiating table and offered to send LSTs from the Pacific to the Mediterranean, with the only string being the British Chiefs' general agreement to "a definite recommendation for an assault on southern or western France."

Americans seemed to have no talent for shaping world affairs, or an interest in doing so. The Italians had just formed their first coalition government as a democracy, and America was nowhere to be found. "You withdraw your good Eisenhower and the sympathetic General Smith, and General Wilson, whom I esteem, takes over," Pietro Badoglio complained. "It leaves my people with an impression that the U.S. is abandoning Italy to Great Britain and the Soviet Union."

In his State of the Union address, Roosevelt promised, "We shall not repeat the tragic errors of ostrich isolationism." But now Roosevelt seemed intent on alienating the man who US intelligence had concluded was the only Frenchman with any hope of being a consensus leader after the fall of Vichy. And while the Americans were abandoning France to Great Britain and the Soviet Union, Churchill was presiding over the first-ever Commonwealth Prime Ministers' Conference, bringing the political leadership from Canada, Australia, New Zealand, South Africa, Southern Rhodesia, and India together in London to coordinate the Empire's common future.

Keith Murdoch

CHAPTER 38

THE MORNING OF May 15, the *Bayonet* pulled into London's Addison Road station. Eisenhower had spent the weekend meeting some of the British and Canadian forces under his command. He made a point of wearing a British overcoat when inspecting British soldiers, which did not help his reputation as an Anglophile. But like Alexander the Great following the conquest of the Persians, Eisenhower understood that a general seeking the loyalty of armies who had taken oaths to a foreign king should do what he could to look less foreign.

It was a cool spring day, and Kay was waiting to drive Eisenhower to Monty's headquarters at Saint Paul's School. The occasion for Eisenhower's visit was the final planning conference for Operation Overlord, marking the transition from planning to execution, and the beginning of the end of the war against Hitler. The same day, the First US Army Planning Group officially cleaned out their desks at their guest offices at Monty's 21st Army headquarters and returned to Bristol.

The conference was convened in what had been a students' lecture auditorium during peacetime. It was a giant crescent-shaped room, paneled in pitch pine, with benches circling up around a central well. All along the outer walls were maps and tables and charts, reducing life spans' worth of painstaking effort to visual aids, as well as a vestigial sign advertising a scholarship available to the sons of clergymen. In the well, there were two short rows of armchairs lined up for the dignitaries, leaving the rest of the room to practice their posture like fidgety schoolboys as they peered down at a massive scale map of the Normandy coast, color-coded with the most valuable secrets the Allies had to protect.

The proceedings were scheduled down to the minute and quickly became a showcase for the continuing preeminence of the British Empire. Passes for 138 men were distributed, along with seven dignitaries: King George IV, Winston Churchill, Field Marshal Jan Smuts from South Africa, Pug Ismay, and the three British Chiefs: Charles Portal, Alan Brooke, and Andrew Cunningham.

Churchill arrived shortly before nine with Jan Smuts. The prime minister always made an entrance, and on this day, he entered like a mafia don, dressed in a black frock coat and munching a cigar. King George was the last to enter, and when he did, the whole of the room—British and American—rose to their feet. Churchill gave one of his usual awkward, almost ironic, bows. King George sat at the center of the front row, with Eisenhower on his left and Churchill next to Eisenhower.

The mood was brightened by that morning's papers, which reported the first major progress in Italy since January. The French soldiers under the command of Wayne Clark had fought with particular distinction. And the only thing to dampen the mood was De Gaulle taking the opportunity to rename the French Committee the "Provisional Government of the French Republic." A subtler choice would have been to rename the French Committee the "Franklin Roosevelt Can Go to Hell Committee."

At nine sharp, the doors were closed and guarded by the biggest and meanest-looking American MPs who could be found for the job. Eisenhower called everyone to attention, by announcing, "We're going to have a briefing on the invasion of France."

"Here we are on the eve of a great battle, to deliver to you the various plans made by the different force commanders," he said simply. "I would emphasize but one thing, that I consider it to be the duty of anyone who sees a flaw in the plan not to hesitate to say so. I have no sympathy with anyone, whatever his station, who will not brook criticism. We are here to get the best possible results and you must really make a co-operative effort."

Eisenhower then turned the floor over to Monty. The hero of El Alamein was born for the moment, right down to the crease in his trousers that had been pressed sharp enough to slit the throat of any man who said otherwise.

"General Eisenhower has charged me with the preparation and conduct of the land battle," Monty began. He emphasized how he had taken the measure of Rommel whom he had defeated at El Alamein and would defeat again. Even those who could not stand Monty had to admire it. His charisma filled the room.

"Last February, Rommel took command from Holland to the Loire. It is now clear that his intention is to deny penetration; Overlord is to be defeated on the beaches. To this end Rommel has:

"(a) thickened up the coastal crust.

"(b) Increased the number of infantry divisions not committed to beach defence, and allotted them in a lay back to seal off any break in the coast crust.

"(c) Redistributed his armoured reserve. There are now sixty enemy divisions in France, of which ten are Panzer type.

"Rommel is an energetic and determined commander; he has made a world of difference since he took over. He is best at the spoiling attack; his forte is disruption; he is too impulsive for the set-piece battle. He will do his level best to 'Dunkirk' us—not to fight the armoured battle on ground of his own choosing, but to avoid it altogether by preventing our tanks landing by using his own tanks well forward.

"The problem: The enemy is in position, with reserves available. There are obstacles and minefields on the beaches; we cannot gain contact with the obstacles and recce them. There are many unknown hazards. After a sea voyage, and a landing on a strange coast, there is always some loss of cohesion.

"The solution: We have the initiative. We must then rely on:

"(a) the violence of our assault.

"(b) our great weight of supporting fire, from the sea and air.

"(c) Simplicity.

"(d) Robust mentality. We must blast our way on shore and get a good lodgment before the enemy can bring sufficient reserves up to turn us out."

Churchill interjected to second Monty's call for aggression. "At Anzio, we had put ashore 160,000 men and 25,000 vehicles and had advanced only twelve miles," the prime minister reminded everyone. "To take a risk occasionally would certainly do no harm."

Monty then turned to the massive terrain map of Normandy on the floor. He had taped phase lines across the British sector that showed his prediction that Caen would be captured on D-Day, and how he would drive southward from there. He spoke in his usual quiet, emphatic way, repeating the most important part of a sentence. "It is intended to move toward Caen, toward Caen," he said.

"We shall have to send the soldiers in to this party 'seeing red,'" he concluded. "We must get them completely on their toes; having absolute faith in the plan; and embued with infectious optimism and offensive eagerness. Nothing must stop them. If we send them in to battle in this way—then we shall succeed. Plans and preparations are now complete in every detail. All difficulties have been foreseen and provided against. Nothing has been left to chance."

With an unsubtle callback to Henry V's Saint Crispin's Day speech, Monty announced that he preferred the company of the men in this students' lecture room to the company of anyone who worried that Operation Overlord might fail. "This is a perfectly normal operation which is certain of success. If anyone has any doubts in his mind, let him stay behind."

All the commanders in chief were given a turn to try to follow Monty's call to arms that morning, as were Tooey Spaatz and Arthur Harris, who took the occasion to remind everyone that they could have won the war with airplanes had Operation Overlord not intruded. Last to speak was King George VI, who stuttered a bit, but hit the right note. The stakes, he reminded everyone, were "the fate of the Empire and the free world." He then concluded, "With God's help this great operation would be brought to a successful conclusion."

The conference broke for lunch and King George had to leave. As he departed, Eisenhower thanked the king for gracing them with his presence, and reminded him that they had assembled the greatest armada in human history. All that was left was for the men on the ground to "capture some villas for the hot shots, particularly one to accommodate the king, who would be as welcome in France as he had been in North Africa."

AT LUNCH, PATTON and Churchill found themselves across the table from one another. The two had met once before at a dinner held during the Casablanca Conference. Patton had arrived late and ordered a glass of orange juice and water. He didn't drink, and at that point in the war, had done nothing to distinguish himself. As far as Churchill could tell, Patton was just another novice American general, who was not even man enough to handle an evening libation. It being after ten at night, and having already had a few libations of his own, Churchill had gotten snide.

Over the intervening year and a half, Churchill had grown to like Patton in his own way. When Eisenhower had told him of Patton's gaffe about the Russians, Churchill just shrugged. Patton had, as far as the prime minister was concerned, "simply told the truth."

Do you remember meeting me? Churchill asked Patton across Saint Paul's dining table.

I do, Patton replied. How could Patton forget meeting such a fat, drunk, rude little Brit?

Churchill then called to the waiter, demanding with a wry wink, Get this man a glass of whiskey!

Patton returned the smile like a secret handshake.

THE AFTERNOON'S PROCEEDINGS were a bit slow, as lower-ranking British and American commanders described their pieces of the operation. But then Churchill took the floor. He began slowly and built as he gained momentum.

"At the risk of hurting the feelings of my dear friend, General De Gaulle," he joked, "we are worrying too much about governing France before conquering it." He then reminded them all that "bravery, ingenuity and persistence" were far more valuable than any military equipment.

Gripping his lapels, Churchill announced, "I am hardening on this enterprise. I repeat, I am now hardening toward this enterprise."

To the room, it was a rousing call to arms. But Eisenhower felt those words like a kick to the solar plexus. Everyone, and certainly everyone in that room, knew that Churchill had to be dragged into the invasion of Normandy as if it were a marriage to Petruchio. But at lunch the previous week, Eisenhower thought Churchill had finally committed to its success, his doubts by then having been well-preserved for history. It was just the two of them. "I am in this thing with you to the end," Churchill had said with tears welling up in his eyes. "If it fails, we will go down together."

Now, though, here Churchill was reminding everyone that he had opposed it all along and was, only now, coming around to the idea. It was a backhanded show of support that gave Churchill the space to cover himself if this invasion turned sour like Gallipoli. Responsibility was truly on Eisenhower's shoulders, and defeat would be his alone.

The energy just drained right out of Eisenhower. There was a conspicuous softness to his voice as he wrapped up the afternoon. He joked that Field Marshal Smuts's presence was a good omen, since Smuts had been there at a similar conference ahead of the invasion of Sicily.

"In a few moments," he continued, trying to keep things light, "Hitler will have missed his last chance to wipe out all the leaders of the invasion by a well-placed bomb." He then concluded saying that those present "should all regard themselves as members of the staff college of the future. It should be a college in which there was neither Navy, Army, nor Air Force, British nor American, but only fighting men there to instruct and to be instructed in the art of war."

Alan Brooke all but rolled his eyes. "Eisenhower was a swinger," he wrote of his presentation that day, "and no real director of thought, plans, energy or direction! Just a coordinator—a good mixer, a champion of interrelated cooperation, and in those respects few can hold a candle to him. But is that enough? Or can we not find all the qualities of a commander in one man?"

No one leaving Saint Paul's School that evening doubted that America would continue to grow as the arsenal of democracy in war and as the free world's factory floor in peace. But equally, no one could doubt that the voice leading that free world still had a distinctly English accent.

THE NEXT MORNING, Eisenhower's first meeting of the day was with an Australian news mogul who had come to England earlier that month to network at the Commonwealth Prime Ministers' Conference. Keith Murdoch would never count as one of Churchill's great friends. Launching his career by exposing the folly of Gallipoli made sure of that. And Murdoch would grouse that, in London, "the food is appalling." But he remained as ardent a subject of the empire as King George could want.

In the 1920s, Murdoch had leveraged his fame as a journalist into fortune as a publisher and conservative kingmaker in Australia with a simple formula for success. Tell people what they already wanted to hear, on the principle, "You cannot run counter violently to the habits of the community." He loved the news business, and his thirteen-year-old son, Rupert, was just beginning to get a feel for it. Like Eisenhower, Murdoch relished sharing a common calling with his boy.

Murdoch had met with the Australian prime minister, John Curtin, the Friday before. Despite having spent years bagging Australia's Labor government for every real or perceived sin, Murdoch was all praise for Curtin's recent efforts to strengthen the empire. Curtin had come to London to propose the creation of a Commonwealth Secretariat to greater centralize policy and planning across the empire.

Murdoch was circling the globe. He had toured His Majesty's realm all the way from Australia and had been heartened that "the splendid masculine strength of the British Empire had restored British prestige to a high peak." The next leg of his journey was to the United States, where he had a full dance card of meetings with almost everyone important. Roy Howard, the head of the Scripps-Howard newspaper company and the all-around macher in the Republican Party behind Wendell Willkie's presidential run in 1940, had invited Murdoch to Chicago for that year's Republican National Convention, so he could see American democracy in action.

Murdoch's meeting with Eisenhower fell on the last day of the Commonwealth Prime Ministers' Conference. In 1923, London had hosted the first Imperial Conference, which Canadian Prime Minister McKenzie King had touted as the grand occasion to "safeguard the permanence of the empire." That year, it would turn out, the empire would reach the peak of its size over the surface of the earth. A lot, though, had changed in the ensuing two decades, and Churchill had convened the Commonwealth Prime Ministers' Conference to reinvigorate the Pax Britannica just as the Imperial Conference had done twenty years before. But even Murdoch had to admit, it may have done the opposite.

The Australian proposal to further integrate the empire had failed in the face of opposition from none other than Canadian Prime Minister Mackenzie King. The Canadians had opposed tighter integration for the same reason that Murdoch was keen for the next leg of his trip: the United States had become too important to ignore.

Just before the war, Roosevelt had negotiated a free trade deal with Canada. Given the size of its economy, the United States rapidly overtook Britain as Canada's largest trading partner. The significance of that shift was not simply economic. The British Empire had been built as a closed trading zone. Free trade within, high tariffs without, and London at the center. Within the empire, British manufacturers could secure commodities from around the world at discount prices and sell their goods protected from competition. And the British government could enjoy unrivaled global influence and financial rewards by being at the hub of it all.

Two world wars, however, had driven the empire to the brink of insolvency in what the British economist John Maynard Keynes would warn was becoming a "financial Dunkirk." The metaphor was apt. The British had successfully evacuated more than 300,000 men from Dunkirk, but left the lions' share of their military hardware behind. Through Lend-Lease, Roosevelt had given Britain a way to "borrow" billions of dollars of needed equipment and supplies without having to dip into its strategic currency reserves.

Lend-Lease had begun the most extraordinary period of political, military, and economic cooperation between two great powers in human history. Churchill had even started to fantasize about the creation of a "Sterling Dollar," presenting Roosevelt a doodle of the symbol that could be used for this new world currency. But over four years of war, British government debt was soon more than double the size of the entire British economy.

In January 1944, just as Eisenhower was returning to London, Keynes wrote a report for the British government concluding, "Special post-war financial assistance from the U.S. on a major scale seems inescapable." But this posed an extraordinary danger to the empire that was more political than it was economic. "It is not the quantity of the accommodation about which we need worry," Keynes wrote. "It is the terms and the consequences of losing our financial independence which should deeply concern us." As the Lend-Lease tab grew, the British government was increasingly unable to resist American demands for free trade. As the United States shoved its massive economy into the empire's tight protectionist bubble, the whole empire was in danger of going the way of Canada.

The irony was that Nazi economists had been the first to see it all coming. An article in Germany's leading economics journal, published in 1941, predicted that soon a "Pax Americana" would consume the British Empire. The author's goal was to inveigh against Roosevelt's postcolonial vision of democracy, equality, and free trade, in favor of German-style ethnonationalism. "What the U.S. has to offer the world," the article warned, "is ruthless absorption and exploitation by an economic imperialism." And it both faulted and ridiculed the British for bringing it all on themselves by opposing Hitler. "In an effort to perpetuate European powerlessness, England will lose its empire to its partner across the Atlantic."

As loyal as he was to the empire, Keith Murdoch had been early to the idea that America would play a decisive role in the future of the world. That was hardly a sure bet when he made it in the early 1940s. Yes, the United States had a massive economy. But its politics were a mess. It was a conglomeration of forty-eight little governments, which had gone to war with each other just eighty years earlier. Its national government was bridled by courts that were fanatical about the protection of private property. And the isolationist faction of Roosevelt's own party tended to think, in an honest moment, that Hitler had a point. For all the grand talk about the United States becoming the "Arsenal of Democracy," it was hard to see how Roosevelt could harness America's common market into a commonwealth.

By 1944, though, the United States was producing twice as many guns, twice as many airplanes, three times as many tanks, and seven times as many ships as the whole British Empire. It did so by mobilizing a smaller percentage of its economy. And, of greatest significance, it had developed a global logistics network to put all that stuff to good use, often by trading Lend-Lease aid for US military outposts on British possessions like Bermuda. In just the previous year, the Arsenal of Democracy had shipped twenty million tons of war matériel all around the world. "It had to be seen to be believed," Murdoch wrote to his Australian readers. America, the reclusive land of cowboys and immigrants, "had become an immense and effective war power with an astonishing speed."

Murdoch saw no conflict between his affection for America and his loyalty to his king. Upon arriving in London, he published a piece in the *Daily Mail*, saying, "Australia's main body of sentiment is stoutly and uncompromisingly British, but geographical and biological facts are hard and unbending. The truth is clear that in the Pacific Ocean British, Americans, and Australians—those who live and think our way—can survive and develop only by working together." And Murdoch came away keenly impressed by Eisenhower, who made that vision a reality. "British and Americans are put together at the same desk," he crowed, and working for a common cause. It had to be seen to be believed.

THAT EVENING, EISENHOWER tried to put the French question to bed once and for all by promising General Marshall, yet again, that he would "carefully avoid anything that could be interpreted as an effort to influence the character of the future government of France." But he could not resist adding that "so far as I am able to determine from information given to me through agents, and through escaped prisoners of war, there exists in France today only two major groups, of which one is the Vichy gang and the other seems to be almost idolatrous in its worship of De Gaulle."

This was, based on those same intelligence sources, an overstatement. De Gaulle was popular across France's partisan divides because he was an empty uniform, who meant something to no one, and therefore nothing to everyone beyond opposing Germany. But three weeks out from D-Day, that was more than enough for Eisenhower's purposes. The alternative was trying to mediate the competing interests of passionate, and prolix, Frenchmen over the future of a country whose significance to Eisenhower was solely that it stood between his army and Hitler.

Nevertheless, Eisenhower promised General Marshall (and therefore Roosevelt) not to give De Gaulle the "exclusive right to deal with me in the handling of French liberated territories." He just wanted the authority to officially deal with somebody.

Happily, the next day, the Soviets came through and approved. "May" won the day, making no firm promises to De Gaulle, but giving Eisenhower discretion to coordinate officially with the "French Committee of National Liberation."

The timing was auspicious, following close on the heels of a disappointing intelligence assessment of the Transportation Plan's progress. There had been tremendous physical damage, and while that might have had some impact on German rail traffic, analysts concluded that the effects were "very largely falling on the French, as is almost inevitable."

Eisenhower believed in the Transportation Plan, but the momentum was turning against it. French cardinals had just made an appeal to the world's Catholics to oppose Allied bombing. "Thousands of civilians have been killed or wounded, and their homes, churches, schools, and hospitals destroyed." The plea could be dismissed as enemy propaganda. But the Allies were developing a reputation for indiscriminate bombing. Swiss newspapers were now denouncing the Allies and the Vatican was calling for an end to the bombing in Italy.

Roosevelt had backed Eisenhower against Churchill's objections, despite his "distress at the loss of life among the French population." Roosevelt, though, could be mercurial, particularly in an election year. Following the Vatican, the Knights of Columbus were now calling for the bombing of Rome to stop, threatening Roosevelt's support among working-class Catholics. A sharp shift in public opinion could weaken not just the Transportation Plan, but also Eisenhower's "direction" of the strategic air forces just when he needed them most.

But then Eisenhower got a peculiar note from General Marshall. Antoine Béthouart, De Gaulle's chief of staff in Algiers, had offered Marshall a suggestion. Now that Eisenhower had the official authority to coordinate with the French Committee, he should ask Koenig for a list of targets. Doing so, Marshall indicated, would "assure the French that we are doing our very best to keep civilian casualties to a minimum." It would also show that it was not the United States bombing France from England, but the United States providing military assistance to its French allies in the fight against Nazi occupation. If the Transportation Plan's targets came from the French, then what standing did the British have to object?

That afternoon, with things now official, Eisenhower sent Beetle to Koenig to do as Béthouart suggested. It was a risk to be sure. The French Committee's protests had been emphatic. There was no reason to think that a list of targets chosen by the French would look anything like Eisenhower's target list. And once the French had made their list of acceptable targets known, Eisenhower would have little room to deviate from it.

Beetle came back wide eyed. Koenig had been happy to see him. When it came to choosing targets, Koenig said that Eisenhower's team had studied the problem more closely than he ever could. He trusted Eisenhower to make the best decisions.

Beetle had raised the controversy over civilian casualties with Koenig. The French Committee had been quite ardent in its protests about the effect of the bombing on innocent French civilians.

"*C'est la guerre.*" Koenig shrugged with sangfroid. "It must be expected that people will be killed. We will take the anticipated loss to be rid of the Germans." *C'est tout.*

Elliott Roosevelt

CHAPTER 39

WITH THREE WEEKS to go, Eisenhower officially set June 5 as D-Day. The timing of the invasion was one of the most sensitive secrets someone with a BIGOT clearance could know. Keeping that and the many other secrets was becoming more difficult, both because of leaks and what had been done to prevent leaks. De Gaulle remained incensed over the diplomatic communication ban and was constantly agitating over the "indignity" as the "chief of state" of being "denied private and secret communications with his own government." The Foreign Office was, in turn, incensed that they were having to deal with a diplomatic crisis.

But secrecy became vital as the dangers grew. There was fresh intelligence that the Germans might be preparing to use anthrax and botulinum. About a hundred X-ray films had become inexplicably fogged at a hospital in Cheltenham. The German air defenses were thickening to the point that they could fill the sky over Normandy with flak, which for a paratrooper meant leaping into a cloud of razor blades. The latest estimates suggested that the Nazis had 750,000 men in France, not including the forces in Belgium or Holland, who could be redeployed to Normandy at a moment's notice. And if the Russians failed to make good on their promised offensive in June, the Germans could draw even more forces from Norway, Denmark, and the Balkans.

Unlike the French, the Russians had been kept informed of the date of the invasion. The sharing of such sensitive intelligence was a source of worry, because dealing with the Soviets was like playing with a new bridge partner. There was no way of knowing how well they knew the game, what risks or strategies or habits they might have. Were their bids too aggressive, too conservative? What kind of hand would make them bid no trumps? It was the opposite of playing with someone like Kay, where the flash of an Irish eyebrow across the table could set up the whole hand.

That uncertainty forced a return to fundamentals. Nothing too tricky, no misdirection. If the Russians bid six spades, you could be damn sure they had every spade in the deck. But what if they were playing you as a mark? Would they cut a deal to throw the game for a share of the pot? That risk grew if they doubted that you had the skills to win. It was among the reasons that Roosevelt had been so dead set against canceling Operation Anvil. Promising a pincer maneuver on the continent of Europe was a jump bid. Calling it off made Roosevelt a dummy with a weak hand.

Earlier that month, Averell Harriman, who had spent the past six months as the ambassador in Moscow, had come to London. Over dinner, Harriman assured Eisenhower that the Russians were all in on mounting a "full-out attack" to correspond with the invasion of Normandy. That conviction was shared by Elliott Roosevelt, who had spent most of May in Moscow and paid a visit to Eisenhower on his way back for an evening of drinks and bridge.

"Stalin was a stickler for keeping his word," Elliott said. The main thing he was worried about was the British and the Americans cutting a side deal for peace themselves.

Eisenhower said he was confident the Russians would come through. He was fascinated by Russia and eager to hear what life under communism was like.

The Russians, Elliott explained, made sure everyone was equal, but had come up with a system of discounts to reward merit. A private in the army got 25 percent off. A general, 75 percent, which was the same discount a top ballet dancer received. It was like Eisenhower's Order of Suvorov entitling him to free rides on the Moscow subway. The thing that had impressed Elliott the most, though, was the scale of everything. "The government buildings in Moscow made the Pentagon look like a play house." And then there was the opera. It put the Met to shame.

Was it awkward being the president's son in Russia? Butch asked.

Elliott didn't think so. The Russians seemed almost deliberately indifferent to that kind of thing. Stalin's own son had enlisted as a private in the Red Army, and been killed. It was impossible to imagine what the Russians had gone through. Elliott said that the estimates were sixteen million dead, civilians and military, against four million German soldiers dead.

Why were the casualties so high?

Part of it, Elliott thought, was that Russia was not the most organized place. Everyone was always waiting for official approval. Getting around was a mess. All the cars were ten-year-old Buicks and Ford Model As. Their planes were slow and they literally ran their pilots until they died, so you couldn't find a pilot with more than thirty missions to his name. The Russians, it had to be remembered, were fighting to the death. Civilians would stay behind after the military withdrew and just fight the Germans until there was nothing left.

Elliott had sensed there was a lot of good feeling between the Russians and the Americans. At one of the air bases he visited, the Russian soldiers had initially been standoffish, saying they had not been given permission to fraternize. But once the official permission had been forthcoming, they had a great time. All friendship, vodka, and smiles. Not so much the British. The Russians seemed to harbor an ancient distrust for the British.

Eisenhower wanted to like the Russians, who could do a lot to improve his chances of victory. Their most immediate contributions would be felt in a matter of weeks. The more the Soviets committed to their offensive in the east following D-Day, the less the Germans would have in counterattacking Eisenhower's forces to the west. The same was true of the "shuttle bombing" initiative. One of the inherent limitations of Operation Pointblank was that the Germans could move strategically valuable targets beyond the range a fully loaded heavy bomber could safely travel before needing to turn around. If the Russians opened their air bases, the strategic air forces flying out of England could bomb deeper into German territory on one-way missions into Russia, where they could refuel, rearm, and return.

There were also longer-term questions. How would occupied German territory be administered? How would the German army be demobilized? How would prisoners of war be exchanged? All those questions would be easier to answer if there was a shared spirit of Russo-Anglo-American cooperation.

It was one of the reasons Eisenhower continued to press General Marshall to ask the president to reconsider the division of Germany. Anticipating the postwar divorce of the United Nations into the Russian, British, and American spheres of influence compromised Eisenhower's ability to win the war in the first place. The mere prospect of it threatened to create the same national jockeying that had disillusioned General Conner during World War I. Each nation had made strategic choices, not to win swift victory, but in pursuit of its own "grandiose ideas" of what prize it would win once the war was won. The result was that the fighting dragged, leaving little left to win by the time all went quiet on the western front.

If the Allies could put their national self-interest aside, there were things they could do collectively to hasten the victory over their common enemy. Some of those things were simple. Intelligence kept coming in that the German army was full of conscripted Russian, Polish, Czech, Norwegian, Dutch, and Belgian soldiers. Taking a page from Abraham Lincoln, Eisenhower asked the Combined Chiefs to coordinate with the Russians to grant an amnesty. Such a move would undoubtedly be unpopular as a matter of the Allies' domestic politics. These soldiers were traitors. But like the Emancipation Proclamation, simply announcing the amnesty would "sow some seeds of distrust in the minds of German associates of these foreigners" and undermine the Germans' ability to fight cohesively.

The biggest thing the Allies could do, though, was to stop demanding Germany's "unconditional surrender." It was a great rallying cry for mobilizing domestic political support for the war. But demanding the unconditional surrender of an entire nation was wholly foreign to international law and the practice of modern, civilized warfare. Even the British, who were nothing if not bloodthirsty toward the Nazis, resisted "unconditional surrender," because it aroused Germany's "Dunkirk spirit" during the war, and, like the humiliations exacted by the Treaty of Versailles, it threatened to undermine Germany's acceptance of peace after the war.

Eisenhower knew Roosevelt would hate the suggestion, but he continued to lobby that the demand be softened to the "unconditional surrender of the Axis Armies, Navies, and Air forces." The Soviets, Eisenhower hoped, might agree. And the Allies could collectively reassure the German people that their goal was the "restoration of peaceful conditions in Europe, including the repatriation of impressed labor and the use of German labor in the restoration of devastated areas." Putting their common cause over the national self-interests could win the war, and win the peace.

King George VI

CHAPTER 40

A STY DEVELOPED in Eisenhower's left eye. His doctor attributed it to stress and prescribed a warm compress and rest. His ear was also still ringing, and given all the uncertainty about the future, it was hardly a surprise that the mental pressure was taking an ever greater physical toll.

Eisenhower did what he could to relax. Summer had come early, and the rides with Kay had become all the more beautiful as Richmond Park burst with rhododendrons, bluebonnets, pheasants, crows, and spring life of every kind. Out on a ride in the open air, he could rest his mind on the "antics of the hordes of rabbits—little bunnies ranging in size from that of a mouse, on up to full grown mamas."

His future with Kay was far from certain. She had become a part of his life, his date at dinners and events. But the peripatetic life they were living together was a temporary kind of life. And it was unclear how she would fit into his life when he inevitably returned to the United States and settled down. Kay, for her part, imagined her future in America. She wanted to become a citizen and Eisenhower asked Edward Betts, his judge advocate general, to figure out the necessary paper-shuffling with the War Department back in Washington.

Eisenhower also missed Mamie. She was home. And he missed home. With his ear ringing and his eye swollen, he panicked when he realized he had forgotten Mother's Day. "Please don't get annoyed with me," he wrote to her. "I depend on you and your letters so much, and I'm living only to come back when this terrible thing is over. So, if any omission of mine gets you irritated, please remember that, after all, you're mine, and all I have—and I am yours, always. Loads of love."

John was only a few weeks from graduation. Eisenhower fantasized about bringing him over to serve by his side in Europe and got excited at the thought that his son's name would be in the new *Army Register*, the index of all active-duty soldiers. Their names would be together, probably right next to each other, on the same page of the same book.

He had two gold Parker Pen sets made for John as a graduation gift. One was simple, or at least as simple as a solid-gold pen could be. The other was decorated with four stars, with each pen inscribed IKE. Eisenhower wasn't sure which to send. If someone had asked for his preference, he would of course have picked the plainest option like a good Kansan. But the etching of those three little letters, "I-K-E," sure did look smart in gold. And he hoped, albeit with some embarrassment, that John would want that one, out of pride for his old man.

Everett Hughes and Georgie Patton had come to chat about home, reporting back on the letters their wives had sent with news of Mamie. Georgie's wife, Beatrice, had been out to lunch with Mamie and had written all about it. He joked about how much national defense information the two of them could figure out if they put their heads together. She even had a new army joke:

An officer came home from the front on rotation and was assigned to the Pentagon. His second day there, he moved his desk. The next day, he moved it again. Then the next day, he moved it again. His commanding officer grew concerned and asked a psychiatrist to evaluate him. Perhaps he had battle anxiety. The psychiatrist ultimately found him at his desk, which he had by now moved to the latrine. Asked why, the soldier replied, "Well, it seemed to be the only place where people know what they are doing."

Georgie could be hilarious. No one would ever guess it, given that old "blood and guts" carried himself with the bearing of a martinet. Yet his voice was so high and his accent so nasal and peculiar that, if you knew him, George S. Patton could be downright silly.

Eisenhower laughed harder than he had in a while. He showed Georgie and Everett the pens and joked that John would probably want the plain one. He was his son, after all. He sent both pens off to Mamie, saying the "Ike" pens might be less ostentatious if she had the words "presented to his son, John," or just "to his son, John" engraved on them as well. Or she could just get John's initials engraved onto the plain set and keep the other one for herself, if she wanted it.

WHENEVER EISENHOWER WAS asked about his future, particularly if there was some suggestion that he might become the military ruler of Germany (if not Europe), he would always say that he was trying to win the war as fast as he could so he could "go home and go fishing." But it seemed increasingly unlikely that when he did go home, he would be left alone to stand in a creek and quietly cast a few lines.

Swede Hazlett had joined the faculty of the Naval Academy as the head of the department of English, History, and Government. He had sent Eisenhower a letter of encouragement, which he hoped "will reach you just about the time you've completed your Broad Jump and are about to start your Marathon." Swede mentioned being contacted by Alden Hatch and Ken Davis, who both seemed to be writing biographies of him with a healthy helping of support from Milton. He attached the letter of reminiscences he had sent to both authors that sketched the story of their friendship and ended by saying "I have been privileged in my close acquaintance with the man I consider to be the outstanding American of today—and I'm sure he will eventually bear comparison with the giants of all time." Back when they were goofing off and boosting ice cream at the Belle Springs Creamery, Eisenhower could never have known that a buddy from the better side of town in Abilene would ever say something like that about him—let alone mean it.

Edgar had also written about being interviewed by Davis. He had been surprised by how much research Davis had done into their family and childhood. But Edgar assured his brother that "the only stories that I related to Davis were those concerning some of the things we did when small kids like floating down Buckeye Avenue in a boat singing 'Marching Through Georgia,' and so forth." Eisenhower wrote back, joking, "if they gave me time and did not check up too closely on fact, I could make you and me look like Tom Sawyer and Huckleberry Finn. Which one would you rather be?"

Davis had just been cleared to come to London as a "recognized correspondent for the purpose of completing a biography of General Eisenhower." Milton assured his brother that Davis was writing a book of "real historical significance" and that he would "review his manuscripts during each revision. Obviously, no member of the family can be officially connected with a book and cannot be quoted, directly, or indirectly, in any way, but by reviewing his work carefully, I think I can guarantee that there will be no errors of consequence."

Milton was carefully cultivating his brother's image, ensuring that Davis did not present their father as weak, their mother as religiously fanatical, or Eisenhower as naive about politics. And he had insisted that "no reference would ever be made to connect Mother up with Russell, Rutherford, etc." Milton had a very specific idea of how the story of Eisenhower, and by extension the story of America, should be told.

"We have progressed from a primitive frontier society to a vast industrial nation whose welfare is bound up with the welfare of all the world," Milton would say. The frontier had created the conditions for American democracy. In an era of "free" land, those disgruntled with their lot in life could venture out and pursue happiness for themselves. But with the closing of the frontier and the rise of industrialization, the government needed to find new ways of providing people the same opportunity to pursue happiness. That was different from the government guaranteeing happiness. If the ideological conflicts of the 1930s had proved anything, it was that guarantees of happiness inexorably descended into tyranny. But it was also tyranny for human beings to be forced into the same predicament as wild animals, trapped in the desperate and all-consuming search for food.

Milton was thinking deeply about how to reframe Roosevelt's economic Bill of Rights in the terms of the frontier. A good government was one that re-created what the frontier had once offered through its abundance—the economic and social space to be free. Government could build roads for those who wanted to venture out into the world. It could build schools to give people the power to think for themselves. It could prevent monopolists from suffocating entrepreneurs. It could guarantee the basics of health, safety, and insurance so that average people were not slaves to their wages, but could work with dignity and pursue their own happiness.

It was a pitch for an American Century that sold not just the allure of individual liberty, but the common good that came from letting ordinary people be free to do all they were capable of achieving. It was an America, Milton would say, that valorized the "average workaday American—the farmer's boy who went into the Army, the machinist at the shipyard, the corner grocer, the city housewife." These were the people who made America great economically and spiritually. It was an argument that a government that fostered individual freedom created the conditions not just for a comfortable life, but the good life. And Milton understood that no one embodied the triumph of that aspiration better than his own brother.

Not coincidentally, Mamie had just gotten a call from Jack Connolly, a movie producer who was taking time off from Hollywood to work in the Roosevelt administration. Connolly had been asking around and thought the movie rights to Eisenhower's life could fetch $150,000, with a $7,500 bonus for Mamie's parents and Eisenhower's mother.

Eisenhower trusted Connolly more than he did other famous entrepreneurs. They had gotten to know each other fifteen years earlier during Eisenhower's year in Paris working on Pershing's memoirs. And $150,000—equivalent to $2.5 million in 2023—was an eye-catching number.

Eisenhower showed the offer to Butch, passing it off as a laugh. But Butch told him to think about it. In four years, there would be another presidential election, and the only certainty was that Roosevelt would not be on the ticket.

Eisenhower balked. He had no interest getting "mixed in any political affairs." Having spent the past two years politically maneuvering, he was "completely fed up on it." But he had been asked the question enough times that he was keeping an open mind if he was, he told Butch, "to find himself being drafted."

Butch encouraged him. If he was drafted, Butch advised, Eisenhower could announce "if elected, he would not run for reelection and devote his attention to the office, just as dispassionately and objectively as he had to that of allied commander in North Africa, and Supreme Commander in England." And Butch was confident that he would be drafted. If D-Day was a success, Butch told him, Eisenhower "will be held in greater esteem than Pershing."

No matter what, Butch thought, the movie could be a good thing for young people to see. Eisenhower was the Horatio Alger myth brought to life. A poor country boy rising to the top of the world. It was the kind of lesson that would inspire kids, who so far as Butch could tell, were all being indoctrinated into believing that the state would take care of them. Traditional American initiative was being lost, Butch feared. "Anything that could be done to reawaken that spirit would benefit America."

AS EISENHOWER TOOK stock of the previous two years, he found himself invited to a private lunch with King George and Queen Elizabeth at Buckingham Palace. It was a Friday and he had spent most of the morning at Wide Wing being interviewed by Hanson Baldwin, the *New York Times*' famed military-affairs reporter. Baldwin was keenly focused at the moment on the Transportation Plan, and he shared the air forces' skepticism—though Baldwin was equally dubious about Operation Pointblank, given that the Luftwaffe appeared as persistent a threat as it had ever been.

Eisenhower got to Buckingham Palace at one thirty in the afternoon and was shown into the Pavilion Breakfast Room, a breathtakingly ornate parlor that overlooked the Victoria Memorial from the northeast corner of the palace's second floor. The room had been built for Queen Victoria in 1849 as a celebration of Chinese architecture following Britain's victorious conquest of Hong Kong in the First Opium War. The walls were papered in a robin's-egg blue that framed enormous *gongbi*-style murals depicting family scenes of Chinese nobility. Six ten-foot-tall oil lamps, each constructed from elaborately decorated Chinese vases, ringed the room like pillars. Winged dragons were carved into the white marble of the fireplace, and gilt bronze dragons flourished throughout the most mundane corners of the room, all overseen in their antics by a massive green dragon that had been painted flying rampant on the ceiling fifteen feet overhead.

There was not a corner of the room that one could look at without a marble, porcelain, gold, or fire-red shock of some orientalist craftsmanship. The room remained exactly as it was when Queen Victoria dined there. The only renovation had been new red curtains, which were crafted from antique Chinese embroideries found in the palace's stores in 1922—though when in such a room, whose exuberant celebration of the empire's first step into the Middle Kingdom was downright giddy, one could be forgiven for not noticing the drapes.

It was a buffet lunch. Eisenhower, the king, and the queen all served themselves. And Eisenhower felt as warmly hosted as if in the company of any old family friends. At one point, King George gestured discreetly to the floor. Eisenhower had dropped his napkin. He reached down, plucked it up, spread it back on his lap, and then continued the conversation, only to be struck a moment later by the realization that he had just made a faux pas in front of the king.

King George didn't make him feel like an embarrassed outsider. Quite the contrary. King George had come to see Eisenhower as a "soldier of the Empire," despite how quintessentially American he was. In fact, being so American was one of Eisenhower's great charms. A farm boy with no family connections rising to lead the free world. In Britain, in the autumn of its greatness, such a story was not only inexplicable, but utterly enchanting. Eisenhower embodied the American promise of a world in which even the most fantastic childhood aspirations could be realized. It gave Eisenhower, the king would say, "the qualities of a little boy which make you love him."

Eisenhower and the royal family all shared a laugh, recalling the first time that Eisenhower had come to visit back in 1942. Queen Elizabeth delighted in telling the story of how Eisenhower had almost caught them "poaching" where they shouldn't have been. Eisenhower and Wayne Clark had been given a private tour of Windsor Castle. King George and Queen Elizabeth happened to be out in the garden. Not dressed to receive guests, the king had exclaimed, "This is terrible, we must not be seen." The king and queen had ducked down behind some shrubs when they heard American voices approaching and shuffled out on their hands and knees like burglars in their own home.

King George had told Eisenhower the story before with the same punch line: "This is terrible, we must not be seen." But they all had a good laugh recounting it again as they nibbled on various cheeses and fresh strawberries that had been put out for dessert. Eisenhower complimented the strawberries and Queen Elizabeth said they were her favorite as well. They were perfect this time of year.

Eisenhower felt as casual as if he were having a buffet luncheon back in Abilene. Though the comfort he felt certainly had little to do with the king and queen of the United Kingdom and the Dominions of the British Commonwealth being just folks. Eisenhower had traveled a great distance from Kansas. He was no longer the kind of person who could be overawed by the antique gravitas of his surroundings the way he had been during his first epic dinner with Churchill at Chequers.

As with everything good and bad in life, Eisenhower had gotten used to it. To say that he felt like he was just back in Abilene meant only that the rarefied world he now inhabited had become as familiar as his hometown had once been. He didn't feel different. No one ever does. But he was larger, even if it seemed to him that the world had become smaller.

On May 31, Eisenhower wrote back to Mamie about the movie deal. He was going to pursue it. If it was made right, it could "encourage kids to work, and depend upon themselves, rather than become too complacent with respect to the state's obligation to the individual." Eisenhower then put Milton on the job, saying that his main conditions were that any money be used to establish the "D.J. and Ida Eisenhower Endowment" at Kansas State, and that the movie not be released during the war. He also emphasized the need for discretion and confidentiality. The only reason he was even entertaining the idea, he told his brother, was to promote "the virtues of the traditional American system, especially as they apply to a family with ambition, energy, and some intelligence."

Anthony Eden

CHAPTER 41

EISENHOWER'S COMFORT IN Buckingham Palace was one thing. But the relationship between the United States and Great Britain was under increasing strain at the very moment cooperation between the two countries had become vital, not just to victory, but to averting the countless opportunities for catastrophe. The Americans' overwhelming presence, and Eisenhower's ultimate say on so many things, had put England in the ironically intolerable position of feeling like a colony.

Back in the summer of 1942, the Allies had agreed to make the United Kingdom the staging area for the invasion of Europe under Operation Bolero. In practical terms, Bolero meant massive inflows of military equipment, Americans to use that equipment, and supplies needed by those Americans, everything from Coca-Cola to shaving mirrors to hot dogs. Two years later, there were more than two thousand military camps and airfields in the United Kingdom stuffed with 1.5 million American soldiers, sailors, and airmen, along with six million tons of supplies that had been shipped through British ports, almost half of which had been crammed through since Eisenhower's arrival that January. This influx grossly distorted the British economy and exacerbated its government's financial and political woes.

Churchill had a long-term plan to stabilize the British economy. The British had helped organize a conference at a resort in Bretton Woods, New

Hampshire, scheduled for that July with representatives from all forty-four of the Allied countries. The goal would be the creation of an international fund for development that many expected would be based in London. John Maynard Keynes, who would be leading the British delegation, designed his plans for the fund around a new international currency called the "bancor," which would come close to realizing Churchill's dream of the "Sterling Dollar" and be tied both to the dollar and the pound. There was, in short, light at the end of the fiscal tunnel.

But that tunnel was long, and, in the meantime, the Americans were sucking Churchill's country dry. Literally. Drought conditions were developing, and Eisenhower had to send out an order directing the American army to economize water and ease the strain on England's aquifers.

The real problem, though, was what Bolero had done to the ports. They were completely jammed. For most of the war, the shipments for Bolero had lagged projections. But since Eisenhower's arrival, the rush to make up the difference had displaced half a million tons of the food, products, natural resources, and other wares that Great Britain had grown accustomed to securing from around the empire to make its little island thrive. Shortages strained the British economy. Inflation was rampant. And with only two weeks to go before the culmination of all those years of struggle, patience was running out. The British people were starving and thirsty.

Churchill invited Eisenhower to lunch, along with the foreign secretary, Anthony Eden. Eisenhower needed to know that His Majesty's government could not keep the ports open to the US Army unless there were guarantees that Roosevelt would compensate the United Kingdom for the shortfalls with more Lend-Lease aid after the invasion.

Eisenhower played for time and promised to lobby General Marshall for help. It was all he could do.

FRICTION AT THE ports was one thing. But there was also serious friction over values. The Smith and Brinson case had reignited concerns about whether America was infecting the empire with its "color problem." British colonial soldiers, who were often Black, had come to believe American laws expressly provided for more severe penalties for Black soldiers than for white soldiers.

Edward Betts's initial investigation into the imposition of death for rape was inconclusive, but far from comforting. The army had sentenced five men to death for rape in the United States over the previous year, but the ethnic breakdown was not recorded in the records. One of the death sentences was commuted, one Betts recognized as an American Indian, and another he said was probably Black given his unit. That left two who appeared to be white, though that was unclear.

Betts also compiled all he could on the punishment for rape. Federal law made it a capital offense, as did the law of many US states. There were also treatises on criminal law that supported death sentences for rape. But Betts had to admit that the Smith and Brinson case broke new ground, because of the seven death sentences imposed by the army in Europe to that point, only murderers had gone to the gallows: four black men, three white.

The controversy over Smith's and Brinson's death sentences might have faded into unimportance with D-Day so close. But then came the case of Leroy Henry, a Black soldier accused of raping a British woman in Bath. The accusations were, on their face, lurid. Henry had supposedly enticed the victim out of her home late at night, claiming to be lost, and the victim agreed to show him the way. When she did not come home, her husband went out searching in a panic only to find his wife in a ditch, saying she had been raped at knifepoint. Henry, picked up nearby, was positively identified as the rapist. He was then questioned for the next fifteen hours and made to sign a prewritten confession the following afternoon.

At his court-martial at the end of May, Henry took the stand in his own defense and repudiated the confession. The truth, he claimed, was that he had known the victim from the local pub and had twice before paid her a pound for sex. He had come to her house that night and she had asked him for two pounds. When he said he didn't have it, she walked away threatening to "get him in trouble."

The press coverage was even uglier than it had been in the Smith and Brinson case. It veered between vilifying Henry and shaming the victim for, as one newspaper put it, going "100 yards in a nightdress," and showing "no visible signs of a woman who had offered physical resistance." Others reported on the victim's reputation around town as a "good-time girl." Civil rights activists were quick to mobilize and letters poured in asking for clemency. One petition from the residents of Bath had 33,000 signatures on it, a quarter of the city's population. The debate roiled Parliament, and Churchill's ministers were being forced to answer why it was that "coloured troops are subject to the death penalty, while white troops are allowed to do what they like?" Labour MPs were even calling for the law to be changed to limit the US Army's ability to impose the death penalty in Britain.

Such controversies were not simply a matter of bad etiquette to a host country, and bad public relations. The Foreign Office had a real say in questions of vital military importance. It was not just Operation Bolero and the ports. Foreign Secretary Eden was now seeking to end the diplomatic communication ban.

Doing so, Eisenhower thought, could be lethal. The most recent intercepts showed that Hitler continued to think the Allies were planning to "establish a beachhead in Normandy or Brittany" as preparations for an all-out assault on Calais. Operation Fortitude was working. Hitler himself was awaiting Patton's First US Army Group and would likely continue to do so even after men started hitting the beaches in the west. If they eased the restrictions on communications now, the Germans would figure out that Georgie was a decoy and then turn all their forces against Normandy.

"I realize," Eisenhower implored Churchill, "that the entire burden of these security measures has been borne by the British Government and public, and that the decision whether this burden is to be borne for a longer period in the interest of continuing security will be influenced by factors of which I know very little." And as a show of his sincerity and willingness to share the burden, Eisenhower forbade all unofficial American travel back home and put a ten-day hold on all American mail.

Then, as if Anglo-American relations were not strained enough, Leigh-Mallory came to Eisenhower. As usual, Leigh-Mallory had concerns. The problem was the planned use of white phosphorus, an incendiary chemical that ignited with incredible heat and dense clouds of blindingly white smoke. Technically, the Allies used white phosphorus for this white smoke, and Patton had asked to have the 4.2-inch chemical mortar shells packed with it during the fighting in North Africa. But white phosphorus had really proved its value in Sicily, which, like the Normandy coast, had been a honeycomb of fortified pillboxes that could withstand even the most smothering barrage of mortar, antitank, and machine gun fire. The Germans were also good at hiding their pillboxes under brush, grass, and other topical features that made it seem as if the earth itself was shooting at you.

White phosphorus, in addition to providing good smoke screens, made all that camouflage the pillboxes' undoing. Firing it directly at a pillbox not only blinded the men inside, it also ignited the camouflage in a mess of smoke, fire, and heat that choked them out or to death. In one battle, white phosphorus was used to set a prairie fire that swept for a mile and a half and turned every pillbox in its path into a human oven.

In an after-action report for the Sicily campaign, Beetle credited white phosphorus as "one of the best weapons we have against all kinds of targets." A direct hit could burn a tank crew "to a crisp." It not only burned and blinded the enemy, but disoriented and terrified those who avoided its immediate effects. "The Germans," the joke was, "are very allergic to white phosphorus."

Leigh-Mallory's concerns were legal. Anthony Eden's Foreign Office had concluded that using white phosphorus as a weapon violated the Geneva Conventions and the 1925 Geneva Protocol on Chemical and Biological Weapons. Using it, in short, was a war crime.

Leigh-Mallory had brought his concerns to Charles Portal, who told Leigh-Mallory that "if he still considered the operational value of the use of white phosphorus against personnel would outweigh its possible grave disadvantages, then he should refer the matter to the Supreme Commander." Leigh-Mallory had therefore come to Eisenhower with his concerns.

Eisenhower might have taken the issue more seriously had it not been brought to him by Leigh-Mallory, whose priggish anticharm had become unusually powerful in its ability to ignite the boyish rosiness of Eisenhower's cheeks into a magmatic red. Eisenhower's doctor had even warned him that he needed to keep his blood pressure under control, and suggested doing so with an occasional stiff drink and by minimizing his exposure to Trafford Leigh-Mallory.

What incensed Eisenhower most was Leigh-Mallory's incessant spotting of concerns without offering solutions, which did nothing except cover Leigh-Mallory's ass. The week before, Leigh-Mallory had also told Eisenhower that he wanted to go "on record" about his concerns over the planned airborne drop behind Utah Beach. Ultra intercepts on the positions of German forces in northern France had revealed two new German divisions in the planned drop zone for the 82nd Airborne. This was on top of significant reinforcements that the Germans had moved into the Cotentin Peninsula. Joe Collins's VII Corps would be facing considerably stronger German resistance on Utah Beach.

Some thought was given to canceling the invasion of Utah Beach altogether. But Omar Bradley ultimately decided to move forward, dropping the 82nd Airborne in the same general area as the 101st Airborne in the hope that together they could provide Collins the needed support. It was, of course, still a massive risk, but one that Brad had calculated and accepted.

Leigh-Mallory went "on record" as having warned Eisenhower in case things went badly. "I cannot guarantee the safe arrival of any definite percentage of troops or equipment, and in my opinion, a large proportion of the force will be lost." Leigh-Mallory was unwilling to be responsible, in other words, if thousands of men dropped to their deaths.

Eisenhower saw through what Leigh-Mallory was doing and so went on the record himself, reminding Leigh-Mallory that "a strong, airborne attack in the region indicated is essential to the whole operation, and it must go on. Consequently, there is nothing for it, but you, the army commander, and the troop carrier commander to work out to the last detail, every single thing that may diminish these hazards."

Eisenhower could dismiss Leigh-Mallory's concerns about the airborne operations because risks to American lives fell on Eisenhower's shoulders and conscience. The suggestion, though, that the Allies were behaving as war criminals was not a problem for him alone. And though not a lawyer, he answered Leigh-Mallory's concerns like one.

White phosphorus was routinely used as a screening agent, and as an incendiary weapon against objects, despite—not because of—the "incidental" effect of harming nearby German soldiers. They had been doing that throughout the war, particularly in Italy, and it had, Eisenhower said, "not heretofore provided the basis for accusations as to the commencement on our part of chemical warfare. You should therefore plan on the use of white phosphorus, wherever it will assist your operational plans in support of Overlord."

Eisenhower's distinction between the use of white phosphorus against things versus its use against people was—technically—correct. That people might be inside those things, or nearby, or close enough to have the hair, skin, clothes, and sweat instantly ignited off of them in a suffocating flash of blinding white death was just collateral damage.

It was also, of course, complete bullshit. There were other ways of generating smoke, such as using hydrocarbons. But, as Patton's men complained after using the alternatives during the Sicily campaign, "it lacked the anti-personnel effect of the white phosphorus grenade."

It was a legalistic fig leaf and a flimsy one. But it worked, at least for the time being. The British Chiefs simply asked Eisenhower that "no orders should be given for the specific use of phosphorus as an anti-personnel weapon, and no reference to its use, as such should be made in any documents, training documents, or orders, liable to fall into the hands of the enemy, and no bombs containing phosphorus should be labeled or known as anti-personnel weapons."

ALL THESE DELICATE diplomatic problems were interconnected and piling up. Eisenhower felt as if he were living "on a network of high tension wires." Each problem made the others worse, so that even the smallest disagreements could ignite with incredible heat.

The last week in May, Frank McCarthy came to London with Thomas Handy and Lawrence Kuter, Hap Arnold's chief of staff, as the advance team for the US Chiefs. The Combined Chiefs were planning on having their first face-to-face meeting since the Cairo Conference the week after D-Day, to decide the future direction of the war, particularly if the invasion failed.

Eisenhower had invited the three of them to Telegraph Cottage for a welcome dinner, where they chatted about progress in Italy, the planned bombing campaign against Japan, and the continuing issues with the B-29s. They were enjoying drinks and jokes and cigarettes and a good time, when a courier came by with an urgent message.

Seeing it was from Churchill, Eisenhower joked to Butch, "The devil himself." He opened it and found the kind of letter you have to hold away from your face so your eyebrows don't get singed.

A reporter from the *Chicago Tribune* had just been allowed to return to the United States, Churchill protested. This was in direct violation of Eisenhower's promised ban on all travel at the very same time he was insisting that the British government enforce an entirely unprecedented ban on diplomatic communications that was probably illegal under international law. "It will not be possible for the British government to agree to an indefinite diplomatic ban after D-Day," Churchill wrote. He would permit it for another week, no longer. And he not so subtly reminded Eisenhower to remember his place.

Eisenhower had laughed it off with his esteemed guests from the Pentagon still there. "The old boy was really in good form," Eisenhower joked. But as soon as they left, Eisenhower rang up Beetle, who sounded as if he were going to rip the phone clean from the wall. The *Chicago Tribune* reporter had been *stopped* from leaving the United Kingdom. Things were working as prescribed.

Eisenhower, with extreme tact, wrote back to Churchill, reiterating that continuing the diplomatic ban was necessary, if only because ending so soon after the invasion would signal to Hitler that the "invasion" of Calais was only a feint. But, Eisenhower dutifully acknowledged, like a good soldier of the Empire, the decision was, of course, committed to the sovereign discretion of His Majesty's Government.

PART FIVE

CRUSADER

Mattie Pinette

CHAPTER 42

ON THE MORNING of June 2, Kay drove Eisenhower and Jimmy Gault to Southwick, a sprawling estate that had been requisitioned for SHAEF nearer to the action in Portsmouth. They drove through the English lawns, manicured English gardens, and English woodlands, where every conceivable type of military equipment was lined up as if in a warehouse. They pulled up to Southwick House, the estate's enormous, three-story white mansion. Bertie Ramsay had claimed Southwick House as the navy's headquarters, and all around the grounds, a small village of tents and trailers had been erected as Monty's "TAC Headquarters."

Eisenhower went to Southwick House's conference room for a short commanders in chief meeting to discuss the weather as well as fresh concerns being raised over the final phase of the Transportation Plan. From Southwick House, Kay drove Eisenhower and Jimmy twenty minutes out to a campsite in the woods that he had chosen for his command post. Originally given the code name "Tuxedo," a wise staff officer quickly changed it to "Sharpener."

Upon seeing Butch, Jimmy told him about the goings-on at Southwick House and laughed that everyone seemed to be a meteorologist. Jimmy even offered Butch a new joke: "What is the definition of a meteorologist? . . . An expert who can look into a girl's eyes and tell whether . . ."

The weather outside had been so pleasant as almost to be an omen. Eisenhower even cabled Marshall that "weather forecasts, while still indefinite, are generally favorable." The trees echoed with the chattering of woodcocks and cuckoos. There was a pond nearby for fishing. And the advance team had connected all the tents and trailers with cinder paths, in case it got muddy.

Eisenhower had Mickey bring his old trailer from North Africa that he liked to call his "circus wagon." The faucets were marked in French and the decoration was limited to two Berber rugs and the pine veneer on its walls. Kay also had succeeded in bringing her circus wagon from North Africa. And the remaining trailer went to Mattie, leaving Butch, Jimmy, and everyone else to make do with standard-issue field tents.

The Lockheed Aircraft Corporation had presented Eisenhower with an enormous chrome, super-deluxe office trailer as a gift. This Lockheed super-deluxe had a mammoth desk situated on what could only be described as a pedestal above a workspace that came complete with built-in filing cabinets, a radio, a safe for secret documents, and phones. Eisenhower had graciously accepted the Lockheed super-deluxe, but gave it to Butch, Mattie, Kay, and Jimmy to use as an Official Family office.

For his own office, Eisenhower opted for a standard-issue field tent, a canvas room of no more than a hundred square feet with four-foot walls on its sides. Its just-to-the-point ornamentation was limited to a carpet and a map of Normandy. Eisenhower's desk, also standard issue, was positioned to give him the full benefit of the eight-foot peak between the tent poles. That left visitors with the awkward choice of standing right in front of the desk, as if in a spotlight, or hunching under the sharply sloping canvas ceiling off to the side, at least until Eisenhower extended the offer to sit in one of the three standard-issue chairs that completed the tent's just-to-the-point furnishings.

The center of life in the campsite, though, was the extra-large mess tent. With enough space for two tables, it was the jealous domain of Corporal Williams, who took pains to ensure that it was a dining room fit for the Supreme Commander, Allied Expeditionary Force.

Eisenhower was invigorated by his surroundings. His ear was still ringing, and his eye still smarted like a pebble in the shoe, but it was looking better. Seeing Corporal Williams, he told him not to bother setting out clean napkins at each meal. Williams looked a bit dejected, and Eisenhower explained that he'd set up camp out there, instead of moving into some nearby manor house, to make sure that he, and everyone else, remembered they were there to fight a war. They were lucky to have napkins at all. He wanted people to remember that. He had even approved a new uniform marking, a narrow green band around the shoulder that only combat officers could wear.

CHURCHILL WAS DUE to come by and after settling in, Eisenhower spent the afternoon playing bridge with the Official Family. Monty had implored Eisenhower to dissuade Churchill from coming to Portsmouth. "If Winnie comes," Monty had told Patton, "he'll not only be a great bore but also may well attract undue attention here. Why in hell doesn't he go and smoke his cigar at Dover Castle and be seen with the Lord Mayor? It would fix the Germans' attention to Calais." It was not a fight, though, that Eisenhower wanted to pick with the prime minister.

Churchill was mad enough at him already. They had been at it all week. There had been the nasty fight over the diplomatic communication ban. And it did not help that this delicate fight over the prestige of the British Empire happened at the very same time Eisenhower was thwarting the prime minister's personal demand to go to Normandy on D-Day aboard a battleship.

Eisenhower had pleaded with Churchill not to go, since they could not very well let the prime minister go down with the ship. Churchill, though, was stubborn. British lives would be lost and he wanted to share their risks. He reminded Eisenhower, again not subtly, that he was still the prime minister of the British Empire. And as such, he retained "certain rights and objections not subject to 'yes' or 'no' of even an Allied Supreme Commander."

Eisenhower quietly went to King George, since His Majesty was the only person in the world to still have the power of yes and no over Winston Leonard Spencer Churchill.

King George, with typical regal indirection, sent Churchill a suggestion. "We should both," the king wrote, "I know, love to be there, but in all seriousness I would ask you to reconsider your plan." Bertie Ramsay then called to let Eisenhower know that apparently, after having considered the king's suggestion, Churchill had declined it. He was still poking around to get himself on a battleship.

Eisenhower and Beetle had worked behind the scenes to persuade King George to elevate the sternness of his suggestion, which that very day, the king had done. "If the King cannot do this," he scolded Churchill, "it does not seem to me right that his Prime Minister should take his place." Churchill was finally cowed.

Churchill arrived a little after seven with Field Marshal Smuts along for the ride. He was in a peevish mood and stayed only a half hour. In addition to everything else, he had wasted nearly the whole day shuttling from port to port, trying to see the troops off, but kept missing their departures.

Upon seeing Eisenhower, he grumbled that the king had somehow gotten word of his intention to be close to the action. It only made sense, Churchill hastened to add, that Eisenhower not go to the battlefront either. If the prime minister was too valuable, certainly the supreme commander presented all the same risks of undue distraction.

WHEN CHURCHILL DEPARTED, Eisenhower headed out for an eight p.m. dinner with Monty. A few days earlier, Monty had taken up residence at Broomfield House, a smaller manor that had been built at the end of the eighteenth century on the periphery of the estate. It was a quiet meal with just the two of them. And they hadn't left much time for it, since they were both due at Southwick House at nine thirty for a commanders in chief meeting on the weather.

The only business to discuss was the newest controversy between the airmen over the Transportation Plan. Fifty-eight thousand tons of bombs had been dropped on ninety targets throughout France. For diplomatic reasons, Eisenhower had ordered the air forces to defer high-casualty targets until right before D-Day. Now Leigh-Mallory was planning a massive bombardment of the French villages and towns leading to Normandy with the goal of establishing "a belt of bombed routes" that could impede any German counterattack.

The French casualties were likely to be astronomical, and Arthur Tedder was opposed to going through with it. As the author of the Transportation Plan, Tedder had believed in the value of bombing the railroad system to prevent the Germans from rapidly redeploying from southern and eastern Europe to northwest France. The most recent intelligence did not paint an encouraging picture of its effectiveness. But the chance to delay the Germans by even a few days as they attempted to move dozens of divisions thousands of miles had been worth the risks to ordinary Frenchmen.

Leigh-Mallory's newest plan, though, was not targeting railroads and was not intended to inhibit the large-scale movement of German divisions. Leigh-Mallory was planning to use heavy bombers to destroy roads. He was applying the continental-scale logic of the Transportation Plan to small-scale German troop movements over a few miles. It made no sense. It would be an extraordinary waste. And the chance of slowing the Germans down by a few hours, at most, hardly seemed worth the risk of killing all the civilians who lived, drove, and walked along something as common as a road.

The week before, Churchill had called Tedder in to scold him about the Transportation Plan again, saying that he was unsure whether "the air forces had done more good than harm." Tedder reminded the prime minister not to believe everything he read in the Vichy-controlled press and assured him that the bombing campaign against the railways was nearly complete. Confidentially, though, Tedder shared his concerns about Leigh-Mallory's plan to use the heavy bombers against Normandy's roads.

Churchill had Leigh-Mallory dragged before a secret meeting of the War Cabinet, at which Anthony Eden had called for a stop to the bombing entirely. Leigh-Mallory assured Eden that the bombing campaign was 95 percent complete and with the invasion imminent, now was not the time to take the pressure off. Churchill left the decision in Eisenhower's hands.

That morning, Eisenhower had sided with Leigh-Mallory—though he was planning on going to Wide Wing the following day to discuss it all further. Monty, who had not been at the commanders in chief meeting that morning, offered his agreement with Eisenhower's decision to support Leigh-Mallory. They needed as much air support as they could get on D-Day. And Eisenhower promised to pass Monty's views along.

Eisenhower and Monty had known each other for two years at that point, ever since Monty had scolded him for smoking. But they had only grown to trust and even like one another over the past six months.

Monty had done some great work. A week earlier, he had sent Eisenhower the speech he was giving to the troops in advance of D-Day. "After four and a half years of war the Allies have, by hard fighting on sea, land, and in the air, worked themselves into a position where they cannot lose," Monty would say. "That is a very good position to reach in any contest; but the good player is never content 'to draw'—he wants to win. And so we must now win, and defeat Germany.

"We are a great team of allies, British and American. As a British general I regard it as an honour to serve under American command; General Eisenhower is captain of the team and I am proud to serve under him."

Monty would then conclude by saying, "Everyone must go all-out. And as we enter battle, let us recall the words of a famous soldier, spoken many years ago: He either fears his fate too much, or his deserts are small, who dare not put it to the touch to win or lose it all."

Eisenhower thought the speech was perfect.

Monty came away from the dinner feeling just as warmly toward Eisenhower, writing in his diary, "Eisenhower is just the man for the job; he really is a 'big' man and is in every way an Allied Commander." Monty continued, "I like him immensely; he has a generous and lovable character and I would trust him to the last gasp."

They left together for Southwick House and arrived a bit late. With everyone assembled in Southwick House's library, Eisenhower got to the point.

"Well, Stagg, what have you for us this time?"

Seeing Stagg present his forecasts each week for the past three months, Eisenhower had learned all of Stagg's tells and could almost predict the weather from the look of the man's face. This time, Stagg looked worried.

"The whole situation from the British Isles to Newfoundland has been transformed in recent days and is now potentially full of menace," Stagg warned. "In the last 24 hours there has been no clear indication how it will go, better or worse, but, at the best, weather in the Channel for the next three or four days at least will be very different from what we hoped for. Until at least Tuesday or Wednesday, there will be much cloud; at times skies will be completely overcast especially in the west of the area and winds will be from a westerly point, often force 4 and up to force 5 at times."

The room was quiet. What will the weather be on Tuesday and Wednesday, Eisenhower asked.

Stagg stood interminably silent. "If I answered that, sir, I would be guessing, not behaving as your meteorological adviser."

Stagg was dismissed.

"OK, gentlemen," Eisenhower said. "I guess you are all agreed that we can carry on until the next meeting."

Eisenhower went back to camp. His mood was hard to conceal. Butch and Mattie were still up. He told everyone that he needed to go to bed. He had to be up early, but he found it difficult to sleep. He got up a few times and milled about until past midnight.

THE NEXT MORNING, Kay drove Eisenhower back to Wide Wing. He had a meeting with Lieutenant General William Simpson, a West Point classmate and longtime friend of Patton, who had come to England a few weeks earlier as commander of the Eighth Army. Simpson had spent the war stateside and Eisenhower knew him a little, the way one did in the army. The biggest issue to date was that the Eighth Army was also the name of Monty's army in

North Africa. Eisenhower thought it best to have it changed, so now Simpson was the head of the Ninth Army.

With D-Day so close, Eisenhower was thinking ahead to the next phase of the war. Assuming they got to shore and were no longer afraid of being "kicked into the sea," he needed to think seriously about how they would drive across the European continent. He had spent so much time thinking about LSTs and the unique complexities of amphibious warfare that he had only begun to think about what a ground offensive might actually look like.

If the eastern front was any guide, the scale of the fighting and the logistics needed to support it would be incredible. The War Department had recently done an audit and confided to Eisenhower that Cliff Lee's staff was "not the tops." They were "learning" though, and Eisenhower was assured that he had enough supplies on hand for ninety days of battle. But who would do the fighting?

For all Monty's virtues, the British did not have enough men or hardware to wage a ground war on that scale. It would therefore fall to the United States to take the lead, not just with Eisenhower at the helm, but on the ground. The natural division between the armies, with Omar Bradley commanding the American forces and Monty commanding the British forces, would be inevitable. There would be army groups. Brad had long favored this. "An American sector with an American mission" supported by American supply lines, he would say.

Eisenhower could see that Brad was about to get his wish. Once they were established in France, the Ninth Army, along with Patton's Third Army, would join the First Army as part of Brad's army group.

Eisenhower had hoped to avoid the division of the alliance in this way. It was one of the reasons he had gone out on a limb the week before, sending yet another message to General Marshall asking him to press Roosevelt to reconsider the postwar division of Germany. Under the integrated Allied command setup he had worked so hard to foster, American and British forces would be distributed basically at random throughout Germany by the time the fighting stopped. With a hard line on a map, dividing the British and Americans into sectors would be a logistical nightmare and create inevitable opportunities for political friction within the alliance.

Eisenhower's plea had no effect, and may have even been counterproductive. The very same day, Roosevelt sent Churchill a message reiterating his demand that Germany be divided and that the Americans get its northwest slice. An argument between Churchill and Roosevelt had ensued. That certainly went a long way to explaining why Churchill had directed so much ire at Eisenhower over the past few days.

With so many cross-cutting pressures, Eisenhower did what he always did when he needed to think clearly. He wrote. One thing after another, in no particular order, he listed out his biggest worries: the French, the weather, the Germans, the use of airpower, and the growing division within the alliance. These were the things he had to understand right now. And so, he wrote himself a long memo to think through it all, telling himself, "Probably no one that does not have to bear the specific and direct responsibility of making the final decision on what to do can understand the intensity of these burdens."

In meeting with the airmen that afternoon, Eisenhower stood by his decision to back Leigh-Mallory's closing salvo for the Transportation Plan. The previous day, Tedder had proposed dropping leaflets on D-Day to warn the civilians to take shelter, which Eisenhower thought was reasonable.

Tedder, though, remained bothered by the reputation airmen, like himself, were getting as indiscriminate butchers. He drafted a directive entitled "Air Attacks on Civilians." It noted that the Germans had been spreading propaganda that "Allied airmen are willfully shooting harmless civilians in the course of their fighter sweeps and tactical bombing attacks." The directive therefore reminded airmen, "Humanity and the principles for which we fight demand from our pilots scrupulous care to avoid any but military targets. The Air Forces of the United Nations are privileged to be the spearhead of the forces fighting for freedom and the herald to the oppressed peoples of Europe of our approach. Be careful that nothing is done to betray this trust or to prejudice our good name in the eyes of our friends still dominated by the Nazi tyranny."

Tedder asked if Eisenhower would send out the directive under his own name. Eisenhower agreed. "Nothing," Eisenhower instructed Leigh-Mallory, "must be done to prejudice our good name in the eyes of our friends."

EISENHOWER LEFT WIDE Wing for the last time before D-Day and got back to Southwick around six in the evening, where he discovered that his whole command post had been strung elaborately with camouflage netting. Seeing Butch, Eisenhower said, "Dammit all. How many man-hours were wasted on this job?"

Butch mollified him, explaining that it had been done as part of a training exercise for the camouflage teams. Apparently they'd done such a good job that the entire camp was now invisible from five hundred feet.

"All right, as long as it was only practice," Eisenhower grumbled. "But I don't want any time wasted making a fuss over me."

Churchill returned for another visit soon after, this time bringing an extensive entourage, in addition to Field Marshal Smuts. Butch welcomed him and played party host by opening up some scotch.

Churchill had something sensitive to discuss, and so Eisenhower showed the prime minister to his office tent and Field Marshal Smuts tagged along.

De Gaulle, the prime minister revealed, was on his way to London. Churchill was unenthusiastic about the idea, but Anthony Eden had persuaded him that it was better to have De Gaulle in London before D-Day, if only to keep him under control. It had been a tiresome negotiation, as it always was. De Gaulle had insisted that he would come to London only if the discussions were done on a "tripartite" basis. Roosevelt obviously refused to do anything of the kind and said Eisenhower should just work it out with Koenig.

Churchill, though, had gotten behind the idea that De Gaulle should at least feel as if he were being consulted, and so had made it all happen. He expected the Frenchman to arrive the following day.

Eisenhower was glad. De Gaulle was not perfect. But he was someone Eisenhower believed he could work with. And Eisenhower needed someone to work with.

It was around eight in the evening when Churchill and his entourage took their leave. Eisenhower had another commanders in chief conference at Southwick House scheduled for nine thirty to check on the state of the weather.

Corporal Williams had set out dinner and Eisenhower got to enjoy a quiet Official Family meal with just Butch, Mattie, Kay, and Jimmy. The conversation turned to favorite poems. Mattie made her case for William Cullen Bryant's "Thanatopsis." She recited the closing stanza, which, given that they were living in a caravan of trailers and tents, was fitting to the moment.

So live, that when thy summons comes to join
The innumerable caravan, which moves
To that mysterious realm, where each shall take
His chamber in the silent halls of death,
Thou go not, like the quarry-slave at night,
Scourged to his dungeon, but, sustained and soothed

By an unfaltering trust, approach thy grave,
Like one who wraps the drapery of his couch
About him, and lies down to pleasant dreams.

Jimmy had never heard it before and asked what it was about.

It was like the line from *Julius Caesar*, Eisenhower said, act 2, scene 2, "The coward dies a thousand deaths, the brave man dies but once."

Mattie corrected him. Shakespeare's actual line was "Cowards die many times before their deaths; the valiant never taste of death but once."

Eisenhower said that, in his opinion, the greatest poem ever written was Thomas Gray's "Elegy Written in a Country Churchyard." It was a long meditation on the dignity of a life of modest hard work, an ode to those like his own father, who died with greatness having passed them by, unaware of how important they really were. He then recited its final stanzas, "the Epitaph":

Here rests his head upon the lap of Earth
A youth to Fortune and to Fame unknown.
Fair Science frown'd not on his humble birth,
And Melancholy mark'd him for her own.

Large was his bounty, and his soul sincere,
Heav'n did a recompense as largely send:
He gave to Mis'ry all he had, a tear,
He gain'd from Heav'n ('twas all he wish'd) a friend.

No farther seek his merits to disclose,
Or draw his frailties from their dread abode,
(There they alike in trembling hope repose)
The bosom of his Father and his God.

Mattie said the poem reminded her of Kipling's "If—." She tried to remember a few lines:

If you can keep your head when all about you
Are losing theirs and blaming it on you,
If you can trust yourself when all men doubt you,
But make allowance for their doubting too;

If you can wait and not be tired by waiting,
Or being lied about, don't deal in lies,
Or being hated, don't give way to hating,
And yet don't look too good, nor talk too wise:

Mattie was frustrated that she couldn't remember the rest. But she did love the poem.

Eisenhower then picked it up and continued right through to the end.

If you can dream—and not make dreams your master;
If you can think—and not make thoughts your aim;
If you can meet with Triumph and Disaster
And treat those two impostors just the same;
If you can bear to hear the truth you've spoken
Twisted by knaves to make a trap for fools,
Or watch the things you gave your life to, broken,
And stoop and build 'em up with worn-out tools:

If you can make one heap of all your winnings
And risk it on one turn of pitch-and-toss,
And lose, and start again at your beginnings
And never breathe a word about your loss;
If you can force your heart and nerve and sinew
To serve your turn long after they are gone,
And so hold on when there is nothing in you
Except the Will which says to them: "Hold on!"

If you can talk with crowds and keep your virtue,
Or walk with Kings—nor lose the common touch,
If neither foes nor loving friends can hurt you,
If all men count with you, but none too much;
If you can fill the unforgiving minute
With sixty seconds' worth of distance run,
Yours is the Earth and everything that's in it,
And—which is more—you'll be a Man, my son!

Eisenhower got up. It was time to find out about the weather.

EISENHOWER ARRIVED IN the library at Southwick House on time and got to it. Stagg came in with some of his fellow meteorologists. They were thirty-six hours out from when the invasion was due to commence that Monday.

"Gentlemen," Stagg began, "the fears my colleagues and I had yesterday about the weather for the next three or four days have been confirmed. The whole weather set-up over the British Isles and, even more so, to the west over the north-east Atlantic, is very disturbed and complex. We cannot have much confidence in what will happen and how it will happen from day to day. Even for tomorrow the details are not clear. But we do know now that the extension of the Azores anticyclone towards our south-west shores, which some of us thought might protect the Channel from the worst effects of the Atlantic depressions, is now rapidly giving way."

Stagg continued going through seemingly all the meteorological details. Eisenhower listened with his head resting on his hand. When Stagg finished, it was as if he had used the last of the air left in the room.

It took a moment, but then Bertie Ramsay asked, "Are the force 5 winds along the Channel to continue Monday and Tuesday?"

"Yes, sir."

"And the cloud on those days?"

"As the situation is at the moment I could not attempt to differentiate one day from another in regard to cloudiness though the whole period from tomorrow till Wednesday when we expect the clearing front to pass through." But he estimated that over the next few days, "skies will be overcast with cloud down to 500 feet at times as on our side."

"Now let me put this one to you," Eisenhower said. "Last night you left us, or at least you left me, with a gleam of hope. Isn't there just a chance that you might be a bit more optimistic again tomorrow?"

"No, sir. As I had hoped you would realize yesterday, I was most unhappy about the prospects for Monday and Tuesday. Even then the whole weather situation was extremely finely balanced and slow to show which way it would develop. Last night, it is true, we thought there might be the slightest tip towards the favorable side; but tonight the balance has gone too far to the other side for it to swing back again overnight tonight."

Stagg was getting ready to leave the room, but Tedder stopped him.

"Before you go, Stagg," Tedder asked, "will you tell us whether all the forecasting centers are agreed on the forecast you have just given us?"

"Yes, sir, they are."

Everyone knew what this meant. If they went on Monday in that kind of weather, it would be a disaster. High tides, heavy winds, dense clouds. The only advantage they would have would be the element of surprise, because no rational commander would launch an amphibious invasion in those conditions. But timing was everything. Each day they postponed, the tides would be higher, making it harder to get vehicles on shore and making the tangle of submerged obstacles near-impossible to destroy. And the tides and the moon would only be right until June 7. After that, it would be weeks until they could try again.

If they delayed until the end of June, who knew what might happen? The Dieppe Raid had been delayed by nearly a month due to weather back in the summer of 1942. The men were demoralized. Security got lax. The Germans were waiting for them and the Allied defeat was total within about six hours of the first men going ashore. And that was before Irwin Rommel was manning the Atlantikwall.

Eisenhower said they should wait "in order not to abandon the original D-Day, unless absolutely mandatory." They had another conference scheduled for four thirty that morning. They would make a final decision then, since "sailing orders could be cancelled by 0600."

Eisenhower returned to his command post at 10:45. Mattie asked if everything was all right. "Reports coming in were not very favorable," he said. "In fact, definitely unfavorable for the contemplated operation." He then went to his trailer to try to get some sleep.

LESS THAN SIX hours later, they were all back in Southwick House's library. Eisenhower was too tired to do more than simply nod at Stagg.

The prediction, Stagg said, was the same.

"The sky outside here at the moment is practically clear and there is no wind," Bertie Ramsay all but shouted at Stagg. "When do you expect the cloud and wind of your forecast to appear here?"

"In another four or five hours from now, sir."

"No part of the air support plan would be practicable," Leigh-Mallory said.

Bertie Ramsay strongly favored postponing. "We had only accepted a daylight assault on the understanding that overwhelming air and naval bombardment would be available to overcome the enemy coast and beach defences." But regardless of the decision, Ramsay reminded Eisenhower, they needed to make the decision now. "If Overlord is to proceed on Tuesday, I must issue provisional warning to my forces within the next half-hour."

"In that case, Gentlemen," Eisenhower interjected, "it looks to me as if we must confirm the provisional decision we took at the last meeting. Compared with the enemy's forces ours are not overwhelmingly strong: we need every help our air superiority can give us. If the air cannot operate we must postpone. Are there any dissentient voices?"

Monty spoke up. He favored going. The men had already been at sea for two or three days. They had been packed in tight given the paucity of LSTs. What would delay mean to them?

"Jesus!" Eisenhower snapped. "You've been telling us for the past three or four months that you must have adequate air cover and that the airborne operations are essential to the assault, and now you say you will do without them? No. We will postpone Overlord for twenty-four hours."

The cable went out to all commanders: "Exercise Hornpipe, ripcord one day; Halcyon now designated Yoke plus five, repeat, Yoke plus five. Acknowledge Receipt. Eisenhower."

Kay was waiting for him outside to drive him back to his circus wagon. His body was heavy as he got to the car. And the sun was just rising into a clear sky.

James Martin Stagg

CHAPTER 43

London, June 3 (AP)—General Eisenhower's headquarters announced tonight that allied forces had landed in France.

Withhold publication London FLASH Eisenhower acknowledges landings France.

London Kill the flash and bulletin from London announcing allied landings in France.

THE SKY WAS still clear and the wind was barely a breeze. Eisenhower was bleary eyed. He had come back to camp around six, laid down for an hour, and then gotten up when Mickey brought him coffee.

Butch was up and eager. The Associated Press had announced the invasion of France. It happened overnight. Apparently, an AP operator in London was practicing setting type and accidentally announced an invasion. They'd sent out a kill message about twenty minutes later. But the bell was rung. CBS had sent it out and so had German radio.

Eisenhower gazed at Butch for a moment and grunted. He went back to his circus wagon and was doing his best to rest, when Beetle came by with his cocker spaniel. Mattie also popped in, saying that there had been a phone call from 10 Downing Street. De Gaulle would be having lunch with

Churchill on his train and asked Eisenhower to come to Southwick House around three that afternoon.

Eisenhower told Beetle to make the necessary arrangements. He then went to lie back down and close his eyes. But it wasn't too long before Mattie was at his door again. There was a very important "eyes only" message waiting for him at Southwick House.

Eisenhower gave up trying to sleep, got out of bed, and had some breakfast. The wind was picking up and the clouds were rolling in.

The US Chiefs had replied to his request for more Lend-Lease aid to make up for the shortages caused by Operation Bolero. Their answer: "We'll see." Given the amount of Lend-Lease already sent, the US Chiefs were about as sympathetic to Britain's plight as the ant was to the grasshopper. "However," it added, "you may assure the prime minister that increased shipping assistance later in the year will be forthcoming to the extent of the loss in imports suffered as a direct result of the discharge of Bolero ships in excess of agreed numbers." Just the sort of thing to put Churchill in a good mood.

Eisenhower went back to his command post to wait for the prime minister to arrive with De Gaulle. He passed the time by playing a few hands of bridge with Mattie, Butch, and Kay. At half past one, he was interrupted by a phone call from the head of operations at SHAEF. Bertie Ramsay was now insisting that the invasion be postponed by another day. Force U, which made up the assault elements scheduled to attack Utah Beach, was scattered all over the Channel. Ramsay had sent along the message, "Additional time was absolutely essential" and wanted to meet with Eisenhower that afternoon.

Eisenhower agreed to meet after his meeting with De Gaulle. But then, a half hour later, Ramsay called up personally. Things were not as bad as feared. He said he would know for sure by six that evening.

Eisenhower went to wait for De Gaulle in Beetle's office tent, which had been set up on the grounds around Southwick House. It was conspicuously large, much larger than Eisenhower's office tent. Churchill was late, leaving Eisenhower to pace about in the cold for forty-five minutes as the weather had begun to turn.

When he finally arrived, Churchill still had Field Marshal Smuts along, as well as Pug Ismay. De Gaulle would be there in ten minutes and Churchill got quickly to the point. He thought De Gaulle should broadcast a message to the French. To do that, though, they would have to tell him the invasion was about to launch, which technically the Combined Chiefs had decided against doing. But Churchill wanted to bring him in. So he had briefed De Gaulle on the plan.

Within minutes, a sedan pulled up and out of the back unfolded the overly long limbs of Charles de Gaulle. They had not seen each other since the previous December, and De Gaulle had his usual look of discontent.

Eisenhower beamed his broad smile as he threw his hand into De Gaulle's palm. De Gaulle pursed his lips, receded his chin, and somehow managed to protrude his nose even farther as he peered down at Eisenhower and then farther down still at Churchill.

De Gaulle had arrived with Koenig and other officials from the French Committee. Eisenhower invited them all into the war room in Southwick House, where the invasion plan was on full display.

The ships, the planes, and hundreds of thousands of men were all in motion, ready to land as soon as Eisenhower said go. Sensing De Gaulle's discontent over his not having been consulted on the invasion of the country over which he declared himself head of state, Eisenhower mentioned the problems with the weather and asked, "What do you think I should do?"

De Gaulle's face brightened.

"Whatever decision you make, I approve in advance and without reservation. I will only tell you that in your place I should not delay."

Eisenhower asked if Koenig could help fold the Free French Forces into the invasion force once they landed.

De Gaulle readily agreed.

Eisenhower then took De Gaulle on a walk around the grounds, while Beetle stayed behind and explained the plans in more detail to Koenig. De Gaulle gestured broadly as he talked, his arms sweeping about, offering critiques of Allied strategy.

"De Gaulle only sees his own point of view," Eisenhower thought. And so, he used that insight. He took every suggestion with an I-wish-I-had-thought-of-that and made sure to be apologetic about the debate over who was entitled to govern France.

"I prefer not to have anything to do with it," Eisenhower assured De Gaulle, adding, "I am a soldier and not a politician." He then told De Gaulle that his orders gave him discretion and that De Gaulle was the only man he had any intention of dealing with. He then asked De Gaulle to make a broadcast on D-Day, to rally his country.

Flattered, De Gaulle said yes. He would draft something to meet the occasion "on purely military lines." He then asked Eisenhower for a copy of the broadcast he was going to make to ensure they harmonized.

Eisenhower was happy to provide one.

Would Eisenhower be open to edits? De Gaulle asked.

The speech had already been recorded, Eisenhower explained, but he would be happy to take suggestions if there was time.

When Eisenhower and De Gaulle returned to Southwick House, the room was cleared of all but the highest officials, and they discussed the themes De Gaulle should mention in his statement. De Gaulle had been won over.

Eisenhower dictated a message to Mattie to send back to the Combined Chiefs. He gave it to Churchill to review, and then sent it. "General de Gaulle and his chief of staff are anxious to assist every possible way and to have the lodgment effected as soon as possible."

WHEN EISENHOWER RETURNED to his command post, he and Kay partnered up for a drink and a few hands of bridge against Butch and Jimmy before an anxious dinner. The wind and rain were now drumming down on the canvas, confirming Stagg's bleakest predictions from earlier that morning.

Back in the Southwick House library, Stagg was shown in.

"Gentlemen," Stagg said with an excitement he had never mustered before. "Since I presented the forecast last evening some rapid and unexpected developments have occurred over the north Atlantic. In particular a vigorous front—a cold front—from one of the depressions has been pushed more quickly and much farther south than could have been foreseen." He then continued on explaining the interaction of various weather systems and air temperatures and how that all would affect cloud cover and precipitation. He finished with the expression of someone who had just delivered amazing news to a group of men who had understood only half of it.

The issue had not been that there was a storm in the Channel. It was that there were five storms all swirling and interacting in the Atlantic and they were each small enough to jet into the Channel. But then, the miraculous had happened.

Over the previous month the US Navy had dedicated eight ships to the collection of weather data across the Atlantic, and that week, the Royal Navy had dedicated another two ships to sharpen the lens even further. All that data showed that there was a massive storm brewing farther west that would start sucking all the smaller storms in the Channel back out into the Atlantic. If conditions persisted, there would be a small window of maybe forty-eight hours around Tuesday, June 6, when the Channel might be entirely clear.

"Can you say anything about the weather beyond Friday?" Eisenhower asked.

"No, sir, from the way we think things are going in the Atlantic and from the fact that we are now in June not January despite what has happened—both those aspects suggest that if the weather turns out as we expect until Friday, then there should be a fair chance of improvement again after that. But after the shake-up in the whole weather situation which we are going through it cannot be expected to re-settle itself quickly: conditions must continue to be regarded as very disturbed."

"What confidence have you in the forecast you have given us?" Tedder asked.

"I am quite confident that a fair interval will follow tonight's front. Beyond that I can only repeat that the rates of development and speeds of movement of depressions in the Atlantic have been exceptional for the time of year. I cannot therefore have much confidence in this state of affairs quieting down immediately after Tuesday."

Eisenhower wanted to know what everyone thought.

"Let's be clear about one thing to start with," Bertie Ramsay said. "If Overlord is to proceed on Tuesday I must issue the provisional warning to my forces within the next half-hour. But if they do restart and have to be recalled again there can be no question of continuing on Wednesday."

"With the cloud conditions Stagg has given us," Leigh-Mallory added, "there's certain to be difficulty in getting the markers down accurately and the bombing will therefore suffer."

"Yes," Tedder agreed, "the operations of the heavy and medium bombers will probably be a bit chancy."

Eisenhower looked at Monty. "Do you see any reason why we should not go on Tuesday?"

"No," Monty said. "I would say—Go."

"It's a helluva gamble," Beetle said. "But it's the best possible gamble."

"The question," Eisenhower said to no one in particular. "Just how long can you hang this operation on the end of a limb and let it hang there." After a few more moments, "I'm quite positive we must give the order. . . . I don't like it, but there it is. . . . I don't see how we can possibly do anything else." They would proceed as planned for Tuesday, and they would reconvene at four that morning, when Eisenhower would make the final decision.

Eisenhower walked out and saw Stagg in the hallway. "Well, Stagg," he said, "we're putting it on again. For heaven's sake hold the weather to what you told us and don't bring any more bad news."

AT 4:15 A.M., Eisenhower was back, again, in Southwick House's library. Rain was pouring down and the wind was whipping through the evergreens. He arrived last, dressed in his battle jacket. There was coffee being offered by young lieutenants and a fire going. Monty looked as if he had been sleeping in his baggy corduroy trousers and sweater, while Bertie Ramsay and the naval staff looked as crisp as a spring morning.

Eisenhower took a seat alone on a couch in front of an empty bookshelf. "Go ahead, Stagg," he said.

"Gentlemen, no substantial change has taken place since last time but as I see it the little that has changed is in the direction of optimism. The fair interval that has now reached here and will extend through all southern England during the night will probably last into the later forenoon or afternoon of Tuesday."

"Well, Stagg," Eisenhower said with a broad smile, "if this forecast comes off, I promise you we'll have a celebration when the time comes."

Tedder, though, was incredulous. How had things changed so quickly?

"Twenty-four hours ago," Stagg tried to explain, "a front from north-west Scotland through north Ireland had trailed away westward into the next Atlantic depression. This front, or part of it, has been pushed quickly south and east so that it swept through Ireland and is now traversing England." It was, in short, the weather.

Eisenhower turned to Bertie Ramsay. "What do you think?"

"I'd like to hear the 'air' give his views before making my final decision," Ramsay said, gesturing to Leigh-Mallory.

Leigh-Mallory talked all through the concerns meticulously, but was willing to "gamble on the predictions of the weather experts."

"All right," Ramsay said. "If the 'air' thinks he can do it, the navy certainly can!"

Eisenhower flashed a smile. But then his face grew heavy. He looked around at Ramsay and Leigh-Mallory, Monty and Tedder, Beetle. He sat for a long moment on the couch, looking at nothing in particular. No one said a word. The fireplace crackled. The rain and wind thundered against the window.

No one, not even he, would remember the precise words he said next.

Ramsay recalled that it was "some quaint American expression." It wasn't poetry. It wasn't meant to be etched into the pedestal of a statue. It was something like what his old football coach at West Point might say when it was time to get on the field.

All right. Let's go.

It was like a whistle being blown. Everyone was on their feet, rushing out. Monty was first through the door, then Leigh-Mallory and Tedder, then Ramsay. Everyone was running.

"Good luck," Eisenhower shouted behind them.

Eisenhower found himself alone, amid the empty bookshelves and the awkwardly placed furniture. Rain and wind were still drumming at the window. The fireplace still crackled. The hallway bustled. There was only one more thing he needed to do.

Eisenhower grabbed a felt-tip pen and a slip of notepaper. "Our landing in Cherbourg—have over hours failed to gain satisfactory foothold and the troops have been withdrawn. This particular operation . . ." He stopped. Enough of this political, passive voice. He owned this. He crossed out what he had been writing and continued.

"I have withdrawn the troops. My decision to attack at this time and place was based upon the best information available and . . ." He stopped again. No excuses. He'd made the decision. It was the best decision. Sometimes the best decision is wrong, just as a bad decision can turn out right. That was all there was to it. He crossed out the "and" and started a new sentence.

"The troops, the air and the navy did all that I asked . . ." He stopped again. The blame was his, but if he had to give this speech, it could not be about him. It had to be about them. It was about the young men who had taken off into a cloudy sky and leapt to their deaths because he had taken a gamble. The ones who stepped fully loaded into tremulous landing craft and were gored on obstacles he had chosen not to bomb, drowned in tides that he had guessed would be smoother, or torn apart by God-knows-what the Germans had devised to mortar the bricks of the Atlantikwall, and from which he had not protected them.

They did it because he told them to do it, but they did not do it for him. They might not have known all the risks. They might have been too young to understand that they only had one death to give. But they had given up every comfort, every dream, every love they might have known back home, for the common good of people on the other side of the world who did not even speak their language.

So, he crossed out the words "I asked" and finished the thought by saying that these men "did all that Bravery and devotion to duty could do. If any blame or fault attaches to the attempt it is mine alone."

Bleary eyed he drew a line under it. That was all that needed to be said. And then he scrawled the date, which his sleep deprived fingers wrote down as "July 5." He folded up the paper, put it in his wallet, and headed out into the storm.

James "Jimmy" Gault

CHAPTER 44

Exercise Hornpipe. Halcyon Y +5 finally and definitely confirmed.

THE SUN CAME up over Southwick the morning of June 5, 1944, behind the clouds. Kay drove Eisenhower and Jimmy to the pier in Portsmouth to see British soldiers off as they loaded up onto LCIs. Everywhere he went, the Tommies seemed glad to see him. And no translation from Jimmy was necessary, when they said, "Good old Ike."

Portsmouth was so jammed with every kind of naval vessel, you could walk across the sea for miles. It was as if the mammoth gears of some impossibly colossal machine had begun to turn. There were 7 battleships, 23 cruisers, 93 destroyers, 142 escorts, 236 LSTs, 837 LCTs, and 2,970 other ships of all kinds. There were 2,395 aircraft loads of paratroopers and 867 gliders. And 8,268 bombers and fighters of all sizes were ready to take flight. Each LST had been packed by the medics with 100 litters, 320 blankets, 4 splint sets, 3 boxes of surgical dressing, and 96 units of plasma. Eighty cargo vessels were being sunk in the shallow waters of the Channel to form breakwaters for the Mulberries. In all, 1,931,855 soldiers were poised to surge forth from the United Kingdom and through the Atlantikwall. And 176,475 of them were geared up with rations, ammunition, and mementos from home, as well as orders to be in France by June 7, 1944.

Eisenhower returned to his command post for lunch. He and Butch played a game of hounds and fox, and then checkers. Butch lost both, though these may have been tactical losses on Butch's part, given Eisenhower's temper and the weight of the decision he had made that morning.

That afternoon, Eisenhower made his way to Southwick House. He noticed the clouds and wind were picking up again and so dropped into Stagg's office wondering where the good weather was.

"They are coming along, sir: good breaks in the cloud by dark tonight and reduced winds." Stagg showed him the chart as if the answer was obvious to anyone who looked at it.

"Good, Stagg, keep it up a little longer."

There was also another storm brewing with De Gaulle. Koenig had been by Southwick House with revisions to Eisenhower's statement to the people of France. "When France is liberated from her oppressors, you yourselves will choose your representatives, and the government under which you wish to live," Eisenhower's statement said. De Gaulle wanted it replaced with the promise that "French authorities would re-establish civil government."

Beetle had told Koenig that there simply was not enough time to get another statement approved by the Combined Chiefs, and it was unclear what De Gaulle would do. The latest intelligence suggested that De Gaulle was becoming increasingly paranoid and megalomaniacal. He was convinced that he was being marginalized because the Americans were cutting secret deals for Morocco's railroads and natural resources. And over the previous few weeks, he had overseen a brutal crackdown in Algiers against anyone who betrayed a hint of Arab nationalism. Who knew what he would do?

Eisenhower returned to the office tent back at his command post, where he sat for a small press conference. "The button had been pushed," he announced. The invasion was now irrevocably set for 6:40 the following morning. This would be, he told them, "the greatest operation we have ever attempted."

Are you nervous? he was asked.

"Nervous," Eisenhower replied. "I'm so nervous I'm boiling over."

Almost on cue, the tent door flapped, flashing in a ray of sunlight.

"By George," Eisenhower interrupted himself, "there is some sun!"

Eisenhower stepped out into a clearing sky only to get a call from Beetle back at Southwick House. De Gaulle was now refusing to do the broadcast.

"To hell with him," Eisenhower said. "If he doesn't come through, we'll deal with someone else." Eisenhower had Beetle call over to the political warfare folks. They should tell De Gaulle that his presence in England will be announced and that people will "wonder why he did not speak." Eisenhower would offer no explanation. He would simply let rumors circulate.

Eisenhower went to the Lockheed super-deluxe trailer, where Butch, Mattie, Jimmy, and Kay were playing bridge. Butch asked if he wanted to play, but Eisenhower declined. There was not enough time. And so, he just sat quietly to the side, watching to see who would win.

Corporal Williams put dinner out early, so that Eisenhower could go out to airfields in Newbury to see off the 101st Airborne. Butch did what he could to lighten the mood as they ate, kibitzing about his old friend Pat Harrison, who was an up-and-coming congressman. Butch joked that Pat's supporters wanted him to play more dirty tricks, recounting the fable of the papa skunk, who upon arriving home one day, smelled something just awful, and said, "I don't know what it is, Mama skunk and children dear, but whatever it is, we must get some of it."

Jimmy joked that there were "no proper skunks in England, only human ones." Eisenhower forced a laugh.

KAY DROVE HIM out to Newbury. It was still before seven, and at that time of year, there were hours left before the sun would set. He stopped at three different rallying points over the next three hours. With the stars on his car covered, it usually took a few seconds after he got out of the back seat to be recognized. But with a three-car entourage, his arrival was hard to overlook.

The men seemed grim but determined. Some had shaved mohawks into their hair or blackened their faces with a war paint made from cocoa and linseed oil, which made them look like coal miners at the end of a shift.

Eisenhower walked slowly, stepping over packs and equipment, shaking hands, saying his usual things.

"Where are you from?"

"From Kansas?"

"How long have you been in the army?"

"Are you a good shot?"

"That's the stuff. That's what will win for you tonight."

Eisenhower struggled to look them all in the eyes. It was different than his usual glad-handing. If Leigh-Mallory was right, every other young man on the other side of every handshake was a young man that Eisenhower had sent to die against advice.

"Don't worry, General," one young man said, looking back at him. "We'll take care of this."

The sky was clear when it was time to load up. The wind had died down, creating a calm in the glow from the setting sun as the men filed with their packs past the jumpmaster and into the hatch of the C-47s that would take them over Normandy.

"Good luck," Eisenhower shouted to them.

On the radio, the BBC inserted a peculiar phrase into its evening news broadcast. "Eileen is married to Joe. Repeat Eileen is married to Joe. The compass points north. The compass points north." It was the signal to the French Resistance. The Eighth Air Force was commencing bombing runs along the Channel coast. And the RAF began bombing coastal batteries along Normandy's beaches.

Eisenhower went to the roof of the 101st Airborne Division headquarters to watch the planes take off in the dark. It was shortly after ten thirty that night and the air was cool and vibrating with the drone of 437 C-47s taking flight, many with gliders being towed behind. The sparkling green-and-red navigation lights streamed through the air among the stars.

Eisenhower stood for half an hour just looking up into it. There was so much of it.

"War is a renunciation and a denial of human brotherhood," Eisenhower would write, reflecting on the experience. But, as Walter White had predicted, it also had an almost mystical power to bring people selflessly together. "In the assembly area before a dawn assault, on the ready line of a forward airfield, there was no thought of a man's antecedents, creed, or race. It was enough then that he was an American—that his heart was strong, his spirit willing—that he was big enough to place the cause above himself."

Eisenhower went back to the Packard with Kay. "Well, it's on," he said.

He tried to lie down as she drove back to the command post. He looked out the window at the sky.

"Nothing can stop it now."

"Black John Smith"

CHAPTER 45

IT WAS NOT a night for sleep. Eisenhower puttered around his circus wagon, chain-smoking, and flipped through the pile of westerns Mickey had procured for him. Mickey knew he preferred the ones with lots of action and shooting. Max Brand was particularly good. It was tragic what had happened to him. Eager to take in the sting of real battle, Brand had embedded a few weeks earlier as a war correspondent with the Fifth Army on the front line in Italy. He was killed by German artillery half an hour after the shooting started.

James Hendryx could also spin a good yarn. He had recently published a collection of his Black John stories called *The Czar of Halfaday Creek*. Its cover, depicting a Yukon man peering through a door with a shotgun, certainly looked promising.

The first chapter was entitled "The Man Who Looked over His Shoulder." Its opening line was intriguing: "He was an innocuous little man with soft, brown eyes, mild and confiding as a setter dog's, yet, with the haunting, hurt look in them, that spoke of confidence betrayed." This man is the newcomer, and he has walked into the saloon in Halfaday Creek, an outpost deep in the Yukon Territory on the border with Alaska, at the turn of the twentieth century.

There is only one other man in the saloon, besides the bartender, and when the newcomer introduces himself as "John Smith," the man, whose bushy black beard James Hendryx has noted a few times, laughs and tells him that "sixteen, seventeen other folks arrived at the same solution—me included—before you come. Of course, we ain't none of us got no patent on the alias, but further indulgence in it would lead to monotony an' confoosion."

Everyone in Halfaday Creek has an alias and nearly everyone arrived saying his name was John Smith. It was a funny conceit for a western. And it leads the man with the black beard to introduce himself as Black John. A Red John is mentioned as living in a cabin nearby. But with so many John Smiths, Black John explains that newcomers have to take their alias from a hat. The newcomer draws out the name George Cornwallis, provoking Black John to say, "This here Cornwallis, I rec'lect, was a general that made a famous retreat."

Around six thirty in the morning, Eisenhower's reading was interrupted by the phone. It was Bertie Ramsay. The news, while still preliminary, was all good. "The sky was clear, thank God, so that night, dawn, and day bombing was going well. Surprise seems to have been achieved up to the time that paratroops had been dropped at 0200." And despite the worst fears of disaster for the airborne divisions, "Only 29 Transport aircraft were lost out of 1300." Things were going according to plan.

Eisenhower returned to his reading. Black John is the outlaw king, hence the title *The Czar of Halfaday Creek*. He explains to Cornwallis that in Halfaday, there are no judgments for things past, but any "murder, claim jumpin', an' larceny" as well as any "skullduggery" that a man commits in Halfaday garners that man a hangin'. Nearly the whole book was dialog, and to hear Black John tell it, hangin's were a routine affair on Halfaday Creek. But there was not much in the way of action, at least, for the first twenty pages.

The first woman to make an appearance is Goldie. Cornwallis shrieks at the sight of her as she makes her way to the saloon, Goldie being his wife. Cornwallis then tells his own tale to Black John, about how Goldie tricked him into marrying her, pretending to be a kind, rich widow only to turn around and try to rob and murder him, as she had done with all her previous betrothed.

When Goldie finally makes her appearance, she demands hot whiskey and lives up to her reputation. Black John plays dumb about the whereabouts of her misbegotten husband but offers to let Goldie stay in a cabin that has recently been vacated after a hanging for skullduggery. Forty pages in, there was still no action. It was a funny story, more in the vein of O. Henry than Max Brand. Except then the story jumps to Black John dashing back into the saloon with a hot rifle in his hand.

Butch popped his head into the circus wagon. Eisenhower looked up from his reading. Butch had just gotten off the phone with Leigh-Mallory. Things were looking much better than predicted, with only twenty-nine of the 1,250 C-47 transport planes reported lost. A report from a pilot who had watched the British drop said that it had gone off smoothly. Apparently, the Germans had put nearly all of their night fighters in Calais. Leigh-Mallory's quote to mark D-Day: "Thank God, that is over."

Eisenhower suppressed a smile and cooly thanked Butch for the update. He then returned to his reading.

Goldie storms into the saloon. Someone has tried to shoot her. This, though, was all part of Black John's plan. He pretends to be shocked and tells Goldie that the gunman must be the man staying in Cornwallis's cabin, whom Black John says is "a-a philanthropist, which that's the scientifical name fer a woman hater." Bushwhacking is skullduggery, he assures her, and he tells her to come back the following afternoon, when justice will be done. But this is all still part of Black John's plan.

The next day, Black John ties Cornwallis up to the rafters, gives him some drops of "Siwash" to knock him unconscious, and then loops the rope around his neck to make it look as though he has been hanged until dead. When Goldie arrives, she declares that Cornwallis was her husband, Hubert Morningstar. She is furious that she missed the trial. And all the more furious that she has missed that hangin'. But with her husband dead, she takes her leave of Halfaday Creek, though not before a quick scuffle with the bartender, whom she attempts to dragoon into a fresh marriage. Black John then pours himself a whiskey and tells everyone not to forget to get Cornwallis down, since he will need a drink too, once he wakes up.

At seven in the morning, the BBC announced a German radio report of an Allied landing from Le Havre to Cherbourg. Eisenhower continued to read.

The next story seemed more promising in terms of action. Black John is out camping in the Yukon along the White River, when he is come upon by four prospectors, "Cheechakos," as he calls them. The Cheechakos don't think much of Black John, mistaking his amiability as a sure sign that he is just some rube. They hire Black John to help them get down the river, but before too long, two bandits jump out from the bushes with rifles. Finally, the story seemed to be picking up. “Put ’em up an’ keep ’em up!” says the bandit. “An’ anyone that tries any monkey work will git blow’d to hell.”

Mickey popped his head into Eisenhower’s circus wagon. It was 7:15, his usual time to check in. Eisenhower looked up at Mickey, whose eyes went to the ashtray, which was by then piled high. Eisenhower flashed him a half smile.

How are you feeling? Mickey asked.

“Not too bad, Mickey.” Eisenhower returned to his reading.

There is no shoot-out at the White River. Black John instead uses his wits. Once the bandits relieve the Cheechakos of their gold, he promises to take them to Halfaday Creek, where they can trade their ill-gotten gold for cash. This double cross is even more convoluted than the one that duped Goldie, involving as it does the Canadian police, forged tax receipts, and another near hangin’. But soon the two bandits are taken off by the law, and Black John is sipping whiskey again, albeit with a healthy portion of the Cheechakos’ gold.

Black John was a fun western character. He lives by a code and is much smarter than everyone takes him for. He knows how to use a bit of subterfuge, if not skullduggery, to make the right thing happen. Although, for a book that speaks so often and so casually about all manner of shootin’ and hangin’, there was not much of that in the story.

Mickey came back with breakfast and then backed out of the trailer. “I’ll be right around if you want me, sir.” Eisenhower reached over and drank some of the juice and then took a sip of coffee. He looked at the food but did not have an appetite. It was almost eight.

Eisenhower got himself up, shaved, and stepped out into the clear morning air refreshed. Butch was outside too and they shared the moment. A GI came by with the morning papers. There on the cover: “Nazis Flee North of Rome.” Eisenhower looked up at the GI and smiled broadly. “Good morning, GOOD morning!”

Eisenhower made his way to the Lockheed super-deluxe, where Mattie was waiting for him. The First Army had still sent no reports. He asked Mattie to take down an update for General Marshall.

“Local time is now eight in the morning,” he said. “I have as yet no information concerning the actual landings nor of our progress through beach obstacles.” He then ran through what little he did know, which was all encouraging, and then concluded: “Yesterday, I visited British troops about to embark and last night a great portion of a United States airborne division just prior to its take off. The enthusiasm, toughness and obvious fitness of every single man was high and the light of battle was in their eyes. I will keep you informed."

At quarter past nine, Eisenhower and the rest of the Official Family crowded into the Lockheed super-deluxe to listen to the radio. His message to the people of France was about to play. At 9:32, the BBC's John Snagge broke into the broadcast: "This is a broadcast from Supreme Headquarters Allied Expeditionary Force. Communique Number 1, which has just been issued by this Headquarters, will be read in five seconds from now."

Five seconds of dead air followed.

"Communique No. 1 issued by Supreme Headquarters Allied Expeditionary Force 'Under the command of General Eisenhower Allied Naval Forces, supported by strong air forces, began landing Allied Armies this morning on the northern coast of France.'"

Then Eisenhower's voice came over the air. "Citizens of France: I am proud to have again under my command the gallant forces of France. Fighting beside their allies, they will play a worthy part in the liberation of their homeland." He then continued, "As France is liberated from her oppressors, you yourselves will choose your representatives and the government under which you wish to live."

Eisenhower's order of the day had been distributed the previous evening. He had not submitted an order of the day to the unforgiving editorial scrutiny of General Fox Conner for two decades. Yet, had Conner reviewed it, he would have been loath to find a single word needing revision.

"Soldiers, sailors, and airmen of the Allied Expeditionary Forces: You are about to embark on the great crusade, toward which we have striven these many months," Eisenhower wrote. He had initially closed by saying, "I have full confidence in your courage, hardihood and skill in battle. We can, and we will win. Good Luck! And may the blessings of Almighty God rest upon us." But then he thought better of it. These would be the last words many of those crossing the Channel would ever hear from the man who sent them there. And so, he ended with something humbler, but nobler. "I have full confidence in your courage, devotion to duty, and skill in battle. We will accept nothing less than full victory! Good luck! And let us all beseech the blessing of Almighty God upon this great and noble undertaking."

Roosevelt and King George both offered prayers that echoed Eisenhower's order of the day. The king broadcast a plea for a "nation-wide perchance world-wide, vigil of prayer as the great crusade sets forth." And

Roosevelt prayed "Give us Faith in Thee; Faith in our sons; Faith in each other; Faith in our united crusade."

When he was a boy, the Bible Students taught that the Crusaders were a corrupt and savagely violent band of mercenaries in the service of a papal Antichrist. But Churchill, who never wavered in his Victorian confidence in Christendom had long invoked the spirit of the Crusades whenever praising an endeavor of great difficulty and nobility. When Roosevelt was elected in 1933 in the depths of the Great Depression, Churchill had wished him Godspeed by saying, "With earnest best wishes for the success of the greatest crusade of modern times."

British propaganda had followed Churchill's lead in championing the Second World War as the "Greatest Crusade." Roosevelt's prayer had cast those crossing Normandy's beaches that morning as crusaders for peace because "they fight not for the lust of conquest. They fight to end conquest. They fight to liberate. They fight to let justice arise, and tolerance and good will among all Thy people."

Eisenhower reclaimed the mantle of crusader as liberator. He would make it a defining theme of his life. The son of religious pacificists wore a flaming crusader's sword emblazoned on his shoulder patch because, in this life, there were times when only a man of arms could cut light through the darkness.

KAY DROVE EISENHOWER and Mattie to Southwick House, so he could send out congratulatory messages to Wayne Clark, Jumbo Wilson, and Alex for the capture of Rome. He ran into Freddie Morgan and congratulated him for the "great plan." Freddie graciously returned the compliment, saying, "Well, you finished it."

As it happened, Jimmy Doolittle had just come back from Normandy. In arguable defiance of Eisenhower's direct orders, Doolittle had commandeered a P-38 to see the action firsthand. He had flown up and down the beaches for more than an hour. "It was," Doolittle remarked, "the most impressive and unforgettable sight I could have possibly imagined."

Eisenhower was forgiving of Doolittle's insubordination, since his was the first eyewitness account Eisenhower had that morning. "Everything was going relatively smoothly," as far as Doolittle could tell. "Everyplace except Omaha. At Omaha Beach I saw landing craft after landing craft suffer a direct hit and blow up right in front of my face."

Eisenhower had Kay drive him out to Bloomfield House. Monty was milling about in the garden, looking pleased. He was planning to cross the Channel himself later that day to set up his headquarters on the other side.

By all lights, everything was going according to plan and, in some cases, better. The losses so far for the airborne flights were under 2 percent. In the British sector, the RAF had dropped the paratroopers with precision and had secured all the relevant bridges by 8:50 that morning. The British forces landing at Sword and Gold beaches had broken right through and had seized the defensive German batteries. The Canadians had taken a bit of a beating on Juno Beach, but they had also broken through, secured the beaches, and were at that very moment pressing inland toward Caen.

Lightning Joe Collins was living up to his nickname. VII Corps was making rapid progress on Utah Beach. The bulk of the force had landed southeast of its target, which turned out to be a happy accident, since the Germans had left it largely undefended. The only outstanding question was Gee Gerow's V Corps. There was nothing back from Omaha Beach yet. Eisenhower was growing worried.

AT NOON, CHURCHILL addressed Parliament. He had been running late and so was a little out of breath when he took the floor. "The House should, I think, take formal cognisance of the liberation of Rome by the Allied Armies under the Command of General Alexander, with General Clark of the United States Service and General Oliver Leese in command of the Fifth and Eighth Armies respectively. This is a memorable and glorious event, which rewards the intense fighting of the last five months in Italy." As soon as he mentioned Alex, the whole of Parliament erupted into cheers.

Churchill took several minutes to describe the long, hard-fought battle from Anzio to victory, before he turned to Normandy. The barometric pressure inside Westminster seemed to change as everyone waited to hear what the prime minister knew.

"The battle that has now begun will grow constantly in scale and in intensity for many weeks to come, and I shall not attempt to speculate upon its course," Churchill said soberly. "This I may say, however. Complete unity prevails throughout the Allied Armies. There is a brotherhood in arms between us and our friends of the United States. There is complete confidence in the supreme commander, General Eisenhower, and his lieutenants, and also in the commander of the Expeditionary Force, General Montgomery. The ardour and spirit of the troops, as I saw myself, embarking in these last few days was splendid to witness. Nothing that equipment, science or forethought could do has been neglected, and the whole process of opening this great new front will be pursued with the utmost resolution both by the commanders and by the United States and British Governments whom they serve."

The exuberant roar from all sides of the House that followed made it seem as if Westminster might shake to the ground.

At five thirty p.m. Charles de Gaulle finally broadcast a message to the people of France. But not until after a day's worth of intransigent chaos-making. Soon after declaring his refusal to broadcast the night before, he declared that the French "liaison officers" the Allies had been preparing to bring to France could not participate until the Americans acknowledged his political authority.

The Combined Chiefs had considered and rejected the idea of including a French division in the D-Day landings. But Eisenhower and Beetle had negotiated with Koenig over many months, agreeing to terms under which a few hundred French "liaison officers" would assist with civil affairs. They had been trained in England for a year at great expense by the British. Even Churchill had enough, saying that if De Gaulle was planning on acting as a spoiler, "an aeroplane would be ready to take him back to Algiers forthwith."

De Gaulle blinked, though as slowly and defiantly as eyelids could close. At four the previous morning, he had agreed to make a speech, but then insisted that he would do it live. No prerecording. The censors were never going to let that happen and so it looked like another stalemate until some magus from the political warfare office was inspired to remind De Gaulle, "We must have a record for posterity." If there was one thing De Gaulle cared more about than France's sovereign dignity, it was the way his voice would carry into posterity. And so, he gave in. *D'accord.*

"The supreme battle has been joined," De Gaulle began. "It is of course the Battle of France, and the battle for France! For the sons of France, wherever they are, whatever they are, the simple and sacred duty is to fight the enemy by every means in their power. The orders given by the French government and by the leaders which it has recognized must be followed precisely. From behind the cloud so heavy with our blood and our tears, the sun of our greatness is now appearing."

IT WAS AFTER six in the evening before Eisenhower received the first official word about Omaha Beach. The news was not good. High swells had resulted in the loss of half the assault tanks. They had a beachhead but were meeting determined resistance. They needed air support against German artillery. The Eighth Air Force was supposed to be conducting heavy bombing operations but overcast skies had made the bombers shy. And while more than 4,500 tons of bombs had been dropped, few of them landed anywhere near the German positions behind Omaha Beach.

Alan Kirk also sent up his first report on behalf of the US Navy. "Considerable mortar and artillery falling on beaches. Foot elements of approximately four regiments ashore. At latest report, no artillery or anti-aircraft ashore. Many stranded landing craft, due to certain obstacles, which were not initially cleared. Destroyers giving close gunfire support to stranded landing craft on Omaha beach. Utah beach latest reports indicate progress. No radio report from either airborne divisions. No hostile attack yet."

Eisenhower went back over to Broomfield House to talk to Monty. Given the progress, Monty was getting ready to set sail for Normandy at nine thirty that night. Eisenhower, though, remained worried by what he was hearing about Omaha Beach. Eisenhower wanted to know what Monty was planning to do about it. Owing to the progress in the British sector, could V Corps be redeployed there? That way they could do an end run around the German defenses at Omaha.

Monty cabled Miles Dempsey, who was commanding the British and Canadian Armies on Normandy's eastern beaches.

"Can you take V Corps?"

"No," Dempsey replied, "unless you want to leave our people out because it is too crowded for my people and V Corps to go in together."

Gee Gerow's men would just have to keep grinding it out.

AFTER DINNER THAT night, Butch set up a movie in the Lockheed superdeluxe. It was an eminently forgettable installment from the Fibber McGee and Molly series. When it was over, Eisenhower sent Butch and Jimmy to Southwick House to get the latest updates. Eisenhower was scheduled to board a destroyer early the next morning to see the front for himself, and the time couldn't pass quickly enough.

By 11:15, Butch and Jimmy had still not returned, so Eisenhower had Mattie call over. Just then, Butch and Jimmy came through the door. They had messages from Bradley and Gerow. The "news was not good" but "it was not desperate."

"Flow of information slow," Bradley reported. There was no information about the 82nd Airborne, but there were reports that the 101st Airborne had captured Saint-Martin Sade Darreville. Utah Beach was, surprisingly, well in hand. "Obstacles not serious. Surf not too bad." Omaha Beach, however, was seeing some trouble. "Progress slow. Obstacles are mined." But things were improving. V Corps had control of a strip that ran 10,000 yards at a depth of 1,200 to 3,000 yards.

The strategic air forces had dropped 10,395 tons of bombs to slow the advance of German reinforcements over the course of the day. There was little sign of French Resistance activity, except some damage to a railway viaduct outside Paris. The action messages to the French Resistance had been sent, but the Germans had been jamming the radio frequency.

Despite the cancellation of Operation Anvil, there had been a successful invasion of sorts in the South of France that day. Tough, no one was allowed to know about it.

General Marshall had wanted Eisenhower to try a new and spectacular airborne maneuver on D-Day, like what George Kenney had done. It made for great press, with journalists around the world, such as Keith Murdoch, continuing to tout the "brilliant generalship of General Kenney" and his "spectacular use," his "historic use," of airborne forces as a credit to American grit and ingenuity.

Eisenhower had opted instead to try a new maneuver with the Office of Strategic Services, code-named "Jedburgh." It was a joint covert operation of British, American, and French commandos, whose job in the months to come would be to coordinate guerrilla warfare from the Pyrenees to Belgium, from Brittany to Monte Carlo. As the 82nd and 101st Airborne Divisions were dropping behind Utah Beach, the first Jedburgh team, code-named "Hugh," had been dropped in the South of France. The drop was a success. The commandos were in France. There were no indications yet, however, of whether they got any ice cream.

WHILE EISENHOWER SPENT the day anxiously ferreting out the latest updates from across the Channel, John graduated from West Point. Mamie and her parents were there to celebrate. Eisenhower had sent a short message of congratulations to the graduates, who by the time they heard it, already knew that the march to Berlin had begun.

Eisenhower had written his son a more personal note to be opened once he received his diploma. Unlike his usual letters, in which he spoke to John like the same little boy with whom he had shared the bathtub, he found himself compelled to mark the moment with formality; a sign of respect to let his son know that he knew his boy was a man.

"Second Lieutenant John S.D. Eisenhower, U.S. Army. I hope you know how happy I am that both you and I are now officers in the great U.S. Army," he began. "I know that your actions will be characterized by firmness based upon knowledge and leadership based upon human understanding. My sincere congratulations together with the assurance that although you will be following your own individual path through life you will always have the enthusiastic support, love, and admiration of your mother and me. Devotedly, Dad."

Patton took a moment on D-Day to write to his own son, who was still two years from graduation at West Point. He reflected on what it meant to be a successful leader. "What you must know is how a man reacts. Weapons change but the man who uses them changes not at all," he advised his son. "The influence one man can have on thousands is a never ending source of wonder to me."

Dwight "Ike" Eisenhower, self-portrait

EPILOGUE

WHAT WERE THE signs of a cholera outbreak?

Thousands of people served in SHAEF, spending day and night anticipating every horror the Germans might contrive. None of the secret weapons they had all spent so much time preparing to counteract materialized, however. There were no reports of foggy film, and an investigation into the fogged film discovered at the hospital in Cheltenham a few weeks earlier had turned up no conclusive cause. There had been none of the difficulty swallowing to be expected with botulism or the kinds of blistering that might suggest an anthrax outbreak.

The Canadians urged mass inoculation against botulism as a precaution. The Combined Chiefs decided against it. There were no signs the Germans had crossed that particular line and medical personnel had not found any indication of inoculation against botulism in the blood samples taken from captured Germans, which suggested that they were not planning to cross that line anytime soon. The Combined Chiefs did, though, decide to maintain a stockpile of botulinum in the United Kingdom in case the need to retaliate arose. And General Marshall suggested the morning after D-Day that Eisenhower warn the medical and intelligence personnel proceeding inland to be on guard for signs of biological warfare.

No one, however, had anticipated the Germans' use of cholera, a bacterium that caused uncontrollable diarrhea, dehydration, and possible death. But then, shortly after the invasion, German propaganda announced, "A typhoid and cholera epidemic threatens to break out in the invasion area on the coast of Normandy." It attributed the outbreak to the Allies' inability "to bury the many thousands of their dead."

The point of the broadcast was to convince listeners that Allied soldiers were being torn to pieces on the Atlantikwall. But saying that the Allied siege of Fortress Europe had caused a cholera outbreak seemed oddly specific. The broadcast might have been written off had it not also been for the discovery in German bunkers of bottles labeled "*Cholera-Imfpstoff Schering*." Medical personnel conducted further blood tests on German POWs and discovered unusually high rates of cholera inoculation. Were the Germans using the broadcast as cover for the use of cholera as a biological weapon?

The bottles, it turned out, were doses of the cholera vaccine, and the high rates of cholera inoculation were associated with Germans who had fought in Russian territory, where cholera was endemic. It was a relief that offered little in the way of relief, because the previously unanticipated threat was now an anticipated one. The Pentagon had issued warnings as far back as February to be on the lookout for biological-weapon attacks on the water supply. Now alerted to the risk of cholera, it was no longer responsible to trust the local water in Normandy. Strict water discipline was therefore imposed, meaning the Allies now had to ship their drinking water across the Channel. That in turn would further slow the buildup of men and matériel, which was already going slower than expected.

In the first week after the invasion, the Allies had gotten about 28,000 of the nearly 37,000 vehicles they had planned to get ashore. The British were behind in getting men across as well. Eisenhower was paying close attention to the turnaround times. The landing craft were supposed to load and unload in four hours. It was possible to do it in three and a half. On the Normandy beaches, it was taking seven.

While the German propaganda was a lie, it was nevertheless true that the evacuation of casualties was also extremely slow. Because of the lessons of Gallipoli, the British surgeon general had insisted on ample hospital ships in the Channel. The problem, though, was that they could not land onshore, which created even more bottlenecks until Eisenhower's chief medical officer started using LSTs to simply transport the injured across the Channel to hospitals in England.

On June 7, Eisenhower and Jimmy boarded the HMS *Apollo* and sailed to the Normandy coast. Eisenhower was anxious to get a sense of progress from Brad and Monty. Brad had gone ashore earlier that morning and had to rush back to meet with Eisenhower. Brad was impatient that he was there, treating Eisenhower's arrival as a meddlesome distraction. And that was fair. Eisenhower had made the trip out of impatience, not because there was anything useful he could do.

The sky had been murky, and the sea was rough. Eisenhower did not even touch land, at least not deliberately. His over-eagerness to get closer to the beach for a better view led the captain of the HMS *Apollo* to run aground, requiring another destroyer to come to Eisenhower's rescue and take him safely back to England for the night.

Eisenhower returned to his camp at a little after ten. Corporal Williams knew he would be getting in late and had saved dessert for him. Strawberries.

There was also an update from Monty waiting for him. "General situation very good and am well satisfied with results of today's fighting." Monty had taken initiative and ordered VII Corps to change direction and press east to join up with V Corps. It slowed down VII Corps' charge toward the port of Cherbourg, but it took the pressure off Omaha Beach and they were now making progress. The best thing, indeed the only thing, that Eisenhower could do that night was enjoy his strawberries.

EISENHOWER SENT HIS first message to Mamie on June 9, the day Omaha Beach linked up with Utah Beach to its west and Gold Beach to its east. "Due to previous engagement, it was impossible to be with you and John Monday but I thought of you." It was the kind of ostentatious understatement that would make his mother proud, just as it made his son's eyes roll. John was due to arrive in London in four days and Eisenhower was "as excited as a bride" to see him.

Eisenhower then wrote Mamie a more personal letter. "When I go through these intense periods of strain and effort," he wrote, "I think of you, I want you here, and try to write to you—but I'm afraid that even my short notes are rather incoherent! Anyway, we've started. Only time will tell how great our success will be. But all that can be done by human effort, intense devotion to duty, and courage in execution, all by thousands and thousands of individuals, will be done by this force."

Over the next fourteen months, Eisenhower stopped complaining to Mamie about the "eternal pound, pound, pound" and feeling like a "Jack-in-the-Box." He would occasionally mention how busy he was, but always by way of an excuse for "not writing with my usual frequency, but it's not because I don't want to do so."

The success of Operation Overlord had not relieved him of his reasons to worry. If anything, the problems were larger and more ambiguous in their solution. Should they seek to control the entire coast of northwest France and Belgium, or should they race the Soviets to Berlin? Should they divert south to liberate Paris? How should he govern France? What might Hitler do with the world closing in on him? Breaking through the Atlantikwall simply presented these questions. It did not answer them.

Eisenhower's roiling mind, however, seemed to grow quieter. No one could miss it, even if they could not precisely pinpoint what was different about him. He raised a few eyebrows when he stopped wearing a helmet during his tours of the front lines. But he wasn't cocky exactly. There was no puffing swagger. It was just something about the way he stood, the way he held his face.

For fifty-three years, Eisenhower had wrestled his nerves to stay below the surface, but they were only ever just below. He could only smile the strain away to a point, and those who knew him well could see the tightness around his boyish blue eyes. It was one of the reasons, no doubt, that General Marshall was always nagging him to take a vacation, to get more exercise, to relax. But in the days and months ahead, Eisenhower carried himself more and more with the ease-in-the-face-of-anything cool befitting a character named Ike.

D-DAY'S SUCCESS GAVE Eisenhower the special worries that come with being one of the most famous people in the world. The flood of congratulations became so overwhelming that Eisenhower had to set up a system for replying to it all. Replies to labor groups, for example, should emphasize the "dependence of the soldier upon that particular organization." And though everything would be signed under his name, the pronoun "we" should always be used instead of "I."

To some congratulations, Eisenhower gave his personal attention. Wayne Clark cabled to say that he was looking forward to fighting alongside him again. Georgie Patton had called, following up with a short note, expressing the "great admiration I have for the tenacity of purpose which you have shown during the last two and a half years." And Jacob Devers sent a letter, saying, "I know I have no claim to any credit in it, but nevertheless as the advance continues and the plan unfolds, I feel as if I at least was on the right track, as the plan is very much the same as the one which started when I was in England in which I so firmly believed." He then offered to help with the invasion of southern France, "if we can get landing craft."

On D-Day, Milton had written to him that "mother's telephone at Abilene, and mine here have been ringing all day—newspaper men calling from all parts of the country." Milton assured him that "the answer is always the same: 'no member of the family wishes to comment.'" But the main reason Milton was eager to write was that he needed Eisenhower's signature, authorizing Milton as his agent for the movie deal.

The following day, Eisenhower sent Milton a teletype, authorizing him "to secure additional information on the matter and to carry on such discussions, as in his judgment, seem desirable." He remained emphatic that he would not touch a cent of any money. And Milton got right to work sending a producer a letter marked "Confidential" and including as a term of any deal that "no intimation would ever be given . . . that the picture was produced with the help of the family."

Mamie was distraught when she learned that Eisenhower was giving the rights to his life story away for free. The amounts on offer were more than they had made in their entire lives. But Eisenhower had the presence of mind to see that the money was poison. Profiting would come at the cost of honor. He wrote back to her, "We don't need it anyway—it's fun to be poor!"

Eisenhower avoided postwar poverty, in part, by writing a best-selling memoir of the war, *Crusade in Europe*. He sent a copy to General Conner with the inscription, "To whom I shall always be indebted." He then wrote Conner a letter, saying, "I doubt very much that I should ever have been in a position to prepare such a memoir, had it not been for the guidance and counsel I got from you."

The movie Milton sought to broker never materialized, but the biography from his protégé, Ken Davis, was published in 1946 under the title *Soldier of Democracy*. Comparing Eisenhower to Lincoln, Davis described Eisenhower as "the most perfect embodiment in our time of America's national ideal," who "signifies the universal validity of what is best and highest in the American dream." Milton could not have written it better himself. And the *New York Times* review began by ruminating, "We came out of the war with soldiers talking more effectively for peace than most of the statements on record. Oustanding among these soldiers is General of the Army Dwight D. Eisenhower."

In November 1951, the "Draft Eisenhower" movement within the Republican Party kicked off at a time when Eisenhower was, publicly, coy about his partisan leanings and still in command of the newly formed North Atlantic Treaty Organization. Keith Murdoch's old friend Roy Howard sent Eisenhower polling showing him a path to victory and shared the opposition research being circulated by his likely rival for the nomination, the isolationist Robert Taft. Eisenhower, in turn, asked Howard to use the finger he had on the American political pulse to tell him the "five or six matters of policy of outstanding public interest."

Howard had cultivated a chummy relationship with Eisenhower after the war and was ever eager to discuss politics. He was among many in the Republican-leaning press to both lobby Eisenhower to run and create momentum within the party for his nomination. Others included Charles Harger, the publisher of the *Abilene Daily Reflector*, who wrote a profile of Eisenhower in the November issue of *The American* magazine, describing his upbringing in a "staunch Republican family."

When the delegates were split between Eisenhower and Taft at the Republican National Convention in Chicago, Howard was the first major journalist to call the race. Eisenhower opened his address accepting the nomination by saying, "Ladies and Gentlemen, you have summoned me on behalf of millions of your fellow Americans to lead a great crusade—for Freedom in America and Freedom in the world."

AS KOENIG HAD predicted, the French people welcomed freedom in their little part of the world and intelligence reports were startled to find that the British were also being "cheered and embraced, flowers were showered on them." While the people of Normandy seemed "unanimous in their questions as to what is the French Government," in the week after D-Day, there were no signs that an incipient civil war was about to tear the country apart. Once towns and villages came under Allied control, French civilians kept doing their day jobs, and French children flashed the V-sign. "Everywhere," the report concluded, "the reception is friendly."

This was despite the massive human costs of the Transportation Plan, which did appear to be achieving the desired results. The "Das Reich" armored division had started mobilizing from southern France the day after D-Day but had to leave its tanks behind due to the lack of rail transport.

The thing was, though, it was not clear that the Transportation Plan deserved the credit. The French Resistance, with plenty of support from the Office of Strategic Services, had sprung into action and appeared to be doing at least as much, if not more, using "technical sabotage," to disrupt the French railway system "by mis-routing trains, mis-signaling and general obstructionism." The night of the D-Day invasion, thousands of Frenchmen with packages of TNT sabotaged railroad tracks and telephone relay stations across the country. They littered the roads with so-called "tire-busters," small mines made to look like horseshit that could blow the wheel clear off a German truck.

The Transportation Plan carried extraordinary costs in bombs, fuel, airpower, political capital, and civilian lives. The persistent sabotage by covert agents, by contrast, was doing the messy work of sludging the German Blitzkrieg down into a Matschkrieg without making a mess.

The Maquis were also increasingly active in northern France, including a group of White Russians in Brittany. Open guerrilla warfare with the German army was spreading like so many little fires. After seeing a few communiqués talking about "captured" territory in France, Eisenhower sent a note to Beetle. All future communications should use the word "liberated."

The only Frenchman who seemed intent on doing battle against the Allies was Charles de Gaulle, who spent the week after D-Day throwing one tantrum after another and complaining that he had been handed a fait accompli like some Anglo-American quisling. To make his point, De Gaulle sent word out that the new French currency the Allies had printed was "*un faux-monnaie*." The French Committee had worked closely with the US Treasury to create this new currency to replace the Vichy government's Banque de France notes. De Gaulle, though, was now insisting that he, as the leader of the Provisional Government of France, accorded no legal value to the "stamped paper" and warned of the dire "political, moral and financial consequences" that would follow if such notes made it into circulation.

Eisenhower, with Roosevelt and Churchill's backing, called De Gaulle's bluff and went ahead and used the currency anyway. Soon, Roosevelt started dangling the prospect of an official visit to Washington, and De Gaulle dropped his complaints about the *faux-monnaie*. De Gaulle would travel to Normandy on June 16 and enter Paris victorious on August 25.

Despite Roosevelt's fears, and Churchill's hopes, perhaps, De Gaulle resigned from the French government in January 1946, after failing to assemble a coalition government. He returned to office in 1958, to a French government in crisis, following imperial humiliations at the Suez Canal and Dien Bien Phu, as well as the success of independence movements across its former empire. Following a half-decade of brutal civil war, De Gaulle would offer independence to Algeria, the last of France's North African territories, in 1959, prompting future president Eisenhower to laud "General de Gaulle's courageous and statesman like declaration. It is our hope that it will lead to an early peace."

SO MUCH OF the planning for D-Day had turned on Eisenhower's ability to hoard precious landing craft in England. "The destinies of two great empires," Churchill would bemoan, "seem to be tied up in some goddamned things called LSTs." But soon after D-Day, Eisenhower had too many landing craft and, within a week, even the coveted LSTs were being rerouted to the Mediterranean for the long-awaited invasion of southern France.

When General Marshall asked Eisenhower if Jacob Devers or Wayne Clark should be given command of the invasion, Eisenhower looked at the situation coolly. The truth was that Devers had done nothing but succeed where many others had failed in Italy. And so he supported Devers, writing back to Marshall without any irony or backhanded discouragement, "I would accept the decision cheerfully and willingly." Wayne was an old friend. But Devers had proved himself in the battle for Rome. As far as Eisenhower was concerned, merit was merit.

Operation Dragoon, as Operation Anvil would be renamed, was finally launched in August. Churchill continued to lobby against it almost to the end. It was one of several strains in the Anglo-American alliance that not only persisted but deepened after D-Day.

Another was the diplomatic communication ban. Eisenhower lobbied Churchill to keep it in place, at least through the end of June, to maintain the fiction that Patton was poised to charge into Calais. Enormous resources had been poured into Operation Fortitude at that point. And the feint worked. Air reconnaissance in the days after the invasion showed the Germans building up their air forces in Calais. And Ultra intercepts showed that the German high command simply could not believe that George S. Patton would not be at the front of the main battle.

Georgie could hardly believe it either, going so far as to offer Eisenhower $1,000 a week to go fight in the line before he had to command the Third

Army. Georgie may have been kidding. But Eisenhower did not even take him up on the joke, seeing how much more value he had as the boogeyman in Hitler's dreams.

Churchill's patience for allowing the diplomatic relations of His Majesty's Government to continue to be dictated by a general from one of its former colonies, however, had run out. The diplomatic ban was formally lifted on June 19, 1944.

This fight over Britain's diplomatic prestige happened just as the Foreign Office was raising new objections to the use of white phosphorus. Anthony Eden judiciously waited until June 7 to bring it up, but he was unsparing when he did. "If these bombs are used primarily against personnel," Eden chided Churchill, "their use is certainly illegal."

The issue was, by then, not theoretical. White phosphorus had been openly dropped throughout the Normandy invasion, and not simply to set the massive white smoke screen the landing forces used as cover when getting ashore on D-Day. The battalions that had been firing it from 4.2-inch mortars, "goon guns," had received a citation "for extraordinary heroism and outstanding performance of duty in action." White phosphorus was used all over Omaha Beach. And Joe Collins directed his forces to fire white phosphorus into enemy positions before demanding surrender over a loudspeaker, a tactic he christened "hog calling."

Upon reading Eden's letter, Churchill forwarded it to the British Chiefs, adding, "Place this serious minute before the Chiefs of Staff and ask them what reply they wish to make." Negotiations continued throughout June and into July, with the British Chiefs asking Eisenhower to reconsider how his forces were using white phosphorus. But rather than looking to end the negotiations on a point of agreement, if only so everyone could save face, Eisenhower stuck to a hard line.

Eisenhower's reasons were sound. The Allies had been using white phosphorus for more than a year and the Germans had never accused them of resorting to chemical weapons. In fact, the Germans had recently taken to using white phosphorus in their shells too. But Eisenhower's unwillingness to compromise, even a little, was an early sign of a much-deeper shift in the Anglo-American balance of power.

In December 1941, Britain's confident place as the senior partner in the Anglo-American alliance was obvious. But a year into the war, it became a cliché for Americans in the know, like Harry Hopkins, to start asking, "Who's senior partner, and who's junior?" The answer wasn't obvious. By the eve of the Cairo Conference, the answer was no longer obvious to Churchill either. Churchill's obsessions with eccentric operations in the Mediterranean were a sign of desperation for something that would save the dignity of the British Empire, such as a "purely British theater when the laurels would be all ours . . . Austria or the Balkans." Alan Brooke would write in the notes to his diary that Churchill's "new feelings of spitefulness" leading into the Cairo Conference had been provoked by the realization that "the strength of the American forces were now building up fast and exceeding ours. He hated having to give up the position of the dominant partner."

After D-Day, the answer was again obvious as the United States increasingly dictated the direction of the war in Europe and as Britain's financial troubles spiraled out of control. By the end of June, one of Churchill's own cabinet ministers would be declaring the country "broke." At the Bretton Woods conference the next month, John Maynard Keynes failed to persuade the world to go along with the bancor as the new global currency. Instead, it went with the dollar, and the headquarters of what would become the International Monetary Fund and the World Bank officially opened for business the following year in Washington, DC.

Keynes's dire warnings about the political costs of Britain's economic woes soon proved optimistic. Over the ensuing years, the economic glue holding places as disparate as Palestine, India, Malta, Malaya, and Sudan together cracked.

A decade later, Great Britain, France, and Israel invaded Egypt with designs on retaking control of the Suez Canal. The action was arguably illegal under the Charter of the United Nations and certainly contrary to its purposes, as the United States asserted before the United Nations Security Council. A cease-fire was quickly in place after future president Dwight Eisenhower brought future prime minister Anthony Eden to heel. Eisenhower did not need to send the 101st Airborne. He just had to cut off Britain's supply of dollars. There would be no conquest of Egypt's sovereign territory, and to ensure the cease-fire held, the Security Council deployed the first-ever United Nations Emergency Force, or "peacekeepers."

EISENHOWER WOULD BE the first American president to be regularly called the "leader of the free world." During the war, Churchill and Roosevelt shared the title. Eisenhower wore the mantle as a duty, saying in his inaugural address, "Freedom is pitted against slavery; lightness against the dark." The sentiment echoed his order of the day on June 6, 1944, official copies of which were embossed with SHEAF's crusader sword emblem, and in which he exhorted those crossing the Channel to seek "the elimination of Nazi tyranny over the oppressed peoples of Europe, and security for ourselves in a free world." But within days of D-Day, Eisenhower would be again forced, as he would be many times in the years ahead, to answer the question: Free for whom?

On June 9, Edward Betts came to Eisenhower with court-martial cases, including the paperwork to finalize the case of Smith and Brinson. Betts advised him to approve the death sentences. As far as Betts was concerned, the "color problem" was a mirage. The claimed disparity in the sentences given for rape, Betts's staff had concluded, "does not show prejudice against colored soldiers, but that the somewhat more severe sentences are justified by the frequency of such crimes, and the more aggravated accompanying circumstances."

The only loose end was Brinson's mother. She had written, first to Roosevelt, and then to the War Department, claiming that her son had been showing signs of mental illness and asked that his life be spared, at least until doctors could evaluate him for insanity. Cliff Lee ordered a psychiatric evaluation of Brinson, but Betts advised Eisenhower to go ahead and approve the death sentences. The evidence, the nature of the crime, and the vigorous defense the men had received, Betts said, warranted the first death sentence for rape the army would impose in England. Eisenhower signed off and Smith and Brinson were hanged on August 11, 1944.

That same day, however, the Leroy Henry case leapt to even greater international attention. The *Tribune* published the full transcript of Henry's trial under the title "The Trial of a Negro." An accompanying editorial stated that it was publishing it verbatim "at this critical stage of the war, because one of the purposes for which our men are fighting is for the restoration of the dignity and equality of all individuals—whatever their colour or creed." It then mentioned without flourish that Henry's fate rested in Eisenhower's hands.

Thurgood Marshall, the legal director of the NAACP, had just written to Eisenhower seeking a stay of Henry's execution and an opportunity to review the record in the case. Marshall was already one of the foremost civil rights attorneys in the United States. The year before, he had persuaded the US Supreme Court to unanimously throw out similarly dubious rape charges against Black soldiers in Louisiana and that very April had persuaded a near-unanimous Supreme Court to invalidate racial discrimination in voting, landing the first hard blow against the previously undefeated

Jim Crow. Thurgood Marshall's request to Eisenhower was a prelude to the NAACP taking up Henry's case, all the way to the Supreme Court if necessary. The League of Colored Peoples also asked Eisenhower to review the record, which prompted Eisenhower to reply immediately and promise that he would conduct a thorough inquiry.

Under this pressure, Betts offered a more sympathetic view of Henry's case. Unlike the victim in the Smith and Brinson case, Betts reasoned, the woman whom Henry allegedly attacked had a poor reputation. His staff lawyers initially concluded that the conviction should be affirmed, but since "this was not an aggravated case of rape," that Henry's sentence should be commuted to life imprisonment.

Eisenhower had a long meeting with Betts a few days later and decided to throw the case out altogether. Betts had one of his assistants draw up another memorandum explaining that the charges should be dropped because the evidence was weak, Henry's confession appeared coerced, and the victim was not credible. With the memorandum justifying the decision in hand, Betts paid a short visit to Eisenhower's office in Wide Wing with the paperwork to sign. Leroy Henry was back on duty by the end of June.

Omar Bradley was far from alone in thinking that "the negro has no place in this theater." Brad saw his job as winning battles and objected that "anything that interferes or complicates that effort is injurious to our national well being." Though, he dutifully—if begrudgingly—agreed to incorporate a division of Black soldiers into the First Army once its foothold in Europe was established.

Around 1,700 Black soldiers landed in the first wave on D-Day, including the 320th Anti-Aircraft Balloon battalion, a combat unit. It had constituted some of the only anti-aircraft defense on Omaha Beach that day. A team of four Black medics was also one of the first to land on Omaha Beach, receiving medals for valor after saving hundreds of lives over thirty sleepless hours.

For the rest of his life, Eisenhower's relationship to America's "color problem" would be marked by the same vacillation between wariness and resolve. During the Battle of the Bulge, Eisenhower would initially approve a plan advanced by Cliff Lee, and supported by both Bradley and Patton, to train 2,500 Black soldiers to fight in integrated units. When Beetle sent word of the plan to Washington, however, General Marshall balked at this naked violation of the army's segregation policy. Rather than abandon the plan, however, Eisenhower eked out a compromise, creating segregated

Black platoons to fight alongside white platoons in the final battle against fascism.

But then, as army chief of staff, Eisenhower would refuse to go further and came out against the integration of the army below the platoon level. Testifying before Congress, Eisenhower said, "If we attempt merely by passing a lot of laws to force someone to like someone else, we are just going to get into trouble." This prompted Walter White to express dismay at "believing he had courage to tackle prejudice as valiantly as he did the Nazis."

But then, after Thurgood Marshall knocked Jim Crow to the mat with his victory in *Brown v. Board of Education*, Eisenhower would be the first president since Ulysses S. Grant to invoke the Insurrection Act against a southern state. And to back up his words, he would deploy the 101st Airborne Division to ensure that Black children could walk safely to school in Little Rock, Arkansas.

AS EISENHOWER WAS deliberating over the fates of Willie Smith, Eliga Brinson, and Leroy Henry, General Marshall arrived in London with Ernest King and Hap Arnold. The following afternoon, Saturday, June 10, Kay drove Eisenhower to the private house General Marshall had been given just outside Staines.

Monty had sent Eisenhower a progress report that morning. The Allies now controlled a unified beachhead that ran sixty miles from Franceville to fifteen miles southeast of Cherbourg. A cable had also come in from Moscow announcing, "Red Army started an offensive on Leningrad front at 0600 today."

General Marshall was serene. He had kept close tabs on progress. Twenty-four hours after photos of the beaches on D-day were taken, they had been on his desk in Washington, DC. That week the army had securely transmitted six hundred photographs from Normandy over its new global "telephoto net," which had been developed in collaboration with Acme Newspictures. In just seven minutes, a photo could be sent across the world. It was something of a marvel.

Now that he was in England, General Marshall wanted Eisenhower to know, in person, of his "satisfaction with what had been accomplished." He estimated that the war against Germany would be won in a year and showed Eisenhower the draft of a report he was planning to send to Roosevelt. "I think we have the Huns at the top of the toboggan slide and the full crash of the Russian offensive should put the skids under them." Marshall told Eisenhower that in the war ahead, from here on out, he would give his protégé complete discretion to choose his own personnel. Marshall might offer the names he collected in his little book. But it was always going to be Eisenhower's call. It was the greatest vote of confidence that George C. Marshall could—or had—ever given to anyone.

The next day, Eisenhower awoke to good news that Monty had sent overnight. The British had mounted a counterattack against the Germans that, if successful, would press the Allied line thirteen miles deep.

Eisenhower ate breakfast in his circus wagon and sent a message to his Russian counterpart, Field Marshal Aleksandr Vasilevsky. "We wish for you the great successes that your courage, endurance and determination so richly deserve and we are proud that we are bringing daily into the fighting line more and more of your comrades in arms to help in the final destruction of Nazi tyranny."

Midmorning, he got into the olive-green Packard and Kay drove the hours-long trip to Wide Wing. A convoy that stretched for miles of tanks, DUWKs, and trucks passed on the opposite side of the road, all heading toward Portsmouth. The tanks bore the black bull of the British Eleventh Armored Division.

Eisenhower reached Wide Wing a little after noon, where Marshall, King, and Arnold were waiting for him. Churchill was also there. Roosevelt had sent Churchill two IBM Electric Executive typewriters as something of a victory present. IBM had released the model that year, as the first typewriter with proportionally spaced text. Churchill had been struck after receiving a letter from the War Department that had been typed on one of the machines. It looked as if a printer had set it. For a literary man, having such a typewriter on his desk was a delightful marvel, and Churchill happily accepted. Churchill also took great pleasure in sharing a telegram he had just received from Uncle Joe offering well wishes from Moscow. The brotherly love in the room made it easy to forget that a brawl had nearly broken out the last time all these men were together.

Eisenhower gave his first briefing on the status of operations since Cairo and General Marshall was impressed by how "cool and confident" he was.

"Allied progress continues," he wrote in the accompanying report, "along the whole of the beach head." The enemy position in Cherbourg was weakening, but the fighting continued to be brutal. The Seventeenth Panzer Division was the most capable of the elements they had encountered, though the Third Paratroopers Division was made up of men "very young and thoroughly indoctrinated with Nazi ideology." The rest of the German divisions in Cherbourg were poorly organized and tended to surrender before things got too intense. And contrary to Stalin's predictions, many were Russian.

Fighting was the most intense in the east. Monty had not yet captured Caen and the Germans were mounting an armored counteroffensive, in which the German Panzer and Tiger tanks were proving indomitable. None of the Allied ammunition had the punch needed to crack into them from the front. They could use some of William Borden's "super guns."

American casualties were much better than feared. The most up-to-date figures showed 4,619 men killed, wounded, or missing on Omaha Beach, and 1,679 on Utah Beach. The airborne figures were grimmer, with 2,261 casualties for the 82nd Airborne and 3,501 for the 101st Airborne. In the case of the 101st Airborne, 1,926 of those men were still reported missing. But there were 440 confirmed dead thus far.

On the naval side of things, E-boats had come out the previous night. But the navy was ready for them and there were no reported Allied casualties. The biggest issue was that the buildup was behind schedule. Eisenhower had visited Bertie Ramsay the night before to discuss the delays, and he was assured things were getting on track. By that evening, 367,142 Allied troops, 50,228 vehicles, and 59,961 tons of supplies would be ashore.

There were still risks, of course. But Eisenhower could confidently report that progress had reached the point that the following morning, he would lead them all on a personal tour of the sixty-mile hole that was now gaping in the Atlantikwall.

EISENHOWER LEFT WIDE Wing around four thirty in the afternoon. He and Kay went to Telegraph Cottage nearby to relax for a while. They were back on the road around half past seven, and, after making a quick stop at Southwick House, finally got back to camp late that night.

Eisenhower was eager to get to bed. But then the phone rang. It was Beetle. Churchill was sending over an urgent message for Eisenhower's eyes only. He should stay up until it arrived. Eisenhower did his best, but when midnight finally struck, he told Butch to wake him up when it came in. He needed a little rest. The message from Churchill came in around two in the morning, but Butch and Jimmy made the call to give him a few more hours of sleep.

Eisenhower was up before dawn and read over Churchill's message. There were new Ultra intercepts. The Germans were trying to assess whether the

Allies had brought gas masks. Knowing that in just a few hours he would be escorting the elders of America's war council onto Normandy's beaches, it was the kind of thing to make the blood cold. He told Butch to contact Monty first thing to make sure the front lines were prepared for potential gas attacks.

Kay drove Jimmy and Eisenhower to Cosham Station at 5:40 a.m. Half an hour later, Churchill's train pulled in and out stepped the prime minister, Marshall, King, Arnold, and their entourage. Eisenhower greeted them all warmly and offered helmets and gas masks for the trip as if handing out life preservers to those boarding a pleasure cruise.

No one was particularly alert that morning. Churchill had treated Marshall, King, and Arnold to dinner the previous night. The prime minister had called an end to the evening at the unusually early hour of eleven, since they all needed to be up early. There was only time, he then said, for another drink, meaning that dinner did not break up until near midnight.

Eisenhower led them all to the destroyer USS *Thompson*, where they bid their farewell to Churchill. The prime minister would be boarding a vessel of His Majesty's Navy to visit the British beaches.

The morning was clear, the first since D-Day. Eisenhower had worn his service cap to keep the sun out of his eyes, which made him look incongruously more official than Marshall, who had opted for an ill-fitting field cap. The visibility made the scale of human activity around Portsmouth incredible to behold. As the USS *Thompson* charted course to Omaha Beach, they passed hundreds of ships of every kind and size in every direction until they reached open water.

After four hours at sea, the Channel again grew dense with ships that were packed with increasing density along the Normandy coast. Eisenhower and his party disembarked on one of the famous Mulberries off Omaha Beach, where they boarded a subchaser for a tour of the coastline. The scene made one reflexively keep an eye on the sky, so inviting a target it would be for the Luftwaffe. Occasional explosions in the water were never quite threatening, but also not reassuring, since they were usually the sound of a newly discovered German mine.

The volume of activity rivaled any dockyard. LSTs, DUWKs, Crocodiles, Liberty Ships, and every manner of landing craft streamed in every direction with so many signal lights flashing as to be a silent cacophony all their own. LSTs beached themselves, dumping men, cargo, tanks, trucks, and everything else to make room for everything heading in the opposite direction all to the rhythm of pops, cracks, thuds, small arms fire, and accidents happening. There were men everywhere, an uncountable number, emptying out from landing craft, walking in columns up the beach, lazing on a break with a K ration, hauling, driving, and milling about like longshoremen.

Eisenhower's party ended their tour of the coast back at the Mulberry. They boarded one of the DUWKs and drove from the water onto land through a path that the sappers had cut through the hedgehogs, tetrahedra, and all the other nasty obstacles that still peeked up through the surf.

Up close, Omaha Beach was a wall of red, brown, and green hills and gray cliffs that jutted a hundred feet up from the waterline. It was a warren of pillboxes, and just beyond were hedgerows and the occasional sign: "Achtung, Minen!"

Blood does not stain sand for very long. The tides, the breeze, the tumble of sea life, refresh any beach to its former serenity after a little while. But the scars of battle remained in the debris, the burned-out wrecks of anything too large for the tide to have yet dragged away. And there was nothing serene about Omaha Beach. It hummed, rattled, and clamored with the mechanical din of traffic, bulldozers, tanks, DUWKs, splashing, shouts, truck engines, and men grunting, shouting, and bullshitting as they offloaded millions of pounds of everything into piles.

Eisenhower climbed out of the DUWK. France was beneath his feet. Looking back out to the sea, the vast armada he commanded stretched to the horizon.

That day, Eisenhower would see Bradley, Gerow, Collins, and even the famous war correspondent Ernie Pyle. When Pyle asked for the latest, Eisenhower joked, "Good god, you're the people we are expecting news from!" He visited the wounded aboard a C-47 hospital plane. He inspected the pens holding prisoners of war. He toured Bradley's command post, a former German bunker in the middle of an apple orchard that had been bitterly won by the Rangers. He passed fields of sprouting poppies and Rommel's "asparagus." Refugees walked inland pushing baby carriages and fishermen milled about in the same broad-brimmed black hats that their grandfathers had worn. Cows grazed amidst it all, indifferent to the fact that their cud was the greatest battlefield the world had ever known.

There were trees stripped nude by fire and Long Tom, the massive German battery that had rained death down onto Gerow's men at Omaha Beach. Some French cottages still smoldered, and in one field, the German dead still lay under the sun. Mounds of life belts were everywhere, wherever soldiers had discarded them, confident they would be on firm ground for the foreseeable future.

Eisenhower returned to Omaha Beach later that afternoon. The rubble of the Atlantikwall was all around. Paris was to his south, Berlin to his east, Britain behind him, and history ahead. The newest issue of *Life* magazine had just hit the stands, featuring aerial photographs of Normandy under the headline "Invasion by Air." Eisenhower appeared only once, in a group photo on page 5, where he sat at a baize-topped conference table, flanked by Bradley, Ramsay, Tedder, Montgomery, Leigh-Mallory, and Beetle.

A week later, *Life* would immortalize him on its cover. Inside that issue were the images of soldiers wading past obstacles onto flaming beaches that would soon come to define D-Day as concisely as the photograph of Marines raising the flag would define the Battle of Iwo Jima. *Life* would not—and could not—run stirring photographs of the worries over risks that turned out to be nothing, the regrets over dangers not foreseen, the memos written to calm his mind and organize his thoughts, the reports, charts, letters, phone calls, cables, tables, lunches, dinners, drinks, bridge games, essay contests, handshake deals, backroom deals, broken deals, empty promises, conferences, arguments, speeches, compromises, and cigarettes that it had taken to put those men on that beach.

Eisenhower would not have had it any other way. D-Day was about the men on those beaches and what they did. "The soldiers, sailors, and airmen are indescribable in their elan, courage, determination and fortitude," he wrote. "They inspire me." Yet still, standing on that beach, in the quiet gaps between the clamor all around, he noticed that young men were staring at him from a distance, saying to one another, "That's Ike."

AUTHOR'S NOTE

A search of the New York Public Library catalog turns up 3,349 books about D-Day and 1,950 about Eisenhower. If you've read this far, I hope that means you enjoyed this one. But given these numbers, you deserve an explanation of why and how I chose to write yet another.

The why comes down to Eisenhower's underappreciated role in America's rise as a superpower. "Underappreciated" may seem like a strange word for someone who became president. But in the histories that explore how the United States displaced the British Empire after World War II, it is rare to find Eisenhower in anything more than a cameo. And while a biographer will always have a warped sense of their subject's importance, I find it difficult to overstate the significance of Roosevelt's selection of Eisenhower over Marshall as Supreme Allied Commander in shaping Britain's, France's, and America's most fateful strategic choices.

Some of those choices were military decisions. There is no reason to think, for example, that once in command of Operation Overlord, Marshall would have immediately thrown out the COSSAC plan, which he had personally approved on the Combined Chiefs. But the most fateful choices were diplomatic decisions. By early 1944, the United States had realized a degree of economic and military potential that should have put every other world power on defensive edge, the British Empire most of all. The British should have been as paranoid as De Gaulle was. Had they been, they could have stifled the growth of American influence, and potentially better preserved their own, by allying more closely with the French, curtailing America's use of British ports and air bases, and using America's investment in Operation Bolero as leverage to drive a harder bargain on Lend-Lease terms. But they didn't.

There were good, indeed noble, reasons the British did not behave as cynically as De Gaulle did. But a major reason was that the British continued to assume that Americans had few grand strategic interests of their own. "They have enormous power, but it is the power of the reservoir behind the dam," a now infamous Foreign Office memorandum surmised. "It must not be our purpose to balance our power against America, but to make use of American power for ends which we regard as good." It concluded, "If we go about our business in the right way, we can help to steer this great unwieldy barge, the United States of America, into the right harbour. If we don't, it is likely to continue to wallow in the ocean, an isolated menace to navigation."

This memo was written in March 1944, when Eisenhower was the face of America in the United Kingdom. It is difficult to imagine this memo having been written if Marshall had come to London instead, particularly so soon after repudiating Churchill's request for American support in the eastern Mediterranean by bellowing "not one American solider is going to die on that goddamned beach!"

From Britain to France to Australia to Algeria, people faced a choice between acquiescence or resistance to America's sudden, gargantuan, and potentially terrifying influence as a global power. For all his great virtues, Marshall's stoic grimace would have had a far harder time becoming the face of the American Century than Eisenhower's smile did. By avoiding the grandiosity associated with great power, Eisenhower made it easy to believe that there was nothing to fear. He wore ambition lightly. He eschewed dogmas in favor of a gut-level commitment to pragmatism, decency, and service to a cause greater than himself. And beamed American optimism, openness, and opportunity. The United States became a superpower without meaningful peer competition, in part, because people are disarmed by what they like. And Ike, if nothing else, was liked.

TO THOSE ACCUSTOMED to, or at least desirous of, Olympian heroes, Eisenhower's likability can be disappointing. Ken Davis, Milton's protégé who wrote *Soldier of Democracy*, would later grouse that Eisenhower had "almost no interest in ideas" and acted with only the slightest "sense of the historical implications of the work he was doing." When trying to write his heroic portrait of Eisenhower in 1945, Davis fretted, "He is in a heroic position without being himself a hero. None of that moody grandeur, depth, et cetera, which inspires men to be better than themselves. No creative will. There is no beyondness in him."

The accusation that Eisenhower lacked an interest in ideas or historical perspective is so bizarrely wrong that it is easy to dismiss such critics as arrogant or ideologically motivated. But part of Davis's complaint is true. Eisenhower did lack the "moody grandeur" and "beyondness" one sees in many of his contemporaries. He valued his privacy and had an almost compulsive eagerness to fit in; the Dale Carnegie strategy for success often deployed by the truly self-made. If this all conspired to make him superficially blander than the romantic heroes of his era, that is likely why far more books have been written about them. A search of the New York Public Library catalog, for example, returns 11,137 books about Churchill, 4,655 about De Gaulle, and 2,285 about Patton.

Even Eisenhower's admirers have tended to sentimentalize an artificially bland image of him. Thanks largely to his brother Milton, the first half of Eisenhower's life was carefully curated into the Horatio Alger tale of an earnest Kansan from the wrong side of the tracks, who reached the heights of global power through hard work and a wholesome common sense reared into him by a close-knit, God-fearing family. Some of this is true enough in the details. But if it sounds like something from the *Saturday Evening Post*, that is because it was a myth spun to launch the political career of a man whose voters were the readers of the *Saturday Evening Post*.

Merriman Smith, UPI's White House correspondent from Franklin Roosevelt through Lyndon Johnson, wrote two books about Eisenhower's presidency. Asked in 1968 for his impressions, Smith said, "Eisenhower was a gravely misunderstood man. He is perhaps the most complex individual I've ever known in my life, and yet other people who know him don't see him that way at all." Smith joked that "to a great many people he gave the facade of sort of a Kewpie doll, a man who had undergone ossification very early in life, as far as his brain was concerned." But, Smith continued, "Underneath was a man who could be quite, quite sensitive, and a man who really did himself a disservice, in that there were aspects of his character, of his personality, which almost never surfaced." The reason they never surfaced, in Smith's estimation: "I don't know of a man I've ever seen in better control of his will, better control of his emotions."

Eisenhower's self-discipline, which his famous temper shows he struggled to cultivate, was central not just to his personality, but also to his conspicuous ability to wield power inconspicuously. Eisenhower grasped—as Caesar Augustus and George Washington had before him, but as few others did in his era—that appearing disinterested in power was the surest strategy for accumulating it, and that being underestimated was the surest strategy for outmaneuvering ambitious competitors. As a result, Merriman Smith observed, "You never knew when Eisenhower was being dumb or whether he could see through things."

Eisenhower therefore presents a unique challenge for biographers in that it is never clear when to take him at face value. Recognizing this difficulty, I have tried to follow three principles in the research and writing process of this book.

The first principle is rigor with sourcing. There is a massive amount of archival material, which would lead you to believe that many different portraits of Eisenhower would have emerged by now. As the historian and biographer John Lewis Gaddis described it, such variation is almost a natural law of biography: "Different books will contain different facts, even if they are about the same person." This book, for example, could easily have been three or four times as long, based just upon the eighty thousand pages of archival documents that I distilled down into this still rather long book.

This natural law has largely held in the diverse portraits of Eisenhower's presidency that have been written over the decades. Yet a surprising amount of what is written about Eisenhower's time as the Supreme Allied Commander relies near-exclusively upon the same few dozen published memoirs and secondary sources. There are major exceptions, such as Forrest Pogue's *The Supreme Command*, David Eisenhower's monumental *Eisenhower at War*, and Carlo D'Este's *Decision in Normandy*. But there is an unusual degree of conventional wisdom for such a routinely trod historical period.

In writing this book, therefore, I treated Eisenhower's daily logs and desk diaries as the bones of the story, then built out the muscles and organs from the vast archive of contemporaneous documentation, then used oral histories and memoirs as connective tissue (so long as the accounts were credible and corroborated), and then sought out secondary sources only where a skin of context was needed. This book therefore leaves out material found in other accounts. But it also includes a lot of new material, including whole events and controversies that were significant at the time, but which soon fell out of the story's standard telling.

The second principle was to try and understand Eisenhower through his influences, rather than his self-descriptions. Some of these influences are people. But there are also cultural and intellectual influences that are surprisingly neglected in other biographical portraits, such as the books and magazines he is known to have read. The excellent scholarship of Timothy Rives, an archivist at the National Archives in Kansas, is a notable exception.

The third principle was to narrow the central timeline to the period between the Cairo Conferences and D-Day. My main reason for doing this was that, with Eisenhower, details mattered. In understanding the person, as well as the significance of the accomplishment, close attention to the "how" is far more revealing than even the accomplishment itself.

This period was also the pivot point of Eisenhower's life, and to a great extent, America's rise as a superpower. Eisenhower seems to have sensed this himself, returning to it repeatedly in his later years, including in an unfinished memoir he drafted under the working title "Churchill & Marshall." The challenges of this period required him to draw upon nearly every major influence on his life to that point. And he encountered, often for the first time, nearly every major issue that would define his presidency. By focusing on just this half year, we can see that what culminated on D-Day was not the mechanical progression of the Horatio Alger myth, but the combined ruthlessness, self-discipline, and luck that a poor boy from Kansas needed to master the art of power politics and become one of the preeminent world figures of the twentieth century.

A FINAL NOTE is warranted on Eisenhower's relationship with Kay Summersby. It has been a subject of prurient fascination since the 1940s. To me, at least, whether and how often Eisenhower and Kay had sex is neither anyone's business, nor especially interesting. But their relationship is. In this book, therefore, I have tried to present what seems to have mattered most about their relationship, relying only upon sources that credibly recount contemporaneous, firsthand experiences.

Among the things that mattered is that almost everyone around Eisenhower thought he was having a romantic relationship with Kay. Franklin Roosevelt is both an obvious and significant example. Roosevelt's personal correspondence during this period has barely a mention of Eisenhower because he did not know him that well. As the president mulled whom he should send to London to lead Operation Overlord, however, one of the few things Roosevelt knew about Eisenhower was his rumored affair with Kay.

Eisenhower's relationship with Kay also reveals a lot about him. In July 1944, he wrote to Milton that there were only four people he trusted to write the story of "my life since leaving Washington": Beetle, Butch, Tex Lee, and Kay. There were dozens of loyal people around him nearly every day, including Jimmy Gault and Mattie Pinette. But Kay was among the four—and the only woman—whom Eisenhower believed understood him.

What can be said for sure is that Kay was an unusually intimate form of what we might now call a "work wife," or what was then called a "girl Friday." Not coincidentally, the original title of Kay's memoir, published in 1948, was

"Eisenhower's Girl Friday." By that point, they had become estranged, and Eisenhower saw the book as nothing but trouble for his nascent political career. Butch saw trouble too and helped Kay get it into the hands of an editor he knew, a decision he defended to Eisenhower on the ground that "you must realize that her stories might have been worse if I hadn't." Butch thought she was writing "from need of money and, also from pique," and left to her own devices, "I can only wonder how bad the results might have been."

Why Eisenhower and Kay became so estranged, after being so close, has fueled considerable speculation. What is known for sure is that in the fall of 1945, Eisenhower was recalled to Washington to succeed Marshall as the army chief of staff and Kay stayed in Europe. "I am terribly distressed," he wrote her in a long letter saying goodbye, "first because it has become impossible any longer to keep you as a member of my personal official family, and secondly because I cannot come back to give you a detailed account of the reasons."

The most widely circulated gossip is that they became estranged after Eisenhower abandoned a plan to divorce Mamie and marry Kay. The main source of this rumor was a book written in 1974 by Merle Miller, in which Harry Truman is quoted as saying that Eisenhower wrote to Marshall of his plan, and that Marshall wrote back, threatening that he would "not only bust him out of the Army, he'd see to it that never for the rest of his life would he be able to draw a peaceful breath." Truman is then quoted as claiming, "One of the last things I did as President, I got those letters from his file in the Pentagon and I destroyed them."

Given the extreme circumspection with which Marshall communicated, such a response would have been wildly out of character, and no direct evidence of this correspondence has ever surfaced. In the 1990s, Merle Miller was exposed as a fabulist, seeming to confirm the denials issued in the 1970s by Joe Collins, whom Truman ostensibly ordered to pull the correspondence from Eisenhower's file. But even on its own terms, the suggestion that Truman pulled it from a "file in the Pentagon" is implausible for several reasons, not the least being that any communication through government channels—which would be the only reason such documents would be in a folder in the Pentagon—would have resulted in carbon copies all over the world. No such copies have ever been found.

A more plausible version of the rumor was circulated by Truman's longtime aide, who claimed that Eisenhower asked Marshall more obliquely what "a change in his marriage relations would have on his future career," to which Marshall replied that it would be "very unwise." The tenor of this supposed exchange is more consistent with how Eisenhower and Marshall communicated. But there is also no evidence of this correspondence either.

The source of this rumor appears to be a gossipy elaboration of correspondence from July 1944 that I discovered in the papers of Marshall's longtime assistant, Frank McCarthy. Eisenhower, at this time, was trying to get Kay commissioned as an officer in the WACs, based upon Edward Betts's advice on how to get Kay American citizenship. Soon after returning to Washington in June 1944, Marshall got wind of Eisenhower's efforts and intervened to stop it. According to a letter McCarthy wrote to the head of the War Department's personnel section, Marshall wanted a memo sent to Eisenhower that explained "as strongly as possible" the official reasons why he should rescind his request. Marshall then added that there was a "personal side" that he would have McCarthy explain in person to Tex Lee, Eisenhower's aide-de-camp, who was briefly in Washington.

There is no record of what this "personal side" was. Tex Lee never published a memoir. But the War Department's personnel section did send Eisenhower a discouraging cable soon after. A week after that, following Tex Lee's return to England, Eisenhower rescinded his request, telling the personnel section, "[I] now understand difficulties and possible embarrassments which I formerly did not realize. Please drop the matter."

Perhaps the "personal side" was Marshall's rumored threat to end Eisenhower's career. Or perhaps, it was simply a heads-up that the request risked fomenting rumors. Or perhaps, it was something else entirely. All that is known for sure is that Eisenhower cared enough for Kay to try. And whatever the nature of their private relationship, it is yet more evidence of Eisenhower treating Kay with a degree of genuine concern that was uncommon for powerful men of the era (to include several who succeeded him in the White House).

The superficially strongest evidence of both Eisenhower and Kay's romantic relationship, and his desire to run away with her, comes from *Past Forgetting*, a tell-all memoir published under Kay's name in 1977. Many Eisenhower historians have relied extensively on this book. I have not, save for two exceptions, where the material in the book is corroborated, because *Past Forgetting* cannot be taken at face value, even as a memoir.

Kay did not write *Past Forgetting*. Two ghostwriters did. The first, Sigrid Hedin, was a longtime friend, whom Kay purportedly told about having had a romantic relationship with Eisenhower around the time of his death in 1969. Kay was soon diagnosed with cancer and Hedin encouraged Kay to sell a tell-all to cover her medical bills. After Kay died in 1975, Hedin largely abandoned the project. But then it was taken up by the ghostwriter Barbara Wyden, who wrote several books on love and sex, including a biography of William Masters and Virginia Johnson and the bodice-ripping romance novel *A Rich Wife*. The credibility of the romantic details in the memoir is impossible to assess, even as the words of Kay Summersby, because neither Wyden nor Hedin preserved records of any interviews. And, while a subjective assessment to be sure, those parts of the book also sound stylistically more like Barbara Wyden than they do Kay Summersby.

This is not to say, of course, that *Past Forgetting* is a fabrication. It is just not credible. And it is undermined by a candid, unpublished interview with Harry Butcher and Mollie Ford ("The Red Cross Girl") from 1976. In it, Mollie claimed that Eisenhower was "infatuated" with Kay, but that their wartime affair was inhibited from blossoming into a lifelong romance by Kay's mourning for Dick Arnold. Butch was more circumspect, though agreed that Kay and Eisenhower's relationship was, at bottom, "a diversion, a long diversion which lasted three years." There was "no great love affair." Butch then concluded, "If Ike had really been in love with her, if Ike really wanted to marry her, then he would've gotten a divorce and married her. That's what I did. I was really in love with Mollie. Still am."

ACKNOWLEDGMENTS

In addition to my family and the other giants on whose shoulders I stand, the credit for making a vaguely sketched idea into a rather long book goes foremost to my superagent Rachel Vogel, my wise and patient editor, Nick Amphlett, as well as Peter Hubbard and Alex Littlefield, who got behind this project at its inception, and Katie Tull and Sharyn Rosenblum, who have made sure that people have the chance to discover it.

Credit for the beauty of this book goes to Carol Wong, who created the illustrations that begin most of the chapters; David Eisenhower, who permitted me to use his father's artwork; and the great team of graphic designers at HarperCollins.

Credit for the content of this book goes to my research assistants, Lyubomir Avdzhiyski, Andrew Bortey, Graham Glusman, Carson Macik, Gabriela Flores Romo, and Douglas Seip, as well as the dozens of people who helped me understand things (often just by humoring me in conversation). They include, first and foremost, Aaron O'Connell, who dedicated days of his life to such discussions, as well as (in alphabetical order) Scott Anderson, Steve Anderson, Frederic Borch, Wesley Clark, Kellam Conover, Mark Copeland, Edward Cox, Melissa Davis, Sharon Delmendo, Elisabeth Dyssegaard, George Fletcher, James Ginther, William Goldstein, Karen Greenberg, Colin Harrison, Scott Johnston, David Kennedy, Kate Klonick, Erik Lamont, Colleen Lawrie, Alex Lovelace, Norm MacDonald, Aaron MacLean, Michael Neiberg, Jason Otaño, Don Patton, Todd Pierce, Shane Reeves, Tu Rinsche, Timothy Rives, Cody Shearer, Russ Stayanoff, Michael Tigar, John Tofanelli, Weike Wang, Matthew Waxman, Benjamin Wittes, and Jason Wright. They also include countless archivists and librarians who helped me find what I was looking for as well as many things I had not been, including Christopher Blythe, Steve Bye, Alejandro Garcia, Vicki Glantz, Andrea Hill, Zoe Hill, Kyle Hovious, Mary Jones, Robert Kelly, Jared Maxwell, Darby Nisbett, Claudia Rivers, Linda Smith,

Sydney Soderberg, Katherine Terry, Lauren Theodore, Ariel Turley, and Abbie Weiser.

The blame for anything and everything not to like about this book, including the absence of any names that should have been included in the previous three paragraphs, goes to me.

NOTES

ABBREVIATIONS

Arnold Papers	Library of Congress, Washington, DC, Henry Arnold Papers
AFHRA	Air Force Historical Research Agency, Maxwell Air Force Base, Alabama
Butcher Diary	Eisenhower Library, Abilene, Kansas, Pre-Presidential Papers, Principal File, boxes 167–68
Cairo & Tehran Papers	William M. Franklin and William Gerber, *Foreign Relations of the United States: Diplomatic Papers, The Conferences at Cairo and Tehran, 1943* (Washington, DC: US Government Printing Office, 1961)
Churchill Papers	Churchill Archives Centre, Churchill College, Cambridge, England
Davis Papers	Kansas State University, Manhattan, Kansas, Kenneth Davis Papers
Eckstam Papers	Betsey B. Creekmore Special Collections and University Archives, University of Tennessee, Knoxville, Eugene E. Eckstam Exercise Tiger Collection
Eisenhower Papers	*The Papers of Dwight David Eisenhower*, ed. Alfred D. Chandler Jr. (Baltimore: Johns Hopkins University Press, 1970–2003)
EL	Dwight D. Eisenhower Presidential Library, Abilene, Kansas
FDR	Franklin D. Roosevelt Presidential Library and Museum, Hyde Park, New York
FRUS	US Department of State, Office of the Historian, Foreign Service Institute, *Foreign Relations of the United States*, available at https://history.state.gov/historicaldocuments
GCM	George C. Marshall Library, Lexington, Virginia
Hughes Papers	Library of Congress, Washington, DC, Everett Hughes Papers
HST	Harry S. Truman Library, Independence, Missouri
IWM	Imperial War Museum, London, England
JCPML	John Curtin Prime Ministerial Library, Curtin University, Perth, Australia
KHS	Kansas Historical Society, Topeka, Kansas

NAACP	Library of Congress, Washington, DC, National Association for the Advancement of Colored People Records
NARA	National Archives and Record Administration, College Park, Maryland
NARA-SL	National Archives and Record Administration, Saint Louis, Missouri
NAUK	National Archives of the United Kingdom, Richmond, England
NAUK-Kew	National Archives of the United Kingdom, Kew, Surrey, England
NLA	National Library of Australia, Canberra, Australia
Patton Papers	Library of Congress, Washington, DC, George S. Patton Papers
Pershing Papers	Library of Congress, Washington, DC, John J. Pershing Papers
Pogue Papers	Murray State University, Murray, Kentucky, Forrest Pogue Papers
Pre-Pres. Misc.	Eisenhower Library, Abilene, Kansas, Pre-Presidential Papers, Miscellaneous File
Pre-Pres. Principal	Eisenhower Library, Abilene, Kansas, Pre-Presidential Papers, Principal File
Sherwood Papers	Harvard University, Cambridge, Massachusetts, Robert Emmet Sherwood Papers
SLAM	University of Texas, El Paso, Samuel Lyman Atwood Marshall Papers
Smith Papers	Eisenhower Library, Abilene, Kansas, Walter Bedell Smith Papers
Stimson Papers	Yale University, New Haven, Connecticut, Henry Lewis Stimson Papers
USAHEC	US Army Heritage and Education Center, Carlisle, Pennsylvania
Vincennes	Château de Vincennes, Vincennes, France
VMI	Virginia Military Institute, Lexington, Virginia

EPIGRAPH

vii *"Today, war—and even":* Dwight Eisenhower, Material on Military History Lecture, Pre-Pres. Principal, box 193.

PROLOGUE

1 *Anyone ever asked:* Peter Liddle, interview with John Grimshaw, February 1970, University of Leeds, Peter Liddle Papers; Ainsley Talbot to Tom Slingsby, May 2, 1915, in *The History of the English Language*, 2nd ed. (Routledge, 2000), 362–64; Steuart Hare, diary, April 25, 1915, IWM, Private Papers of Stuart Hare, catalogue no. 18385.

1 *under a canopy:* Ellis Ashmead-Bartlett, *The Uncensored Dardanelles* (Hutchinson & Co., 1928), 62–75.

1 *Since before dawn:* Ashmead-Bartlett, 75.

1 *a shrubby cove:* J. C. Latter, *The History of the Lancashire Fusiliers, 1914–1918* (Gale & Polden, 1949), 1:51.

1 *The cliffs ahead:* Latter, 1:51.

1 *cast in shadow:* Hare, diary, April 25, 1915.

1 *red clay seeped out:* George Patton, "The Defense of Gallipoli," August 31, 1936, Army Headquarters, Hawaiian Department, Fort Shater.

1 *Everything was silent:* Richard Willis, diary, quoted in Michael Ashcroft, "Gallipoli Landing VCs: The 'Six Before Breakfast,'" *Sunday Telegraph*, February 2, 2014.
1 *there was a shot:* Talbot to Slingsby.
2 *slumbering cliffs erupted:* Harold Shaw, "Gallipoli: The Landings, View from the Beach, 25 April 1915," in *Brief History of the First World War: Eyewitness Accounts of the War to End All Wars, 1914–1918,* ed. John E. Lewis (Robinson, 2014), 93.
2 *sea seemed to boil:* Liddle interview with Grimshaw.
2 *in their crowded boats:* Talbot to Slingsby.
2 *Six weeks earlier:* Latter, *History of the Lancashire Fusiliers*, 1:46.
2 *Rudyard Kipling's poem:* Talbot to Slingsby.
2 *Major Thomas Frankland:* Harold Farmer to Violet Farmer, June 5, 1915, quoted in Katherine Davies, "The Landing at W Beach: A Staff Officer's Perspective," *Gallipolian*, no. 137, 2015.
2 *Their boat was:* Hare, diary, April 25, 1915.
2 *seventy-pound packs:* Latter, *History of the Lancashire Fusiliers*, 1:50-51.
2 *coils of barbed wire:* Willis, diary, quoted in Ashcroft, "Gallipoli Landing VCs: The 'Six Before Breakfast'."
2 *As one man drowned:* Ashmead-Bartlett, *Uncensored Dardanelles*, 82.
3 *On the right:* Latter, *History of the Lancashire Fusiliers*, 1:51.
3 *washed-up garbage:* Hugh Tate, memorandum, n.d., quoted in Peter Hart, *Gallipoli* (Oxford, 2011), 138.
3 *dyed the ocean:* "Gallipoli: The Landings, View from the Beach, 25 April 1915," in *Brief History of the First World War* (Robinson, 2014), 93.
3 *Seeing the massacre:* Farmer to Farmer.
3 *He had been commissioned:* The Official Army List 1902, NAUK-Kew, 932.
3 *His soft chin:* Photograph, Thomas Hugh Colville Frankland, n.d., IWM, Lives of the First World War, https://livesofthefirstworldwar.iwm.org.uk/lifestory/5315347.
3 *a military family: Burke's Peerage, Baronetage & Knightage*, 107th ed. (Burkes Peerage & Gentry Books, 2003), 3:4292.
3 *his pilot's certification:* Thomas Frankland, Royal Aero Club Aviators' Certificate No. 679, November 5, 1913, Royal Aero Club Records, Royal Air Force Museum, London, England.
3 *Hare rallied his men:* Hare, diary, April 25, 1915.
3 *shot three Turks:* Farmer to Farmer, June 5, 1915, quoted in Davies, "Landing at W Beach."
3 *through the calf:* Hare, diary, April 25, 1915.
3 *Frankland helped drag:* Hare.
3 *Frankland raced back:* Farmer to Farmer.
3 *the wounded lay about:* Richard Haworth, "Capt. Haworth at the Dardanelles," *The Carthusian*, July 1915, pp. 477–78.
3 *out of their rifles:* Liddle interview with Grimshaw.
3 *"Lancs getting on":* Thomas Frankland to Royal Fusiliers, April 25, 1915, IWM, Private Papers of Stuart Hare.
4 *The cliffs had been dug:* Ashmead-Bartlett, *Uncensored Dardanelles*, 64–80.
4 *Frankland pulled out:* Farmer to Farmer, June 5, 1915, quoted in Davies, "Landing at W Beach."
4 *nine in the morning:* Harold Farmer to Stuart Hare, May 22, 1915, IWM, Private Papers of Stuart Hare.
4 *As the day wore on:* Lancashire Fusiliers, First Battalion, War Diary and Intelligence Summary, April 24–30, 1915, NAUK, WO 95/4310.
4 *The air grew cold:* Farmer to Farmer.
4 *Snipers took potshots:* Haworth, "Capt. Haworth at the Dardanelles," 477–78.
4 *The day of the invasion:* Winston Churchill, *The World Crisis, 1911–1918* (Scribner, 1923), 2:327.
4 *"Dig in and stick":* Churchill, 2:336.
4 *The British plan:* Ashmead-Bartlett, *Uncensored Dardanelles*, 75–76.
4 *On a map:* Ashmead-Bartlett, 9; Churchill, *World Crisis*, 2:32–34; Stuart Hare, manuscript, 1936, IWM, Private Papers of Stuart Hare, catalogue no. 18385.
4 *"Any fool can see":* Hare, manuscript, 1936.
4 *Britain's War Office:* Churchill, *World Crisis*, 2:277.
5 *"a giant shipwreck":* Ashmead-Bartlett, *Uncensored Dardanelles*, 69.
5 *Donald MacCarthy-Morrogh:* Alec Riley, *Gallipoli Diary, 1915* (Little Gully, 2021), 286.
5 *"I am off":* "Some of the OS at the Front or in the Forces," *The Stonyhurst Magazine*, July 1915, pp. 1247, 1271.
5 *While his wife:* Eighth Manchester Regiment, War Diary, 1915, NAUK-Kew, WO 95; Riley, *Gallipoli Diary*, 286.
5 *an unembarrassed champion:* Tom D. C. Roberts, *Before Rupert* (University of Queensland Press, 2015), 36–49; Ronald M. Younger, *Keith Murdoch* (Harper, 2003), 58–70.

5 *twenty-five-page letter:* Keith Murdoch to Andrew Fisher, September 23, 1915, NLA, ms2823-2.
5 *Murdoch made sure:* Keith Murdoch to H. H. Asquith, September 25, 1915, NLA, ms2823-2.
6 *Churchill derided Murdoch's letter:* Roberts, *Before Rupert*, 36–49.
6 *forced to resign:* Churchill, 2:526–27.
6 *"a cold hard day":* Eighth Manchester Regiment, War Diary, 1915, NAUK-Kew, WO 95.
6 *Churchill bore the blame:* Ashmead-Bartlett, *Uncensored Dardanelles*, 12.
6 *"leave the past":* Foreign Affairs, January 23, 1948, Hansard House of Commons, vol. 446, p. 557.
6 *"The sea":* Forrest Pogue, interview with Lord Ismay, October 18, 1960, GCM, Forrest Pogue Interviews.
6 *Ships against forts:* Churchill, *World Crisis*, 2:95.
7 *"folly of follies":* John T. Mason, *The Reminiscences of Alan Goodrich Kirk, 1962*, no. 455, Oral History Research Office, Columbia University, p. 300; Pogue interview with Ismay; Theodore Gatchel, *At the Water's Edge: Defending against the Modern Amphibious Assault* (Naval Institute Press, 2013), 24.
7 *detailed study of Gallipoli:* Patton, "Defense of Gallipoli."
7 *Patton's bleak conclusion:* Jeter Isley, *US Marines and Amphibious Warfare* (Princeton University Press, 1951), 20–21.
7 *doctrine on amphibious warfare:* Aaron O'Connell, *Underdogs: The Making of the Modern Marine Corps* (Harvard University Press, 2012), 13–14; Arthur Nevins to Jeter Isely, January 25, 1950, Pre-Pres. Principal, box 59.
7 *The Marines, whose very:* Gatchel, *At the Water's Edge*, 24; Isley, *US Marines and Amphibious Warfare*, 5.
7 *the Marines' solutions:* U.S. Marine Corps, "Tentative Manual of Landing Operations" (1933), Combined Arms Research Library, Leavenworth, KS, N17315.492.
7 *"There is one line":* Reproduced in Dwight Eisenhower, *At Ease* (Doubleday, 1967), 246–47.
8 *a field marshal:* Dwight Eisenhower, diary, July 1, 1937, in *Eisenhower: The Pre-War Diaries and Selected Papers*, ed. Daniel Holt and James Leyerzapf (Johns Hopkins University Press, 1998), 325–26.
8 *"better showing":* Dwight Eisenhower, diary, January 13, 1942, EL, Diaries, box 1.

CHAPTER 1

11 *being on time:* Michael McKeogh and Richard Lockridge, *Sgt. Mickey & General Ike* (Putnam, 1946), 59.
11 *gotten up before dawn:* Butcher Diary, A-898.
11 *That September, the British:* John Erhmann, *Grand Strategy* (Her Majesty's Stationery Office, 1956), 5:88–114.
12 *Churchill had asked:* Winston Churchill to Dwight Eisenhower, October 2, 1943, Pre-Pres. Principal, box 22.
12 *area of authority:* George Marshall to Dwight Eisenhower, October 7, 1943, Pre-Pres. Principal, box 132.
12 *"All I am asking for":* Winston Churchill to Dwight Eisenhower, October 7, 1943, Pre-Pres. Principal, box 22.
12 *"I do not want":* Marshall to Eisenhower.
12 *kept at it:* George Marshall to Dwight Eisenhower, October 9, 1943, Pre-Pres. Principal, box 132.
12 *No decision had yet:* George Marshall to Dwight Eisenhower, November 4, 1943, Pre-Pres. Principal, box 132.
12 *left for Malta:* C. L. Sulzberger, "British Lose Lateros in Five-Day Battle," *New York Times*, November 18, 1943, p. 1.
12 *stop over in Algiers:* Butcher Diary, A-898.
12 *Hence, the hunting trip:* Butcher Diary, A-895.
12 *Malta was a strategic:* George Patton, "The Flight into Egypt," 1944, Patton Papers, box 64.
13 *his own stopover:* Robert H. Ferrell, ed., *The Eisenhower Diaries* (Norton, 1981), 103–4.
13 *gotten to know Harriman:* Robert E. Sherwood, *Roosevelt and Hopkins* (Harper, 1948), 582.
13 *"speaking for the president":* Forrest Pogue, *George C. Marshall: Interviews and Reminiscences for Forrest C. Pogue* (George C. Marshall Foundation 1996), 582.
13 *War Plans Division:* Ray Cline, *Washington Command Post: The Operations Division*, CMH Pub. 1-2 (US Government Printing Office, 1951), 107–39.
14 *two-stage strategic plan:* Dwight Eisenhower, Notes on BOLERO Organization Charts, May 11, 1942, Pogue Papers, box 157.
14 *The real juicy piece:* Dwight Eisenhower, Memorandum, December 6, 1943, in Butcher Diary, A-929.
14 *West Point class ring:* Susan Eisenhower, *Mrs. Ike* (Farrar, Straus and Giroux, 1996), 35.
14 *a long letter:* Dwight Eisenhower to Mamie Eisenhower, November 1, 1943, private collection.
15 *Mamie had first hired:* McKeogh & Lockridge, 3.
15 *Rounding things out:* Dwight Eisenhower to Mamie Eisenhower.
15 *Chief among those:* Mattie Pinette, Diary, 1944, EL, George Hall Papers, box 1.
15 *Sergeant John Moaney:* Mattie Pinette, Eisenhower I, undated, EL, George Hall Papers, box 1.

15 *"That is the whole group"*: Dwight Eisenhower to Mamie Eisenhower.

15 *Everett Hughes:* Alexander G. Lovelace, "Hughes' War" (master's thesis, George Washington University, 2013), 33–46.

15 *The folks back in Kansas:* Swede Hazlett, Milton Eisenhower, to Kenneth Davis, 1944, Davis Papers, box 61.

15 *enjoying a highball:* "A Day with General Eisenhower," June 20, 1944, EL, Harry C. Butcher Papers, box 3.

15 *honor that Eisenhower dreaded:* Dwight Eisenhower, memorandum, December 6, 1943, in Butcher Diary, A-929.

15 *survive in the job:* Butcher Diary, A-885.

16 *threat of promotion:* Robert E. Sherwood, *Roosevelt and Hopkins* (Harper, 1948), 582.

16 *created that job:* Dwight Eisenhower to George Marshall, May 11, 1942, Eisenhower Papers, 1:292–93.

16 *"It is necessary"*: Eisenhower, Diary, June 4, 1942, EL, Diaries, box 1.

16 *at his desk:* Dwight Eisenhower, Manuscript, "Churchill & Marshall," November 17, 1966, Post-Presidential Papers, A-WR Series, box 8.

16 *"If U.S. and U.K.":* Dwight Eisenhower, Diary, June 8, 1942, in *The Eisenhower Diaries* (Norton 1981), at 62

16 *second in command:* Dwight Eisenhower, "Notes on BOLERO Organization Charts," May 11, 1942, Pogue Papers, box 157.

16 *When asked:* Dwight Eisenhower to George Marshall, July 29, 1942, Pre-Pres. Principal, box 80.

17 *"well trained"*: Forrest Pogue, Notes on Frederick Morgan, manuscript, "OVERLORD by the Under-Dog-in-Chief," 1946, Pogue Papers, box 157.

17 *"very reluctant"*: Butcher Diary, A-930.

17 *"We have the"*: Sherwood, *Roosevelt and Hopkins*, 759.

17 *Even his wife:* Forrest Pogue, interview with Eleanor Roosevelt, March 17, 1958, GCM, Forrest Pogue Interviews.

17 *when he finally arrived:* Butcher Diary, A-904.

17 *incubating a cold:* Alan Brooke, *War Diaries, 1939–1945* (Phoenix Press, 2001), 473.

17 *keen to relish:* Dwight Eisenhower, manuscript, "Churchill & Marshall," November 17, 1966, Post-Presidential Papers, A-WR Series, box 8.

18 *same room together:* Henry Stimpson, Diary, December 20, 1941, Stimpson Papers, series XIV, box 74.

18 *Washington Conference:* Memorandum by the United States Chiefs of Staff, January 14, 1942, FRUS, *The Conferences at Washington, 1941–1942, and Casablanca, 1943*, doc. 121; Ray Cline, *Washington Command Post: The Operations Division*, CMH Pub. 1-2 (US Government Printing Office, 1951), 97–104.

18 *British Empire claimed:* Paul Kennedy, *The Rise and Fall of the Great Powers* (Random House, 1988), 290.

18 *"In an illiberal age"*: W. K. Hancock, *Argument of Empire* (Penguin, 1943), 13.

18 *first supreme commander:* Report by the United States and British Chiefs of Staff, December 30, 1941, FRUS, *The Conferences at Washington, 1941–1942, and Casablanca, 1943*, doc. 161; Andrew Roberts, *Masters and Commanders* (Penguin, 2009), 79–82.

18 *The first time:* Sherwood, *Roosevelt and Hopkins*, 582.

19 *guest of honor:* Dwight Eisenhower, Diary, July 5, 1942, EL, Diaries, box 1.

19 *The Chequers estate:* Norma Major, *The Chequers Estate* (Harper Collins, 1996); Plantagenet Somerset Fry, *Chequers* (HMSO, 1977); J. Gilbert Jenkins, *Chequers* (Pergamon, 1967).

19 *His room was dominated:* Dwight Eisenhower, Diary, July 5, 1942, EL, Diaries, box 1.

20 *Mickey had forgotten:* Michael McKeogh & Richard Lockridge, *Sgt. Mickey & General Ike* (Putnam, 1946), 44.

20 *That night:* Dwight Eisenhower, Diary, July 5, 1942, EL, Diaries, box 1.

20 *In his first week:* Eisenhower, Diary, June 25–July 4, 1942, EL, Diaries, box 1.

20 *"a bit of a"*: Eisenhower to Mamie Eisenhower, August 26, 1942.

20 *furious at Mickey:* Michael McKeogh and Richard Lockridge, *Sgt. Mickey & General Ike* (Putnam, 1946), 44.

20 *Eisenhower awoke:* Dwight Eisenhower, Diary, July 5, 1942, EL, Diaries, box 1.

20 *bore the snarl:* Major, *Chequers Estate*, 145.

21 *guard of honor:* Dwight Eisenhower, Diary, July 5, 1942, EL, Diaries, box 1.

21 *"As we said"*: Everett Hughes, Diary, November 18, 1944, Hughes Papers, box I-1.

21 *received a cable:* Franklin Roosevelt to Dwight Eisenhower, November 17, 1943, FRUS, The Conferences at Cairo and Tehran, 1943, doc. 137.

21 *Eisenhower recommended:* Prime Minister Churchill to President Roosevelt, November 18, 1943, FRUS, *The Conferences at Cairo and Tehran, 1943*, doc. 141.

21 *The original plan:* "Final Report of the Combined Chiefs of Staff to the President and the Prime Minister," January 23, 1943, FRUS, *The Conferences at Washington, 1941–1942, and Casablanca, 1943*, doc. 416.

22 *Churchill confided:* Dwight Eisenhower, manuscript, "Churchill & Marshall," November 17, 1966, Post-Presidential Papers, A-WR Series, box 8l; Butcher Diary, A-929.

22 *Roosevelt had reopened:* Sherwood, *Roosevelt and Hopkins*, 758.
22 *Churchill had readily agreed:* Brooke, *War Diaries*, 442.
22 *Churchill mentioned:* Eisenhower, "Churchill & Marshall."
22 *One idea:* Butcher Diary, A-929.
22 *Another idea:* The Joint Chiefs of Staff to the President, November 11, 1943, Cairo & Tehran Papers, doc. 226.
22 *Churchill added:* Butcher Diary, A-929.
22 *"needed more":* David Lawrence, "Transfer of Gen. Marshall to European Command Would Not be a Demotion, Says Lawrence," US News (syndicate), September 21, 1943.
22 *"With General Marshall":* Eisenhower, "Churchill & Marshall."
23 *remained unconvinced:* Butcher Diary, A-898.
23 *"Channel tides":* Dwight Eisenhower to Hastings Ismay, December 3, 1960, EL, Whitman Name File, box 19.
23 *"soft underbelly":* Elliott Roosevelt, *As He Saw It* (Duell, Sloan & Pearce, 1946), 93.
23 *Churchill was preparing:* Butcher Diary, A-898.

CHAPTER 2

24 *"Will proceed":* President Roosevelt to Prime Minister Churchill, November 19, 1943, Cairo & Tehran Papers, doc. 143.
24 *Eisenhower's cold:* Dwight Eisenhower to George Patton, November 19, 1943, Pre-Pres. Principal, box 91.
24 *Henry Morgenthau:* Butcher Diary, A-883.
24 *"Don't tell":* Franklin Roosevelt to Dwight Eisenhower, October 11, 1943, Pre-Pres. Principal, box 100.
24 *flew to Oran:* Butcher Diary, A-901.
25 *Transporting all this brass:* Frank McCarthy, Memorandum for Colonel McCauley, November 11, 1943, GCM, McCarthy Papers, box 4.
25 *"Operation Adult":* Memorandum for Chief of Staff, Operation "ADULT," November 11, 1943, GCM, McCarthy Papers, box 4.
25 *"This is not a drill":* White House Files, Log of the Trip, November 11 to 17, 1943, Cairo & Tehran Papers, doc. 245.
25 *The* Iowa: White House Files, Log of the Trip, November 11 to 17, 1943, Cairo & Tehran Papers, doc. 245.
25 *Eisenhower was intent:* Butcher Diary, A-901.
25 *Eisenhower stood:* Roosevelt, *As He Saw It*, 124–33.
25 *Elliott had a reputation:* George W. Goddard, U.S. Air Force Oral History Program, Interview of Lt. Gen. James Doolittle, July 20, 1967, University of Texas, Dallas, James H. Doolittle Papers, Series XVII, box 1, D021-95-14-93-3.
25 *regularly scold Doolittle:* Leish, interview with Jimmy Doolittle, April 1960, James H. Doolittle Papers, Series XVII, box 1, D021-95-14-93-3, p. 34.
25 *Through binoculars:* Roosevelt, *As He Saw It*, 133.
25 *Even at a distance:* Henry Arnold, Diary (Trip to SEXTANT), Arnold Papers, reel 222.
26 *next twenty minutes:* White House Files, Log of the Trip, November 11 to 17, 1943, Cairo & Tehran Papers, doc. 245.
26 *"Roosevelt weather!":* Elliot Roosevelt, *As He Saw It*, 133.
26 *motorcade thundered:* Arnold, Diary (Trip to SEXTANT).
26 *"The war—":* Roosevelt, *As He Saw It*, 133.
26 *"I think":* Oral History Research Office, Eisenhower Administration: John S. D. Eisenhower, 1973, Columbia Center on Oral History, p. 13.
26 *Their first meeting:* Dwight Eisenhower, Diary, June 22, 1942, EL, Diaries, box 1.
26 *They had met again:* Robert E. Sherwood, *Roosevelt and Hopkins* (Harper, 1948), 676.
26 *daylong tours:* Roosevelt, *As He Saw It*, 106.
27 *"neck was in":* Sherwood, *Roosevelt and Hopkins*, 676.
27 *Even General Marshall:* Larry I. Bland, ed., *George C. Marshall Interviews and Reminiscences for Forrest C. Pogue* (George C. Marshall Foundation, 1996), 582.
27 *imposed censorship:* Sherwood, *Roosevelt and Hopkins*, 676.
27 *Darlan affair:* Arthur L. Funk, "Negotiating the 'Deal with Darlan,'" *Contemporary History* 8, no. 2 (April 1973); Sherwood, *Roosevelt and Hopkins*, 649–663; G. Ward Price, *Giraud and the African Scene* (MacMillan, 1944), 141–65; Rick Atkinson, *An Army at Dawn* (Holt, 2002), 198–200; Mark Clark, *Calculated Risk* (Harper 1950), 90–132; Dwight Eisenhower, *At Ease* (Doubleday 1967), 254–258; George Howe, *Northwest Africa*, CMH Pub. 6-1-1 (GPO 1957), 262–274.

27 *"extremely legalistic"*: Kenneth Davis, interview with General Eisenhower, August 11, 1944, Davis Papers, box 94.
27 *the Oxbridge set:* Sherwood, *Roosevelt and Hopkins*, 655.
27 *Wayne Clark had negotiated:* Funk, "Negotiating the 'Deal with Darlan.'"
27 *"You are learning"*: Dwight Eisenhower to John Eisenhower, December 20, 1942, Pre-Pres. Principal, box 173.
27 *"Generals could be"*: Robert Sherwood, Talk with General Eisenhower at His Office in the Pentagon Building, January 14, 1947, Sherwood Papers, box 40.
28 *Darlan's assassination:* George Patton, Memorandum to General Eisenhower, "Synopsis of Matters Discussed by General Nogues upon the Occasion of his visit on December 31," January 2, 1943, Patton Papers, box 32.
28 *"How long'll it take"*: Roosevelt, *As He Saw It*, 100–1.
28 *"when there was some"*: Sherwood, *Roosevelt and Hopkins*, 689.
28 *"I spent many hours"*: Franklin Roosevelt, Address to the White House Correspondents' Association Dinner, February 13, 1943, FDR, Speeches of Franklin D. Roosevelt, box 71.
28 *"Mission accomplished"*: Omar Bradley to Dwight Eisenhower, Cable, May 9, 1943, Pre-Pres. Principal, box 13.
28 *a quarter-million:* Atkinson, *An Army at Dawn*, 480–529; George Howe, *Northwest Africa*, CMH Pub. 6-1-1 (GPO 1957), 359–668.
28 *unlike Churchill:* Robert Sherwood, Additional Notes, undated, Sherwood Papers, box 75. Churchill had a peculiar aversion to nicknames. Only his wife, "Clemmie," was given a sobriquet.
29 *"Can I call"*: Jerry N. Hess, Oral History Interview with Felix E. Larkin, September 18, October 23, 1972, HST, Oral History Interviews.
29 *devised code names:* Sherwood, *Roosevelt and Hopkins*, 606.
29 *When they arrived:* Arnold, Diary (Trip to SEXTANT).
29 *Within fifteen minutes:* White House Files, Log of the Trip, November 11 to 17, 1943, Cairo & Tehran Papers, doc. 245.
29 *tracked the coast:* Arnold, Diary (Trip to SEXTANT).
29 *The flight:* White House Files, Log of the Trip, November 11 to 17, 1943, Cairo & Tehran Papers, doc. 245.
29 *And from overhead:* Arnold, Diary (Trip to SEXTANT).
29 *sizing him up:* Eisenhower, "Churchill & Marshall."
29 *"British girl"*: Kay Summersby, *Eisenhower Was My Boss* (Dell, 1948), 89.
29 *The presidential aero-cade:* Arnold, Diary (Trip to SEXTANT).
29 *littered the tarmac:* White House Files, Log of the Trip, November 11 to 17, 1943, Cairo & Tehran Papers, doc. 245.
29 *wheeled down:* Butcher Diary, A-901.
29 *"You can't drive"*: Summersby, *Eisenhower Was My Boss*, 89.
29 *It was twelve miles:* White House Files, Log of the Trip, November 11 to 17, 1943, Cairo & Tehran Papers, doc. 245.
30 *Roosevelt asked:* Roosevelt, *As He Saw It*, 133.
30 *pulled up to a villa:* Henry Arnold, Diary (Trip to SEXTANT).
30 *rechristened the "White House"*: White House Files, Log of the Trip, November 11 to 17, 1943, Cairo & Tehran Papers, doc. 245.
30 *Roosevelt in town:* Memorandum for Chief of Staff, Operation "ADULT," November 11, 1943, GCM, McCarthy Papers, box 4.
30 *Butch came in:* Summersby, *Eisenhower Was My Boss*, 90.
30 *gravitated toward fireplaces:* Michael McKeogh & Richard Lockridge, *Sgt. Mickey & General Ike* (Putnam, 1946), 39.
30 *Kay had just driven:* Summersby, *Eisenhower Was My Boss*, 90.
30 *Tall and slim:* Kenneth Davis, interview with Kay Summersby, 1944, Davis Papers, box 94.
30 *"I want to"*: Everett Hughes, Diary, December 30, 1942, Hughes Papers, box I-1 ("He says he wants to hold her hand").
30 *a poker face:* Louise Locke to George Hall, November 8, 1977, EL, George Hall Papers, box 1.
30 *"Irish, How about"*: Dwight Eisenhower to Kay Summersby, June 1944, Sotheby's, Sale 6188, Fine Books and Manuscripts, June 13, 1991, lot 174.
30 *one of the closest people:* Dwight Eisenhower to Milton Eisenhower, July 10, 1944, Pre-Pres. Principal, box 174.
30 *"Mr. President"*: Summersby, *Eisenhower Was My Boss*, 90.
31 *Marshall was not invited:* White House Files, Log of the Trip, November 11 to 17, 1943, Cairo & Tehran Papers, doc. 245.

31 *a shyness:* Eisenhower, "Churchill & Marshall."
31 *called him "Ike":* Forrest Pogue, interview with Dwight Eisenhower, June 28, 1962, GCM, Forrest Pogue Interviews.
31 *Times Square:* Butcher Diary, A-905.
31 *keen to gossip:* Eisenhower, "Churchill & Marshall."
31 *a single glass:* Butcher Diary, A-907.
31 *"This is the President's decision":* Eisenhower Project: Dwight D. Eisenhower, 1970, Oral History Research Office, Columbia University, p. 42.
31 *thought little:* Dwight Eisenhower, Diary, March 14, 1942, EL, Diaries, box 1.
31 *"One thing":* Eisenhower, Diary, March 10, 1942, EL, Diaries, box 1.
31 *"We now have":* Eisenhower, "Churchill & Marshall."
32 *Marshall was feeling pressed:* Edward Cray, *General of the Army* (Cooper Square Press, 2000), 85.
32 *King boozily apologized:* Eisenhower, "Churchill & Marshall."
32 *change the subject:* Eisenhower, "Churchill & Marshall."
32 *Eisenhower flashed:* Harry C. Butcher, *My Three Years with Eisenhower* (Simon & Schuster, 1946), 445.
32 *Dinner was:* White House Files, Log of the Trip, November 11 to 17, 1943, Cairo & Tehran Papers, doc. 245.
32 *Roosevelt was keen:* Summersby, *Eisenhower Was My Boss*, 92.
32 *She had driven:* Kenneth Davis, interview with Kay Summersby, 1944, Davis Papers, box 94.
32 *Her father:* "Some of the OS on the Front or in the Forces," *The Stonyhurst Magazine*, July 1915, pp. 1247, 1271.
32 *the last time:* Davis, interview with Summersby.
32 *"Mr. President":* Summersby, *Eisenhower Was My Boss*, 92.
33 *"A night flight":* Roosevelt, *As He Saw It*, 135.
33 *Eisenhower got back:* Butcher Diary, A-908-A-909.
34 *"By god":* Forrest Pogue, interview with Dwight Eisenhower, June 28, 1962, GCM, Forrest Pogue Interviews.
34 *"did not necessarily":* Eisenhower, "Churchill & Marshall."
34 *issue with Mark Clark:* Butcher Diary, A-909.
34 *A year earlier:* "General 'Ike' Eisenhower," *Life*, November 9, 1942, pp. 112–24.
35 *secret mission:* Mark Clark, *Calculated Risk* (Harper 1950), 67–91.
35 *"Mark always wears":* "General Clark's Famous Pants Find Home," Associated Press, September 11, 1943.
35 *"General Clark lost his":* Juanita Wecksung, "Mrs. Mark Clark Calls for Unity," *Iowa City-Press Citizen*, December 1, 1943.
35 *"Publicity":* Butcher Diary, A-908.
35 *Around noon:* White House Files, Log of the Trip, November 11 to 17, 1943, Cairo & Tehran Papers, doc. 245.
35 *his usual spot:* Dwight Eisenhower to Vera McCarthy-Morrogh, June 12, 1943, Sotheby's, Sale 6188, Fine Books and Manuscripts, June 13, 1991, lot 161.
35 *all smiles:* Summersby, *Eisenhower Was My Boss*, 94.
35 *American presence:* Henry Arnold, Diary (Trip to SEXTANT).
35 *originally promised:* Butcher Diary, A-909.
35 *Among the groves:* Henry Arnold, Diary (Trip to SEXTANT).
35 *how few scars:* White House Files, Log of the Trip, November 11 to 17, 1943, Cairo & Tehran Papers, doc. 245.
36 *Like a mine:* Kay Summersby, *Eisenhower Was My Boss*, 84.
36 *Telek was an active:* Michael McKeogh & Richard Lockridge, *Sgt. Mickey & General Ike*, 41.
36 *first got to London:* Kenneth Davis, interview with Harry Butcher, 1944, Davis Papers, box 94.
36 *Butch found:* Michael McKeogh & Richard Lockridge, *Sgt. Mickey & General Ike*, 41.
36 *Kay brought:* Kay Summersby, *Eisenhower Was My Boss*, 35–36.
36 *"Tele-K":* Kay Summersby, *Past Forgetting* (Simon & Schuster, 1977), 67.
36 *sat together:* Kay Summersby, *Eisenhower Was My Boss*, 94.
36 *"We've lost Tunis!":* Kenneth Davis, interview with Walter B. Smith, 1944, Davis Papers, box 94.
37 *The "bloody nose":* Kenneth Davis, interview with General Eisenhower, August 11, 1944, Davis Papers, box 94.
37 *there was Hill 609:* Elliot Roosevelt, *As He Saw It*, 138.
37 *shrubby near-mountain:* George F. Howe, *United States Army in World War II, Mediterranean Theater of Operations, Northwest Africa* (US Government Printing Office, 1957), 627.
37 *they continued south:* White House Files, Log of the Trip, November 11 to 17, 1943, Cairo & Tehran Papers, doc. 245.
37 *"That's an awfully":* Summersby, *Eisenhower Was My Boss*, 94.

37 *Kay was madly in love:* Lloyd Shearer, "The Eisenhower-Summersby Love Affair (Draft)," October 28, 1976, University of Wyoming, Harry Butcher Papers, box 3.

37 *Eisenhower had personally approved:* Dwight Eisenhower, R. R. Arnold, Marriage, March 22, 1943, Pre-Pres. Principal, box 112.

37 *Eisenhower wandered off:* Summersby, *Eisenhower Was My Boss*, 94.

37 *a squadron of fifty-one:* White House Files, Log of the Trip, November 11 to 17, 1943, Cairo & Tehran Papers, doc. 245.

37 *"Ike, if, one year":* Dwight Eisenhower, *Crusade in Europe* (Doubleday, 1948), 195.

38 *with a horseshoe:* White House Files, Log of the Trip, November 11 to 17, 1943, Cairo & Tehran Papers, doc. 245.

38 *"Mr. President, we've":* Eisenhower, *Crusade in Europe*, 214.

38 *Kay turned west:* Butcher Diary, A-909.

38 *And Roosevelt wondered:* Robert Sherwood, Talk with General Eisenhower at His Office in the Pentagon Building, January 14, 1947, Sherwood Papers, box 40.

38 Life of Hannibal: Joe W. Howe, "Dwight D. Eisenhower," undated, Davis Papers, box 22.

38 *locked his books:* Dwight Eisenhower, *At Ease* (Doubleday, 1967), 39–42.

38 *"written about only":* Dwight Eisenhower, Material on Military History Lecture, Pre-Pres. Principal, box 193.

38 *was as keenly interested:* Elliot Roosevelt, *As He Saw It*, 136–37.

38 *They speculated:* Dwight Eisenhower, *Crusade in Europe*, 214.

39 *"Ike," he said:* Robert Sherwood, Talk with General Eisenhower at his Office in the Pentagon Building, January 14, 1947, Sherwood Papers, box 40.

39 *weighed on him:* Robert Sherwood, Memorandum of Interview with William Leahy, September 13, 1943, Sherwood Papers, box 38.

39 *acting chief of staff:* Sherwood, *Roosevelt and Hopkins*, 770.

39 *brief the Combined Chiefs:* Eisenhower, manuscript, "Churchill & Marshall," November 17, 1966, Post-Presidential Papers, A-WR Series, box 8.

39 *back at the White House:* Butcher Diary, A-909.

39 *"You know, Ike":* Roosevelt, *As He Saw It*, 136–37.

39 *aloft for Cairo:* White House Files, Log of the Trip, November 11 to 17, 1943, Cairo & Tehran Papers, doc. 245.

CHAPTER 3

40 *"Wide publicity":* George Marshall to Dwight Eisenhower, November 23, 1943, Pre-Pres. Principal, box 132.

40 *On August 3, 1943:* H. S. Clarkson, Report of Investigation, Treatment of Certain Mentally Ill Hospital Patients by Lieutenant General George S. Patton, Jr., September 18, 1943, Pre-Pres. Principal, box 91; Alex Lovelace, "Slap Heard around the World," *Parameters*, Vol. 49, No. 3 (2019), 79–91.

40 *"You're going back":* Henry J. Taylor, "General Patton's Version of the Sicilian Slapping Incident," in *Deadline Delayed* (Dutton, 1947), 149–65.

41 *"God damned coward":* Clarkson, Report of Investigation.

41 *"curse and say a hymn":* Larry I. Bland, ed., *George C. Marshall Interviews and Reminiscences for Forrest C. Pogue* (George C. Marshall Foundation, 1996), 582.

41 *oldest friends:* Dwight Eisenhower, *At Ease* (Doubleday 1967), at 169–175; Carlo D'Este, *Patton* (HarperCollins 1995), 285–303; Jean Edwards Smith, *Eisenhower in War and Peace* (Random House, 2012), 53–55; Jonathan Jordan, *Brothers, Rivals, Victors* (Penguin, 2011), at 19–21.

41 *during the Great War:* Dwight Eisenhower, *At Ease: Stories I Tell My Friends* (Doubleday, 1967), 132–33.

41 *Camp Colt in Gettysburg:* Dwight Eisenhower, *At Ease*, at 148–150.

41 *been stationed with:* Carlo D'Este, *Patton* (HarperCollins 1995), at 187–266; Hubert Essame, *Patton* (Scribner, 1975), at 8–18; Jesse L. Thompson, Lecture Delivered on Tanks to the Students, Army Center of Artillery, 1919, Patton Papers, box 47.

41 *Wild Bill Hickok:* Tom Clavin, *Wild Bill* (St. Martin's, 2019).

41 *self-styled cowboy:* Timothy Rives, "Eisenhower and the Remnants of the Western Past," *Great Plains Traverse*, Vol. 1, No. 1 (January 2018); "From Plebe to President (Ike as His Classmates Remember Him)," *Colliers*, June 10, 1955 at 92–97; Alexander Weyand, "The Athletic Cadet Eisenhower," *Assembly*, Spring 1968, at 65.

41 *Legend had it:* Tom Clavin, *Wild Bill*, 432.

42 *the name Dwight:* Oral History Research Office, Eisenhower Administration: Milton Eisenhower, 1973, Columbia Center on Oral History, p. 72; interview with Edgar Eisenhower in Bela Kornitzer, *The Great American Heritage* (Farrar, Straus and Cudahy, 1955), 251; Charles Gans to Dwight Eisenhower, May 28, 1947,

Pre-Pres. Principal, box 45; Anna Young Walters to Eisenhower, May 12, 1945, Pre-Pres. Principal, box 119; Leila Grace Picking, OH-7, January 27, 1965, EL, Oral Histories; Joe W. Howe, "Dwight D. Eisenhower," undated, Davis Papers, box 22.

42 *Abilene had reformed:* Tim Rives, "Eisenhower and Three Remnants of the Western Past," *Great Plains Traverse,* Vol. 1, No. 1 (January 2018); Earl Endacott, "Abilene—Land of Boom and Bust 1883-1895", EL, Earl Endacott Papers, box 4.

42 *Young Dwight:* Kenneth Davis, interview with Edgar Eisenhower and Charlie Chase, 1944, Davis Papers, box 61.

42 *At Camp Meade:* Smith, *Eisenhower in War and Peace*, 53–55.

42 *looked out for Eisenhower:* George Patton to Dwight Eisenhower, July 9, 1926, Pre-Pres. Principal, box 91.

42 *Eisenhower jumped:* Dwight Eisenhower to George Patton, September 17, 1940, Pre-Pres. Principal, box 91.

42 *made Eisenhower more abrupt:* George S. Patton, Diary, July 5, 1943, Patton Papers, box 3.

43 *he visited the Seventh Army's:* Patton, Diary, July 12, 1943, Patton Papers, box 3.

43 *On a single day:* Fred Borch, "War Crimes in Sicily," *The Army Lawyer* (March 2013), 1–6.

43 *Two reporters:* Kenneth Davis, interview with General Eisenhower, August 11, 1944, Davis Papers, box 94.

44 *"acting like a madman":* Everett Hughes, Diary, August 20, 1943, Hughes Papers, box I-1.

44 *"as a friend":* Kenneth Davis, interview with General Eisenhower, August 11, 1944, Davis Papers, box 94.

44 *"the only General":* George S. Patton, Diary, September 14, 1943, Patton Papers, box 3.

44 *"I do not see":* Dwight Eisenhower to George Marshall, September 6, 1943, Pre-Pres. Principal, box 80.

44 *"There are men":* Kenneth Davis, interview with Eisenhower, August 11, 1944.

44 *handed him a letter:* George S. Patton, Diary, August 29, 1943, Patton Papers, box 3.

45 *"putting on an act":* Clarkson, Report of Investigation.

45 *"could not understand":* Forrest Pogue, interview with Omar N. Bradley, July 19, 1957, GCM Library, Forrest Pogue Interviews.

45 *"made him see red":* Clarkson, Report of Investigation.

45 *Eisenhower broke the news:* George S. Patton, Diary, September 6, 1943, Patton Papers, box 3.

45 *Georgie had joined:* Patton, Diary, October 16, 1943, Patton Papers, box 3.

45 *"she must be":* Patton, Diary, September 10, 1943, Patton Papers, box 3.

45 *"always acting":* Patton, Diary, October 16, 1943, Patton Papers, box 3.

45 *"Here is a story":* "Eisenhower Squelches Pearson for Slur on Patton," Associated Press, November 22, 1943.

45 *"A very vicious":* Dwight Eisenhower to George Patton, November 23, 1943, Pre-Pres. Principal, box 91.

46 *The* New York Times *ran it:* "Patton Struck Ailing Soldier, Apologized to Him and Army," *New York Times*, November 23, 1944.

46 *Charles Kuhl's parents:* "Soldier Told Family Patton Kicked Him," United Press, November 23, 1943.

46 *Senator Claude Pepper:* "Congress May Probe General's Actions," United Press, November 24, 1943.

46 *Drew Pearson called:* "Drew Pearson Calls for Senate Probe," Associated Press, November 22, 1943.

46 *"not to supply":* Merrill Mueller, NBC Broadcast, November 23, 1943.

46 *"we will support":* George Marshall to Dwight Eisenhower, November 23, 1943, Pre-Pres. Principal, box 132.

46 *Joseph McNarney:* Ray S. Cline, *The War Department Washington Command Post: The Operations Division*, CMH Pub. 1–2 (GPO, 1951), 91–95.

46 *"silent one":* William Morrison, Interview with Henry Aurand, February 25, 1977, USAHEC, Henry S. Aurand Papers, Folder 1, at 11.

46 *"hatchet man":* Larry I. Bland, ed., *George C. Marshall Interviews and Reminiscences for Forrest C. Pogue* (George C. Marshall Foundation, 1996), 626.

46 *McNarney also expected:* Forrest Pogue, interview with Joseph T. McNarney, February 2, 1966, GCM, Forrest Pogue Interviews.

46 *McNarney was poised:* George S. Patton, Diary, November 28, 1943, Patton Papers, box 3.

46 *encouraged his boss:* Butcher Diary, A-915.

46 *"General Patton has never":* "Eisenhower Squelches Pearson for Slur on Patton," Associated Press, November 22, 1943.

46 *exposed as such:* C. R. Cunningham, "Army Now Admits Patton Struck Soldier, Was Censured by Eisenhower, Apologized," United Press, November 23, 1943.

46 *"Well, I certainly":* Kenneth Davis, interview with Walter B. Smith, 1944, Davis Papers, box 94.

46 *"For God's sake":* Davis, interview with General Eisenhower, August 11, 1944, Davis Papers, box 94.

47 *"Oh, well, Beedle":* Davis, interview with Walter B. Smith, 1944, Davis Papers, box 94.

47 *The irony was:* Davis, interview with Smith; George S. Patton, Diary, October 27, 1943, Patton Papers, box 1.

47 *"full and complete amends":* Dwight Eisenhower to George Patton, November 23, 1943, Smith Papers, box 15.

47 *"mercilessly castigated"*: Tear Sheet, November 23, 1943, Pre-Pres. Principal, box 91.

47 *"It is my judgement"*: Dwight Eisenhower to George Patton, November 24, 1943, Smith Papers, box 15.

CHAPTER 4

48 *The last time:* Meeting of the Combined Chiefs of Staff, January 15, 1943, FRUS, *The Conferences at Washington, 1941–1942, and Casablanca, 1943*, doc. 342.

48 *first met Alan Brooke:* Dwight Eisenhower, manuscript, "Churchill & Marshall," November 17, 1966, Post-Presidential Papers, A-WR Series, box 8; Dwight Eisenhower, *Crusade in Europe* (Doubleday, 1947), at 30.

49 *the second time:* Alan Brooke, *War Diaries, 1939–1945* (Phoenix Press, 2001), 276.

49 *Brooke remained convinced:* Brooke, 343.

49 *What if:* Meeting of the Combined Chiefs of Staff, January 15, 1943, FRUS, *The Conferences at Washington, 1941–1942, and Casablanca, 1943*, doc. 342.

49 *"throat [was] about"*: George S. Patton, Diary, January 15, 1943, Patton Papers, box 3.

49 *"I am afraid"*: Brooke, *War Diaries*, 351.

49 *Alan Brooke proposed:* Brooke, 365.

50 *The intervening reality:* Dwight Eisenhower, Memorandum, June 11, 1943, Pre-Pres. Principal, box 137.

50 *Alex was an aristocrat:* Forrest Pogue, interview with Hastings Ismay, December 17, 1946, Murray State, Forrest Pogue Papers, box 161.

50 *His only flaw:* Dwight Eisenhower, Memorandum, June 11, 1943, Pre-Pres. Principal, box 137.

50 *"fills me with gloom"*: Brooke, *War Diaries*, 473.

50 *Eisenhower flew to Cairo:* Elliott Roosevelt, *As He Saw It* (Duell, Sloan & Pearce, 1946), 140.

50 *something of a vacation:* Kay Summersby, *Eisenhower Was My Boss* (Dell, 1948), 98.

51 *"going full swing"*: Ernest Lee, Diary, December 1, 1944, EL, Ernest R. Lee Papers, box 1.

51 *The prices, though:* Dwight Eisenhower to Vera McCarthy-Morrogh, December 2, 1943, Sotheby's, Sale 6188, Fine Books and Manuscripts, June 13, 1991, lot 169.

51 *Kids hitched rides:* Lee, Diary, December 1, 1944.

51 *Beggars, suffering from:* George Patton, "The Flight into Egypt," 1944, box 64.

51 *The Nile itself:* Lee, Diary, December 1, 1944.

51 *Thursday was Thanksgiving:* Meeting of the Combined Chiefs of Staff, November 24, 1943, FRUS, *The Conferences at Cairo and Tehran, 1943*, doc. 265.

51 *That night, there was:* Henry Arnold, Diary (Trip to SEXTANT), Arnold Papers, reel 222.

51 *Even the weather:* White House Files, Log of the Trip, November 11 to 17, 1943, Cairo & Tehran Papers, doc. 245.

51 *Roosevelt had met:* Meetings of Roosevelt, Churchill, Chiang, and Madame Chiang, Afternoon, November 22, 1943, FRUS, *The Conferences at Cairo and Tehran, 1943*, doc. 249.

51 *Eisenhower asked why:* Dwight Eisenhower, manuscript, "Churchill & Marshall," November 17, 1966, Post-Presidential Papers, A-WR Series, box 8.

51 *the president's suite:* White House Files, Log of the Trip, November 11 to 17, 1943.

51 *The Legion of Merit:* Fred Borch, *Medals for Soldiers and Airmen* (MacFarland, 2013), 123–25; Charles P. McDowell, *Military and Naval Decorations of the United States* (Quest, 1984), 133–34.

51 *Legion of Honor:* Dwight Eisenhower to Frances Curry, April 3, 1943, Pre-Pres. Principal, box 29.

52 *"You deserve this"*: Roosevelt, *As He Saw It*, 166.

52 *The Combined Chiefs meeting:* Combined Chiefs of Staff Minutes, November 26, 1943, FRUS, *The Conferences at Cairo and Tehran, 1943*, doc. 277.

52 *Alex would:* Dwight Eisenhower, *Crusade in Europe* (Doubleday, 1947), 217.

52 *"had the forces"*: Meeting of the Combined Chiefs of Staff with Roosevelt and Churchill, November 24, 1943, FRUS, *The Conferences at Cairo and Tehran, 1943*, doc. 263.

52 *Rhodes to the Dardanelles:* Combined Chiefs of Staff Minutes, November 26, 1943.

52 *"a common front"*: Roosevelt, *As He Saw It*, 141.

52 *"Overlord remained"*: Meeting of the Combined Chiefs of Staff with Roosevelt and Churchill, November 24, 1943.

52 *"The Channel will be"*: Robert Sherwood, "Meeting with Admiral Ernest J. King in his Office at the Navy Department," May 24, 1946, Sherwood Papers, box 40.

52 *Alan Brooke had pulled:* Eisenhower, "Churchill & Marshall."

53 *British strategic doctrine*: Eugenia Keisling, "Military Doctrine and Planning in the Interwar Era," in *The Cambridge History of War* (Cambridge University Press), 4:346–47; David French, "Doctrine and Organization of the British Army, 1919–1932," *The Historical Journal* 44, no. 2 (2001): 497–515.

53 *"Thrust and peck"*: Dwight Eisenhower to Hastings Ismay, December 3, 1960, EL, Whitman Name File, box 19.

53 *Alan Brooke was convinced:* Eisenhower, "Churchill & Marshall."
53 *"Eisenhower does not":* Brooke, *War Diaries*, 413.
53 *"established in the Balkans":* Forrest Pogue, interview with Hastings Ismay, December 17, 1946, Pogue Papers, box 161.
53 *"We must realize":* Joint Chiefs of Staff Minutes, November 28, 1943, Cairo & Tehran Papers.
53 *"The way to kill":* Roosevelt, *As He Saw It*, 185.
54 *"His Majesty's Government":* Larry Bland, ed., *George C. Marshall: Interviews and Reminiscences for Forrest C. Pogue* (George C. Marshall Research Foundation, 1991), 622.
54 *"God forbid, if I":* Larry I. Bland, ed., *George C. Marshall Interviews and Reminiscences for Forrest C. Pogue* (George C. Marshall Foundation, 1996), 622.
54 *He recounted the year's:* Combined Chiefs of Staff Minutes, November 26, 1943, FRUS, *The Conferences at Cairo and Tehran, 1943*, doc. 277; Butcher Diary, A-932.
54 *"almost resulted in":* Arnold, Diary (Trip to SEXTANT).
54 *"the father and mother":* Brooke, *War Diaries*, 481.

CHAPTER 5

55 *Friday-evening drinks:* Alan Brooke, *War Diaries, 1939–1945* (Phoenix Press, 2001), 481.
55 *General Marshall ordered:* Dwight Eisenhower, *Crusade in Europe* (Doubleday, 1947), 220.
55 *Arthur Tedder, had told:* Kay Summersby, *Eisenhower Was My Boss* (Dell, 1948), 100.
55 *assigned Eisenhower a villa:* Summersby, 98.
56 *That night:* Elliott Roosevelt, *As He Saw It* (Duell, Sloan & Pearce, 1946), 167.
56 *His mother would:* Oral History Research Office, Eisenhower Administration: The Reminiscences of Milton Eisenhower, 1979, Columbia Center on Oral History, 27–29.
56 *he despised fun:* Interview with Arthur Eisenhower, in Bela Kornitzer, *The Great American Heritage* (Farrar, Straus and Cudahy, 1955), 18–19.
56 *bottle of whiskey:* Reminiscences of Milton Eisenhower, 5.
56 *obsessed with Egypt:* Oral History Research Office, Eisenhower Administration Project: Edgar N. Eisenhower, 1968, Columbia Center on Oral History, 19.
56 *"In that day":* Isaiah 19:19–20 (King James Version).
56 *Eisenhower's father:* Kenneth Davis, Kansas Research on General Dwight David Eisenhower, 1944, Davis Papers, box 94.
56 *The River Brethren:* Interview with the Rev. R. I. Witter, OH-5, August 28, 1964, EL, Oral Histories.
56 *"possession of property":* Earl Endacott, "Home and Family Introduction and Early History", EL, Earl Endacott Papers, box 4.
57 *Eisenhower clan moved:* Davis, Kansas Research on General Dwight David Eisenhower.
57 *David Eisenhower attended:* Carlo D'Este, *Eisenhower* (Holt, 2002), 16; Dwight Eisenhower, *At Ease* (Doubleday, 1967), at 77–78.
57 *That business failed:* Thomas Braniger, "No Villains—No Heroes," *Kansas History* (1992): 173–74.
57 *in a house:* Earl Endacott, "Abilene—Land of Boom and Bust 1883-1895," EL, Earl Endacott Papers, box 4.
57 *a man convinced:* Interview with Edgar Eisenhower, in Kornitzer, *Great American Heritage*, 13–35.
57 *"I find a very strong":* "Populism Is Dead, Candidate Debs Says Its Mission Is Ended," *Abilene Weekly Reflector*, October 19, 1900, p. 1.
57 *In 1903, David ran:* "Cowen Is Mayor, Handsome Victory for Republican Candidates," *Abilene Weekly Reflector*, April 9, 1903, p. 6.
57 *worked as a technician:* Interview with Dwight Eisenhower, in Kornitzer, *Great American Heritage*, 32.
57 *a venture:* Earl Endacott, "Home and Family Introduction and Early History," EL, Earl Endacott Papers, Box 4.
57 *Once assembled:* Interview with Eisenhower, in Kornitzer, 32.
57 *Church was not:* Davis, Kansas Research on General Dwight David Eisenhower.
57 *allowed to play sports:* Interview with Eisenhower, in Kornitzer, *Great American Heritage*, 29.
57 *Sunday school:* Interview with Rev. R. I. Witter, OH-5, August 28, 1964, EL, Oral Histories.
57 *"It isn't a religion":* Kenneth Davis, interview with Dr. Thayer, 1944, Davis Papers, box 61.
58 *John Taylor:* John Taylor, *The Great Pyramid: Why Was It Built and Who Built It?* (Longman, Green, Longman, & Roberts, 1859).
58 *Charles Piazzi Smyth:* Charles Piazzi Smyth, *Our Inheritance in the Great Pyramid* (Strahan, 1864).
58 *"The Pyramid witnesses":* Charles Taze Russell, *Studies in the Scriptures, The Divine Plan of the Ages* (Watch Tower Bible and Tract Society, 1886), 42.
58 *David copied the chart:* Kenneth Davis, interview with Arthur Eisenhower, 1944, Davis Papers, box 94.

58 *a very certain man:* Interview with Arthur Eisenhower, in Kornitzer, *Great American Heritage*, 19.
58 *his father was arrested:* Braniger, "No Villains—No Heroes," 173.
58 *"His face was":* Dwight Eisenhower, *At Ease: Stories I Tell to Friends* (Doubleday, 1967), 36–37.
59 *"weak":* Kenneth Davis, interview with Edgar Eisenhower and Charlie Chase, 1944, Davis Papers, box 61.
59 *searching for an answer:* Interview with Edgar Eisenhower, in Kornitzer, *Great American Heritage*, 134–135.
59 *"the floor-line":* Russell, *Studies in the Scriptures*, 341.
59 *David unsuccessfully lobbied:* David Eisenhower to Joseph Bristow, August 6, 1913, KHS, Joseph Bristow Papers, box 68.
59 *went to work:* Kornitzer, *Great American Heritage*, 18.
59 *"he couldn't go along":* Interview with Edgar Eisenhower, in Kornitzer, 134–135.
59 *a Witness funeral:* Kenneth Davis, interview with Mrs. David J. Eisenhower and Naomi Engle, 1944, Davis Papers, box 61.
59 *The ceremony was conducted:* "Rites for D. J. Eisenhower," *Abilene Daily Reflector*, March 13, 1942, 6.
59 *Dr. J. L. Thayer: Abilene Weekly Reflector*, May 29, 1902, p. 9.
59 *"Millions Now Living":* "Local Bible Students Active," *Abilene Daily Chronicle*, December 7, 1920, p. 3.
59 *"Jehovah God":* "Dr. Thayer to Speak," *Manhtan Mercury*, October 11, 1928, p. 1.
59 *A local paper:* "D. J. Eisenhower Dies," *Morning Chronicle*, March 13, 1942, p. 8.
59 *"connected with":* "D. J. Eisenhower Dead," *Abilene Daily Reflector*, March 10, 1942, p. 8.
60 *Ernest King had driven:* Dwight Eisenhower, Diary, March 10, 1942, EL, Diaries, box 1.
60 *He got the call:* Mamie Eisenhower to John Douds, March 13, 1942, in Susan Eisenhower, *Mrs. Ike* (FSG, 1996), at 178.
60 *"Father died":* Eisenhower, Diary, March 10, 1942.
60 *"I loved":* Eisenhower, Diary, March 11, 1942, EL, Diaries, box 1.
60 *"I am proud":* Eisenhower, Diary, March 12, 1942, EL, Diaries, box 1.
60 *The following day:* Summersby, *Eisenhower Was My Boss*, 100.
60 *"The Joint Chiefs":* Roosevelt, *As He Saw It*, 168.
61 *a Franciscan priest:* Kenneth Davis, interview with Mickey McKeogh, 1944, Davis Papers, box 94.
61 *As a religious:* Ernest Lee, Diary, December 1, 1944, EL, Ernest R. Lee Papers, box 1; George Patton, "The Flight into Egypt," 1944, Patton Papers, box 64.
61 *The monks:* Summersby, *Eisenhower Was My Boss*, 104.
61 *"a bouncing":* Davis, interview with Mickey McKeogh.
61 *"Guess I've got":* Summersby, *Eisenhower Was My Boss*, 104.
61 *River Brethren Sunday school:* Oral History Research Office, Eisenhower Administration Project: Edgar N. Eisenhower, 1968, Columbia Center on Oral History, 18.
61 *could not resist:* Summersby, *Eisenhower Was My Boss*, 104.
61 *Mount of Olives:* Patton, "Flight into Egypt."
62 *They left Jerusalem:* Summersby, *Eisenhower Was My Boss*, 104.
62 *Eisenhower was relieved:* Everett Hughes, Diary, December 1, 1943, Hughes Papers, box I-1.

CHAPTER 6

63 *Eisenhower returned:* Harry Butcher, *My Three Years with Eisenhower* (Simon & Schuster, 1946), 451.
63 *Eisenhower joked:* Butcher Diary, A-926.
63 *writing discreetly:* Harry Butcher to Steve Early, December 5, 1943, University of Wyoming, Harry Butcher Papers, box 3.
63 *middle of quicksand:* Dwight Eisenhower to John Doud, December 3, 1943, Pre-Pres. Principal, box 171.
63 *most urgent task:* Butcher Diary, A-934.
64 *"eternal pound, pound":* Dwight Eisenhower to Mamie Eisenhower, November 6, 1942, private collection.
64 *He first noticed:* Dwight Eisenhower to Mamie Eisenhower.
64 *"nervous wreck":* Dwight Eisenhower, *Letters to Mamie* (Doubleday, 1977), 159.
64 *"Our new":* Mamie Eisenhower to Dwight Eisenhower, November 13, 1943, Pre-Presidential Papers, Principal File, box 173.
64 *"Gee! I'm crazy":* Dwight Eisenhower to Mamie Eisenhower, September 25, 1917, EL, Pre-Pres. Misc., box 22.
64 *Mamie had named:* Susan Eisenhower, *Mrs. Ike* (Farrar, Straus and Giroux, 1996), 51.
64 *The most brutal:* Dwight Eisenhower, *At Ease: Stories I Tell to Friends* (Doubleday, 1967), at 148–150.
64 *After the first wave:* "Influenza Takes More Soldiers," *Gettysburg Times*, October 11, 1918, 1.
65 *the nursing staff:* Percy Eichelburger & Paul Falk, *Adams County in the World War* (The Evangelical Press, 1921); "Red Cross Takes Important Steps," *Gettysburg Times*, October 3, 1918, 1.
65 *"kindness":* "Influenza Takes More Soldiers," *Gettysburg Times*, October 11, 1918, 1.

65 *camp under lockdown*: Jon Tracey, "Spanish Influenza and Eisenhower's Leadership in Gettysburg," *American Battlefield Trust,* September 20, 2021.
65 *he was terrified*: Dwight Eisenhower, *At Ease: Stories I Tell to Friends* (Doubleday, 1967), 148–150.
65 *Nearly two hundred*: Percy Eichelburger & Paul Falk, *Adams County in the World War* (The Evangelical Press, 1921).
65 *The mortality rate*: Joseph Siler, *The Medical Department of the United States Army in the World War* (GPO, 1928), 138.
65 *"I miss you"*: Dwight Eisenhower, *Letters to Mamie* (Doubleday, 1977), 158.
65 *Eisenhower consoled himself*: Butcher Diary, A-926.
65 *Elliott Roosevelt skipped:* Butcher Diary, A-923.
65 *Churchill kept reproposing*: Elliott Roosevelt, *As He Saw It* (Duell, Sloan & Pearce, 1946), 184.
65 *Roosevelt had asked:* Minutes of the First Plenary Meeting, November 28, 1943, FRUS, *The Conferences at Cairo and Tehran, 1943*, doc. 361.
66 *According to Elliott*: Roosevelt, *As He Saw It*, 206.
66 *On the last:* The Military Agreement, FRUS, *The Conferences at Cairo and Tehran, 1943*, doc. 424.
66 *Stalin liked it:* Roosevelt, *As He Saw It*, 194.
66 *The latest rumors*: Butcher Diary, A-923.
66 *his exhausted stenographers:* Kenneth Davis, interview with Margaret Shick, 1944, Davis Papers, box 94; Forrest Pogue, "Interviewing General Eisenhower and His Friends," 1970, Pogue Papers, box 36.
66 *"Shit, I don't"*: Michael McKeogh & Richard Lockridge, *Sgt. Mickey & General Ike* (Putnam, 1946), 51 (In the direct quote, Eisenhower is reported as having said "damn it," but Mickey is quick to add, "but he really didn't just say damn it.").
66 *recommending a book:* George Patton to Dwight Eisenhower, November 28, 1943, Patton Papers, box 32.
67 *Eisenhower welcomed:* Dwight Eisenhower to George Patton, December 1, 1943, Patton Papers, box 32.
67 *wrote to Kay's mother*: Dwight Eisenhower to Vera McCarthy-Morrogh, December 2, 1943, Sotheby's, Sale 6188, Fine Books and Manuscripts, June 13, 1991, lot 169.
67 *"in education lies"*: Dwight Eisenhower to Milton Eisenhower, December 3, 1943, Pre-Pres. Principal, box 174.
67 *wrote to his son:* Dwight Eisenhower to John Eisenhower, December 3, 1942, Pre-Pres. Principal, box 173.
67 *wrote to Mamie's father*: Dwight Eisenhower to John Doud, December 3, 1943, Pre-Pres. Principal, box 171.
67 *wrote to Mamie:* Eisenhower, *Letters to Mamie*, 156–159.
67 *Eisenhower was up:* Butcher Diary, A-937.
67 *The water and gas:* Harry Butcher, *My Three Years with Eisenhower* (Simon & Schuster, 1947), 199.
67 *dreary charm:* Kay Summersby, *Eisenhower Was My Boss* (Dell, 1948), 52–55.
68 *A cable:* Butcher Diary, A-937.
68 *"The possibility"*: George Marshall to Dwight Eisenhower, December 6, 1943, Smith Papers, box 15.
68 *Roosevelt landed:* White House Files, Log of the Trip, November 11 to 17, 1943, Cairo and Tehran Papers, doc. 245; Robert Sherwood, Chronology, Sherwood Papers, box 41.
68 *"Well, Ike"*: Robert Sherwood, Talk with General Eisenhower at His Office in the Pentagon Building, January 14, 1947, Sherwood Papers, box 40.
68 *"You are going"*: Dwight Eisenhower, *Crusade in Europe* (Doubleday, 1947), 227.
68 *The Combined Chiefs had agreed:* Combined Chiefs of Staff Minutes, December 4, 1943, FRUS, *The Conferences at Cairo and Tehran, 1943*, doc. 461.
68 *"Mr. President"*: Eisenhower, *Crusade in Europe*, 227.
68 *"I cannot spare"*: Dwight Eisenhower, manuscript, "Churchill & Marshall," November 17, 1966, EL, Post-Presidential Papers, A-WR Series, box 8.
68 *That night, Roosevelt invited:* Robert Sherwood, Chronology, Sherwood Papers, box 38.
68 *Scenes from the*: Carl Spaatz, Diary, December 7, 1943, LOC, Carl Spaatz Papers, box 12.
68 *Roosevelt held forth:* Roosevelt, *As He Saw It*, 209.
68 *Roosevelt waxed:* Butcher Diary, A-938.
69 *The following day:* White House Files, Log of the Trip, November 11 to 17, 1943.
69 *Roosevelt confided:* Robert E. Sherwood, *Roosevelt and Hopkins* (Harper, 1948), 803.
69 *"Poor dear old Winney"*: George S. Patton, Diary, December 8, 1943, Patton Papers, box 3.
69 *"the office open"*: John T. Mason, The Reminiscences of Alan Goodrich Kirk, no. 455, 1962, Oral History Research Office, Columbia University, p. 264.
69 *"Empire ideas"*: Roosevelt, *As He Saw It*, 155.
69 *Eisenhower stayed in Tunis:* Butcher Diary, A-939.
69 *"I enjoyed our day"*: Franklin Roosevelt to Dwight Eisenhower, December 10, 1943, Pre-Pres. Principal, box 100.

69 *"The date for the capture"*: Dwight Eisenhower to Franklin Roosevelt, December 10, 1943, Pre-Pres. Principal, box 100.

CHAPTER 7

70 *he went east:* Butcher Diary, A-944.

70 *"GCM"*: George Marshall to Dwight Eisenhower, December 7, 1943, GCM, Marshall Papers, box 66.

70 *"For your very private"*: Dwight Eisenhower to John Eisenhower, December 14, 1942, Pre-Pres. Principal, box 173.

71 *The previous February:* Rick Atkinson, *An Army at Dawn* (Holt, 2002), 359–392; George Howe, *Northwest Africa*, CMH Pub. 6-1-1 (GPO, 1957), 438-458.

71 *"The front"*: Dwight Eisenhower to George Marshall, December 17, 1943, Pre-Pres. Principal, box 80.

71 *French sports car:* Mattie Pinette, Diary, June 4, 1944, EL, George Hall Papers, box 1.

71 *great aviation heroes:* Forrest Pogue, interview with Arthur Tedder, February 13, 1947, Murray State, Forrest Pogue Papers, box 161.

71 *taught Eisenhower:* Kenneth Davis, interview with Arthur Tedder, 1944, Davis Papers, box 94.

71 *Tedder was understated:* Kenneth Davis, interview with Arthur Tedder, 1944, Davis Papers, box 94.

71 *most trusted friends:* Forrest Pogue, interview with James Gault, February 13, 1947, Murray State, Forrest Pogue Papers, box 161.

72 *British-American line:* Eisenhower, Memorandum, June 11, 1943, Pre-Pres. Principal, box 137.

72 *A steel-trap mind:* Dwight Eisenhower, *Crusade in Europe* (Doubleday, 1947), 232; Brian Izzard, *Mastermind of Dunkirk and D-Day* (Casemate, 2020); W.S. Chalmers, *Full Cycle* (Hodder & Stoughton, 1959).

72 *Gallipoli campaign:* John T. Mason, The Reminiscences of Alan Goodrich Kirk, no. 455, 1962, Oral History Research Office, Columbia University, p. 351.

72 *Cunningham had personally:* Andrew Cunningham, *A Sailor's Odyssey* (Hutchinson, 1951), 585.

72 *"did the dirty"*: Larry I. Bland, ed., *George C. Marshall Interviews and Reminiscences for Forrest C. Pogue* (George C. Marshall Foundation, 1996), 627.

72 *He had dropped:* D. K. R. Croswell, *Beetle* (University of Kentucky, 2010), 109–201.

72 *"Staff is an extension"*: Kenneth Davis, interview with Walter B. Smith, 1944, Davis Papers, box 94.

72 *of the most value:* Oral History Research Office, An Interview with Brigadier General John S.D. Eisenhower Concerning the Eisenhower Presidency, 1982, Columbia Center on Oral History, 5.

72 *joined the Official Family:* Forrest Pogue, interview with James Gault, February 13, 1947, Murray State, Forrest Pogue Papers, box 161.

72 *An Eton- and Cambridge-educated:* Kenneth Davis, interview with James Frederic Gault, 1944, Davis Papers, box 94.

73 *"a sure sign"*: Dwight Eisenhower, *At Ease* (Doubleday, 1967), 1.

73 *exhausted stenographers:* Kenneth Davis, Interview with Mattie Pinette, 1944, Davis Papers, box 94.

73 *submit to a test:* Mattie Pinette, "Eisenhower I," undated, EL, George Hall Papers, box 1.

74 *Churchill arrived Saturday:* Butcher Diary, A-946.

74 *After the Casablanca Conference:* Final Report of the Combined Chiefs of Staff to the President and the Prime Minister, January 23, 1943, FRUS, *The Conferences at Washington, 1941–1942, and Casablanca, 1943*, doc. 416; SHAEF, History of COSSAC, May 1944, HMC 8-3.6 CA, 1–11.

74 *Roosevelt and Churchill had personally:* Report to the President and Prime Minister of the Final Agreed Summary of Conclusions Reached by the Combined Chiefs of Staff, August 24, 1943, FRUS, *Conferences at Washington and Quebec, 1943*, doc. 523.

74 *COSSAC had been building:* SHAEF, History of COSSAC, May 1944, HMC 8-3.6 CA, 30–32.

75 *meant a demotion:* Kenneth Davis, interview with Frederick E. Morgan, August 6, 1944, Davis Papers, box 94.

75 *Another protégé:* James Scott Wheeler, *Jacob L. Devers: A General's Life* (University of Kentucky Press, 2015), 126–139.

75 *Marshall had sent Devers:* Wheeler, 288.

75 *"I must be"*: Jacob Devers to Dwight Eisenhower, July 29, 1943, Pre-Pres. Principal, box 34.

75 *Devers's heart:* Devers to Eisenhower, December 27, 1943, Pre-Pres. Principal, box 34.

75 *Omar Bradley was in command:* Forrest Pogue, interview with Omar N. Bradley, July 19, 1957, GCM, Forrest Pogue Interviews.

75 *Eisenhower was not convinced:* Butcher Diary, A-938.

75 *"supreme operations"*: Report of the Combined Chiefs of Staff to the President and the Prime Minister, December 6, 1943, FRUS, *The Conferences at Cairo and Tehran, 1943*, doc. 499.

75 *Too much was at stake:* Butcher Diary, A-938.

75 *to Sicily and asked:* Patton, Diary, December 8, 1943.
75 *Patton and Devers:* Wheeler, *Jacob L. Devers*, 35–49.
75 *Georgie presented him:* George Patton to Beatrice Patton, December 4, 1943, Patton Papers, box 18.
75 *Eisenhower assured him:* George Patton, Diary, December 4, 1943, Patton Papers, box 3.
76 *Marshall having promoted Devers:* Wheeler, *Jacob L. Devers*, 35–49.
76 *Eisenhower figured:* Dwight Eisenhower to George Marshall, December 17, 1943, Pre-Pres. Principal, box 80.
76 *Eisenhower wrote a lengthy:* Eisenhower to Marshall.

CHAPTER 8

77 *landings at Salerno:* Martin Blumenson, *Salerno to Cassino*, CMH_Pub_3-3-1 (US Government Printing Office, 1969), 73–153.
77 *"Modern battle":* Henry Arnold, Diary (Trip to SEXTANT), Arnold Papers, reel 222.
78 *Eisenhower flew:* Butcher Diary, A-948.
78 *Wayne was eager:* Mark Clark, *Calculated Risk* (Harper, 1950), 250–252.
79 *The rat had holed:* Butcher Diary, A-951; Michael McKeogh and Richard Lockridge, *Sgt. Mickey & General Ike* (Putnam, 1946), 95.
79 *As he closed:* Butcher Diary, A-951.
80 *"Goddamn":* Butcher Diary, A-948.
80 *The day after:* Butcher Diary, A-954.
81 *It was not long:* Butcher Diary, A-955.
81 *Marshall was insisting:* George Marshall to Dwight Eisenhower, December 21, 1943, Smith Papers, box 19.
81 *Eisenhower and Beetle:* Dwight Eisenhower to George Marshall, December 23, 1943, Smith Papers, box 19.
81 *so well balanced:* Dwight Eisenhower, Memorandum, June 11, 1943, Pre-Pres. Principal, box 137.
81 *"Please inform":* Franklin Roosevelt to Dwight Eisenhower, December 22, 1943, Pre-Pres. Principal, box 100.
81 *ordered the arrest:* "Flandin, Boisson Held as Traitors," *New York Times*, December 22, 1943.
82 *Eisenhower was stunned:* Dwight Eisenhower to George Marshall, December 22, 1943, Smith Papers, box 15.
82 *"I am shocked":* Winston Churchill to Franklin Roosevelt, December 21, 1943, Pre-Pres. Principal, box 100.
82 *The previous summer:* Statement by the British Government, August 26, 1943, FRUS, *Conferences at Washington and Quebec*, doc. 530; Statement by the Canadian Government, August 26, 1943, FRUS, *Conferences at Washington and Quebec*, doc. 531; French Committee of National Liberation (Russian Representation), Hansard House of Commons, September 22, 1943, vol. 392, 174.
82 *Roosevelt had refused:* Statement by the British Government, August 26, 1943, FRUS, *Conferences at Washington and Quebec*, doc. 529.
82 *"There was a chance":* Forrest Pogue, interview with Walter B. Smith, May 8, 1947, Pogue Papers, box 161.
82 *devised a plan:* Pogue, interview with Smith.
82 *"I can visualize":* Dwight Eisenhower to Robert Murphy, December 22, 1943, Smith Papers, box 15.
82 *"profoundly disturbed":* Dwight Eisenhower to Franklin Roosevelt, December 22, 1943, Pre-Pres. Principal, box 100.
83 *"a very capable":* George Marshall to Dwight Eisenhower, December 23, 1943, GCM, Marshall Papers, box 66.
83 *blocked his request:* Franklin Roosevelt to Winston Churchill, December 23, 1943, Smith Papers, box 15.
83 *he had hoped:* Dwight Eisenhower to George Marshall, December 23, 1943, Smith Papers, box 19.
83 *his final decision:* Roosevelt to Churchill, December 23, 1943.
83 *Eisenhower knew this:* Eisenhower to Marshall, December 23, 1943.
83 *Monty's greatest patron:* Forrest Pogue, interview with Andrew Thorne, January 28, 1947, Pogue Papers, box 161.
83 *Brooke had been grooming:* Alan Brooke, *War Diaries, 1939–1945* (Phoenix Press, 2001), 454.
83 *"Monty":* Kenneth S. Davis, "Ike's Identification with Kansas," October 12, 1990, delivered at Eisenhower and Kansas Symposium, October 12, 1990, Davis Papers, box 19.

CHAPTER 9

84 *a goodwill trip:* Kay Summersby, *Eisenhower Was My Boss* (Dell, 1948), 115; Michael McKeogh and Richard Lockridge, *Sgt. Mickey & General Ike* (Putnam, 1946), 95–96; Arnold, Diary (Trip to SEXTANT), Arnold Papers, reel 222.
84 *a palace:* Carl Spaatz, to Discuss with Eisenhower and General Smith, undated, LOC, Carl Spaatz Papers, box 12.
84 *"Whose is that?":* Summersby, *Eisenhower Was My Boss*, 115.

85 *"Things are not going"*: Dwight Eisenhower, Diary, February 28, 1933, in Daniel Holt and James Leyerzapf, eds., *Eisenhower: The Pre-War Diaries and Selected Papers* (Johns Hopkins University Press, 1998), 246–49.

85 *"an able administrator"*: Dwight Eisenhower, Diary, September 3, 1939, in Daniel Holt and James Leyerzapf, eds., *Eisenhower: The Pre-War Diaries and Selected Papers* (Johns Hopkins University Press, 1998), 446.

85 *The scion of a storied:* For some excellent biographies of MacArthur, see Arthur Herman, *Douglas MacArthur* (Random House, 2016); Mark Perry, *The Most Dangerous Man in America* (Basic Books, 2014); William Manchester, *American Caesar* (Little, Brown, 2008); Geoffrey Perret, *Old Soldiers Never Die* (Random House, 1996).

85 *angled his way*: William Morrison, Interview with Henry Araund, May 3, 1974, USAHEC, Henry S. Aurand Papers, Folder 11, 18.

85 *Eisenhower was enthralled:* Dwight Eisenhower, Diary, June 15, 1932, in Holt and Leyerzapf, *Pre-War Diaries and Selected Papers*, 224–31; Dwight Eisenhower to Elvira Doud, John Doud, and Eda Carlson, November 12, 1931, in Holt and Leyerzapf, 201–2.

85 *summer of 1932:* Report from the Chief of Staff, United States Army to the Secretary of War, On the Employment of Federal Troops in Civil Disturbance in the District of Columbia, July 28–30, 1932, August 15, 1932, in Holt and James Leyerzapf, 233–47; George Moseley, manuscript, "The Bonus March 1932," LOC, George Moseley Papers, box 9; Paul Dickson and Thomas B. Allen, *The Bonus Army* (Walker Books, 2004).

85 *would later claim:* Dwight Eisenhower, *At Ease: Stories I Tell to Friends* (Doubleday, 1967), 216.

86 *"As Gen. MacA's"*: Dwight Eisenhower, Diary, August 10, 1932, in Holt and Leyerzapf, *Pre-War Diaries and Selected Papers* , 233.

86 *had happily followed:* The best accounts of Eisenhower's time in the Philippines are, by far: Jean Edwards Smith, *Eisenhower in War and Peace* (Random House, 2012), for a well-composed human portrait of Eisenhower's development during this period; Carlo D'Este, *A Soldier's Life* (Holt, 2002), for his examination of Eisenhower's professional thinking; and Geoffrey Perret, *Eisenhower* (Random House, 1999) for the most incisive and balanced evaluation of Eisenhower and MacArthur's relationship. But for those interested in a deeper dive, the period comes across most vividly in Eisenhower's own diaries and correspondence, which are collected in Holt and Leyerzapf, eds., *Pre-War Diaries and Selected Papers*.

86 *a field marshal*: Dwight Eisenhower, Diary, July 1, 1937, in Holt and Leyerzapf, *Pre-War Diaries and Selected Papers*, 325–26.

86 *"conceited little monkey"*: Eisenhower, Diary, October 8, 1937, in Holt and Leyerzapf, 360–61.

86 *Eisenhower left the Philippines*: Dwight Eisenhower, Diary, March 9, 1939, in Daniel Holt and James Leyerzapf, eds., *Eisenhower: The Pre-War Diaries and Selected Papers* (Johns Hopkins University Press, 1998), 422.

86 *The only thing*: Dwight Eisenhower to John Eisenhower, August 7, 1943, Pre-Pres. Principal, box 173.

86 *racked with self-pity:* D. Clayton James, General John H. Chiles Oral History Interview, July 27, 1977, HST, Oral History Interviews.

86 *"superior professional ability"*: Douglas MacArthur to Dwight Eisenhower, December 9, 1939, Pre-Pres. Principal, box 74.

87 *MacArthur took it:* Forrest Pogue, interview with Dwight Eisenhower, June 28, 1962, GCM, Forrest Pogue Interviews.

87 *"abolish all personally assigned"*: Dwight Eisenhower to Mark Clark, December 27, 1943, Pre-Pres. Principal, box 23.

CHAPTER 10

88 *Churchill was looking:* John Colville, *The Fringes of Power* (Hodder & Stoughton, 1985), 75–76.

88 *The only concern:* Walter B. Smith to Dwight Eisenhower, January 5, 1944, Smith Papers, box 19.

88 *Eisenhower left after lunch:* Butcher Diary, A-970.

88 *Beetle had spent:* Walter B. Smith to George Marshall, December 24, 1943, Smith Papers, box 15.

88 *As far as Roosevelt:* Elliott Roosevelt, *As He Saw It* (Duell, Sloan & Pearce, 1946), 89.

88 *Roosevelt's suspicions:* Roosevelt, 113–15.

89 *"a direct slap"*: Smith to Marshall, December 24, 1943.

89 *very first time:* Dwight Eisenhower, *At Ease: Stories I Tell to Friends* (Doubleday, 1967), 208–209.

89 *This disagreement over:* Butcher Diary, A-964.

90 *Everything felt off:* Dwight Eisenhower, *Letters to Mamie* (Doubleday, 1977), 159.

90 *Mamie's parents:* Dwight Eisenhower to John Doud, December 26, 1943, 1943-12-26, *9, Pre-Pres. Principal, box 171.

90 *vodka and cigarettes:* Walter B. Smith to Aleksandr Vasilevsky, December 20, 1943, Pre-Pres. Principal, box 109.

90 *Roosevelt agreed:* Franklin Roosevelt to Dwight Eisenhower, December 26, 1943, Pre-Pres. Principal, box 100.

90 *a lengthy cable*: Dwight Eisenhower to George Marshall, December 27, 1943, in Butcher Diary, A-964.
90 *last press conference*: Transcript of Press Conference, December 27, 1943, NARA, RG 331, 1, box 14.
92 *Eisenhower's quirks:* SHAEF, Verbatim Transcript of General Eisenhower's Press Conference, 1100 Hours 20 Grosvenor Square, January 17, 1944, *110, Davis Papers, box 59.
92 *shared with Roosevelt*: David Kennedy, *Freedom from Fear* (Oxford University Press, 1999), 138.
93 *pulled him aside:* Butcher Diary, A-970.
93 *meeting with De Gaulle*: D. K. R. Croswell, *Beetle: The Life of Walter Bedell Smith* (University of Kentucky Press, 2010), 546.
93 *Alex's instructor:* Conference with General Eisenhower, April 24, 1947, Pre-Pres. Principal, box 68.
93 *met Monty*: Dwight Eisenhower, Diary, May 27, 1942, in *The Eisenhower Diaries* (Norton, 1981), 59.
93 *reached for a Camel*: Mark Clark, *Calculated Risk* (Harper 1950), 19.
94 *"German communications"*: Kenneth Davis, interview with Arthur Tedder, 1944, Davis Papers, box 94.
94 *assess Monty objectively:* Eisenhower, Memorandum, June 3, 1944, *27, Pre-Pres. Principal, box 137.
94 *Monty was, despite:* Forrest Pogue, interview with Miles Dempsey, March 12-13, 1947, Pogue Papers, box 161; Forrest Pogue, interview with Charles L. Bolte, May 28, 1958, GCM, Forrest Pogue Interviews.
94 *to remind everyone:* George S. Patton, Diary, September 29, 1943, Patton Papers, box 3.
94 *"down to the last shoelace"*: Robert Sherwood, "Meeting with Admiral Ernest J. King in His Office at the Navy Department," May 24, 1946, Sherwood Papers, box 40.
94 *asked Monty:* Dwight Eisenhower to George Marshall, February 8, 1944, Smith Papers, box 27; Dwight Eisenhower to Hastings Ismay, December 3, 1960, EL, Whitman Name File, box 19.
94 *villa in Marrakesh:* Butcher Diary, A-981.
94 *greatest patron:* Forrest Pogue, interview with Andrew Thorne, January 28, 1947, Pogue Papers, box 161.
94 *The previous May:* Memorandum by the Combined Staff Planners, May 25, 1943, FRUS, *Conferences at Washington and Quebec 1943*, Doc. 99.
95 *"Atlantikwall"*: Headquarters, First US Army, After Action Against Enemy, Reports After/After Action Report, August 6, 1944, EL, U.S. Army, First Army Headquarters: Records, 1943–55, box 2; Anthony Saunders, Hitler's Atlantic Wall (Sutton, 2001); Chris McNab, *Hitler's Fortifications* (Osprey Press, 2014), 136.
95 *142 million square meters*: Saunders, *Hitler's Atlantic Wall*, 22.
95 *lead sentry: Erwin Rommel:* Theodore Gatchel, *The Water's Edge* (Naval Institute Press, 2013), 24.
95 *Freddie Morgan's planners:* Operation "OVERLORD," J.C.S. 442, August 5, 1943, GCM, George Elsey Papers, Box 1; Dwight D.Eisenhower, *Report by the Supreme Commander*, 1–2.
96 *Freddie Morgan's concept:* Kenneth Davis, interview with Frederick E. Morgan, August 6, 1944, Davis Papers, box 94.
96 *the COSSAC plan:* Operation "OVERLORD," J.C.S. 442, August 5, 1943, GCM, George Elsey Papers, box 1.
96 *had first seen:* Dwight Eisenhower to George Marshall, February 8, 1944, Smith Papers, box 27; Dwight Eisenhower, Memorandum, February 7, 1944, in Butcher Diary, A-1062.
96 *"fairly weak"*: SLA Marshall, Interview with Dwight Eisenhower, June 3, 1946, Pogue Papers, box 161.
96 *the wrong lessons:* Dwight Eisenhower to George Marshall, February 8, 1944, Smith Papers, Box 27; Dwight D. Eisenhower, *Report by the Supreme Commander*, 3.
97 *The assumption that the Germans:* "Operation Overlord—Outline Plan, Annex: Comparison of Our Own Build-up with the German Rate of Reinforcement," August 10, 1943, NARA, RG 331, entry 1, box 76.
97 *bigger and wider:* Eisenhower to Marshall, February 8, 1944.
97 *Beetle felt:* Forrest Pogue, interview with Walter B. Smith, May 9, 1947, Pogue Papers, box 161.
97 *Monty arrived:* Bernard Montgomery to Alan Brooke, December 28, 1943, in *Master of the Battlefield* (McGraw Hill, 1983), 475–76.
98 *Churchill wanted:* Carlo D'Este, *Decision Normandy* (Konecky & Konecky, 1983), 57.
98 *"head soldier"*: Montgomery to Brooke, December 28, 1943.
98 *The COSSAC plan:* COSSAC, Operation "OVERLORD," J.C.S. 4421, August 6, 1943, GCM, George Elsey Papers, box 1.
98 *"British and Canadian"*: Franklin Roosevelt to Winston Churchill, December 23, 1943, Smith Papers, box 15.
98 *Monty loved:* Montgomery to Brooke, December 28, 1943.
98 *"War is history"*: Lord Taylor, Interview with Field Marshall Montgomery, Memorial University of Newfoundland, Media & Data Center, No. L-3606.
98 *"fairly weak"*: Dwight Eisenhower to Hastings Ismay, December 3, 1960, EL, Whitman Name File, box 19.
98 *"I'd like to"*: Walter B. Smith, *Eisenhower's Six Great Decisions* (Longmans, 1956), 30.
98 *Monty's reputation:* Forrest Pogue, interview with Sir Arthur Cunningham, February 14, 1947, Pogue Papers, box 161.
99 *"No risks"*: Kenneth Davis, interview with Arthur Tedder, 1944, Davis Papers, box 94.

99 *winning the loyalty:* Forrest Pogue, interview with Dwight Eisenhower, June 28, 1962, GCM, Forrest Pogue Interviews.
99 *in the trenches:* Nigel Hamilton, *The Full Monty* (Penguin, 2002), 50–124.
99 *His only son:* Nigel Hamilton, *The Full Monty*, 254–276, 424–25, 495.
99 *"wasn't interested":* Lord Taylor, Interview with Field Marshall Montgomery, Memorial University of Newfoundland, Media & Data Center, No. L-3606.
99 *"his chaplains":* Colville, *Fringes of Power*, 79.
99 *"to take complete":* Bernard Montgomery, *The Memoirs of Field Marshal Montgomery* (The World Publishing, 1958), 184–85.
99 *work with Beetle:* Walter B. Smith, *Eisenhower's Six Great Decisions* (Longmans, 1956), 30.
99 *Commander's "deputy":* Montgomery to Brooke, December 28, 1943.
99 *Beetle left for London:* Croswell, *Beetle*, 546–47.
99 *Eisenhower caught up:* Dwight Eisenhower, Assorted Letters, December 28, 1943, Pre-Pres. Principal, box 91.
99 *"has full confidence":* Charles de Gaulle to Dwight Eisenhower, December 28, 1943, Pre-Pres. Principal, box 34.
99 *"I do hope":* Dwight Eisenhower to Charles de Gaulle, December 29, 1943, Pre-Pres. Principal, box 34.
100 *"personalities or plans":* Dwight Eisenhower to Jacob Devers, December, 27, 1943, Pre-Pres. Principal, box 34.
100 *"I am looking":* Jacob Devers to Dwight Eisenhower, December 27, 1943, Pre-Pres. Principal, box 34.
100 *"my conceptions":* Dwight Eisenhower to George Marshall, December 28, 1943, Smith Papers, box 19.
100 *an intelligence report:* Butcher Diary, A-968.

CHAPTER 11

101 *"You got everything":* Butcher Diary, A-972.
101 *Marshall's message:* George Marshall to Dwight Eisenhower, December 28, 1943, Smith Papers, box 19.
102 *"With regard":* Dwight Eisenhower to George Marshall, December 29, 1943, Eisenhower Papers, 3:1631.
102 *"Thank you":* Dwight Eisenhower to Jacob Devers, December 29, 1943, Pre-Pres. Principal, box 34.
102 *a second cable:* Dwight Eisenhower to George Marshall, December 29, 1943, Eisenhower Papers, 3:1630.
102 *"You will":* George Marshall to Dwight Eisenhower, December 29, 1943, Smith Papers, box 19.
102 *Before leaving:* The Acting American Representative to the French Committee of National Liberation Algiers (Chapin) to the Secretary of State, June 10, 1944, FRUS 1944, vol. III, doc. 641.
102 *He had met:* Charles de Gaulle, *The Complete War Memoirs of Charles de Gaulle* (Carroll & Graf, 1950), 312.
103 *Eisenhower understood:* Dwight Eisenhower to Lyman L. Lemnitzer, June 17, 1966, private collection.
103 *"War is politics":* Forrest Pogue, interview with Charles de Gaulle, January 14, 1947, Pogue Papers, box 161.
103 *"a most definite":* Charles de Gaulle to Dwight Eisenhower, December 26, 1942, Pre-Pres. Principal, box 34.
103 *Over the previous year:* De Gaulle, *Complete War Memoirs*, 432.
103 "Je suis ici": Charles de Gaulle, *Mémoires de Guerre* (Plon, 1956), 2:115.
103 *From Eisenhower's perspective:* Robert Sherwood, Talk with General Eisenhower at His Office in the Pentagon Building, January 14, 1947, Sherwood Papers, box 40; Dwight Eisenhower to Henri Giraud, December 15, 1943, Smith Papers, box 12.
103 *France under Vichy:* Edwin Wilson, "Policy re Establishment of French Civil Administration in Continental France after Liberation," January 20, 1944, NARA, RG 107, entry 183, box 55.
103 *French army's only tactical victories:* Julian Jackson, *De Gaulle* (Belknap Press, 2018), 103–107; Ray Argyle, *The Paris Game* (Dundurn, 2014), 71–75; Jonathan Fenby, *The General: Charles de Gaulle and the France he Saved* (Skyhorse, 2012), 124–128.
103 *successfully rallied:* Jackson, *De Gaulle*, 145–150; Fenby, *The General*, 150–158.
104 *a death sentence:* Jackson, *De Gaulle*, 157.
104 *the only man:* Edwin Wilson, "Policy re Establishment of French Civil Administration in Continental France after Liberation," January 20, 1944, NARA, RG 107, entry 183, box 55.
104 *"love fest":* Harry Butcher, *My Three Years with Eisenhower* (Simon & Schuster, 1946), 473.
104 *Eisenhower reminisced:* The Acting American Representative to the French Committee of National Liberation Algiers (Chapin) to the Secretary of State, June 10, 1944, FRUS 1944, doc. 641.
104 *"You are a man":* De Gaulle, *Mémoires de Guerre*, 2:647–76.
104 *De Gaulle pledged:* Dwight Eisenhower to George Marshall, December 31, 1943, Pre-Pres. Principal, box 80.
104 "la situation": De Gaulle, *Mémoires de Guerre*, 2:647–76.
104 *Stalling, he spent:* Michael McKeogh and Richard Lockridge, *Sgt. Mickey & General Ike* (Putnam, 1946), 95.
105 *British Chiefs of Staff:* Walter B. Smith to Dwight Eisenhower, December 30, 1943, Pre-Pres. Principal, box 109.

105 *personnel debates:* Dwight Eisenhower to Walter B. Smith, December 31, 1943, Smith Papers, box 27.
105 *All he wanted:* Dwight Eisenhower to George Marshall, December 31, 1943, Pogue Papers, box 154.
105 *As he soaked:* McKeogh and Lockridge, *Sgt. Mickey & General Ike*, 96.
105 *At eleven thirty:* McKeogh and Lockridge, 95.
105 *It was six:* Butcher Diary, A-981.
105 *"The Prime Minister":* SHAEF, Verbatim Transcript of General Eisenhower's Press Conference, 1100 Hours 20 Grosvenor Square, January 17, 1944, Davis Papers, box 59.
105 *Churchill was jovial:* Butcher Diary, at A-981.
106 *"My ADCs":* John Colville, *The Fringes of Power* (Hodder & Stoughton, 1985), 79.
106 *Churchill dominated:* Butcher Diary, A-981.
106 *"acclaimed in the future":* Dwight Eisenhower, manuscript, "Churchill & Marshall," November 17, 1966, EL, Post-Presidential Papers, A-WR Series, box 8.
106 *made Eisenhower uneasy:* Butcher Diary, A-981.
106 *"eccentric operations":* Robert Sherwood, "Meeting with Admiral Ernest J. King in His Office at the Navy Department," May 24, 1946, Sherwood Papers, box 40.
106 *"masterpieces of military art":* Churchill, *World Crisis*, 2:5.
106 *Eisenhower warned Churchill:* Dwight Eisenhower to George Marshall, February 9, 1944, Pre-Pres. Principal, box 80.
106 *If landing craft:* Butcher Diary, A-981.
106 *"balancing the scales":* Dwight Eisenhower, "Churchill & Marshall."
106 *After dinner:* Bernard Montgomery, *The Memoirs of Field Marshal Montgomery* (The World Publishing, 1958), 190.
106 *his prerogative:* Colville, *Fringes of Power*, 459.
106 *Eisenhower left before:* McKeogh and Lockridge, *Sgt. Mickey & General Ike*, 95.
106 *They left Marrakesh:* Butcher Diary, A-982.
107 *"Goodbye, Honey":* Susan Eisenhower, *Mrs. Ike* (Farrar, Straus and Giroux, 1996), 182.
107 *"Because of you":* Dwight Eisenhower, *Letters to Mamie* (Doubleday, 1977), 26.
107 *"Delighted to receive":* Dwight Eisenhower to Mamie Eisenhower, teletype message, December 14, 1943, Pre-Pres. Principal, box 173.
107 *For day-to-day things:* Dwight Eisenhower to Mamie Eisenhower.
107 *he would mention it:* Dwight Eisenhower to John Eisenhower, December 14, 1942, Pre-Pres. Principal, box 173.
107 *"Happy Birthday!!!":* Dwight Eisenhower to Mamie Eisenhower, November 1, 1943, Private Collection.
108 *"Irish":* Dwight Eisenhower to Kay Summersby, June 1944, Sotheby's, Sale 6188, Fine Books and Manuscripts, June 13, 1991, lot 174.
108 *"It was the best":* Dwight Eisenhower to Mamie Eisenhower, November 1, 1943.
108 *"the irrepressible":* "Women in Lifeboats," *Life*, February 22, 1943.
108 *"Don't go bothering":* Eisenhower, *Letters to Mamie*, 97–99.
108 *"Now, Miss Doud":* Susan Eisenhower, *Mrs. Ike*, 34.

CHAPTER 12

111 *the potbellied stove:* Interview with Earl Eisenhower, in Bela Kornitzer, *The Great American Heritage* (Farrar, Straus and Cudahy, 1955), 31.
111 *"Boys!":* Interview with Edgar Eisenhower, in Kornitzer, 31–32.
111 *Mamie's father:* Susan Eisenhower, *Mrs. Ike* (Farrar, Straus and Giroux, 1996), 11.
112 *spent the summer:* E.V. Cutter, Inclosed Charges, October 13, 1921, NARA, RG 159, PC-51 26, box 665.
112 *big man on campus:* Dwight Eisenhower, *At Ease: Stories I Tell to Friends* (Doubleday, 1967), 181.
112 *neighbor's dog:* Mamie Eisenhower to John Doud, January 1921, in Susan Eisenhower, *Mrs. Ike*, 69.
112 *"See you later":* Mamie Eisenhower to John Doud, September 1920, in Susan Eisenhower, 66.
112 *that September:* Mamie Eisenhower to John Doud, September 1920, in Susan Eisenhower, 65–66.
112 *child-size uniform:* Dwight Eisenhower, *At Ease*, 181.
112 *"based on those elements":* S. D. Rockenbach to Dwight Eisenhower, November 15, 1920, Pre-Pres. Misc., box 22.
112 *hired a nanny:* Eisenhower, *At Ease*, 180–181.
112 *They hosted Sunday:* Susan Eisenhower, *Mrs. Ike*, 64.
112 *Eisenhower carried his son:* Mamie Eisenhower to Barbara Thompson, October 21, 1979, in Susan Eisenhower, 67.

113 *Camp Meade's hospital:* Sick Officer's Quarters, Base Hospital, Camp Meade, Maryland, June 12, 1916, NARA, RG 165, Entry 165-WW, box 249.
113 *The hospital put him:* Mamie Eisenhower to Barbara Thompson, October 21, 1979, in Susan Eisenhower, *Mrs. Ike*, 67–68.
113 *Eisenhower's little brothers:* Kenneth Davis, interview with Earl and Kay Eisenhower, 1944, Davis Papers, box 61.
113 *brain of the family:* Interview with Milton Eisenhower in Kornitzer, *Great American Heritage*, 121–22.
113 *developed tonsillitis:* State of Maryland, Certificate of Death, Doud Dwight Eisenhower, January 2, 1921.
113 *She went home:* Mamie Eisenhower to Barbara Thompson, October 21, 1979, in Susan Eisenhower, *Mrs. Ike*, 67–68.
113 *As things turned:* Dwight Eisenhower, *At Ease*, 181.
113 *It was ten p.m.:* Certificate of Death, Doud Dwight Eisenhower.
113 *He raged:* Dwight Eisenhower, *At Ease*, 181.
114 *Mamie couldn't talk:* Mamie Eisenhower to Barbara Thompson, October 21, 1979, in Susan Eisenhower, *Mrs. Ike*, 67.
114 *arrived back home:* Mamie Eisenhower to John Doud, January 1921, in Susan Eisenhower, *Mrs. Ike*, 68.
114 *The bitterest one:* Dwight Eisenhower to John Doud, January 29, 1921, in Susan Eisenhower, 69.
114 *Eisenhower started working:* Mamie Eisenhower to John Doud, January 31, 1921, in Susan Eisenhower, 70.
114 "Insurmountable": Dwight Eisenhower to Louis Marx, January 27, 1948, Pre-Pres. Papers, Box 81.
114 *He would come:* Mamie Eisenhower to John Doud, January 31, 1921, in Susan Eisenhower, *Mrs. Ike*, 70.
114 *was abruptly closed:* Eli Helmick to Chief of Staff, December 12, 1921, NARA, RG 159, PC-51 26, box 665.
114 *"for duty as executive officer":* John J. Pershing, Order, December 7, 1912, Pre-Pres. Principal, box 190.
115 *Mamie hated it:* Virginia Conner, *What Father Forbade* (Dorrance, 1951), 120.
115 *sat atop:* Panama Canal Zone—Camp Gaillard, 1924, NARA, RG 18, entry 18-AA-106-59, box 106.
115 *The only road:* Fox Conner, Camp Gaillard—Pedro Miguel Road, December 18, 1923, NARA, RG 395, NM-94, box 4.
115 *its brown wood:* Camp Gaillard, NARA, RG 18, entry 18-AA-106-59, box 106.
115 *Mamie was pregnant:* Susan Eisenhower, *Mrs. Ike*, 75–77.
115 *Their unhappiness together:* Conner, *What Father Forbade*, 120.
115 *Mamie had enough:* Susan Eisenhower, *Mrs. Ike*, 78.
115 *Camp Gaillard's clinic:* Clark Blance, Repairs of Hospital, September 19, 1924, NARA, RG 395, NM-94, box 4.
115 *Mamie was concerned:* Conner, *What Father Forbade*, 120.
115 *most of all, boring:* Farrand Sayre to Commanding General, June 28, 1921, Pre-Pres. Misc. box 22.
115 *first Marine encampments:* Russ Stayanoff, "MG Fox Conner: Soldier, Mentor, Enigma," Masters Thesis, Norwich University, 2007, 74–75.
116 *decommissioned USS* Iowa: James Totten, Firing on U.S.S. ex-Iowa, March 13, 1923, NARA, RG 395, NM-94, box 4.
116 *All sorts of people:* Farrand Sayre to Commanding General, June 28, 1921, Pre-Pres. Misc. box 22.
116 *sodomy "crisis":* James Totten, "Courts-Martial—Offenses Involving Abnormal Sexual Relations," September 13, 1924, NARA, RG 395, NM-94, box 1.
116 *A rigid man:* Russ Stayanoff, "MG Fox Conner: Soldier, Mentor, Enigma," Masters Thesis, Norwich University, 2007, 71–72.
116 *the Confederate army:* Stephen Rabalais, *General Fox Conner* (Casemate, 2016), at 12–18.
116 *"If you don't vote":* George Chynoweth to George Pappas, October 24, 1967, USAHEC, Chynoweth Papers, box 3.
116 *"hatchet man":* Russ Stayanoff, "MG Fox Conner: Soldier, Mentor, Enigma," Masters Thesis, Norwich University, 2007, 71.
116 *daily chore:* Cole Kingseed, "Mentoring General Ike," *Military Review*, PB 100-90-10, vol. 70, no. 10 (October 1990): 28.
116 *never called him:* Dwight Eisenhower to Fox Conner, January 3, 1949, Pre-Pres. Principal, box 27.
117 *"I'll tell you":* George Chynoweth to George Pappas, October 24, 1967, USAHEC, Chynoweth Papers, box 3.
117 *Army War College:* William Aldrich, "Fox Conner," Military Studies Program Paper, 1993, 18.
117 *"Shakespeare undoubtedly":* Eisenhower, *At Ease*, 187.
117 *a massive library:* Edward Cox to Michel Paradis, June 8, 2021, private collection.
117 *As they chatted:* Eisenhower, *At Ease*, 182–87.
118 *Nearly every day:* Conner, *What Father Forbade*, 120.
118 *They both chain-smoked:* Stephen Rabalais, *General Fox Conner*, 24–26.

118 *In the evenings:* Dwight Eisenhower to Mamie Eisenhower, June 3, 1922, in Susan Eisenhower, *Mrs. Ike*, 78.
118 *Eisenhower redecorated:* Relam Morin, interview with Dwight Eisenhower, August 5, 1965, EL, 1965 Principal File, box 2.
118 *Frederick the Great's 1757 victory:* Eisenhower, *At Ease*, 182–87.
119 *Eisenhower studied:* Dwight Eisenhower et al., "War and its Principles, Methods, and Doctrines: Course at the Army War College, 1927–1928," February 27, 1928, USAHEC, AWC Curricular Archives, Command Course, File 347, 1–4.
119 *"It is an art":* Johannes von Seeckt, *Command and Combat Use of Combined Arms, German Field Service Regulations, September 1, 1921* (N&M Press, 2021/1925), 5, 151.
119 *It all illustrated:* Eisenhower et al., "War and its Principles."
119 *One of the titles:* Eisenhower, *At Ease*, 182–87.
119 *The journo-pugilist:* Jennifer Ratner-Rosenhagen, *American Nietzsche* (University of Chicago Press, 2012), 58–74.
119 *"Convictions are more dangerous":* H. L. Mencken, *Gist of Nietzsche* (Luce & Co., 1910), 2–3.
119 *"Warfare prepares":* Mencken, 25–26.
120 *"Always take":* Eisenhower, *At Ease*, 182–87.
120 *"A few men":* Press Relations Section, G-2, Hq., "First Corps Area, U.S. Army, General Fox Conner, New England's Army Commander, Completes Forty Years Service Friday," June 15, 1934, Pershing Papers box 52.
120 *"In spite of":* Ralph Ernest Jones, *Principles of Command* (Riker's, 1922), 3.
120 *"General":* Dwight D. Eisenhower, "Command in War," Speech Delivered to the National War College, October 30, 1950, EL, Pre-Presidential Speeches.
120 *Conner had planned:* Aldrich, "Fox Conner," 16; "General Fox Conner, New England's Army Commander, Completes Forty Years Service"; Russ Stayanoff, "MG Fox Conner: Soldier, Mentor, Enigma," Masters Thesis, Norwich University, 2007, 40–49.
120 *He had been wounded:* "General Fox Conner, New England's Army Commander, Completes Forty Years Service."
120 *arrived in Europe:* Fox Conner, "Divisional Organization," *Infantry Journal* 39, no. 2 (May–June 1933).
121 *"The ulterior motives":* Fox Conner, "The Allied High Command and Allied Unity of Direction," March 19, 1934, USAHEC, AWC Curricular Archives, Conduct of War Course, 29–30.
121 *"how do you get":* Charles Brown, Interview with Dwight Eisenhower, in Charles Brown, "Fox Conner: A General's General," *Journal of Mississippi History,* Vol. 49, No. 3 (Aug. 1987), at 179–202.
121 *The Great War:* Russ Stayanoff, "MG Fox Conner: Soldier, Mentor, Enigma," Masters Thesis, Norwich University, 2007, 45–46.
121 *"nothing short of a genius":* Dwight Eisenhower, *At Ease*, at 195.
121 *"When war comes":* Forrest Pogue, interview with Dwight Eisenhower, June 28, 1962, GCM, Forrest Pogue Interviews.
121 *"The Treaty of Versailles":* Oral History Research Office, Eisenhower Administration: John S.D. Eisenhower, 1973, Columbia Center on Oral History, p. 22.
121 *"Goddammit":* Pogue, interview with Eisenhower, June 28, 1962.
121 *Eisenhower felt a lifelong:* Dwight Eisenhower to Fox Conner, October 7, 1948, Pre-Pres. Principal, box 27; Dwight Eisenhower to Fox Conner, January 3, 1949, Pre-Pres. Principal, box 27.
121 *returned from Panama:* Dwight D. Eisenhower 201 File (copy), EL, Howard Snyder Papers, box 2.
121 *used his magic:* Fox Conner to Adjutant General, August 15, 1924, Pre-Pres. Misc. box 22.
121 *It was where:* Mark Bender, *Watershed at Leavenworth* (CSI Special Studies 1990), 51.
122 *"You will recall":* Eisenhower, *At Ease*, 201.
122 *writing to Georgie:* George Patton to Dwight Eisenhower, July 9, 1926, Pre-Pres. Principal, box 91.
122 *"Gee" Gerow was also:* Bender, *Watershed at Leavenworth*, 45.
122 *in San Antonio:* Kenneth Davis, interview with Jim Broym, 1944, Davis Papers, box 94.
122 *"woman hater":* Susan Eisenhower, *Mrs. Ike*, 34.
122 *"the prettiest girl":* Cole Kingseed, "Ike and Gladys—The Summer of 1915," *Assembly* 52, no. 1 (September 2009): 18–20.
122 *intense summer romance:* Gladys Harding, Diary, EL, Gladys Harding Papers, box 1.
122 *Eisenhower introduced him:* Davis, interview with Broym, 1944.
122 *Back together at Leavenworth:* Bender, *Watershed at Leavenworth*, 45.
122 *"Congratulations":* John Doud, Telegram to Dwight Eisenhower, June 16, 1926, Pre-Pres. Principal, box 171.
122 *"stop thinking":* Patton to Eisenhower, July 9, 1926.
122 *deny studying:* Bender, *Watershed at Leavenworth*, 51.
122 *He was plagued:* Dwight D. Eisenhower, Medical Records, EL, Howard Snyder Papers, box 2.

122 *"a neurotic element"*: Dwight D. Eisenhower, Medical Records, November 11, 1932, EL, Howard Snyder Papers, box 2.
122 *"a dying frog"*: Howard Snyder, "Manila, P.I.—1938," August 13, 1959, EL, Howard Synder Papers, box 2.
123 *regular social circle:* Kenneth Davis, interview with Milton and Helen Eisenhower, 1944, Davis Papers, box 61.
123 *"Club Eisenhower"*: Susan Eisenhower, *Mrs. Ike*, 128.
123 *"Has someone gone"*: Dwight Eisenhower, manuscript, "Churchill & Marshall," November 17, 1966, Post-Presidential Papers, A-WR Series, box 8.
123 *drove together:* Butcher Diary, A-982-A-983.

CHAPTER 13

124 *old Munitions Building:* Ray S. Cline, *The War Department Washington Command Post: The Operations Division* (GPO, 1951), 166.
124 *To maintain secrecy:* Butcher Diary, A-983.
124 *"This is something"*: Forrest Pogue, interview with Dwight Eisenhower, June 28, 1962, GCM, Forrest Pogue Interviews.
124 *Marshall wanted it:* Robert Sherwood, Memorandum of Interview with William Leahy, September 13, 1943, Sherwood Papers, box 38.
124 *McCarthy was scheduled:* Forrest Pogue, interview with Frank McCarthy, September 29, 1958, GCM, Forrest Pogue Interviews.
125 *"wholeheartedly"*: Robert E. Sherwood, *Roosevelt and Hopkins* (Harper, 1948), 803.
125 *to appoint Eisenhower:* Robert Sherwood, interview with Henry Lewis Stimson, October 23, 1946, Sherwood Papers, box 40; Pogue, interview with Harry Truman, November 14, 1960, GCM, Forrest Pogue Interviews; Pogue, interview with Eleanor Roosevelt, March 17, 1958, GCM, Forrest Pogue Interviews.
125 *Eisenhower had kept:* Dwight Eisenhower to George Marshall, December 17, 1943, Pre-Pres. Principal, box 80.
125 *"Well, you're not"*: Dwight Eisenhower, manuscript, "Churchill & Marshall," November 17, 1966, Post-Presidential Papers, A-WR Series, box 8.
125 *matter least*: Henry Stimson, diary, December 17, 1943, Yale University, Henry Lewis Stimson Papers, MS 456, Series 14, Reel 8U.
125 *always admired most:* Ed Edwin, Eisenhower Project: Dwight D. Eisenhower, 1970, Oral History Research Office, Columbia University, p. 43.
125 *"all out"*: Butcher Diary, A-1132.
125 *"Any questions"*: Eisenhower, "Churchill & Marshall."
126 *the Alibi Club:* Butcher Diary, A-983.
126 *George Kenney:* George C. Kenney, *General Kenney Reports* (Duell, Sloan and Pearce, 1949), 342–43.
126 *Bernard Baruch:* Butcher Diary, A-983.
126 *met Baruch:* Dwight Eisenhower, "War Policies," *Cavalry Journal* 45, no. 168 (December 1931): 25–298.
126 *had come to Washington*: Dwight D. Eisenhower, 201 File (copy), EL, Synder Papers, box 2.
126 *War Policies Commission*: Pub. Res. No. 98, 71st Cong., June 27, 1930.
126 *two weeks' worth of testimony:* Hearing before the Commission appointed under the authority of public resolution no. 98, 71st Congress, 2d session (H.J. Res. 251) March 5–18, 1931.
127 *Marshall interrupted:* Butcher Diary, A-983.
127 *"I truly don't"*: Kenney, *General Kenney Reports*, 287–94.
127 *about the ice cream:* Butcher Diary, A-983.
128 *4.5 million man-days*: Byron Fairchild & Jonathan Grossman, *The Army and Industrial Manpower*, CMH Pub. 1-8 (GPO, 1959), 74–75.

CHAPTER 14

129 *That night, Eisenhower's buzz:* Frank McCarthy to Joseph Brown, January 5, 1944, GCM, McCarthy Papers, Box 10; Butcher Diary, A-986.
129 *But in 1942:* Dwight Eisenhower to John Eisenhower, September 24, 1942, Pre-Pres. Principal, box 173.
129 *Eisenhower had first pulled:* Dwight Eisenhower, *At Ease* (Doubleday, 1967), 4.
129 *a tall, gawky:* Relman Morin, interview with Dwight Eisenhower, August 5, 1965, EL, 1965 Principal File, box 2.
129 *a free education:* Dwight Eisenhower, *At Ease*, 104.
129 *he had dreamed:* John Long to Earl Endacott, March 21, 1966, EL, Endacott Papers, box 4.

129 *"I had never"*: SLA Marshall, Eulogy for Eisenhower, 1969, SLAM Papers, box 71.
129 *"not a decision"*: Dwight Eisenhower to Walter B. Smith, July 5, 1947, SLAM Papers, box 95.
130 *"plebe life"*: Charles King, "West Point As It Was and Is," *Saturday Evening Post* 173, no. 31 (February 2, 1901).
130 *"was dominated"*: "The Cry for Football Reform," *Literary Digest*, January 13, 1906, p. 41.
130 *No one from Abilene*: Morin, interview with Eisenhower, August 5, 1965.
130 *Howe had given*: Kenneth Davis, interview with Paul Royer, 1944, Davis Papers, box 61.
130 *"the small town"*: Joe W. Howe, Dwight D. Eisenhower, undated, Davis Papers, box 22.
130 Life of Hannibal: Joe W. Howe, "Dwight D. Eisenhower," undated, Davis Papers, box 22.
130 *"Knights of Honor"*: Davis, interview with Royer, 1944.
130 *"Bums of the Lawsy Lou"*: Leila Grace Picking, OH-7, January 27, 1965, EL, Oral Histories.
130 *In his senior year*: Frank Hodges, Banquet of the Young Men's Democratic Club, November 9, 1909, Abilene, KS, HST, President's Secretary's Files, Frank Hodges File.
130 *"The Student in Politics"*: Dwight Eisenhower, "The Student in Politics," *Dickinson County News*, November 18, 1909.
131 *a handshake agreement*: Kenneth Davis, Interview with Edgar Eisenhower and Charlie Chase, 1944, Davis Papers, box 61.
131 *That left Eisenhower*: Swede Hazlett, to Alden Hatch, 1944, Pre-Pres. Principal, box 56.
131 *still playing football*: Walter Barbash, Interview with Orin Snider, October 6, 1964, EL Oral Histories.
131 *Eisenhower remained friends*: Kenneth Davis, interview with Paul Royer, 1944, Davis Papers, box 61.
131 *By chance, an old*: Swede Hazlett to Alden Hatch, 1944, Pre-Pres. Principal, box 56.
131 *Swede traveled*: Eisenhower to Swede Hazlett, October 11, 1941, Pre-Pres. Principal, box 56.
131 *indirectly known Harger*: Charles Harger, "The Eisenhower I Know," *The American Magazine* 152, no. 5 (November 1951).
132 *"What chance"*: Swede Hazlett to Alden Hatch, 1944, Pre-Pres. Principal, box 56.
132 *Eisenhower gave it a shot*: Dwight Eisenhower to Joseph Bristow, August 20, 1910, Kansas Historical Society, Joseph Bristow Papers, box 31. The correspondence with Bristow is largely well-preserved likely because Bristow ultimately did give him the appointment. No records have been found reflecting his correspondence with the other Kansas congressmen, such as Representative Reeder who gave his appointment to John H. Dykes, the son of the head of Kansas State Medical Board. "Two Kansas Boys are New Eligible for West Point," *Salina Semi-Weekly Journal*, February 16, 1911, 1.
132 *went to local businessmen*: George Sterl to Joseph Bristow, August 23, 1910, Pre-Pres. Misc. box 22.
132 *"your application"*: Secretary to Senator Brisow to Dwight Eisenhower, August 22, 1910, Kansas Historical Society, Joseph Bristow Papers, box 3.
132 *competitive exam*: "Competitive Exams for Two Academies," *Topeka Daily Capital*, August 26, 1910, p. 4.
132 *sent another letter*: Dwight Eisenhower to Joseph Bristow, September 3, 1910, Kansas Historical Society, Joseph Bristow Papers, box 3.
132 *Bristow wrote back*: Joseph Bristow to Dwight Eisenhower, September 5, 1910, Kansas Historical Society, Joseph Bristow Papers, box 31.
132 *would forever credit*: Eisenhower to Hazlett, October 11, 1941.
132 *He scored second*: G. T. Fairchild to Joseph Bristow, October 22, 1910, Kansas Historical Society, Joseph Bristow Papers, box 32.
132 *"as my nominee"*: Joseph Bristow to Dwight Eisenhower, October 24, 1910, Kansas Historical Society, Joseph Bristow Papers, box 32.
133 *"not looking"*: Swede Hazlett to Kenneth Davis, 1944, Davis Papers, box 61.
133 *He left Abilene*: Oral History Research Office, Eisenhower Administration: The Reminiscences of Milton Eisenhower, 1979, Columbia Center on Oral History, p. 24.
133 *the largest class*: "164 West Point Grads," *Washington Post*, June 13, 1915, p. 1.
133 *"the class the stars"*: Michael Haskew, *West Point 1915* (Zenith Press, 2014).
133 *When he reached*: Morin, interview with Eisenhower, August 5, 1965.
133 *"What am I"*: Dwight Eisenhower, *At Ease: Stories I Tell to Friends* (Doubleday, 1967), 62.
133 *His clothes were cheap*: Kenneth Davis, Interview with Edgar Eisenhower and Charlie Chase, 1944, Davis Papers, box 61.
133 *march in time*: Dwight Eisenhower, *At Ease*, 8.
134 *acquired a swagger*: Alexander Weyand, "The Athletic Cadet Eisenhower," *Assembly*, Spring 1968, at 65.
134 *crooned*: "From Plebe to President (Ike as His Classmates Remember Him)," *Colliers*, June 10, 1955, 92–97.
134 *With his gang*: Joe W. Howe, "Dwight D. Eisenhower," undated, Davis Papers, box 22.
134 *inseparable as kids*: Oral History Research Office, Eisenhower Administration: Milton Eisenhower, 1973, Columbia Center on Oral History, p. 72.

134 *minstrel characters:* "Aunt Sukie's Santa Claus," *New York Evening Post*, December 13, 1902.
134 *Cotter published:* Joseph Cotter, *A White Song and a Black Song* (Bradley & Gilbert Co., 1909), 56.
134 *"Little Ike"*: Helianthus '09 (Yearbook), 1909, EL, Museum Manuscripts Transferred to the Library, 1969–1981, box 3.
134 *At West Point:* Interview with Edgar Eisenhower in Bela Kornitzer, *The Great American Heritage* (Farrar, Straus and Cudahy, 1955), 251.
134 *The quintessential Ike:* Ralph Connor, *The Prospector* (Revell, 1904).
134 *Eisenhower relished:* Eisenhower, *At Ease*, 22, 89; "From Plebe to President (Ike as His Classmates Remember Him)," *Colliers*, June 10, 1955, 92–97.
135 *"Nothing was said"*: Carlo D'Este, *Eisenhower* (Henry Holt, 2002), 65.
135 "he loved": William Morrison, Interview with Henry Araund, February 25, 1977, USAHEC, Henry S. Aurand Papers, Folder 1, 11.
135 *the academic side:* Dwight Eisenhower to J. Franklin Bell, February 14, 1967, Post-Presidential Papers, Convening File, 1945–1969, box 1.
135 *F Company:* Kenneth Davis, interview with John Eisenhower, 1944, Davis Papers, box 61.
135 *played in Abilene:* Walter Barbash, Interview with Orin Snider, October 6, 1964, EL Oral Histories; Kenneth Davis, Interview with John Eisenhower, 1944, Davis Papers, box 61; Helianthus 1909, EL, Museum Manuscripts Transferred to the Library, 1969–1981, box 3.
135 *as a sophomore:* Eisenhower, *At Ease*, 13.
135 *West Point won:* West Point, *The Howitzer*, 1913 (West Point yearbook), Davis Papers, box 61.
135 *reputation as a line smasher:* "Eisenhower Can't Play," *Abilene Weekly Chronicle*, October 8, 1913, p. 8.
135 *Army v. Carlisle:* David Maraniss, *Path Lit by Lightning* (Simon & Schuster, 2022), 183–199; Steve Sheinkin, *Undefeated* (Roaring Brook, 2017), at 199–207; Lars Anderson, *Carlisle vs. Army* (Random House, 2007).
135 *"athletic marvel"*: "Thorpe's Indians Crush West Point," *New York Times*, November 10, 1912, p. S1.
136 *"high-low"*: Kenneth Davis, interview with Earl and Kay Eisenhower, 1944, Davis Papers, box 61.
136 *knocked their heads:* Ann Whitman, Diary, 1960, EL, Whitman Diary, box 11.
136 *Carlisle won:* "Thorpe's Indians Crush West Point."
136 *His hero was Honus:* Michael Beschloss, "Eisenhower's Baseball Secret," *New York Times*, July 18, 2014.
136 *poorly guarded secret:* Robert L. Schilz, Memo, EL, Ann Whitman File, box 19.
136 *knocked in the knee:* Morin, interview with Eisenhower, August 5, 1965.
136 *"Blue Devils"*: Dwight Eisenhower to Ruby Norman, November 24, 1913, EL, Ruby Norman Lucier Papers, box 1.
137 *to Argentina after graduation:* Oral History Research Office, Eisenhower Administration: Milton Eisenhower, 1973, Columbia Center on Oral History, p. 104.
137 *"entrancing than Europe"*: Morin, interview with Eisenhower, August 5, 1965.
137 *"people—Gauchos"*: T. C. Harbaugh, "The Pampas Hunters," *Beadle's Boy's Library of Sport, Story and Adventure*, no. 48 (December 3, 1899).
137 *"Pan-American Era"*: John Barrett, "The Pan-American Era," *Saturday Evening Post*, October 10, 1914, 12.
137 *As he recovered:* Eisenhower, *At Ease*, 23–26.
137 *His best friend:* Davis, interview with John Eisenhower, 1944.
137 *developed a reputation:* Oral History Research Office, Recollections of Dwight Eisenhower by Omar Bradley, 1966, Columbia Center on Oral History.
137 *"At one time"*: West Point, *The Howitzer*, 1915.
137 *He coached:* Eisenhower, *At Ease*, 23–26.
137 *rumors circulated:* Dwight Eisenhower to Charles Harger, December 4, 1946, Pre-Pres. Principal, box 55.
137 *West Point's quick adoption:* Eisenhower, *At Ease*, 23–26.
137 *made an assistant coach: Annual Report of the Army Athletic Council, 1913–1916*, 1916.
138 *turn a blind eye:* Morin, interview with Eisenhower, August 5, 1965.
138 *"football, perhaps more"*: Eisenhower, *At Ease*, 16.
138 *"A football team"*: Brigadier General Edward L. King, Lecture Delivered by Brigadier General Edward L. King, Commandant, the General Service Schools to the Command and General Staff School, Fort Leavenworth, Kansas, September 11, 1925 (Fort Leavenworth, KS: GS Schools, September 22, 1925), 201.
138 *"The all important"*: Ernest Graves, *The Line Man's Bible* (1921), 23, 133–34, 148.
138 *"Master every detail"*: Walter Camp, *Football Without a Coach* (Appleton, 1920), 21, 37–38, 41–42.
138 *"All right"*: Graves, *Line Man's Bible*, 150.
138 *son at West Point:* Dwight Eisenhower to John Eisenhower, November 20, 1942, Pre-Pres. Principal, box 173.
138 *Doolittle's son:* Dwight Eisenhower to Jimmy Doolittle, March 3, 1943, Pre-Pres. Principal, box 35.
139 *a surrogate father:* Swede Hazlett, Milton Eisenhower to Kenneth Davis, 1944, Davis Papers, box 61.
139 *"This place made"*: Kenneth Davis, interview with John Eisenhower, 1944.

139 *"I want you"*: Forrest Pogue, interview with Dwight Eisenhower, June 28, 1962, GCM, Forrest Pogue Interviews.
139 *The indignity of it:* Dwight Eisenhower, diary, March 21, 1942, in *The Eisenhower Diaries* (Norton, 1981), at 52.
139 *gone to visit John:* Oral History Research Office, Eisenhower Administration: John S. D. Eisenhower, 1973, Columbia Center on Oral History, p. 22.
139 *running a fever:* Susan Eisenhower, *Mrs. Ike* (Farrar, Straus and Giroux, 1996), 181.
139 *"What's your job"*: Oral History Research Office, Eisenhower Administration: John S. D. Eisenhower, 1973, Columbia Center on Oral History, p. 24.
140 *Eisenhower was giddy:* Dwight Eisenhower to John Eisenhower, July 24, 1941, Pre-Pres. Principal, box 173.
140 *John would say:* Oral History Research Office, Eisenhower Administration: John S. D. Eisenhower, 1973, Columbia Center on Oral History, p. 6.
140 *Eisenhower was delighted:* Dwight Eisenhower to John Eisenhower, September 20, 1943, Pre-Pres. Principal, box 173.
140 *to share and offered:* Dwight Eisenhower to John Eisenhower, September 20, 1943.
140 *"The only unforgivable"*: Dwight Eisenhower to John Eisenhower, May 22, 1943, Pre-Pres. Principal, box 173.
140 *"because someday"*: Dwight Eisenhower to John Eisenhower, November 20, 1942, Pre-Pres. Principal, box 173.
140 *Marshall's private train:* Davis, interview with John Eisenhower, 1944.
140 *bring him some whiskey:* Frank McCarthy to Richard Harris, January 5, 1944, GCM, McCarthy Papers, box 10.
140 *Francis Wilby:* Dwight Eisenhower to Francis Wilby, May 24, 1944, Pre-Pres. Principal, box 124.
140 *fresh haircut:* Frank McCarthy to Joseph Brown, January 5, 1944, GCM, McCarthy Papers, box 10.
140 *John had not been told:* Butcher Diary, A-986.
140 *two inches taller:* Eisenhower to Hazlett, October 11, 1941.
140 *few pounds leaner:* Davis, interview with John Eisenhower, 1944.
140 *chronic ear issue:* John Eisenhower to Dwight Eisenhower, December 3, 1942, Pre-Pres. Principal, box 173.
140 *His eyesight:* Davis, interview with John Eisenhower, 1944.
140 *gained some weight:* Dwight Eisenhower, *Letters to Mamie* (Doubleday, 1977), 162.
140 *tended to tense up:* Davis, interview with John Eisenhower, 1944.
140 *"little afraid"*: Davis, interview with John Eisenhower, 1944.
141 *Eisenhower's temper:* John Eisenhower, *Strictly Personal*, 8–9.
141 *"Mother makes the house"*: Davis, interview with John Eisenhower, 1944.
141 *"Please don't take"*: Dwight Eisenhower to John Eisenhower, December 1, 1942, Pre-Pres. Principal, box 173.
141 *incurably impatient:* John Eisenhower, *Strictly Personal* (Doubleday, 1974), 8–9.
141 *"Infantry or artillery"*: Davis, interview with Mamie Eisenhower, 1944, Davis Papers, box 94.
141 *John was almost reticent:* Davis, interview with John Eisenhower, 1944.
141 *The only thing:* Dwight Eisenhower to John Eisenhower, September 14, 1943, Pre-Pres. Principal, box 173.
141 *Mamie thought he:* Interview with Mamie Eisenhower, OH-12, July 20, 1972, EL, Oral Histories.
141 *"Hell"*: Susan Eisenhower, *Mrs. Ike*, 217.
142 *whiskey was delivered:* Frank McCarthy to Richard Harris, January 5, 1944, GCM, McCarthy Papers, box 10.
142 *B&O Railroad's chef:* Frank McCarthy to Joseph Brown, January 5, 1944, GCM, McCarthy Papers, box 10.
142 *As they dined:* Butcher Diary, A-986.

CHAPTER 15

143 *The president's schedule:* Grace Tully, Note, FDR, President's Secretary's File, box 83; White House Appointment Diary, January 5, 1944, FDR, PPF 1-500, 1933-1945, box 83. The Butcher Diary incorrectly records this meeting as taking place on Monday, January 3, 1944. Butcher Diary, at A-983.
143 *into the president's bedroom:* Butcher Diary, A-983.
143 *"flu germ"*: Relman Morin, interview with Dwight Eisenhower, August 5, 1965, EL, 1965 Principal File, box 2.
143 *"My God"*: SHAEF, Verbatim Transcript of General Eisenhower's Press Conference, 1100 Hours 20 Grosvenor Square, January 17, 1944, Davis Papers, box 59.
143 *Roosevelt had signed:* Dwight Eisenhower to Edwin Watson, December 30, 1943, Pre-Pres. Principal, box 112.
143 *suspecting the rumors:* Anna Roosevelt Boettiger to John Boettiger, December 19, 1943, FDR, Anna Roosevelt Halstead Papers, box 6.
144 *Eisenhower stayed:* White House Appointment Diary, January 5, 1944, FDR, PPF 1-500, 1933-1945, box 83.
144 *"The French just had"*: Morin, interview with Eisenhower, August 5, 1965.

144 *"The poor Indo-Chinese"*: Lord Halifax to Anthony Eden, December 19, 1943, NAUK, FO 371/35921.

144 *"I am sure"*: Elliott Roosevelt, *As He Saw It* (Duell, Sloan & Pearce, 1946), 113–15.

144 *meeting with Hap Arnold:* Henry Arnold to Dwight Eisenhower, January 1944, NARA, RG 331, E1, box 14. David Eisenhower describes this meeting as having taken place over the telephone because Arnold was on the West Coast. David Eisenhower, *Eisenhower at War* (Random House, 1986), 116. However, both in Eisenhower and Arnold's correspondence, cited above, and in Kenney's recollection of the meeting in his memoir, the meeting is described as in person. Though, in the correspondence between Eisenhower and Arnold, both men mention that the meeting was "cut short" by Arnold needing to fly to the West Coast.

144 *They had spent:* Carlo D'Este, *Eisenhower: A Soldier's Life* (Henry Holt, 2002), 292.

144 *Marshall was emphatic:* Butcher Diary, A-986.

144 *Since the summer:* See, e.g., Richard Overy, *The Bombing War* (Penguin, 2014), 302–14; Robert Frank Futrell, *Ideas, Concepts, Doctrine: Basic Thinking in the United States Air Force, 1907–1984* (Air University Press, 1989), 137–138.

145 *At Leavenworth:* Mark Bender, *Watershed at Leavenworth* (CSI Special Studies, 1990), 34; Robert Frank Futrell, *Ideas, Concepts, Doctrine: Basic Thinking in the United States Air Force, 1907–1984* (Air University Press, 1989), 84–89.

145 *separate from Britain's army:* Barry Posen, *The Sources of Military Doctrine* (Cornell University Press, 1985), 142–146; Eugenia Keisling, "Military Doctrine and Planning in the Interwar Era," in *The Cambridge History of War* (Cambridge University Press), Vol. 4, 346–347.

145 *"he intended"*: Lord Tedder, *With Prejudice* (Little Brown, 1966), 499.

145 *promised to win:* Forrest Pogue, Interview with Leslie Scarman, February 25, 1947, Pogue Papers, box 161.

145 *"No longer"*: William Mitchell, *Winged Defense* (Putnam, 1925), at xv-xvi.

146 *Mitchell became:* Craig Morris, *The Origins of American Strategic Bombing Theory* (Naval Institute Press, 2017), 144–159; Richard Overy, *The Bombing War* (Penguin, 2014), 43–47; Wesley Craven & James Cate, *Army Air Forces in World War II* (University of Chicago Press, 1949), Vol. I, 22–53; Robert T. Finney, "History of the Air Corps Tactical School 1920–1940," USAF Historical Division, No. 100, 1955, 62–71; Robert Frank Futrell, *Ideas, Concepts, Doctrine: Basic Thinking in the United States Air Force, 1907–1984* (Air University Press, 1989), 51–53.

146 *At the Casablanca Conference:* Memorandum by the Combined Chiefs of Staff, January 21, 1943, FRUS, *The Conferences at Washington, 1941–1942, and Casablanca, 1943*, Doc. 412.

146 *In May 1943:* Report of the Combined Chiefs of Staff to President Roosevelt and Prime Minister Churchill, May 25, 1943, FRUS, *Conferences at Washington and Quebec, 1943*, Doc. 150; Wesley Craven & James Cate, *Army Air Forces in World War II* (University of Chicago Press, 1949), Vol. II, 366–376; Richard Overy, *The Bombing War* (Penguin, 2014), 598.

146 *Then, at Cairo:* Memorandum by the United States Chiefs of Staff, November 18, 1943, FRUS, The Conferences at Cairo and Tehran, 1943, Doc. 230.

146 *a great choice:* Henry Arnold, Diary (Trip to SEXTANT), Arnold Papers, reel 222.

146 *A year ahead:* Richard Davis, *Carl A. Spaatz and the Air War in Europe* (Center for Air Force History, 1993); C.V. Glines, "Carl A. Spaatz: An Air Power Strategist," HistoryNet, June 29, 2017.

146 *Eisenhower admired Spaatz:* Conference with General Eisenhower, April 24, 1947, Pre-Pres. Principal, box 68.

146 *trusted his judgment:* Eisenhower, Memorandum, June 11, 1943, Pre-Pres. Principal, box 137.

146 *evangelical believer:* Carl Spaatz, Diary, January 21, 1944, LOC, Carl Spaatz Papers, Box 12

146 *If Eisenhower needed:* Dwight D. Eisenhower, *Report by the Supreme Commander to the Combined Chiefs of Staff on the Operations in Europe of the Allied Expeditionary Force: 6 June 1944 to 8 May 1945*, CMH Pub. 70-58 (US Government Publishing Office, 1946), 14.

146 *Harris had a reputation:* Lord Tedder, *With Prejudice*, 501–502.

146 *given free rein:* The United States Strategic Bombing Survey, Summary Report (European War), September 30, 1945, 3; Richard H. Kohn and Joseph P. Harahan, "Strategic Air Warfare: An Interview with Generals Curtis E. LeMay, Leon W. Johnson, David A. Burchinal, and Jack J. Catton," Office of Air Force History 1988, pp. 40–41; Carl Spaatz, Diary, January 21, 1944, LOC, Carl Spaatz Papers, box 12; Butcher Diary, A-910; Henry Arnold, *Global Mission* (Harper & Bros., 1949), 235.

147 *"The air people"*: Larry I. Bland, ed., *George C. Marshall Interviews and Reminiscences for Forrest C. Pogue* (George C. Marshall Foundation, 1996), 619.

147 *one of the reasons:* George Marshall to Dwight Eisenhower, December 28, 1943, Smith box 19.

147 *The Army Air Forces:* Budgets for the Military and Departmental Activities of the War Department, and for the Office of Strategic Services, for the Fiscal Year 1944, May 20, 1943, 78th Cong., 1st Sess., Doc. 205.

147 *which still fell:* John Millet, *The Organization and Role of the Army Service Forces* CMH Pub 3-1 (GPO, 1954), 123–137.

147 *procurement budget*: Robert Palmer, *Mobilization of the Ground Army*, AGF Study No. 4, 1946, 10–11.
147 *airplanes were expensive*: Irving Brinton Holley, *Buying Aircraft*, CMH Pub. 11-2 (GPO, 1964), 557.
147 *glare of the Truman Committee*: Drew Pearson, "Washington Merry-Go-Round," November 30, 1943; Steve Drummond, *The Watchdog* (Hanover, 2032), 146–48, 250–84.
147 *contracts had been cut*: Irving Brinton Holley, *Buying Aircraft*, CMH Pub. 11-2 (GPO, 1964), 325, 546–547; Henry Arnold, *Global Mission* (Harper & Bros., 1949), 476–478; Thomas Coffey, *Hap: The Story of the U.S. Air Force and the Man who Built It, General Henry H. "Hap" Arnold* (Viking, 1982), 334–337.
147 *He was prepared*: Butcher Diary, A-986.
147 *The Sicily campaign*: Walter B. Smith, Training Memorandum, no. 50, "Lessons from the Sicilian Campaign," November 20, 1943, Patton Papers, box 44 (357), p. 61.
147 *As just one example*: Edith Rogers, "The Reduction of Pantelleria and Adjacent Islands, 8 May-14 June 1943," May 1947, AAFHS-52, Air Historical Office.
147 *the same flexibility*: Eisenhower, *Report by the Supreme Commander*, 14.
148 *"When a battle"*: Dwight Eisenhower, *Crusade in Europe* (Doubleday, 1947), 334.
148 *Arnold agreed*: Henry Arnold to Dwight Eisenhower, January 1944, NARA, RG 331, E1, box 14; *see also* War Department Field Manual 100-20, Command and Employment of Air Power, July 21, 1943, 1–2.
148 *hand-anointed acolyte*: Henry Arnold, *Global Mission*; James Tate, *The Army and Its Air Corps* (Air University Press, 1998), 161–179; Thomas Coffey, *Hap: The Story of the U.S. Air Force and the Man who Built It, General Henry H. "Hap" Arnold*, 128–129.
148 *"necessary drive"*: Meeting of the Combined Chiefs of Staff, December 4, 1943, FRUS, *The Conferences at Cairo and Tehran, 1943*, doc. 439.
148 *at Cairo, the understanding*: Memorandum by the United States Chiefs of Staff, Control of Strategic Air Forces in Northwest Europe and in the Mediterranean, C.C.S. 400/2, December 4, 1943, FRUS, The Conferences at Cairo and Tehran, 1943, Doc 478; Combined Chiefs of Staff Minutes, December 7, 1944, FRUS, The Conferences at Cairo and Tehran, 1943, Doc. 461.
148 *Arnold had been*: Arnold, Diary (Trip to SEXTANT).
148 *United States was producing*: Paul Kennedy, *The Rise and Fall of the Great Powers* (Random House, 1988), 455–58.
148 *more of the risks*: The United States Strategic Bombing Survey, Summary Report (European War), September 30, 1945, 3–5, 71–74; Richard Overy, *The Bombing War* (Penguin, 2014), 43–55; Butcher Diary, A-1036.
148 *would be key*: Henry Arnold to Dwight Eisenhower, January 1944, NARA, RG 331, E1, box 14.
148 *General Marshall then called*: George C. Kenney, *General Kenney Reports* (Duell, Sloan and Pearce, 1949), 342–43.
149 *"spark plugs"*: Henry Arnold to Dwight Eisenhower, March 8, 1944, NARA, RG 331, entry 1, box 14.
149 *Kenney offered*: Kenney, *General Kenney Reports*, 342–43.
149 *"I am leaving"*: Dwight Eisenhower to Walter B. Smith, January 6, 1944, Smith Papers, box 27.
149 *"Montgomery insists"*: Walter B. Smith to Dwight Eisenhower, January 6, 1944, Smith Papers, box 27.

CHAPTER 16

150 *For two days*: Butcher Diary, A-986.
150 *those same two days*: Walter B. Smith to Dwight Eisenhower, January 9, 1944, Smith Papers, box 19.
150 *Frank McCarthy landed*: Frank McCarthy, Memorandum for Miss Thomas, January 14, 1944, GCM, McCarthy Papers, box 10.
150 *see his mother*: Dwight Eisenhower to George Marshall, December 31, 1943, Pogue Papers, box 154.
150 *June 1941*: "Great in War, Just 'My Son' to His Mother," *Salina Journal*, June 27, 1942.
150 *family portrait*: Mark Bender, *Watershed at Leavenworth* (CSI Special Studies, 1990), 57.
150 *more of an effort*: Eisenhower to Swede Hazlett, October 11, 1941, Pre-Pres. Principal, box 56.
150 *wanted to go home*: Dwight Eisenhower, Diary, March 11, 1942, EL, Diaries, box 1.
150 *losing her memory*: Edgar Eisenhower to Dwight Eisenhower, March 24, 1942, Pre-Pres. Principal, box 172.
150 *His older brother*: Dwight Eisenhower to Edgar Eisenhower, May 1, 1942, Pre-Pres. Principal, box 172.
151 *Roy was*: Kenneth Davis, interview with Earl and Kay Eisenhower, 1944, Davis Papers, box 61.
151 *died suddenly*: Kenneth Davis, Kansas Research on General Dwight David Eisenhower, 1944, Davis Papers, box 94.
151 *"I feel lost"*: "Great in War, Just 'My Son' to His Mother."
151 *tried to imagine*: Dwight Eisenhower to Ida Stover Eisenhower, October 25, 1943, Pre-Pres. Principal, box 172.
151 *regular touch*: Naomi Engle to Dwight Eisenhower, June 16, 1944, Pre-Pres. Principal, box 38.
151 *"He sounds"*: Frances Curry to Dwight Eisenhower, September 8, 1943, Pre-Pres. Principal, box 29.

151 *Mamie opted to stay:* Kenneth Davis, interview with Mamie Eisenhower, 1944, Davis Papers, box 94.
151 *flight got delayed:* Frank McCarthy, Memorandum for Major Davenport, January 8, 1944, GCM, McCarthy Papers, box 10.
151 *landed at Fort Riley:* McCarthy, Memorandum for Miss Thomas.
151 *mother from Abilene:* Butcher Diary, A-986.
151 *"You know":* Oral History Research Office, Eisenhower Administration: The Reminiscences of John S.D. Eisenhower, 1979, Columbia Center on Oral History, p. 129.
151 *Though she worried:* Frances Curry to Dwight Eisenhower, November 22, 1943, Pre-Pres. Principal, box 29.
151 *"I hate war":* "Great in War, Just 'My Son' to His Mother."
152 *"Well, since they":* Frances Curry to Dwight Eisenhower, June 23, 1944, Pre-Pres. Principal, box 29.
152 *Mamie's parents flew:* Arthur Eisenhower to Mamie Eisenhower, February 7, 1944, Pre-Pres. Principal, box 171.
152 *gracious host:* Edgar Eisenhower to Dwight Eisenhower, May 13, 1944, Pre-Pres. Principal, box 172.
152 *Junior the puppy:* Dwight Eisenhower to Milton Eisenhower, January 20, 1944, Pre-Pres. Principal, box 174; Butcher Diary, A-983.
152 *Anglo-British friendship:* Davis, Kansas Research.
152 *Born when Eisenhower:* Stephen E. Ambrose and Richard H. Immerman, *Milton S. Eisenhower: Educational Statesman* (Johns Hopkins University Press, 1983), 15–24.
152 *insatiably ambitious:* Interview with Milton Eisenhower in Bela Kornitzer, *The Great American Heritage* (Farrar, Straus & Cudahy, 1955), 122.
152 *he was appointed:* Ambrose and Immerman, *Milton S. Eisenhower*, 39–52.
152 *Agriculture Department*: David Kennedy, *Freedom from Fear* (Oxford University Press, 1999), 202–213.
152 *10 percent:* Message of the President of the United States Transmitting the Budget 1930 (U.S. Government Printing Office 1928), vi.
152 *The age gap:* Milton Eisenhower to Dwight Eisenhower, June 10, 1940, Pre-Pres. Principal, box 173.
152 *Milton had a house:* Kornitzer, *Great American Heritage*, 118.
152 *Milton was a natural:* "Notes of Social Activities in New York and Elsewhere," *New York Times*, May 12, 1932, p. 16.
152 *invitations to the White House:* Kornitzer, *Great American Heritage*, 225.
153 *friendly older brother:* Oral History Research Office, Eisenhower Administration: John S.D. Eisenhower, 1973, Columbia Center on Oral History, p. 18.
153 *War Relocation Authority:* "'Work Corps' Set Up for Coast Aliens," *New York Times*, March 19, 1942, 14; Ambrose and Immerman, *Milton S. Eisenhower*, 59–66; Milton Eisenhower, *The President is Calling* (Doubleday, 1974), 95–127.
153 *"purely a military":* Interview with Milton Eisenhower in Kornitzer, *Great American Heritage*, 233.
153 *"living in an atmosphere":* Milton Eisenhower to Franklin Roosevelt, April 22, 1943, Roosevelt Papers.
153 *Director of War Information:* Milton Eisenhower, *The President Is Calling*, at 128–132.
153 *"science of propaganda":* Milton Eisenhower to H. W. Lunow, Proposal for an Institute of Citizenship, 1944, Davis Papers, box 22.
153 *Milton's key insight:* Milton Eisenhower, "Toward World Democracy," Honors Day Address at the University of Nebraska, April 18, 1944, Davis Papers, box 22.
153 *Voice of America:* Joseph Nye, "Public Diplomacy and Soft Power," *Annals of the American Academy of Political and Social Science*, no. 616 (2008): 98.
153 *Milton gloated:* Milton Eisenhower, "Toward World Democracy."
153 *Kansas State University*: Milton Eisenhower, *The President Is Calling*, 150–151.
153 *Institute of Citizenship:* Milton Eisenhower to H. W. Lunow, "Proposal for an Institute of Citizenship," 1944, Davis Papers, box 22.
153 *had opened a letter:* Charles M. Harger to Dwight Eisenhower, November 20, 1943, Pre-Pres. Principal, box 55.
154 *"It will take":* Dwight Eisenhower to Charles M. Harger, December 26, 1943, Pre-Pres. Principal, box 55.
154 *"if the home folks":* Joe W. Howe, Dwight D. Eisenhower, undated, Davis Papers, box 22.
154 *Ostentatious modesty:* Kenneth S. Davis, "Ike's Identification with Kansas," October 12, 1990, delivered at the Eisenhower and Kansas Symposium, Davis Papers, box 19.
154 *"Go into any":* William Allen White, "What's the Matter with Kansas?," *Emporia Gazette*, August 15, 1896, p. 5.
154 *"as a cowpuncher":* Harry Butcher, "General Dwight David Eisenhower," Allied Force Headquarters, Information and Censorship Section, Public Relations Branch, EL, Harry C. Butcher Papers, box 3.
154 *"it is easy":* Dwight Eisenhower to John Eisenhower, December 20, 1942, Pre-Pres. Principal, box 173.
154 *"I have been":* Dwight Eisenhower to John Eisenhower, April 8, 1943, Pre-Pres. Principal, box 173.

155 *the way Milton dressed:* "Ike, Milton Are First Brothers on Best-Dressed List," International News Service, January 11, 1954; Bela Kornitzer, *Great American Heritage*, 120.
155 *reports of bad weather:* Butcher Diary, A-987.
155 *So, Sunday morning:* McCarthy, Memorandum for Miss Thomas.

CHAPTER 17

156 *"The operation is":* Walter B. Smith to Dwight Eisenhower, January 9, 1944, Smith Papers, box 19.
156 *army running brothels:* Frank McCarthy, Memorandum for Major Davenport, January 10, 1944, GCM, McCarthy Papers, box 10.
156 *"If we do":* Bernard Montgomery to Dwight Eisenhower, January 10, 1944, Pre-Pres. Principal, box 83.
156 *After two days:* McCarthy, Memorandum for Major Davenport.
157 *had an appointment:* B. W. Davenport, Memorandum for Commander Butcher, January 11, 1944, GCM, McCarthy Papers, box 10.
157 *At ten thirty*: White House Appointment Diary, January 12, 1944, FDR, PPF 1-500, 1933-1945, Box 83.
157 *looking much better:* Butcher Diary, A-987.
157 *"the ring of":* Dwight Eisenhower, *At Ease* (Doubleday, 1967), 268.
157 *"This nation":* Franklin Roosevelt, State of the Union Address, January 11, 1944, in *The Public Papers and Addresses of Franklin D. Roosevelt, 1944–1945* (Harper, 1950), at 32.
157 *"Freedom from fear":* Franklin Roosevelt, State of the Union Address, January 11, 1944, in *The Public Papers and Addresses of Franklin D. Roosevelt, 1944–1945*, 32.
157 *three lucky coins:* Kenneth Davis, *Soldier of Democracy* (Konecky & Konecky, 1945), 1.
157 *Britain in 1944:* For a persuasively presented case of hegemonic convergence, see Kori Schake, *Safe Passage: The Transition from British to American Hegemony* (Harvard University Press, 2017).
158 *"long tirade":* Alan Brooke, *War Diaries, 1939–1945* (Phoenix Press, 2001), 472.
158 *"It was better":* William Louis, *Imperialism at Bay* (Oxford, 1986), 6–7.
158 *His favorite book:* Kenneth Davis, Interview with John Eisenhower, 1944, Davis Papers, box 61.
159 *"So they lived":* Arthur Conan Doyle, *The White Company* (Dodd, Mead, and Company, 1927), 362.
159 *a few American eyebrows:* Edgar Eisenhower to Ida Stover Eisenhower, December 4, 1942, Pre-Pres. Principal, box 172; George S. Patton, Diary, October 16, 1943, Patton Papers, box 3; Forrest Pogue, interview with James Gault, February 13, 1947, Pogue Papers, box 161; Pogue, interview with Leslie Scarman, February 25, 1947, Pogue Papers, box 161.
159 *"I wish to God":* George S. Patton, Diary, August 26, 1943, Patton Papers, box 3.
159 *The British loved:* Pogue, interview with Gault, February 13, 1947; Pogue, interview with Sir Arthur Cunningham, February 14, 1947, box 161.
159 *Even Alan Brooke:* Alan Brooke, *War Diaries, 1939–1945* (Phoenix Press, 2001), 365.
159 *"peacemaker":* Franklin Roosevelt to Grace Tully, November 1943, FDR, Grace Tully Papers, box 4.
159 *"It seems pretty clear":* Elliott Roosevelt, *As He Saw It* (Duell, Sloan & Pearce, 1946), 209.
159 *thought better*: Memorandum by the United States Chiefs of Staff, December 4, 1943, FRUS, The Conferences at Cairo and Tehran, 1943, Doc. 477.
159 *"The Southwest":* Dwight Eisenhower, manuscript, "Churchill & Marshall," November 17, 1966, Post-Presidential Papers, A-WR Series, box 8.
159 *"It's none of my":* Relman Morin, interview with Dwight Eisenhower, August 5, 1965, EL, 1965 Principal File, box 2; Dwight Eisenhower, *At Ease* (Doubleday, 1967), 208–209.
160 *"Do not be too free":* Dwight Eisenhower to John Eisenhower, September 20, 1943, Pre-Pres. Principal, box 173.
160 *Eleanor Roosevelt dropped in:* Susan Eisenhower, *Mrs. Ike* (Farrar, Straus and Giroux, 1996), 217.
160 *blur of meetings:* Frank McCarthy, Memorandum for the Chief of Staff, January 17, 1944, GCM, McCarthy Papers, box 10.
160 *"Drones":* Henry Arnold, Diary (Trip to England June 8, 1944–June 21, 1944), Arnold Papers, reel 222.
160 *"You make":* Henry Stimson, diary, January 12, 1944, Yale University, Henry Lewis Stimson Papers, MS 456, Series 14, Reel 8U.
160 *good movies:* George Marshall to Dwight Eisenhower, January 5, 1944, NARA, RG 331, E1, box 8.
161 *"People demand action":* ed. Larry I. Bland, *George C. Marshall Interviews and Reminiscences for Forrest C. Pogue* (George C. Marshall Foundation, 1996), 622.
161 *"actual combat scenes":* George Marshall to Dwight Eisenhower, January 5, 1944, NARA, RG 331, E1, box 8.
161 *"There are now":* Combined Chiefs of Staff Minutes, November 29, 1943, FRUS, *The Conferences at Cairo and Tehran, 1943*, doc. 364.
161 *understand logistics:* Larry I. Bland, ed., *George C. Marshall Interviews and Reminiscences for Forrest C. Pogue* (George C. Marshall Foundation, 1996), 582.

161 *Bill recommended:* Butcher Diary, A-987.
161 *Everyone was receptive:* Dwight Eisenhower to Walter B. Smith, January 13, 1944, Smith Papers, box 27.
161 *"large, slow targets":* Nigel Lewis, *Exercise Tiger* (Prentice Hall, 1990), 23.
162 *"Beetles":* Jeter Isley, *U.S. Marines and Amphibious Warfare* (Princeton University Press, 1951), 20–21.
162 *thought about tanks:* Dwight Eisenhower, "Tanks with Infantry," in Daniel Holt and James Leyerzapf, eds., *Eisenhower: The Pre-War Diaries and Selected Papers* (Johns Hopkins University Press, 1998), 35–42.
162 *In assessing the failures:* George Patton, "The Defense of Gallipoli," August 31, 1936, Army Headquarters, Hawaiian Department, Fort Sher.
162 *That changed with:* Jeter Isley, *U.S. Marines and Amphibious Warfare*, 15–16; Gordon Rothman, *Landing Ship Tank (LST) 1942–2002* (Bloomsbury, 2005); Theodore Gatchel, *At the Water's Edge* (Naval Institute Press, 2013), 34; Richard Leighton & Robert Coakley, *Global Logistics and Strategy: 1940 –1943*, CMH Pub. 1-5 (U.S. Government Printing Office, 1955), 682–686.
162 *late January 1942:* Dwight Eisenhower, Diary, January 24, 1942, EL, Diaries, box 1.
162 *"Who is responsible":* Eisenhower, Diary, May 6, 1942, EL, Diaries, box 1.
163 *single-minded Bill Somervell:* John Ohl, *Supplying the Troops : General Somervell and American Logistics in* WWII (Northern Illinois University Press, 1994), 181–193; John Millet, *The Army Service Forces*, CMH Pub. 3-1 (U.S. Government Printing Office, 1953), 80–81; Richard Leighton & Robert Coakley, *Global Logistics and Strategy: 1940–1943*, CMH Pub. 1-5 (U.S. Government Printing Office, 1955), 376–382; David Kennedy, *Freedom from Fear* (Oxford University Press, 1999), 621–628.
163 *development of the LCI:* Forrest Pogue, interview with J. Hughes Hallett, February 11–12, 1947, Pogue Papers, box 161.
163 *had manufactured 9,488:* "Navy Enters Fourth War Year with Fleet of 61,045 Vessels," Bureau of Naval Personnel, Information Bulletin, February 1945, at 43.
163 *Eisenhower's meetings:* Dwight Eisenhower to Walter B. Smith, January 13, 1944, Smith Papers, box 27.
164 *A simultaneous amphibious invasion:* David Kennedy, *Freedom from Fear*, 699–701.
164 *"desirability of strengthening":* Eisenhower to Bernard Montgomery, January 13, 1944, Pre-Pres. Principal, box 83.
164 *They needed to keep:* Eisenhower to Smith, January 13, 1944.

CHAPTER 18

167 *boarded a C-54:* Butcher Diary, A-988.
167 *Things with Mamie:* Dwight Eisenhower to Mamie Eisenhower, January 16, 1944, Pre-Pres. Principal, box 173.
167 *In time, she:* Michael Beschloss, *Eisenhower: A Centennial Life* (HarperCollins, 1990), 61.
167 *She felt jilted:* Susan Eisenhower, *Mrs. Ike* (Farrar, Straus and Giroux, 1996), 217.
167 *Mamie gave him:* Eisenhower to Mamie Eisenhower, January 16, 1944.
167 *The fog in London:* Butcher Diary, A-988; Bertram Ramsay, *The Year of D-Day* (University of Hull, 1994), 9.
168 *Eisenhower noticed:* Eisenhower to Mamie Eisenhower, January 16, 1944.
168 *London was always dark:* Kay Summersby, Desk Diary, January 16, 1944, EL, Wyden Papers, box 1.
168 *"a real pea souper":* Kay Summersby, *Eisenhower Was My Boss* (Dell, 1948), 121–22.
168 *Eisenhower recognized:* Dwight Eisenhower to Vera McCarthy-Morrogh, June 27, 1943, Sotheby's, Sale 6188, Fine Books and Manuscripts, June 13, 1991, lot 162.
168 *"Irish tantrum":* Lloyd Shearer, "The Eisenhower-Summersby Love Affair" (draft), May 28, 1976, University of Wyoming, Harry Butcher Papers, box 3.
168 *He helped her get:* Dwight Eisenhower to Vera McCarthy-Morrogh, October 10, 1943, Sotheby's, Sale 6188, Fine Books and Manuscripts, June 13, 1991, Lt 167.
168 *find a job:* Eisenhower to Vera McCarthy-Morrogh, August 7, 1943, Sotheby's, Sale 6188, Fine Books and Manuscripts, June 13, 1991, lot 163.
168 *He gave her time:* Shearer, "Eisenhower-Summersby Love Affair."
168 *So he shared:* Dwight Eisenhower to Vera McCarthy-Morrogh, August 27, 1943, Sotheby's, Sale 6188, Fine Books and Manuscripts, June 13, 1991, lot 165.
168 *"very necessary":* Shearer, "Eisenhower-Summersby Love Affair."
168 *things to do:* Kenneth Davis, interview with Kay Summersby, 1944, KSU, Davis Papers, box 94.
168 *good at them:* Dwight Eisenhower to John Eisenhower, August 22, 1944, Pre-Presidential Papers, Principal File, box 173.
168 *"philosophical about it":* Dwight Eisenhower to Louis Marx, January 27, 1948, Pre-Pres. Papers, Box 81.
168 *Over time, Kay:* Eisenhower to McCarthy-Morrogh, August 27, 1943.
168 *only contemplative spot:* Summersby, *Eisenhower Was My Boss*, 105.

168 *"Good night!"*: Reproduced in Kay Summersby, *Past Forgetting* (Simon & Schuster, 1977), 161.
168 *"Now I know"*: Summersby, *Eisenhower Was My Boss*, 121–22.
169 *"Eisenhower Platz"*: Kenneth Davis, interview with Harry Butcher, 1944, Davis Papers, box 94.
169 *Eisenhower went to:* Summersby, *Eisenhower Was My Boss*, 121–22.
169 *Hayes Lodge:* Michael McKeogh and Richard Lockridge, *Sgt. Mickey & General Ike* (Putnam, 1946), 101.
169 *"acting"*: Dwight D. Eisenhower, *Report by the Supreme Commander to the Combined Chiefs of Staff on the Operations in Europe of the Allied Expeditionary Force: 6 June 1944 to 8 May 1945*, CMH_Pub_70-58 (GPO, 1946), 3.
169 *Photographers swarmed:* US Army Photograph, Dwight Eisenhower, January 18, 1944, Pogue Papers, box 136.
169 *Mattie, who typed:* Kenneth Davis, interview with Mattie Pinette, 1944, Davis Papers, box 94.
169 *"I have complete"*: "Eisenhower in Britain," Pathé Gazette, January 20, 1944, Film ID: 1350.02.
170 *Eisenhower met with:* Mattie Pinette, Eisenhower I, undated, EL, George Hall Papers, box 1.
170 *Beetle was back:* Everett Hughes, Diary, January 18, 1944, Hughes Papers, box I-1.
170 *new emblem made:* Harry C. Butcher, *My Three Years with Eisenhower* (Simon & Schuster, 1946), 592.
170 *black sable:* Forrest Pogue, *The Supreme Command* (US Government Printing Office, 1954), 518.
170 *"While our visit"*: Eisenhower to Mamie Eisenhower, January 16, 1944.
170 *"I will always"*: Dwight Eisenhower to Jacob Devers, CABLE, January 16, 1944, Pre-Pres. Principal, box 34.
170 *sent another cable:* Eisenhower to Devers.
170 *"I offer you"*: Butcher Diary, A-1000, 1039–40.
170 *the cancellation of Operation Anvil:* BCOS to Prime Minister, January 14, 1944, NARA, RG 331, entry 1, box 76.
171 *"I came home"*: Butcher Diary, A-1011.
171 *first press conference:* Daily Appointment Log, January 17, 1944, Pre-Pres. Principal, box 127.
171 *The room:* Walter White, Notes, January 17, 1944, NAACP, Box II A603.
171 *"Because none of you"*: SHAEF, Verbatim Transcript of General Eisenhower's Press Conference, 1100 Hours 20 Grosvenor Square, January 17, 1944, Davis Papers, box 59.
172 *a bit punchy:* Butcher Diary, A-993.
172 *Eisenhower assured Beetle:* Butcher Diary, A-1000.
173 *not a team player:* Butcher Diary, A-993.
173 *second full day:* Daily Appointment Log, January 18, 1944, EL, Pre-Pres. Principal, box 127.
173 *sign a card:* Butcher Diary, A-993.
173 *Eisenhower introduced himself:* James Martin Stagg, *Forecast for Overlord* (Norton, 1971), 17.
173 *Beetle had an altercation:* Butcher Diary, A-993.
174 *"It was grand"*: Franklin Roosevelt to Dwight Eisenhower, January 18, 1944, Pre-Pres. Principal, box 100.
174 *regiment to Dakar:* Relman Morin, interview with Dwight Eisenhower, August 5, 1965, EL, 1965 Principal File, box 2.
174 *Eisenhower ordered:* Dwight Eisenhower to Franklin Roosevelt, February 1, 1944, Pre-Pres. Principal, box 100.
174 *so many uncertainties:* Dwight Eisenhower to George Marshall, January 17, 1944, Pre-Pres. Principal, box 80.
174 *The press' newest:* Butcher Diary, A-996.
174 *"my boy"*: "Mother, 82, Helped Cook Ike's Dinner," Associated Press, January 17, 1944.
174 *He seethed at:* Dwight Eisenhower to Milton Eisenhower, January 20, 1944, Pre-Pres. Principal, box 174.

CHAPTER 19

175 *On Friday:* SHAEF, Minutes of Meeting Convened by Supreme Commander Allied Expeditionary Force in Room 126, Norfolk House 1030 Hours on Friday 21st January 1944, EL, Raymond Barker Papers, box 1.
175 *Norfolk House:* "St. James's Square: No 31, Norfolk House," in *Survey of London* (London County Council, 1960), vols. 29 and 30, 187–202.
175 *Parking was reserved:* Kay Summersby, *Eisenhower Was My Boss* (Dell, 1948), 124.
175 *Taking command:* Carlo D'Este, *Decision in Normandy* (Konecky & Konecky, 1983), 66.
175 *Monty's specific role:* Bertram Ramsay, *The Year of D-Day* (University of Hull, 1994), 2.
175 *British were running:* Bernard Montgomery, "Notes Taken at a Meeting of Army Commanders and Their Chiefs of Staff, HQ 21 Army Group, 7 Jan. 1944," NAUK, WO 205 16.
176 *"command his administration"*: Frederick Morgan, Administrative Command, COSSAC/3110/Sec., January 5, 1944, NARA, RG 331, Entry NM8 3, box 123.
176 *Over the course:* Bertram Ramsay, *The Year of D-Day*, 1–4; Nigel Hamilton, *Master of the Battlefield* (McGraw Hill, 1983), 492.
176 *A massive buildup:* Walter B. Smith to Dwight Eisenhower, January 5, 1944, Smith Papers, box 19.

176 *"chaps, who went"*: Forrest Pogue, interview with J. Hughes Hallett, February 11–12, 1947, Pogue Papers, box 161.
176 *places like Sandhurst:* Brian Bond, *British Military Policy between the Two World Wars* (Oxford University Press, 1980), 62–70; David French, "Doctrine and Organization of the British Army," 1919–1932, *Historical Journal*, Vol. 44, No. 2 (2001), 513–515.
176 *retreat at Dunkirk:* Pogue, interview with Hallett, February 11–12, 1947.
176 *Monty had been:* Lord Taylor, Interview with Field Marshall Montgomery, Memorial University of Newfoundland, Media & Data Center, No. L-3606.
177 *giving him carte blanche:* Forrest Pogue, Interview with J. Hughes Hallett, February 11–12, 1947, Pogue Papers, box 161; Alan Brooke, *War Diaries 1939–1945* (Phoenix Press, 2001), 188–189; Nigel Hamilton, *The Full Monty* (Penguin, 2002), 373–380.
177 *For the three days:* Hamilton, *Master of the Battlefield*, 492.
177 *The COSSAC planners:* COSSAC, Operation "OVERLORD," J.C.S. 4421, August 6, 1943, GCM, George Elsey Papers, box 1; D'Este, *Decision in Normandy*, 66.
177 *He wanted to divide:* Dwight Eisenhower to George Marshall, January 22, 1944, Smith Papers, box 27.
177 *near a port:* Forrest Pogue, interview with Walter B. Smith, May 9, 1947, Pogue Papers, box 161.
177 *Freddie Morgan credited:* Kenneth Davis, interview with Frederick E. Morgan, August 6, 1944, Davis Papers, box 94.
177 *preposterously grandiose:* Forrest Pogue, interview with Hastings Ismay, December 20, 1946, Pogue Papers, box 161.
177 *As a result:* COSSAC, Operation "OVERLORD," J.C.S. 4421, August 6, 1943, GCM, George Elsey Papers, box 1.
177 *was unpersuaded:* SHAEF, Minutes of Meeting Convened by Supreme Commander Allied Expeditionary Force in Room 126, Norfolk House 1030 Hours on Friday 21st January 1944.
177 *he proposed:* Hamilton, *Master of the Battlefield*, 492.
178 *Dieppe was chosen:* C. P. Stacey, *Official History of the Canadian Army in the Second World War* (Dept. of National Defence, 1956), 1:326.
178 *"the first offensive"*: Dwight Eisenhower to George Marshall, June 26, 1942, Pre-Pres. Principal, box 80.
178 *Royal Air Force's performance*: W.M. (42) 115th Conclusions, Minute 1, Confidential Annex, August 20, 1942, NAUK, CAB 65/31/18; War Cabinet 118(42), August 25, 1942, NAUK, CAB 65/27/34.
178 *The plan had been:* Chief of Combined Operations, "Raid on Dieppe: Report on Lessons Learnt," September 1942, NAUK, WO 106/4115; Stacey, *Official History*, Vol. I, 1:332; David O'Keefe, *One Day in August* (Icon, 2013), 221–233.
178 *The invasion of Dieppe:* "Dieppe Raid (Combined Report)," October 1942, NAUK, ADM 234/447; Battle Summary No. 33, "Raid on Dieppe, August 19th 1942," C.B. 3081(26), February 1946, NAUK, ADM 234/354; Raid on Dieppe: Report by Chief of Combined Operation on Lessons Learnt, September 1942, NAUK, WO 106/4115; Stacey, *Official History*, 1:339.
178 *answer was "DIEPPE"*: Val Gilbert, "MI5 Never Had a Clue about the D-Day Crosswords Puzzle," *Daily Telegraph*, May 3, 2004.
178 *"Very heavy casualties"*: Stacey, *Official History*, 1:386.
179 *COSSAC's planners had drawn:* SHAEF, History of COSSAC, May 1944, HMC 8-3.6 CA, 27-29; Operation "OVERLORD", J.C.S. 442, August 5, 1943, GCM, George Elsey Papers, box 1; Hamilton, *Master of the Battlefield*, 49.
179 *The farthest west:* Dwight Eisenhower to George Marshall, January 22, 1944, Smith Papers, box 27.
179 *code-named Utah and Omaha:* Dwight D. Eisenhower, *Report by the Supreme Commander to the Combined Chiefs of Staff on the Operations in Europe of the Allied Expeditionary Force: 6 June 1944 to 8 May 1945*, CMH Pub. 70-58 (GPO, 1946), 6.
179 *verged on suicidal:* Operation "OVERLORD", J.C.S. 442, August 5, 1943, GCM, George Elsey Papers, box 1; SLA Marshall, "History and the Post-War Situation," May 13, 1946, NAUK, AIR 37/784; Dwight D. Eisenhower, *Report by the Supreme Commander to the Combined Chiefs of Staff on the Operations in Europe of the Allied Expeditionary Force: 6 June 1944 to 8 May 1945*, CMH Pub. 70-58 (GPO 1946), 1–6.
179 *taking the Cotentin:* Dwight Eisenhower to CCS, January 23, 1944, Pre-Pres. Principal, box 130.
179 *He could divide:* Montgomery, "Notes Taken at a Meeting of Army Commanders."
179 *Monty's 21st Army Group*: Dwight D. Eisenhower, *Report by the Supreme Commander*, 7.
179 *"prevent any interference"*: Montgomery, "Notes Taken at a Meeting of Army Commanders."
180 *messy three days:* Walter B. Smith to Dwight Eisenhower, January 5, 1944, Smith Papers, box 19; D'Este, *Decision in Normandy*, 66; Hamilton, *Master of the Battlefield*, 492.
180 *"Montgomery Plan"*: D. K. R. Croswell, *Beetle: The Life of Walter Bedell Smith* (University of Kentucky Press, 2010), 554.

180 *Eisenhower assembled:* SHAEF, Minutes of Meeting Convened by Supreme Commander Allied Expeditionary Force in Room 126, Norfolk House 1030 Hours on Friday 21st January 1944.

180 *They posed together:* "Allied Chiefs Meet in London," British Pathé, 1944, Film ID: 1350.18; "Allied Chiefs Meet," British Pathé, 1944, Film ID:1819.04.

180 *"strike hard":* SHAEF, Minutes of Meeting Convened by Supreme Commander Allied Expeditionary Force in Room 126, Norfolk House 1030 Hours on Friday 21st January 1944.

181 *"The Mulberry":* Bernard Montgomery, "Notes for the Commander-in-Chief's Meeting with the Supreme Commander on Friday 21st January 1944," NAUK, WO 205 16.

181 *medieval maps:* SHAEF SGS File, Meeting to Discuss the Geological Nature of OVERLORD Beaches, November 19, 1943, Pogue Papers, box 157.

181 *Monty concluded:* SHAEF, Minutes of Meeting Convened by Supreme Commander Allied Expeditionary Force in Room 126, Norfolk House 1030 Hours on Friday 21st January 1944.

182 *recently demobilized:* Gordon A. Harrison, "Were We Duped by the British?," SLAM, box 94.

182 *"Our resources":* SHAEF, Minutes of Meeting Convened by Supreme Commander Allied Expeditionary Force in Room 126, Norfolk House 1030 Hours on Friday 21st January 1944.

182 *As the only commander:* Pogue, interview with Hallett, February 11–12, 1947.

182 *Leigh-Mallory proposed:* SHAEF, Minutes of Meeting Convened by Supreme Commander Allied Expeditionary Force in Room 126, Norfolk House 1030 Hours on Friday 21st January 1944.

182 *The parking space:* Summersby, *Eisenhower Was My Boss,* 124.

182 *appointment with Churchill:* Winston Churchill, Engagement Diary, January 1944, Churchill Papers, CHAR 20/19/03.

182 *Eisenhower's stomach:* Dwight Eisenhower, *Letters to Mamie* (Doubleday, 1977), 164.

183 *so many unknowns:* First United States Army, Report of Operations, Annex no. 2, 9, RG 165, entry NM-84 79, box 1991.

183 *The previous October:* Dwight Eisenhower to CCS, October 29, 1943, Pre-Pres. Principal, box 130.

183 *"The cross-channel":* Dwight Eisenhower to George Marshall, January 22, 1944, Smith Papers, box 27.

183 *Eisenhower persuaded:* SHAEF, Minutes of Meeting Convened by Supreme Commander Allied Expeditionary Force in Room 126, Norfolk House at 1030 Hours on Friday 21st January 1944, EL, Raymond Barker Papers, box 1.

184 *Patton was ordered:* CINC to George Patton, January 22, 1944, Patton Papers, box 44.

184 *Georgie cabled:* George Patton to Dwight Eisenhower, January 23, 1944, Patton Papers, box 44.

184 *have to be approved:* Jacob Devers to Dwight Eisenhower, January 16, 1944, Pre-Pres. Principal, box 34.

184 *"Landing was":* Henry Wilson to Dwight Eisenhower, January 23, 1944, Pre-Pres. Principal, box 124.

184 *"has got absolutely":* Alan Brooke, *War Diaries, 1939–1945* (Phoenix Press, 2001), 516.

184 *Mamie had finally:* Eisenhower, *Letters to Mamie,* 164.

184 *Gault had convinced:* Butcher Diary, A-1001.

184 *Sunday night:* Butcher Diary, A-1049.

184 *"This operation marks":* Dwight Eisenhower to CCS, January 23, 1944, Pre-Pres. Principal, box 130.

185 *"Whatever my orders":* Dwight Eisenhower, Memorandum, January 24, 1944, in Kay Summersby, SHAEF Desk Calendar, January 24, 1944, EL, Wyden Papers, box 1.

CHAPTER 20

186 *Monday morning:* SHAEF, Minutes of Supreme Commander's Conference, Room 105, Norfolk House, 1000 Hours, 24 January 1944, Meeting No. 3, in Butcher Diary, A-1049.

187 *That afternoon:* Butcher Diary, A-1016.

187 *Beetle became the butt:* Butcher Diary, A-1119.

187 *Churchill had requisitioned:* Michael McKeogh and Richard Lockridge, *Sgt. Mickey & General Ike* (Putnam, 1946), 102–3.

187 *"syndicate":* Headquarters, First US Army, After Action against Enemy, Reports After/After Action Report, August 6, 1944, EL, U.S. Army, First Army Headquarters Records, box 2.

187 *Given the fears:* John Mason, "The Reminiscences of Alan Goodrich Kirk," no. 455, 1962, Oral History Research Office, Columbia University, p. 276.

187 *First US Army Planning Group:* Headquarters, First US Army, After Action Against Enemy, Reports After/After Action Report, August 6, 1944.

187 *Coordinating the two army:* Interview with Goronwy Rees, in ed. Richard Holmes, *The World at War* (Ebury, 2008), 365–366.

188 *Initial Joint Plan:* Initial Joint Plan, Neptune, February 1, 1944, IWM, Papers of Field Marshal Viscount Montgomery of Alamein, box 101.

188 *"stage lines"*: 21st Army Group, Stage Lines for OVERLORD, NARA, RG 331, entry 31, box 208.
188 *combined exercises:* Arthur Nevins to Jeter Isely, January 25, 1950, Pre-Pres. Principal, box 59.
188 *different schemes:* Mason, "Reminiscences of Alan Goodrich Kirk," 247.
188 *Culture, though:* Mason, 261; Brian Izzard, *Mastermind of Dunkirk and D-Day* (Casemate, 2020), 213.
188 *When Bertie Ramsay:* Paul Kennedy, *The Rise and Fall of the Great Powers* (Random House, 1988), 29.
189 *The Anglo-American alliance:* Robert Gilpin, *War and Change in World Politics* (Cambridge University Press, 1981), 196.
189 *It tripled*: Richard Overy, *Blood and Ruins* (Random House, 2021), 530–531.
189 *the Kriegsmarine*: Stephen Roskill, *The War at Sea* (H.M.S.O., 1954), Vol. II, 354–347; Jonathan Dimbleby, *The Battle of the Atlantic* (Oxford, 2016), 77–102; David White, *The Bitter Ocean* (Simon & Schuster, 2006), 297–301; David Kennedy, *Freedom from Fear* (Oxford University Press, 1999), 566–590.
189 *In 1943 alone*: Richard Overy, *Blood and Ruins* (Random House, 2021), 530–531; Donald Nelson, *Arsenal of Democracy* (Harcourt, Brace & Co., 1946), 237–238; Alan Gropman, *Mobilizing U.S. Industry in World War II*, McNair Paper 50 (August 1996), 96.
189 *eager to innovate:* Mason, "Reminiscences of Alan Goodrich Kirk," 285.
189 *This left Alan Kirk:* Mason, 218.
189 *Eisenhower's bonhomie:* Forrest Pogue, interview with A. W. Kenner, June 1, 1945, Pogue Papers, box 161.
189 *asked for plans:* Forrest Pogue, interview with J. Hughes Hallett, February 11–12, 1947, Pogue Papers, box 161.
189 *those who liked:* Forrest Pogue, interview with Philip Wigglesworth, April 1, 1947, Pogue Papers, box 161.
189 *Spaatz complaining:* Butcher Diary, A-1036.
189 *"assignments can no"*: Dwight Eisenhower to Jacob Devers, February 1, 1944, Pre-Pres. Principal, box 34.
190 *"a bit puzzled"*: Dwight Eisenhower to George Marshall, January 29, 1944, Pre-Pres. Principal, box 80.
190 *"Sorry we could"*: Jacob Devers to Dwight Eisenhower, February 2, 1944, Pre-Pres. Principal, box 34.
190 *"This is just"*: Butcher Diary, A-1074.
190 *"a flea on"*: Dwight Eisenhower, *Letters to Mamie* (Doubleday, 1977), 165.
190 *did not write:* Dwight Eisenhower to Milton Eisenhower, July 24, 1942, Pre-Pres. Principal, box 174.
190 *his only family:* Dwight Eisenhower, Diary, July 24, 1942, EL, Diaries, box 1.
190 *"just jumping around"*: Dwight Eisenhower to Edgar Eisenhower, July 24, 1942, Pre-Pres. Principal, box 172.
190 *"I find it"*: Dwight Eisenhower to Fox Conner, July 4, 1942, Pre-Pres. Principal, box 27.
190 *"Organization"*: Fox Conner to Dwight Eisenhower, August 21, 1942, Pre-Pres. Principal, box 27.
190 *as did Butch:* Dwight Eisenhower to Milton Eisenhower, July 24, 1942.
190 *grew more confident:* Dwight Eisenhower to John Eisenhower, September 24, 1942, Pre-Pres. Principal, box 173.
190 *he told Tex:* Butcher Diary, A-1010.
190 *He also knew:* Dwight Eisenhower to George Marshall, February 9, 1944, Pre-Pres. Principal, box 80.

CHAPTER 21

191 *the end of January:* Daily Appointment Log, January 27, 1944, EL, Pre-Pres. Principal, Box 127.
191 *a beach community:* Nigel Lewis, *Exercise Tiger* (Prentice Hall, 1990), 6–34.
191 *The reason:* Edwin Hoyt, *The Invasion before Normandy: The Secret Battle of Slapton Sands* (Stein & Day, 1985), 82.
191 *constructed mock-ups:* Dwight Eisenhower to George Marshall, February 9, 1944, Pre-Pres. Principal, box 80.
191 *On the day:* Lewis, *Exercise Tiger*, 34.
192 *Brad was less enthusiastic:* Forrest Pogue, interview with Omar N. Bradley, May 27, 1957; July 19, 1957, GCM, Forrest Pogue Interviews.
192 *low-tech ferries:* John Mason, "The Reminiscences of Alan Goodrich Kirk," no. 455, 1962, Oral History Research Office, Columbia University, p. 302.
192 *Eisenhower thought the world:* Dwight Eisenhower, Memorandum, June 11, 1943, Pre-Pres. Principal, box 137.
192 *the same company:* Oral History Research Office, Recollections of Dwight Eisenhower by Omar Bradley, 1966, Columbia Center on Oral History.
192 *"His most prominent"*: Quoted in Carlo D'Este, *Eisenhower: A Soldier's Life* (Holt, 2002), 82.
192 *"his weapon of command"*: John Mason Brown, *Many a Watchful Night* (McGraw-Hill, 1944), 181.
192 *"That's not how"*: Oral History Research Office, An Interview with Brigadier General John S.D. Eisenhower Concerning the Eisenhower Presidency, 1982, Columbia Center on Oral History, p. 28–29.
192 *Brad thought little:* Walter B. Smith to Dwight Eisenhower, April 1, 1948, SLAM Papers, box 95.
192 *one of the few:* Kenneth Davis, "Portrait of a General, Some Personal Impressions of Eisenhower," 1944, Davis Papers, box 94.

192 *Even Beetle admired:* Forrest Pogue, interview with Walter B. Smith, May 8, 1947, Pogue Papers, box 161.
192 *cantankerous as ever:* George S. Patton, Diary, January 26, Patton Papers, box 3.
192 *"God Bless Us":* George S. Patton to Beatrice Patton, January 23, 1944, Patton Papers, box 18.
192 *Eisenhower broke:* George S. Patton, Diary, January 26.
192 *The plan was:* Dwight D. Eisenhower, *Report by the Supreme Commander to the Combined Chiefs of Staff on the Operations in Europe of the Allied Expeditionary Force: 6 June 1944 to 8 May 1945*, CMH Pub. 70-58 (GPO, 1946), 7.
192 *"nothing for Sicily":* George S. Patton to Beatrice Patton, January 12, 1944, Patton Papers, box 18.
192 *"is a man":* George S. Patton, Diary, January 17, 1944, Patton Papers, box 3.
193 *Eisenhower invited Georgie:* George S. Patton, Diary, January 26, 1944.
193 *Official Family dinner:* George Hall, interview with Mattie Pinette, January 5, 1977, EL, George Hall Papers, box 1.
193 *Growing up*: George Hall, Notes, undated, EL, George Hall Papers, box 1.
193 *no patience*: Kenneth Davis, Interview with Mattie Pinette, 1944, Davis Papers, box 94.
193 *teased Jimmy*: Mattie Pinette, Eisenhower I, undated, EL, George Hall Papers, Box 1.
193 *handsome and charming*: Mattie Pinette, Diary, June 2, 1944, EL, George Hall Papers, box 1.
193 *arguing politics*: Kenneth Davis, Interview with Mattie Pinette, Davis Papers, box 94.
193 *George S. Patton show:* Butcher Diary, A-1017.
193 *Georgie misquoted:* Hall, interview with Pinette, January 5, 1977.
193 *Kay was there:* Patton, Diary, January 26, 1944.
194 *"Jesus Christ Himself":* Hank Cox, *The General Who Wore Six Stars: The Inside Story of John C. H. Lee* (University of Nebraska Press, 2018), xvi.
194 *Lee had arrived:* Eisenhower, *Report by the Supreme Commander*, 12; Cox, 55–56.
194 *a prime example:* Butcher Diary, A-1017.
194 *On the first of February:* JSM Wasington to WCO London, February 1, 1944, NARA, RG 331, entry 1, box. 76.
194 *The following day:* Butcher Diary, A-1052.
194 *"Politics":* Alan Brooke, *War Diaries, 1939–1945* (Phoenix Press, 2001), 518.
194 *the cover plan:* Frederick Morgan to ACoS, G-3, February 3, 1944, NARA, RG 331, entry 1, box 23; Thaddeus Holt, *The Deceivers* (Scribner, 2014), 477–591; Rick Beyer, *The Ghost Army of World War II* (Princeton Architectural Press, 2015), 58; Anthony Brown, *Bodyguard of Lies* (Harper & Row, 1975), 459–499; Eric Hresko, "Quicksilver IV: The Real Operation Fortitude," June 2010, thesis, School of Advanced Air and Space Studies, Air University.
194 *"There is required":* Winston Churchill, *The World Crisis* (Scribner, 1923), 2:5.
194 *"truth deserves a":* Third plenary meeting, November 30, 1943, FRUS, *The Conferences at Cairo and Tehran, 1943*, doc. 373.
194 *Freddie Morgan's planners:* COSSAC, Outline of Cover Operation (Pas de Calais), November 26, 1943, NARA, RG 331, entry 1, box 78.
195 *"Messpot":* Frederick Morgan to ACoS, G-3, February 3, 1944, NARA, RG 331, entry 1, box 23.
195 *"Why break the":* Brooke, *War Diaries*, 518.
195 *Churchill continued:* Butcher Diary, A-1052.
195 *"Very well if":* Forrest Pogue, interview with Hastings Ismay, December 17, 1946, Pogue Papers, box 161.
195 *"when did William cross?":* John Mason, "The Reminiscences of Alan Goodrich Kirk," no. 455, 1962, Oral History Research Office, Columbia University, p. 297.
195 *King George took:* Brooke, *War Diaries*.
195 *called him back:* Butcher Diary, A-1052.
195 *so much promise*: Hastings Ismay to Averell Harriman, March 17, 1944, LOC, Averell Harriman Papers, Box 1102.

CHAPTER 22

196 *trip to Plymouth:* Butcher Diary, A-1055.
196 *Under the plan:* Initial Joint Plan, Neptune, February 1, 1944, IWM, Papers of Field Marshal Viscount Montgomery of Alamein, box 101.
196 *Woodruff had briefly:* Stephen Taaffe, *Marshall and His Generals* (University Press of Kansas, 2013), 176–177.
196 *Marshall had sent:* Dwight Eisenhower to George Marshall, January 29, 1944, GCM, Marshall Papers, box 66.
196 *Eisenhower was desperate:* Eisenhower to Marshall, January 18, 1944, Eisenhower Papers, 3:1664–65.

197 *"exceptionally well-experienced"*: Dwight Eisenhower to Jacob Devers, January 16, 1944, Pre-Pres. Principal, box 34.
197 *studying the problem:* Lucian Truscott, Overcoming Beach Obstacles, August 10, 1942, GCM, Lucian Truscott Papers, box 10.
197 *refused to let go:* Jacob Devers to Dwight Eisenhower, January 19, 1944, Pre-Pres. Principal, box 34.
197 *Beetle doubted:* Forrest Pogue, interview with Walter B. Smith, May 9, 1947, Pogue Papers, box 161.
197 *Marshall also had:* George Marshall to Dwight Eisenhower, January 24, 1944, GCM, Marshall Papers, box 66.
197 *his own favorites:* Marshall to Eisenhower, December 28, 1943, Smith box 19.
197 *Gee had done:* Eisenhower to Marshall, January 18, 1944.
197 *took the time:* Dwight Eisenhower to Leonard Gerow, September 19, 1944, VMI, Leonard T. Gerow Papers, box 1.
197 *"big push"*: Butcher Diary, A-885.
197 *"to lead it"*: Dwight Eisenhower to Leonard Gerow, July 26, 1943, VMI, Leonard T. Gerow Papers, box 1.
197 *Eisenhower discussed:* Dwight Eisenhower to George Marshall, January 29, 1944, Pre-Pres. Principal, box 80.
197 *Eisenhower's train arrived:* Butcher Diary, A-1063.
197 *V Corps was made:* Joseph Balkoski, *Beyond the Beachhead* (Stackpole Books, 1989), 2–25.
198 *The only part:* Dwight Eisenhower to George Marshall, February 9, 1944, Pre-Pres. Principal, box 80.
198 *"You are the ones"*: Kenneth Davis, "Portrait of a General, Some Personal Impressions of Eisenhower," undated, Davis Papers, box 94.
198 *provoke an ovation:* Butcher Diary, A-1065.
198 *break ranks:* Davis, "Portrait of a General."
198 *"I wonder whether"*: Dwight Eisenhower, "Remarks before ECAD and SHAEF Officer Personnel, May 9, 1944," Pre-Presidential Papers, Principal File, box 167.
198 *a leadership trick:* Stephen Ambrose, *The Supreme Commander* (Anchor Books, 2012), 347.
198 *Eisenhower envied:* Forrest Pogue, interview with Dwight Eisenhower, June 28, 1962, GCM, Forrest Pogue Interviews.
198 *folksy patter:* Mattie Pinette, Eisenhower I, undated, EL, George Hall Papers, box 1.
198 *"Is there anyone"*: Kenneth S. Davis, "Ike's Identification with Kansas," October 12, 1990, delivered at Eisenhower and Kansas Symposium, Davis Papers, box 19.
198 *He'd pick men:* Davis, "Portrait of a General."
198 *He'd ask how:* Michael McKeogh and Richard Lockridge, *Sgt. Mickey & General Ike* (Putnam, 1946), 59.
198 *the mess halls:* Kenneth Davis, interview with General Eisenhower, August 11, 1944, Davis Papers, box 94.
198 *The most important:* Dwight Eisenhower to John Eisenhower, November 2, 1944, Pre-Pres. Principal, box 173.
198 *when he sensed:* Kenneth Davis, interview with James Frederic Gault, 1944, Davis Papers, box 94.
199 *"plenty in the contingent fund"*: Butcher Diary, A-1063.
199 *Getting out of London:* Davis, interview with Gault, 1944.

CHAPTER 23

200 *"that General De Gaulle"*: Dwight Eisenhower to Combined Chiefs of Staff, January 19, 1944, Eisenhower Papers, 3:1667.
200 *"informally"*: John McCloy to Dwight Eisenhower, January 25, 1944, Eisenhower Papers, 3:1668n.2 (summarizing the cable).
200 *He quietly set up:* Henri d'Astier de la Vigerie to Dwight Eisenhower, February 7, 1944, Vincennes, GR/1/K/237/2.
201 *Koenig was one:* Lowell Rooks to Walter B. Smith, April 2, 1944, Smith Papers, box 15.
201 *In 1942, Koenig achieved:* Marie Joseph Pierre François Koenig, *Bir-Hakeim* (Laffont, 1971); Dominque Lormier, *Koenig: L'homme de Bir Hakeim* (Toucan, 2012), 177-270; Susan Travers, *Tomorrow to Be Brave* (Free Press, 2001), 138; Jonathan Fenby, *The General: Charles de Gaulle and the France he Saved* (Skyhorse, 2012), 182–183; Benjamin Jones, *Eisenhower's Guerrillas* (Oxford University Press, 2016), 69–70.
201 *"La Miss"*: Travers, 255.
201 *Koenig carried himself:* Travers, 139; Lormier, 11-29.
201 *they laid out:* Koenig to Eisenhower, February 7, 1944.
201 *mobilize the Maquis:* Memorandum, ANVIL, March 19, 1944, NARA, RG 331, entry 53A, box 16; Office of Strategic Services, "The Secret Army," undated (1944), NARA, RG 226, Entry A1 201, box 312; SHAEF, Weekly Intelligence Summary No. 3, April 8, 1944, Smith Papers, box 30; Benjamin Jones, *Eisenhower's Guerrillas*, 5–8.

202 *Koenig was confident:* Koenig to Eisenhower, February 7, 1944.
202 *air-dropping aid:* OSS, Summary of French Resistance, 6 June–31 August 1944, September 1944, NARA, RG 226, entry 1991, box 16.
202 *The casualties were astronomical:* Martin Blumenson, *Salerno to Cassino*, CMH_Pub_3-3-1 (US Government Printing Office, 1969), 424.
202 *The men were stuck:* Blumenson, 375.
202 *The planning:* Butcher Diary, A-1062.
202 *"I believe that":* Dwight Eisenhower to George Marshall, February 6, 1944, Pre-Pres. Principal, box 132.
202 *The same day:* Winston Churchill to Franklin Roosevelt, February 6, 1944, in *Churchill and Roosevelt: The Complete Correspondence* (Princeton University Press, 1987), 2:705.
203 *"Anvil is doomed":* Dwight Eisenhower, Memorandum, February 7, 1944, in Butcher Diary, A-1062.
203 *"private war":* Butcher Diary, A-1010.
203 *pressing the Combined Chiefs:* Alan Brooke, *War Diaries, 1939–1945* (Phoenix Press, 2001), 359.
203 *In the summer of 1942:* Richard Leighton & Robert Coakley, *Global Logistics and Strategy: 1940–1943*, CMH Pub. 1-5 (U.S. Government Printing Office, 1955), 483–484.
203 *That November, when:* Aaron O'Connell, *Underdogs* (Harvard University Press, 2012), at 48–60; Theodore Gatchel, *The Water's Edge* (Naval Institute Press, 2013), 73; Amphibious Operations During the Period August to December 1943, COMINCH P-001, April 22, 1944, USAHEC, D773.A46, 1-1; James Stockman, *The Battle for Tarawa*, Historical Section, Division of Public Information, U.S. Marine Corps (1947).
203 *"critical phase":* Eisenhower, Memorandum, February 7, 1944.
203 *They were proposing:* Walter B. Smith to Thomas Handy, February 10, 1944, Smith Papers, box 23.
203 *"should have every":* Eisenhower, Memorandum, February 7, 1944.
203 *As things stood:* SHAEF, Operation OVERLORD—Assault Lift, February 10, 1944, NARA, RG 331, entry 1, box 76.
203 *Eisenhower just wanted:* Eisenhower, Memorandum, February 7, 1944.
204 *"localitis":* George Marshall to Dwight Eisenhower, February 8, 1944, Pre-Pres. Principal, box 132.
204 *Patton had even:* George S. Patton, Diary, July 12, 1943, Patton Papers, box 3.
204 *"this thing is":* Dwight Eisenhower to George Marshall, February 8, 1944, Pre-Pres. Principal, box 132.
204 *That afternoon:* George Marshall, Memorandum for Admiral Leahy and Admiral King, February 9, 1944, in *The Papers of George Catlett Marshall* (Johns Hopkins University Press, 1996), 4:273–75.
204 *trust the British numbers:* Marshall, ibid.
204 *Handy told Beetle:* SHAEF, OVERLORD and ANVIL—Meeting with General Eisenhower, February 11, 1944, NARA, RG 331, NM8 3, box 126.
204 *"merely in the interests":* Dwight Eisenhower to George Marshall, February 9, 1944, Pre-Pres. Principal, box 80.
204 *Beetle made another:* Smith to Handy, February 10, 1944.
205 *Handy told Beetle:* Marshall, Memorandum for Admiral Leahy and Admiral King.
205 *sent a note:* Marshall, ibid.
205 *"assist Eisenhower":* George Marshall, ibid.
205 *He went that afternoon:* COS(44), OVERLORD and ANVIL—Meeting with General Eisenhower, February 11, 1944, NARA, RG 331, entry NM8 3, box 126.
206 *Cooke and Hull arrived:* Butcher Diary, A-1085.
206 *Beetle then took:* SHAEF, Special Meeting held in Room 126, Norfolk House 1000 hours, February 13, 1944, NARA, RG 331, entry 1, box 76.
206 *Hull handed Eisenhower:* Butcher Diary, A-1090.
206 *"My dear Eisenhower":* George Marshall to Dwight Eisenhower, February 10, 1944, Pre-Pres. Principal, box 80.
207 *Eisenhower thought the proposal:* Dwight Eisenhower to George Marshall, February 19, 1944, Pre-Pres. Principal, box 80.
207 *Monday morning, Eisenhower sat:* SHAEF, Special Meeting held in Room 126, Norfolk House 1000 hours, February 14, 1944.
207 *some numbers:* SHAEF, Comparison of Available Lift for OVERLORD with that Used for Planning Purposes the Present Time, February 13, 1944, NARA, RG 331, entry 1, box 76.
208 *Eisenhower asked Bertie:* SHAEF, Special Meeting held in Room 126, Norfolk House 1000 hours, February 14, 1944.
209 *"already the great value":* Dwight Eisenhower to George Marshall, February 14, 1944, Pre-Pres. Principal, box 132.
209 *"unceasing pressures":* Dwight Eisenhower, *Letters to Mamie* (Doubleday, 1977), 167.

209 *not heard anything:* Dwight Eisenhower to John Eisenhower, February 19, 1944, Pre-Pres. Principal, box 173.

209 *"brought out the":* Eisenhower, *Letters to Mamie*, 167.

CHAPTER 24

210 *seen cable traffic:* Butcher Diary, A-1092.

210 *"I am absolutely":* President Roosevelt to the British Prime Minister (Churchill), February 7, 1944, FRUS 1944, vol. 1, doc. 89.

210 *broker a compromise:* Dwight Eisenhower to George Marshall, February 15, 1944, Pre-Pres. Principal, box 80.

211 *That same week:* Butcher Diary, A-1092.

211 *Georgie came by:* Daily Appointment Log, February 16, 1944, EL, Pre-Pres. Principal, box 127.

211 *"I'm afraid you":* George S. Patton, Diary, February 16, 1944, Patton Papers, box 3.

212 *Within a day:* Butcher Diary, A-1092.

212 *The US Chiefs rejected:* The Joint Chiefs of Staff to the Secretary of State, February 17, 1944, FRUS 1944, vol. 3, doc. 587.

212 *Before leaving:* R. E. Cummings to CINC, November 18, 1943, Patton Papers, box 44.

212 *The American soldiers:* John McCloy to Dwight Eisenhower, December 13, 1943, NARA, RG 331, entry 1, box 14.

212 *internecine violence:* Kenneth Davis, interview with General Grisette [*sic*, Lt. Gen. Sir A. E. Grasett], 1944, Davis Papers, box 94.

212 *"the Jew-Arab question":* Kenneth Davis, interview with General Eisenhower, August 11, 1944, Davis Papers, box 94.

212 *million and a half:* Dwight D. Eisenhower, *Report by the Supreme Commander to the Combined Chiefs of Staff on the Operations in Europe of the Allied Expeditionary Force: 6 June 1944 to 8 May 1945*, CMH_Pub_70-58 (GPO 1946), 12.

212 *a reputation for hassling:* Edward Betts, Memorandum, "Relationships between the Civil Population and Members of the U.S. Forces," 1944, NARA RG 498, entry UD 1028, box 4719.

213 *the condom controversy:* Edward Betts, Memorandum, "Disposition of Contraceptives by Military Personnel," January 21, 1944, NARA RG 498, entry UD 1028, box 4719.

213 *twenty-one-year-old private: United Steats v. Leherberry*, ETO no. 1621, *European Theater Operations Board of Review Opinions* (Office of the Judge Advocate General, 1945), 5:103.

213 *"the Negro question":* Walter White, Draft Article for *Life* Magazine, February 1944, NAACP, box II A-76.

213 *first press conference:* "Duty in England for Negro WAACS," *New York Times*, August 16, 1942; Dwight Eisenhower to John Marshall, September 1, 1942, Eisenhower Papers, 1:519–21.

213 *"Might just as well":* Harry C. Butcher, *My Three Years with Eisenhower* (Simon & Schuster, 1946), 59.

213 *"darkies":* Dwight Eisenhower to Mamie Eisenhower, November 1, 1943, Private Collection.

213 *General Conner:* Russ Stayanoff, "MG Fox Conner: Soldier, Mentor, Enigma," Masters Thesis, Norwich University, 2007, 11.

214 *forcibly deported, detained:* George Moseley, Memorandum for the Assistant Secretary of War, October 9, 1930, LOC, George Moseley Papers, box 3.

214 *"defective": Sterilize Refugees*, United Press, May 13, 1938.

214 *"In my opinion":* George Moseley, Statement, August 12, 1939, LOC, George Moseley Papers, box 15.

214 *"a very dangerous":* George Moseley, to Tiffany Blake, March 30, 1939, LOC, George Moseley Papers, box 3.

214 *Hitler had a point:* George Moseley, Hitler, March 29, 1938, LOC, George Moseley Papers, box 9.

214 *Hitler always revolted him:* Dwight Eisenhower, diary, September 3, 1939, in Daniel Holt and James Leyerzapf, eds., *Eisenhower: The Pre-War Diaries and Selected Papers* (Johns Hopkins University Press, 1998), 446.

214 *Jews in Manila:* Dwight Eisenhower/Alex Frieder correspondence, Pre-Pres. Principal, box 43. In *At Ease*, Eisenhower recounts having many Jewish friends in the Philippines, being generally revolted by the era's antisemitism, and even being offered (though declining) a lucrative job resettling Jewish refugees in Asia. Dwight D. Eisenhower, *At Ease: Stories I Tell to Friends* (Doubleday & Company, 1967), 230. There is also popular legend that Eisenhower played a pivotal role in the Philippine resettlement of 1,300 Jewish refugees in the late 1930s. While Eisenhower's rejection of antisemitism is well-supported by the documentary record, recent scholarship into the plight of the Jewish refugees in the Philippines has persuasively concluded that there is little evidence to support much of this lore. Sharon Delmendo, "Ike and the Jews: Was Dwight D. Eisenhower involved in Jewish refugee rescue in the Philippines during the Holocaust?" manuscript, undated; Bonnie M. Harris, *Philippine Sanctuary: A Holocaust Odyssey* (University of Wisconsin Press, 2021), 73.

214 *"Little Brown Brothers"*: Oral History Research Office, Eisenhower Administration: John S.D. Eisenhower, 1973, Columbia Center on Oral History, p. 15.
214 *"What time are"*: Oral History Research Office, Eisenhower Administration: John S.D. Eisenhower, 1973, Columbia Center on Oral History, p, 15.
214 *"I am not"*: Dwight Eisenhower to George Moseley, April 26, 1937, in Daniel Holt and James Leyerzapf, eds., *Eisenhower: The Pre-War Diaries and Selected Papers* (Johns Hopkins University Press, 1998), 330–331.
214 *wrong side of Abilene's tracks:* Kenneth Davis, interview with Edgar Eisenhower and Charlie Chase, 1944, Davis Papers, box 61.
215 *About 10 percent:* J. Robert Lilly and J. Michael Thomson, "Executing U.S. Soldiers in England, World War II: Command Influence and Sexual Racism," *British Journal of Criminology* 37, no. 2 (Spring 1997): 262–88.
215 *refuse service to Black soldiers:* F.A. Newsom to Dwight Eisenhower, August 31, 1942, NAUK, HO 45/25604.
215 *"any discrimination"*: F.A. Newsom to the Chief Constable, September 4, 1942, NAUK, HO 45/25604; Ulysses Lee, *United States Army in World War II, The Employment of Negro Troops* (US Government Printing Office, 1966), 625.
215 *"this policy"*: John Dahlquist to F.A. Newsom, September 3, 1942, NAUK, HO 45/25604.
215 *"the presence"*: Dwight Eisenhower to Commanding Generals and Commanding Officers, July 16, 1942, in Lee, *The Employment of Negro Troops*, 623.
215 *Eisenhower worried about:* Graham Smith, *When Jim Crow Met John Bull* (I. B. Tauris, 1987), 106.
215 *He prohibited:* Dwight Eisenhower, Order, July 16, 1942, NARA, RG 332, Add. Hist. 218.
215 *"It is absolutely essential"*: Dwight Eisenhower to John Lee, September 15, 1942, in Lee, *Employment of Negro Troops*, 625.
215 *"People that were"*: Forrest Pogue, interview with John Lee, March 21, 1947, Pogue Papers, box 161.
216 *When Jacob Devers took over:* Smith, *When Jim Crow Met John Bull*, 114, 164–165; Lee, *Employment of Negro Troops*, 630.
216 *Before the war:* James Scott Wheeler, *Jacob L. Devers* (University of Kentucky Press, 2015), 201.
216 *"Colored soldiers"*: Leadership of Colored Troops, July 15, 1943, Inspector General Section Investigation Reports, 1942-47, NARA, RG 498, entry 372, box 32.
216 *The memo provoked:* Smith, *When Jim Crow Met John Bull*, 114.
216 *the previous September:* Kate Werren, *An American Uprising in Second World War England* (Pen & Sword History, 2020); Bernard Nalty, *Strength for the Fight* (Simon & Schuster, 1986), 154–57.
216 *"Blacks Tuesday"*: Smith, *When Jim Crow Met John Bull*, 106; Jacob Devers to John Lee, October 25, 1943, NARA, RG 498, box 32.
216 *introduced him to Walter White:* Daily Appointment Log, February 18, 1944, EL, Pre-Pres. Principal, box 127.
216 *"one of the foremost"*: Wendell Willkie to Dwight Eisenhower, September 15, 1943, Veterans Affairs File, box II-G5.
217 *White was of mixed:* Walter White, *A Man Called White* (Arno Press, 1959); see also A. J. Baime, *White Lies* (Mariner Books, 2022); Robert Zangrando and Ronald Lewis, *Walter F. White* (West Virginia University Press, 2019); Kenneth Janken, *Walter White* (University of North Carolina Press, 2006); Thomas Dyja, *Walter White* (Ivan R. Dee, 2008).
217 *press pass to report:* Walter White to the Editors, NAACP, January 7, 1944, NAACP, General Office File, box II-A603.
217 *He had arrived:* Walter White to "Folks," January 15, 1944, NAACP, General Office File, box II-A603.
217 *"We may"*: Walter White, "Observations and Recommendations of Walter White on Racial Relations in the ETO," February 11, 1944, NAACP, General Office File, box II-A604.
217 *"fighting a war"*: Walter White, "Address over the Columbia Broadcasting System Network," April 30, 1944, NAACP, Miscellany-General 1941- Jan 31, 1946, box II-G12.
217 *Cliff Lee arrived:* Daily Appointment Log, February 18, 1944.
218 *"He told me"*: Walter White, *A Rising Wind* (Doubleday, 1945), 62–66.
218 *"overwhelming majority of the white"*: White, "Observations and Recommendations."
219 *"assigned to service units"?*: White, "Address over the Columbia Broadcasting System Network."
219 *"It is hard"*: White, "Observations and Recommendations."
219 *"None of the glamour"*: Walter White, notes, "Recommendations," undated, NAACP, box II A603.
219 *"As men approach"*: White, "Address over the Columbia Broadcasting System Network."
219 *He mentioned to White:* White, *A Rising Wind*, 62–66.
219 *White suggested:* White, "Observations and Recommendations."
219 *Look at how Black soldiers:* White, *A Rising Wind*, 62–66.
219 *positions of leadership:* White, "Observations and Recommendations."
220 *"a Negro"*: Walter White, notes, "Recommendations," undated, NAACP, box II A603.

220 *Eisenhower promised White:* Walter White to Eleanor Roosevelt, February 23, 1944, NAACP, General Office File, box II-A603.
220 *Cliff Lee gave:* White, *A Rising Wind*, 62–66.
220 *He suggested:* White, "Observations and Recommendations."
220 *invited White:* John C. H. Lee to Walter White, April 3, 1944, NARA, RG 498, entry UD 1028, box 4719.
220 *The meal was:* White, "Address over the Columbia Broadcasting System."
221 *A survey:* War Department, Command of Negro Troops, February 29, 1944, EL, WWII Participants, box 56.
221 *"Negro problem":* Lee to White, April 3, 1944.

CHAPTER 25

222 *Friday evening, Eisenhower:* SHAEF, Minutes of Meeting Held in Room 126, Norfolk House, 1700 Hours, February 18, 1944, Smith Papers, box 21.
222 *That plan would have:* 21st Army Group, Memorandum on Implications of the SHAEF Proposal to Reduce the Allocation of Landing Ships and Landing Craft, February 17, 1944, Pogue Papers, box 154.
222 *"The 21st Army":* SHAEF, Minutes of Meeting Held in Room 126, Norfolk House, 1700 Hours, February 18, 1944.
223 *lunch with Churchill:* Butcher Diary, A-1102.
223 *"I recommend":* Bernard Montgomery to Dwight Eisenhower, February 19, 1944, Pre-Pres. Principal, box 83.
223 *The next morning:* COS(44), OVERLORD/ANVIL—Meeting with General Eisenhower, February 19, 1944, NARA, RG 331, entry NM8 3, box 126.
225 *"emphatically recommended":* Copy of Minute Dated 19th February 1944 to the Prime Minister from General Ismay, NARA, RG 331, entry 1, box 76.
225 *reported back:* Dwight Eisenhower to George Marshall, February 19, 1944, Pre-Pres. Principal, box 132.
225 *"I will use":* George Marshall to Dwight Eisenhower, February 8, 1944, Pre-Pres. Principal, box 132.
225 *"I agree thoroughly":* Eisenhower to Marshall, February 19, 1944.
225 *He had spent:* Daily Appointment Log, February 16, 1944, EL, Pre-Pres. Principal, box 127.
225 *The main issue:* Eisenhower to Marshall, February 19, 1944.

CHAPTER 26

227 *call him Ike:* Forrest Pogue, interview with Mark Clark, November 17, 1959, GCM, Forrest Pogue Interviews.
227 *Back at the start:* Forrest Pogue, interview with Dwight Eisenhower, June 28, 1962, GCM, Forrest Pogue Interviews.
227 *Beetle too:* Forrest Pogue, interview with Walter Bedell Smith, July 29, 1958, GCM, Forrest Pogue Interviews.
228 *"I wouldn't even":* Dwight Eisenhower to George Marshall, September 6, 1943, Pre-Pres. Principal, box 80.
228 *"Man up":* Carlo D'Este, *Eisenhower: A Soldier's Life* (Holt, 2002), 341–42.
228 *"friendliness in welding":* Dwight Eisenhower, Memorandum, February 7, 1944, in Butcher Diary, A-1063.
228 *newspaper columnists:* Wes Gallagher, "Failure to Exploit Successes after Anzio Landings Costly," Associated Press, February 9, 1944; Butcher Diary, A-1081.
228 "All your": Dwight Eisenhower to Maitland Wilson, February 11, 1944, Pre-Pres. Principal, box 124.
228 *arrived that weekend:* Everett Hughes, Diary, February 20, 1944, Hughes Papers, box I-1.
228 *A few years older:* Alexander G. Lovelace, "Hughes' War" (master's thesis, George Washington University, 2013), 3–4.
228 *Hughes's role as:* Lovelace, 33–46.
229 *Marshall had intervened:* George Marshall to Dwight Eisenhower, February 10, 1944, Pre-Pres. Principal, box 80.
229 *was a buddy:* Everett Hughes, Diary, December 31, 1942, Hughes Papers, box I-1.
229 *dogged by a cold:* Hughes, Diary, February 23, 1944, Hughes Papers, box I-1.
229 *get used to:* Dwight Eisenhower, *Letters to Mamie* (Doubleday, 1977), 168.
229 *Eisenhower offered him:* Lovelace, "Hughes' War," 74.
229 *"Red Cross girl":* Everett Hughes, Diary, February 21, 1944, Hughes Papers, box I-1.
229 *Butch planned to divorce:* Lloyd Shearer, "The Eisenhower-Summersby Love Affair" (draft), October 28, 1976, Wyoming, Harry Butcher Papers, box 3.
229 *running away to Tahiti:* Lloyd Shearer, "Butch and Ike—Different Roads," *Parade*, July 21, 1985.
229 *"Why are you":* Shearer, "Eisenhower-Summersby Love Affair."
230 *"worn out wolf":* Harry Butcher to John Burns, December 6, 1943, Wyoming, Harry Butcher Papers, box 3.

230 *Eisenhower got annoyed:* Everett Hughes, Diary, May 24, 1944, Hughes Papers, box I-1.
230 *"Sit tight":* Thomas Handy to Dwight Eisenhower, February 21, 1944, Pre-Pres. Principal, box 54.
230 *"We are committed":* William Leahy to Dwight Eisenhower, February 21, 1944, Smith Papers, box 27.
230 *"You were delegated":* George Marshall to Dwight Eisenhower, February 21, 1944, Smith Papers, box 27.
230 *US Chiefs rejected:* JCS to Dwight Eisenhower, February 21, 1944, Pre-Pres. Principal, box 63.
230 *"If the decision":* Bernard Montgomery to Dwight Eisenhower, February 21, 1944, Pre-Pres. Principal, box 83.
230 *Eisenhower attempted:* Dwight Eisenhower to Bernard Montgomery, February 21, 1944, Pre-Pres. Principal, box 83.
231 *Eisenhower returned:* COS(44) 55th Meeting, February 22, 1944, NARA, RG 331, entry NM8 3, box 126.
232 *Eisenhower tried to sell:* Dwight Eisenhower to George Marshall, February 22, 1944, Pre-Pres. Principal, box 133.

CHAPTER 27

233 *went to dinner:* Dwight Eisenhower to Andrew Cunningham, February 23, 1944, Pre-Pres. Principal, box 29.
233 *"Today":* Andrew Cunningham, "Speech by the First Sea Lord on the Occasion of the Presentation of a Signed Salver to General Eisenhower," February 22, 1944, Pre-Pres. Principal, box 29.
234 *"I feel that":* Andrew Cunningham, *The Cunningham Papers* (Routledge, 1996), 2:88.
234 *silver salver:* Dwight Eisenhower, *Letters to Mamie* (Doubleday, 1977), 170.
234 *"General Dwight":* Butcher Diary, A-1102.
234 *On the back:* James Gault to H. P. R. Hoar, February 29, 1944, Pre-Pres. Principal, box 46.
234 *The churlish part:* Eisenhower, *Letters to Mamie*, 170.
234 *He thanked everyone:* Dwight Eisenhower to Andrew Cunningham, February 23, 1944, Pre-Pres. Principal, box 29.
234 *Eisenhower awoke early:* Butcher Diary, A-1108.
234 *felt embarrassed:* Eisenhower to Cunningham, February 23, 1944.
234 *Parker Pen Company:* Eisenhower to Cunningham, February 26, 1944, Pre-Pres. Principal, box 29.
235 *"In your own":* Dwight Eisenhower, Memorandum to Kay Summersby, March 29, 1944, Sotheby's, Sale 6188, Fine Books and Manuscripts, June 13, 1991, lot 171.
235 *"I have so":* Dwight Eisenhower to Walter B. Smith, February 26, 1944, Pre-Pres. Principal, box 109.
235 *That Saturday:* SHAEF, Minutes of Meeting Held in Room 126, Norfolk House, 1000 Hours, February 26, 1944, NAUK, WO 205 12.
235 *"Conclusions":* CCS to Dwight Eisenhower, February 26, 1944, Pre-Pres. Principal, box 130.
235 *Beetle read:* SHAEF, Minutes of Meeting Held in Room 126, Norfolk House, 1000 Hours, February 26, 1944.
236 *"saw wood":* Butcher Diary, A-1119.
236 *Leigh-Mallory had concerns:* SHAEF, Minutes of Meeting Held in Room 126, Norfolk House, 1000 Hours, February 26, 1944.
236 *"Big Week":* Mark Copeland, *The Mighty Eighth* (Griffon International, 2021), 56.
236 *"an increased effort":* SHAEF, Minutes of Meeting Held in Room 126, Norfolk House, 1000 Hours, February 26, 1944.
237 *"The Air Plan":* SHAEF, Minutes of Meeting Held in Room 126, Norfolk House, 1000 Hours, February 26, 1944 ("The Air Plan [will] would not not be ready for a few days").
237 *Ramsay spoke:* John Mason, "The Reminiscences of Alan Goodrich Kirk," no. 455, 1962, Oral History Research Office, Columbia University, 351.
237 *Monty fully agreed:* SHAEF, Minutes of Meeting Held in Room 126, Norfolk House, 1000 Hours, February 26, 1944.

CHAPTER 28

238 *The month of February:* Dwight Eisenhower, *Letters to Mamie* (Doubleday, 1977), 168.
238 *drinking more:* George S. Patton, Diary, March 1, 1944, Patton Papers, box 3.
238 *three packs a day:* Michael McKeogh and Richard Lockridge, *Sgt. Mickey & General Ike* (Putnam, 1946), 40.
238 *He knew the smoking:* Eisenhower, *Letters to Mamie*, 167.
238 *He had experimented:* Tobin, "A Day with General Eisenhower," June 20, 1944, EL, Harry C. Butcher Papers, box 3.
238 *He liked rapping:* McKeogh and Lockridge, *Sgt. Mickey & General Ike*, 39.
238 *London's winters:* Bertram Ramsay, *The Year of D-Day* (University of Hull, 1994), 34.

238 *air raids:* Conclusions of a Meeting of the War Cabinet held 10 Downing Street, SW 1, on Monday, February 28, 1944, NAUK, CAB 65/41/26.
238 *Churchill invited Eisenhower:* Butcher Diary, A-1119.
238 *a foul mood:* Alan Brooke, *War Diaries, 1939–1945* (Phoenix Press, 2001), 526.
238 *The Italian campaign:* Harold Alexander to Alan Brooke, February 28, 1944, NARA, RG 331, entry 1, box 76.
239 *The British had sent:* Martin Blumenson, *Salerno to Cassino*, CMH_Pub_3-3-1 (US Government Printing Office, 1969), 322–351; Butcher Diary, A-1119; Robert Barlow, et al., "Battle Analysis: Rapido River Crossing, Offensive, Deliberate Attack, River Crossing," May 1984, Combat Studies Institute, Fort Leavenworth, KS.
239 *ten that evening:* Chiefs of Staff, Record of a Staff Conference Held in the Prime Minister's Map Room, on Monday, 28th February, 1944 10 p.m., NARA, RG 331, NM8 3, box 126.
239 *Churchill had been heartened:* Winston Churchill, COS, 54th Meeting, February 25, 1944, Annex I, EL, Smith Papers, box 21.
239 *Bertie Ramsay's solution:* Chiefs of Staff, Record of a Staff Conference held in the Prime Minister's Map Room, on Monday, 28th February.
239 *the delay in one:* Corrigendum to C.O.S. (44) 86th Meeting (O) Minutes, March 15, 1944, NARA, RG 331, NM8 3, box 126.
239 *time to make:* Dwight Eisenhower to George Marshall, March 3, 1944, Pre-Pres. Principal, box 80.
239 *A memo on:* Trafford Leigh-Mallory, "'OVERLORD'—Employment of Bomber Forces in Relation to the Outline Plan," February 13, 1944, AFHRA, reel A5099.
240 *Arthur Tedder deserved:* Forrest Pogue, interview with James Robb, February 3, 1947, Pogue Papers, box 161; Lord Tedder, *With Prejudice* (Little Brown, 1966), 503.
240 *The Allies had refined:* Harold R. Bull, Diary & Notes, EL, Harold R Bull Papers, box 2.
240 *"What attack would":* Forrest Pogue, interview with James Robb, February 3, 1947, Pogue Papers, box 161.
240 *air planners estimated:* Leigh-Mallory, "'OVERLORD.'"
240 *Churchill balked at:* Butcher Diary, A-1119.
240 *"Why did we":* Eisenhower to Marshall, March 3, 1944.
241 *Eisenhower played for:* Eisenhower to Arthur Tedder, February 29, 1944, Pre-Pres. Principal, box 124.
241 *reduce German production:* Lord Tedder, *With Prejudice*, 510.
241 *"succession of dust":* Eisenhower, Report on Trans-Continental Trip, November 3, 1919, EL, Records as President, President's Personal File, box 967.
241 *"in this thing":* Eisenhower to Tedder, February 29, 1944.
241 *That meeting began:* Chiefs of Staff, COS (44) 70th Meeting War Cabinet, Chiefs of Staff, Record of a Staff Conference Held in the Prime Minister's Map Room, on Monday, 29th February, 1944 10p.m., NARA, RG 331, NM8 3, box 126.
241 *"We hoped to":* Brooke, *War Diaries*, 527; Hastings Ismay to Averell Harriman, March 17, 1944, LOC, Averell Harriman Papers, box 1102.
241 *To help the whale:* Chiefs of Staff, Record of a Staff Conference Held in the Prime Minister's Map Room, on Monday, 29th February, 1944.
241 *Churchill's position:* Butcher Diary, A-1121.
241 *"Control of the":* Memorandum by the United States Chiefs of Staff, Control of Strategic Air Forces in Northwest Europe and in the Mediterranean, C.C.S. 400/2, December 4, 1943, FRUS, *The Conferences at Cairo and Tehran, 1943*, doc. 478; Combined Chiefs of Staff Minutes, December 7, 1944, FRUS, *The Conferences at Cairo and Tehran, 1943*, doc. 461.
242 *Portal had opposed:* Combined Chiefs of Staff Minutes, December 4, 1942, FRUS, *The Conferences at Cairo and Tehran, 1943*, doc. 439.
242 *"to go home":* Chiefs of Staff, Record of a Staff Conference held in the Prime Minister's Map Room, on Monday, 29th February, 1944.
242 *The main problem:* Eisenhower to Marshall, March 3, 1944.
242 *would ever agree:* Carl Spaatz to Henry Arnold, draft, February 7, 1944, LOC, Carl Spaatz Papers, Box 12; Carl Spaatz, Diary, February 15, 1944, LOC, Carl Spaatz Papers, box 12.
242 *Would that be:* Butcher Diary, A-1121.
242 *"Leigh-Mallory was":* Conference with General Eisenhower, April 24, 1947, Pre-Pres. Principal, box 68.
242 *generous to Leigh-Mallory:* Forrest Pogue, interview with Philip Wigglesworth, April 1, 1947, Pogue Papers, box 161.
243 *Leigh-Mallory was happy:* Butcher Diary, A-1121.
243 *"the continuation":* Charles Portal to Dwight Eisenhower, March 7, 1944, Pre-Pres. Principal, box 93
243 *"supreme operations":* Report of the Combined Chiefs of Staff to the President and the Prime Minister, December 6, 1943, FRUS 1943, doc. 499.

243 *"hot shot"*: Henry Arnold to Dwight Eisenhower, March 8, 1944, NARA, RG 331, entry 1, box 14.
243 *reminding Jimmy Doolittle:* Leish, interview with Jimmy Doolittle, April 1960, James H. Doolittle Papers, Series XVII, box 1, D021-95-14-93-3, p. 34.
243 *he did best:* James Doolittle to Joe Doolittle, April 5, 1944, James H. Doolittle Papers, Series IX, box 113, D022-84.
243 *Eisenhower called Tedder:* George S. Patton, Diary, March 6, 1944, Patton Papers, box 3.
243 *three points:* Butcher Diary, A-1001.
244 *"Now listen"*: George S. Patton, Diary, March 8, 1944, Patton Papers, box 3.
244 *"In that case"*: Forrest Pogue, interview with Leslie Scarman, February 25, 1947, Pogue Papers, box 161.
244 *"responsibility for supervision"*: Charles Portal to Dwight Eisenhower, March 9, 1944, Pre-Pres. Principal, box 93.
244 *"exactly what we"*: Dwight Eisenhower to Charles Portal, March 10, 1944, Pre-Pres Principal, box 93.
244 *"I think this"*: Walter B. Smith to Dwight Eisenhower, March 10, 1944, Pre-Pres Principal, box 93.
244 *orders for D-Day*: SHAEF to Bernard Montgomery, Bertram Ramsay, and Trafford Leigh-Mallory, Operation OVERLORD, March 10, 1944, IWM, Papers of Field Marshal Viscount Montgomery of Alamein, box 105.
244 *Omar Bradley*: Walter Smith, Memorandum for Omar Bradley, Operation OVERLORD, March 10, 1944, IWM, Papers of Field Marshal Viscount Montgomery of Alamein, box 105.
244 *A courier*: Goronwy Rees, *Sketches in Autobiography* (University of Wales Press, 2001), 266.

CHAPTER 29

247 *"No man ever"*: SLA Marshall, Eisenhower on Lee, SLAM Papers, box 71.
247 *like city living:* Butcher Diary, A-1132.
247 *"country"*: Dwight Eisenhower to Mamie Eisenhower, March 4, 1944, private collection.
247 *the same complex*: Walter B. Smith to Dwight Eisenhower, January 1, 1944, Pre-Pres. Principal, box 109.
248 *incessant flow:* Dwight Eisenhower to Mamie Eisenhower, March 4, 1944.
248 *Kingston 7777*: ETO, Roster of Key Officers, June 1, 1944, Pre-Pres. Principal, box 154.
248 *All week, he:* Butcher Diary, A-1132.
248 *the fresh air:* Eisenhower, *Letters to Mamie*, 167.
248 *back in Algeria:* Dwight Eisenhower to Mamie Eisenhower, November 1, 1943, private collection.
248 *a few times:* Kay Summersby, *Eisenhower Was My Boss* (Dell, 1948), 62.
248 *North African sun:* Dwight Eisenhower to Mamie Eisenhower, June 30, 1943, private collection.
248 *the vast, flat:* McKeogh and Lockridge, *Sgt. Mickey & General Ike*, 60.
248 *often come along:* Summersby, *Eisenhower Was My Boss*, 62.
248 *had a workhorse:* Oral History Research Office, Eisenhower Administration: The Reminiscences of Milton Eisenhower, 1979, Columbia Center on Oral History, p. 5.
248 *named Blackie*: Dwight Eisenhower, *At Ease: Stories I Tell to Friends* (Doubleday, 1967), 188–92.
248 *no one else wanted:* Relman Morin, interview with Dwight Eisenhower, August 5, 1965, EL, 1965 Principal File, box 2.
248 *Over weeks:* Eisenhower, *At Ease*, 188–92.
249 *The groundskeeper's horse:* Butcher Diary, A-1132.
249 *a single filing cabinet*: Mack Teasley, Interview with Sue Sarafian Jehl, February 13, 1991, EL, Oral Histories, 9.
249 *Old acquaintances:* Dwight Eisenhower to Florence Northcott, February 28, 1944, Pre-Pres. Principal, box 85.
250 *personally respond*: Mack Teasley, Interview with Sue Sarafian Jehl, February 13, 1991, EL, Oral Histories.
250 *"I begin to"*: Eisenhower, *Letters to Mamie*, 172.
250 *Four different biographers:* Arthur Eisenhower to Mamie Eisenhower, February 7, 1944, Pre-Pres. Principal, box 171.
250 *"human interest"*: Dwight Eisenhower to Edgar Eisenhower, April 10, 1944, Pre-Pres. Principal, box 172.
250 *"interested in the entire"*: Eisenhower, Material on Military History Lecture, Pre-Pres. Principal, box 193.
250 *books would be written:* Eisenhower to Milton Eisenhower, August 2, 1944, Pre-Pres. Principal, box 16.
250 *Butch was in talks:* H.S. Latham to Harry Butcher, January 10, 1944, EL, Harry C. Butcher Papers, box 3.
250 *Milton was keen:* Milton Eisenhower to Harry Butcher, March 10, 1944, Wyoming, Harry Butcher Papers, box 3.
250 *"Let the biographers"*: Harry Butcher to Milton Eisenhower, April 10, 1944, Wyoming, Harry Butcher Papers, box 3.
250 *thinking far bigger:* J. P. Didier to Kenneth Davis, February 23, 1944, Davis Papers, box 94.
250 *"spiritual greatness"*: Milton Eisenhower, "The Foundation of America, Address at a Patriotic Rally," February 22, 1944, Davis Papers, box 22.

250 *"American Century"*: Henry Luce, "The American Century," *Time*, February 17, 1941.
251 *"Our intellectual heroes"*: Milton Eisenhower, "Foundation of America."
251 *reaching out to publishers:* Didier to Davis, February 23, 1944.
251 *"drama in the fact"*: Milton Eisenhower to Kenneth Davis, October 13, 1944, Davis Papers, box 61.
252 *"a book of character"*: Kenneth Davis, interview with Milton Eisenhower, 1944, Davis Papers, box 61.
252 *Milton had asked:* Milton Eisenhower to Kenneth Davis, February 3, 1944, Davis Papers, box 22.
252 *"more literary quality"*: Kenneth Davis to Ruth Boyd, February 26, 1944, Davis Papers, box 94.
252 *Doubleday ultimately offered:* Kenneth Davis, "Summary of Telephone Conversion with Elise McKeogh," February 29, 1944, Davis Papers, box 94.
252 *serialize the finished product:* Elise Boyd to Kenneth Davis, March 1, 1944, Davis Papers, box 94.
252 *"for the family"*: Kenneth Davis to Elise McKeogh, March 11, 1944, Davis Papers, box 94.
252 *"I hope you"*: Milton Eisenhower to Dwight Eisenhower, March 10, 1944, Pre-Pres. Principal, box 174.
252 *Eisenhower still preferred:* Harry Butcher to Milton Eisenhower, April 10, 1944, Wyoming, Harry Butcher Papers, box 3.
252 *Eisenhower's fame was:* Program of "Passing Out Parade" at No. 100 Royal Armoured Corps Officers Cadet Training Unit, Royal Military College, Sandhurst, in Butcher Diary, A-1132.
253 *Eisenhower stood:* Dwight Eisenhower, March 20, 1944, British Pathé, Film ID: 1354.05.
253 *"I'm keenly sensible"*: "Transcript of Extemporaneous Remarks, Sandhurst, England," March 11, 1944, Wyoming, Harry Butcher Papers, box 3.
254 *"One would feel"*: Eisenhower, *Letters to Mamie*, 172.
254 *Kay was mobbed:* Summersby, *Eisenhower Was My Boss*, 140.
254 *"I think, at times"*: Dwight Eisenhower to George Marshall, March 15, 1944, Pre-Pres. Principal, box 80.
254 *"translantic essay contest"*: Butcher Diary, Harry C. Butcher, *My Three Years with Eisenhower* (Simon & Schuster, 1946), 37.
254 *By March, everyone:* COMNAVEU to OPNAV, March 14, 1944, NARA, RG 331, entry 1, box 76.
254 *Things had become:* Henry Wilson to British Chiefs of Staff, March 20, 1944, NARA RG 331, entry 1, box 76.
255 *tried to prepare:* Dwight Eisenhower to George Marshall, March 20, 1944, Pre-Pres. Principal, box 133.
255 *He had overcome:* British Chiefs of Staff, Control of Strategic Bombing for Overlord, March 17, 1944, AFHRA, reel A5049.
255 *"responsibility for supervision"*: Charles Portal to Dwight Eisenhower, March 9, 1944, Pre-Pres. Principal, box 93.
255 *a cable came:* J.S.M. Washington to W.C.O London, March 17, 1944, NARA, RG 331, entry 1, box 76.
255 *Arnold remained opposed:* David Eisenhower, *Eisenhower at War* (Random House, 1986), 49–50, 180.
255 *"he did not"*: J.S.M. Washington to W.C.O London, March 17, 1944.
255 *"astonished"*: Dwight Eisenhower to George Marshall, March 21, 1944, Pre-Pres. Principal, box 133.
255 *Monty's condescending tirades:* SHAEF, Minutes of Meeting Held in Room 126, Norfolk House, 1000 Hours, March 10, 1944, NAUK, WO 205 12.
255 *On Monday, March 20:* Kay Summersby, Diary, March 20, 1944, EL, Barbara Wyden Papers, box 1.
255 *lunch in London:* Winston Churchill, Engagement Diary, March 1944, Churchill Papers, CHAR 20/19/03.
255 *Churchill was irate:* Butcher Diary, A-1148-49.
256 *"the first of"*: Joseph Dynan, "Pucheu Condemned to Die as Traitor," Associated Press, March 11, 1944.
256 *close to agreeing:* The Secretary of State to the Ambassador in the Soviet Union (Harriman), April 8, 1944, FRUS 1944, vol. 3, doc. 609.
256 *In September:* The Under Secretary of State (Stettinius) to the Secretary of State, May 22, 1944, FRUS 1944, vol. 3, doc. 1.
256 *operated from Algiers:* Duff Cooper to Anthony Eden, March 24, 1944, NAUK, FO-954-16B-531.
256 *"mediocre men who"*: Edwin Wilson, "Policy re Establishment of French Civil Administration in Continental France After Liberation," January 20, 1944, NARA, RG 107, entry 183, box 55.
257 *"I get so weary"*: Butcher Diary, A-1146.
257 *Letters Eisenhower had written:* Dwight Eisenhower to George Marshall, March 21, 1944, Pre-Pres. Principal, box 80.
257 *a long memo:* Dwight Eisenhower, Memorandum, March 22, 1944, in Butcher Diary, A-1156.
258 *"Amen!"*: Butcher Diary, A-1158.
258 *Eisenhower began:* Butcher Diary, A-1160.
258 *new intelligence:* Bryan Conrad to Clayton Bissell, March 23, 1944, Smith Papers, box 23.
258 *"certain materials"*: George Marshall to Dwight Eisenhower, March 22, 1944, NARA RG77, Subfile 7D.
258 *"At least twelve"*: Clayton Bissell to Dwight Eisenhower, March 24, 1944, Smith Papers, box 27.
258 *The first stop:* Kay Summersby, Diary, March 23, 1944, EL, Barbara Wyden Papers, box 1.

258 *been a fascination:* Dwight Eisenhower to George Marshall, February 19, 1944, Pre-Pres. Principal, box 80; Eisenhower to Marshall, September 20, 1943, Pre-Presidential Papers, Principal File, box 80.
258 *Patton queasy:* George Patton to George Patton Jr., April 19, 1944, Patton Papers box 19.
258 *Churchill led:* "Churchill and Eisenhower Visit Paratroopers," British Pathé, undated, Film ID: 1973.11.
258 *looking more worn down:* Everett Hughes, Diary, March 23, 1944, Hughes Papers, box I-1.
259 *regards to Kay:* Kay Summersby, *Eisenhower Was My Boss* (Dell, 1948), 140–141; Barney Oldfield, *Never a Shot in Anger* (Van Rees, 1956), 45.
259 *"This 81":* Oldfield, *Never a Shot in Anger*, 44.
259 *Churchill stood before:* Summersby, Diary, March 23, 1944.
259 *"Soon you will":* "Churchill in Inspection of Air Borne Units," United Press, March 23, 1944.
259 *"I thank God":* "Churchill Tells American Troops Showdown Near," United Press, March 23, 1944.
259 *A little after six:* Kay Summersby, Diary, March 23, 1944, EL, Barbara Wyden Papers, box 1.
259 *They were joined:* Omar Bradley, *A General's Life* (Simon & Schuster, 1983), 231–32.
260 *"back General Eisenhower":* Kay Summersby, Diary, March 24, 1944, EL, Barbara Wyden Papers, box 1.
260 *There was brandy:* Bradley, *A General's Life*, 231–32.
260 *to regale everyone:* Dwight Eisenhower, manuscript, "Churchill & Marshall," November 17, 1966, Post-Presidential Papers, A-WR Series, box 8.
260 *grill Joe Collins:* Summersby, *Eisenhower Was My Boss*, 141.
260 *chance to let loose:* Bradley, *A General's Life*, 231–32.
260 *always got dour:* Eisenhower, "Churchill & Marshall."
260 *"casualty conscious":* Dwight Eisenhower to Hastings Ismay, December 3, 1960, EL, Whitman Name File, box 19.
260 *"haunted by the twin":* Hastings Ismay to Dwight Eisenhower, December 30, 1960, EL, Whitman Name File, box 19.
261 *"My dear General":* Dwight Eisenhower, "Churchill & Marshall."
262 *"The drums!":* Bradley, *A General's Life*, 231–32.

CHAPTER 30

263 *"War is essentially":* Fox Conner, "Organization and Functioning of G-3, A. E. F," September 18, 1931, USAHEC, AWC Curricular Archives, G-3 Course 8.
263 *"The only constant":* Eisenhower, Material on Military History Lecture, Pre-Pres. Principal, box 193.
264 *Operation Pointblank culminated:* Kay Summersby, Diary, March 25, 1944, EL, Barbara Wyden Papers, box 1.
264 *Tedder made:* SHAEF, Final Minutes of a Meeting Held on Saturday March 25th to Discuss the Bombing Policy in the Period before Overlord, CAS/Misc./61, March 25, 1944, EL Pre-Pres. Principal, box 139.
264 *"The first five":* SHAEF, Final Minutes of a Meeting Held on Saturday March 25th to Discuss the Bombing Policy.
265 *"Everything I have read":* SHAEF, Final Minutes of a Meeting Held on Saturday March 25th to Discuss the Bombing Policy.
265 *"approximately 80%":* Carl Spaatz, Employment of Strategic Air Forces in Support of Overlord, March 24, 1944, Pre-Pres Principal, box 136.
266 *"I entirely agree":* SHAEF, Final Minutes of a Meeting Held on Saturday March 25th to Discuss the Bombing Policy.
266 *decision on landing craft:* George Marshall to Dwight Eisenhower, March 25, 1944, Pre-Presidential Papers, Principal File, box 133.
266 *Eisenhower would get:* Dwight Eisenhower to George Marshall, March 25, 1944, Pre-Presidential Papers, Principal File, box 133.
266 *sense of purpose:* Dwight Eisenhower to Walter B. Smith, July 5, 1947, SLAM Papers, box 95, folder 1559.

CHAPTER 31

267 *A routine developed:* Mattie Pinette, Eisenhower I, undated, EL, George Hall Papers, box 1.
267 *sprawl out:* Dwight Eisenhower to Mamie Eisenhower, June 30, 1943, private collection.
267 *come to realize:* Dwight Eisenhower, "On Military History," April 22, 1947, SLAM Papers, box 94; Dwight Eisenhower, *Crusade in Europe* (Doubleday, 1947), 261–262.
267 *particularly grueling trip:* Kay Summersby, *Eisenhower Was My Boss* (Dell, 1948), 142.
267 *First Infantry Division:* Summersby, Diary, April 2, 1944, EL, Barbara Wyden Papers, box 1.
267 *"Private Arthur Goodwin":* E. C. Biehnke, "Experience of a Replacement with a Veteran Combat Unit," undated, EL, Harry C. Butcher Papers, box 3.

268 *his voice started:* Butcher Diary, A-1177.
268 *"You know you're":* Mattie Pinette, Eisenhower I, undated, EL, George Hall Papers, box 1.
268 *"If he can":* Dwight Eisenhower to Leonard Gerow, April 3, 1944, Pre-Pres. Principal, box 46.
268 *been looking forward:* Kay Summersby, Diary, March 18, 1944, EL, Barbara Wyden Papers, box 1.
269 *Eisenhower shipped off:* Susan Eisenhower, *Mrs. Ike* (Farrar, Straus and Giroux, 1996), 136, 143, 153, 166.
269 *that in 1941:* Ray S. Cline, *The War Department Washington Command Post: The Operations Division* (US Government Printing Office, 1951), 54–55.
269 *One of Gee's deputies:* Dwight Eisenhower, *Crusade in Europe* (Doubleday, 1947), 17.
269 *"How long?":* Forrest Pogue, interview with Dwight Eisenhower, June 28, 1962, GCM, Forrest Pogue Interviews.
269 *Eisenhower left that day:* Kenneth Davis, interview with Earnest R. ("Tex") Lee, 1944, Davis Papers, box 94.
269 *"Look, there are":* Pogue, interview with Eisenhower, June 28, 1962.
270 *Wayne Clark had recommended:* Forrest Pogue, interview with Mark Clark, November 17, 1959, GCM, Forrest Pogue Interviews.
270 *kept a list:* Larry I. Bland, ed., *George C. Marshall Interviews and Reminiscences for Forrest C. Pogue* (George C. Marshall Foundation, 1996), 626.
270 *"Divine Destiny":* George S. Patton to Beatrice Patton, November 11, 1943, Patton Papers, box 18.
270 *"worked closely with":* "Eisenhower as War Plans Chief Completes Army Staff Recasting," *New York Times*, February 20, 1942.
270 *Gee's departure:* Cline, *War Department Washington Command Post*, 75–77.
270 *two messages:* Joint Committee on the Investigation of the Pearl Harbor Attack, 79th Cong. 2nd Sess., doc. no. 244, 1946, 209–25.
271 *Beetle had been:* Forrest Pogue, interview with Walter Bedell Smith, July 29, 1958, GCM, Forrest Pogue Interviews.
271 *The fourteenth part:* Joint Committee on the Investigation of the Pearl Harbor Attack, 209–25.
271 *Gee willingly took:* Joint Committee on the Investigation of the Pearl Harbor Attack, 128.
271 *political vulnerability:* Forrest Pogue, Interview with Mark Clark, November 17, 1959, GCM, Forrest Pogue Interviews; Forrest Pogue, Interview with LT Gerow, February 24, 1958, GCM, Forrest Pogue Interviews; Jade Hinman, "When the Japanese Bombed the Huertgen Forest," monograph, AY 2011, School of Advanced Military Studies.
271 *Back in London:* Winston Churchill, Engagement Diary, April 1944, Churchill Papers, CHAR 20/19/03.
271 *Conversation dwelled:* Butcher Diary, A-1177.
271 *confidence vote:* Education Bill (Question of Confidence), March 29, 1944, *House of Commons Hansard*, 398:1480–524.
272 *The press, though:* "Confidence," *Observer* (London), April 2, 1944.
272 *didn't get it:* Butcher Diary, A-1180.
272 *easily survived:* Central Direction of the War, July 2, 1942, *House of Commons Hansard*, 381:527–611.
272 *"It is an axiom":* Quentin Reynolds, "Invasion," *Collier's* 113, no. 15 (April 8, 1944).
272 *"British propagandists":* "Demand to Beat 'Japan First' Sweeping the Nation," *Pittsburg Sun-Telegraph*, March 26, 1944, 3.
272 *"Sometimes":* Dwight Eisenhower, manuscript, "Churchill & Marshall," November 17, 1966, Post-Presidential Papers, A-WR Series, box 8.
272 *Eisenhower was adamant:* Butcher Diary, A-1177.
273 *Churchill showed Eisenhower:* Dwight Eisenhower to George Marshall, April 3, 1944, Pre-Presidential Papers, Principal File, box 133.
273 *the French question:* Butcher Diary, A-1179.
273 *only viable partner:* Dwight Eisenhower to Combined Chiefs, January 19, 1944, Eisenhower Papers, 3:1667; Butcher Diary, A-1185; Lowell Rooks to Walter B. Smith, April 2, 1944, Smith Papers, box 15; Dwight Eisenhower to George Marshall, May 16, 1944, Pre-Pres. Principal, box 133; Drew Pearson, "Washington Merry Go Round," February 1, 1944.
273 *the spill:* Clayton Bissell to Dwight Eisenhower, March 29, 1944, Smith Papers, box 27; Butcher Diary, A-1177.
273 *Eisenhower took:* Dwight Eisenhower to Ceil Gans, April 3, 1944, Pre-Pres. Principal, box 45; Dwight Eisenhower to Frances Curry, April 3, 1944, Pre-Pres Principal, box 29; Dwight Eisenhower to Ida Stover Eisenhower, March 31, 1944, Pre-Pres Principal, box 172.
273 *wrote to Mamie:* Dwight Eisenhower, *Letters to Mamie* (Doubleday, 1977), 174.
273 *wrote to John:* Dwight Eisenhower to John Eisenhower, March 31, 1944, Pre-Pres. Principal, box 173.
273 *The biggest decision:* Butcher Diary, A-1185.
273 *got a letter:* Butcher Diary, A-1182.

273 *"In view of"*: Winston Churchill to Dwight Eisenhower, April 3, 1944, Pre-Pres. Principal, box 22.
274 *worked with Teddder*: Lord Tedder, *With Prejudice* (Little Brown, 1966), 522.
274 *"made feasible"*: Eisenhower to Churchill, April 5, 1944, Pre-Pres. Principal, box 22.
274 *an afternoon ride*: Butcher Diary, A-1185.

CHAPTER 32

275 *General William Borden*: George Marshall to Dwight Eisenhower, April 1, 1944, GCM, Marshall Papers, box 66.
275 *Borden had spent*: Marshall to Douglas MacArthur, September 14, 1943, in *The Papers of George Catlett Marshall* (Johns Hopkins University Press, 1996), 4:125–26.
275 *battle for Kwajalein*: Philip A. Crow and Edmund G. Love, *Seizure of the Gilberts and Marshalls*, CMH _Pub_5-6-1 (US Government Printing Office, 1955), 245.
275 *"super guns"*: Lida Mayo, *The Ordinance Department*, CMH Pub 10-11 (US Government Printing Office, 1968), 336.
275 *Edward Stettinius*: Kay Summersby, Diary, April 12, 1944, EL, Barbara Wyden Papers, box 1.
275 *persuade Stettinius*: The Under Secretary of State (Stettinius) to the Secretary of State, April 13, 1944, FRUS 1944, vol. 1, doc. 276.
276 *"tidiness inspection"*: Dwight Eisenhower to George Marshall, April 17, 1944, Pre-Pres. Principal, box 80.
276 *Exercise Thunderclap*: Kay Summersby, Diary, April 7, 1944, EL, Barbara Wyden Papers, box 1.
276 *"Allied Team"*: Bernard Montgomery, "Brief Summary of Operation 'Overlord' as Affecting the Army," April 7, 1944, IWM, Papers of Field Marshal Viscount Montgomery of Alamein, box 74.
276 *"This is an invasion"*: George S. Patton, Diary, April 7, Patton Papers, box 3.
276 *"Germans will suffer"*: Winston Churchill to Franklin Roosevelt, April 12, 1944, Churchill Papers, CHAR 20/161.
276 *six at night*: Summersby, Diary, April 7, 1944.
276 *"A shortage of"*: George S. Patton, Diary, April 7, Patton Papers, box 3.
276 *"off again"*: Butcher Diary, A-1205.
276 *"The End Run"*: Butcher Diary, A-1162.
277 *Eisenhower thought*: Dwight Eisenhower to George Marshall, April 8, 1944, Pre-Pres. Principal, box 80.
277 *machine called Colossus*: David A. Price, *Geniuses at War* (Knopf, 2021), 151.
277 *agreed to share*: George Marshall to Dwight Eisenhower, March 15, 1944, GCM, Marshall Papers, box 66.
277 *Code-named "Ultra"*: Frederick Winterbotham, *The Ultra Secret* (Harper and Row, 1974), 119–130; David A. Price, *Geniuses at War*, at 131; Peter Caddick-Adams, *Sand and Steel* (Oxford, 2019), 294–297.
277 *One of the first messages*: Price, *Geniuses at War*, 151.
277 *In response, the Nazis*: Everett Hughes, Diary, March 18, 1944, Hughes Papers, box I-1.
277 *There were stakes*: Alfred Beck, et al., *The Corps of Engineers*, CMH Pub. 10-22 (GPO, 1985), 300–302; GSI 21st Army Group, Weekly Neptune Review, No. 10, April 23, 1944, NARA, RG 331, Entry 262A, Box 17; T. J. Waldron and James Gleeson, *The Frogmen* (Evans, 1951), 114–120; A.J. Leibling, "Cross-Channel Trip, Part I," *The New Yorker*, June 23, 1944.
277 *In an ideal world*: John Mason, "The Reminiscences of Alan Goodrich Kirk," no. 455, 1962, Oral History Research Office, Columbia University, p. 295.
278 *the sappers*: Forrest Pogue, interview with E.T. Williams, May 30-31, 1947, Pogue Papers, box 161.
278 *But at low tide*: Mason, "Reminiscences of Alan Goodrich Kirk," 295.
278 *"of the highest order"*: George Marshall to Dwight Eisenhower, March 22, 1944, NARA, RG77, Subfile 7D.
278 *It was a Saturday*: Daily Appointment Log, April 8, 1944, EL, Pre-Pres. Principal, box 127.
278 *A rather bookish-looking major*: Vincent C. Jones, *Manhattan* (Center for Military History, 1985), 195.
278 *keen to explain*: A. V. Peterson, "Nature of Problem and Plan of Operation of Operation Peppermint," NARA, RG77, Subfile 7D.
279 *German physicists*: Anthony Brown and Charles MacDonald, *The Secret History of the Atomic Bomb* (Dell, 1977), 223.
279 *And in September 1941*: Brown and MacDonald, 210; Thomas Powers, *Heisenberg's War* (Knopf, 1993), 117–25.
279 World Set Free: H. G. Wells, *The World Set Free* (MacMillan, 1914).
279 *"la bomba"*: "Las Nuevas Armas de esta Guerra," *Hoja Oficial Del Lunes*, December 1, 1941, at 1.
279 *"the development"*: George Strong, Memorandum for General Eisenhower, September 8, 1942, NARA, RG 77, Subfile 7D.
280 *"It was possible"*: Peterson, "Nature of Problem and Plan of Operation."

280 *"Manual on Use"*: A. V. Peterson, "Manual on the Use of Radioactive Materials in Warfare," NARA, RG 77, Subfile 7D.

280 *Scientists working for:* Leslie Groves, "Radioactive Warfare," RSD 322.115, February 15, 1948, NARA, RG 218, entry 206, box 206.

280 *warned General Marshall:* Leslie Groves to George Marshall, July 23, 1943, NARA, RG 77, Subfile 7D.

280 *conducted experiments:* Groves, "Radioactive Warfare."

280 *The good news:* J. P. Conant, A. H. ComPatton, and H. C. Urey, "The Use of Radioactive Materials as a Military Weapon," September 4, 1943, U.S. Department of Energy Office of Scientific and Technical Information, ACHl.000003.006e.

281 *"The roentgen"*: Peterson, "Nature of Problem and Plan of Operation."

281 *though, could kill:* Joseph G. Hamilton, "Radioactive Warfare," December 31, 1946, NARA, RG 218, entry 206, box 206.

281 *Experiments showed:* Harold C. Hodge, "Practical Tests of the Application of Highly Radioactive Sprays and Dusts to Level Ground and to Buildings," August 6, 1943, NARA, RG 77, Subfile 7D.

281 *"One day's exposure"*: Peterson, "Nature of Problem and Plan of Operation."

281 *Chemical companies connected:* Brown and MacDonald, *Secret History of the Atomic Bomb*, 215.

281 *"no moral issue"*: A. V. Peterson, "Military Use of Radio-active Materials and Organization for Defense," NARA, RG77, Subfile 7D.

281 *Experts inside:* Harold C. Urey to James Conant, September 8, 1943, NARA, RG 77, Subfile 7D.

282 *Peterson's experiments:* Peterson, "Nature of Problem and Plan of Operation."

282 *Peterson revealed: Report on Action Taken for Defense against Possible use of Radioactive Material by the Enemy*, NARA, RG 77, Subfile 7D.

282 *Every time a German:* George S. Eyster, "Operation 'Peppermint,'" May 1, 1944, NARA, RG 77, Subfile 7D.

282 *had the discretion:* Eyster.

282 *personal signature:* Walter B. Smith, Receipt of Material, April 8, 1944, NARA, RG 331, entry 1, box 14.

282 *A big one:* Everett Hughes, Diary, April 6, 1944, Hughes Papers, box I-1.

283 *"to the lower"*: Everett Hughes to Dwight Eisenhower, April 5, 1944, Pre-Pres. Principal, box 58.

283 *"special additional duties"*: George Marshall to Jacob Devers, December 1943, NARA, RG 77, Subfile 7D.

283 *Even Edward Betts:* Dwight Eisenhower to George Marshall, March 26, 1944, Harrison-Bundy Files Relating to the Development of the Atomic Bomb, National Archives Microfilm Publication, M1108, Folder 56.

283 *distributed no further:* A. V. Peterson to Leslie R. Groves, "Operation 'Peppermint,'" NARA, RG77, Subfile 7D.

283 *Eisenhower decided:* R. B. Lovett, Operation Peppermint, May 1, 1944, NARA, RG 77, Subfile 7D; Eyster, "Operation 'Peppermint'"; Dwight Eisenhower to George Marshall, May 11, 1944, Pre-Pres. Principal, box 80.

283 *"A few cases"*: J. H. McNinch, "Report of an Epidemic Disease," May 1, 1944, NARA, RG 77, Subfile 7D.

283 *"A survey is"*: W. W. Jerway to Photo Officer (Tebow), FUSAG, April 27, 1944, NARA, RG 77, Subfile 7D.

284 *Similarly vague messages:* W. W. Jerway, Memorandum, January 7, 1944, NARA, RG 77, Subfile 7D.

284 *a few reports:* McNinch, "Report of an Epidemic Disease."

284 *just another bullet:* "President Says Atom Bomb Would Be Used Like 'Bullet,'" *New York Times*, March 17, 1955, p. A1.

284 *without any logic:* Memorandum of Discussion, the 471st Meeting of the National Security Council, December 22, 1960, FRUS, 1958–1960, National Security Policy; Arms Control and Disarmament, Vol. III, doc. 133.

CHAPTER 33

285 *The US Chiefs:* George Marshall to Dwight Eisenhower, March 25, 1944, in *The Papers of George Catlett Marshall* (Johns Hopkins University Press, 1996), 4:374–376.

285 *"falling between two"*: George Marshall to Dwight Eisenhower, April 13, 1944, Pre-Presidential Papers, Principal File, box 133.

285 *blamed the British:* Butcher Diary, A-1217.

285 *He then worked:* Dwight Eisenhower to Hastings Ismay, April 17, 1944, Pre-Pres. Principal, box 60.

285 *US Chiefs walked away:* George Marshall to Dwight Eisenhower, April 19, 1944, Pre-Presidential Papers, Principal File, box 133.

286 *"History will never"*: Alan Brooke, *War Diaries, 1939–1945* (Phoenix Press, 2001), 541.

286 *"Pacific First"*: Butcher Diary, A-1214.

286 *political gossip:* Butcher Diary, A-1192.

286 *The newspapers had been:* "Asked to Run in '44, M'Arthur Upholds Critic of New Deal," *New York Times*, April 14, 1944.
286 *"If Overlord failed":* Butcher Diary, A-1214.
286 *admired him:* Dwight Eisenhower, manuscript, "Churchill & Marshall," November 17, 1966, Post-Presidential Papers, A-WR Series, box 8.
286 *Churchill revealed:* Kay Summersby, Diary, April 24, 1944, EL, Barbara Wyden Papers, box 1.
286 *The British Admiralty:* COS(44) 93rd Meeting, March 23, 1944, RG 331, entry NM8 3, box 126.
286 *Two massive caissons:* S. H. Negrotto, "Mulberry 'B' 10 June to 31 October 1944," undated, NARA, RG 331, E31, box 211.
287 *"You think you":* Edwin Hoyt, *The Invasion before Normandy: The Secret Battle of Slapton Sands* (Stein & Day, 1985), 79.
287 *behind schedule:* COS(44) 93rd Meeting, March 23, 1944.
287 *"Of course":* Eisenhower, "Churchill & Marshall."
287 *As planned, Churchill:* SHAEF, COS Brief & Action Report, 144th Meeting, May 4, 1944, RG 331, entry NM8 3, box 126; Butcher Diary, A-1223; Eisenhower, "Churchill & Marshall."
288 *"Everything was on":* Eisenhower, "Churchill & Marshall."
288 *letters to relatives:* Dwight Eisenhower to John Eisenhower, April 16, 1944, Pre-Pres. Principal, box 173.
288 *"instances that have":* Edgar Eisenhower to Dwight Eisenhower, March 1, 1944, Pre-Pres. Principal, box 172.
288 *championship football:* Kay Summersby, Diary, April 15, 1944, EL, Barbara Wyden Papers, box 1.
288 *The crowd:* Butcher Diary, A-1204.
288 *Eisenhower presented:* Summersby, Diary, April 15, 1944.
288 *"Baghdad, Rangoon":* Dwight Eisenhower, *Letters to Mamie* (Doubleday, 1977), 175.
289 *run for president:* Kay Summersby, Diary, April 10, 1944, EL, Barbara Wyden Papers, box 1.
289 *"No wartime soldier":* Dwight Eisenhower, *Letters to Mamie*, 176.
289 *"We are not":* Dwight Eisenhower to James Somerville, April 4, 1944, Pre-Pres. Principal, box 109.

CHAPTER 34

290 *He fixed that problem:* Harold R. Bull, "Behind the Scenes with the 'Overlord' Weathermen," undated, 1944, EL, Harold R Bull Papers, box 3.
290 *"minimum operating weather":* Bull.
290 *The navy needed:* David Eisenhower, *Eisenhower at War* (Random House, 1986), 227–28.
290 *those conditions:* Sverre Petterson, Memoirs, EL, WWII Participants, box 104.
291 *For the weekly:* SHAEF, Minutes of Meeting Held in the Conference Room (C4–Room 8) Wide Wing 1145 hours, April 17, 1944, NAUK, WO 205 12.
291 *He wanted the weathermen:* Bull, "Behind the Scenes."
291 *"As you all":* James Martin Stagg, *Forecast for Overlord* (Norton, 1971), 46.
291 *a quiet brogue:* Walter B. Smith, *Eisenhower's Six Great Decisions* (Longmans, 1956), 43.
291 *He predicted:* Bull, "Behind the Scenes."
291 *"Whenever you see":* Stagg, *Forecast for Overlord*, 46.
291 *Eisenhower announced that:* Arthur Nevins to Harold Bull, September 27, 1960, EL, Harold R. Bull Papers, box 3.
291 *"Many thousands":* Carl Spaatz to Dwight Eisenhower, April 22, 1944, LOC, Carl Spaatz Papers, box 12.
292 *remained unmoved:* Carl Spaatz, Diary, April 22, 1944, LOC, Carl Spaatz Papers, box 12.
292 *"Enemy secret developments":* SHAEF, Minutes of Meeting Held in the Conference Room (C4–Room 8) Wide Wing 1145 hours, April 24, 1944.
292 *Stagg was then called:* Stagg, *Forecast for Overlord*, 47.
292 *Exercise Tiger was about:* Clifford L. Jones, "Neptune: Training, Mounting, the Artificial Ports," March 1946, *The Administrative and Logistical History of the ETO*, 8-3.1 AA, Vol. 6, 251–263; W.R. Pierce, "Exercise Tiger," April 1,1944, Eckstam Papers, Box 3.
292 *The most recent estimates:* John Rogers to A. W. Kenner, April 26, 1944, NARA, RG 331, entry 65, box 3.
292 *The three miles:* Nigel Lewis, *Exercise Tiger* (Prentice Hall, 1990), 20.
292 *embedded mock pillboxes:* Hoyt, *Invasion before Normandy*, 87.
292 *"Aren't you sticking":* James Martin Stagg, *Forecast for Overlord* (Norton, 1971), 45.
292 *The following evening:* Kay Summersby, Diary, March 23, 1944, EL, Barbara Wyden Papers, box 1.
292 *He stopped in Wilton:* Butcher Diary, A-1225.
292 *was the hub:* Ronald Ruppenthal, *Logistical Support of the Armies*, CMH Pub. 7-2-1 (US Government Printing Office, 1952), 1:86.
293 *The man had built:* For a superb biography of Lee, which makes a convincing case for him as an unsung hero

of the Second World War, see Hank Cox, *The General Who Wore Six Stars: The Inside Story of John C. H. Lee* (University of Nebraska Press, 2018).

293 *Everything was systematized*: Richard Leighton & Robert Coakley, *Global Logistics and Strategy: 1943–1945*, CMH Pub. 1-6 (U.S. Government Printing Office, 1968), 143–156; Daniel Immerwahr, *How to Hide an Empire* (FSG, 2019), 216–224, 293–295, 305–310; David Kennedy, *Freedom from Fear* (Oxford University Press, 1999), 647–649.

293 *American truck parts*: Richard Leighton & Robert Coakley, *Global Logistics and Strategy: 1940–1943*, CMH Pub. 1-5 (U.S. Government Printing Office, 1955), 639–641.

293 *The weather was beautiful:* Nigel Lewis, *Exercise Tiger* (Prentice Hall, 1990), 65.

293 *There would be:* Dwight D. Eisenhower, *Report by the Supreme Commander to the Combined Chiefs of Staff on the Operations in Europe of the Allied Expeditionary Force: 6 June 1944 to 8 May 1945*, CMH_Pub_70-58 (US Government Printing Office, 1946), 7.

293 *orders for Operation Neptune*: Bertram Ramsay, "Operation Neptune: Naval Operations Orders," April 10, 1944, NARA, RG 331, entry 262A, box 19.

294 *Don P. Moon*: Bertram Ramsay, *The Year of D-Day* (University of Hull, 1994), 40.

294 *"actual war conditions"*: William F. Spragro, ADM #131 Exercises, April 30, 1945, NARA, RG 18, entry NM6 7, box 5834.

294 *two-day operation:* Clifford L. Jones, "Neptune: Training, Mounting, the Artificial Ports," March 1946, *The Administrative and Logistical History of the ETO*, 8-3.1 AA, Vol. 6, 251–63; W.R. Pierce, "Exercise Tiger," April 19, 1944, Eckstam Papers, box 3.

294 *"GMC jumps"*: Edwin Hoyt, *The Invasion before Normandy: The Secret Battle of Slapton Sands* (Stein & Day, 1985), 84.

294 *"upon beach obstacles"*: W. R. Pierce, Exercise Tiger, April 19 1944, Eckstam Papers, box 3.

294 *All told, Moon's armada:* Lewis, *Exercise Tiger*, 73.

294 *an inauspicious start:* Hoyt, *Invasion before Normandy*, 89.

294 *up before dawn:* Kay Summersby, Diary, April 27, 1944, EL, Barbara Wyden Papers, box 1.

295 *At 6:50 a.m.*: USS *Bayfield*, G-3 Journal, April 27, 1944, NARA, RG 338, entry P 50119, box 2.

295 *Fifteen minutes later:* Summersby, Diary, April 27, 1944.

295 *In dribs and drabs:* USS *Bayfield*, G-3 Journal, April 27, 1944.

295 *At 8:21 a.m.*: Hoyt, *Invasion before Normandy*, 90.

295 *Before long, a ribbon:* Butcher Diary, A-1225.

295 *"tommyrot"*: Kirke Simpson, "Interpreting the War News," Associated Press, April 8, 1944.

296 *call from Beetle:* Walter B. Smith to George Marshall, cable, April 27, 1944, Pre-Pres. Principal, box 91.

296 *"Newspapers today"*: George Marshall to Dwight Eisenhower, April 26, 1944, Pre-Pres. Principal, box 91.

296 *British Welcome Club:* George S. Patton to Everett Hughes, May 25, 1944, Hughes Papers, box II-2.

296 *"Until today, my only"*: Patton to Hughes, April 30, 1944, Everett Hughes Papers, II-2.

296 *"the whole question"*: The Ambassador in the United Kingdom (Winant) to the Secretary of State, March 23, 1944, FRUS 1944, vol. 3, doc 596.

296 *The Soviets were justifiably:* The British Embassy to the Department of State, FRUS 1944, March 31, 1944, vol. 3, doc. 602.

296 *recently awarded Eisenhower:* Frank McCarthy to Dwight Eisenhower, April 27, 1944, NARA, RG 331, E1, box 14.

297 *the best part:* Tobin, "A Day with General Eisenhower," June 20, 1944, EL, Harry C. Butcher Papers, box 3.

297 *Eisenhower told Beetle:* Smith to Marshall, cable, April 27, 1944.

297 *call Georgie:* George S. Patton, Diary, April 27, 1944, Patton Papers, box 3.

297 *Brad agreed:* Omar Bradley, *A General's Life* (Simon & Schuster, 1983), 231.

297 *The mood was:* Butcher Diary, A-1225.

298 *All he wanted:* Forrest Pogue, interview with Omar N. Bradley, May 27, 1957; July 19, 1957, GCM, Forrest Pogue Interviews.

298 *Gee was also fretting:* Butcher Diary, A-1225.

CHAPTER 35

299 *Dr. Eugene Eckstam:* Eugene Eckstam, "The Tragedy of Exercise Tiger," *Navy Medicine* 85, no. 3 (May–June 1994), 5–7.

300 *On April 24:* Interview with James F. Murdock, August 16, 1944, at 2, Eckstam Papers, box 3.

300 *There was little:* Nigel Lewis, *Exercise Tiger* (Prentice Hall, 1990), 63–72.

300 *gone to bed:* Eckstam, "Tragedy of Exercise Tiger."

300 *But then at 1:35:* Interview with James F. Murdock, August 16, 1944, at 2, Eckstam Papers, box 3.

300 *"They had better"*: Eckstam, "Tragedy of Exercise Tiger."

300 *"I guess they're"*: Lewis, *Exercise Tiger*, 79–82.
300 *The general-quarters alarm:* J. H. Doyle, "Report from Commanding Officer, LST 515 to the commander in Chief Relating to LST 515 and Action on Night of 28 April 1944," LST515/A16/A9-8, May 3, 1944, Eckstam Papers, Box 3; B.H. Grundborg, Report of Enemy Naval Action, April 30, 1944, Eckstam Papers, box 3.
300 *It was so sudden:* Eckstam, "Tragedy of Exercise Tiger."
301 *The stern and bow*: Interview with James F Murdock, August 16, 1944, Eckstam Papers, Box 3.
301 *"Why are you"*: Ed Panter, "LST-289 & 507," LST Scuttlebutt (2002), available at ExerciseTiger.org.uk (https://perma.cc/8P2E-RZP2).
301 *Men hung in rings:* Interview with James F. Murdock, August 16, 1944, at 2, Eckstam Papers, box 3; Lewis, *Exercise Tiger*, 81–102.
302 *A few flashes:* Lewis, 131.
302 *Eckstam went numb:* Eckstam, "Tragedy of Exercise Tiger."
302 *In the dawn light:* Lewis, *Exercise Tiger*, 105–113.
302 *Dr. Eckstam analyzed:* Eckstam, "Tragedy of Exercise Tiger."
302 *choice to launch:* Interview with James F. Murdock, August 16, 1944, at 2, Eckstam Papers, box 3.
302 *Someone from the British navy:* Lewis, 74–75.
302 *at 4:35 a.m.:* B. W. Wahlberg, LST 151–Deck Log, April 28, 1944, Eckstam Papers, box 4.
303 *the E-boats hit:* Doyle, "Report from Commanding Officer," Eckstam Papers, box 3.
303 *saved 132 men:* Wahlberg, LST 151–Deck Log.
303 *an early meeting:* Winston Churchill, Engagement Diary, April 1944, Churchill Papers, CHAR 20/19/03.
303 *"there were too many"*: Winston Churchill, "Reactions to Allied Air Raids on W. Seaboard of Europe," April 29, 1944, NARA, RG 331, entry 1, box 66.
303 *He could not justify:* Winston Churchill to Franklin Roosevelt, May 7, 1944, FDR, Map Room Papers, 1941–1945, box 6.
303 *"a high degree"*: SHAEF, G-2, Weekly Intelligence Summary no. 6, April 29, 1944, Smith Papers, box 30.
303 *zero sum:* Dwight Eisenhower to Winston Churchill, May 2, 1944, Pre-Pres. Principal, box 22.
303 *"bases, troop concentrations"*: Eisenhower to George Marshall, May 6, 1944, Pre-Pres. Principal, box 80.
303 *chatting with Butch:* Butcher Diary, A-1230.
304 *At 4:10:* VII Corps, Message no. 90, G-3 Journal, USS *Bayfield*, April 28, 1944, NARA, RG 338, entry 950119, box 2.
304 *"This reduces our reserve"*: Butcher Diary, A-1230.
304 *"was not a restful"*: Dwight Eisenhower to George Marshall, April 29, 1944, Eisenhower Papers, 3:1138.
304 *Bertie Ramsay followed:* Butcher Diary, A-1231.
304 *The investigation was:* Lewis, *Exercise Tiger*, 126.
304 *the 243 men:* Butcher Diary, A-1231.
304 *Ten of the missing:* Charles MacDonald, "Slapton Sands: The Cover-Up That Never Was," *Army* 38, no. 6 (1988): 64–67.
304 "Gefangennahme": Lewis, *Exercise Tiger*, 131.

CHAPTER 36

305 *General Henry Miller:* Kay Summersby, Diary, April 19, 1944, EL, Barbara Wyden Papers, box 1.
305 *Miller had been:* E. L. Sibert to Omar Bradley, April 19, 1944, Pre-Pres. Principal, box 13.
305 *"hell of a"*: Kenneth Davis, interview with General Eisenhower, August 11, 1944, Davis Papers, box 60.
305 *The ten officers:* Nigel Lewis, *Exercise Tiger* (Prentice Hall, 1990), 132; Edwin Hoyt, *The Invasion before Normandy: The Secret Battle of Slapton Sands* (Stein & Day, 1985), 157; Charles MacDonald, "Slapton Sands: The Cover-Up That Never Was," *Army* 38, no. 6 (June 1988).
306 *a dozen copies:* John Eisenhower, *Allies* (Doubleday, 1982), 461; Gilles Perrault, *The Secrets of D-Day* (Little Brown, 1965), 148.
306 *A memo circulated:* E. C. Biehnke, "SHAEF Officers Who Have Complete Knowledge of OVERLORD," May 15, 1944, EL, Harry C. Butcher Papers, box 3.
306 *"Between now and"*: "A Letter from the Publisher," *Time*, May 8, 1944.
306 *The phones were*: Horace Franklin, memo, May 5, 1944, Patton Papers, box 44.
306 *"An alleged serious"*: George Patton, memo, "Security Violations," May 4, 1944, Patton Papers, box 44.
306 *Eisenhower drafted:* Daily Appointment Log, April 30, 1944, EL, Pre-Pres. Principal, box 127.
307 *"Why can't he"*: Everett Hughes, Diary, April 28, 1944, Hughes Papers, box I-1.
307 *"a nervous, fidgety"*: Everett Hughes to Kate Hughes, April 28, 1944, Hughes Papers, box II-2.
307 *Everett then pulled:* Everett Hughes, Diary, April 28, 1944, Hughes Papers, box I-1.
307 *Two full pages:* George Patton to Everett Hughes, April 30, 1944, Hughes Papers, box II-2.

307 *"Oh hell"*: Everett Hughes, Diary, April 28, 1944, Hughes Papers, box I-1.
307 *SHAEF had created:* Harold Bull, "Plan 'Fortitude'—Commanders," May 4th, 1944, NARA, RG 331, entry 58, box 18; Thadius Holt, *The Deceivers: Allied Military Deception in the Second World War* (Scribner, 2014); Joshua Levine, *Operation Fortitude: The Story of the Spy Operation That Saved D-Day* (Collins, 2011); Michael Howard, *Strategic Deception in the Second World War* (Norton, 1995); Anthony Brown, *Bodyguard of Lies* (Harper, 1975).
307 *In support of FUSAG:* E. J. King-Salter, "Report on the Wireless Deception & Security Measures Taken by the Three Services in Connection with Operation Neptune," July 1944, NARA, RG 457, entry 9 11, box 161.
307 *all the more menacing:* Bull, "Plan 'Fortitude.'"
308 *as anybody knew:* George S. Patton to Beatrice Patton, May 19, 1944, Patton Papers, box 18.
308 *drive to victory:* Rick Atkinson, *An Army at Dawn* (Holt, 2002), 441–487; Carlo D'Este, *Patton* (HarperCollins, 1995), 456–503; Hubert Essame, *Patton* (Scribner, 1975), 64–102; Jonathan Jordan, *Brothers, Rivals, Victors* (Penguin, 2011), 135–208.
308 *Back in 1921:* E. F. McGlachlin, "Report in the Case of Major Dwight D. Eisenhower, Inf., Tanks," June 21, 1921, NARA, RG 159, entry PC-51 26, box 665; H. H. Pritchett to Commanding General, 3rd Corps Area, Fort Howard, MD, October 4, 1921, NARA, RG 159, entry PC-51 26, box 665.
308 *turned himself in:* Eli Helmick, "Investigation Concerning the Drawing of Commutation of Quarters, Heat and Light by Major Dwight D. Eisenhower, Infantry," June 18, 1921, NARA, RG 159, entry PC-51 26, box 665.
308 *an assistant inspector:* Eli Helmick to the Adjutant General, July 6, 1921, 1921-07-06, RG 159, entry PC-51 26, box 665.
308 *In October 1921:* Charge Sheet, Dwight D. Eisenhower, October 3, 1921, NARA, RG 159, entry PC-51 26, box 665.
308 *double jeopardy:* S. D. Rockenbach to Commanding General, 3rd Corps Area, Fort Howard, MD, October 21, 1921, NARA, RG 159, entry PC-51 26, box 665.
308 *That technicality was:* H. F. Hodges to Commanding General, 3rd Corps Area, Fort Howard, MD, October 24, 1921, NARA, RG 159, entry PC-51 26, box 665.
308 *The assistant inspector general:* Eli Helmick to Chief of Staff, December 12, 1921, NARA, RG 159, entry PC-51 26, box 665.
308 *In the middle:* John Pershing, Diary, November 14, 1921, Pershing Papers, box 1.
308 *Two days later:* Fox Conner to John Pershing, November 16, 1921, Pre-Pres. Misc. box 22.
309 *when Georgie prayed:* Virginia Conner, *What Father Forbade* (Dorrance, 1951), 109.
309 *"charged with offenses"*: Helmick to Chief of Staff, December 12, 1921.
309 *the order came:* John J. Pershing, Order, December 7, 1912, Pre-Pres. Principal, box 190.
309 *assistant inspector general:* Helmick to Chief of Staff, December 12, 1921.
309 *The biggest obstacle:* George Marshall to Dwight Eisenhower, April 29, 1944, Pre-Pres. Principal, box 91.
309 *"I have warned"*: Dwight Eisenhower to George Patton, April 29, 1944, Pre-Pres. Principal, box 91.
309 *"investigation shows that"*: Eisenhower to George Marshall, April 29, 1944, Pre-Pres. Principal, box 91.
309 *Marshall had known:* John Pershing, Diary, September 14, 1919, Pershing Papers, box 1; Jonathan Jordan, *Brothers, Rivals, Victors*, 32–34; Hubert Essame, *Patton*, 30–31; David Roll, *George Marshall* (Dutton, 2019), 123. Carlo D'Este, who is ordinarily one of the most meticulous historians, inexplicably says that George Marshall "barely knew" Patton until the early 1940s, Carlo D'Este, *Patton*, 376. As the Pershing Diary entries just cited show, the two were regularly in close contact socially as well as professionally, as early as 1919.
310 *tour of Camp Meade:* John Pershing, Diary, November 14, 1919, Pershing Papers, box 1.
310 *Eisenhower called Beetle:* Kay Summersby, Diary, April 30, 1944, EL, Barbara Wyden Papers, box 1.
310 *Georgie's choice:* George S. Patton, Diary, April 30, 1944, Patton Papers, box 3.
310 *"On all of the"*: Dwight Eisenhower to George Marshall, April 30, 1944, Pre-Pres. Principal, box 91.
310 *Monday morning, Georgie:* Marty Snyder, *My Friend Ike* (Fell, 1956), 53.
310 *"George, you have"*: George S. Patton, Diary, May 1, 1944, Patton Papers, box 3.
311 *"Incidentally, the numerous"*: George Marshall to Dwight Eisenhower, May 2, 1944, Pre-Pres. Principal, box 91.
311 *Eisenhower called Georgie:* Everett Hughes, Diary, May 3, 1944, Hughes Papers, box I-1.
311 *an admonishing letter:* George S. Patton, Diary, May 3, 1944, Patton Papers, box 3.
311 *The cable was stern:* Dwight Eisenhower to George Patton, May 3, 1944, Pre-Pres. Principal, box 91.
311 *"judicial poise"*: Henry Stimson to Dwight Eisenhower, May 5, 1944, Pre-Pres. Principal, box 111.
312 *"any person subject"*: Dwight Eisenhower, General Eisenhower Sends "Personal Message" to All Americans in ETOUSA, March 2, 1944, Davis Papers, box 94.
312 *"The Command of Negro"*: War Department, Command of Negro Troops, February 29, 1944, EL, WWII Participants, box 56.

312 *200,000 copies:* Walter White to John H. C. Lee, May 19, 1944, NAACP, General Office File, box II-A644.

312 *"double V campaign":* Matthew Delmont, *Half American: The Epic Story of African Americans Fighting World War II at Home and Abroad* (Viking, 2022), 90–93.

312 *In early April:* Arthur Green, Review of the Record of Trial by General Court Martial, NARA, RG 498, Entry UD 1028, Box 4719; *United States v. Turner, et al.*, ETO No. 2566, *European Theater Operations Board of Review Opinions* (Office of the Judge Advocate General, 1945), Vol. 7, 151.

313 *court-martialed for disorder:* Arthur Green, "Review of the Record of Trial by General Court Martial," May 19, 1944, NARA, RG 498, entry UD 1028, box 4719.

313 *Some commands:* Everett Hughes, Memorandum to Dwight Eisenhower, April 5, 1944, Pre-Pres. Principal, box 58.

313 *Since Eisenhower first took:* E. C. McNeil to Dwight Eisenhower, July 29, 1944, NARA, RG 498, entry UD 1028, box 4716.

313 *Willie Smith and Eliga Brinson:* FDC 817 to ETO, April 29, 1944, NARA, RG 498, entry UD 1028, box 4722.

313 *The evidence pointing: United States v. Smith & Brinson*, ETO No. 2686, *European Theater Operations Board of Review Opinions* (Office of the Judge Advocate General, 1945), Vol. 7, 295.

313 *had criminal records:* Evidence of Previous Convictions in the Case of Smith, Willie, 34565556, March 24, 1944, *United States v. Smith & Brinson*, Record of Trial, Ex. 30, NARA-SL, Army Record V151125, Eliga Brinson, No. 34052175; Evidence of Previous Convictions in the Case of Brinson, Eliga, 34052175, March 24, 1944, *United States v. Smith & Brinson*, Record of Trial, Ex. 29, NARA-SL, Army Record V151125, Eliga Brinson, No. 34052175.

313 *In one case: United States v. Allen*, ETO no. 1644, *European Theater Operations Board of Review Opinions* (Office of the Judge Advocate General, 1945), 5:233.

314 *conducted executions:* J. Robert Lilly and J. Michael Thomson, "Executing U.S. Soldiers in England, World War II: Command Influence and Sexual Racism," *British Journal of Criminology* 37, no. 2 (Spring 1997): 262–88.

314 *the local paper:* "Two U.S. Soldiers on Court-Martial," *Gloucestershire Echo*, April 29, 1944.

314 *across the United Kingdom:* "Death Sentence on Two U.S. Soldiers," *Derby Evening Telegraph*, April 29, 1944.

314 *abolished the death penalty:* "Clemency Urged," *Gloucestershire Echo*, May 10, 1944.

314 *"People who live":* "Stern Necessity," *Gloucestershire Echo*, May 10, 1944.

314 *"American negroes":* "Protecting Women," *Gloucestershire Echo*, May 10, 1944.

314 *spread their "color problem":* Allison J. Gough, "'Messing Up Another Country's Customs:' The Exportation of American Racism During World War II," World History Connected (2008).

314 *"racial persecution":* "Mr Eden and U.S. Sentence," *The Citizen*, May 10, 1944.

314 *Eisenhower asked:* McNeil to Eisenhower, July 29, 1944.

314 *draft personal responses:* Dwight Eisenhower to Edward Betts, May 15, 1944, NARA, RG 498, entry UD 1028, box 4719.

CHAPTER 37

315 *That old, familiar tension:* Dwight Eisenhower to James Somerville, April 4, 1944, Pre-Pres. Principal, box 109.

315 *The pressure inside:* Butcher Diary, A-1300.

315 *Ultra intercept:* David A. Price, *Geniuses at War* (Knopf, 2021), 151.

315 *The Germans were:* SHAEF, G-2, Weekly Intelligence Summary no. 8, May 13, 1944, Smith Papers, box 30.

315 *"one of the":* Thomas Davis, "Memorandum for General Henry: Botulinus Toxin," May 8, 1944, NARA RG 331, entry 66, box 3.

316 *"new and surprising":* GSI 21st Army Group, Weekly Review, Appendix B, May 14, 1944, NARA, RG 331, Entry 262A, box 17.

316 *"most colossal":* COS Brief & Action Report, 139th Meeting, May 6, 1944, RG 331, entry NM8 3, box 126.

316 *"I have assumed":* Dwight Eisenhower to George Marshall, May 11, 1944, Pre-Pres. Principal, box 80.

316 *Eisenhower was weary:* Butcher Diary, A-1252.

316 *needed to compartmentalize:* Dwight Eisenhower to George Marshall, April 17, 1944, Pre-Pres. Principal, box 80.

316 *one piece of paper:* George Hall, interview with Mattie Pinette, January 5, 1977, EL, George Hall Papers, box 1.

316 *protecting time:* Dwight Eisenhower to John Eisenhower, March 31, 1944, Pre-Pres. Principal, box 173.

316 *After a few weeks:* Butcher Diary, A-1232.

316 *Butch's dirty jokes:* Harry Butcher to John Charles Daly, May 15, 1944, University of Wyoming, Harry Butcher Papers, box 3.

316 *good news:* Butcher Diary, A-1232.

316 *Exercise Fabius:* Clifford L. Jones, "Neptune: Training, Mounting, the Artificial Ports," March 1946, *The Administrative and Logistical History of the ETO*, 8-3.1 AA, vol. 6, pp. 263–65.

317 *two reported casualties:* Nigel Lewis, *Exercise Tiger* (Prentice Hall, 1990), 133.

317 *The weather had been:* Historical Section, COMNAVEU, United States Naval Administrative History of World War II #147E, United States Naval Forces Europe, vol. 5, *The Invasion of Normandy, Operation Neptune*, 1946, 365.

317 *Stagg had predicted:* James Martin Stagg, *Forecast for Overlord* (Norton, 1971), 47.

317 *He assured Churchill:* Dwight Eisenhower to Winston Churchill, May 2, 1944, Pre-Pres. Principal, box 22.

317 *"selection of targets":* Walter B. Smith to Carl Spaatz, May 5, 1944, Pre-Pres. Principal, box 22.

317 *Cabinet voted against:* Winston Churchill to Dwight Eisenhower, April 29, 1944, NARA, RG 331, entry 1, box 66.

317 *"The War Cabinet":* Churchill to Franklin Roosevelt, May 7, 1944, FDR, Map Room Papers, 1941–1945, box 6.

317 *They believed they:* Richard H. Kohn and Joseph P. Harahan, "Strategic Air Warfare: An Interview with Generals Curtis E. LeMay, Leon W. Johnson, David A. Burchinal, and Jack J. Catton," Office of Air Force History 1988, pp. 40–41.

317 *such as Alan Brooke:* COS(44) 164th Meeting, Held May 23, 1944, NARA, RG 331, entry 1, box 66.

317 *extraordinary civilian casualties:* The United States Strategic Bombing Survey: over-all report (European war), September 30, 1945, 95.

318 *"the losses and damage":* Commissariat for Foreign Affairs, "Memorandum with Respect to Allied Bombing of France," May 5, 1944, NARA, RG 331, E1, box 66.

318 *Combined Chiefs had permitted:* Dwight Eisenhower to Combined Chiefs of Staff, April 20, 1944, Smith Papers, box 23.

318 *"Which hat":* Robert Sherwood, "Meeting with Admiral Ernest J. King in His office at the Navy Department," May 24, 1946, Sherwood Papers, box 40.

318 *Beetle leaned:* Butcher Diary, A-1150.

318 *only acceptable terms:* The Secretary of State to the Acting American Representative to the French Committee of National Liberation Algiers (Chapin), April 21, 1944, FRUS 1944, vol. 3, doc. 613.

318 *Eisenhower kept Koenig:* FCNL, Compte Rendu de la Reunion du Mardi 29 Fevrier 1944 au Ministry of Economic Warfare, March 1, 1944, Vincennes, GR/1/K/237/2.

318 *"absurd allegation":* Dwight Eisenhower to George Marshall, March 27, 1944, Pre-Presidential Papers, Principal File, box 133.

318 *"countries whose troops":* Eisenhower to Alan Brooke, April 9, 1944, Pre-Pres. Principal, box 3.

318 *Churchill had relented:* Eisenhower, *Report by the Supreme Commander*, 14.

319 *De Gaulle exploded:* Charles de Gaulle, *The Complete War Memoirs* (Carroll & Graf 1998), 551–553; Julian Jackson, *De Gaulle* (Belknap Press, 2018), 306–308; Jonathan Fenby, *The General: Charles de Gaulle and the France He Saved* (Skyhorse, 2012), 237.

319 *Eisenhower hosted Koenig:* Kay Summersby, Diary, May 6, 1944, EL, Barbara Wyden Papers, box 1.

319 *The conversation involved:* Dwight Eisenhower, *Letters to Mamie* (Doubleday, 1977), 177.

319 *"the name of the":* Eisenhower to Combined Chiefs of Staff, May 8, 1944, Eisenhower Papers, vol. III, 1852–53.

319 *"the limitations under":* Eisenhower to Combined Chiefs of Staff, May 11, 1944, Eisenhower Papers, Vol. 3, at 1857–1858.

319 *provoked Roosevelt:* Walter B. Smith to George Marshall, May 14, 1944, Pre-Pres. Principal, box 133.

319 *middle of April:* Walter Giblin, "Military Control of the Office of Strategic Services," April 24, 1944, RG 226, entry UD 190, box 230.

319 *Orders of magnitude:* Dwight Eisenhower to George Marshall, May 6, 1944, Smith Papers, box 23.

319 *remind the world:* Secretary of State to the Acting American Representative to the French Committee of National Liberation Algiers (Chapin), April 21, 1944.

319 *By June, American aid:* "Summary of French Resistance, 6 June–31 August 1944," September 1944, RG 226, entry 1991, box 16.

319 *process of dropping:* Paul Van Der Strict, "Progress Report, 27 April to 27 May 1944," May 27, 1944, RG 226, entry A1 99, box 2.

319 *"Green Plan":* Blake Clark, manuscript, 1945, entry 1991, box 16; Benjamin Jones, *Eisenhower's Guerrillas* (Oxford University Press, 2016), 76–77.

320 *embedding agents:* Van Der Stricht, "Progress Report."

320 *801st Bomb Group:* Martin Harris, "Progress Report for the Month of April, May 9, 1944," RG 226, entry A1 99, box 2.

320 *trust with Koenig:* Walter B. Smith to George Marshall, May 14, 1944, Pre-Pres Principal, box 167.

320 *After World War I*: Matthew Parker, *One Fine Day* (PublicAffairs, 2023), 47–48.
320 *new operation:* Hastings Ismay, for COS Committee, undated, Pre-Pres. Principal, box 22.
320 *"a definite recommendation"*: John Erhmann, *Grand Strategy* (Her Majesty's Stationery Office, 1956), 5:260–61.
320 *Americans seemed to have no talent:* Alan Dudley, "The Essentials of an American Policy," March 21, 1944, UKNA, FO 371/38523/AN1538.
320 *"You withdraw your"*: The American Representative on the Advisory Council for Italy (Murphy) to the Secretary of State, April 22, 1944, FRUS 1944, vol. 3, doc. 1017.
321 *"We shall not"*: Franklin Roosevelt, State of the Union Address, January 11, 1944, in *The Public Papers and Addresses of Franklin D. Roosevelt, 1944–1945* (Harper, 1950), 32.
321 *intelligence had concluded:* Louis Marlo, memorandum, March 17, 1944, RG 107, entry 183, box 55.
321 *Churchill was presiding: The Mackenzie King Record* (University of Toronto Press, 1960), Vol. I, 678–687; William Louis, *Imperialism at Bay* (Oxford, 1986), at 337–350; Robert O'Shea, "Not Foreign to Each Other," Oxford University, DPhil Thesis, Hilary 2016, 62–73.

CHAPTER 38

322 *spent the weekend:* Kay Summersby, Diary, May 13, 1944, EL, Barbara Wyden Papers, box 1.
322 *British overcoat:* Everett Hughes, Diary, April 21, 1944, Hughes Papers, box I-1.
322 *Alexander the Great:* Andrew Collins, "The Royal Costume and Insignia of Alexander the Great," *American Journal of Philology* 133, no. 3 (Fall 2012): 317–402.
322 *Saint Paul's School:* Kay Summersby, Diary, May 15, 1944, EL, Barbara Wyden Papers, box 1.
322 *The occasion for:* James Holland, *Nomandy '44* (Grove, 2019), 1–5; Peter Caddick-Adams, *Sand and Steel* (Oxford, 2019), 247–250; David Eisenhower, *Eisenhower at War* (Random House, 1986), 231–234; Max Hastings, *Overlord* (Simon & Schuster, 1984), 55–56; Carlo D'Este, *Decision at Normandy* (Konecky & Konecky, 1983), 82–89.
322 *The same day:* Headquarters, First US Army, After Action Against Enemy, Reports After/After Action Report, August 6, 1944, EL, U.S. Army, First Army Headquarters Records, box 2.
322 *The conference was convened:* Trafford Leigh-Mallory, AEAF, Daily Reflections on the Court of the Battle, 1944, NAUK, AIR 37/784.
323 *down to the minute:* SHAEF, "Program: Presentation of 'OVERLORD' Plans," May 15, 1944, NARA, RG 331, entry 1, box 78.
323 *Passes for 138 men:* SHAEF, "Allotment of Passes to Presentation of Plan," May 10, 1944, NARA, RG 331, entry 1, box 78.
323 *Churchill arrived:* Leigh-Mallory, AEAF, Daily Reflections on the Court of the Battle.
323 *King George sat:* R. E. Baker, "Presentation of Overlord Plans," May 3, 1944, RG 331, entry 1, box 78.
323 *The mood was:* Butcher Diary, A-1255.
323 *At nine sharp:* Leigh-Mallory, AEAF, Daily Reflections on the Court of the Battle.
324 *"General Eisenhower has"*: Bernard Montgomery, "Address Given by General Montgomery to the General Officers of the Four Field Armies on 15 May 1944, Brief Presentation of Plans before the King," May 15, 1944, IWM, Papers of Field Marshal Viscount Montgomery of Alamein, Box 104.
324 *He emphasized how:* Leigh-Mallory, AEAF, Daily Reflections on the Court of the Battle.
324 *His charisma filled:* Alan Brooke, *War Diaries, 1939–1945* (Phoenix Press, 2001), 546.
324 *"Last February, Rommel"*: Montgomery, "Address Given by General Montgomery to the General Officers," May 15, 1944.
324 *"At Anzio, we"*: Leigh-Mallory, AEAF, Daily Reflections on the Court of the Battle.
324 *He had taped:* J. Lawton Collins, *Lightning Joe* (Louisiana State University Press, 1979), 192; Omar Bradley, *A General's Life* (Simon & Schuster, 1983), 233.
325 *"It is intended"*: Leigh-Mallory, AEAF, Daily Reflections on the Court of the Battle.
325 *"We shall have"*: Montgomery, "Address given by General Montgomery to the General Officers."
325 *"Plans and preparations"*: Bernard Montgomery, Note, in *Master of the Battlefield* (McGraw Hill, 1983), 582–89.
325 *stuttered a bit:* Leigh-Mallory, AEAF, Daily Reflections on the Court of the Battle.
325 *"the fate"*: John Mason, "The Reminiscences of Alan Goodrich Kirk," no. 455, 1962, Oral History Research Office, Columbia University, p. 300.
325 *"With God's help"*: Leigh-Mallory, AEAF, Daily Reflections on the Court of the Battle.
325 *"capture some villas"*: Butcher Diary, A-1254.
325 *At lunch, Patton:* George S. Patton, Diary, May 15, 1944, Patton Papers, box 3.
325 *gotten snide:* Patton, Diary, January 22, 1943, Patton Papers, box 2.

326 *"simply told the"*: Patton, Diary, May 1, 1944, Patton Papers, box 3.
326 *Do you remember:* Patton, Diary, May 15, 1944.
326 *took the floor:* Butcher Diary, A-1254.
326 *"At the risk"*: Patton, Diary, May 15, 1944 ("the risk of hurting the feelings of my [his] dear friend, General De Gaulle," he joked, "We are [were] worrying too much about governing France before conquering it.").
326 *"bravery, ingenuity"*: Butcher Diary, A-1254.
326 *But Eisenhower felt:* S. L. A. Marshall, interview with Dwight Eisenhower, June 3, 1946, Pogue Papers, box 161.
326 *"I am in"*: Butcher Diary, A-1237.
326 *Responsibility was truly:* Marshall, interview with Eisenhower, June 3, 1946. The historian Carlo D'Este has suggested that Eisenhower's reaction to Churchill may have been based on a misunderstanding of a peculiar English idiom. According to D'Este, "to harden toward" an enterprise meant to become increasingly confident of its success, rather than persuaded of its merits. Perhaps Eisenhower and Churchill were divided by their common language. But there is no question Eisenhower felt the way he did, as he remembered and made a point of mentioning the perceived slight in a debriefing by the army historian in 1946. Carlo D'Este, *Decision at Normandy* (Konecky & Konecky, 1983), 86.
327 *"In a few"*: Leigh-Mallory, AEAF, Daily Reflections on the Court of the Battle.
327 *"Eisenhower was a"*: Brooke, *War Diaries*, 546.
327 *The next morning:* Kay Summersby, SHAEF Desk Calendar, May 16, 1944, EL, Wyden Papers, box 1.
327 *"the food is"*: Keith Murdoch, "Town Hall Reception Speech," July 21, 1944, NLA, Keith Murdoch Papers, MS 2823.
327 *"You cannot run"*: Tom D. C. Roberts, *Before Rupert* (Queensland Press, 2015), 128.
327 *He loved:* "Censorship Down Under," *Time*, December 30, 1940.
327 *Like Eisenhower:* Ronald M. Younger, *Keith Murdoch* (HarperCollins, 2003), 179.
327 *Murdoch had met:* Prime Minister's Visit to England via USA, Itinerary and Engagements 1944, JCPML, Records of Frederick McLaughlin, JCPML00129/1.
327 *spent years bagging:* Younger, *Keith Murdoch*, 282.
327 *Curtin had come:* "Empire Affairs, The London Conference," *Western Australian*, May 13, 1944.
328 *"the splendid"*: "Sir Keith Murdoch in London," *The Herald*, May 4, 1944, p. 2.
328 *The next leg:* Keith Murdoch, "Visits to Washington and New York," June 1944, NLA, Keith Murdoch Papers, MS 2823, File 27.
328 *Roy Howard, the head:* Roy Howard to Keith Murdoch, April 26, 1944, NLA, Keith Murdoch Papers, MS 2823, File 21.
328 *"safeguard the permanence"*: Matthew Parker, *One Fine Day* (PublicAffairs, 2023), 45.
328 *done the opposite:* William Louis, *Imperialism at Bay* (Oxford, 1986), 337–350; Robert O'Shea, "Not Foreign to Each Other," Oxford University, DPhil Thesis, Hilary 2016, 62–73.
328 *The Australian proposal:* "Empire Affairs, The London Conference."
328 *the size of its:* Gregory P. Marchildon, "From Pax Britannica to Pax Americana and Beyond," *Annals of the American Academy of Political and Social Science* 538 (March 1995): 151–68.
328 *closed trading zone:* Richard Overy, *Blood and Ruins* (Random House, 2021), 551.
328 *brink of insolvency:* David Kennedy, *Freedom from Fear* (Oxford University Press, 1999), 465–468.
328 *"financial Dunkirk"*: John Maynard Keynes, "Our Overseas Financial Prospects," August 13, 1945, in *The Collected Writings of John Maynard Keynes* (Macmillan, 1979), 24: 410.
328 *from Dunkirk:* David Kennedy, *Freedom from Fear*, 439.
328 *Through Lend-Lease:* Jeremy Green, *The Political Economy of the Special Relationship* (Princeton University Press, 2020), 77; Overy, *Blood and Ruins*, 554; David Kennedy, *Freedom from Fear*, 460–476.
329 *most extraordinary period:* Richard Gardner, *Sterling-Dollar Diplomacy: Anglo-American Collaboration in the Reconstruction of Multilateral Trade* (2nd ed., Oxford University Press, 1969), 165–178; David Kennedy, *Freedom from Fear*, 465–498, 809–10; Kori Schake, *Safe Passage: The Transition from British to American Hegemony* (Harvard University Press, 2017), 254–270.
329 *"Sterling Dollar"*: Winston Churchill, Signed Art: The "Sterling Dollar," Washington, DC: May 28, 1943, Bauman Rare Books, Item 103058.
329 *British government debt:* Benn Steil, *The Battle of Bretton Woods*, (Princeton University Press, 2013), 3.
329 *"Special post-war"*: John Maynard Keynes, "Notes on External Finance in the Post-Japanese-Armistice Transitional Period," January 11, 1944, in *The Collected Writings of John Maynard Keynes* (Cambridge, 2012), 24:10.
329 *"What the U.S. has"*: Hans Kaiser, "Pax Britannica und Pax Americana," *Zeitschrift für Politik* 31, no. 7 (July 1941): 389–410.
329 *As loyal as:* Roberts, *Before Rupert*, 241.

330 *By 1944, though:* Mark Harrison, *The Economics of World War II* (Cambridge University Press, 1998), 27–34.
330 *military outposts:* Daniel Immerwahr, *How to Hide an Empire* (FSG, 2019), 216–224.
330 *"It had to be seen":* Murdoch, "Town Hall Reception Speech."
330 *"Australia's main body":* Keith Murdoch, "Hard Going: The Italian Campaign," *West Australian*, May 6, 1944.
330 *"British and Americans":* Murdoch, "Town Hall Reception Speech."
330 *"carefully avoid anything":* Dwight Eisenhower, Cable to Marshall, May 16, 1944, Pre-Pres. Principal, box 133.
331 *the Soviets came through:* The Chargé in the Soviet Union (Hamilton) to the Secretary of State, May 17, 1944, FRUS 1944, vol. 3, doc. 622.
331 *"very largely falling":* SHAEF, G-2, Weekly Intelligence Summary no. 8, May 13, 1944, Smith Papers, box 30.
331 *"Thousands of civilians":* "Bombing of France, Plea by Cardinals," *The Age*, May 15, 1944, p. 1.
331 *Swiss newspapers:* Confidential Annex, "Conclusions of a Meeting of the War Cabinet Held at 10 Downing Street, SW 1, on Tuesday, 30th May, 1944, 6:30pm," NAUK, CAB 65/46/12.
331 *Allies and the Vatican:* Butcher Diary, A-1188.
331 *"distress at the":* Franklin Roosevelt to Winston Churchill, May 11, 1944, NARA, RG 331, E1, box 66.
331 *Knights of Columbus:* "K. of C. Ask Religious Freedom in Countries Allies Liberate," *Boston Globe*, May 10, 1944.
331 *"assure the French":* George Marshall to Bedell Smith, May 16, 1944, in *The Papers of George Catlett Marshall* (Johns Hopkins University Press, 1996), 4:454–56.
332 "C'est la guerre": Walter B. Smith to George Marshall, May 17, 1944, Smith Papers, box 27.

CHAPTER 39

333 *set June 5:* Dwight D. Eisenhower, *Report by the Supreme Commander to the Combined Chiefs of Staff on the Operations in Europe of the Allied Expeditionary Force: 6 June 1944 to 8 May 1945*, CMH Pub. 70-58 (US Government Printing Office, 1946), 5.
333 *"denied private":* Cordell Hull to the Chief of Mission, May 20, 1944, EL, Harry C. Butcher Papers, box 3.
333 *anthrax and botulinum:* SHAEF 710-21 MED, Biological Warfare, May 17, 1944, NARA RG 331, entry 66, box 3.
333 *X-ray films:* X-Ray Department, 317th Station Hospital to Theater Surgeon, ETO, May 24, 1944, NARA, RG 77, Subfile 7D.
333 *German air defenses:* Dwight Eisenhower, memorandum, May 22, 1944, Pre-Pres Principal, box 167.
333 *The latest estimates:* SHAEF, G-2, Weekly Intelligence Summary No. 9, May 20, 1944, Smith Papers, Box 30; Butcher Diary, A-1271.
334 *Unlike the French:* Butcher Diary, A-1188.
334 *source of worry:* Butcher Diary, A-1146, A-1169, A-1188, A-1212, A-1223, A-1238.
334 *Earlier that month:* Dwight Eisenhower to George Marshall, May 6, 1944, Pre-Pres. Principal, box 133.
334 *Harriman assured Eisenhower:* Butcher Diary, A-1238.
334 *drinks and bridge:* Butcher Diary, A-1280.
335 *Eisenhower wanted to like:* Harold Bull to Walter B. Smith, May 19, 1944, RG 331, entry NM8 4, box 121.
335 *"shuttle bombing":* P.J. Sutterlin to F.L. Anderson, May 25, 1944, LOC, Carl Spaatz Papers, box 12; Mark Conversino, *Fighting with the Soviets* (University of Kansas Press, 1997); Headquarters, Mediterranean Allied Air Forces, The History of Frantic, 1944; Carl Spaatz, Diary, February 17, 1944, LOC, Carl Spaatz Papers, box 12; Butcher Diary, A-1076, A-1183; Carl Spaatz, Notes of Meeting with General Wilsch, April 30, 1944, LOC, Carl Spaatz Papers, box 12; Carl Spaatz, Minutes of Meeting, April 29, 1944, LOC, Carl Spaatz Papers, box 12.
335 *continued to press:* Dwight Eisenhower to Walter B. Smith, May 20, 1944, Pre-Pres. Principal, box 109.
336 *"sow some seeds":* Eisenhower to Combined Chiefs of Staff, May 17, 1944, Smith Papers, box 23.
336 *"Dunkirk spirit":* "Unconditional Surrender," *The Observer*, April 2, 1944.
336 *Eisenhower knew Roosevelt:* Eisenhower to Smith, May 20, 1944.

CHAPTER 40

337 *A sty developed:* Butcher Diary, A-1300.
337 *Summer had come early:* Bertram Ramsay, *The Year of D-Day* (University of Hull, 1994), 77–78.
337 *"antics of the hordes":* Dwight Eisenhower, *Letters to Mamie* (Doubleday, 1977), 177.
337 *Eisenhower asked Edward Betts:* Edward C. Betts, memorandum, "Naturalizion of Mrs. Kay Summersby," April 1, 1944, Pre-Pres. Principal, box 112.
337 *"Please don't get":* Eisenhower, *Letters to Mamie*, 177.
338 *Eisenhower fantasized:* Eisenhower to Mamie Eisenhower, May 17, 1944, private collection.

338 *And he hoped:* Everett Hughes to Kate Hughes, May 24, 1944, Hughes Papers, box II-2.
338 *news of Mamie:* Everett Hughes, Diary, May 24, 1944, Hughes Papers, box I-1.
338 *Georgie's wife:* George Patton to Beatrice Patton, May 25, 1944, Patton Papers, box 18.
338 *new army joke:* Everett Hughes, Diary, May 24, 1944.
338 *"Well, it seemed":* Everett Hughes to Kate Hughes, May 24, 1944.
338 *Georgie could be:* Michael McKeogh and Richard Lockridge, *Sgt. Mickey & General Ike* (Putnam, 1946), 55.
338 *a martinet:* George Hall, interview with Mattie Pinette, January 5, 1977, EL, George Hall Papers, box 1.
338 *Eisenhower laughed harder:* George Patton to Beatrice Patton, May 25, 1944.
338 *He showed Georgie:* Everett Hughes to Kate Hughes, May 24, 1944.
338 *"presented to his":* Eisenhower, *Letters to Mamie*, 177.
339 *"go home and":* Butcher Diary, A-1297.
339 *"will reach you":* Swede Hazlett to Dwight Eisenhower, May, 23, 1944, Pre-Pres. Principal, box 56.
339 *"the only stories":* Edgar Eisenhower to Dwight Eisenhower, May 13, 1944, Pre-Pres. Principal, box 172.
339 *"if they gave":* Dwight Eisenhower to Edgar Eisenhower, May 22, 1944, Pre-Pres. Principal, box 172.
339 *"recognized correspondent":* Richard Powell to LeBaron Barker, April 29, 1944, Davis Papers, box 94.
339 *"real historical":* Milton Eisenhower to Dwight Eisenhower, May 2, 1944, Pre-Pres. Principal, box 174.
340 *carefully cultivating:* Kenneth Davis to Milton Eisenhower, 1944, Davis Papers, box 61.
340 *"no reference would":* Swede Hazlett, Milton Eisenhower to Kenneth Davis, 1944, Davis Papers, box 61.
340 *"We have progressed":* Milton Eisenhower, "The Foundation of America," Address at Patriotic Rally, February 22, 1944, Davis Papers, box 22.
340 *trapped in:* Friedrich Nietzsche, *Untimely Meditations,* trans. J.P. Stern (Cambridge University Press, 1983), 157.
340 *terms of the frontier:* Timothy Rives, "Eisenhower, the Frontier, and the New Deal," *Prologue* 47, no. 3 (Fall 2015): 8–15.
340 *"average workaday":* Milton Eisenhower to H. W. Lunow, "Proposal for an Institute of Citizenship," 1944, Davis Papers, box 22.
340 *call from Jack Connolly:* Jack S. Connolly to Mamie Eisenhower, May 19, 1944, Pre-Pres. Principal, box 174.
341 *Eisenhower trusted Connolly:* Dwight Eisenhower to Milton Eisenhower, May 30, 1944, Pre-Pres Principal, box 167.
341 *"mixed in any":* Butcher Diary, A-1313.
341 *Buckingham Palace:* Kay Summersby, Diary, May 26, 1944, EL, Barbara Wyden Papers; Kenneth Davis, "Notes Based on Colonel Gault's Diary," 1944, Davis Papers, box 94.
341 *Hanson Baldwin:* Daily Appointment Log, May 26, 1944, EL, Pre-Pres. Principal, box 127.
341 *keenly focused:* Hanson Baldwin, "The Task Ahead for Allied Airmen," *New York Times*, May 25, 1944.
342 *Pavilion Breakfast Room:* Ashley Hicks, *Buckingham Palace: The Interiors* (Rizzoli, 2021).
342 *buffet lunch:* Butcher Diary, A-1300.
342 *"soldier of the Empire":* Forrest Pogue, interview with Sir Arthur Coningham, February 14, 1947, Pogue Papers, box 161.
342 *quintessentially American:* Pogue, "Notes OVERLORD by the Under-Dog-in-Chief, by Frederick Morgan," 1946, Pogue Papers, box 157.
342 *"the qualities":* Pogue, interview with Coningham, February 14, 1947.
343 *"poaching":* Butcher Diary, A-1300.
343 *"This is terrible":* Dwight Eisenhower, *At Ease* (Doubleday, 1967), 277–278.
343 *King George had told:* Harry C. Butcher, *My Three Years with Eisenhower* (Simon & Schuster, 1946), 17.
343 *felt as casual:* Butcher Diary, A-1300.
343 *"encourage kids":* Eisenhower, *Letters to Mamie*, 177.
343 *"the virtues":* Dwight Eisenhower to Milton Eisenhower, May 30, 1944, Pre-Pres Principal box 167.

CHAPTER 41

344 *Two years later:* Ronald Ruppenthal, *Logistical Support of the Armies*, CMH Pub. 7-2-1 (US Government Printing Office, 1952), 1:231-258; Byron Greenwald, "Why Normandy Still Matters: Seventy-Five Years On, Operation Overlord Inspires, Instructs, and Invites Us to Be Better Joint Warfighters," *Joint Force Quarterly*, no. 95 (2019): 580.
344 *The British had helped:* Jeremy Green, *The Political Economy of the Special Relationship* (Princeton, 2020), 90; Benn Steil, *The Battle of Bretton Woods* (Princeton, 2013), 221; Richard Gardner, *Sterling-Dollar Diplomacy: Anglo-American Collaboration in the Reconstruction of Multilateral Trade* (2nd ed., Oxford University Press, 1969), 77–80.
345 *Drought conditions:* Dwight Eisenhower to Omar Bradley, April 10, 1944, Pre-Pres. Principal, box 13.

345 *The real problem:* Eisenhower to George Marshall, May 23, 1944, Pre-Pres. Principal, box 133.

345 *Churchill invited Eisenhower:* Kay Summersby, SHAEF Desk Calendar, May 22, 1944, EL, Wyden Papers, box 1.

345 *promised to lobby:* Dwight Eisenhower to George Marshall, May 23, 1944, Pre-Pres. Principal, box 133.

345 *British colonial soldiers:* Edward Betts, memorandum, "Article on Military Justice," NARA, RG 498, entry UD 1028, box 4716.

345 *Betts's initial investigation:* E. C. McNeil, memorandum, "Death Sentences for Rape by General Courts-Martial in U.S.," May 12, 1944, NARA, RG 498, entry UD 1028, box 4716.

346 *Betts also compiled:* RF, memorandum, "Federal Laws on Punishment for Rape," May 1944, NARA, RG 498, entry UD 1028, box 4716.

346 *case of Leroy Henry:* Mary Louise Roberts, "The Leroy Henry Case: Sexual Violence and Allied Relations in Great Britain, 1944," *Journal of the History of Sexuality* 26, no. 3 (September 2017): 402–23.

346 *letters poured in:* General Court Martial Record, NARA-SL, *United States v. Leroy Henry*, Court-Martial No. 264262, Record of Trial.

346 *One petition:* Arthur Burgess, Transmittal of Signatures for Clemency, September 20, 1944, NARA-SL, *United States v. Leroy Henry*, Court-Martial No. 264262, Record of Trial.

346 *"coloured troops are":* "Conduct of U.S. Troops Very Good—Morrison," *Citizen* (Gloucester), May 25, 1944, p. 5.

346 *Labour MPs were:* Howard Bucknell to Edward Stettinius, May 30, 1944, NARA, RG 498, entry UD 1028, box 4719.

347 *"establish a beachhead":* David A. Price, *Geniuses at War* (Knopf, 2021), 153.

347 *"I realize":* Dwight Eisenhower to Winston Churchill, May 29, 1944, Pre-Pres. Principal, box 22.

347 *The problem was:* SHAEF, COS Brief & Action Report, 178th Meeting, June 3, 1944, *554, RG 331, entry NM8 3, box 126.

347 *Patton had asked:* Leo P. Brophy and George J. B. Fisher, *The Chemical Warfare Service: Organizing for War*, CMH Pub. 10-1 (US Government Printing Office, 1955), 303.

347 *proved its value:* Walter B. Smith, Training Memorandum no. 50, "Lessons from the Sicilian Campaign," November 20, 1943, Patton Papers, box 44, p. 20.

348 *"one of the best":* Smith, 51.

348 *"The Germans":* Alden H. Waitt, "The 4.2 Chemical Mortar," *Infantry Journal*, March 1944.

348 *"if he still":* COS (444), Brief & Action Report, 178th Meeting, June 3, 1944, RG 331, entry NM8 3, box 126.

348 *Eisenhower's doctor:* Forrest Pogue, interview with A. W. Kenner, June 1, 1945, Pogue Papers, box 161.

348 *"on record":* Trafford Leigh-Mallory to Dwight Eisenhower, May 29, 1944, Pre-Pres Principal, box 167.

348 *Ultra intercepts:* Price, *Geniuses at War*, 152.

348 *Some thought:* Harold Bull, "Implications of Reported Enemy Reinforcements of the Cotentin Peninsula," May 26, 1944, RG 331, entry 1, box 76.

349 *"I cannot guarantee":* Leigh-Mallory to Eisenhower, May 29, 1944.

349 *"a strong, airborne":* Dwight Eisenhower to Trafford Leigh-Mallory, May 30, 1944, Pre-Pres Principal box 167.

349 *"not heretofore":* COS (44), Brief & Action Report, 178th Meeting.

349 *"it lacked":* Brooks Kleber and Dale Birdsell, *The Chemical Warfare Service: Chemicals in Combat*, CMH Pub. 10-3 (US Government Printing Office, 1966), 127.

349 *"no orders":* COS (44), Brief & Action Report, 178th Meeting.

350 *"on a network":* Dwight Eisenhower, *Letters to Mamie* (Doubleday, 1977), 177.

350 *The last week:* Kay Summersby, Diary, May 30, 1944, EL, Barbara Wyden Papers, box 1.

350 *The Combined Chiefs:* Robert Sherwood, "Meeting with Admiral Ernest J. King in His Office at the Navy Department," May 25, 1946, Sherwood Papers, box 40.

350 *Eisenhower had invited:* Butcher Diary, A-1319.

350 *"The devil himself":* Butcher Diary, A-1321.

350 *"It will not":* Winston Churchill to Dwight Eisenhower, May 31, 1944, Pre-Pres Principal, box 167.

350 *rang up Beetle:* Butcher Diary, A-1321.

350 *wrote back:* Dwight Eisenhower to Winston Churchill, June 1, 1944, Pre-Pres. Principal, box 22.

CHAPTER 42

353 *morning of June 2:* Kay Summersby, Diary, June 2, 1944, EL, Barbara Wyden Papers, box 1.

353 *in a warehouse:* James Martin Stagg, *Forecast for Overlord* (Norton, 1971), 68.

353 *Bertie Ramsay had claimed:* Allan Michie, *The Invasion of Europe* (Dodd, Mead, 1964), 118.

353 *short commanders in chief:* Trafford Leigh-Mallory, Historical Record AEAF (June 1944), NAUK, AIR

37/1057; Minutes of Meeting Held in the ANXF Conference Room Southwick House 1000 hours, 2nd June 1944, NAUK, WO 205 12.

353 *a campsite:* Mattie Pinette, Diary, June 2, 1944, EL, George Hall Papers, box 1.

353 *"Sharpener":* E. C. Boehnke to ALCON, May 23, 1944, NARA, RG 331, E1, box 23.

353 *"What is the definition":* Butcher Diary, A-1328.

354 *The weather outside:* Butcher Diary, A- 1301.

354 *"weather forecasts, while":* Dwight Eisenhower to George Marshall, June 1, 1944, Pre-Pres. Principal, box 133.

354 *The trees echoed:* Mattie Pinette, Diary, June 2,1944, EL, George Hall Papers, box 1.

354 *pond neaby for fishing:* Marty Snyder, *My Friend Ike* (Fell, 1956), 60.

354 *cinder paths:* Pinette, Diary, June 2, 1944.

354 *his old trailer:* Snyder, *My Friend Ike*, 50.

354 *"circus wagon":* Michie, *Invasion of Europe*, 120.

354 *Kay also had:* Pinette, Diary, June 2, 1944.

354 *The Lockheed Aircraft:* Michie, *Invasion of Europe*, 119.

354 *Lockheed super-deluxe:* Pinette, Diary, June 2, 1944.

354 *his eye still smarted:* Butcher Diary, A-1326.

354 *Seeing Corporal Williams:* Pinette, Diary, June 2, 1944.

355 *new uniform marking:* Dwight Eisenhower to George Marshall, May 24, 1944, Pre-Pres. Principal, box 80.

355 *spent the afternoon:* Pinette, Diary, June 2, 1944.

355 *"If Winnie comes":* George S. Patton, Diary, June 1, 1944, Patton Papers, box 3.

355 *"certain rights":* Butcher Diary, A-1319.

355 *"We should both":* George VI to Winston Churchill, May 31, 1944, Churchill Papers, box CHAR 20/136.

355 *Ramsay then called:* Bertram Ramsay, *The Year of D-Day* (University of Hull, 1994), 8; Butcher Diary, A-1321.

355 *"If the King":* George VI to Winston Churchill, June 2, 1944, Churchill Papers, box CHAR 20/136.

356 *Churchill arrived:* Summersby, Diary, June 2, 1944.

356 *in a peevish mood:* Butcher Diary, A-1326.

356 *Upon seeing Eisenhower:* Butcher Diary, A-1328.

356 *dinner with Monty:* Summersby, Diary, June 2, 1944.

356 *Broomfield House:* Bernard Montgomery, *The Memoirs of Field Marshal Montgomery* (The World Publishing, 1958), 211.

356 *a quiet meal:* Montgomery, 222.

356 *they were both due:* Trafford Leigh-Mallory, "Historical Record AEAF (June 1944)," NAUK, AIR 37/1057.

356 *Fifty-eight thousand tons:* SHAEF, G-2, Weekly Intelligence Summary no. 11, June 3, 1944, Smith Papers, box 30.

356 *For diplomatic reasons:* Walter B. Smith to Carl Spaatz, May 5, 1944, Pre-Pres. Principal, box 22.

356 *"a belt of bombed":* Trafford Leigh-Mallory, "Minutes of Meeting held Southwick House 1000 hours, 2nd June, 1944," NAUK, AIR 37/1057.

356 *Tedder was opposed:* Notes Taken by General Cabell at Air Commanders Meeting at Stanmore, 3 June, LOC, Carl Spaatz Papers, box 12.

356 *most recent intelligence:* SHAEF, G-2, Weekly Intelligence Summary no. 11.

357 *"the air forces":* Lord Tedder, *With Prejudice* (Little Brown, 1966), 538.

357 *Tedder shared his concerns:* Winston Churchill to Paymaster-General, M. 674/4, June 1, 1944, Churchill Papers, CHAR 20/152/6.

357 *a secret meeting:* Confidential Annex, "Conclusions of a Meeting of the War Cabinet Held at 10 Downing Street, SW 1, on Tuesday, 30th May, 1944, 6:30pm," NAUK, CAB 65/46/12.

357 *Eisenhower had sided:* Leigh-Mallory, "Historical Record AEAF."

357 *They needed as much:* Summersby, Diary, June 2, 1944.

357 *"After four":* Bernard Montgomery, "Before 'OVERLORD,'" May 1944, Pre-Pres. Principal, box 83.

358 *Eisenhower thought the speech:* Dwight Eisenhower to Bernard Montgomery, May 26, 1944, Pre-Pres. Principal, box 83.

358 *"Eisenhower is just":* Bernard Montgomery, Diary, June 2, 1944, in Nigel Hamilton, *Master of the Battlefield* (McGraw Hill, 1983), 596.

358 *They left together:* Summersby, Diary, June 2, 1944.

358 *Stagg's tells:* Interview with James Martin Stagg, in *The World at War* (Thames Television, 1973), Episode 17.

358 *"The whole situation":* Stagg, *Forecast for Overlord*, 86.

358 *His mood was hard:* Summersby, Diary, June 2, 1944.

358 *difficult to sleep:* Mattie Pinette, Diary, June 3, 1944, EL, George Hall Papers, box 1.

358 *back to Wide Wing:* Pinette.

358 *He had a meeting:* Kay Summersby, Diary, June 3, 1944, EL, Barbara Wyden Papers, box 1.

358 *William Simpson:* Thomas R. Stone, "He Had the Guts to Say No" (PhD diss., Rice University, 1974), 1.
359 *"kicked into the sea":* Eisenhower, memorandum, June 3, 1944, Pre-Pres. Principal, box 137.
359 *"not the tops":* LeRoy Lutes to Brehon Somervell, May 9, 1944, in John Millet, *The Army Service Forces*, CMH Pub. 3-1 (U.S. Government Printing Office, 1953), 81.
359 *"An American":* Chester Hansen, Diary, May 4, 1944, USAHEC, Chester Hansen Papers.
359 *the Ninth Army:* Kay Summersby, Diary, June 3, 1944, EL, Barbara Wyden Papers, box 1.
359 *yet another message:* Dwight Eisenhower to George Marshall, May 27, 1944, Pre-Pres. Principal, box 80.
359 *Roosevelt sent Churchill:* President Roosevelt to the British Prime Minister (Churchill), May 27, 1944, FRUS 1944, vol. 1, doc. 113.
359 *An argument:* The British Prime Minister (Churchill) to President Roosevelt, May 31, 1944, FRUS 1944, vol. 1, doc. 114; President Roosevelt to the British Prime Minister (Churchill), June 2, 1944, FRUS 1944, vol. 1, doc. 117.
360 *"Probably no one":* Eisenhower, memorandum, June 3, 1944.
360 *dropping leaflets:* Trafford Leigh-Mallory, Minutes of Meeting held Southwick House 1000 hours, 2nd June, 1944.
360 *"Allied airmen are":* Dwight Eisenhower, "Air Attacks on Civilians," June 2, 1944, NAUK, AIR 37/1057.
360 *"Nothing":* Eisenhower to Leigh-Mallory, Harris, and Spaatz, June 2, 1944, Pre-Pres. Principal, box 161.
360 *left Wide Wing:* Summersby, Diary, June 3, 1944.
360 *back to Southwick:* Pinette, Diary, June 3, 1944.
360 *"Dammit all":* Michie, *Invasion of Europe*, 120.
361 *Churchill returned:* Summersby, Diary, June 3, 1944.
361 *Butch welcomed:* Butcher Diary, A-1328.
361 *Eisenhower showed:* Pinette, Diary, June 3, 1944.
361 *on his way:* Butcher Diary, A-1328.
361 *Churchill was unenthusiastic:* Confidential Annex, "Conclusions of a Meeting."
361 *De Gaulle had insisted:* The Acting American Representative to the French Committee of National Liberation Algiers (Chapin) to the Secretary of State, May 31, 1944, FRUS 1944, Vol. III, doc. 632.
361 *Roosevelt obviously refused:* The Secretary of State to the Acting American Representative to the French Committee of National Liberation Algiers (Chapin), April 21, 1944, FRUS 1944, vol. 3, doc. 633.
361 *behind the idea:* Confidential Annex, "Conclusions of a Meeting."
361 *He expected:* Butcher Diary, A-1328.
361 *Eisenhower needed someone:* Eisenhower, Memorandum, June 3, 1944.
361 *eight in the evening:* Butcher Diary, A-1328.
361 *Eisenhower had another:* Leigh-Mallory, Historical Record AEAF, June 1944.
361 *Official Family meal:* Pinette, Diary, June 3, 1944.
364 *"Gentlemen":* Martin Stagg, *Forecast for Overlord*, 97.
364 *If they went:* Harold R. Bull, "Memorandum for Record," June 4, 1944, EL, Harold R. Bull Papers, box 3.
365 *Each day:* Chester Hansen, Diary, June 4, 1944, USAHEC, Chester Hansen Papers.
365 *The Dieppe Raid:* C. P. Stacey, *Six Years of War: Official History of the Canadian Army in the Second World War*, 1:339–44.
365 *"in order not":* Bull, "Memorandum for Record," June 4, 1944; Bertram Ramsay, *The Year of D-Day* (University of Hull, 1994), 81.
365 *"Reports coming in":* Pinette, Diary, June 3, 1944.
365 *"The sky outside":* Stagg, *Forecast for Overlord*, 100.
365 *"No part of":* Kingston McCloughry, *Direction of War* (Prager, 1955), 138–39.
365 *"We had only":* Bertram Ramsay, *The Year of D-Day*, at 82.
365 *"If Overlord is":* Stagg, *Forecast for Overlord*, 100–14.
366 *Monty spoke up:* Lord Tedder, *With Prejudice* (Little Brown, 1966), 545; Michie, *Invasion of Europe*, 138.
366 *"Jesus!":* McCloughry, *Direction of War*, 138–39.
366 *"Exercise Hornpipe":* Dwight Eisenhower to CCS, June 4, 1944, NARA, RG 331, entry 1, box 76.
366 *Kay was waiting:* Summersby, Diary, June 3, 1944.
366 *And the sun:* Summersby.

CHAPTER 43

367 *"London, June 3":* Teletype, June 3, 1944, EL, WWII Participants and Contemporaries, box 69.
367 *The sky:* James Martin Stagg, *Forecast for Overlord* (Norton, 1971), 104.
367 *back to camp:* Mattie Pinette, Diary, June 4, 1944, EL, George Hall Papers, box 1.
367 *Butch was up:* Butcher Diary, A-1328.

367 *an AP operator:* Harold R. Bull, "Memorandum for Record," June 4, 1944, EL, Harold R. Bull Papers, box 3.
367 *Eisenhower gazed:* Butcher Diary, A-1328.
367 *Beetle came by:* Pinette, Diary, June 4, 1944.
368 *The wind was:* Stagg, *Forecast for Overlord*, 105.
368 *"However":* JCS to Dwight Eisenhower, June 4, 1944, Pre-Pres. Principal, box 63.
368 *Eisenhower went back:* Pinette, Diary, June 4, 1944.
368 *"Additional time":* Bull, "Memorandum for Record," June 4, 1944.
368 *Beetle's office tent:* Pinette, Diary, June 4, 1944.
368 *finally arrived:* Bull, "Memorandum for Record," June 4, 1944.
368 *De Gaulle should broadcast:* Butcher Diary, A-1343.
369 *Churchill wanted:* Dwight Eisenhower to CCS, June 6, 1944, Pre-Pres. Principal, box 130.
369 *Within minutes:* Butcher Diary, A-1343.
369 *De Gaulle had arrived:* Bull, "Memorandum for Record," June 4, 1944.
369 *Eisenhower invited them:* Butcher Diary, A-1343.
369 *"What do you":* Charles de Gaulle, *The Complete War Memoirs of Charles de Gaulle* (Carroll & Graf, 1950), 2:253.
369 *Eisenhower then took:* Bull, "Memorandum for Record," June 4, 1944.
369 *De Gaulle gestured:* Butcher Diary, A-1343.
369 *"De Gaulle only":* Kay Summersby, Diary, June 4, 1944, EL, Barbara Wyden Papers, box 1.
369 *"I prefer not":* The Acting American Representative to the French Committee of National Liberation Algiers (Chapin) to the Secretary of State, June 10, 1944, FRUS 1944, vol. 3, doc. 641 ("He preferred not to have anything to do with it" / "he was a soldier and not a politician").
369 *told De Gaulle:* Confidential Annex, "Conclusions of a Meeting of the War Cabinet Held at 10 Downing Street, SW 1, on Monday, 5th June, 1944, 6:30pm," NAUK, CAB 65/46/15.
370 *The speech:* Walter B. Smith to Winston Churchill, June 5, 1944, Pre-Pres. Principal, box 22.
370 *returned to Southwick House:* Bull, "Memorandum for Record," June 4, 1944.
370 *Eisenhower dictated:* Pinette, Diary, June 4, 1944.
370 *"General de Gaulle":* Dwight Eisenhower to Combined Chiefs of Staff, June 4, 1944, Eisenhower Papers, vol. 3, 1906–7.
370 *When Eisenhower:* Pinette, Diary, June 4, 1944.
370 *"Gentlemen":* Stagg, *Forecast for Overlord*, 110.
370 *Over the previous month:* Stagg, 52.
370 *All that data:* Sverre Petterson, Memoirs, undated, EL, WWII Participants, box 104.
371 *"Can you say":* Stagg, *Forecast for Overlord*, 110.
371 *"It's a helluva":* Allan Michie, *The Invasion of Europe* (Dodd, Mead, 1964), 142.
371 *"The question":* Bull, "Memorandum for Record," June 4, 1944.
371 *"I'm quite":* Gordon A. Harrison, *Cross-Channel Attack*, CMH Pub 7-4-1 (US Government Printing Office, 1951), 274.
372 *"Well, Stagg":* Stagg, *Forecast for Overlord*, 115.
372 *At 4:15 a.m.:* Bull, "Memorandum for Record," June 4, 1944.
372 *Rain was pouring:* Kenneth Strong, *Intelligence at the Top: The Recollections of an Intelligence Officer* (Doubleday, 1969), 184.
372 *He arrived last:* Walter B. Smith, *Eisenhower's Six Great Decisions* (Longmans, 1956), 53.
372 *"Go ahead":* Stagg, *Forecast for Overlord*, 116.
372 *"What do you":* Michie, *Invasion of Europe*, 144.
372 *face grew heavy:* Walter B. Smith, *Eisenhower's Six Great Decisions*, 54–55.
372 *the precise words:* Timothy Rives, "'OK, We'll Go': Just What Did Ike Say When He Launched the D-day Invasion 70 Years Ago?," *Prologue*, Spring 2014, p. 38.
373 *"some quaint American":* Barney Oldfield, *Never a Shot in Anger* (Van Rees, 1956), 72.
373 *Let's go:* Ernest Graves, *The Line Man's Bible* (1921), 150.
373 *"Good luck":* Michie, *Invasion of Europe*, 144.
373 *"Our landing":* Dwight Eisenhower, Draft Message, June 5, 1944, GCM, Marshall Papers, box 66.

CHAPTER 44

375 *"Exercise Hornpipe":* SHAEF to CCS, June 5, 1944, NARA, RG 331, entry 1, box 76.
375 *The sun came up:* James Martin Stagg, *Forecast for Overlord* (Norton, 1971), 119.
375 *Kay drove:* Butcher Diary, A-1331.
375 *"Good old Ike":* Kay Summersby, Diary, June 5, 1944, Pre-Pres. Principal, box 140.

375 *ships of all kinds:* Harold R. Bull, "Forces Available in ETO for Operation 'OVERLORD,'" Pre-Pres. Principal, box 153.

375 *aircraft loads:* Dwight D. Eisenhower, *Report by the Supreme Commander to the Combined Chiefs of Staff on the Operations in Europe of the Allied Expeditionary Force: 6 June 1944 to 8 May 1945*, CMH Pub. 70-58 (US Government Printing Office, 1946), 22.

375 *bombers and fighters:* Bull, "Forces Available in ETO for Operation 'OVERLORD.'"

375 *Each LST:* Headquarters, First US Army, After Action Against Enemy, Reports After/After Action Report August 6, 1944, EL, U.S. Army, First Army Headquarters Records, 1943–55 box 2.

375 *Eighty cargo vessels:* Butcher Diary, 1301.

375 *1,931,855 soldiers:* Bull, "Forces Available in ETO for Operation 'OVERLORD.'"

376 *Eisenhower returned:* Mattie Pinette, Diary, 1944, EL, George Hall Papers, box 1.

376 *played a game:* Butcher Diary, 1332.

376 *"Good, Stagg":* Stagg, *Forecast for Overlord*, 120.

376 *another storm:* Walter B. Smith to Winston Churchill, June 5, 1944, Pre-Pres. Principal, box 22.

376 *latest intelligence:* The Acting American Representative to the French Committee of National Liberation Algiers (Chapin) to the Secretary of State, May 31, 1944, FRUS 1944, vol. 3, doc. 635.

376 *"The button":* Mattie Pinette, Diary, 1944, *97, EL, George Hall Papers, box 1.

376 *"the greatest operation":* Butcher Diary, 1328.

376 *"Nervous":* Kenneth Davis, *Soldier of Democracy* (Konecky & Konecky, 1945), 1.

376 *"By George":* Butcher Diary, 1328.

376 *"To hell with":* Butcher Diary, 1332.

377 *"wonder why":* Robert A. McClure, Diary, 1943–1945, Pogue Papers, box 161.

377 *playing bridge:* Mattie Pinette, Diary, 1944, EL, George Hall Papers, box 1.

377 *the papa skunk:* Butcher Diary, 1332.

377 *"proper skunks":* Mattie Pinette, Diary, 1944, EL, George Hall Papers, box 1.

377 *three different rallying points:* Kay Summersby, Diary, Pre-Pres. Principal, box 140.

377 *grim but determined:* Trafford Leigh-Mallory, "Daily Reflections on the Court of the Battle," 1944, NAUK, AIR 37/784.

377 *blackened their faces:* Allan Michie, *The Invasion of Europe* (Dodd, Mead, 1964), 147.

377 *Eisenhower walked slowly:* Butcher Diary, A-1335.

377 *"Are you a":* Michie, *Invasion of Europe*, 147.

377 *Eisenhower struggled:* Interview with Kay Summersby Morgan, in *The World at War* (Thames Television, 1973), Episode 17.

378 *"Don't worry, General":* Relman Morin, interview with Dwight Eisenhower, August 5, 1965, EL, 1965 Principal File, box 2.

378 *sky was clear:* Stagg, *Forecast for Overlord*, 121.

378 *"Good luck":* Michie, *Invasion of Europe*, 147.

378 *"Eileen is married":* Blake Clark, manuscript, 1945, NARA, RG 226, entry 1991, box 16.

378 *Eighth Air Force:* US War Department, Operations Division, Diary, EL, U.S. War Department, Operations Division: Diaries, 1942–1946.

378 *went to the roof:* Kay Summersby, Diary, 1944, Pre-Pres. Principal, box 140.

378 *shortly after ten thirty:* George Elsey, "Weather During NEPTUNE," GCM, George Elsey Papers, box 1.

378 *sparkling green-and-red:* Leigh-Mallory, "Daily Reflections on the Court of the Battle," 1944.

378 *Eisenhower stood:* Kay Summersby, Diary, 1944, Pre-Pres. Principal, box 140.

378 *"War is a renunciation":* Dwight Eisenhower to Reynolds, February 20, 1946, private collection.

378 *"Well, it's on":* Kay Summersby, *Eisenhower Was My Boss* (Dell, 1947), 147–48.

378 *out the window:* Relman Morin, interview with Dwight Eisenhower, August 5, 1965.

378 *"Nothing can stop":* Summersby, *Eisenhower Was My Boss*, 147–48.

CHAPTER 45

379 *Mickey had procured for him:* Michael McKeogh and Richard Lockridge, *Sgt. Mickey & General Ike* (Putnam, 1946), 117.

379 *action and shooting:* McKeogh and Lockridge, 54.

379 *a war correspondent:* "Author Max Brand Killed on War Front," Associated Press, May 16, 1944.

379 Czar of Halfaday Creek: Meredith Mason Brown deposited a copy of *The Czar of Halfaday Creek* in the Eisenhower Library with the note that it was the book Eisenhower was reading on D-Day. Brown claimed to have received this book from his father, John Mason Brown, who was a writer, serving with the navy on D-Day, who in turn claimed to have received it from Harry Butcher. (Meredith Mason Brown, *Touching*

America's History: From the Pequot War through World War II [Indiana University Press, 2013], 204.) No independent corroboration of this claim has been found. Against it, Mickey McKeogh describes Eisenhower as reading a western "magazine." (McKeogh and Lockridge, *Sgt. Mickey & General Ike*, 116.) However, the illustrated cover of the edition of *The Czar of Halfaday Creek* donated to the Eisenhower library has the illustrated style and typography that would make it look upon a quick glance like a pulp magazine.

379 *"The Man Who"*: James Hendryx, *The Czar of Halfaday Creek* (Triangle Books, 1942), 1.

380 *six thirty in the morning:* Butcher Diary, A-1336.

380 *"The sky"*: Bertram Ramsay, *The Year of D-Day* (University of Hull, 1994), 83.

381 *"Thank God"*: Relam Morin, interview with Dwight Eisenhower, August 5, 1965, EL, 1965 Principal File, box 2.

381 *Eisenhower suppressed:* Butcher Diary, A-1336.

381 *seven in the morning:* George S. Patton, Diary, June 6, 1944, Patton Papers, box 3.

382 *Mickey popped:* McKeogh and Lockridge, *Sgt. Mickey & General Ike*, 116.

382 *"I'll be right"*: McKeogh and Lockridge, 116.

382 *"Nazis Flee North"*: "Nazis Flee North of Rome," *Stars and Stripes*, June 6, 1944.

382 *"Good morning"*: Butcher Diary, A-1337.

382 *Eisenhower made his way:* Mattie Pinette, Diary, June 6, 1944, EL, George Hall Papers, box 1.

382 *The First Army:* Courtney Hodges, War Diary, 1944, EL, Courtney Hodges Papers, box 25.

382 *"Local time"*: Dwight Eisenhower to George Marshall, June 6, 1944, Pre-Pres. Principal, box 133.

383 *quarter past nine:* Pinette, Diary, June 6, 1944.

383 *"Communique No. 1"*: Davidson Taylor to William Paley, June 7, 1944, EL, William Paley Papers, box 1.

383 *"Citizens of France"*: Dwight D. Eisenhower, "D-Day Broadcast to People of Western Europe, June 6, 1944," EL, Pre-Presidential Speeches.

383 *"Soldiers, sailors"*: Dwight D. Eisenhower, Order of the Day, June 6, 1944, EL, Pre-Presidential Speeches.

383 *He had initially closed:* Order of the Day (Draft), EL, Ray W. Barker Papers, 1942–46, box 1.

383 *"nation-wide"*: "King Calls Empire to Prayer," *New York Times*, June 7, 1944, p. 4.

384 *"Give us"*: Franklin Roosevelt, "D-Day Prayer," June 6, 1944, LOC, Printed Ephemera, portfolio 242, folder 42.

384 *When he was a boy:* Charles Taze Russell, *Studies in the Scriptures, The Divine Plan of the Ages* (Watch Tower Bible and Tract Society, 1886), 347–48.

384 *"With earnest best wishes"*: Winston Churchill to Franklin Roosevelt, October 8, 1933, in *Churchill and Roosevelt: The Complete Correspondence* (Collins, 1984), 1:23.

384 *"Greatest Crusade"*: Central Office of Information, "Unity of Strength/The Greatest Crusade," NAUK, INF 3/341; "The Greatest Crusade," *The Guardian*, October 8, 1940; Michael John Horswell, *The Rise and Fall of British Crusader Medievalism* (Routledge, 2018), 186–87.

384 *"they fight"*: Roosevelt, "D-Day Prayer."

384 *"great plan"*: Butcher Diary, A-1340.

384 *Jimmy Doolittle:* Leish, interview with Jimmy Doolittle, University of Texas, Dallas, James H. Doolittle Papers, Series XVII, box 1, D021-95-14-93-3.

384 *In arguable defiance:* James Doolittle, Log Book 11, University of Texas, Dallas, James H. Doolittle Papers, box 143, D022-84.

384 *"It was"*: Mark Copeland, *The Mighty Eighth* (Griffon, 2021), 67.

384 *"Everything was going"*: Leish, interview with Jimmy Doolittle.

385 *Monty was milling:* Butcher Diary, A-1340.

385 *The losses so far:* Pinette, Diary, June 6, 1944.

385 *the British sector:* Dwight D. Eisenhower, *Report by the Supreme Commander to the Combined Chiefs of Staff on the Operations in Europe of the Allied Expeditionary Force: 6 June 1944 to 8 May 1945*, CMH Pub. 70-58 (GPO, 1946), 22–23.

385 *The bulk:* Headquarters, First US Army, After Action Against Enemy, Reports After/After Action Report, August 6, 1944, EL, U.S. Army, First Army Headquarters Records 1943–55, box 2.

385 *There was nothing:* Pinette, Diary, June 6, 1944.

385 *At noon, Churchill:* "Encouragement and a Warning," *The Guardian*, June 7, 1944, p. 6.

385 *"The House should"*: The War Situation, June 6, 1944, *House of Commons Hansard*, 400:1207–10.

386 *The exuberant roar:* "Encouragement and a Warning."

386 *de Gaulle finally broadcast:* Mattie Pinette, Diary, 1944, EL, George Hall Papers, box 1.

386 *he declared that the French:* Confidential Annex, "Conclusions of a Meeting of the War Cabinet Held at 10 Downing Street, SW 1, on Monday, 5th June, 1944, 6:30pm," NAUK, CAB 65/46/15.

386 *Combined Chiefs had considered:* Combined Chiefs of Staff Minutes, December 4, 1943, FRUS 1943, *The Conferences at Cairo and Tehran, 1943*, doc. 461.

386 *agreeing to terms:* Confidential Annex, "Conclusions of a Meeting."
386 *trained in England:* The Ambassador in the United Kingdom (Winant) to the Secretary of State, June 8, 1944, FRUS 1944, Vol. III, doc. 638.
386 *"an aeroplane would be":* Confidential Annex, "Conclusions of a Meeting."
386 *De Gaulle blinked:* Butcher Diary, A-1340.
386 *"We must have":* Forrest Pogue, interview with Robert Bruce Lookhart, February 18, 1947, Pogue Papers, box 161.
386 *"The supreme battle":* Charles de Gaulle, *The Complete War Memoirs of Charles de Gaulle* (Carroll & Graf, 1950), 2:256.
386 *six in the evening:* Pinette, Diary, June 6, 1944.
387 *The Eighth Air Force:* H.W. Putnam, "Report on Memorandum for Lt. Colonel Elbert," August 28, 1944, GCM, George Elsey Papers, box 1.
387 *"Considerable mortar":* "Report from Naval Commander, Western Task Force," June 6, 1944, NARA, RG 331, entry 1, box 62.
387 *talk to Monty:* Pinette, Diary, June 6, 1944.
387 *Given the progress:* Bernard Montgomery, *The Memoirs of Field Marshal Montgomery* (The World Publishing, 1958), 223–24.
387 *Eisenhower wanted to know:* Butcher Diary, A-1342.
387 *"Can you take":* Forrest Pogue, interview with Miles Dempsey, March 12–13, 1947, Pogue Papers, box 161.
387 *After dinner:* Pinette, Diary, June 6, 1944.
387 *"Flow of information":* "Special Sitrep Report on First Army as of 061200B Hours," June 6, 1944, NARA, RG 331, E1, box 62.
388 *"Obstacles not serious":* Hodges, War Diary, 1944.
388 *V Corps:* Headquarters, First US Army, After Action Against Enemy, Reports After/After Action Report, August 6, 1944, EL, U.S. Army, First Army Headquarters Records, box 2.
388 *The strategic air forces:* Eisenhower, *Report by the Supreme Commander*, 20.
388 *little sign:* SHAEF, G-3 Daily Summary of SAS and SF Operations Under SHAEF Control, June 6, 1944, RG 331, entry 262A, box 135.
388 *"brilliant generalship":* Keith Murdoch, "Address to the Foreign Press Association," June 21, 1944, NLA, Keith Murdoch Papers, MS 2823, file 27.
388 *Jedburgh:* SHAEF, G-3 Daily Summary of SAS and SF Operations Under SHAEF Control No. 3, June 10, 1944, NARA, RG 331, Entry 262A, box 135; Butcher Diary, at A-1260; OSS Activities, April 1944, NARA, RG 226, Entry A1 99, box 122; James Graham, Summary of French Resistance, 6 June–31 August, October 7, 1944, NARA, RG 226, Entry 1991, box 16; Albert Lanier, OG Operations in Southern France, September 24, 1944, NARA, RG 226, Entry 1991, box 16; James Graham, Activity of the Jedburgh Teams, September 12, 1944, NARA, RG 226, Entry 1991, box 16; Benjamin Jones, *Eisenhower's Guerrillas* (Oxford University Press, 2016), 134.
388 *"Hugh":* James B. Graham to W. B. Kantack, September 12, 1944, RG 226, entry 1991, box 16.
388 *John had graduated:* Dwight Eisenhower to John Doud, June 27, 1944, Pre-Pres. Principal, box 171.
388 *Eisenhower had sent:* Eisenhower to Francis Wilby, May 24, 1944, Pre-Pres. Principal, box 124.
389 *"Second Lieutenant":* Eisenhower to John Eisenhower, May 24, 1944, Eisenhower Papers, Vol. 3, 1886–1887.
389 *"What you must":* George Patton to George Patton Jr., June 6, 1944, Patton Papers, box 19.

EPILOGUE

390 *The Canadians urged:* Walter B. Smith to Kenneth Stuart, June 6, 1944, NARA, RG 331, entry 66, box 3.
390 *and medical personnel:* Dwight Eisenhower to Clayton Bissell, June 8, 1944, NARA, RG 331, entry 66, box 3.
390 *maintain a stockpile:* George Marshall to Dwight Eisenhower, June 9, 1944, NARA, RG 331, entry 66, box 3.
391 *"A typhoid":* Dwight Eisenhower to Alan Kirk, June 18, 1944, NARA, RG 331, entry 66, box 3.
391 *The Pentagon had issued:* Memorandum, "Defense Against Sabotage Methods of Biological Warfare in a Theater of Operations," February 24, 1944, NARA, RG 331, entry 66, box 3.
391 *Strict water discipline:* Dwight Eisenhower to Alan Kirk, June 18, 1944, NARA, RG 331, entry 66, box 3.
391 *In the first week:* E. Stevens, "American Build Up Progress Report for Period ending 2359hrs," June 12, 1944, RG 331, entry NM8 34, box 10.
391 *paying close attention:* Butcher Diary, A-1366.
391 *the British surgeon general:* Forrest Pogue, interview with A.W. Kenner, June 1, 1945, Pogue Papers, box 161.
391 *On June 7:* Kay Summersby, Diary, June 7, 1944, EL, Barbara Wyden Papers.
392 *Brad had gone ashore:* Chester Hansen, Diary, June 7, 1944, USAHEC, Chester Hansen Papers.

392 *Brad was impatient*: Omar Bradley, *A General's Life* (Simon & Schuster, 1983), 257.
392 *The sky had been*: Courtney Hodges, War Diary, 1944, EL, Courtney Hodges Papers, box 25.
392 *His over-eagerness*: Dwight Eisenhower to Andrew Cunningham, June 23, 1944, Pre-Pres. Principal, box 29.
392 *saved dessert for him*: Mattie Pinette, Diary, 1944, EL, George Hall Papers, box 1.
392 *"General situation very good"*: Bernard Montgomery to Dwight Eisenhower, June 7, 1944, Pre-Pres. Principal, box 83.
392 *Monty had taken the initiative*: Chester Hansen, Diary, June 7, 1944, USAHEC, Chester Hansen Papers; Nigel Hamilton, *Master of the Battlefield: Monty's War Years, 1942–1944* (McGraw Hill, 1983), 613.
392 *"Due to previous"*: Dwight Eisenhower, *Letters to Mamie* (Doubleday, 1977), 189.
392 *son's eyes roll*: Eisenhower, 187.
392 *"excited as a bride"*: Dwight Eisenhower, *Letters to Mamie* (Doubleday, 1977), 190.
392 *"When I go"*: Eisenhower, 189.
393 *"not writing with"*: Eisenhower, 202.
393 *problems were larger*: Eisenhower to Forrest Pogue, March 10, 1947, Pre-Pres. Principal, box 93.
393 *seemed to grow quieter*: Forrest Pogue, interview with James Gault, February 13, 1947, Pogue Papers, box 161; George Marshall to Franklin Roosevelt, June 14, 1944, GCM, McCarthy Papers, box 24; Kenneth Davis to Elsie McKeogh, August 11, 1944, Davis Papers, box 94; Butcher Diary, A-1350-1351.
393 *stopped wearing a helmet*: "Eisenhower Flies over Nazi Lines," *New York Times*, July 6, 1944.
393 *The flood of congratulations*: Dwight Eisenhower to Walter B. Smith, June 9, 1944, Pre-Pres. Principal, box 109.
393 *Wayne Clark cabled*: Mark Clark to Dwight Eisenhower, June 7, 1944, Pre-Pres. Principal, box 23.
393 *"great admiration I have"*: George Patton to Dwight Eisenhower, June 7, 1944, Pre-Pres. Principal, box 91.
394 *"I know I"*: Jacob Devers to Dwight Eisenhower, June 12, 1944, Pre-Pres. Principal, box 34.
394 *"mother's telephone"*: Milton Eisenhower to Dwight Eisenhower, June 6, 1944, Pre-Pres. Principal, box 174.
394 *"Confidential"*: Milton Eisenhower to Leo Morrison, June 1944, Sherwood Papers, box 4.
394 *"We don't need"*: Eisenhower, *Letters to Mamie*, 190.
394 *"To whom I shall"*: Eisenhower, *Crusade in Europe* (Doubleday, 1947) (from the library of Fox Conner, private collection).
394 *"I doubt very much"*: Dwight Eisenhower to Fox Conner, January 3, 1949, Pre-Presidential Papers, Principal File, box 27.
394 *"the most perfect"*: Kenneth Davis, *Soldier of Democracy* (Konecky & Konecky, 1945), 540.
394 "We came out": Charles Poore, "Books of the Times," *N.Y. Times*, November 29, 1945.
395 *"Draft Eisenhower"*: William B. Pickett, *Eisenhower Decides to Run* (Ivan R. Dee, 2000), 118–35; Douglass K. Daniel, "They Liked Ike: Pro-Eisenhower Publishers and His Decision to Run for President," *Journalism & Mass Communication Quarterly* 77, no. 2 (June 2000): 393–404.
395 *Roy Howard sent Eisenhower*: Roy Howard to Dwight Eisenhower, November 6, 1951, Pre-Pres. Principal, box 58.
395 *"five or six"*: Roy Howard to Dwight Eisenhower, April 22, 1952, Pre-Pres. Principal, Box 58.
395 *Republican-leaning press*: Daniel, "They Liked Ike."
395 *"staunch Republican family"*: Charles Harger, "The Eisenhower I Know," *The American Magazine* 152, no. 5 (November 1951): 24–31.
395 *first major journalist*: "Roy Howard Visits Ike, Sees Victory," United Press, July 10, 1944.
395 *"Ladies and Gentlemen"*: Dwight D. Eisenhower, "Address Accepting the Presidential Nomination at the Republican National Convention in Chicago," online by Gerhard Peters and John T. Woolley, the American Presidency Project, https://www.presidency.ucsb.edu/node/275894.
395 *the French people*: D.R. Ellias, Preliminary Report on Recce of British Beach-head, June 12, 1944, NARA, RG 331, Entry 262A, box 13.
395 *"unanimous in their questions"*: Dwight Eisenhower, CAREP 2, June 12, 1944, Smith Papers, box 23.
395 *Once towns and villages*: Eisenhower, CAREP 2, June 12, 1944.
395 *V-sign*: Everett Hughes to Kate Hughes, June 14, 1944, Hughes Papers, box II-2.
395 *"Everywhere"*: D.R. Ellias, Preliminary Report on Recce of British Beach-head, June 12, 1944, NARA, RG 331, Entry 262A, box 13.
395 *appear to be achieving*: E. J. Ford, "Survey of Attacks on the French Railway Centers," November 12, 1944, AFHRA, reel A5166.
395 *"Das Reich" armored division*: "French Resistance during the First Ten Days of the Operations in Normandy," R. 2265, June 16, 1944, RG 226, entry 1991, box 16.
396 *"technical sabotage"*: SHAEF, "Summary of SAS/SF Plans Directed Against Railway Lines from South of France," June 9, 1944, RG 331, entry 58, box 18.
396 *thousands of Frenchmen*: Blake Clark, Manuscript, 1945, NARA, RG 226, Entry 1991, box 16.

396 *the persistent sabotage:* 21st Army Group, Intelligence Summary no. 135, June 23, 1944, RG 226, entry 1991, box 16.

396 *The Maquis were also:* SHAEF, G-3 Daily Summary of SAS and SF Operations Under SHAEF Control no. 3, June 10, 1944, RG 331, entry 262A, box 135.

396 *the word "liberated":* Dwight Eisenhower to Walter B. Smith, June 11, 1944, 1944-06-11, *13, Pre-Pres. Principal, box 109.

396 *handed a fait accompli:* The Acting American Representative to the French Committee of National Liberation Algiers (Chapin) to the Secretary of State, June 10, 1944, FRUS 1944, vol. 3, doc. 641.

396 "un faux-monnaie": Forrest Pogue, interview with Charles de Gaulle, January 14, 1947, Pogue Papers, box 161.

396 *had worked closely:* FCNL, "Note for the Combined Committee for Civil Affairs," May 5, 1944, NARA, RG 107, entry 183, box 55.

396 *"stamped paper":* The Acting American Representative to the French Committee of National Liberation (Chapin) to the Secretary of State, June 8, 1944, FRUS 1944, Vol. III, doc. 639.

396 *called De Gaulle's bluff:* Dwight Eisenhower, CAREP 2, June 12, 1944.

396 *Roosevelt started dangling:* The Acting American Representative to the French Committee of National Liberation Algiers (Chapin) to the Secretary of State, June 13, 1944, FRUS 1944, vol. 3, doc. 651.

397 *"General de Gaulle's courageous":* Dana Adams Schmitt, "Eisenhower Hails de Gaulle Plan," *N.Y. Times*, September 18, 1959, 9.

397 *"The destinies of two":* Bradley, *Soldier's Story*, 23.

397 *But soon after D-Day:* SHAEF, "Release of Shipping and Craft from Operation 'Neptune,'" June 12, 1944, RG 331, entry 58, box 18.

397 *"I would accept":* Dwight Eisenhower to George Marshall, July 12, 1944, Pre-Presidential Papers, Principal File, box 80.

397 *Churchill continued to lobby:* Mattie Pinette, Diary, August 5, 1944, EL, George Hall Papers, box 1; John Erhman, *Grand Strategy* (Her Majesty's Stationery Office, 1956), Vol. 5, 5:362–67; David Eisenhower, *Eisenhower at War* (Random House, 1986), 404–405.

397 *Eisenhower lobbied Churchill:* 77th Meeting War Cabinet, Chiefs of Staff, Record of a Staff Conference Held in the Prime Minister's Map Room, on Monday, 13th June, 1944 6:30 p.m., NAUK, CAB 65/42/35.

397 *Enormous resources:* Harold Bull, "Plan 'Fortitude'—Commanders," May 4th, 1944, NARA, RG 331, entry 58, box 1; E. J. King-Salter, "Report on the Wireless Deception & Security Measures Taken by the Three Services in Connection with Operation Neptune," July 1944, NARA, RG 457, entry 9 11, box 161.

397 *Air reconnaissance:* Trafford Leigh-Mallory, AEAF, "Daily Reflections on the Court of the Battle," 1944, NAUK, AIR 37/784.

397 *Ultra intercepts showed:* Frederick Winterbotham, *The Ultra Secret* (Harper and Row, 1974), 137.

397 *offer Eisenhower $1,000:* Kenneth Davis, interview with General Eisenhower, August 11, 1944, Davis Papers, box 94.

398 *The diplomatic ban:* 80th Meeting War Cabinet, Chiefs of Staff, Record of a Staff Conference Held in the Prime Minister's Map Room, on Monday, 19th June, 1944 5:45 p.m., NAUK, CAB 65/42/38.

398 *"If these bombs":* Anthony Eden to Winston Churchill, June 7, 1944, NAUK, FO-954-18A-155.

398 *been openly dropped:* Brooks Kleber and Dale Birdsell, *The Chemical Warfare Service: Chemicals in Combat*, CMH Pub. 10-3 (US Government Printing Office, 1966), 463.

398 *"for extraordinary heroism":* John Menaugh, "Chemical Mortar," *Chicago Daily Tribune*, October 29, 1944, B1.

398 *White phosphorus was used:* Kleber and Birdsell, *Chemical Warfare Service*, 463.

398 *"hog calling":* Harry C. Butcher, *My Three Years with Eisenhower* (Simon & Schuster, 1946), 597–98.

398 *"Place this serious minute":* Winston Churchill to Hastings Ismay, D. 195/4, June 19, 1944, Churchill Papers, CHAR20/152/6.

398 *stuck to a hard line:* Walter Bedell Smith to Secretary, Chiefs of Staff Committee, June 30, 1944, NAUK, FO-954-18A-190.

398 *In December 1941:* Dwight Eisenhower, manuscript, "Churchill & Marshall," November 17, 1966, Post-Presidential Papers, A-WR Series, box 8.

398 *"Who's senior partner":* Elliott Roosevelt, *As He Saw It* (Duell, Sloan & Pearce, 1946), 151.

399 *"new feelings of spitefulness":* Alan Brooke, *War Diaries, 1939–1945* (Phoenix Press, 2001), 473.

399 *"broke":* John MacCormack, "Britain Is 'Broke,'" *New York Times*, July 7, 1944, p. 7.

399 *Bretton Woods conference:* Benn Steil, *The Battle of Bretton Woods* (Princeton, 2013), 221.

399 *A decade later:* Philip Zelikow, *Suez Deconstructed* (Brookings, 2018); Alex von Tunzelmann, *Blood and Sand* (Harper, 2016); David Nichols, *Eisenhower, 1956* (Simon & Schuster, 2011); Keith Kyle, *Suez* (St. Martin's, 2010).

399 *supply of dollars:* Benn Steil, *The Battle of Bretton Woods* (Princeton University Press, 2013), 332; Evan

Thomas, *Ike's Bluff* (Little Brown, 2012), 221-225; Diane B. Kunz, *The Economic Diplomacy of the Suez Crisis* (University of North Carolina Press, 1991).

399 *"leader of the free world"*: The phrase did not become a stock one until the early 1940s. The Newspapers .com database shows 232 instances of its use over the course of the 1940s, 84 percent of which also contain a reference to the word "president." In the 1950s, the database shows 14,984 instances of the phrase being used, 91 percent of which also contain a reference to the word "president," a whopping 55-fold increase decade over decade. This shift principally occurs between the years 1952 and 1953, in which there is a 2.6-fold increase year over year in the number of instances in which the phrase is found in close proximity to the word "president."

399 *During the war:* "Map a Blow at Hitler," *Des Moines Register*, August 15, 1941, p. 1.

399 *"Freedom is pitted"*: Inaugural Address, January 20, 1953, in *Public Papers of the Presidents: Dwight D. Eisenhower, 1953* (US Government Printing Office, 1960), 1.

400 *On June 9:* Kay Summersby, Diary, June 9, 1944, EL, Barbara Wyden Papers, box 1.

400 *"does not show"*: E.C. McNeil to Eisenhower, July 29, 1944, NARA, RG 498, entry UD 1028, box 4716.

400 *The only loose end:* Queen Brinson to Provost Marshal, May 13, 1944, NARA-SL, Army Record V151125, Eliga Brinson, no. 34052175.

400 *Cliff Lee ordered:* A. H. Corley to Commanding General, Southern Base Command, June 9, 1944, NARA-SL, Army Record V151125, Eliga Brinson, no. 34052175.

400 *Eisenhower signed off*: General Court Martial Orders No. 62, August 4, 1944, NARA-SL, Army Record V151125, Eliga Brinson, No. 34052175.

400 *Smith and Brinson were hanged:* "Two U.S. Soldiers Hanged; Crime Cleeve," *Gloucestershire Echo*, August 12, 1944.

400 *the full transcript:* "The Trial of a Negro," *The Tribune*, June 9, 1944.

400 *seeking a stay:* Thurgood Marshall to Dwight Eisenhower, June 2, 1944, June 8, 1944, NARA-SL, *United States v. Leroy Henry*, Court-Martial No. 264262, Record of Trial.

400 *Black soldiers in Louisiana: Adams v. United States*, 319 U.S. 312 (1943).

400 *racial discrimination in voting: Smith v. Allwright*, 321 US 649 (1944).

401 *League of Colored Peoples:* Graham Smith, *When Jim Crow Met John Bull* (Tauris, 1987), at 185.

401 *Under this pressure:* Edward Betts to W.J. Wenham, June 29, 1944, Pre-Pres. Principal, box 119.

401 *"this was not"*: H.M. Peyton, Review of the Record of Trial by General Court Martial, June 2, 1944, NARA-SL, *United States v. Leroy Henry*, Court-Martial No. 264262, Record of Trial.

401 *long meeting*: Daily Appointment Log, June 14, 1944, Pre-Pres. Principal, box 127.

401 *later and decided*: General Court-Martial Data Sheet, Leroy Henry (signed by Frederick Bertolet, June 16, 1944), Case No. 264262, NARA-SL, *United States v. Leroy Henry*, Court-Martial No. 264262, Record of Trial.

401 *another memorandum*: Frederick Bertolet, *United States v. Henry*, Review by Staff Judge Advocate, undated (signed by Edward Betts June 17, 1944), NARA-SL, *United States v. Leroy Henry*, Court-Martial No. 264262, Record of Trial.

401 *Betts paid a short visit*: Daily Appointment Log, June 17, 1944, Pre-Pres. Principal, box 127.

401 *paperwork to sign*: General Court Martial Order No. 44, Headquarters, European Theater of Operations, U.S. Army, June 17, 1944, NARA-SL, *United States v. Leroy Henry*, Court-Martial No. 264262, Record of Trial.

401 *back on duty*: "Back to duty after Quashed Death Verdict," *Daily Mirror*, June 22, 1944.

401 *"the negro has"*: Chester Hansen, Diary, May 4, 1944, USAHEC, Chester Hansen Papers.

401 *Around 1,700 Black soldiers:* Ulysses Lee, *United States Army in World War II: The Employment of Negro Troops* (US Government Printing Office, 1966), 638.

401 *only anti-aircraft defense:* Report from Naval Commander, Western Task Force, June 6, 1944, NARA, RG 331, entry 1, box 62.

401 *four Black medics:* Linda Hervieux, *Forgotten* (HarperCollins, 2015), 211, 240.

401 *Battle of the Bulge*: Jean Byers, *A Study of the Negro in Military Service*, June 1947, 164–175; Walter White, Eisenhower on Civil Rights, April 1, 1948, Pre-Pres. Principal, box 123.

402 *"If we attempt"*: Testimony of General Dwight D. Eisenhower before the Committee on Armed Services, US Senate, Friday, April 2, 1948, vol. 11, pp. 2591–96.

402 *"believing he had courage"*: Walter White, *The Ku Klux Klan and Civil Rights Legislation*, Graphic Syndicate, April 8, 1944.

402 *knocked Jim Crow: Brown v. Board of Education of Topeka*, 347 U.S. 483 (1954).

402 *The following afternoon:* Kay Summersby, Diary, Pre-Pres. Principal, box 140.

402 *Monty had sent:* Bernard Montgomery to Dwight Eisenhower, June 10, 1944, Pre-Pres. Principal, box 83.

402 *"Red Army started":* John Deane to Combined Chiefs of Staff, June 10, 1944, RG 331, entry NM8 4, box 121.
402 *Marshall was serene:* Eisenhower, "Churchill & Marshall."
402 *Twenty-four hours after:* George Raynor Thompson and Dixie R. Harris, *United States Army in World War II, The Technical Services, The Signal Corps: The Outcome (Mid-1943 Through 1945)* (Center for Military History, 1966), 564.
402 *"telephoto net":* Thompson and Harris, 605.
402 *"satisfaction with what":* Eisenhower, "Churchill & Marshall."
402 *He estimated that:* Kay Summersby, Diary, 1944, EL, Barbara Wyden Papers, box 1.
402 *"I think we":* George Marshall to Franklin Roosevelt, June 14, 1944, GCM, McCarthy Papers, box 24.
403 *discretion to choose:* Eisenhower, "Churchill & Marshall."
403 *Monty had sent overnight:* Butcher Diary, A-1356.
403 *Eisenhower ate breakfast:* Mattie Pinette, Diary, 1944, EL, George Hall Papers, box 1.
403 *"We wish for you":* Dwight Eisenhower to Walter B. Smith, June 11, 1944, Pre-Pres. Principal, box 109.
403 *Midmorning, he got into:* Kay Summersby, Diary, 1944, EL, Barbara Wyden Papers, box 1.
403 *A convoy that stretched:* Mattie Pinette, Diary, 1944, EL, George Hall Papers, box 1.
403 *IBM Electric Executive:* Franklin Roosevelt to Winston Churchill, June 6, 1944, GCM, McCarthy Papers, box 24.
403 *IBM had released:* Wilfred A. Beeching, *Century of the Typewriter* (Bournemouth, 1990), 124.
403 *Churchill had been struck:* Franklin Roosevelt to Winston Churchill, June 6, 1944, GCM, McCarthy Papers, box 24.
403 *For a literary man:* Churchill to Roosevelt, June 16, 1944, Churchill Papers, CHAR 20/137 C.
403 *sharing a telegram:* Butcher Diary, A-1356.
403 *"cool and confident":* George Marshall to Franklin Roosevelt, June 14, 1944, GCM, McCarthy Papers, box 24.
403 *"Allied progress continues":* Dwight Eisenhower, Communique no. 10, June 11, 1944, Smith Papers, box 23.
403 *"very young and":* Headquarters, First US Army, After Action Against Enemy, Reports After/After Action Report, August 6, 1944, EL, U.S. Army, First Army Headquarters Records, 1943–55, box 2.
404 *many were Russian:* Walter B. Smith to European Advisory Commission, June 1944, RG 331, entry 58, box 1.
404 *an armored counteroffensive:* Dwight Eisenhower, Communique no. 10, June 11, 1944.
404 *None of the Allied ammunition:* Eisenhower to George Marshall, July 5, 1944, Pre-Pres. Principal, box 80.
404 *American casualties were:* HQ 21st Army Group, 'A' Sitrep no. 5, June 12, 1944, NARA, RG 331, Entry 1, box 62.
404 *E-boats had come out:* Dwight Eisenhower, Communique no. 10, June 11, 1944.
404 *visited Bertie Ramsay:* Kay Summersby, Diary, 1944, EL, Barbara Wyden Papers, box 1.
404 *By that evening:* US War Department, Operations Division, Diary, EL, U.S. War Department, Operations Division: Diaries, 1942–1946.
404 *Telegraph Cottage nearby:* Mattie Pinette, Diary, 1944, EL, George Hall Papers, box 1.
404 *back on the road:* Kay Summersby, Diary, 1944, EL, Barbara Wyden Papers, box 1.
404 *eager to get to bed:* Kay Summersby, Diary, 1944, Pre-Pres. Principal, box 140.
404 *the phone rang:* Butcher Diary, A-1356.
405 *potential gas attacks:* Butcher Diary, A-1359.
405 *Kay drove Jimmy:* Kay Summersby, Diary, 1944, EL, Barbara Wyden Papers, box 1.
405 *Churchill's train pulled in:* James Gault, "General Eisenhower's Visit to France on 12 June," in Butcher Diary, A-1360.
405 *Eisenhower greeted them:* Henry Arnold, Diary (Trip to England June 8, 1944–June 21, 1944), Arnold Papers, reel 222.
405 *dinner the previous night:* Arnold.
405 *bid their farewell:* Kay Summersby, Diary, June 12, 1944, Pre-Pres. Principal, box 140.
405 *The morning was clear:* Unless otherwise indicated, the descriptions of the Normandy beachhead, along with the particular details of Eisenhower's visit on June 12, 1944, are taken from the contemporaneous accounts available in Chester Hansen, Diary, June 12, 1944, USAHEC, Chester Hansen Papers; Henry Arnold, Diary (Trip to England June 8, 1944 - June 21, 1944), Arnold Papers, Reel 222; Thor Smith, Diary, June 12, 1944, EL, Thor Smith Papers, Box 3; Kay Summersby, Diary, June 12, 1944, EL, Barbara Wyden Papers, Box 1; James Gault, General Eisenhower's Visit to France on 12 June 1944, in Butcher Diary, at A-1361; Everett Hughes to Kate Hughes, June 14, 1944, Hughes Papers, Box II-2; Courtney Hodges, War Diary, 1944, EL, Courtney Hodges Papers, Box 25; Trafford Leigh-Mallory, Historical Record AEAF (June 1944), NAUK, AIR 37/1057; George Marshall to Franklin Roosevelt, June 14, 1944, GCM, McCarthy Papers, Box 24; John T. Mason, The Reminiscences of Alan Goodrich Kirk, 1962, No. 455, Oral History Research Office, Columbia University, at 368; Forrest Pogue, Interview with James Gault, February 13, 1947, Pogue Papers, Box 161; John Mason Brown, *Many a Watchful Night* (McGraw-Hill, 1944), 176–192; Omar Bradley, *A General's Life*

(Simon & Schuster, 1983), at 259; A.J. Leibling, "Cross-Channel Trip, Part III," *The New Yorker*, July 15, 1944, at 36–45; Henry Arnold, *Global Mission* (Harper & Bros., 1949), 506–508.

406 *"Good god, you're"*: Gault, "General Eisenhower's Visit to France."

407 *"Invasion by Air"*: *Life* 16, no. 24 (June 12, 1944).

407 *on its cover*: *Life* 16, no. 25 (June 19, 1944).

407 *"They inspire me"*: Eisenhower, 189.

407 *"That's Ike"*: James Gault, "General Eisenhower's Visit to France."

AUTHOR'S NOTE

409 *"They have enormous power"*: Alan Dudley, "The Essentials of an American Policy," March 21, 1944, UKNA, FO 371/38523/AN1538.

410 *was liked:* As just one example, in the month after the U.S. Army liberated Paris found that only 29 percent of Frenchmen polled agreed the United States "contributed most in the defeat of Germany," with 61 percent giving credit to the Soviet Union. Yet, when asked where they would like to visit after the war, 43 percent said the United States, with only 13 percent eager to celebrate the Soviet Union's contributions in Russia itself. *The Public Opinion Quarterly*, Vol. 8, No. 4 (Winter, 1944-1945).

410 *"sense of the historical"*: Kenneth S. Davis, "Ike's Identification with Kansas," October 12, 1990, Davis Papers, box 19.

410 *bizarrely wrong:* In preparation for a lecture in 1946 on military history, Eisenhower privately ruminated on how America's role in World War II reflected its larger role in the progress of civilization. "War has been growing more complicated as the national economies waging it advance materially, intellectually, spiritually," he wrote. "The only constant is man." In prehistoric times, he mused, war was defined by individual weapons: the rock, the spear, the shield. Then the Greeks invented the phalanx, the organized movement of men to do what no one of them could do. Hannibal domesticated the elephants to terrifying effect. The Romans invented the legion, overseas supply lines, and the ability to wage war at civilizational scale. The Byzantines mastered the use of fire. The British gained dominance with the long bow. The Chinese stunned their enemies with gun powder and the Europeans devised weapons powered by gunpowder. Victory in modern war, he concluded had come to depend upon "troop and national morale, a war-geared economy, accelerated scientific research, international cooperation" and global logistics. Hence, those were the things he believed the United States would need to cultivate if it had any hope of peace and security. Dwight Eisenhower, Material on Military History Lecture, undated, Pre-Pres. Principal, box 193.

411 *"Eisenhower was"*: Oral History Research Office, Eisenhower Administration: Merriman Smith, 1972, Columbia Center on Oral History, pp. 1–2.

411 *"You never knew"*: Merriman Smith, p. 20.

412 *"Different books"*: John Lewis Gaddis, "Spiderman, Shakespeare, and Kennan: The Art of Teaching Biography," *Passport*, Vol. 43, No. 3 (September 2012).

413 *"Churchill & Marshall"*: Dwight Eisenhower, Manuscript, "Churchill & Marshall," November 17, 1966, Post-Presidential Papers, A-WR Series, box 8.

413 *"my life"*: Dwight Eisenhower to Milton Eisenhower, July 10, 1944, Pre-Pres. Principal, box 174.

414 *Eisenhower saw the book:* Dwight Eisenhower to George Bye, July 26, 1948, Pre-Pres. Principal, box 16.

414 *"you must realize"*: Harry Butcher to Dwight Eisenhower, November 1, 1948, Pre-Pres. Principal, box 16.

414 *"I am terribly distressed"*: Dwight Eisenhower to Kay Summersby, November 22, 1945, Pre-Pres. Principal, box 112.

414 *"not only"*: Merle Miller, *Plain Speaking* (Berkley, 1974), at 368–369.

414 *as a fabulist:* Francis Heller & Robert H. Ferrell, "Plain Faking," *American Heritage*, No. 46 (May–June 1995).

414 *by Joe Collins:* J. Lawton Collins, to Forrest Pogue, July 8, 1977, Pogue Papers, box 57.

415 *"a change"*: Harry H. Vaughn, to Forrest Pogue, June 29, 1977, Pogue Papers, box 57.

415 *"as strongly as possible"*: Frank McCarthy to M.G. White, July 7, 1944, GCM, McCarthy Papers, box 23.

415 *briefly in Washington:* Ernest Lee, Diary, July 1, 1944, EL, Ernest Lee Papers, reel 1.

415 *personnel section:* M.G. White to Dwight Eisenhower, July 8, 1944, Pre-Pres. Principal, box 112.

415 *"now understand"*: Ernest Lee to Frank Stoner, July 16, 1944, Pre-Pres. Principal, box 112.

415 *Sigrid Hedin:* Interview with Erik Lamont, June 26, 2023.

416 *unpublished interview:* Lloyd Shearer, "The Eisenhower-Summersby Love Affair (Draft)," October 28, 1976, University of Wyoming, Harry Butcher Papers, box 3.

INDEX